**CONFLICT PREVENTI
POST-CONFLICT RECON!**

Urban Poor Perceptions of Violence and Exclusion in Colombia

Caroline Moser
Cathy McIlwaine

Foreword by Andres Solimano

*Latin America and Caribbean Region,
Environmentally and Socially Sustainable Development
Sector Management Unit
The World Bank
Washington, D.C.*

© 2000 The International Bank for Reconstruction
and Development/THE WORLD BANK
1818 H Street, N.W.
Washington, D.C. 20433

All rights reserved
Manufactured in the United States of America
First printing July 2000
1 2 3 4 04 03 02 01 00

The findings, interpretations, and conclusions expressed in this paper are entirely those of the author(s) and should not be attributed in any manner to the World Bank, to its affiliated organizations, or to members of its Board of Executive Directors or the countries they represent. The World Bank does not guarantee the accuracy of the data included in this publication and accepts no responsibility for any consequence of their use.

The material in this publication is copyrighted. The World Bank encourages dissemination of its work and will normally grant permission to reproduce portions of the work promptly.

Permission to *photocopy* items for internal or personal use, for the internal or personal use of specific clients, or for educational classroom use is granted by the World Bank, provided that the appropriate fee is paid directly to the Copyright Clearance Center, Inc., 222 Rosewood Drive, Danvers, MA 01923, USA.; telephone 978-750-8400, fax 978-750-4470. Please contact the Copyright Clearance Center before photocopying items.

For permission to *reprint* individual articles or chapters, please fax a request with complete information to the Republication Department, Copyright Clearance Center, fax 978-750-4470.

All other queries on rights and licenses should be addressed to the Office of the Publisher, World Bank, at the address above or faxed to 202-522-2422.

Cover photo: Teen gang members "converted" to militias with 7.65 pistols, Medellin, Colombia 1991. Timothy Ross/Imageworks.

Caroline Moser is a head specialist, Social Development, Latin America and Carribean Region at the World Bank.
Cathy McIlwaine is Lecturer at the Department of Geography, Queen Mary and Westfield College, London. She was on a one year sabbatical to the World Bank to carry out this research.
Andres Solimano is Country Director for Colombia, Ecuador, and Venezuela, The World Bank.

ISBN 0-8213-4731-4

Library of Congress Cataloging-in-Publication Data

Moser, Caroline O.N.
  Urban poor perceptions of violence and exclusion in Colombia / Caroline Moser, Cathy McIlwaine.
      p. cm. — (Conflict prevention and post-conflict reconstruction)
  Includes bibliographical references.
  ISBN 0-8213-4731-4
  1. Violence — Colombia — Public opinion. 2. Urban Poor — Colombia — Attitudes. 3. Public opinion — Colombia. 4. Violence — Colombia. 5. Marginality, Social — Colombia. I. McIlwaine, Cathy, 1965-   II. Title. III. Series.

HN310.Z9 V5526 2000
303.6´09861—dc21   00-04632

Contents

Foreword v
Acknowledgments xi
Executive Summary 1
1 Introduction 7
2 Summary Findings: Perceptions of General Problems and Violence 15
3 Social Violence in the Family and Household 31
4 Economic Violence and Drug Consumption 43
5 Unemployment, Exclusion, and Economic Violence ...57
6 Perverse Social Capital and Economic and Political Violence 71
7 Youth, Exclusion, and Violence 93
8 Community Perceptions of Solutions to Violence 99
Notes 113
Annexes 115
Bibliography 121

Foreword

Societies in Crisis, Globalization and Violence

Andres Solimano

Societies in crisis: Concept and scope

A society in crisis presents both a challenge and an opportunity. This is certainly the case in the context of Colombia, now in the fifth decade of its bitter civil war. The crisis in which Colombia finds itself today represents an integral challenge to the economy, the institutions, and the values of its society. At the same time, it provides an opportunity for changing structures that no longer work. Although this may vary according to different interests in society, the needs of the most excluded and poorest are often marginalised. Yet, as this study shows, they have very clear perceptions of those structures that they consider important to change

The elusive concept of crisis that underpins this study has long been an important concern. The German philosopher Jurgen Habermas for instance, provides a useful taxonomy of systemic crisis comprising a fourfold classification of (a) economic crisis, (b) rationality crisis, (c) legitimation crisis, and (iv) motivation crisis (Habermas 1972). An *economic* crisis, termed a "realization crisis" by Habermas, may be a recession, an economic depression, or an inflationary phenomena; a *rationality* crisis, in Habermas's words, is a breakdown of the "rational administrative" practices necessary to maintain the economy in due course. This can be interpreted as the inability of the government in a crisis situation, to properly manage and regulate the economic system. A *legitimation* crisis, in turn, is characterized by a breakdown in the level of public support, credibility, and trust on existing institutions. A *motivation* crisis is a crisis in the realm of values, traditions, and norms in society. Both economic and rationality crises belong to the economic sphere, legitimation crises are political in essence and motivational crises belong to the sociocultural realm. The boundaries may shift, in turn, depending on the specific nature of a crisis in a country during a given historical period.

Thus, a societal crisis is a comprehensive phenomena occurring simultaneously at an economic, political, socio-cultural (value-system) level. It is a systemic, rather than a partial or local, phenomena in which institutions become dysfunctional in terms of their ability to process internal societal conflicts, as both the formal and informal rules that mediate social interaction collapse. Such a breakdown often has far-reaching, mostly negative, effects. At the economic level, the investment climate deteriorates in an environment without well-defined rules (e.g., property rights may not be enforced), with ensuing adverse effects in terms of economic growth and employment creation. Countries in crisis rarely experience economic growth and development is postponed. At the social level conflict erodes trust and social cohesion-the social capital so important in development processes.

Another manifestation of crisis is the emergence of violence, a phenomena linked to a breakdown in rules of behavior (see below). High levels of violence and insecurity not only deteriorate the investment climate, but have economic as well as human, social, and political costs which exacerbate the crisis. In a crisis situation, public objectives may start to be replaced by private interests. Accountability and monitoring of the "agent" (e.g. governments or public officials) by "principals" (parliament, judiciary system, the people) weaken substantially. Often the result is corruption, a phenomenon that has received substantial attention in the 1990s, particularly in the development community. Corruption has a demoralizing effect on the public (and on honest officials in the public sector institutions), eroding social creditability in institutions. In Habermas's framework, corruption, and, to an extent, violence, can be understood from several angles. At one level, corruption is a manifestation of a "rationality crisis". In this sense common administrative practices of sound governments weaken to such an extent that conditions prevail for the acquisition of public assets for private benefit. In turn, when corruption reaches significant proportions a legitimation crisis may develop, eroding trust and confidence in government and other public institutions. Finally, if corruption became an ingrained social practice, affecting the norms and values of society, this then contains the typical features of a motivational crisis. Thus Colombia is experiencing a dirty war, economic recession and high levels of corruption, all of which are affected by and in turn affect the current crisis.

Crisis and Violence: Global and national causes

Since the theme of this book is violence, it may be useful to put the issue into historical perspective. Marx, as well as other 19th century political theorists highlighted the fact that the most important political changes in history were surrounded by violence, sometimes acute and dramatic. Such was the case of the French, Russian and American revolutions- to name a few important examples of radical social change. In a more contemporary context, the post-cold war period of the 1990s has also been characterized by violence and internal armed conflict. Examples of this include the following: the disintegration of the Soviet Union, followed by violence in former soviet states such as the Chechnya war; the dissolution of the former Yugoslavia, leading to the more recent armed conflicts in Bosnia and Kosovo. The degree of violence and armed conflict in Africa in the 1990s, such as in Rwanda and Somalia to name but two of the conflicts affecting the region, have frightened the international community. In Latin America, violence and armed conflict have also been present, such as in Chiapas, Mexico. The long lasting Colombian conflict is probably the most intractable, armed conflict in South-America, given the complex interplay of guerrilla, narcotraffics, paramilitary, and the army. On the positive side, the 1990s in Central America witnessed the signing of peace agreements, and the end of civil wars in El Salvador, Nicaragua and Guatemala. These coincided with the end of the cold war. Yet these countries continue to experience high levels of violence in terms of street violence, social violence and violent crime which pervade all sectors of their societies, thus hampering their post-conflict recovery.

Looking ahead in the early 21st century it seems that political and ethnic violence will, unfortunately, be prevalent phenomena in several regions of the world. The historian Eric Hobsbawn (1999) has recently pointed out that a decade after the dissolution of the Soviet block, the process of state-building in the former soviet republics and former Yugoslavia is still an unfolding process. Needless to say, those processes are far from being peaceful and orderly events. The Andean region of Latin America also turned very volatile in the late 20th century, a trend that is bound to pervade into the early 21st century. Beside war-torn Colombia, traditionally peaceful Ecuador shows the first signs of unrest that could lead to political violence-as a consequence of the tensions accumulating from deep economic crisis, increased regional division, political fragmentation, and the eruption of an active and powerful indigenous movement with a radical economic and political agenda. In addition, Peru is experiencing complex reactions to its current presidential elections, and Venezuela is engaged in an attempt at internal political and institutional change the final outcomes of which still remain uncertain.

Therefore, the end of the cold war and the onset of globalization in the 1990s, contrary to initial expectations, have not been followed by widespread growth and social and political cohesion. Rather the last decade has seen an increase in inequality, exclusion, and violence around the globe. However, the nature of violence has changed when compared to that of the cold-war years. Wars between countries have become less important (almost disappearing), while internal armed conflicts within countries have become a more important source of violence. In addition, internal conflict in countries such as Colombia, have changed their nature from a conflict with a relatively important ideological component to a conflict tied to (and financed by) the large economic rents generated by the drug-industry and kidnapping. It would be interesting to know more about the effects of a globalized (probably illegal) arms market that provides the weapons that sustain such conflicts. Furthermore, as this study shows, Colombia is affected by many different types of violence at different levels that rise from problems not likely to be resolved by any peace process.

Summing-up, several factors can be highlighted as 'new' determinants of violence in the post-cold war, globalized world of the late 20th and early 21st century. These include the reconfiguration of new national states after the collapse of the soviet block, the eruption of underlying ethnic conflicts in several countries, the emergence of an apparently important global arms market, the competition for increasing shares of the large economic rents generated by narco-trafficking, internal social conflict generated by deep economic crisis and the loss of legitimation (Habermas's 'legitimation' crisis) of existing political regimes because of corruption and poor management. In the Latin American context, increasing inequality and social exclusion are leading to higher levels of tension and frustration throughout the region, often resulting in increased levels of violence as countries such as Guatemala, El Salvador, Nicaragua, and Peru fail to move away from the cultures of violence they lived in the 1980s. These will be some of the main challenges facing Colombia in a post-conflict context, a country which has lived through a simmering civil war for half a century, in which unemployment, unequal income distribution, and social exclusion are some of the main determinants of violence, a situation only worsened by its recent unanticipated economic crisis.

Reforms to rebuild societies in crisis and reduce violence

We have seen that crises are a multidimensional phenomena with several manifestations: sluggish economic growth, dysfunctional institutions, corruption, and violence. Interestingly enough, societal crises often accompany and/or trigger important historical transformations. The most recent examples of important political and economic events at a global scale are the end of the cold war in the late 1980s and the process of economic globalization in the 1990s. Overcoming societal crisis require comprehensive economic, institutional, and political reform.

Measured in a historical-time scale, economic reforms can proceed at a faster pace than institutional reforms. In turn, institutional reforms that alter formal rules can take place more rapidly than changes oriented to modify informal rules of human behavior, based on cultural norms, values, traditions, and other historical factors. These considerations are valid when addressing the problem of violence. Its determinants are multiple, and linked to such factors as the occurrence of legitimation and motivational crises, broad historical transformations, and economic crisis. Therefore, a comprehensive strategy to reduce violence must include broad economic and institutional reforms, specific interventions to address factors that propagate violence, and, ultimately, a change in values and cultural norms that certainly underlay the phenomena of violence. In addressing such issues the perceptions of poor communities themselves are essential. Through the participatory research methodology employed in this study the inter-linkages between different types of problems and their relation to different types of violence can be explored from the voices of the poor themselves. In this way the findings from this study complement more widely known economic and statistical data on violence, to show the complex reality of violence and exclusion in poor urban communities. This study follows on from a sector study on violence in Colombia also published in this series (Solimano 2000, World Bank 1999). It provides the next stages of the critical work necessary to better understand the forces involved in violence reduction and the transition to peace in Colombian society in the coming years.

Acknowledgments

This study is based on research conducted during January and February of 1999, using a participatory urban appraisal methodology. The study is part of a larger initiative within the Environmentally and Socially Sustainable Development Department, Latin America and Caribbean Region, World Bank—the Urban Peace Program—directed by Caroline Moser (Lead Specialist Social Development).

The Swedish International Development Authority (SIDA) has provided funding for this program, which also includes a similar study on Guatemala. For her vision in supporting this very new initiative, particular acknowledgment is owed to Eivor Halkjaer.

In Colombia Donny Meertens, of Universidad Nacional de Colombia, was the adviser for the project, and Daniel Selener of the Instituto Internacional de Reconstrucción Rural in Quito was the participatory urban appraisal trainer. The study was carried out by the authors, in collaboration with four teams of researchers from the Universidad Nacional, CEMILLA (Centro Microempresarial del Llano), Fundación Mujer y Futuro, and a group of consultants. They included the following members:

Universidad Nacional
Julián Arturo
Haidí Hernández Córdoba
Lya Yeneth Fuentes Carlos
Maria Eugenia Vásquez

CEMILLA
Santiago Parra Roman
Claudia Zulima Jiménez
Margarita Molina M.
Rafael Roman
Alba Rocío Rosas G.
Titus Moser

Fundación Mujer y Futuro
Isabel Ortiz
Christiane Lelièvre
Carlos Arnulfo Mendoza
José Luis Muñoz
Cathy McIlwaine

Independent consultants
Ana Daza
Angelica Acosta
Juan Pablo Fayad
Francisco Hurtado G.
William Rodriguez

In the World Bank's Colombia Country Management Unit in Washington, D.C., Andres Solimano (Director), Jonathan Parker (Sector Leader), and Connie Luff (Country Officer) provided important commitment and advice to the project. In Bogotá at the World Bank Mission, Felipe Saez (Resident Representative), Jairo Arboleda (Civil Society and Social Development Representative), and Maria Teresa de Henao (Sr. Operations Assistant) all provided invaluable assistance and support. The authors are particularly grateful to the entire mission staff for their interest and help to the project throughout the research process.

World Bank peer reviewers for this study were Norman Hicks (LCSPR), Markus Kostner (SDVPC), Joel Reyes (LCSHE), Lavinia Gasperini (LCSHE), and Anthony Bebbington (SDV). As a member of the Urban Peace Program Team, Carolina Ladino, with assistance from Fiona Clark, made important contributions to the data analysis of this study. Thanks are also due to Barbara Karni, Daphne Levitas, and Carole-Sue Castronuovo of Communications Development for the editing and production of this document.

Cathy McIlwaine would like to thank the Department of Geography, Queen Mary and Westfield College, University of London, for granting her a year's leave of absence to pursue this research.

Above all, the authors thank the many people in the nine communities in Colombia who participated in the research. They not only welcomed us into their lives, shared their time and perceptions, but in some cases took risks in order to contribute to the study. For safety reasons, they must remain anonymous.

Executive Summary

Despite sustained improvements in its social and economic indicators over the past several decades and its rich stock of natural and human resources, Colombia remains plagued by violence. The very high level of violence reflects a variety of factors, including the country's simmering 50-year-old civil war, the increase in armed conflict, the rise in urban and rural crime, and drug cartel–linked violence.

As the government struggles to reach peace agreements with guerrilla and paramilitary groups, political violence and armed conflict have been the primary focuses of political analysts and civil society groups alike. The perceptions of violence by people living in poor communities have received much less attention. This report addresses this issue by providing the results of a participatory study of violence conducted in low-income urban communities in Colombia.

Objectives of the Study

The study documents how people living in poor urban communities in Colombia perceive violence. Specifically, it identifies the categories of violence affecting poor communities, the costs of different types of violence, the effect of violence on social capital, and the causes and effects of social exclusion.

To describe the relationships that produce and sustain this cycle of violence and to begin to identify interventions to break it, the study develops a violence–capital–exclusion nexus—an analytical framework that links different types of violence both to society's capital and to the exclusion of its poor population. To incorporate the rarely heard voices of the poor, the study uses the participatory urban appraisal methodology, which emphasizes local knowledge and enables locals to make their own analysis of the problems they face and identify their own solutions.

Fieldwork was undertaken in nine predominantly low-income communities located in seven cities or towns that are representative of Colombia's urban areas. These communities, identified by pseudonyms, included three *barrios* in Bogotá (Embudo, 14 de Febrero, and Jericó); two *barrios* in cities long connected with the drug cartel (Pórtico, Medellín, and El Arca, Cali); two *barrios* in cities or towns with large numbers of displaced people (Amanecer, Bucaramanga, and Rosario, Girón); and two *barrios* in frontier towns located in areas rich in natural resources (Cachicamo, Yopal, and Colombia Chiquita, Aguazul).

Types of Violence

Violence-related problems emerged as the single most important type of problem facing the urban poor. Within this category, drug use was identified as a major issue in many communities. Lack of physical capital was the second most important type of problem, with unemployment the most frequently cited specific problem. Lack of social capital was identified as a problem more often than lack of human capital. Lack of natural capital was cited as a problem only in recently established settlements.

Focus groups in the nine communities listed an average of 25 different types of violence, with one community distinguishing 60 different types of violence. The various types of violence were grouped into three interrelated categories: political, economic, and social. Economic violence was cited most often (54 percent of all types of violence), followed by social violence (32 percent) and political violence (14 percent).

Perceptions of violence varied across cities and demographic groups. Intrafamily violence emerged as especially important in Bogotá, gang violence as very important in Cali and Medellín, and political violence as important in frontier towns and towns with large numbers of displaced people.

Elderly people were most concerned with insecurity and drugs. Adult women focused on violence against children, whereas adult men were most concerned with political and youth violence. Young people were especially troubled by the drug problem. Young men were also concerned with gang and militia violence, and young women were worried about rape outside the home. Children's perceptions, elicited from drawings, revealed the association between fear and guns.

Costs, Causes, and Consequences of Violence

Different types of violence are interrelated in a highly complex and dynamic manner. Social violence within households and families, for example, may lead young people to take drugs and join gangs, which may in turn lead to economic violence—including robbery and killing—or political violence associated with guerilla or paramilitary groups. Understanding each type of violence is thus critical to understanding the nature of the problems affecting people living in poor communities.

EXECUTIVE SUMMARY 3

Families, Households, and Social Violence

Intrafamily violence is a daily occurrence in Colombia, and it is closely linked to other types of violence. Study participants identified some 20 different types of violence perpetrated within the home, including incest, sexual abuse, and murder. People in the communities associated the level of intrafamily violence with various factors, including changes in the economy and the rate of unemployment, alcohol (and to a lesser extent drug) use, and *machismo* among men and submissiveness among women.

Intrafamily violence was perceived as undermining how households functioned internally in terms of constructing norms, values, and trust. It also eroded social capital networks between households and reduced the human capital endowments of children and young people. Violence within the home was perceived as leading to violence outside the home.

Violence was perceived as permeating the spectrum of social relations within poor urban communities, with the critical nexus being households and families. With trust in the home severely eroded by violence, children spend long periods of time in the street with their friends. Young men often join gangs or military groups associated with political violence. Young women engage in sexual relations at an early age, often becoming pregnant.

Drug Consumption and Economic Violence

Drug consumption, particularly among young men, was perceived as the leading cause of economic violence in most of the communities studied. Children were reported to begin consuming marijuana at age 8, moving on to petrol and glue by age 12. Teenagers began using *bazuco* (a type of cocaine) at 14, later moving on to *perico* (another type of cocaine), the most expensive of the drugs used.

The most frequently cited causes of drug consumption were intrafamily violence and conflict, peer pressure, and parental example. Other causes included the lack of organized recreational opportunities, especially sports and leisure facilities, and unemployment, which made it difficult for young people to fill their days.

Drug consumption eroded the human capital of young people, who often dropped out of school after getting involved with drugs. School dropouts were rarely able to secure employment, leading them to engage in illegal activities, such as drug dealing and robbery. Drug consumption also increased fear in communities, with drug addicts perceived as the perpetrators of assaults and robbery. Many people responded to the perception of danger by remaining indoors in the evenings. The result was an erosion of community-level social capital.

Unemployment, Exclusion, and Economic Violence

Economic violence was also found to be tied to the level of unemployment, which was very high in the communities studied as a result of both the nationwide recession and the large number of people fleeing political violence in the countryside. Employment prospects were also perceived as being reduced by the stigma of coming from the *barrio*, which many people outside the community associate with criminal activity.

High levels of unemployment were closely linked to various types of violence. In some cases violent crime was a last-resort survival response to unemployment. In other cases it reflected desperation and frustration created by lack of economic opportunities. Many people reported that using drugs was a way of dealing with lack of work and that robbing was a way of paying for drugs.

Another factor tied to economic violence (and violence in general) was exclusion of young people, which many young people dealt with by using drugs or becoming involved in violent or criminal activities. A major cause of exclusion was high levels of intergenerational conflict, often the result of intrafamily violence.

Community Level Social Institutions, Perverse Social Capital, and Political Violence

Violence not only affects individuals and households, but communities themselves. Study participants identified 371 social institutions across the nine research communities. These institutions included both institutions that benefited the community (that is, created positive social capital) and institutions that benefited their members while hurting the community as a whole (that is, created perverse social capital).

Women's and childcare groups and state-run social service delivery organizations (primarily schools and health centers) were trusted by most members of the community. Institutions connected with the perpetration or prevention of violence, such as gangs or state security and justice institutions, were the least trusted.

Perverse organizations were the most prevalent membership organizations, with 16 types of illegal groups functioning in the nine communities. Guerrilla and paramilitary groups perpetrating political violence were universally feared in areas where their presence was dominant. Underlying this fear was the lack of trust among community members, who were afraid to talk openly about the problem. The fear of reprisals eroded solidarity, replacing it with the belief that people must look after themselves to survive.

Community Perceptions of Solutions to the Problem of Violence

Study participants identified four types of strategies for dealing with violence: avoidance, confrontation, conciliation, and other strategies. Most people responded to violence by keeping silent about it out of powerlessness or fear of retribution. Many changed their mobility patterns, avoiding taking certain routes or simply staying home in the evening.

People in the communities recognized that the continuum of violence requires that a variety of solutions be implemented simultaneously. Almost half of the interventions proposed involved creating social capital. Within this category, the promotion of family values and dialogue between families and communities was the most frequently mentioned proposal. Other proposed interventions included improving education, establishing more drug and alcohol rehabilitation centers, improving employment opportunities, and integrating young people into society. Many community members also endorsed increasing the resources of community organizations and obtaining external assistance to establish new organizations. Some endorsed social cleansing and harsh police actions to crack down on violence.

Public Policy Recommendations

Local communities identified three national-level binding constraints that policymakers need to address. These include:

- *The pervasive nature of political violence.* Negotiation of peace with the guerrillas, paramilitary organizations, and other groups is an important precondition for the success of other violence reduction interventions.
- *The serious problem of displaced people,* which affects the daily lives of people in all communities.
- *The lack of employment,* which leads to drug use, crime, and violence.

To address these problems, people in the communities suggested the following interventions:

- Create job opportunities in the formal, informal, and self-employment sectors.
- Attack the problem of drug use.
- Reduce society's tolerance for intrahousehold violence.

- Rebuild trust in the police and the judicial system.
- Strengthen the capacity of community-based membership organizations, particularly those run by women.
- Target interventions at young people.

Chapter One
Introduction

Colombia has long been plagued by violence. Despite being one of the most enduring democracies in South America and sustained improvements in its social and economic indicators over the past several decades, the country has one of the highest homicide rates in the world. The very high level of violence reflects the country's 50-year-old simmering civil war, the rise in armed conflict, urban and rural crime, and the presence of drug cartels.

Until the late 1980s, economic development continued unabated in Colombia. Armed conflict affected primarily those involved in the political conflict and marginal populations in remote rural areas. Urban crime and violence affected mainly low-income *barrio* dwellers.

In the past decade the scale and intensity of violence has changed, with violence now dominating the daily lives of most Colombians. Remote guerrilla conflict has turned into a countrywide war that involves other actors, such as paramilitary groups and drug cartels. The causes of violence have also changed. These include external events such as the collapse of the Cold War, which has affected funding sources for guerrilla activity. It also includes internal changes relating to economic liberalization, which have had implications for the demand for labor (and levels of unemployment), and the growing levels of inequality, which are associated with areas of the country in which coal and oil developments have occurred. Since 1982 successive governments have tried to find both military and political solutions for reaching peace with different guerrilla groups. State agencies, nongovernmental organizations (NGOs), and private foundations have spent vast resources attempting to reduce levels of urban crime, while military and police forces have endeavored to break the drug cartels.

The World Bank's 1997 Colombian Country Assistance Strategy (World Bank 1997), which adopted a participatory approach that included consultations with civil society, identified violence as the country's key development constraint. That constraint is now affecting macro- and microeconomic growth and productivity in Colombia, as well as reducing the government's capacity to alleviate the poverty, inequality, and exclusion that affect the majority of its residents in both urban and rural areas. The Country Assistance Strategy recommended a comprehensive intersector policy, with violence reduction—and its counterpart, peace and development—identified as one of six key areas of strategic importance in which the World Bank could assist Colombia in its development process.

In 1999 the Bank completed a sector study on violence based on background papers commissioned from the foremost experts in their fields, most of them Colombians (World Bank 1999). The study included three critical components: a conceptual framework, which identified a continuum of violence, including political, economic, and social violence; an assessment of the costs of violence in terms of its erosion of the country's capital and associated assets (especially its social capital); and a brief framework for a National Strategy for Peace and Development, comprising a national-level peace program, sector-level initiatives to integrate violence reduction into priority sectors, and municipal-level social capital projects.

Objectives and Research Framework of the Study

In studying violence, most journalists and research *violentólogos* (violence experts, a uniquely Colombian discipline) focus on political violence and armed conflict. The perceptions of violence by poor communities have received much less attention. To address this issue, this report provides the results of a recently completed study conducted in poor urban communities in Colombia. The study was undertaken as part of the third stage in the Bank's contribution to developing operational interventions for peace and development.

The objective of the study is to document violence in Colombia as perceived by poor urban communities in terms of the following four questions:

- *What categories of violence affect poor communities?* Is the political violence that dominates the newspapers and preoccupies politicians the only important source of concern for poor people, or are other types of violence also important? Building on the work of violence experts in Colombia and the World Bank Colombia Sector Study (World Bank 1998), the study distinguishes among political, economic, and social violence, identifying each in terms of a particular type of power that consciously or unconsciously uses violence to gain or maintain itself.
- *What are the costs of different types of violence?* What is the financial or psychological cost of violence to poor communities, households, and individuals in terms of the erosion of physical, human, natural, and social capital and their associated assets?

INTRODUCTION

- *Does violence erode or foster the creation of social capital?* Does "social capital for some imply social exclusion for others" (Harriss and De Renzio 1997; p. 926)? In fact social capital may lead to negative outcomes, and social capital itself may be created by activities that do not serve the public good. In examining this issue the study distinguishes between productive, or positive, social capital and unproductive, or perverse, social capital (Rubio 1997).
- *Is violence the cause or consequence of exclusion?* The complex relationship between violence and poverty has been widely debated. Social exclusion (the process through which individuals or groups are excluded from full participation in the society in which they live) may be a more useful concept than poverty for understanding violence, because it involves a more dynamic and multidimensional conceptualization of deprivation. The study thus seeks to identify the causal linkages between violence and exclusion.

In order to identify the relationships that produce and sustain violence in poor urban communities in Colombia and to begin to identify interventions to break this cycle, the study develops a violence–capital–exclusion nexus (figure 1.1). This analytical framework links different types of violence to both society's capital and the exclusion of its poor population.

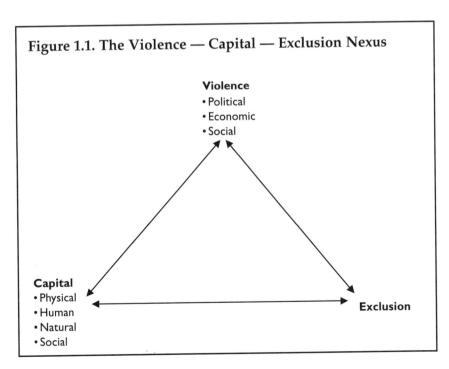

Figure 1.1. The Violence — Capital — Exclusion Nexus

The Participatory Methodology and Its Implications for Policy Recommendations

Like poverty, violence can be measured in different ways (see Baulch 1996 and Moser 1998). Both phenomena can be measured objectively using large, random sample household surveys that use measures of income or consumption as proxies for the variable being measured (Ravaillon 1992). Both can also be understood subjectively using participatory assessments that collect data on multiple indicators that emerge out of the complex and diverse local realities in which the poor live (Chambers 1992, 1995). The same is true of violence.

Extensive statistical and political analyses of Colombia violence exist (World Bank 1999). To complement those findings with the rarely heard voices of the poor, this study uses a participatory urban appraisal methodology. This approach emphasizes local knowledge and enables local people to make their own appraisals, analyses, and plans.[1] Its iterative approach to research is suitable for the investigation of the complex causal relationships that affect violence (Moser and McIlwaine 1999). The reliability of the findings is increased through triangulation—the use of a variety of techniques and sources to investigate the same issues and verify results. Qualitative research such as this study, which relies on indepth investigation of a small number of communities, also uses purposive rather than random sampling. This means selecting communities that are considered representative of the issue under investigation and conducting a participatory urban appraisal with sufficient groups to be representative of each community. (See annex A for a summary of participatory urban appraisal techniques.)

Participatory urban appraisal involves an extensive number of different tools (see annex A). The most important ones used in the current study are listings that provided the basis for the quantitative data analysis, causal impact diagrams that analyze the causes and effects of particular issues, and the institutional mapping diagrams that allow the identification of social institutions perceived as important within communities. All participatory urban appraisal tools are implemented in focus groups facilitated by two researchers and comprising between 2 and 20 people (occasionally they are conducted with one person).

The primary aim of participatory urban appraisal is to allow the people to express their own ideas and perceptions. Therefore, in the focus groups people are encouraged to design the diagrams and provide the associated text themselves. This process often is referred to as "handing over the stick" (in the urban Colombian context it usually involves pens and pencils). The rationale behind this methodology is the transfer of power from the researcher to the researched. Consequently, all the diagrams reproduced in this document were drawn by people in the communities themselves and use their language.[2]

The study describes community perceptions of the causes, costs, and consequences of violence and identifies local perceptions of potential solutions to the problems described. Whether perceptual data can legitimately be used to influence or define violence reduction policies or strategies is currently an issue of debate. The Bank's recently completed report "Global Synthesis: Consultations with the Poor" (Narayan and others 1999) and its endorsement by President James Wolfensohn in his 1999 annual meeting address has certainly given a measure of legitimacy to this approach in international agencies.

During the past decade several innovative interventions have been proposed to reduce violence (table 1.1). All of the approaches reflect different solutions, although in general there has been a shift away from the control of violence toward violence prevention and most recently to rebuilding social capital.

By presenting bottom-up solutions to violence, this study aims to contribute to the search for sustainable solutions. The solutions recommended are those that local communities themselves perceive as appropriate. The approach adopted here, therefore, is one of a number of approaches that can guide policymakers concerned with reducing violence.

Problems Associated with Using a Participatory Urban Appraisal to Study Violence

Determining perceptions of violence in communities deeply affected by violence is difficult for several reasons. First, the law of silence makes many people reluctant to discuss violence directly or indirectly. This unwillingness to speak out was most evident in communities affected by guerrilla and paramilitary activity that had experienced killings or threats to community members. To deal with the problem, the researchers made appointments to talk at safe times, when people were sure that the paramilitaries or guerillas were not present, and conducted focus groups in back rooms of houses rather than in the street.

Second, intrafamily violence is a highly sensitive issue. Young people were often more willing to discuss the issue than older people, and women were more likely to raise the issue than men. The problem of alcohol abuse, a major cause of domestic violence, was often used as a conduit to discuss violence in the home.

To ensure the safety of the people who participated in the study and to prevent retribution, the researchers changed the names of all study participants and communities.[3] To ensure the researchers' safety and help negotiate with gatekeepers, the research teams included people with guaranteed access to the communities.

Table 1.1. Policy Approaches to Violence Intervention

Approach	Objective	Type of violence addressed	Policy/planning intervention	Limitations
Criminal justice	Violence deterrence and control through increased arrest and conviction rates and harsher punishment	Economic	Top-down strengthening of judicial, penal, and police systems and associated institutions	Limited applicability to political and social violence; success highly dependent on enforcement
Public health	Violence prevention through the reduction of individual risk factors	Economic, social	Top-down surveillance; risk factor identification; resultant behavior modification; scaling up of successful interventions	Almost exclusive focus on individual; often imposed top down; highly sensitive to quality of surveillance data; limitations in indicators
Conflict transformation	Nonviolent resolution of conflict through negotiated terms between conflicting parties	Political, social	Negotiations to ensure conflict reduction between different social actors, often using third-party mediation. May be top down or bottom up.	Often long term in its impact; often faces challenges in bringing parties to the table and in mediating conflict
Human rights	Legal enforcement of human rights and documentation of abuses by states and other social actors	Political, social	Top-down legal enforcement reinforced by bottom-up popular participation and NGO lobbying	Legalistic framework often difficult to enforce in a context of lawlessness, corruption, and impunity; documentation of abuse sometimes dangerous
Social capital	Creation of social capital to reduce violence in both informal and formal social institutions, such as families, community organizations, and the judiciary	Political, economic, social	Bottom-up participatory appraisal of violence; institutional mapping to address problems; community participation in violence reduction measures	Less well-articulated than other approaches; fewer indicators developed

Description and Categorization of Communities Studied

Fieldwork was undertaken in nine predominantly low-income settlements or communities, located in seven cities and towns that are broadly representative of Colombia's urban areas (table 1.2). The communities reflect coverage of different geographical areas of the country as well as different types of violence.

The nine communities studied can be categorized into four main urban area types: the capital, large metropolitan areas with a long ties to the drug cartel, medium-size cities or small towns with large numbers of displaced people, and frontier towns located in areas rich in natural resources. In the capital, fieldwork was conducted in three communities: Embudo, Jericó, and 14 de Febrero. Embudo, a colonial settlement, is located in the central area of Santa Fe. Jericó and 14 de Febrero, both established in the 1970s and 1980s, are located in the southern part of Bogotá. Jericó was founded by three families who invaded a large hacienda and then illegally sold off subplots. The community of 14 de Febrero was established following land invasions by the Central Nacional Provivienda, a left-wing party linked to the Colombian Communist Party.

Two communities, Pórtico and El Arca, were selected in cities with ties to the drug cartel. Pórtico is located in Medellín, Columbia's second largest city. El Arca is located in Cali, the third largest city in Colombia. Both cities continue to be dominated by the drug cartel, despite the arrest and later assassination of Pablo Escobar of the Medellín cartel in 1993 and the capture of the Rodríguez Orejuela brothers and other leaders of the main Cali cartel in 1995.

Communities in medium-size cities or small towns included Amanecer and Rosario, both located in Bucaramanga. Amanecer is located within the city limits of the Santander departmental capital. Rosario is located within the jurisdiction of the town of Girón. Metropolitan Bucaramanga has a large number of displaced people, many of them from the Magdalena Medio region. In Rosario, a relatively new, unconsolidated settlement with high levels of squatting and cheap rental housing, displaced people represent more than half of the population.

Two frontier town communities were included in the study. Cachicamo is located in Yopal, the capital of the Department of Casanare. Colombia Chiquita is located in Aguazul. Both towns are located in the oil-producing region of the *Llanos*, which has been affected by the booms and busts associated with oil development. During the mid–1980s the oil boom brought significant economic activity to both communities, as international oil companies constructed facilities. Once the facilities were completed, the economies of both communities collapsed, as demand for labor fell dramatically.

Table 1.2. Descriptions of Urban Communities Studied

Characteristic	Embudo	14 de Febrero	Jericó	Pórtico	El Arca	Amanecer	Rosario	Cachicamo	Colombia Chiquita
Location	Bogotá	Bogotá	Bogotá	Medellín, Antioquia	Cali, Valle de Cauca	Bucaramanga, Santander	Girón, Santander	Yopal, Casanare	Aguazul, Casanare
Type of city	Large metropolitan area/capital city	Large metropolitan area/capital city	Large metropolitan area/capital city	Large metropolitan area with drug cartel history	Large metropolitan area with drug cartel history	Medium-size city with displaced populations	Small town with displaced populations	Frontier town in area rich in natural resources	Frontier town in area rich in natural resources
Socio-economic status	Poor	Poor	Poor	Poor	Poor	Poor	Poor	Poor and middle-income	Poor
Intracity location	Inner-city	Peri-urban	Peri-urban	Peri-urban	Peri-urban	Peri-urban	Peri-urban	Central urban	Peri-urban
Date of establishment	1596	1971	1980	1972	1980	1980	1991	1935	1994
Form of establishment	Colonial residential area	Invasion of private land by Central Nacional Provivienda	Invasion of private farmland and purchase of lots	Purchase of lots on private farmland	Invasion of private land by M-19 guerillas	Purchase of lots on private farmland	Invasion of unused public land	First settlement registered in municipality	Invasion of private farmland

Chapter Two
Summary Findings: Perceptions of General Problems and Violence

Rather than ask respondents specifically about violence, the participatory urban appraisal first focused on people's perceptions of the main problems affecting them and their community. Thus it did not assume that violence would necessarily be an important issue in people's daily lives.

Perceptions of Problems in Poor Urban Communities

Violence was the single most frequently cited problem facing the urban poor (table 2.1). Respondents identified 14 types of violence-related problems, with drugs leading the list. Drug consumption and its associated problems represented 21 percent of all violence problems (annex B, table 1).

Important differences exist in perceptions of violence across communities. In Pórtico, Medellín, the Peace and Conciliation Process of the

Table 2.1. Frequency Listings of Types of Problems Identified in Nine Urban Communities

Type of problem	Percentage of total problems cited
Violence-related	43
Lack of physical capital	28
Lack of social capital	14
Lack of human capital	12
Lack of natural capital	3
Total	100

Source: 159 focus group listings of general problems.

Metropolitan Area of Aburrá, initiated in 1994, reduced the perception of violence. In contrast, in Colombia Chiquita, Aguazul, where 14 people have been assassinated since 1998, the relatively low levels of reported perceptions of violence probably reflect community fear of retaliation.

The perception of drugs as a community problem reflected both the existence of drugs and differences in levels of tolerance of drug consumption. In Rosario, Girón, where tolerance of drug consumption is low, one-third of all violence problems were identified as drug related. In contrast, in Pórtico, Medellín, where drug consumption was widespread but tolerance levels were very high, only 5 percent problems identified were related to drug consumption.

Ranking of Perceived Problems in Poor Communities

Focus groups ranked problems according to their importance (box 2.1). These findings reinforced the frequency findings and revealed the interrelationship among different types of problems. In three communities (Embudo and 14 de Febrero, Bogotá; and Rosario, Girón), drug-related problems were perceived as most important. In another three communities (Pórtico, Medellín; Cachicamo, Yopal; and Colombia Chiquita, Aguazul), unemployment was the most significant problem. In El Arca, Cali, and Jericó, Bogotá, the most important problem cited was insecurity, a catchall term widely used. In Amanecer, Bucaramanga, the leading problem cited was robbery. Problems related to violence were thus identified as the most serious problem facing three of the nine communities. In communities identifying unemployment as the most significant problem, it was invariably linked with violence and insecurity.

Lack of Physical Capital

Lack of physical capital was the second most frequently cited general problem (see table 2.1). Within this category, unemployment problems were mentioned most frequently (annex C, table 1). Aggravated by the recent decline in national economic performance, the lack of employment opportunities was severely undermining the productive capacity of many communities. In El Arca, Cali, the decline in the drug cartel–linked construction industry following the recent capture of key drug traffickers increased unemployment to about 80 percent. In Colombia Chiquita, Aguazul, about 90 percent of the community were reportedly unemployed. The high rate of unemployment was associated with the completion of the exploration phase of the region's oil boom and the resulting decline in demand for construction workers. Recent legislation prohibiting the sale of goods from stalls on the streets was also perceived to have increased unemployment (see chapter 5).

SUMMARY FINDINGS 17

> **Box 2.1. Ranking of Problems in Pórtico, Medellín, Prepared by Mixed Group of Six Adults**
>
> The focus group listed 11 community problems and then prioritized them using an onion diagram. The most serious problems were placed in the center ring of the diagram, with those of lesser importance placed in the outer rings. The most serious problems identified were unemployment and lack of training; the least important problems were lack of parent-child education and lack of information about health services. Problems related to violence were placed in the third ring, although the group indicated that these problems were interrelated with unemployment and lack of unity.
>
>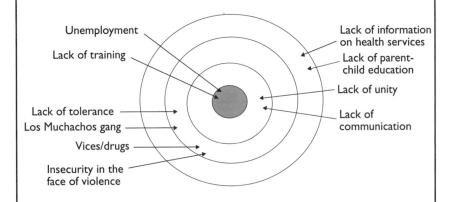
>
> *Note:* "Vices" refers primarily to drug use. It can also refer to alcohol and cigarette use. Throughout the document "mixed group" refers to a group mixed by sex.
> *Source:* Five women and one man, ages 20–45 years.

Even when job opportunities existed, people felt shunned by employers, who stereotyped urban poor communities as seedbeds of guerrilla activity, delinquency, prostitution, and drug consumption. Residents with academic qualifications found the stigma of living in a poor urban area difficult to overcome.

Lack of adequate public service provision, including water, electricity, sanitation, and garbage collection, was also a major preoccupation. While most communities had access to water and electricity, the cost and quality of service were problematic, with a number of households pirating electricity. Housing concerns often related to issues such as overcrowding and high rents charged by landlords.

Lack of Social Capital

Overall lack of social capital was identified as a slightly greater problem than lack of human capital (see table 2.1). Specific problems included lack of unity within the community; lack of trust in social institutions, particularly the police; and a sense of exclusion or discrimination by the *barrio* as a whole or by particular demographic groups. Young men, for example, often mentioned that the rest of the community dismissed their views ("no one takes us into account"). Middle-age and elderly people tended to complain about an increasing sense of isolation in their communities and a lack of communication. In figure 2.1, for instance, social

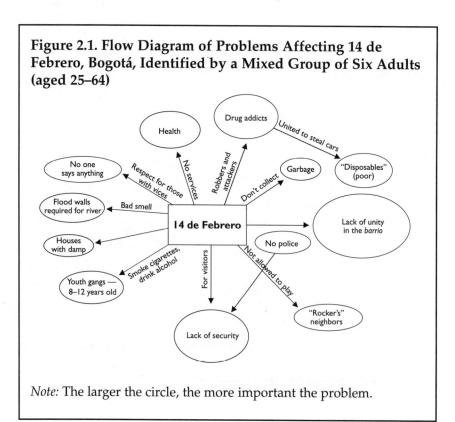

Figure 2.1. Flow Diagram of Problems Affecting 14 de Febrero, Bogotá, Identified by a Mixed Group of Six Adults (aged 25–64)

Note: The larger the circle, the more important the problem.

capital—identified as "lack of unity"—was perceived as the most important problem in 14 de Febrero, Bogotá.

Lack of Human Capital

Concerns over lack of human capital emerged frequently in all communities. Lack of sufficient primary-school places was seen as a particularly serious problem. Because of the current economic crisis, some middle class people are no longer able to afford to send their children to private school, something that was once the norm among the middle class. This increased pressure on the state system means that children from the poorest families often have fewer opportunities. In addition, many people complained about the lack of money to pay matriculation fees. In the case of health care services, complaints related to lack of services, increasing costs, and distances to health posts.

Lack of Natural Capital

The lack of natural capital was cited frequently only in the recently established settlements: Rosario, Girón and Colombia Chiquita, Aguazul. In both communities, the most commonly cited problem was that residents felt threatened by the adjacent river's lack of flood barriers.

Perceptions of Problems by Demographic Group

Perceptions of problems differed across different age and gender groups. Elderly women, for example, cited declining state public services provision, especially health care, as well as the decline in social capital, recalling with nostalgia the days when everyone knew one another and worked together for the good of the community.

Adult women focused on community problems rather than individual concerns. Community mothers (childcare providers employed by the Colombian Family Welfare Institute) frequently cited mistreatment of children, lack of adequate recreation for young people, and lack of community unity.

Teenage girls viewed community problems more from an individual perspective and were more likely than other groups to cite problems such as rape and harassment by men in the street. Teenage girls also cited intrafamily violence regularly. Girls under the age of 12 mentioned intrafamily violence, rape, and fear in the streets as well as problems in school, especially teacher violence and harassment from boys.

In contrast, elderly and adult men focused on employment and taxation. Less directly affected by violence in the community than other groups, they blamed community violence on young people, often describing young men as "full of vices" and young women as "street girls" (*ninas callajeras*).

Young men cited exclusion, unemployment, lack of educational and recreational opportunities, police harassment, and drugs as major issues. Teenage boys cited family discord, drugs, and violence at school. Children and young people were more likely than other groups to raise taboo subjects, including rape, intrafamily violence, and guerilla activity.

Significant differences emerged across socioeconomic lines. Although all the participatory urban appraisals were conducted in low-income communities, a number of the older settlements comprised sections with people of higher socioeconomic status. In Cachicamo, Yopal, for example, several focus groups were conducted with professionals and businesspeople. These groups tended to emphasize the effects of corruption, payment of bribes, and political violence on their businesses.

Perceptions of Violence in Poor Communities

Focus groups in the nine communities listed an average of 25 different types of violence, with one community (Embudo, Bogotá) distinguishing 60 different types of violence. Types of violence ranged from intrafamily violence to fights between rival gangs and local militias to robbery and assassination (table 2.2).

Types of Violence

Listings of violence were grouped together under three rubrics: political, economic, and social violence (World Bank 1999; table 2.3). Social violence was disaggregated into violence within the home, violence outside the home, and either (to categorize rape when it was not clear where it occurred). The types of violence represent a continuum of categories that overlap rather than being mutually exclusive. Drugs, for example, are categorized as economic violence, because drug consumers were perceived mainly as a problem linked to robbery to feed their habit. For drug consumers themselves, taking drugs was linked primarily with seeking an identity, conforming to youth culture, and succumbing to peer pressure, therefore making it a social violence issue.

Together economic and social violence were mentioned more frequently than political violence in all nine communities. Economic violence was most dominant, representing over half of all types of violence. Social violence accounted for about one-third of all violence, with political violence constituting 14 percent (tables 2.3 and 2.4).

Types of violence varied across communities. In Embudo, Bogotá, almost 60 percent of violence was identified as social, despite the fact that drugs (a form of economic violence) dominated the community. In Jericó, Bogotá, intrafamily violence was mentioned more often than in any other

Table 2.2. Types of Violence and Insecurity in El Arca, Cali, Identified by Mixed Group of Six Adults

Sphere of influence	Violence	Insecurity
Individual	Physical and verbal aggression	Fear
Household	Fights between husbands and wives Fights between grown-ups Killing wife and burying her in the yard	Bad neighbors Drug addicts Leaving children alone in the house Deficient housing construction
Interpersonal	Disharmony Armed fights among friends	Hypocrisy Lack of confidence or knowledge to talk to friends
Neighbor	Armed robbery Lack of conscience	Lack of telephone to call in case of emergency Bringing strangers to the *barrio* Dangerous friends Lack of unity
Community	Guerilla confrontations with civilian victims Army accusations of civilians being guerilla members	Naming people from outside the *barrio* as representatives Unknown neighbors Politicians
City	Youth gangs Satanic sects	Policies of Pastrana Government coup

Source: Three women and three men, ages 24–40.

community; in Amanecer, Bucaramanga, and Rosario, Girón, economic violence represented 70–80 percent of all references to violence.

In communities with a history of drug cartels, economic violence predominated, although political violence was also important. El Arca, Cali, for example, was established after members of the now demobilized guerilla group the Movimiento 19 de Abril (M–19) invaded the area. In both Cali and Medellín, levels of violence have escalated as guerilla groups (mainly the National Liberation Army, or ELN), militias, and informal protection forces and gangs have fought with one another within communities (see chapter 6).

Political violence was an important source of violence in Cachicamo, Yopal, and Colombia Chiquita, Aguazul. This violence was tied to the

Table 2.3. Types of Economic, Social, and Political Violence as Percentage of Total Violence in Each Community

Type of violence	Embudo, Bogotá	14 de Febrero, Bogotá	Jericó, Bogotá	Amanecer, Bucaramanga	Rosario, Girón	El Arca, Cali	Pórtico, Medellín	Cachicamo, Yopal	Colombia Chiquita, Aguazul	Total
Economic	31	57	54	71	83	60	51	52	28	54
Drugs	18	22	12	15	33	12	11	9	0	15
Insecurity	4	13	14	15	9	16	11	18	15	13
Robbery	9	17	15	28	15	25	7	16	8	15
Loitering	0	3	3	9	25	0	2	2	3	5
Gangs[a]	0	2	10	3	0	7	18	2	2	5
Prostitution	0	0	0	1	1	0	2	5	0	1
Social	58	40	42	27	16	23	40	18	25	32
Inside the home	11	10	16	6	11	13	5	7	8	10
Intrafamily violence	11	10	16	6	11	13	5	7	8	10
Outside the home	32	28	22	15	1	10	33	11	10	18
Fights	23	20	10	8	1	4	13	4	5	10
Deaths	8	2	2	3	0	0	20	5	0	4
Alcoholism	0	6	4	3	0	5	0	2	2	2
Encapuchados (hooded men)	0	0	0	0	0	1	0	0	0	1
Other[b]	1	0	6	1	0	0	0	0	3	1

Table 2.3. cont.

Type of violence	Embudo, Bogotá	14 de Febrero, Bogotá	Jericó, Bogotá	Amanecer, Bucaramanga	Rosario, Girón	El Arca, Cali	Pórtico, Medellín	Cachicamo, Yopal	Chiquita, Aguazul	Colombia Total
Outside or inside the home	15	2	4	6	4	0	2	0	7	4
Rape	15	2	4	6	4	0	2	0	7	4
Political	11	3	4	2	1	17	9	30	47	14
Police abuses	11	3	2	1	0	8	7	0	2	4
Guerrilla activity	20	0	2	0	0	1	0	2	0	1
War	0	0	0	0	0	1	0	26	0	3
Paramilitary activity	0	0	0	0	0	0	0	2	22	2
Assassination	0	0	0	0	0	1	0	0	18	2
Activity by private security forces	0	0	0	0	0	7	0	0	0	1
Extortion	0	0	0	0	0	0	2	0	0	0
Threats	0	0	0	1	0	0	0	0	0	0
Violence by displaced people	0	0	0	0	0	0	0	0	5	1
Total	100	100	100	100	100	100	100	100	100	100

a. Gangs were classified as an economic form of violence because of the close nexus with theft.
b. Includes *machismo*, discrimination, and mistreatment of children in the street.

Source: 104 focus group listings of types of violence.

Table 2.4. Types of Violence Identified in Nine Urban Communities

Type of violence	Percentage of types of violence identified
Economic	54
Drugs	14
Insecurity	13
Robbery	15
Other	12
Social	32
Inside the home	10
Outside the home	18
Inside/outside the home	4
Political	14
Police abuse	4
War	3
Paramilitary activities	2
Assassination	2
Other	3
Total	100

large guerilla and paramilitary presence associated with the oil boom. Initially, these organizations competed for territory and power; with the collapse of the oil sector they turned to economic extortion and corruption, terrorizing the local population. In Colombia Chiquita, residents were assassinated by paramilitary groups. In Cachicamo the main concern was "war" in general.

Ranking Types of Violence

Focus groups identified the most serious types of violence in their communities. In the seven communities where violence was prioritized, drug-related violence was most important in Embudo and 14 de Febrero, Bogotá, and in Rosario, Girón. In Jericó, Bogotá, intrafamily violence was considered most significant (box 2.2), while in Pórtico, Medellín, killing was viewed as the most serious problem. In El Arca, Cali, mistreatment of children and robbery were identified as particularly severe.

Perceptions of violence also varied by gender and age. Elderly women and men tended to be concerned mainly with insecurity and drugs. Elderly men discussed how young women were involved in violence and drug use, something that represented a new phenomenon for them.

SUMMARY FINDINGS 25

> **Box 2.2. Types of Violence in Jericó, Bogotá, Ranked by a Group of Four 11-Year-Old Girls**
>
> A group of 11-year-old school girls listed the main types of violence affecting their community and ranked each (4 = most serious problem, 3 = next most serious, 2 = third most serious problem). They unanimously identified drug-related violence as the most serious problem, with marijuana, *bazuco* (a form of cocaine), cocaine, and Boxer (a type of glue) the most common drugs used. Three of the four girls had experienced pressure from their friends to take drugs, with one girl noting that a girlfriend said sniffing Boxer was "like being on the moon." Trying drugs was a sign of bravery; refusal meant being called *pollo* (chicken) or *bobo* (fool). The girls were also concerned about rape. They felt most threatened by men they knew (friends, boyfriends, and male relatives).
>
> | *Listing of type of violence* | *Score* | *Prioritization* |
> |---|---|---|
> | Rape | 13 | Drugs |
> | Robbery | 4 | Rape |
> | Fights among gangs | 4 | Robbery |
> | Verbal aggression | 2 | Fights among gangs |
> | Drugs | 16 | Verbal aggression |
> | Family arguments | — | |

Adult women (especially among the community mothers) focused on violence against children and insecurity. In contrast, adult men discussed political violence, as well as violence among young people, especially drug-related violence and delinquency.

Young people were especially concerned with the drug problem. Young men also mentioned gang and militia violence, with most being aware of the illegal and informal organizations operating in their *barrios*. Young women also discussed these themes, but they tended to be more concerned about rape outside the home.

Children's perceptions were elicited not only from group discussions but also from drawings (figure 2.2). Of a total of 244 drawings created in response to the question "What are you afraid of?" almost half (115) dealt with violence with two-thirds of the drawings associating fear with guns. In 80 percent of the drawings, men were depicted as perpetrators of violence. Most of the violence depicted took place outside the home, usually in the streets (82 percent of cases). Several children also depicted

Figure 2.2. Drawing of "What Are You Afraid Of" by 13-year-Old Girl in El Arca, Cali

Note: *Peleas* = fights; *violaciones* = rapes; *borrachos* = drunks; *maltrato* = mistreatment; *pandillas* = gangs.

intrafamily violence, although many were reluctant to do so. In 14 de Febrero, for example, two young boys (ages 7 and 8) refused to draw what they were afraid of. Eventually they admitted that they were afraid of their fathers, who beat them regularly. Drawings of both types of violence invariably showed victims, usually women or children, in tears. Drawings of drugs usually depicted men inhaling cocaine or *bazuco* or smoking marijuana on street corners in the evenings.

Perceptions of the Spatial Nature of Violence

The incidence of violence varied across types of communities (table 2.5). Drug-related violence, insecurity, and robbery were important in all areas. Intrafamily violence was especially important in Bogotá. In the

Table 2.5. Variations in Types of Violence

Urban category/community	Predominant types of violence

Large metropolitan area/ capital city
  Embudo, Bogotá
  14 de Febrero, Bogotá
  Jericó, Bogotá
	Economic and social (drug-related violence, insecurity and robbery, intrafamily violence)

Large metropolitan area with drug cartel history
  El Arca, Cali
  Pórtico, Medellín
	Economic, social, and political (drug-related violence, insecurity and robbery, gang violence)

Intermediate cities and small towns with high levels of displaced populations
  Amanecer, Bucaramanga
  Rosario, Girón
	Economic and social (drug-related violence, insecurity and robbery, loitering)

Frontier towns in natural resource rich areas
  Cachicamo, Yopal
  Colombia Chiquita, Aguazul
	Economic and political (insecurity and robbery, war, paramilitary violence, assassinations)

large metropolitan areas with histories of drug cartel activity, gang violence was especially marked. The effects of political violence in the countryside were experienced in the intermediate towns and cities through displaced populations. Loitering among young people was also perceived as an important problem. In frontier towns rich in natural resources, political violence—including war, paramilitary violence, and assassinations—was most marked.

Political violence by guerilla and paramilitary organizations dominated the area around Aguazul, (shown in figure 2.3 as the city) and the outlying *barrio* of Colombia Chiquita itself. The community was surrounded by guerilla and paramilitary groups, both in the highland area (known as the Piedemonte) and the lowlands (known as the Llanos).

People living in peri-urban communities located on the outskirts of large urban areas often felt ostracized by the city itself due to the "area stigma" associated with perceptions of high concentrations of violence (see chapter 5). In Bucaramanga the city center is located on a plateau, while the community of Amanecer is situated in a lowland area around the city. A 19-year-old woman from Amanecer who had also lived in the city center noted that Amanecer was primarily associated with crime and

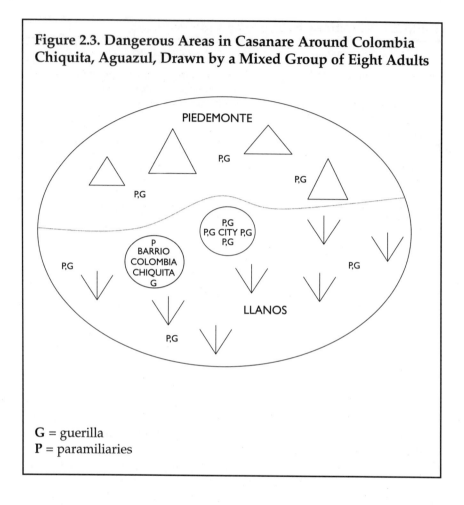

Figure 2.3. Dangerous Areas in Casanare Around Colombia Chiquita, Aguazul, Drawn by a Mixed Group of Eight Adults

G = guerilla
P = paramiliaries

"people who make you afraid." She assumed that it was better to live in the city center.

At the community level, the dangerous areas most commonly cited included street corners, basketball courts, parks, and river banks—all places where drug addicts, sellers, or gangs congregated. In most communities, girls and women feared river banks because of the danger of rape in these secluded locations (see chapter 4).

In El Arca, Cali, residents felt unsafe in most of the *barrio* (figure 2.4). While some areas were dangerous only at night, most were also dangerous during the day. Most places, such as the basketball court, were dangerous for both men and women. Places where drugs were sold and gangs met were perceived as unsafe only for women. Ironically, the police

SUMMARY FINDINGS

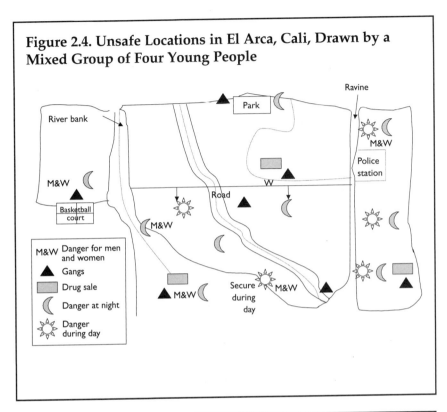

Figure 2.4. Unsafe Locations in El Arca, Cali, Drawn by a Mixed Group of Four Young People

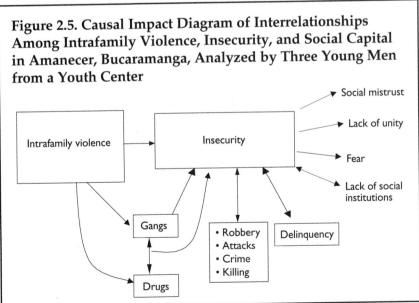

Figure 2.5. Causal Impact Diagram of Interrelationships Among Intrafamily Violence, Insecurity, and Social Capital in Amanecer, Bucaramanga, Analyzed by Three Young Men from a Youth Center

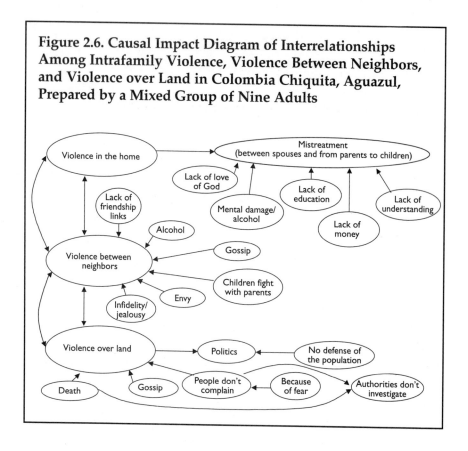

Figure 2.6. Causal Impact Diagram of Interrelationships Among Intrafamily Violence, Violence Between Neighbors, and Violence over Land in Colombia Chiquita, Aguazul, Prepared by a Mixed Group of Nine Adults

station was also perceived as unsafe, reflecting negative attitudes toward the police (see chapter 6).

Interrelationships among Different Types of Violence

Different types of violence are interrelated in a highly complex dynamic manner. In Amanecer, Bucaramanga, intrafamily violence (the primary cause of insecurity) leads family members, especially young people, to take drugs and join gangs (figure 2.5). Drugs and gangs in turn lead to economic violence outside the home, including robbery, attacks, and killing. This ultimately leads to other negative outcomes, including erosion of social capital (social mistrust, lack of unity, fear, and lack of social institutions). In Colombia Chiquita, Aguazul, political violence leads to both social violence between neighbors and intrahousehold violence (figure 2.6).

Chapter Three
Social Violence in the Family and Household

Throughout the communities studied, young and old alike agreed that violence begins in the home. A young boy in 14 De Febrero, Bogotá, noted, "Violence begins in the home. It is one of the most important factors in the [lack of] harmony of the community. It brings about lack of respect in everyone." All communities identified intrafamily violence as a daily occurrence, and all perceived it to be linked to violence in the community.

Because of the "law of silence," however, the frequency with which intrahousehold violence was reported was low (10 percent for the sample as a whole).[4] The topic emerged much more forcefully in focus group, discussions with children, adolescents, and adult women (adult men rarely raised the issue). In El Arca, Cali, a group of community mothers estimated that at least one in three children in the community was mistreated at home. In Cachicamo, Yopal, teachers estimated that intrafamily violence affected 70 percent of the community.

The Nature and Scope of Intrahousehold or Intrafamily Violence

Urban residents identified some 20 different types of intrahousehold violence (box 3.1). Three types of intrafamily violence emerged as most important: violence between spouses, violence against children, and sexual abuse of children.

Violence between Spouses
Violence between spouses was widespread, with husbands more likely than wives to be the perpetrators. Violence, ranging from verbal and physical aggression to murder, occurs on a daily basis in most communities. As a 25-year-old woman from Amanecer, Bucaramanga, noted, "Here it is an everyday thing that husbands beat their wives. Some have been wounded with knives and bottles."

> **Box 3.1. Types of Intrafamily Violence Identified by Urban Residents in Nine Communities**
>
> - Mistreatment of children
> - Physical violence between spouses
> - Verbal violence between spouses
> - Husband killing wife and burying her in the yard
> - Hitting children hard and making them bleed
> - Aggression against children by parents
> - Children hitting parents
> - Mistreatment of the elderly
> - Fighting
> - Violence of husbands towards mothers-in-law
> - Rape of girls by fathers
> - Rape of girls by renters
> - Rape of girls by stepfathers
> - Rape of girls by fathers under the influence of *bazuco*
> - Children having sexual relations with their mothers when they take *bazuco*
> - Mothers raping sons under the influence of drugs
> - Fights between siblings
> - Abandonment of children
> - Physical and emotional trauma
>
> *Source:* 159 focus group listings of general problems and 104 listings of violence.

Violence against Children

Violence against children includes beating, usually by fathers but also by mothers. Miguel, a 10-year-old boy from 14 de Febrero, Bogotá, acknowledged that he was afraid to go home because his father beat him with wooden sticks and a leather cattle whip, particularly when inebriated. Although his mother did not hit him, she did nothing to stop the father's abuse. "I think my mother loves me, but not my father," said the boy, capturing a frequently repeated theme.

Sexual Abuse of Children

Sexual abuse of children, including incest within the home, was cited frequently in focus groups. The most severe abuse was identified in

Box 3.2. Perpetrators of Rape in 14 de Febrero, Bogotá, Identified by a Group of Six Community Mothers

A group of community mothers in 14 de Febrero, Bogotá, identified rape by tenants as the most important problem affecting the children they looked after. According to them, tenants were more likely than relatives, stepfathers, or others to rape children.

Listing	Ranking by votes
Family (father, uncle, relative)	18
Step-father	12
Renter	21
Delinquent	8

Embudo, Bogotá, where it was associated with high levels of drug consumption. Fathers and mothers were identified as raping daughters and sons when under the influence of *bazuco*. Rape of girls by male relatives was mentioned in most communities. A community mother in 14 de Febrero, Bogotá, noted, "One hears a lot about the rights of children, but there is one rape a day of children."

Sexual abuse of children by tenants or lodgers was especially acute in communities with high levels of renting (box 3.2). Thus while housing can be used as a productive asset with which to generate income, the effect on children can be harmful.

Factors Affecting the Level of Intrafamily Violence

Intrafamily violence is considered a permanent feature of life in the communities studied. As a local leader from 14 de Febrero, Bogotá, noted, "Mistreatment within the family has existed since Adam and Eve, and still we have this illness." The level of intrafamily violence appears to be affected by various factors, including changes in the economy and the rate of unemployment, alcohol (and to a lesser extent drug) use, *machismo* among men and submissiveness among women, and the intergenerational transfer of abuse within the home.

Changes in the Economy and the Rate of Unemployment

Residents of all nine communities perceived that intrafamily violence had intensified since the mid–1980s, partly as a result of a decline in the economy and an increase in unemployment. In 14 de Febrero, Bogotá, for example, intrafamily violence has risen since 1985, when unemployment became a problem (figure 3.1). In El Arca, Cali, where male unemployment has increased since 1991, men have spent more time at home and taken out their frustration by abusing their children. Yet in Cachicamo, Yopal, the boom in employment opportunities that began in 1985 also increased intrahousehold violence. People migrated to Yopal to work for the oil companies, often earning good salaries. The combination of money, drugs, prostitutes, and fighting resulted in increases in intrahousehold violence.

Alcohol and Drug Consumption

Alcohol—and to a lesser extent drug use—was identified as a critically important determinant of intrafamily violence. Celebrations and festivals at which large amounts of alcohol are consumed often resulted in violence. A focus group in Amanecer, Bucaramanga, identified the worst periods of the year as Mother's Day in May, the festival of the "Day of Love and Friendship" in September, and Christmas—all occasions of family gatherings. Violence within the home also tended to increase on weekends, when alcohol consumption was greatest.

Machismo *among Men and Submissiveness among Women*

Gender-based violence was caused both by *machismo* among men and submissiveness among women—referring to the manner in which women put up with continual violence or abuse from husbands. Three community mothers from El Arca, Cali, linked *machismo* and female submissiveness to the role of stepfathers, who often created discord within the home and committed both physical and sexual abuse. With the arrival of new father figures in the home, new rules were laid down for children, which mothers rarely opposed. As a consequence, children invariably felt rejected.

Intergenerational Transfer of Abuse

A common perception was that adults who were abused as children abused their own children. In Embudo, Bogotá, a 43-year-old male community leader referred to sexual abuse or rape as "hereditary rape," stating, "He who was raped gets converted into a rapist." Rape was also closely associated with drug use.

Other Types of Violence

In communities affected by high levels of political violence, assassination of family members can lead to family disintegration and conflict. In Colombia Chiquita, Aguazul, a focus group identified how political violence undermines the institution of the family. Family members of two

SOCIAL VIOLENCE IN THE FAMILY AND HOUSEHOLD

Figure 3.1. Time Lines Showing Changes in Intrafamily Violence, 1970–1999, Prepared by Three Groups of Adults in 14 de Febrero, Bogotá, El Arca, Cali, and Cachicamo, Yopal

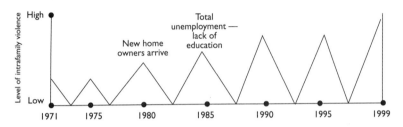

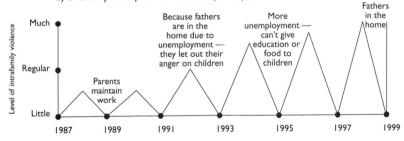

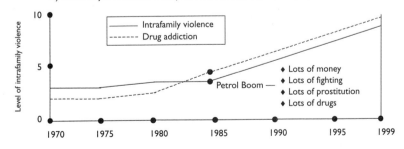

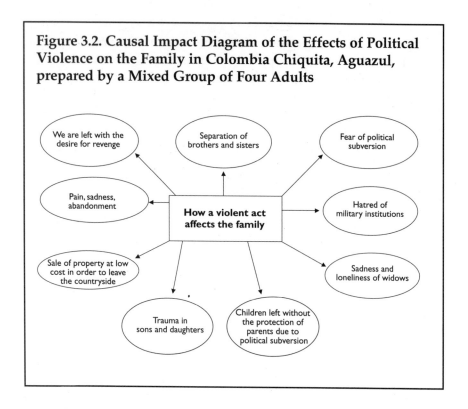

Figure 3.2. Causal Impact Diagram of the Effects of Political Violence on the Family in Colombia Chiquita, Aguazul, prepared by a Mixed Group of Four Adults

women whose brother had been killed by the guerillas or paramilitary had joined the army and the paramilitaries in search of revenge. The two women noted that their families were torn apart by the assassinations in their families. Both women felt hate and fear of all armed groups and worried about their own safety and that of their children. Their emotions caused intense conflict within their households, sometimes erupting in violence (figure 3.2).

Consequences of Intrafamily Violence

Intrafamily violence has several serious consequences. It erodes the social capital endowments of households, increases the level of violence outside the home, and erodes the human capital of young people.

Erosion of Social Capital Endowments within Households

Intrafamily violence undermines the way households function internally in terms of creating norms, values, and trust (social capital). Family disintegration, in turn, increases the level of violence within the home.

SOCIAL VIOLENCE IN THE FAMILY AND HOUSEHOLD

Family relations provide a primary source of cognitive social capital (that is, values, norms, attitudes, and beliefs). Family disintegration thus severely erodes social capital endowments. In Colombia Chiquita, Aguazul, for instance, one group identified "lack of family communication" as the key problem in their community and showed how lack of family communication appears to both generate violence and exacerbate disintegration of the home (figure 3.3).

Erosion of Social Capital

In discussing strategies to cope with intrafamily violence, people noted that their response was often to remain silent or not get involved because of the problems that result when people try to help. Two women from 14 de Febrero, Bogotá, noted that intervening in domestic arguments generated fights among neighbors: "Fights between neighbors arise because one gets involved so that the mother is not hit, or so that the mother doesn't massacre her children. Then one is treated like someone who interferes." They reported that they were actively excluded and stigmatized by neighbors when they tried to stop the abuse.

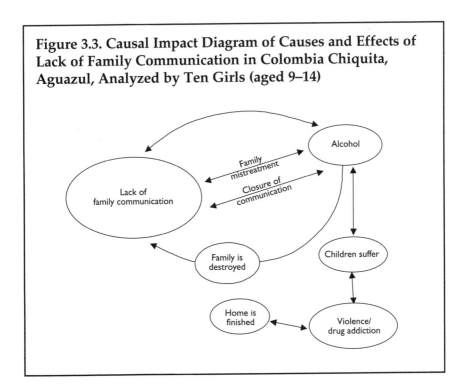

Figure 3.3. Causal Impact Diagram of Causes and Effects of Lack of Family Communication in Colombia Chiquita, Aguazul, Analyzed by Ten Girls (aged 9–14)

Increase in Intrafamily Violence outside the Home

Violence that occurs within the home can lead to violence in the public sphere. According to the urban poor, violence permeates the entire spectrum of social relations within their communities, the critical nexus being households and families. In Jericó, Bogotá, a group of women drew a problem tree through which they noted that a major consequence of intrahousehold violence was "total violence—war," which would create a "country without future." According to them, violence would lead to

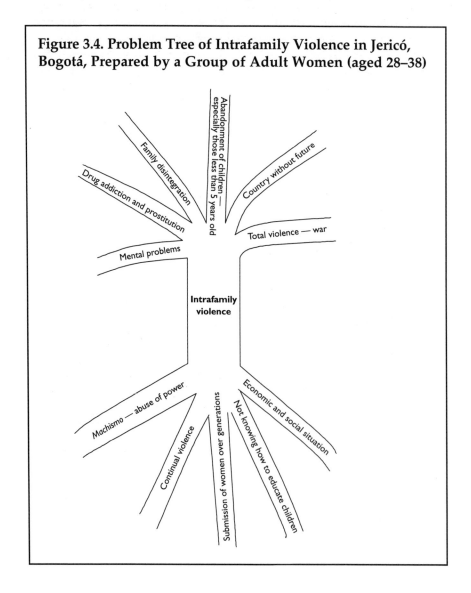

Figure 3.4. Problem Tree of Intrafamily Violence in Jericó, Bogotá, Prepared by a Group of Adult Women (aged 28–38)

further family disintegration, drug addiction, prostitution, mental problems, and the abandonment of children (figure 3.4).

Children and young people experiencing violence in the home—either as victims or as witnesses to violence between their parents—often join gangs and become involved in drug-related crime and violence. With trust in the home environment severely eroded, children spend long periods of time with their friends in the street.

A focus group in Colombia Chiquita, Aguazul, revealed how violence against children, coupled with parental abandonment, had far-reaching effects on children in later life. According to the group, violence toward children can lead to such extreme responses as children killing their stepfathers, children becoming thieves and living on the streets, and children killing people outside the family (figure 3.5).

Several focus groups discussed how violence within the home also leads young women "to the streets." While some young women joined

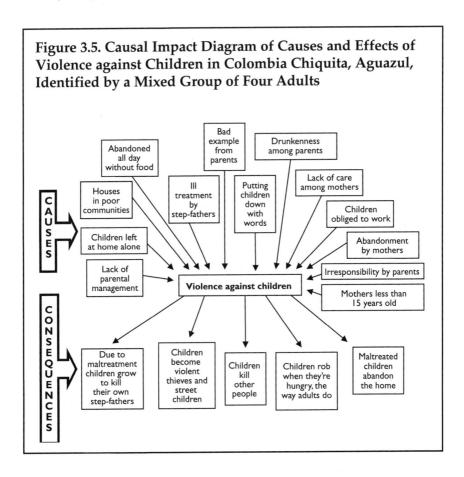

Figure 3.5. Causal Impact Diagram of Causes and Effects of Violence against Children in Colombia Chiquita, Aguazul, Identified by a Mixed Group of Four Adults

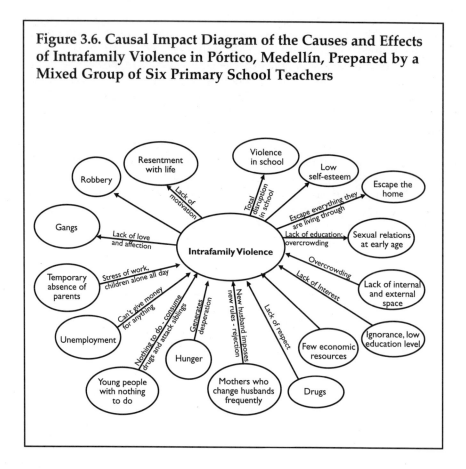

Figure 3.6. Causal Impact Diagram of the Causes and Effects of Intrafamily Violence in Pórtico, Medellín, Prepared by a Mixed Group of Six Primary School Teachers

gangs and used drugs, the more usual pattern was for them to engage in sexual relations at an early age, often resulting in pregnancy. In all of the communities it was common for 14- to 15-year-old women to be mothers.

In Rosario, Girón, a focus group of young women noted how some "street girls" (*muchachas vagas*) took drugs and participated in male-dominated gangs as a result of violent experiences or parental conflict. Drug use and gang membership were seen as having led these girls into early sexual activity, often resulting in pregnancy. In some cases, it was noted that they became prostitutes as well.

Erosion of Human Capital of Children and Young People
Violence in the home influences the behavior of children and young people, which in turn affects their educational attainment and acquisition of skills. Intrafamily violence thus erodes human capital of future generations, something teachers in the community emphasized. A group of 37

> **Box 3.3. The Effects of Intrafamily Violence Identified by Primary School Teachers**
>
> **Seven primary school teachers in 14 de Febrero, Bogotá**
> - Lack of discipline
> - Bad vocabulary
> - Aggression with other pupils
> - Introverted children
> - Low academic achievement
> - Sexual abuse of girls
> - Unhelpful attitude
> - School desertion
>
> **30 primary school teachers in Pórtico, Medellín**
> - Low self-esteem
> - Emotional instability
> - Verbal and physical aggression
> - Lack of respect
> - Aggressive games
> - Antisocial behavior
> - Loneliness
> - Absenteeism
> - Low academic achievement
> - Lack of conflict resolution
> - Abandonment of the home
> - Disarticulation within the community

teachers from 14 de Febrero, Bogotá, and Pórtico, Medellín, identified 13 problems affecting the community, including aggression in the class room, low educational attainment, antisocial behavior, and absenteeism or dropping out of school altogether (box 3.3). According to these teachers, sexual abuse and rape are the most important factors affecting young people's human capital. Dropping out of school was a common outcome of intrafamily violence among children. Low educational attainments and limited employment opportunities meant that many young people turned to gangs, drugs, or, in the case of young women, to early sexual activity (figure 3.6).

Chapter Four
Economic Violence and Drug Consumption

Drug-related problems were a major concern in most of the communities studied, with drugs linked to 21 percent of all violence-related problems. The importance of drugs varied across communities. In Rosario, Girón, for example, drugs were perceived to be related to one-third of violence problems. In contrast, in Colombia Chiquita, Aguazul, drugs were not perceived to affect the community at all (table 4.1). Alcohol-related problems were perceived as significant in only five of the nine communities, representing an average of 2 percent of all violence-related problems (see annex B, table B-1). Although alcohol was a causal factor in other types of violence, especially of intrafamily violence, community members did not perceive it as significant in itself.

Table 4.1. Drug-Related Violence as Proportion of All Violence-Related Problems (percent)

Community	Violence-related problems as a percent of all problems	Drug-related violence as a percent of all violence-related problems
Embudo, Bogotá	58	27
14 de Febrero, Bogotá	63	28
Jericó, Bogotá	49	13
Amanecer, Bucaramanga	52	20
Rosario, Girón	35	33
El Arca, Cali	41	22
Pórtico, Medellín	21	23
Cachicamo, Yopal	34	10
Colombia Chiquita, Aguazul	23	0
Total	43	23

Source: 159 focus group listings of general problems.

Drugs represented 15 percent of all types of violence across the nine communities, with Rosario, Girón, and 14 de Febrero, Bogotá, the most affected. The figure understates the actual extent of drug-related violence, however. In Embudo, Bogotá, for example, where drug use is widespread, fights made up 5 percent of the violence-related incidents cited. Many of these fights were related to drug consumption and sale.

Types of Drug-Related Problems

People in the communities identified 24 types of problems related to drugs (box 4.1). These problems ranged from the presence of drug

---

Box 4.1. Types of Drug-Related Problems Identified in Nine Communities

- Presence of drug addicts, including female addicts
- Presence of *viciosos* (people with vices, usually referring to drugs)
- Robbing for drugs
- Killing for drugs
- Drug use among children
- Parents forcing their children to obtain drugs
- Fathers under the influence of *bazuco* raping their daughters
- Children under the influence of *bazuco* having sexual relations with their mothers
- Mothers under the influence of drugs raping their sons
- Violence by women anxious to get drugs
- Drug addicts making others leave the basketball court
- Drug addicts mistreating people in the community
- Sex offered in exchange for drugs
- Husbands killing wives who don't give them money for drugs
- Police belief that everyone is a drug addict and/or *desechable* (disposable)
- Young women forced to smoke drugs against their will
- Smoking and sale of drugs
- Drug trafficking
- Youth under the influence of marijuana
- Many people using marijuana
- Easy access to drugs
- Death from drugs

Source: 159 focus group listings of general problems.

addicts to murder. The most common problem identified was "there are lots of drug addicts" or "lots of people with vices," a term in Colombia that refers to drugs. In all communities with high levels of drug use the most commonly cited consequence was robbery. In Rosario, Girón, a 13-year-old girl noted, "The people who take marijuana rob, they rob from houses." Drugs were also associated with other types of violence, including intrafamily and sexual violence. Young women frequently blamed drug addicts for rapes in their *barrio*, both in the street and at home.

Drug consumption was also linked to death. Some people killed to obtain drugs or while under the influence of drugs; others were killed by the physiological or psychological effects of drug use. In Embudo, Bogotá, a male addict noted, "We were all born to die." A focus group of drug addicts—a man and woman who had just been released from prison and two other men who robbed to feed their drug habits—described the inevitability and acceptance of death (figure 4.1).

Drug consumption in most communities was a relatively new phenomenon. While community members noted that alcohol consumption had negatively affected their *barrios* for as long as they could remember, drug consumption began mainly in the 1980s, with marked increases in the 1990s. Alcohol was associated with intrafamily violence; drugs were closely linked with insecurity. Drug use had become more widespread over time. A timeline drawn in 14 de Febrero, Bogotá, showed how in the past insecurity was linked with police harassment in the neighborhood

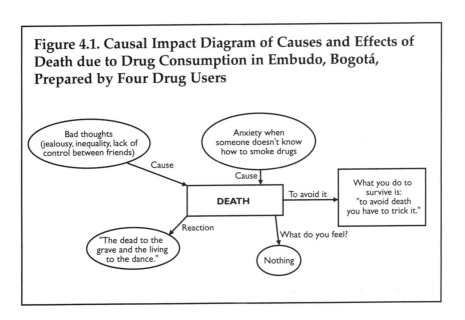

Figure 4.1. Causal Impact Diagram of Causes and Effects of Death due to Drug Consumption in Embudo, Bogotá, Prepared by Four Drug Users

and a policy of "social cleansing." But since 1990 there has been an increase in the perception of insecurity as a result of the increased levels of drug consumption (figure 4.2). Before 1990 drugs tended to be consumed in the home or "hidden from view," while in the past few years the number of "open" drug users (using drugs in public view), has increased considerably.

Attitudes toward drug traffickers were mixed. In Embudo, Bogotá, it was noted that the sale of drugs decreased following the death of Pablo Escobar. In both Medellín and Cali, however, the drug cartels were often seen in a very positive light. Pórtico, Medellín, for example, benefited from a basketball court built with money donated by Pablo Escobar. The period during which the Medellín cartel was most active (the early 1980s) was viewed favorably because of its economic benefits. As one man in the community pointed out, "When the drug traffickers left, the situation became very difficult. Everyone was left worse off." In Cali the economic fortunes of the El Arca community declined with the capture of Los Rodriguez of the Cali cartel. As one community leader stated, "The drug traffickers helped us to a certain extent. They produced an increase in employment and allowed the people to build their own homes."

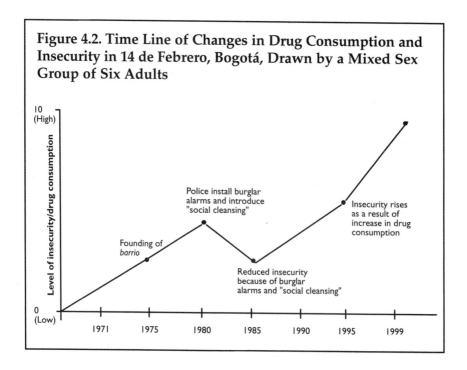

Figure 4.2. Time Line of Changes in Drug Consumption and Insecurity in 14 de Febrero, Bogotá, Drawn by a Mixed Sex Group of Six Adults

Types of Drugs Available and Tolerance Levels

A variety of drugs was available in low-income communities (box 4.2). Marijuana was most commonly mentioned, followed by *bazuco* and *perico/a*, both forms of crack cocaine that are usually smoked rather than injected.

Drug consumption is so common in poor urban communities in Colombia that many young people immediately identified themselves in terms of whether or not they consumed drugs. Those who did not consume drugs called themselves *sanos* (healthy) or *zanahórios* (healthy). Drug users were referred to by nonusers as *drogadictos* (drug addicts), *viciosos* (people with vices), *marihuaneros* (marijuana smokers), *colinos*, or *sopladores* (drug addicts). Estimates of drug use varied widely across communities (table 4.2).

In 14 de Febrero, Bogotá, where tolerance of drug use is moderate, residents were resigned to the fact that 40–50 percent of their community used drugs. A group of seven community leaders (six women and one

---

Box 4.2. Types of Drugs Available

- Cocaine
- Marijuana
- *Marimba* (type of marijuana)
- *Perico/a* (type of cocaine)
- *Bazuco* (type of cocaine sometimes mixed with ground brick or broken glass)
- Crack
- *Pepas* (generic name for tablets, usually uppers)
- *Piola* (tablets, usually uppers)
- *Ruedas* (tablets for epilepsy)
- *Roche* (tablets for epilepsy)
- *Exstasis* (Ecstasy)
- Boxer (type of glue)
- Antiseptic alcohol (mixed with Coca-Cola-or other soft drink—known as *chamberlai*)
- Gasoline
- *Tiner* (paint thinner)
- *Escama de pezcado* (cocaine-based fish flakes)
- *Bicha* (joint of marijuana)

Source: Focus groups in nine communities.

man) estimated that there were 500 users of whom only 50 used drugs openly. The remaining users, known as "closed" users, were usually adults, who consumed drugs in their homes. The "open" users were often also drug distributors for the "closed" users. Drug addicts from the community estimated that there were 30–40 hard-core users and 100 young people who took drugs on a less regular basis, getting the regular users to buy drugs for them.

In Pórtico, Medellín, where the level of tolerance and visibility of drug use was highest, 60 percent of the population was estimated to smoke marijuana. This marijuana use was viewed as a hobby, and a way to "relax, sleep, pass the time, and keep your mind elsewhere." One young man stated that everyone took drugs—children as young as 8 or 10, boyfriends and girlfriends, and parents and relatives. Although consumption of marijuana was high, *bazuco* was rarely consumed, because it was associated with the "war" from which the city is just emerging.

Table 4.2. Tolerance and Visibility of Drug Consumption in Four Communities, Identified by Focus Groups

Community	Level of tolerance	Percentage of population consuming drugs/ age range of users	Visibility	Main type of drug
14 de Febrero, Bogotá	Moderate	40–50 percent/ young people	Visible among young people, hidden among adults	Marijuana and *bazuco* among young people, marijuana and cocaine among adults
Pórtico, Medellín	High	60 percent/ young people and adults	Visible	Cocaine, marijuana and *roches*
Cachicamo, Yopal	Very low	Floating population of 3–4/ young people	Visible	Marijuana and *bazuco*
Rosario, Girón	Very low	5 percent/ young people	Visible	Marijuana and *bazuco*

Source: Various focus groups in nine communities.

Characteristics of Drug Consumers

Young people, primarily young men, were reported to make up the bulk of drug consumers, with women representing about a third of consumers in those communities in which estimates were obtained (see table 4.2). Most users were identified as young, with the majority between 15 and 30 (table 4.3). All communities noted that parents often used drugs. Children as young as 8 also reportedly used drugs, with different drugs taken at different ages. Children began with marijuana at the age of 8, moving on to gasoline and glue at the age of 12. The use of *bazuco* came at the age of 14, with *perico*, the most expensive drug, used later.

There were marked generational differences between drug and alcohol consumers. According to a group of young women from Amanecer, Bucaramanga, drug use was associated primarily with the young, while alcohol use was linked with middle-age and elderly people (box 4.3). Alcoholics were also more likely than drug users to be male. Drug users were perceived as more dangerous to society than alcoholics because of their loss of control when under the influence of drugs as well as their stealing to feed their habits. At least in the public sphere, alcoholics were better able to control themselves and were not associated with acts of delinquency.

The Cost of Drugs

Drugs were noted to be considerably less expensive than alcohol (table 4.4). One joint of marijuana, for example, cost 300–500 pesos ($.19–$.30)—much less than a small bottle of beer (800 pesos, or $.50). A bottle of brandy cost more than a gram of the most expensive hard drugs (cocaine and *perico*). A gram of *bazuco* was not much more expensive than a bottle of beer.

Table 4.3. Distribution of Drug Consumers by Age in 14 de Febrero, Bogotá, Identified by Seven Community Leaders

Age range	Estimated number of consumers	Percentage of total
10–20 years	100	20
21–30 years	250	50
31–40 years	100	20
Over 40	50	10
Total	500	100

> **Box 4.3. Characteristics of Drug Addicts and Alcoholics Reported by Five Young Women**
>
> **Drug addicts**
> - Act without thinking
> - Think only about doing bad things
> - Act without conscience
> - Rob from houses
> - Are dangerous
> - Are mainly adolescents
> - 7 out of 10 are male
>
> **Alcoholics**
> - Despite everything, they know what they're doing
> - Mainly fall asleep under the effects of alcohol
> - Fall over
> - Mainly middle-age and elderly
> - 9 out of 10 are male
>
> *Source:* Five women ages 12–16, in Amanecer, Bucaramanga.

Several focus group members also estimated how much they spent a day on drugs (box 4.4). In 14 de Febrero, Bogotá, a young male addict reported spending 10,000–20,000 pesos ($6.20–$12.50) a day on drugs. Three other users reported spending an average of 15,000 pesos ($9.40) a day, with a low of 5,000 ($3.10) when their daily earnings were low. In Pórtico, Medellín, nine young men from the Los Muchachos gang estimated that they each smoked 10 marijuana joints a day, at a cost of 3,000–5,000 pesos ($1.90–$3.10).

Table 4.4. Costs of Drugs and Alcohol in 14 de Febrero, Bogotá, and Pórtico, Medellín (pesos)

Type of drug or alcohol	14 de Febrero	Pórtico
Marijuana	300–1,000 per joint	300–500 per joint
Bazuco	1,000–2,000 per gram	
Perico	5,000 per gram	4,000–8,000 per gram
Pepas		1,500 per tablet
Cocaine		4,000–8,000 per gram
Antiseptic alcohol	800 per half bottle	
Beer		800 per small bottle
Spirits		6,000 per bottle of rum
		9,000 per bottle of brandy

Note: Exchange rate: US$1 = 1,604 pesos.
Source: Six focus groups in both communities.

Box 4.4. Household Drug Expenditures in Pórtico, Medellín, Reported by Two Adult Groups

The household expenditures shown below were provided by Elvira, a mother from Pórtico, Medellín, in a focus group discussion. Her household comprises nine people, including Alfonso, a painter, who earns 350,000 pesos ($218) a month and spends 540,000 pesos a month on alcohol, drugs, and gambling. The household's monthly shortfall of 744,300 pesos ($464) is made up by Alfonso working extra hours or asking for salary advances.

Expenditure item	Cost per month (pesos)	Cost per month ($)	Percent of total
Alcohol, drugs, gambling	540,000	336.7	49.3
Food	400,000	249.3	36.6
Transport	95,800	59.7	8.8
Services	50,000	31.2	4.6
Education	8,500	5.3	0.8
Total	1,094,300	682.2	100.0

The household expenditure patterns shown below are aggregated estimates from a focus group of four women (19–40) and two young men (17 and 23). Expenditures on drugs—74,000 pesos a month ($46)—exceeded expenditures on education. Drugs and alcohol combined were the second largest expenditure item after food.

Expenditure item	Cost per month (pesos)	Cost per month ($)	Percent of total
Food	200,000	124.7	30.7
Services	100,000	62.3	15.3
Rent and credit	85,000	53.0	13.0
Transport	60,000	37.4	9.2
Education	50,000	31.2	7.7
Bazuco	40,000	24.9	6.1
Parties	40,000	24.9	6.1
Alcohol	30,000	18.7	4.6
Cocaine/*perico*	20,000	12.5	3.1
Gambling	12,000	7.5	1.8
Marijuana	8,000	5.0	1.2
Pepas	6,000	3.7	0.9
Total	651,000	405.9	100.0

Source: Group of four women ages 25–40 and a mixed group of adults ages 17–40.

Causes of Drug Consumption

Drug consumption among young people, the primary users, was closely linked with intrafamily violence and conflict (see chapter 3). The problem tree drawn by community mothers from Rosario, Girón, focused on nonviolent conflict within the home that could cause young people to turn to drugs (figure 4.3). Key factors they cited included "lack of comprehension of parents toward children," "lack of interest" on the part of parents, and "lack of love and dialogue within the family." Young men were more likely than young women to turn to drugs and gangs when family life becomes untenable. Young women tended to get involved in early sexual relationships, often becoming pregnant or turning to prostitution.[5]

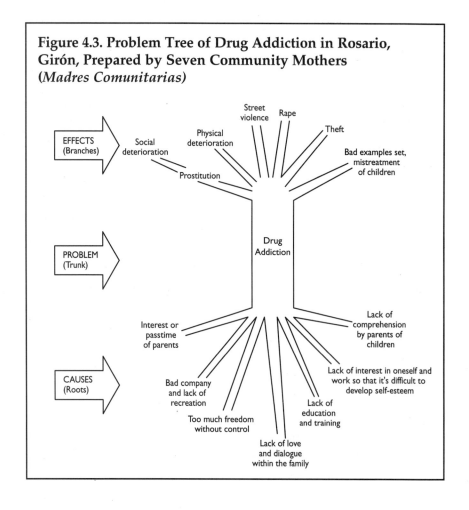

Figure 4.3. Problem Tree of Drug Addiction in Rosario, Girón, Prepared by Seven Community Mothers (*Madres Comunitarias*)

Another important cause of drug consumption was peer pressure, which was noted by children as young as 10. In Jericó, Bogotá, for instance, a group of four 11-year-old girls said that they had been pressured to smoke cigarettes and then use drugs (starting with Boxer glue).

Often, gangs of drug pushers stood outside the school gates trying to entice students into trying drugs by offering the first consignment free of charge. Pressure also came from friends. In all communities *malas amistades* (bad friendships) or *malas companias* (bad company) was cited as a cause of drug use.

Finally, some parents not only provided bad examples but actually taught their children to smoke marijuana. A group of three adults in El Arca, Cali, noted that with so many parents using drugs, children learn to accept drug consumption as normal.

Consequences of Drug Consumption

Lack of physical and human capital was both a cause and an effect of drug use. Community members often blamed the drug problem on lack of recreational opportunities, especially sports and leisure facilities. It is important to note, however, that both basketball courts and football fields were among the most popular sites for consuming drugs. Some people suggested that it was the lack of organized sports clubs or youth clubs that generated boredom and discontent among young people, leading them to take drugs.

With unemployment one of the major problems in all of the communities, people become desperate and turn to drugs as a way to fill their time or soften the edge of their despair. As figure 4.4, drawn by three Communist Party members who founded 14 de Febrero, illustrates, stress related to having nothing to do can lead people to take drugs. In their highly politicized view, lack of employment was also linked with lack of workers' conscience, lack of professional training, and unfair labor laws. Lack of education was also cited as both a cause and effect of drug consumption.

Drug consumption tends to erode physical and human capital. When young people become involved in drugs, they usually leave school, according to the focus groups. Once they become involved in drugs, they are rarely able to secure employment other than drug dealing and robbery. Young people claimed that they were increasingly succumbing to drugs because of lack of alternatives. The combination of deteriorating physical and human capital meant that the quality of the labor force within these communities was extremely low.

In all communities, it was mainly teachers who linked drug consumption among students with gang membership. One teacher complained

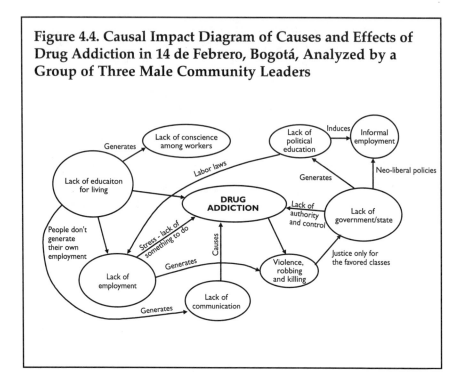

Figure 4.4. Causal Impact Diagram of Causes and Effects of Drug Addiction in 14 de Febrero, Bogotá, Analyzed by a Group of Three Male Community Leaders

that teachers were unable to cope with these types of problems: "We are not trained to deal with drug addiction nor with gang culture. For this we need special training. The *pandillas* (gangs) are very frightening." Thus while drugs affect all strata of society in the nine communities, the ramifications were most severe for young people.

A second important consequence of drug consumption was the increase in fear and insecurity in the communities. People were afraid of drug addicts, both because they were perceived as muggers and robbers and because drugs are illegal and therefore feared, at least by older people. "[Drugs] create fear" was a constant rejoinder. Discussing marijuana users, two women and a man from Rosario, Girón, noted, "People can't go out in the evening …. One can't send a girl or even a boy out alone because they'll get caught-up with them."

In many communities, people feared areas where drugs were sold or used. The most commonly cited dangerous places in 14 de Febrero, Bogotá, for example, were the basketball courts, where young people consumed drugs; the banks of the river, where young women had reportedly been raped by drug addicts; a park, which was dark and attracted

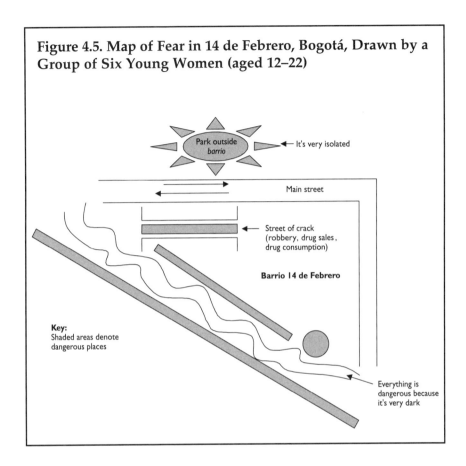

Figure 4.5. Map of Fear in 14 de Febrero, Bogotá, Drawn by a Group of Six Young Women (aged 12–22)

drug addicts; a street on which crack was sold; and a house from which drugs were sold (figure 4.5). These patterns were found in other communities as well.

The reduced mobility as a result of fear eroded trust and collaboration—cognitive social capital—within the community. A woman from 14 de Febrero, Bogotá, noted that "before," people were more united and "one didn't see young people smoking [marijuana] because there was more communication." In contrast, "now," there was no collaboration, people no longer respected one another, and members of the community were afraid to confront others about the problems facing the *barrio*.

There was also a strong gender dimension to fear. While men of all ages were afraid of robbery and mugging, levels of fear among women of all ages were higher and related to fear of attack, especially rape, by drug addicts.

Chapter Five
Unemployment, Displacement, Area Stigma, and Economic Violence

Colombia's current economic crisis has increased unemployment, which community members perceived as a major cause of violence and insecurity. As a man in Cali pointed out, "In a poor country with hunger and without work, there's no peace." Unemployment was a major contributing factor in many types of violence, and it was closely linked to the large-scale displacement of people fleeing political violence in rural areas. This displacement exacerbated unemployment in urban areas. "Area stigma"—sometimes referred to as "bad reputation"—attached to low-income communities was also perceived as a major obstacle to securing employment.

Nature and Scope of Unemployment

In five of the nine communities studied, unemployment was the leading problem cited under the rubric of lack of physical capital. Unemployment constituted 13 percent of all problems in Pórtico, Medellín, and 11 percent in 14 de Febrero, Bogotá; Cachicamo, Yopal; and Colombia Chiquita, Aguazul. Unemployment represented about a third of all problems related to the lack of physical capital (table 5.1).

Estimates of the rate of unemployment in the sample communities were very high. In Colombia Chiquita, Aguazul, a group of three women and one man estimated that 90 percent of the *barrio* was unemployed. In Pórtico, Medellín, a group of two men and six women estimated that 70 percent of the population had no work. Similar figures were estimated in El Arca, Cali, where a group of three men estimated that unemployment stood at 80 percent. Estimates of unemployment by age reveal that younger people have higher rates of employment than older people (table 5.2). Unemployment among all age groups is very high, however, with two of three 15- to 25-year-olds unemployed.

Table 5.1. Relative Importance of Lack of Physical Capital and Unemployment (percent)

Community	Lack of physical capital as a percentage of all problems	Unemployment as a percentage of problems related to lack of physical capital
Embudo, Bogotá	15	33
14 de Febrero, Bogotá	23	46
Jericó, Bogotá	33	19
Amanecer, Bucaramanga	21	30
Rosario, Girón	27	24
El Arca, Cali	28	32
Pórtico, Medellín	37	34
Cachicamo, Yopal	34	33
Colombia Chiquita, Aguazul	36	30
Total	28	31

Unemployment also varies by gender, with unemployment higher among men than among women. It is easier for women to find informal sector work, and in many communities women were the primary income earners. As one man from El Arca, Cali, pointed out, "Today there are more women working and they are maintaining us." Another man explained that he was now taking care of the home, cooking, cleaning, and caring for his children.

Types of Employment Available

Employment opportunities lacked stability in all nine communities. Men tended to work in construction, either as laborers or in skilled trades; as guards; as drivers; or in a host of informal sector activities, particularly

Table 5.2. Unemployment by age range, El Arca, Cali

Age range	Percentage unemployed
15–25	66
26–35	77
36–45	78
46–60	82
Over 60	50–100

Source: Six focus groups in El Arca, Cali.

street vending. Women were employed as community mothers, as domestic servants, or in a range of informal activities, such as selling cooked food and dressmaking.

Many people made ends meet through *rebusque* (literally, careful searching), engaging in different work activities every day. One man from Jericó, Calixto, who earned his living from *rebusque* pointed out, "I'm not ashamed to say that I would sell anything, even a pregnant woman.... I have to get enough to eat every day."

Child labor was also noted in most communities. In Jericó, Bogotá, one community leader estimated that 20 percent of all children worked, selling newspapers and lottery or bus tickets. Even higher proportions were noted in Pórtico, Medellín, where a group of four women and two men estimated that 60 percent of 10- and 14-year-olds worked, usually engaging in some form of selling activity (table 5.3).

Types of Violence Caused by Unemployment

High levels of unemployment and economic hardship are closely linked with various types of violence. In some cases, violence is a survival response to unemployment; in other cases, it is the outcome of desperation and frustration created by lack of economic opportunities. As suggested by a group of adolescents in 14 de Febrero, Bogotá, violent crime is often a last-resort survival strategy and often an integral element of *rebusque*. The most common type of crime committed was theft, especially street robbery and robbery of trucks delivering soft drinks.

One man from Jericó, Bogotá, noted: "If they don't let us work, we are pushed into robbing. You can't let yourself die from hunger, and less so your children." Other survival strategies include prostitution (mainly among women but also among men) and small-scale drug dealing (figure 5.1).

The frustration of being unemployed also led to violence. Drug use was frequently cited as a way of dealing with the lack of work. To purchase drugs, unemployed people often robbed. Unemployed men tended to feel inadequate when they could not fulfil their role of breadwinner, often turning to alcohol and intrafamily abuse to vent their feelings.

The national recession has forced more and more workers to become casual workers. The resulting instability has increased insecurity and violence. In 14 de Febrero, Bogotá, a group of young men who had worked intermittently over the year in construction activities noted that they usually worked four months a year (June-July and November-December). During the slack periods, they hung about making money from illegal means, usually by robbery.

Table 5.3. Economic Activity Matrix by Age Group, Pórtico, Medellín

Item	0–10	11–14	15–25	26–35	36–45	45–55	Over 55
Number in group	396	500	700	500	300	400	300
Number of people who work	100 (all boys)	300 (all boys)	200 (50% male, 50% female)	150 (50% male, 50% female)	150 (60% male, 40% female)	100 (60% male, 40% female)	50 (60% male, 40% female)
Type of activity	• Selling sweets • Street vending • Recycling	• Selling • From age 13, stealing	• Stealing • Construction • Street vending • Domestic servant	• Construction • Dressmaking • Domestic servant	• Construction • Street vending • Domestic servants	• Construction • Street vending • Domestic servants	• Construction • Street vending • Domestic servants • Begging
Estimated monthly earnings in pesos (in dollars)	30,000 ($18.7)	40,000 ($25)	180,000 ($112)	240,000 ($150)	240,000 ($150)	240,000 ($150)	200,000 ($125)

Note: $1 = 1,600 pesos.
Source: Focus group of women (ages 19–56) and men (ages 27–34).

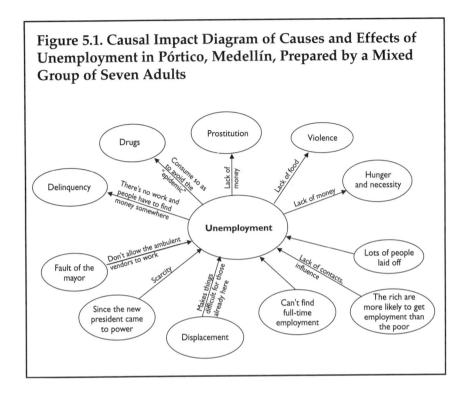

Figure 5.1. Causal Impact Diagram of Causes and Effects of Unemployment in Pórtico, Medellín, Prepared by a Mixed Group of Seven Adults

Causes of Economic Violence

Unemployment in the communities studied was tied to a variety of factors, including the national recession, local constraints, legislation regulating the informal sector, political violence in the countryside, area stigma, and the collapse of the oil industry. Economic violence was tied to all of these factors.

Changing Economic Circumstances
Colombia's economy is in recession. In the first quarter of 1999 (when the study was conducted), GDP was projected to contract by 4–7 percent. The worst-affected sectors include manufacturing, construction, and retailing, all concentrated in urban areas. Urban unemployment in the seven largest cities reached 19.5 percent in March 1999, up from 14.4 percent the previous year, according to the national statistics department. Urban unemployment was highest in Medellín, where 22.6 percent of the economically active population had no work (Oxford Analytica 1999).

In all of the communities the national economic recession as well as changing political circumstances were viewed as causes of violence and insecurity. An 18-year-old construction worker from Rosario, Girón, explained that because of the economic crisis, there was no work and therefore no money. With no money, there was little food, especially in urban areas. In addition, people, especially young people, had nothing to do and got involved with bad company, which led to drug use and robbery. These sentiments were repeated throughout the nine communities (figure 5.2).

Constraints Faced by Local Economies

Local urban economies experienced the economic crisis in different ways. In Bogotá, especially in 14 de Febrero and Jericó, both located close to large industrial zones, residents complained about factory closures and layoffs. Discussing the bankruptcy of the local factories in 14 de Febrero, Maritza, the treasurer at a communal action group, predicted that the future held only further economic crisis, war, and violence if nothing was done to deal with unemployment. In her words, "A member of the family who has no work and has to respond to their obligations often has to turn to robbery."

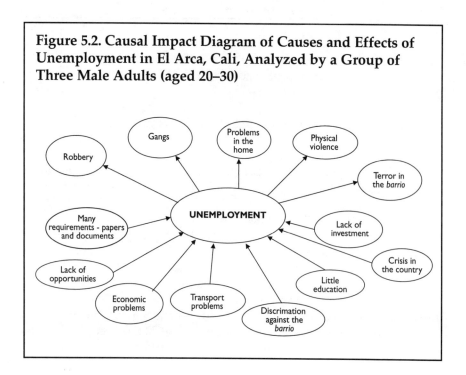

Figure 5.2. Causal Impact Diagram of Causes and Effects of Unemployment in El Arca, Cali, Analyzed by a Group of Three Male Adults (aged 20–30)

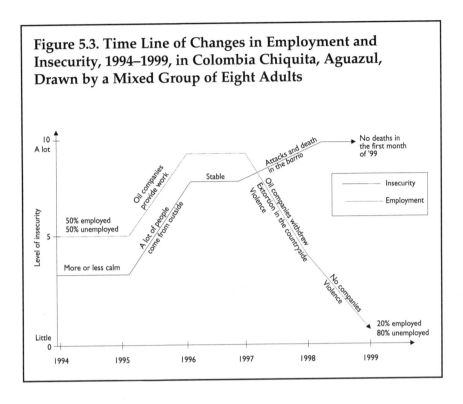

Figure 5.3. Time Line of Changes in Employment and Insecurity, 1994–1999, in Colombia Chiquita, Aguazul, Drawn by a Mixed Group of Eight Adults

A timeline from Colombia Chiquita, Aguazul (figure 5.3), illustrates the complex relationship between insecurity and employment in oil-rich areas. Between 1995 and 1997, the level of insecurity increased as people arrived from outside the area in search of work in the oil industry. Although employment was high, increased guerilla and paramilitary activity linked to corruption and extortion meant that insecurity rose. After 1997, as demand for labor in the companies declined, people lost jobs that paid two and a half times what they could earn elsewhere ($312 a month in the oil industry versus $125 in farming). The loss of employment created resentment among the population and increased the level of crime. With fewer sources of extortion among the oil companies, the paramilitaries and guerillas turned on the local residents instead.

In Cali and Medellín unemployment was associated with the collapse of the construction industry, once associated with the drug cartels. The cartels had laundered large amounts of money through the construction industry which, in turn, employed large numbers of the urban poor. The national economic downturn and the capture of leading drug cartel figures have caused the construction industry to contract. According to a group of middle-age men in El Arca, Cali, the employment situation would improve 100 percent if the Rodríguez brothers were released from prison. With the capture of the Rodríguez brothers, "money did not move." The main effects were an increase in armed attacks, the proliferation of gangs, a 100 percent increase in insecurity, and a rise in homicides.

Legislation Regulating the Informal Sector

Municipal legislation has recently been passed restricting street vending in public areas. Although the intent of the law was to curb the sale of drugs, the effect has been to increase unemployment in some communities. Ironically, the law has led to increased insecurity, according to residents. One woman from 14 de Febrero, Bogotá, said that the main solution to reducing violence was to rescind this law and permit street vendors to work. She noted that 25 percent of the working population in the *barrio* worked as traders and that many were forced to rob and engage in illegal activities because of the restrictions imposed by the mayor.

Political Violence in the Countryside

Communities perceived political violence in the countryside as a major cause of the economic crisis. Many felt that the government was allocating scarce resources to the army and the war rather than to the economy. A 13-year-old boy in Pórtico, Medellín, commented, "The only people that are paid are the soldiers, and when they are killed the mother is left rich."

The most important effect of the civil war on poor urban areas has been the influx of people fleeing political violence in rural areas. The phenomenon is occurring throughout the country, with the highest levels of flight in Urabá, Magdalena Medio, and Ariari. Recent estimates by the World Bank suggest that 1.2 million people in Colombia had fled their home areas by 1998 (World Bank 1999). Displaced populations were identified in all of the study communities except Embudo, Bogotá. The highest proportions of displaced persons were found in Rosario, Girón, where about 50 percent of the population had fled from other areas—mainly the Magdalena Medio—and in Colombia Chiquita, Aguazul, where 50–60 percent of the population were displaced. A group of six men and two women in Colombia Chiquita, Aguazul, identified three types of displaced people in the *barrio*: people who had fled political violence in the rural areas of Casanare, people who had fled political violence in other departments, and people who sought employment with the oil companies.

Displaced people are in desperate need of employment. Two couples who had fled political violence in San Vicente Chucurá, leaving their small farm, aspired to nothing more than "finding a fixed job that paid the minimum wage." They survived by eating unwanted vegetables they collected from the Centro de Abastos. Most of the displaced people in Rosario, Girón, felt grateful to have escaped political violence and found the *barrio* very peaceful. One displaced woman was relieved to be able to live without constant fear because "in César they kill many people for doing nothing, only for the sake of killing."

The influx of displaced people affects employment of the local population, who blame the newcomers for putting pressure on the labor market. In Cachicamo, Yopal, displacement was perceived as a major factor in unemployment, exacerbating an already difficult economic situation. "No work for those who arrive, nor those who are already here," commented one resident (figure 5.4). Although displaced people were not necessarily actively excluded within their new communities, they were blamed for contributing to unemployment.

In Pórtico, Medellín, unemployment was also perceived to be tied to racial discrimination. A group of four Afro-Colombian men and one woman who had migrated from the coast to find work in the city blamed their unemployment on various forms of discrimination. These included

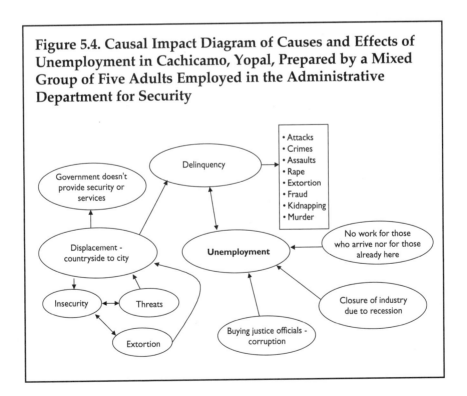

Figure 5.4. Causal Impact Diagram of Causes and Effects of Unemployment in Cachicamo, Yopal, Prepared by a Mixed Group of Five Adults Employed in the Administrative Department for Security

"not being a native," "being a person of color—racism," and "living in Pórtico" as well as a range of factors linked with lack of networks and the fact that jobs are secured only through contacts.

Many displaced people and migrants noted the lack of job and welfare assistance networks. In Rosario, Girón, two displaced women who had recently fled from Puerto Wilches listed potential sources of assistance. They noted that neighbors gave them food occasionally and that the communal action committee gave them money once, but they complained that shopowners and money-lenders gave credit only to those able to prove they work. The only source of assistance available to them was Centro de Abastos, where free food and merchandise were available. "It is the only thing we have to cook," they noted.

Collapse of the Oil Industry

The collapse of the oil industry in Casanare had ramifications beyond the loss of employment. With the decline in oil operations, guerilla and paramilitary groups, which extorted the oil companies for years, increasingly turned to the local population as sources of funding. According to residents of Colombia Chiquita, Aguazul, and Cachicamo, Yopal, in addition to suffering directly from political violence at the hands of these groups, they suffer economically through a range of extortion and kidnapping activities (table 5.4). According to three cattle farmers, the paramilitaries are the worst perpetrators of extortion, with the guerillas targeting large organizations rather than small business people. Organized crime rings have now joined the guerillas and paramilitaries in their activities.

Extortion has had severe effects on local economies. In rural areas, violence, killings, and "taxes" imposed by paramilitary and guerila groups have forced some farmers to abandon their land (figure 5.5). "Vaccinations" (protection money) have to be paid for harvests every six months, or annually, or in the case of cattle ranching, per head of cattle. Urban areas have not fared much better. A clothing manufacturer in Yopal reported having to pay $60–$125 for every suit it makes. Transport companies have to pay extortion money for every trip they make (see table 5.4). These additional business expenses have led to widespread bankruptcies, which affect both the business owners and employees, who lose their jobs.

The story of Don Pedro, a truck driver from Cachicamo, Yopal, reveals the economic hardship imposed by extortion and corruption (box 5.1). Everyone involved in the process of driving a truck has to be paid. In addition, Don Pedro has to pay bribes to the authorities because he lacks proper transportation papers (which he cannot afford). He also pays the guerilas when they stop him on the road. So extensive are the bribes and

Table 5.4. Cost of Extortion Activities in Yopal and Aguazul, in pesos (in dollars)

Target group	Payment
Rice growers	15,000 per harvest every 6 months ($9)
Cattle farmers	1,500–2,500 ($1.00–$1.60)
Butchers	100,000 ($62) every 3–4 months
Taxi drivers	30,000 ($19) a day
Salesperson (clothes and shoes)	100,000–200,000 ($62–$125) per complete outfit sold
Commercial nursery (plants)	200,000 ($125) per produce load
Transport/haulage	50,000 ($31) per carload per day
Banana farmer	150,000 ($94) per hectare per year
Cattle farmers, businesspeople	5–10 million ($3,121–$6,242) ransom per person kidnapped
Foreigners	($5,000–$10,000) ransom per person kidnapped

Source: Focus group discussions in Yopal and Aguazul.

Figure 5.5. Causal Impact Diagram of the Effects of Extortion in Cachicamo, Yopal, Prepared by a Group of Three Male Cattle-Ranchers

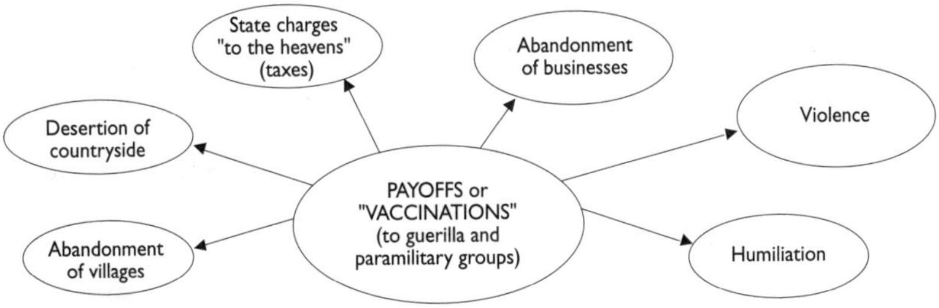

PAYOFFS or "VACCINATIONS" (to guerilla and paramilitary groups) lead to:
- State charges "to the heavens" (taxes)
- Abandonment of businesses
- Violence
- Humiliation
- Abandonment of villages
- Desertion of countryside

> **Box 5.1. Extortion of Truck Drivers in Cachicamo, Yopal: The Case of Don Pedro**
>
> Don Pedro, a truck driver from Cachicamo, Yopal, complained that he paid so many "taxes," legal and illegal, to so many sources that he was beginning to feel that it was not worth his while to work. "I have a truck for working and from that I make my living. The man who gives me the cargo takes 10 percent for giving me the goods, the company that owns the cargo takes 40 percent, the cargo handlers take 30 percent, the owner of the truck takes 5 percent, and the driver takes 5 percent. Besides that I have to pay for gas, oil, tires, in other words, maintenance for the truck.
>
> "When I'm on the road I have to bribe the authorities when I'm stopped because I don't have all the transportation papers. Sometimes I'm attacked and stopped by guerillas, to whom I have to give more contributions—more expenses. As a result, I'm working at a loss. I can't pay the taxes for the truck and I'm charged a fine of 35,000 pesos per month. I therefore don't have enough money to maintain the truck, and much less to maintain my family.
>
> "The war between the paramilitaries and guerillas is killing everyone because of the distrust among the people who constantly accuse each other. With the extortion, everyone has to give money, and besides that, one has to remain silent. This generates mistrust among everyone. There is lots of death and confusion. I think that disarmament is for fools, because when the authorities stop me it's to confiscate my machete, as they think I'm going around armed. But for me, it's a tool that I use to chop logs, to cut branches. In contrast, when I'm attacked by the paramilitaries and guerillas, they have all the most modern weapons and nobody says anything. For that reason, for me the most important thing would be to be able to work and live in peace."

payments that Don Pedro must make that he feels it is hardly worth his while to work at all.

Area Stigma

Area stigma, or prejudice against people who live in the *barrio*, is another important constraint limiting employment opportunities, especially formal sector jobs, for people from poor urban settlements. Pablo, a young high-school graduate from Amanecer, Bucaramanga, reported that every time he applied for a job he was automatically dismissed because he came from the Ciudad Norte, which many people associate with delinquency, drug consumption, and robbery. "Just because we are from Ciudad Norte no one will give us work. They think that all of us here are

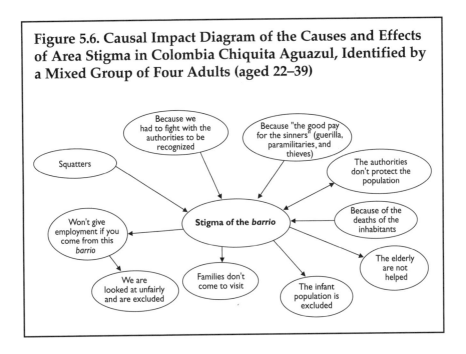

Figure 5.6. Causal Impact Diagram of the Causes and Effects of Area Stigma in Colombia Chiquita Aguazul, Identified by a Mixed Group of Four Adults (aged 22–39)

thieves." Similar situations were noted in other communities. In Pórtico, Medellín, residents cited "discrimination against people from the communities." Following gang wars and widespread killings, employers reportedly dismissed employees who came from these communities, identifying them all as gang members or murderers.

This sense of territorial exclusion was particularly marked in areas affected by political violence. In Colombia Chiquita, Aguazul, for example, many residents complained that they were treated like guerilla members, thieves, prostitutes, or drug addicts. Not only had this characterization made their community a target for paramilitaries, resulting in 14 assassinations, but it also undermined their ability to secure employment. In Colombia Chiquita, members reported being stigmatized as guerilla members (figure 5.6). As they noted, "The good pay for the sinners—guerillas, paramilitaries, and thieves."

Chapter Six
Perverse Social Capital and Economic and Political Violence

Violence not only affects individuals and households but communities themselves, by producing particular social institutions and their associated social capital. Structural social capital, the main focus here, refers to interpersonal relationships in formal or informal organizations or networks. Cognitive social capital refers to values, norms, attitudes, and beliefs. The two kinds of capital are intricately linked, with attitudes affecting interpersonal relationships (Uphoff 1997).

Prevalence and Importance of Social Institutions

Community members identified 371 social institutions in the nine communities studied (table 6.1). The number of institutions identified was used as a proxy for perceptions of the prevalence of social institutions. The number of times an institution was cited was used as a proxy for perceptions of its importance (Groothaert 1999). The study distinguished between membership groups, in which people participate, either formally or informally, in the functioning of the organization, and service delivery organizations, in which community members do not make decisions. Information on individual organizational membership was not gathered since the participatory urban appraisal methodology does not use questionnaire surveys (see, for example, Groothaert 1999; Narayan 1997). However, a particular advantage of the participatory urban appraisal is its ability to identify illegal or criminal violence-related groups in a context of anonymity. For instance, a gang member may not admit to membership in a gang in a one-to-one interview situation, yet when asked in a group context which institutions are important in a community, the gang member may find it be easier to identify the existence of the gang in which he or she is a member. In other words, participatory urban appraisal tools are often more effective in identifying violence-related or illegal institutions than conventional questionnaire-based research techniques.

Service delivery organizations (mainly education and health services) were perceived as the most prevalent institutions within the communities. The role of the state in providing services, both directly and indirectly (through funding of neighborhood or other groups) emerged as important. Gangs, guerilla groups, and paramilitary organizations were also identified as prevalent local institutions.

Prevalence patterns varied across the nine communities. In 14 de Febrero and Jericó, Bogotá, many NGOs, private institutions, and government agencies had established pilot projects and interventions. El Arca, Cali, had many neighborhood organizations and youth and recreation groups; it also boasted the highest number of drug rehabilitation centers. In contrast, many organizations had abandoned Pórtico, Medellín, because of widespread gang and militia violence in the *barrio*.

In Cachicamo, Yopal, and Colombia Chiquita, Aguazul, a high number of social institutions were linked to the political situation in the area, which has attracted government institutions and NGOs. Residents in both communities noted the high number of state security and justice organizations and violence-related groups.

Similar patterns emerged in terms of the importance of organizations (table 6.2). Social service delivery organizations were perceived as the most important institutions, with neighborhood committees viewed as more important than state and government institutions. Violence-related groups were among the most important institutions cited.

Areas of intense conflict, such as Yopal and Aguazul, had few membership organizations, perhaps because of residents' reluctance to participate in organizations in which ideas are shared for fear of reprisals. In contrast, service delivery organizations involved little danger for those receiving services. Among membership organizations, violence-related groups, including gangs, militias, drug dealers and users, and guerilla and paramilitary groups, were perceived as most prevalent. In Cachicamo, Yopal, for instance, such organizations represented more than half of all membership organizations. In Jericó, Bogotá, violence-related groups represented a quarter of all membership organizations; in 14 de Febrero, Bogotá, they constituted a third.

One out of five organizations cited was involved in the prevention or perpetration of violence. In Colombia Chiquita, Aguazul, state security and justice organizations were perceived as the most important of all service delivery institutions. Neighborhood committees were perceived as the most important type of membership organization overall, although violence-related groups were viewed as more important in Jericó, Bogotá, and Cachicamo, Yopal (see table 6.2).

Table 6.1. Number of Social Institutions Identified by Community Members, by Type

Type of institution	Embudo, Bogotá	14 de Febrero, Bogotá	Jericó, Bogotá	Amanecer, Bucaramanga	Rosario, Girón	El Arca, Cali	Pórtico, Medellín	Cachicamo, Yopal	Colombia Chiquita, Aguazul	Total
Membership organizations										
Violence-related groups	4	10	9	0	0	6	1	8	4	42 (23.7)
Neighborhood committees	2	7	9	2	2	7	3	1	5	38 (21.5)
Religious groups[a]	4	5	7	3	2	1	3	3	5	33 (18.6)
Women's and childcare organizations	4	3	7	5	2	3	3	1	4	32 (18.6)
Youth, sports, and recreational organizations	0	4	3	1	2	7	3	1	1	22 (12.4)
Organizations for elderly people	0	4	1	0	0	3	1	1	0	10 (5.6)
Subtotal	14	33	36	11	8	27	14	15	19	177

Table 6.1. cont.

Type of institution	Embudo, Bogotá	14 de Febrero, Bogotá	Jericó, Bogotá	Amanecer, Bucaramanga	Rosario, Girón	El Arca, Cali	Pórtico, Medellín	Cachicamo, Yopal	Colombia Chiquita, Aguazul	Total
Service delivery organizations										
Social service organizations	3	9	3	5	1	12	4	11	6	54 (27.8)
State/government organizations	1	4	7	5	5	0	2	12	9	45 (23.2)
NGOs	3	2	6	1	0	9	0	10	3	34 (17.5)
State security/ justice institutions	2	3	0	2	2	2	1	5	5	22 (11.3)
Private sector organizations	1	0	0	1	1	1	0	5	8	17 (8.8)
Productive service organizations	1	0	0	1	4	1	1	1	3	12 (6.2)
Drug rehabilitation centers	3	0	2	1	0	4	0	0	0	10 (5.1)
Subtotal	14	18	18	16	13	29	8	44	34	194
Total	28	51	54	27	21	56	22	59	53	371

Note: Figures in parentheses represent percent of total.
a. Religious groups refers to churches and prayer groups only. Religious organizations that provide social services are included in the appropriate service delivery category.
Source: 92 focus groups.

Table 6.2. Perceived Importance of Social Institutions Identified by Community Members, by Type

Type of institution	Embudo, Bogotá	14 de Febrero, Bogotá	Jericó, Bogotá	Amanecer, Bucaramanga	Rosario, Girón	El Arca, Cali	Pórtico, Medellín	Cachicamo, Yopal	Colombia Chiquita, Aguazul	Total
Social service organizations	8	20	4	7	3	17	13	21	16	109 (15.5)
Neighborhood committees	2	26	10	5	12	21	6	4	12	98 (13.9)
State/government organizations	3	4	8	6	7	0	2	33	19	82 (11.7)
Violence-related groups	5	11	13	0	0	11	6	15	10	71 (10.1)
State security/justice institutions	3	7	0	4	2	4	2	22	21	65 (9.2)
Women's and childcare organizations	7	3	8	7	7	7	5	1	12	57 (8.1)
Religious groups[a]	4	10	10	3	6	1	3	8	10	55 (7.8)
NGOs	4	2	7	1	0	19	0	13	3	49 (7)

Table 6.2. cont.

Type of institution	Embudo, Bogotá	14 de Febrero, Bogotá	Jericó, Bogotá	Amanecer, Bucaramanga	Rosario, Girón	El Arca, Cali	Pórtico, Medellín	Cachicamo, Yopal	Colombia Chiquita, Aguazul	Total
Private sector organizations	1	0	0	1	5	3	0	14	17	41 (5.8)
Youth, sports, and recreational	0	5	3	2	4	11	3	1	3	32 (4.6)
Organizations for elderly people	0	7	2	0	0	5	1	2	0	17 (2.4)
Drug rehabilitation centers	7	0	2	1	0	5	0	0	0	15 (2.1)
Productive service organizations	1	0	0	1	4	1	1	1	3	12 (1.7)
Total	45	95	67	38	50	105	42	135	126	703

Note: Figures in parentheses represent percent of total.
a. Religious groups refers to churches and prayer groups only. Religious organizations that provide social services are included in the appropriate service delivery category.
Source: 92 focus groups.

Trust in Social Institutions

Study participants were asked to indicate whether they viewed each institution positively (interpreted as indicating a high level of trust) or negatively (interpreted as indicating a low level of trust). Among membership organizations, women's and childcare groups received the highest percentage of positive rankings (88 percent; table 6.3). Neighborhood committees also received high ratings (75 percent). Among the service delivery organizations, drug rehabilitation centers and NGOs were the most highly trusted, followed by social service delivery organizations, a category that includes primarily schools and health centers.

The least trusted institutions were those associated with perpetrating or preventing violence. Eighty-two percent of respondents viewed violence-related groups unfavorably, and half of all respondents lacked confidence in the state security and justice institutions (the police, the army, the Administrative Security Department, and the judicial system).

Table 6.3. Trust in Social Institutions Identified by Community Members (percent of respondents)

Type of institution	High level of trust	Low level of trust
Membership organizations		
Women's and childcare organizations	88	12
Youth, sports, and recreational organizations	86	14
Religious groups	79	21
Neighborhood committees	75	25
Organizations for elderly people	67	33
Violence-related groups	18	82
Total membership	64	36
Service delivery organizations		
Drug rehabilitation centers	100	
NGOs	91	9
Social service organizations	87	13
Private sector organizations	72	28
Productive service organizations	67	33
State/government organizations	70	30
State security/justice institutions	49	51
Total service delivery	74	26

Source: 92 focus groups.

Characteristics of Productive and Perverse Social Institutions

The study distinguished between productive and perverse institutions. Productive institutions aim to provide benefits in order to improve the well-being of the community. Perverse institutions benefit their members but are usually detrimental to the community or society at large (see Rubio 1997).

Most productive institutions were linked to the state. These included central government institutions, such as the Instituto Colombiano de Bienestar Familiar (Colombian Institute of Family Welfare), local government organizations, and the communal action committees, which received some funding from local governments but retained automony in their decisionmaking.

An institutional map drawn by 20 residents of Pórtico, Medellín, reveals that the majority of the institutions identified by this group were influenced by the state (figure 6.1). Both the school and the health center

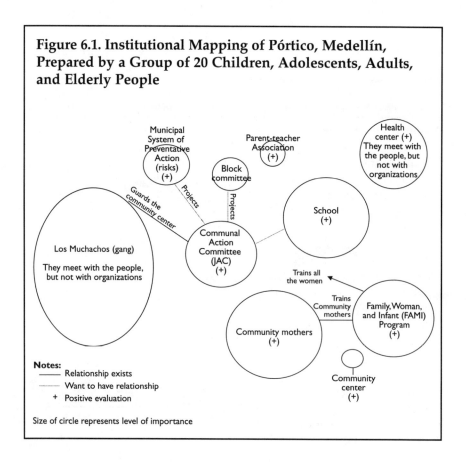

Figure 6.1. Institutional Mapping of Pórtico, Medellín, Prepared by a Group of 20 Children, Adolescents, Adults, and Elderly People

Box 6.1. Perverse Social Institutions in the Nine Barrios by Type of Violence

Type of violence	Institution
Social	*Parche:* A place or group of teenagers that meet to converse, drink, or consume drugs. May also involve acts of crime and violence. Usually based on flexible association and spontaneous congregation. Male-dominated but may have female members.
	Combo: A place or group that commits acts of crime and violence. Less open and more organized than a *parche*. Male-dominated but may have female members.
	Gallada: A gang of primarily male teenagers or adolescents that congregates in a *parche*. May commit crimes and acts of violence. May form into a *pandilla* if an identity and symbols are developed.
	Pandilla: A gang with a strong internal organizational structure. Uses symbols and markings to denote gang identity. Comprises mainly men (usually in their early 20s) involved in delinquency, territorial disputes, and drug use.
Economic	*Raponeros:* Petty thieves or snatchers who steal from people in the streets. Operate individually or in groups and mainly comprise male children and adolescents.
	Atracadores: Thieves armed with guns or knives. Usually mug people in the streets, although some groups specialize in particular types of attacks, such as attacks on taxis. Less organized than *ladrones*.
	Ladrones: Generic name for thieves. Some groups of *ladrones* specialize in particular types of theft or robbery.
	Apartamenteros: Thieves who specialize in theft from apartments.
	Banda: Group of male delinquents organized to commit crimes, primarily robbery and other acts of violence. A *banda* may offer its services to others. May specialize in a particular good, such as jewelry.
	Oficina: Group of organized male drug dealers or businesspeople that hires others to commit acts of crime or violence.

Box 6.1. Cont.	
Type of violence	*Institution*
Political	*Encapuchados:* Literally, hooded people. Generic name for those who commit acts of crime and violence. May be *sicarios*, militia members, or guerillas.
	Sicarios: Paid assassins, usually contracted to kill for revenge. Often linked to social cleansing.
	Milicias populares: Organized militias that commit violence, mainly through use of delinquents. Usually informal protection/justice forces. Some linked to guerillas.
	Grupos de limpieza social: Social cleansing groups. Also known as *paperos* in Cali, *rayas* in Bogotá, and *capuchos* in Medellín. Highly organized, male professional killers. Target groups are delinquents, beggars, drug addicts, petty thieves, street children, and prostitutes. Usually have links with the police, the military, or state security forces.
	Paramilitares/pájaros: Paramilitary organizations known locally as the "birds." Usually linked with the extreme right. Includes a range of civil defense groups funded by landowners, emerald magnates, and drug traffickers and thought to be linked to the military and government. Ostensibly aim to protect civilians and eradicate the two main guerilla organizations. Highly organized, male-dominated structure.
	Guerilla/gatos: Guerilla organizations known locally as "cats." Includes the FARC (Fuerzas Armadas Revolucionarias de Colombia—Armed Revolutionary Forces of Colombia), a pro-Soviet guerilla group, and the ELN (Ejército de Liberación Nacional—National Liberation Army), a pro-Cuban guerilla group. Highly sophisticated organizations that control large areas of the national territory.

were state run. The Communal Action Committee, the community mothers, and the FAMI Program (Family, Mother, and Child Program) received funds from the municipality. Indeed, the only institution not linked with the state was the Los Muchachos gang, which was seen as an informal protection group. Los Muchachos was perceived as the most important perverse social institution in the community as well as the most influential. However, its only formal ties with other community organizations was through guarding the community center run by the Communal Action Committee.

Gangs and Other Violent Organizations

Respondents identified 15 types of organized groups that fostered perverse social capital. Most of organizations were cohesive hierarchical units headed by a leader and governed by internal rules to which their members strictly adhered. Box 6.1 lists each of these groups by type of violence.

Much of the violence committed by these groups was social in nature, involving the pursuit of power. As one community leader in Jericó, Bogotá, noted, the reasons for joining a gang are "often not economic. It's the desire for leadership, the force of power."

Groups involved in economic violence were involved mainly in robbery and delinquency. Some groups, such as the *apartamenteros*, who steal from apartments, specialize in certain types of crime. Others, such as the *bandas* and *oficinas*, were organized based on Mafia-style structures. The *bandas* sold their services, while the *oficinas* contracted to others to commit crimes for them. The least organized group was the *raponeros*, usually street children or adolescents involved in "snatching" in the streets.

Organizations that commit political violence often had links with guerilla groups. In El Arca, Cali, for instance, some militias were closely associated with the National Liberation Army (ELN). A community leader noted, "The militias have the same components as the guerillas. The state views them as guerillas, the *barrio* views them as militias … the militias have more power here than the guerillas." Such groups were widely known and identified by all members of the community, including children (figure 6.2).

The most extreme violence-related organizations, the paramilitaries, or *pájaros*, and guerilla groups, or *gatos*, had the greatest influence on *communities*.[6] In Colombia Chiquita, Aguazul, the paramilitaries and guerillas dominated the daily lives of the population. Between 1996 and 1999, 2 community leaders and 12 other community members were killed, 2 people disappeared, and 10 families that had been threatened fled the *barrio*. One community leader noted, "The people have become accustomed to take away their dead." By 1999 the main threat was the paramilitaries. Every Friday at 7 p.m. the *carros lujosos* (literally "luxury cars") arrived and terrorized the population. People suspected of talking to or having links to the guerillas were threatened and sometimes assassinated. In El Arca, Cali, a variety of perverse institutions dominated the insti-

Perverse Institutions Involved in Drug Sale

Organizations selling or distributing drugs were critically important in the communities. These networks were extremely hierarchical, with patterns of authority rigidly and violently enforced.

The most complex network of drug vendors and their accomplices was found in Embudo, Bogotá. According to one woman, networks were

Figure 6.2. Drawings of Guerillas by a 13-year-old Girl in El Arca, Cali

Note: Ancillo ayudenme — help me. ELN, FARC — guerilla groups (see text).

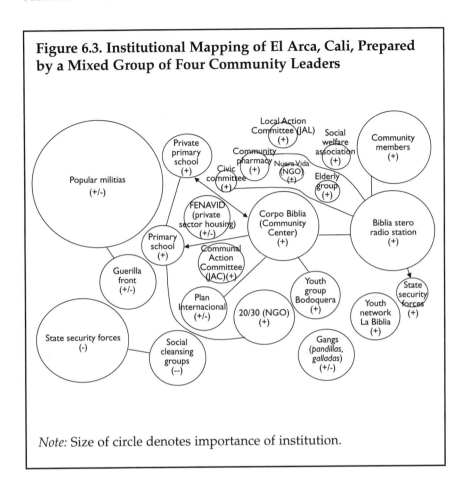

Figure 6.3. Institutional Mapping of El Arca, Cali, Prepared by a Mixed Group of Four Community Leaders

Note: Size of circle denotes importance of institution.

organized vertically, with authority maintained through violence (figure 6.4). Men held the positions of authority, with women usually playing supportive roles. Each street invariably had two male *cabezas* (heads), who lived outside the *barrio*. The *cabezas* distributed drugs through three male or female intermediaries know as *jibaros* (peasants), who also lived outside the community. *Jibaros* rigorously maintained their authority, killing those who broke their contracts. *Jibaros* controlled taquilleros (clerks), who sold the drugs to users. *Taquilleros* rarely consumed drugs or committed murder, but they did employ force—punching consumers who did not pay up on time. The *taquilleros* received 10 percent of what they sold in 24 hours (known as a turn), earning about 30,000 pesos ($18.70) a day. *Taquilleros* employed mainly women and children as lookouts, advising them of police movements or the arrival of strangers.

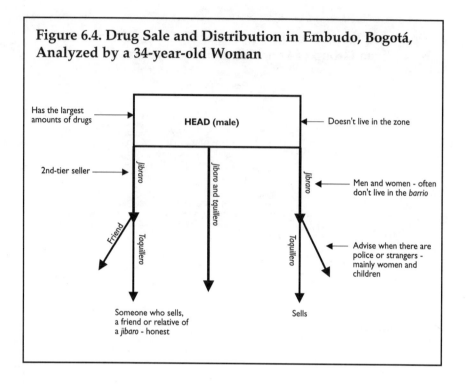

Figure 6.4. Drug Sale and Distribution in Embudo, Bogotá, Analyzed by a 34-year-old Woman

Drugs were sold in certain areas referred to as *ollas* (literally, stew-pot). *Ollas* were usually rented rooms within larger dwellings where drug sale and consumption occurred. Two female sex workers from Embudo, Bogotá, noted that *ollas* were linked not only to drugs but also to attacks, murder, sexual violence, and the abandonment of children (figure 6.5). Often run by *jibaros*, *ollas* were also used to sell stolen goods, and many served as brothels for adult and child prostitutes.

Causes of Perverse Social Institutions

The prevalence and importance of gangs, militias, and other violent organizations are an important indicator of the high level of distrust of state security and justice systems. This is closely associated with the long history of internal conflict in the country. Fifty-one percent of respondents distrusted such organizations as the police, the military, the Administrative Security Department (which includes the secret police), and judicial institutions. Members of communities noted that informal, illegal organizations filled the gap left by lack of state intervention or the inability of the state to protect poor urban communities.

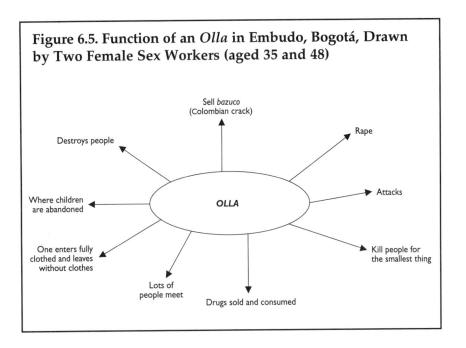

Figure 6.5. Function of an *Olla* in Embudo, Bogotá, Drawn by Two Female Sex Workers (aged 35 and 48)

Perceptions of the Police Force

The least trusted institution was the police force, with people in all communities holding negative views of the police. A man in Pórtico, Medellín, thought that the police were untrustworthy and exacerbated bad situations. As a result, "If I see someone getting killed here and the police arrive and ask questions, I say nothing. Here it's better that way." The police were often identified as major perpetrators of violence and were held in contempt in most communities. They were also perceived as having little authority.

In Amanecer, Bucaramanga, a group of young men described the relationship between the police and the residents of the *barrio* as highly antagonistic (figure 6.6). According to these young men, the police enter the *barrio* only to harass the population. They make about 10 rounds a day, constantly asking for papers from people they know. The police were perceived as highly corrupt and interested only in obtaining money through bribery and extortion. Occasionally, they arrive and fire shots to frighten residents. As a result, many children were afraid of them.

People in Embudo, Bogotá, held the most extreme views of the police and perceived them as major perpetrators of violence who promote rather than curtail the sale and consumption of drugs. According to community members, the police run a well-organized system of extortion

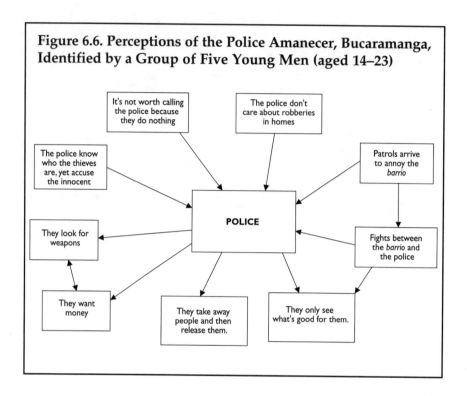

Figure 6.6. Perceptions of the Police Amanecer, Bucaramanga, Identified by a Group of Five Young Men (aged 14–23)

from drug dealers, resorting to violence when necessary. Eight-man police patrols work three shifts a day, each officer receiving 2,680 pesos ($1.70) per shift. Drug dealers and consumers usually met the police's demands because the police threatened them with violence or death through social cleansing.

Perceptions of the Judicial System and the Government

Distrust of the judicial system was also widespread. Most people in the *barrios* believe that the police immediately release people after arrest and that even if a case gets to court, justice is not served. The local justice institution, House of Justice in Bucaramanga, Santander, located near Amanecer, is illustrative. This was located within the *barrio* in an effort to improve access to conciliation and legal services for low-income people. Figure 6.7, drawn by the institution's director and two of his functionaries, shows the functions and components of the program in terms of their institutional links with other entities. Figure 6.8, drawn by a woman from the community, reveals a lack of knowledge of the program, associating it only with the police, a banking facility, the family

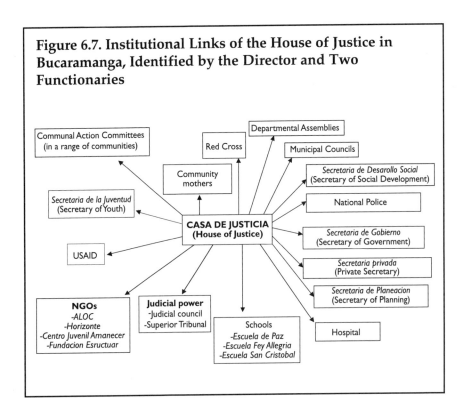

Figure 6.7. Institutional Links of the House of Justice in Bucaramanga, Identified by the Director and Two Functionaries

commissary (where domestic violence cases can be reported), and judicial services.

A group of young men who knew more about the institution held predominantly negative views, noting, "No one trusts the House of Justice.... It is the same as the police; it plays the same role." The men went on to say that the only justice in the *barrio* was *ley de defensa* (law of defense), the use of arms and force. The concept of justice by force was mentioned in most of the communities, where it was referred to as the "law of the strongest" and the "law of knives." In all cases, it related to the lack of alternatives in the absence of faith in the state judicial system and the presence of high levels of impunity.

All perverse organizations were associated with the use of arms and informal justice systems, particularly social cleansing. In El Arca, Cali, for instance, a member of the M–19 guerilla group who had been "reinserted" into the community described how justice by force had become more violent over time. In the past, organized conflict-resolution procedures based on a system of warnings and community

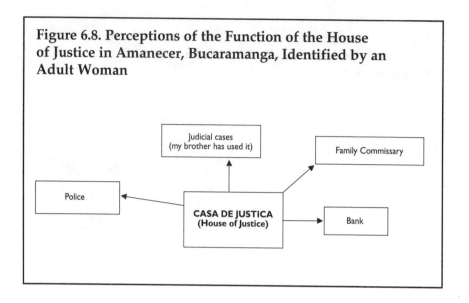

Figure 6.8. Perceptions of the Function of the House of Justice in Amanecer, Bucaramanga, Identified by an Adult Woman

meetings were used. For the most part, only informers were killed. Now, he reported, militias and *bandas* killed as a way of sending messages to the community.

Underlying the rapid growth in perverse social institutions was the perception that the power of the government as an effective law enforcement and welfare institution was declining. This was graphically illustrated by an 11-year-old boy in Jericó, Bogotá, who identified the government as a "killer" and "squeezer," diminishing in its importance and presence to the point of being a mere skeleton (figure 6.9).

Perverse social institutions perpetrating political violence generated greatest fear in the frontier communities of Cachicamo, Yopal, and Colombia Chiquita, Aguazul. Although a minority of community members condoned the actions of these groups, most people feared them. In Colombia Chiquita, Aguazul, in particular, paramilitary organizations were associated with a range of negative consequences that undermined cognitive social capital (figure 6.10). Fear of reprisals from paramilitaries or guerillas made it impossible to talk openly in the community. As a result, solidarity was eroded and distrust created. This in turn created a society in which people had to look out for themselves to survive. Perceptions of the military were mixed in this community. Although relations with the army have deteriorated, as the army was perceived to be doing little to prevent political violence, it was nevertheless looked to as a source of protection.

PERVERSE SOCIAL CAPITAL 89

Figure 6.9. Depiction of the Government by an 13-year-old Boy in Jericó, Bogotá

Note: Lo mato el gobierno: the government kills; Gobierno exprimidor: government squeezer.

Reconstruction of Productive Social Institutions and Female-Dominated Organizations

Which community organizations are the best vehicles for rebuilding cognitive social capital? As table 6.3 shows, the most trusted institutions were women's and childcare groups. In five of the eight communities in which these organizations existed, all were evaluated positively (100 percent trust level). Childcare organizations consist largely of state-run community homes, while women's organizations include small NGOs and locally formed women's self-help groups.

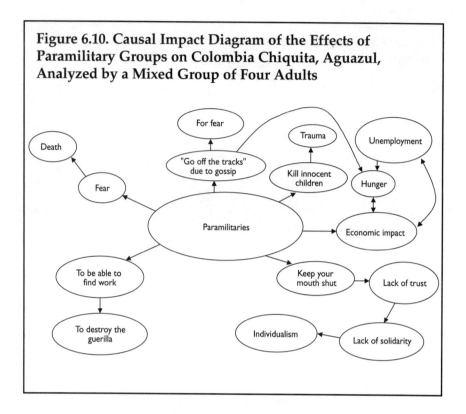

Figure 6.10. Causal Impact Diagram of the Effects of Paramilitary Groups on Colombia Chiquita, Aguazul, Analyzed by a Mixed Group of Four Adults

Community Homes

Two main types of community homes provide care. Social Welfare Homes (*Hogares de Bienestar Social,* HOBIS) provide childcare for children up to five years. The Family, Mother, and Child Programs (*Programa Familia, Mujer, e Infancia del Instituto Colombiano de Bienestar Familiar, FAMI*) provide care for pregnant and lactating women. These organizations existed in all of the communities except Cachicamo, Yopal.

The community homes are run entirely by women known as community mothers, who operate these childcare groups from their own homes. As many as eight or nine homes function in each community. People trusted the community homes because they are operated by local women hiring inside the community. Overall levels of trust were high among all groups of people, even young men, who identified community mothers as extremely important and a positive force in the community (figure 6.11).

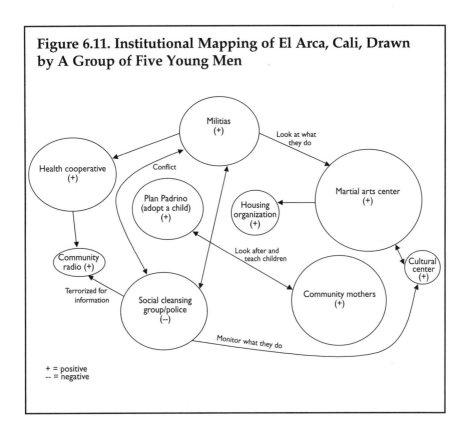

Figure 6.11. Institutional Mapping of El Arca, Cali, Drawn by A Group of Five Young Men

Women's Organizations

Women's organizations were found to be extremely important institutions in some communities, especially those experiencing high levels of violence. In Colombia Chiquita, Aguazul, for example, a group of adult men and women identified the Women's Association (a local women's self-help group) as the most important positive institution in the community (figure 6.12). The only other influential organization was the Communal Action Committee, which the focus group believed had lost sight of its origins and no longer kept its promises.

Focus groups described the Women's Association as "successful," "trustworthy," and "well-functioning." One woman, who had been displaced from another department because of violence, decided to form the organization after experiencing violence at the hands of the paramilitaries and guerillas in Aguazul. The organization's aim was to reunite a

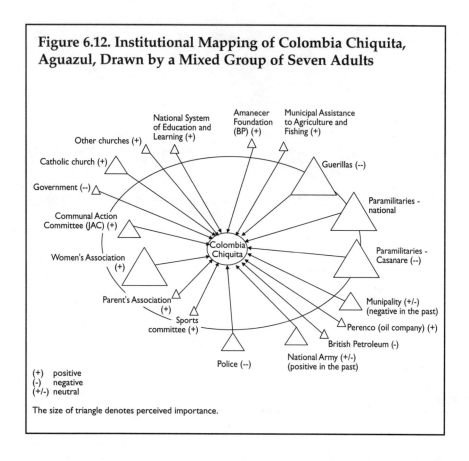

Figure 6.12. Institutional Mapping of Colombia Chiquita, Aguazul, Drawn by a Mixed Group of Seven Adults

community whose social fabric had been destroyed by violence by training women to maintain their families, mainly by setting up their own small businesses. In this woman's view, women were more likely than men to be heard by the authorities because "there is always truth and sincerity in the eyes of women." The organization also managed to change the image of the *barrio* in the eyes of the authorities, who no longer view it as "full of thieves, drug addicts, and guerrilla members." Despite the obstacles that faced her, the woman felt confident about the future. "I continue to lead the association without worrying what the macho men think. Maybe that's why they call me the mad woman."

Chapter Seven
Youth, Exclusion, and Violence

Young people are at the apex of the nexus of violence, social exclusion, and the creation of perverse social institutions. If interventions to reduce violence are to be sustainable in the longer term, they must address the problem of youth exclusion.

Perceptions of Exclusion

Young people, particularly men, felt excluded, both from particular groups and organizations within their communities and from their communities themselves. Many young people complained that "no one takes us into account" and repeatedly mentioned rejection (*rechazo*). A group of young men in 14 de Febrero, Bogotá, highlighted the following sources of exclusion.

- Parents, especially mothers, who they claimed tried to prevent them from having friends and going out.
- The Communal Action Committee, which never listened to them.
- The police, who harassed them daily and engaged in social cleansing (killing young people in the *barrio* on the pretense that they are drug addicts). "They look at you as the worst. They don't come in peace but to fight."
- The community in general, who blamed them for the drug problem in the *barrio*. As one man noted: "When the people begin to talk badly of you ... they invent that you are involved with vices [drugs]."

Several young women also complained of discrimination. A group of five 14- to 17-year-old girls from Rosario, Girón, identified their main problem as "people talking badly of young people" and especially of young unmarried women who did not work. They discussed how a group of elderly women in the *barrio* called them *muchachas vagas* (lazy, corrupt young women), implying that they took drugs and hung around with men.

> **Box 7.1. Exclusion of Young Women in Rosario, Girón**
>
> The group listed stereotypes used in the community, which they felt contributed to social exclusion. Although they saw themselves as *muchachas alegres*, they were constantly called *vagas*, which they viewed as discrimination.
>
> | *muchacha vaga* (lazy, corrupt girl) | *Muchacha alegre* (happy girl) | *Muchacha sana* (healthy girl) |
> |---|---|---|
> | • Unemployed | • Happy | • Works |
> | • Spends all day in the street | • Uncomplicated | • Studies |
> | • Smokes marijuana | • Wears sporty clothes | • Stays home |
> | • Wears tennis shoes | • Wears tennis shoes | • Wears clothes similar to her mother's |
> | | • Wears necklace (with friends' names on it) | • Should not have a boyfriend (although may have one in secret) |
> | | • Has boyfriends | |
>
> *Source:* Five young women.

Young women felt that people in the community labeled young women as either *muchachas vagas* or *muchachas sanas* (healthy girls), refusing to acknowledge young women such as themselves, *muchachas alegres* (happy girls) (box 7.1). Although they admitted that "we are not nuns," they resented being blamed for things they did not do. They also resented the fact that young men in the *barrio* who engaged in some of the same behaviors were not condemned.

Causes and Effects of Exclusion

A major cause of exclusion among young people was high levels of intergenerational conflict. Channels of communication between parents and their children were broken—often as a result of witnessing or being victimized by intrafamily violence resulting in family disintegration and feelings of isolation. As children turned away from their parents, the older generation began to blame young people for the ills of society.

This intergenerational conflict was especially widespread in 14 de Febrero, Bogotá, particularly among male community leaders of the Communist Party–influenced Provivienda committee, whose sons rejected the principles of collective action. Indeed, one group of three *jóvenes sanos* (healthy young people), including the son of a community leader, disparaged communism, stating that individualism was much better.

YOUTH, EXCLUSION, AND VIOLENCE

Some sons of Communists had become involved in drugs and gangs as way of rejecting their fathers' teaching.

This type of conflict was not confined to 14 de Febrero or to fathers. In Jericó, Bogotá, a group of five female community leaders noted that some gang members were the sons of leaders. One woman whose son was in a gang pointed out, "I work for the community, and my son damages the community."

Intergenerational conflict contributed to exclusion by the community as a whole. In many cases, young people withdrew from mainstream society, exacerbating their exclusion. In 14 de Febrero, Bogotá, a group of male rock or punk musicians who dressed in black, shaved their heads, and espoused an ideology of anarchic communism were acutely aware of their exclusion. In their words, "The people don't like us. We are looked on as drug addicts and are associated with satanic cults." These young men gained strength from their music, embracing their exclusion, and what they call the intolerance of the community, as a coping strategy.

For many young people another response to exclusion was drug use or involvement in crime and violence, often through gang membership. A group of six 14- to 18-year-old men in Rosario, Girón, identified the fact that "we're not recognized or taken into account" as a major issue (figure 7.1). They associated their exclusion with lack of educational and

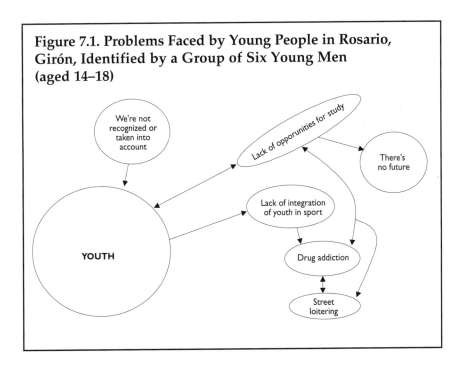

Figure 7.1. Problems Faced by Young People in Rosario, Girón, Identified by a Group of Six Young Men (aged 14–18)

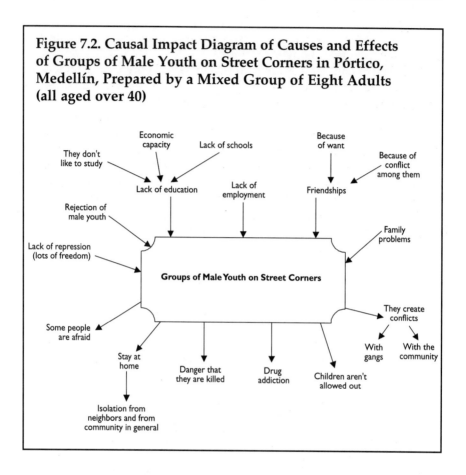

Figure 7.2. Causal Impact Diagram of Causes and Effects of Groups of Male Youth on Street Corners in Pórtico, Medellín, Prepared by a Mixed Group of Eight Adults (all aged over 40)

recreational opportunities, noting that football tournaments in the *barrio* were organized either for children or adults. Exclusion led to drug use and loitering, as well as the lack of a promising future.

Older people identified similar problems faced by young people in the *barrios*. In Pórtico, Medellín, a group of eight adults analyzed the problem of young men on street corners, providing a sophisticated account of the nexus of violence, exclusion, and social capital (figure 7.2). The causal factors they identified included rejection, lack of education and employment opportunities, family problems, and the influence of friends ("bad company"). Young men got involved in drugs and gangs, which led to violence. As a result, the community became afraid of them, contributing to the erosion of cognitive social capital.

Exclusion was often exacerbated as a result of involvement in violence. For instance, a member of the Los Muchachos gang in Pórtico, Medellín,

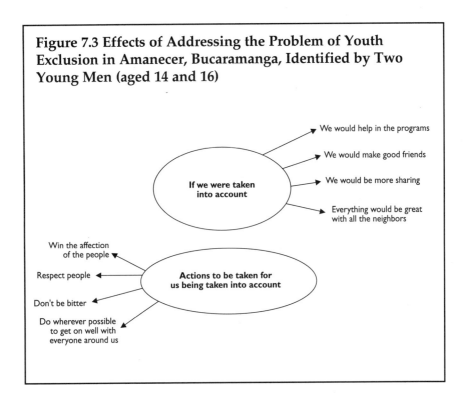

Figure 7.3 Effects of Addressing the Problem of Youth Exclusion in Amanecer, Bucaramanga, Identified by Two Young Men (aged 14 and 16)

noted that he felt rejected by the community because people ran away when he went by their houses. A drug addict from 14 de Febrero, Bogotá, said he felt "rejected because of drugs" and wanted to give up drugs, have a family, and become part of the community again.

Young men and, to a lesser extent, young women destroyed trust in their communities by generating fear within their communities and failed to lay the groundwork for social capital. Indeed, young people's exclusion from the functioning of the community undermined the creation of ties and networks within communities—except those that developed within perverse institutions.

Two young men from Amanecer, Bucaramanga, who felt acutely excluded from their community, outlined what actions needed to be taken to include young people in the community (figure 7.3). They felt that if affection and respect toward young people were established, there would be more sharing, and community programs would be more efficient. As it stood, they did not participate in any community activities because of the conflict between young people and the rest of the population.

Chapter Eight
Community Perceptions of Solutions to Violence

Strategies for coping with violence can be divided into four types: avoidance, confrontation, conciliation, and other strategies (Moser 1996, 1998) (table 8.1).

Most people reported adopting *avoidance mechanisms*, with "ignoring the situation" the most prevalent. Fear of retribution, powerlessness, and fear of exacerbating the situation prompted these responses. Particularly marked was the silence surrounding intrafamily violence (see chapter 3). Neighbors and friends did not intervene in this type of conflict, and family members maintained silence. One young man from Pórtico, Medellín, noted that he watched television when his father beat his mother, mainly because he felt he could do little to help. Responses to political violence were also dominated by silence. In communities in which the level of political violence was high, "keeping one's mouth shut" was often necessary to avoid being killed.

Another important avoidance strategy involved changes in mobility patterns. Many people avoid places where drug addicts or gangs congregate, changing their walking routes or staying home in the evening. Two *jóvenes sanos* (healthy young people) from 14 de Febrero, Bogotá, noted how they avoided drug addicts by taking a long route home. Many people also restricted their movements after dark, locking themselves in their homes in the evening when the incidence of violence increased. Women reported being particularly afraid to go out in the evenings. A group of young women from Rosario, Girón, identified the danger of going out at night as a major restriction in their lives. Some, for example, wanted to continue their education at night school but were afraid to leave their homes in the evening.

Other community members noted that they avoided speaking to people involved in violence-related activities. Young people avoided falling into bad company or getting involved with friends who would lead them astray, particularly with respect to drugs. People avoided being robbed by not carrying valuables. A group of three adults from El Arca, Cali,

Table 8.1. Strategies for Coping with Violence (percent of total)

Strategy	Percentage of total strategies cited
Avoidance strategies	
Avoid bad company	4
Avoid people involved in violence-related activities	7
Remain silent/ignore situation	21
Avoid dangerous areas	11
Don't go out at night	10
Flee from attackers	11
Don't carry valuables	3
Avoid gossip	2
Leave *barrio*	2
Lock house/put bars on windows	4
Confrontation strategies	
Confront person causing problem	2
Carry weapons	2
Use violence	2
Conciliation strategies	
Develop relations with people involved in violence	2
Turn to religion; pray for those involved	2
Other strategies	
Report violence to family members or teachers	5
Report violence to police	2
Submit, cry, abort (in the case of rape)	5
Total	**100**

Note: Violence-related activities include drugs, insecurity, intrafamily violence, perverse social institutions (gangs, militias), rape, robbery, murder, and fights in the street.
Source: 133 focus group listings.

noted that one had to go out "without rings, without a watch, without luxury shoes, and without brand name clothes." Another basic avoidance strategy was to flee from thieves or gangs. Flight was also significant as a way of coping with intrafamily violence for both victims of and witnesses to intrafamily violence.

Confrontation strategies were much less common than avoidance strategies because of fear of violence. Indeed, the few community members who cited confrontation as a response were either gang members or drug users. According to a member of the Los Muchachos gang in Pórtico, Medellín, "killing them first" was a way of dealing with murder in the community. A few people suggested that "hitting back" was an appropriate way of dealing with intrafamily violence.

Conciliation strategies were rare. In a few cases, young people got to know drug addicts or gang members, both to protect themselves and to make the addicts and gang members feel less excluded. Most people, especially women and the elderly, were afraid of these groups, however. Some said that they prayed for people committing acts of violence.

The *other mechanisms* for dealing with violence were to report conflicts to the authorities or to family members or teachers (in the case of children and young people). Few people felt that reporting violence solved the problem, however. Most people felt that the only thing to do was to submit. A group of four 11-year-old girls in Jericó, Bogotá, noted that they were afraid to tell their parents about rape for fear of rejection and could talk about it only with their friends. Their main strategy was to have an abortion and "be brave and deal with it as it comes."

Three women in Colombia Chiquita, Aguazul, summarized many of the coping and conciliation strategies, including forgiveness and trusting in God (figure 8.1). With alcoholism a major problem in the community, they also suggested that the bars be closed early to prevent intrafamily violence and street fights among drunks. As this community was severely affected by political violence, confrontation was not an option for fear of assassination.

Interventions to Reduce Violence

People in the communities had a variety of ideas for reducing violence. Almost half of the solutions were associated with social capital (tables 8.2 and 8.3). Within this category, the promotion of family values and dialogue between family members and community members was the most important strategy (see table 8.3). Improving human capital represented almost a third of the interventions cited, while increasing physical capital represented just a fifth of all proposed interventions.

Increasing Social Capital

Social capital interventions were the most important type of intervention in seven of the nine communities. Productive social capital interventions (building trust, integrating young people into society, and reforming policy) outnumbered perverse social capital interventions (social cleansing, harsher police behavior) by a factor of three to one. The most important productive solutions were the generation of dialogue among both family and community members, the promotion of family values, and the building of trust. In Jericó, Bogotá, for example, a family felt that the most appropriate solution to the problem of insecurity was "to unite the com-

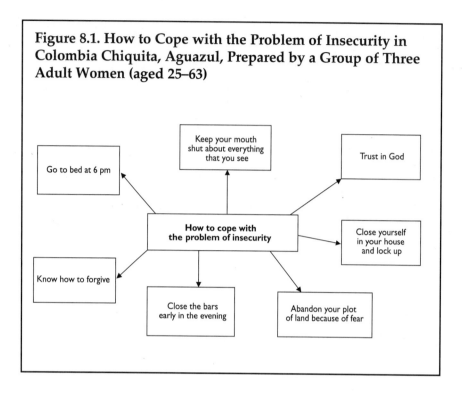

Figure 8.1. How to Cope with the Problem of Insecurity in Colombia Chiquita, Aguazul, Prepared by a Group of Three Adult Women (aged 25–63)

munity to make everyone alert" (figure 8.2). Education in conflict resolution techniques was suggested in 14 de Febrero, Bogotá, and Pórtico, Medellín.

Community organizations were an important solution for addressing violence. Some community members suggested increasing the resources of existing organizations, such as the Communal Action Committees. Others suggested seeking external assistance in order to establish new organizations, which would be run and controlled from within the *barrio*.

A group of seven community mothers in Jericó, Bogotá, identified a series of solutions to the problem of violence. They stressed the importance of bottom-up solutions, noting, "Peace is not [attained by] throwing resources around without building projects from below, from families and community organizations." Their proposed solutions involved building both structural social capital (through community-based organizations) and cognitive social capital (by building trust among those involved in violence) (box 8.1).

Almost a third of the social capital interventions involved repressive activities, such as social cleansing. Community members who endorsed

COMMUNITY PERCEPTIONS OF SOLUTIONS TO VIOLENCE   103

Table 8.2. Interventions for Reducing Violence, by Type of Capital and Community (percent of total)

Intervention	Embudo, Bogotá	14 de Febrero, Bogotá	Jericó, Bogotá	Amanecer, Bucaramanga	Rosario, Girón	El Arca, Cali	Pórtico, Medellín	Cachicamo, Yopal	Colombia Chiquita, Aguazul	Total
Increase physical capital	16	17	17	23	28	21	11	20	45	21
Create jobs	5	6	4	9	8	9	11	6	24	8
Provide housing	3	0	2	2	0	5	0	0	3	1
Improve infrastructure	0	1	11	8	0	5	0	2	0	3
Build more prisons	0	6	0	2	0	0	0	2	0	2
Increase household security (locks, bars)	0	2	0	2	8	2	0	0	0	2
Implement land reform in rural areas	2	1	0	0	4	0	0	6	12	2
Improve urban planning	6	0	0	0	0	0	0	0	0	1
Other[a]	0	1	0	0	8	0	0	4	6	2
Increase human capital	30	35	23	14	20	45	35	39	34	31
Improve academic and vocational education	13	9	15	5	12	22	17	24	9	14
Provide more drug and alcohol rehabilitation	10	10	0	2	4	5	3	2	3	5
Provide drug and sex education	2	4	4	0	0	2	10	0	7	3
Provide self-esteem training	5	2	2	2	0	2	0	4	3	3
Provide sports and recreational opportunities	0	3	0	5	4	2	0	2	9	3
Improve health care	0	2	0	0	0	10	0	4	0	1
Provide conflict resolution education	0	5	2	0	0	0	5	0	0	1
Provide family counseling	0	0	0	0	0	2	0	2	3	1

Table 8.2. cont.

Intervention	Embudo, Bogotá	14 de Febrero, Bogotá	Jericó, Bogotá	Amanecer, Bucaramanga	Rosario, Girón	El Arca, Cali	Pórtico, Medellín	Cachicamo, Yopal	Colombia Chiquita, Aguazul	Total
Increase social capital	54	48	60	63	52	33	54	41	21	48
Productive social capital										
Promote family values and dialogue among family and community members	20	11	21	12	4	17	32	7	3	14
Endorse effective peace process	0	0	0	0	0	0	0	2	6	1
Help community organizations get started	10	7	2	9	20	0	0	6	0	6
Develop programs to integrate young people into society	0	1	11	7	0	2	7	0	0	3
Build trust	5	2	13	9	12	2	7	12	12	7
Reform the police	0	7	4	9	8	2	0	0	0	4
Perverse social capital										
Tighten police control over communities	3	8	4	5	4	2	0	0	0	4
Increase social cleansing	11	6	4	7	4	5	7	0	0	6
Increase military protection/strengthen state presence	4	6	0	5	0	2	0	12	0	4
Provide arms to citizens	0	0	0	0	0	0	0	2	0	1
Total	100	100	100	100	100	100	100	100	100	100

a. This includes solutions such as reporting violent incidents to authorities (Girón), leaving the country (Cachicamo), disarming offenders (Cachicamo), and prohibiting sale of alcohol (Colombia Chiquita).

Source: 133 focus group listings.

COMMUNITY PERCEPTIONS OF SOLUTIONS TO VIOLENCE

Table 8.3. Interventions for Reducing Violence, by Type of Violence (percent of total)

Intervention	Percentage of all solutions
Increase social capital	48
Productive	35
Perverse	13
Increase human capital	31
Increase physical capital	21
Total	100

social cleansing groups had lost faith in the police and army and believed that social cleansing represented the only hope for dealing with violent offenders. As a community leader from El Arca, Cali, noted, "Often the people are in favor of social euthanasia because the state doesn't respond."

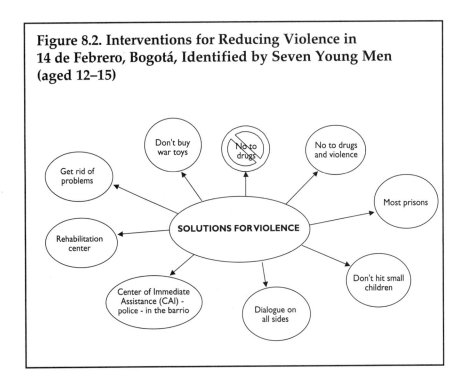

Figure 8.2. Interventions for Reducing Violence in 14 de Febrero, Bogotá, Identified by Seven Young Men (aged 12–15)

> **Box 8.1. Seven Community Mothers' Approach to the Problem of Violence**
>
> **What do they do?**
> - Recognize violent people.
> - Listen to them.
> - Make them participate in peace building.
> - Do not reject them.
> - Pacify them.
> - Provide moral support.
> - "Orientation."
>
> **Solution**
> - Create schools for parents on peace building.
> - Generate income.
> - Bring public and private resources within the community together, without institutional corruption.
> - Increase participation of community organizations in decisionmaking.
> - Ensure that peace begins in the family, in the nursery, and in the school.

While social cleansing was a repressive social capital solution in response to the absence of the state, the other types related to greater presence of the state security forces to deal with violence. In Cachicamo, Yopal, many people endorsed a greater military presence coupled with state provision of arms to help ordinary citizens defend themselves. Two small-scale cattle farmers called for "paid official protection from the state" as well as training the army in international humanitarian laws and human rights.

Men favored repressive interventions much more often than women. Among the female-only and male-only focus groups that discussed interventions, only one group of women favored social cleansing. Of 11 single-sex focus groups that suggested various types of repressive solutions, nine were male.

Increasing Human Capital

Education and drug and alcohol rehabilitation centers dominated the human capital interventions proposed by community members. In El Arca, Cali, human capital solutions were viewed as the most significant (see table 8.2). Also notable was the need for drug and alcohol rehabilitation in Embudo and 14 de Febrero, Bogotá, and for drug and sex education interventions in Pórtico, Medellín.

Increasing Physical Capital

Increasing physical capital was less important than increasing social or human capital in most of the nine communities. Such solutions were perceived as critical in Colombia Chiquita, Aguazul, however, where they represented almost half of all interventions. They were also important in Rosario, Girón, where they represented 28 percent of all solutions. Better

Table 8.4. Recommended Interventions, by Type of Violence (percent)

Type of violence	Physical capital intervention	Human capital intervention	Social capital intervention
Economic violence			
Drugs	20	32	48
Insecurity	26	17	57
Gangs	17	36	47
Robbery	28	16	56
Delinquency	14	43	43
Social violence			
Alcoholism	0	0	100
Fights	20	0	80
Murder	19	13	68
Violence against women	18	55	27
Domestic violence	18	45	37
Rape	9	39	52
Verbal abuse	11	22	67
Disputes between neighbors	14	0	86
Killings	14	29	57
Political violence			
Police abuses	0	50	50
Hooded gunmen/militias	0	0	100
Intimidation	50	0	50
War	43	30	27
Total			

Source: Focus groups.

community infrastructure, especially community centers, was also perceived as important.

Interventions by Type of Violence

Community members proposed different types of interventions to different types of violence. Social capital interventions were suggested most often to address economic and social violence; physical capital interventions were suggested most often to address political violence (tables 8.4 and 8.5). This was especially marked in Colombia Chiquita, Aguazul, where job creation was viewed as the most important solution to political violence.

More than half the interventions proposed for reducing violence against women involved human capital. These interventions involved consciousness-raising activities for women as well as training to help women find jobs that would allow them to leave their husbands. Training and workshops for male perpetrators of violators were also suggested.

Probably the most critical issue raised by local communities was their recognition that dealing with the continuum of violence in their communities required implementing a variety of solutions simultaneously. This was illustrated by a group of members of the Los Muchachos gang, who identified a range of impacts, strategies, and solutions to socially motivated murder (box 8.2).

Constraints and Recommendations

The perceptions of the poor can help policymakers formulate public policy. Local communities identified three national-level constraints to solving the problems of violence:

- *The extensive nature of political violence.* Negotiating peace among the guerrillas, paramilitaries, and other violence groups was perceived as

Table 8.5. Recommended Interventions, by Type of Violence (percent of all interventions)

Type of violence	Physical capital	Human capital	Social capital
Economic	22	26	52
Social	16	34	50
Political	40	27	33

> **Box 8.2. Impact, Strategies, and Solutions to Gang Murder Suggested by Three Young Gang Members in Pórtico, Medellín**
>
> **Impact**
> - Shock and restraint.
> - Personal insecurity.
> - Lack of trust among friends.
> - Negative psychological and moral effects.
> - Negative atmosphere in the *barrio*.
> - You look after yourself more.
> - Community is shocked—no one goes out into the street, children aren't allowed out.
>
> **What do you do?**
> - Talk with the young men, searching for the why and for what.
> - Confront the problem.
> - Make sure the problem doesn't get worse.
> - Try to solve the problem in the friendliest way.
> - Try to prevent the problem from affecting the whole community.
> - Secure justice.
>
> **What would you like to do?**
> - Maintain dialogue with other gangs.
> - Try to make sure the young people keep busy in their free time.
> - Establish educational or night center in the school.
> - Create employment.

an important precondition for the success of many other violence reduction interventions.

- *The problem of displaced people,* which affects the daily lives of all communities. Local people perceive newly arrived displaced people as competitors for employment and income-generating opportunities, provoking economic and social violence. Even the basic needs of many displaced people are not being met, highlighting the importance of a policy and program agenda on displaced people.
- *Unemployment.* All of the communities were concerned about government reforms necessary to pull the economy out of the worst recession in decades. While poor urban communities recognized that violence is not simply a consequence of the downturn in the economy, they understood that high levels of unemployment and stagnant local economies exacerbate political, economic, and social violence.

Local community recommendations for reducing violence can be summarized in terms of seven priorities:

- *Create job opportunities in the formal, informal, and self-employment sectors.*
- *Attack the problem of drug consumption.* The high level of drug consumption was one of the most important concerns in most communities. A comprehensive strategy must include drug (and to a lesser extent alcohol) consumption, both prevention and rehabilitation. Implementing such a solution requires collaboration among education, health, social welfare, and other sectors as well as between the government and NGOs.
- *Reduce society's tolerance for intrahousehold violence.* All communities acknowledged that violence begins at home. Dealing with high levels of physical and mental abuse requires a strategy that encompasses both prevention and rehabilitation. Many agencies have already struggled long and hard to address different aspects of intrahousehold violence. A holistic approach, with extensive interagency, media, and NGO collaboration, may help meet the demand from communities to address this issue.
- *Rebuild trust in the police and judicial system.* The severe lack of confidence in the government's capacity to provide adequate police or judicial protection fosters the development of alternative informal justice systems and social cleansing and raises the level of fear and insecurity. Despite extensive measures to address this issue (through, for instance, the introduction of local houses of justice), fundamental measures are still needed to rebuild trust at the local level in order to eliminate informal justice and social cleansing.
- *Strengthen the capacity of community-based membership organizations,* particularly those run by women. Childcare organizations run by women in the community and neighborhood associations are highly trusted by people in the communities. Both types of organization need to be strengthened to help reduce violence.
- *Target intervention for young people.* Involving young people in the community was perceived as critical to overcoming violence-related problems (table 8.6). The most frequently cited intervention was workshops and talks with young people, usually about drugs and self-esteem. Establishing rehabilitation centers for gang members was also perceived as an important step toward reducing violence. One innovative solution to address the inclusion of young people into society suggested by community members was the development of small locally based community centers for young people, based on

COMMUNITY PERCEPTIONS OF SOLUTIONS TO VIOLENCE

Table 8.6. Community Solutions to Including and Excluding Young People (percent of total)

Interventions for including youth	Percent of all solutions cited	Interventions for excluding youth	Percent of all solutions cited
Offer workshops and talk to young people.	24	Have the police chase them.	5
Integrate young people into society.	14	Don't give any charity to drug addicts.	5
Provide rehabilitation for gang members.	14	Remove them from the *barrio*.	5
Advise young men of dangers, establish dialogue with them.	10	Ignore them.	15
Increase job opportunities for all young people.	8	Kill them all.	15
Provide young men with vocational and technical training.	8	Clean the streets of sources of aggression.	5
Employ gang members and drug addicts.	6	Send them to the military.	10
Provide more education for teenagers.	4	Don't mix with them. Mix only with "healthy people."	10
Provide psychological help/therapy.	4	Do not get involved with drug addicts.	5
Develop relationships with young drug-addicted men.	4	Build houses to displace drug-addicted men.	5
Give them work in community-related type jobs.	2	Keep young men occupied somewhere else.	15
Acknowledge drug addicts as human beings.	2	Don't allow children from other *barrios* here.	5
Total	100	**Total**	100

Source: 155 focus group listings.

the "community mother" model and run directly by local men, women, and young people.

People living in poor urban communities recognize that the problem of violence is so complex that it requires cross-sectoral solutions. They also recognize that local ownership is crucial if the sense of fear, powerlessness, and lack of trust is to be overcome. Given the conventional sector divisions in line ministries and NGOs alike, developing such solutions is likely to prove challenging.

Notes

1. Development practitioners use participatory urban appraisal as a research tool for sharing local people's knowledge and perceptions with outsiders. Chambers (1994a, 1994b, 1994c) provides comprehensive detailed reviews of the participatory rural appraisal approach. The techniques used in that methodology are also applicable in urban settings and are used here. The World Bank's Participation Sourcebook (World Bank 1995) includes participatory appraisals as one of the techniques currently being integrated into the Bank's operational work. The methodology has already been incorporated into several recent Bank studies, including country poverty assessments in Zambia, Ghana, and South Africa (World Bank 1994). The first study on urban poverty and violence using this methodology was undertaken in Jamaica in 1996 (Moser and Holland 1997).

2. For both translation and production purposes, the diagrams have been transferred into computerized form.

3. One of the participatory urban-appraisal ground rules is ownership of visual outputs through named acknowledgment. Given the nature of the issue being studied, however, anonymity was considered essential.

4. The terms "intrafamily" and "intrahousehold" are used interchangeably in this report.

5. Prostitution among young men was also noted in Pórtico, Medellín. A group of four teachers noted that when young men wanted to buy something or find money (which could be used for drugs), they sold sexual favors.

6. The term *pájaro* dates back to the Liberal/Conservative conflict that resulted in La Violencia (1949–53). It purportedly refers to the way the Liberals threw the Conservatives out of airplanes, making them "fly."

Annexes

Annex A. Participatory Urban Appraisal Tools Used in Study

Annex B. Importance of Social Institutions

Annex C. Problems Identified by Community Members

Annex A. Participatory Urban Appraisal Tools Used in Study

Participatory urban appraisals are usually based on focus group discussions, semistructured interviews, direct observation, ethnocentric histories, and biographies and case studies of community members. Discussions with community members take place in local community centers, communal buildings, or in the street (on street corners, at football or basketball fields, outside people's houses).

Various tools were used to gather information on the following themes: community characteristics; the history of the community and violent events; general problems and types of violence as perceived by communities; poverty; well-being and violence; changes in levels of violence over time; social capital and exclusion; causes and consequences of different types of violence; social capital and mapping social institutions; and strategies and solutions for dealing with and reducing violence (Moser and McIlwaine 1999). The specific tools used in the study included the following:

- Matrix of general data.
- Matrix of social organization.
- Listing of general problems.
- Ranking of general problems (scoring, onion diagram, flow diagram).
- Listing of types of violence.
- Ranking of types of violence (scoring, onion diagram, flow diagram).
- Map of institutional relationships.
- Preference matrix on social institutions.
- Participatory map of the community.
- Participatory map of secure and insecure places.
- Matrix on history of the community.
- Matrix on trends of general problems.
- Matrix on trends of types of violence.
- Daily, weekly, monthly, and annual time lines.
- Causal flow diagram on types of violence and/or other problems.
- Problem tree.
- Listing of strategies to cope with violence.
- Diagram of strategies to cope with violence.
- Listing of solutions to reduce violence.
- Diagram of solutions to reduce violence.
- Drawings.

Annex B. Importance of Social Institutions

Table B.1. Importance of Social Institutions (percent of all institutions cited)

Problem	Embudo, Bogotá	14 de Febrero, Bogotá	Jericó, Bogotá	Amanecer, Bucaramanga	Rosario, Girón	El Arca, Cali	Pórtico, Medellín	Cachicamo, Yopal	Colombia Chiquita, Aguazul	All communities
Neighborhood committees	2	26	10	5	12	21	6	4	12	14 (98)
Women's and childcare groups	7	3	8	7	7	7	5	1	12	8 (57)
Institutions for the elderly	7	7	2			5	1	2		2 (17)
Youth, sports, and recreational organizations	5	5	3	2	4	11	3	1	3	5 (32)
NGOs	4	2	7	1		19		13	3	7 (49)
Violence-related groups	5	11	13			11	6	15	10	10 (71)
State security/justice	3	7	4	4	2	4	2	22	21	9 (65)
Social services	8	20		7	3	17	13	21	16	16 (109)
Drug rehabilitation	7		2	1		5				2 (15)

Table B.1. cont.

Problem	Embudo, Bogotá	14 de Febrero, Bogotá	Jericó, Bogotá	Amanecer, Bucaramanga	Rosario, Girón	El Arca, Cali	Pórtico, Medellín	Cachicamo, Yopal	Colombia Chiquita, Aguazul	All communities
State/government institutions	3	4	8	6	7		2	33	19	12 (82)
Religious groups	4	10	10	3	6	1	3	8	10	8 (55)
Private organizations	1			1	5	3		14	17	6 (41)
Productive services	1			1	4	1	1	1	3	2 (12)
Total number of institutions	(45)	(95)	(67)	(38)	(50)	(105)	(42)	(135)	(126)	(703)

Note: Figures in parentheses represent number of institutions.
Source: 92 institutional listings, institutional mapping/Venn diagrams, and institutional preference matrices.

Annex C. Problems Identified by Community Members

Table C.1. Problems Identified by Community Members (percent of all problems cited)

Problem	Embudo, Bogotá	14 de Febrero, Bogotá	Jericó, Bogotá	Amanecer, Bucaramanga	Rosario, Girón	El Arca, Cali	Pórtico, Medellín	Cachicamo, Yopal	Colombia Chiquita, Aguazul	All communities
Violence	58	63	49	52	35	41	21	34	23	43
Drug use	16	18	6	10	12	9	5	3	0	9
Insecurity	11	12	21	10	3	8	3	7	4	9
Robbery	5	11	3	14	5	13	0	6	1	6
Intrafamily violence	5	4	10	3	4	3	2	2	4	4
Loitering	0	4	0	6	9	1	3	1	1	3
Fights	5	6	2	2	0	1	0	2	1	2
Gangs	0	2	6	1	0	3	6	1	1	2
Killing	11	2	0	1	0	0	2	2	3	2
Rape	5	1	0	1	1	0	0	0	2	1
Alcoholism	0	4	0	2	0	3	0	1	1	1
Prostitution	0	0	0	1	1	0	1	2	0	1
Paramilitary groups	0	0	0	0	0	0	0	1	5	1
Threats	0	0	0	0	0	0	0	5	0	1
Guerrilla	0	0	2	0	0	0	0	1	0	0
Lack of physical capital	15	23	33	21	27	28	37	34	36	28
Unemployment	5	11	6	6	7	9	13	11	11	9
Lack of public services	0	2	13	9	9	7	7	8	11	7
Poverty	5	8	10	1	2	5	6	5	6	5

Table C.1. cont.

Problem	Embudo, Bogotá	14 de Febrero, Bogotá	Jericó, Bogotá	Amanecer, Bucaramanga	Rosario, Girón	El Arca, Cali	Pórtico, Medellín	Cachicamo, Yopal	Colombia Chiquita, Aguazul	All communities
Housing problems	5	1	2	1	2	3	9	7	5	4
Transport problems	0	1	3	4	8	4	3	3	3	3
Lack of social capital	16	8	10	19	9	18	14	17	13	14
Lack of unity	0	2	6	10	5	3	13	12	0	5
Absence of the state	0	0	3	1	2	2	2	2	11	3
Discrimination/stigma	5	2	0	3	1	4	0	3	0	2
Corruption	11	3	0	1	0	0	0	0	3	2
Distrust of police	0	2	0	3	1	9	0	1	0	2
Lack of human capital	10	6	8	6	16	11	27	12	17	12
Lack of education	5	0	6	4	10	7	13	6	7	6
Lack of health services	5	0	0	0	4	3	6	4	6	3
Lack of recreation	0	4	2	2	2	0	8	1	4	2
Hunger	0	2	0	0	0	2	1	1	0	1
Lack of natural capital	0	1	0	2	13	2	1	3	10	3
River (flooding)	0	1	0	1	13	1	0	1	7	2
Environmental hazards	0	0	0	0	0	1	1	1	1	1
Erosion	0	0	0	1	0	0	0	1	1	0
Natural disasters	0	0	0	0	0	0	0	0	1	0
Total	100	100	100	100	100	100	100	100	100	100

Source: Focus groups.

Bibliography

Baulch, B. 1996. "The New Poverty Agency: A Disputed Consensus." *IDS Bulletin* 27 (1): 1–10.

Chambers, R. 1992. *Rural Appraisal: Rapid, Relaxed and Participatory.* IDS Discussion Paper 311. Brighton.

———. 1994a. "The Origins and Practice of Participatory Rural Appraisal." *World Development* 22 (7): 953–69.

———. 1994b. "Participatory Rural Appraisal (PRA): Analysis of Experience." *World Development* 22 (9): 1253–68.

———. 1994c. "Participatory Rural Appraisal (PRA): Challenges, Potentials and Paradigms." *World Development* 22 (10): 1437–54.

———. 1995. *Poverty and Livelihoods: Whose Reality Counts?* IDS Discussion Paper 347. Brighton.

Chernick, M. 1997. "Changing Perceptions of Violence in Colombia and Its Implications for Policy." Washington, D.C.

Coleman, J.S. 1990. *Foundations of Social Theory.* Cambridge, Mass.: Harvard University Press.

Collier, P. 1999. "Social Capital and Poverty." Social Capital Initiative Working Paper 4. Washington, D.C.: World Bank.

De Haan, A. 1998a. "'Social Exclusion': An Alternative Concept for the Study of Deprivation." *IDS Bulletin* 29 (1): 10–19.

———. 1998b. "Social Exclusion in Policy and Research: Operationalising the Concept." In J. Figueredo and A. de Haan, eds., *Social Exclusion: The Way Forward in Policy and Research.* Geneva: International Labour Organization.

De Haan, A., and S. Maxwell. 1998. "Poverty and Social Exclusion in the North and South." *IDS Bulletin* 29 (1): 1–9.

Faynzylber, P., D. Lederman, and N. Loayza. 1998. "What Causes Violence Crime?" Washington, D.C.: World Bank, Office of the Chief Economist, Latin America and the Caribbean.

Feldman, T.R., and S. Assaf. 1999. "Social Capital: Conceptual Frameworks and Empirical Evidence: An Annotated Bibliography." Social Capital Initiative Working Paper 5. Washington, D.C.: World Bank.

Fukuyama, F. 1995. *Trust: The Social Virtues and the Creation of Prosperity.* London: Penguin Books.

Gore, C., with contributions from J.B. Figueiredo and G. Rodgers. 1995. "Introduction: Markets, Citizenship and Social Exclusion." In G. Rodgers, C. Gore, and J.B. Figueiredo, eds., *Social Exclusion: Rhetoric, Reality, Responses.* Geneva: International Institute for Labour Studies/United Nations Development Programme/International Labour Organization.

Groothaert, C. 1998. "Social Capital: The Missing Link?" Social Capital Initiative Working Paper 3. Washington, D.C.: World Bank.

———. 1999. "Local Institutions and Service Delivery in Indonesia." Local Level Institutions Working Paper 5. Washington, D.C.: World Bank.

Habermas, J. 1972. *Legitimation Crisis.* Beacon Press.

Harriss, J., and P. De Renzio. 1997. "An Introductory Bibliographic Essay. 'Missing link' or Analytically Missing? The Concept of Social Capital." *Journal of International Development* 9 (7): 919–37.

Hobsbawn, E. 1999. *On the Edge of a New Century,* Free Press.

IILS/UNDP (International Institute for Labour Studies/United Nations Development Programme). 1996. *Social Exclusion and Anti-Poverty Strategies.* Geneva: International Institute for Labour Studies.

Krishna, A. and N. Uphoff. 1999. "Mapping and Measuring Social Capital: A Conceptual and Empirical Study of Collective Action for Conserving and Developing Watersheds in Rajasthan, India." Social Capital Initiative Working Paper 13. Washington, D.C.: World Bank.

Lederman, D., N. Loayza, and A.M. Menéndez. 1999. "Violent Crime: Does Social Capital Matter?" World Bank, Poverty Reduction and Economic Management Network, Washington, D.C.

Moser, C. 1996. *Confronting Crisis: A Comparative Study of Household Responses to Poverty and Vulnerability in Four Urban Poor Communities.* Environmentally Sustainable Studies and Monograph Series 8. Washington, D.C.: World Bank.

———. 1998. "The Asset Vulnerability Framework: Reassessing Urban Poverty Reduction Strategies." *World Development* 26 (1): 1–19.

Moser, C., and J. Holland. 1997. "Urban Poverty and Violence in Jamaica." World Bank Latin American and Caribbean Studies Viewpoints. Washington, D.C.: World Bank.

Moser, C., and C. McIlwaine. 1999. "Participatory Urban Appraisal and its Application for Research on Violence." *Environment and Urbanization* 11.

Narayan, D. 1997. *Voices of the Poor: Poverty and Social Capital in Tanzania.* Environmentally and Socially Sustainable Development Studies and Monograph Series 20. Washington, D.C.: World Bank.

———. 1999. "Complementarity and Substitution: The Role of Social Capital, Civic Engagement and the State in Poverty Reduction." Washington, D.C.: World Bank, Poverty Reduction and Economic Management Network, Poverty Group.

Narayan, D., C. Chambers, M. Shah, and P. Petesch. 1999. "Global Synthesis: Consultations with the Poor." Washington, D.C.: World Bank, Poverty Reduction and Economic Management Network, Poverty Group.

North, D. 1990. *Institutions, Institutional Change, and Economic Performance.* New York: Cambridge University Press.

Olson, M. 1982. *The Rise and Decline of Nations: Economic Growth, Stagflation and Social Rigidities.* New Haven, Conn.: Yale University Press.

Oxford Analytica. 1999. [www.oxan.com].

Portes, A. 1998. "Social Capital: its Origins and Applications in Modern Sociology." *American Review of Sociology* 24 (1): 1–24.

Putnam, R. 1993. *Making Democracy Work: Civic Traditions in Modern Italy.* Priceton, N.J.: Princeton University Press.

Putzel J. 1997. "Accounting for the 'Dark Side' of Social Capital: Reading Robert Putnam on Democracy." *Journal of International Development* 9 (7): 939–49.

Ravaillon, M. 1992. *Poverty Comparisons: A Guide to Concepts and Measures.* Living Standards Measurement Study Working Paper 64. Washington D.C.: World Bank.

Rodgers, G. 1995. "What is Special about a Social Exclusion Approach?" In G. Rodgers, C. Gore, and J.B. Figueiredo, eds., *Social Exclusion: Rhetoric, Reality, Responses.* Geneva: International Institute for Labour Studies/United Nations Development Programme/ International Labour Organization.

Rubio, M. 1997. "Perverse Social Capital: Some Evidence from Colombia." *Journal of Economic Issues* 31 (3): 805–16.

Serageldin, I. 1996. *Sustainability and the Wealth of Nations: First Steps in an Ongoing Journey.* Environmentally Sustainable Studies and Monograph Series 5. Washington, D.C.: World Bank.

Serageldin, I., and Steer A., eds. 1994. *Making Development Sustainable: From Concepts to Action.* Washington, D.C.: World Bank.

Silver, H. 1995. "Reconceptualizing Social Disadvantage: Three Paradigms of Social Exclusion." In G. Rodgers, C. Gore, and J.B. Figueiredo, eds., *Social Exclusion: Rhetoric, Reality, Responses.* Geneva: International Institute for Labour Studies/United Nations Development Programme/ International Labour Organization.

Solimano, A. (ed.). 1998. *Social Inequality: Values, Growth and the State.* The University of Michigan Press.

Solimano, A. (ed.). 2000. *Essays on Peace and Development: the case of Colombia and International Experience,* Conflict Prevention and Post Conflict Reconstruction Series, The World Bank, Washington, DC.

Solimano, A., E. Aninat, and N. Birdsall, (eds.). 2000. *Distributive Justice and Economic Development,* The University of Michigan Press.

Uphoff, N. 1997. "Giving Theoretical and Operational Content to Social Capital." Ithica, N.Y.: Cornell University, Government Department.

Vanderschueren, F. 1996. "From Violence to Justice and Security in Cities." *Environment and Urbanization* 8: 93–112.

Woolcock, M. 1998. "Social Capital and Economic Development: Toward a Theoretical Synthesis and Policy Framework." *Theory and Society* 27 (2): 151–208.

World Bank. 1995. "World Bank Participation Sourcebook." Environment Department Papers. Washington, D.C.

———. 1997. *Country Assistance Strategy for the Republic of Colombia.* Washington, D.C.

———. 1998. "Violence in Colombia: Towards Peace, Partnerships and Sustainable Development." World Bank Sector Study. Washington, D.C.

———. 1999. "Violence in Colombia: Building Sustainable Peace and Social Capital." Environmentally and Socially Sustainable Development Sector, Management Unit Report 18652–CO. Washington, D.C.

World Bank. 2000. *Violence in Colombia: Building Sustainable Peace and Social Capital,* The World Bank, Washington, DC.

THE SOCIETY OF SINGULARITIES

The Society of Singularities

Andreas Reckwitz

Translated by Valentine A. Pakis

polity

First published in German as *Die Gesellschaft der Singularitäten* © Suhrkamp Verlag Berlin 2017
This English edition © Polity Press, 2020

The translation of this work was funded by Geisteswissenschaften International – Translation Funding for Work in the Humanities and Social Sciences from Germany, a joint initiative of the Fritz Thyssen Foundation, the German Federal Foreign Office, the collecting society VG WORT, and the Börsenverein des Deutschen Buchhandels (German Publishers & Booksellers Association).

Polity Press
65 Bridge Street
Cambridge CB2 1UR, UK

Polity Press
101 Station Landing
Suite 300
Medford, MA 02155, USA

All rights reserved. Except for the quotation of short passages for the purpose of criticism and review, no part of this publication may be reproduced, stored in a retrieval system, or transmitted, in any form or by any means, electronic, mechanical, photocopying, recording, or otherwise, without the prior permission of the publisher.

ISBN-13: 978-1-5095-3422-7

A catalogue record for this book is available from the British Library.

Library of Congress Cataloging-in-Publication Data

Names: Reckwitz, Andreas, author. | Pakis, Valentine A., translator.
Title: Society of singularities / Andreas Reckwitz ; translated by Valentine A. Pakis.
Other titles: Gesellschaft der Singularitäten. English
Description: Cambridge ; Medford, MA : Polity, [2020] | "First published in German as Die Gesellschaft der Singularitäten © Suhrkamp Verlag Berlin 2017"-- Title verso. | Includes bibliographical references and index. | In English, translated from the original German. | Summary: "In this major new book, Andreas Reckwitz examines the causes, structures and consequences of the society of singularities in which we now live"-- Provided by publisher.
Identifiers: LCCN 2019033278 (print) | LCCN 2019033279 (ebook) | ISBN 9781509534227 (hardback) | ISBN 9781509534241 (epub)
Subjects: LCSH: Social change. | Individualism. | Culture. | Postmodernism.
Classification: LCC HM831 .R425 2020 (print) | LCC HM831 (ebook) | DDC 303.4--dc23
LC record available at https://lccn.loc.gov/2019033278
LC ebook record available at https://lccn.loc.gov/2019033279

Typeset in 10.5 on 11.5 pt Times New Roman MT
by Fakenham Prepress Solutions, Fakenham, Norfolk NR21 8NL
Printed and bound in Great Britain by TJ International Limited

The publisher has used its best endeavors to ensure that the URLs for external websites referred to in this book are correct and active at the time of going to press. However, the publisher has no responsibility for the websites and can make no guarantee that a site will remain live or that the content is or will remain appropriate.

Every effort has been made to trace all copyright holders, but if any have been overlooked the publisher will be pleased to include any necessary credits in any subsequent reprint or edition.

For further information on Polity, visit our website:
politybooks.com

Contents

Acknowledgments	*page* ix
Introduction: The Proliferation of the Particular	1

I Modernity Between the Social Logic of the General and the Social Logic of the Particular

1 The Social Logic of the General	19
Modernity and Generality	19
Typifications and Rationalizations	21
Standardization, Formalization, Generalization	23
Objects, Subjects, Spaces, Times, and Collectives in the Social Logic of the General	25
Industrial Modernity as a Prototype	28
2 The Social Logic of the Particular	32
The General-Particular, Idiosyncrasies, Singularities	33
Objects, Subjects, Spaces, Times, and Collectives in the Social Logic of Singularities	39
Practices of Singularization I: Observation and Evaluation	43
Practices of Singularization II: Production and Appropriation	46
Performativity as a Mode of Praxis and Automated Singularization	48
3 Culture and Culturalization	52
Culture as a Sphere of Valorization and De-Valorization	52
Culturalization versus Rationalization	58
Qualities of Cultural Praxis: Between Sense and Sensibility	61
4 The Transformation of the Cultural Sphere	65
Premodern Societies: The Fixation and Repetition of the Singular	66

Bourgeois Modernity: The Romantic Revolution of the Unique	68
Organized Modernity: Mass Culture	70
Late Modernity: Competitive Singularities, Hyperculture, and Polarization	72

II The Post-Industrial Economy of Singularities

Beyond Industrial Society	81
Unleashing the Creative Economy	83

1 Unique Goods in Cultural Capitalism — 87

The Culturalization of Goods	87
Singular Goods: Originality and Rarity	91
Things as Singular Goods	93
Services, Media Formats, and Events as Singular Goods	95
Features of Singular Goods I: The Performance of Authenticity	98
Features of Singular Goods II: Moment and Duration	101
Features of Singular Goods III: Circulation and Hyperculture	102

2 Cultural Singularity Markets — 106

Attractiveness Markets as Markets of Attention and Valorization	106
The Cultural Economization of the Economy and Society	108
Overproduction and Winner-Take-All Competitions	111
Buzz Effects and the Struggle for Visibility	114
Valorization Techniques and Reputation	118
Singularity Capital	120
Quantifying the Unique	124

III The Singularization of the Working World

The Cultural Economization of Labor and Its Polarization	131

1 Practices of Labor and Organization in the Creative Economy — 135

Cultural Production as Creative Labor	135
Projects as Heterogeneous Collaborations	138
Organizational Cultures and Networks	141

2 The Singularization and Self-Singularization of Working Subjects — 145

Beyond the Formalization of Labor	145
The Profile Subject: Competencies and Talents	147
Labor as Performance	150

The Singularization Techniques of Labor	153
Fields of Tension in Highly Qualified Labor: Between the Artist's Dilemma and the Superstar Economy	156

IV Digitalization as Singularization: The Rise of the Culture Machine

From Industrial Technics to Digital Technology	163
1 The Technology of Culturalization	166
Algorithms, Digitality, and the Internet as Infrastructures	166
The Digital Culture Machine and the Ubiquity of Culture	168
Culture Between Overproduction and Recombination	172
2 Cultural and Automated Processes of Singularization	176
The Digital Subject: Performative Authenticity and Visibility	177
Compositional Singularity and the Form of the Profile	179
Big Data and the Observation of Profiles	183
The Personalized Internet and Softwarization	186
Digital Neo-Communities and the Sociality of the Internet	188
Fields of Tension in Online Culture: From the Pressure to Create Profiles to Extreme Affect Culture	191

V The Singularistic Life: Lifestyles, Classes, Subject Forms

The Late-Modern Self Beyond the Leveled Middle-Class Society	199
The Cultural Class Divide and the "Paternoster-Elevator Effect"	201
1 The Lifestyle of the New Middle Class: Successful Self-Actualization	207
Romanticism and Bourgeois Culture: The New Symbiosis	207
Self-Actualization and the Valorization of Everyday Life	210
The Curated Life	214
Culture as a Resource and Cultural Cosmopolitanism	216
Status Investment and the Prestige of the Unique	219
2 Elements of the Singularistic Lifestyle	224
Food	225
Homes	228
Travel	232
Bodies	235
Parenting and Early Education	238
Work–Life Balance, Urbanity, Juvenilization, Degendering, and New Liberalism	242

Fields of Tension in the Lifestyle of the New Middle Class: The Inadequacy of Self-Actualization	246
3 The Culturalization of Inequality	252
The Underclass's Way of Life: Muddling Through	252
Cultural Devaluations	255
Singularistic Counter-Strategies of the Underclass	258
The Tableau of Late-Modern Classes and Their Relations	261

VI Differential Liberalism and Cultural Essentialism: The Transformation of the Political

The Politics of the Particular	269
1 Apertistic–Differential Liberalism and the Politics of the Local	272
From the Social-Democratic Consensus to New Liberalism	272
The Competition State and Diversity: The Two Sides of New Liberalism	274
The Politics of Cities I: New Urbanism and the Global Attractiveness Competition	277
The Politics of Cities II: Culturally Oriented Governmentality and Singularity Management	281
2 The Rise of Cultural Essentialism	286
Collective Identities and Particular Neo-Communities	286
Ethnic Communities Between Self-Culturalization and External Culturalization	291
Cultural Nationalism	294
Religious Fundamentalism	296
Right-Wing Populism	299
Cultural Conflicts Between Essentialism, Hyperculture, and Liberalism	301
The Politics of Violence: Terrorism and Mass Shootings as Celebrations of the Singular Act	305
Conclusion: The Crisis of the General?	310
Notes	320
Bibliography	371
Index	398

Acknowledgments

Although books seem to stand on their own in the cultural sphere, they are in fact nodal points within networks and are made possible by infrastructures. This book, too, owes much to many. Over the past few years, I have had the opportunity to present the building blocks of this work at many conferences and workshops held at various universities and institutions. Without exception, these presentations led to lively debates with colleagues, both known and unknown to me, whose advice and objections improved this book considerably. Special thanks are due to the members of my research colloquium and my department at the Viadrina European University in Frankfurt an der Oder. I would like to mention in particular those who took the time to read the manuscript in whole or in part: Martin Bauer, Michael Hutter, Hannes Krämer, Jan-Hendrik Passoth, Hilmar Schäfer, and Klaus Schlichte. Stefan Wellgraf provided me with many helpful references for Part V. I am indebted to Wiebke Forbrig, Julien Enzana, and especially Moritz Plewa for their reliable research assistance and for their help in preparing the manuscript for publication. Eva Gilmer at the Suhrkamp Verlag edited my original German text with her usual authoritative and critical eye. The early stages of my research on this topic were facilitated by a fellowship from the Institute for Advanced Studies at the University of Freiburg, and this book never could have been written without the generous assistance of the Volkswagen Foundation, which supported my research with its "magnum opus initiative" during the years 2015 to 2017. Heartfelt thanks to everyone!

Introduction: The Proliferation of the Particular

Wherever we look in today's society, what has come to be expected is not the *general* but the *particular*. Rather than being directed toward anything standardized or regular, the hopes, interests, and efforts of institutions and individuals are pinned on the unique and singular.

Travelers, for instance, are no longer satisfied with the uniform vacation destinations associated with mass tourism. Instead, it is the uniqueness of a location, the authentic atmosphere of a particular city, an exceptional landscape, or a particular local culture that piques the interest of tourists. And this is only one example among many, for this development has encompassed late modernity's entire global economy. In the case of both services and material goods, the mass production of uniform products has been replaced by events and objects that are not the same or identical for everyone but are rather intended to be unique – that is, *singular*. People have thus become passionate about extraordinary occasions such as live concerts and music festivals, sporting events and art shows, but also about lifestyle sports and the imaginary worlds of computer games. The so-called ethical consumer has developed discerning tastes for different types of bread and coffee in a way that had previously, at best, been typical of wine connoisseurs. Instead of buying a new sofa "off the rack" (so to speak), many people prefer to search for a vintage piece, and a brand such as Apple offers not only the latest technology but a whole environment that is attractive and unique, and that the user would be unwilling to trade for any other. Finally, various forms of psychological treatment offer tailored therapeutic or spiritual services.

More and more, the late-modern economy has become oriented toward singular things, services, and events, and the goods that it produces are no longer simply functional. Instead, they also – or even exclusively – have cultural connotations and appeal to the emotions. We no longer live in the age of industrial capitalism but in that of *cultural capitalism*.[1] This has profound consequences for the professional world as well. Whereas industrial society focused on clearly defined formal qualifications and performance requirements, in today's knowledge and culture economy the working subject has to develop a "profile" that is out of the ordinary. Now those who achieve, or promise to achieve, something extraordinary – something far above average – are rewarded, while employees who perform routine tasks lose out.

Without a doubt, the economy sets the pace of society, but by now the shift from the general to the particular has taken place in many other areas as well – for instance, in education.[2] Unlike 20 years ago, it is no longer enough for schools successfully to teach the curriculum required by the state. Every school has and wants to be different, has and wants to cultivate its own educational profile and provide pupils (and their parents) with the opportunity to forge a unique educational path. And parents, at least those in the educated middle class, regard their individual children as people whose particular talents and characteristics should be fostered and encouraged.

Another area in which the rise of the singular has been observable for some time is architecture. With its repetitive structures, the International Style seems rather monotonous, and it has largely been neglected since the 1980s in favor of unique designs, so much so that it seems necessary for today's museums, concert halls, flagship stores, and apartment buildings to be built in an original style (sometimes these styles are striking, sometimes merely odd). Hidden behind all of this lies a fundamental transformation of spatial structures. In globalized and urbanized late modernity, the interchangeable spaces of classical modernity are to be replaced with recognizable individual *places*, each with a unique atmosphere that can be associated with specific narratives and memories. In the name of so-called cultural regeneration, cities large and small have thus made concerted efforts to develop their own local logic, one that promises a particular quality of life and has its own unique selling points. And the new middle class has flocked to these teeming cities, while other, less attractive, regions (be they in the United States or France, Great Britain or Germany) are in danger of becoming deserted altogether.

It is no surprise, then, that the late-modern subjects who move in these environments seek satisfaction in the particular. The type of subject that predominated in the West up to the 1970s – that is, the average employee with an average family in the suburbs, whom David Riesman described as being "socially adjusted"[3] – has become, in Western societies, an apparently conformist negative foil to be avoided by the late-modern subject. In this regard, Ulrich Beck and others have written a great deal about individualization – meaning that subjects have been liberated from general social expectations and freed to practice self-responsibility.⁴ Singularization, however, means more than independence and self-optimization. At its heart is a more complex pursuit of uniqueness and exceptionality, which has not only become a subjective desire but also a paradoxical social *expectation*. This is especially pronounced in the new, highly qualified middle class – that is, in the social product of educational expansion and post-industrialization that has become the main trendsetter of late modernity. Here, everything in one's lifestyle is measured according to the standard of "specialness": how one lives, what one eats, where and how one travels, and even one's own body and circle of friends. In the mode of singularization, life is not simply lived; it is *curated*. From one situation to the next, the late-modern subject *performs* his or her particular self to others, who become an audience, and this self will not be found attractive unless it seems authentic. With their profiles, the omnipresent social media are one of the central arenas for crafting this particularity. Here, the subject operates within a comprehensive social market governed by attractiveness, in which there is an ongoing struggle for visibility that can only be won by those who seem exceptional. Late modernity has turned out to be a *culture of the authentic* that is simultaneously a *culture of the attractive*.

Finally, the displacement of industrial society's logic of the general by late modernity's logic of the particular has had extraordinarily profound effects on the social, collective, and political forms of the early twenty-first century. It is not only individuals and objects that have been singularized: collectives have been singularized as well! Of course, formal organizations, political parties, and the bureaucratic state exist further in the background, yet even they are on the defensive against particular and temporary forms of the social that promise higher degrees of identification. The latter undermine universal rules and standard procedures by cultivating worlds of their own, each with its own identity. This is true of collaborations and projects in the professional and political world that, as affective entities with particular participants and fixed deadlines, are each unique. And it is also true of the scenes, political subcultures, leisure clubs, and consumer groups in the real and virtual worlds that, as aesthetic or hermeneutic voluntary communities with highly specific interests and world views, distance themselves quite far from popular culture and mainstream politics.

The singularization of the social also applies to the ubiquitous political and sub-political *neo-communities* in which a given historical, geographical, or ethical peculiarity is taken as the basis of a commonly imagined culture. This is a broad field that includes the identity politics of ethnic communities and diasporas that have formed over the course of global migration flows. In many places, too, new religious and fundamentalist communities (mostly

Christian or Muslim) have begun to spread that lay claim to a sort of religious exceptionalism. Within this context, the right-wing political populism that has arisen since the turn of the millennium has invoked the cultural authenticity of one's own people and their national culture. At the same time, but in a different way, "cultural diversity" became a guiding principle of liberal social and cultural politics around the beginning of the twenty-first century.

Like the shapes and colors in a kaleidoscope, the phenomena of present-day society discussed above, which at first seem to be highly heterogeneous, form a pattern, and it is this pattern that I intend to outline in the present book. My main thesis is as follows: in late modernity, a structural transformation has taken place in society, a transformation in which the dominance of the social logic of the general has been usurped by the dominance of a *social logic of the particular*. In what follows, this exceptionality or uniqueness – in other words, that which seems to be nonexchangeable and incomparable – will be circumscribed with the concept of singularity.[5] My theory of late modernity, and of modernity in general, thus hinges on the distinction between the general and the particular. This distinction is not uncomplicated, but it opens up a perspective that helps us to unlock the present. Originally a philosophical matter, the difference between the general and the particular was subjected to a systematic analysis by Kant.[6] Here, however, I would like to free it from the corset of epistemology and discuss it in sociological terms. In the human world, of course, the general and the particular always coexist; it is a matter of perspective. According to Kant, "concepts" are always general, whereas "intuition" (*Anschauung*) is directed toward the particular. Thus, it is possible to interpret every element of the world either as a specific individual entity or as an example of a general type. As far as sociology is concerned, this is trivial. The sociologically interesting question is entirely different: there are social complexes and entire forms of society that systematically promote and prefer the creation of the general while inhibiting and devaluing the particular. And, conversely, there are other social complexes and societies that encourage, value, and actively engage in the practice of singularization at the expense of the general. *The general* and *the particular* do not simply exist. They are both social fabrications.

Late-modern society – that is, the form of modernity that has been developing since the 1970s or 1980s – is a *society of singularities* to the extent that its predominant logic is the social logic of the particular. It is also – and this cannot be stressed enough – the first society in which this is true in a comprehensive sense. In fact, the social logic of the particular governs *all* dimensions of the social: things and objects as well as subjects, collectives, spaces, and

Introduction: The Proliferation of the Particular

temporalities. "Singularity" and "singularization" are cross-sectional concepts, and they designate a cross-sectional phenomenon that pervades all of society. Although the thought may seem unusual at first, it must be emphasized that singularization has affected *more* than just human subjects, and it is for this reason that the concept of individuality, which has traditionally been reserved for human beings, is no longer applicable. Singularization also encompasses the fabrication and appropriation of things and objects as particular. It applies to the formation and perception of spaces, temporalities, and – not least – collectives.

To be sure, the structure of the society of singularities is unusual and surprising, and it appears as though we are lacking suitable concepts and perspectives for understanding its complexity. How can a society organize itself in such a way as to be oriented toward the seemingly fleeting and antisocial factor of the particular? Which structures have given shape to the society of singularities, and which forms have been adopted by its economy and technology, its social structure and lifestyles, its working world, cities, and politics? And how can and should a sociological investigation proceed that wishes to subject the social logic of singularization to a detailed analysis? From the outset, it is important for such an investigation to avoid two false approaches: mystification and exposure.

Those who maintain a *mystifying* attitude toward singularities – which is widespread in the social world of art viewers, religious worshippers, admirers of charismatic leaders, lovers, music fans, brand fetishizers, and unwavering patriots – presume that the things that are valuable and fascinating to them are, in their very essence and independent of their observer, *genuinely* authentic and unique phenomena. In response to this tendency to mystify the authentic, the function of sociological analysis is to clarify matters. It should not be supposed that singularities are pre-social givens; rather, it is necessary to reconstruct the processes and structures of the social logic of singularities. "Social logic" means that singularities are not, without any ado whatsoever, objectively or subjectively present but are rather *socially fabricated* through and through. As we will see, that which is regarded and experienced as unique arises exclusively from social practices of perception, evaluation, production, and appropriation in which people, goods, communities, images, books, cities, events, and other such things are *singularized*. That it is possible to analyze *general* practices and structures, which themselves revolve around the production of *singularities*, is not a logical contradiction but rather a genuine paradox. That is precisely the objective of this book: to figure out the patterns, types, and constellations that have emerged from the social fabrication of particularities. Singularities are therefore anything but antisocial or pre-social; in this context, any metaphor suggesting that they are in some way isolated or separated from society would be entirely out of place. On the contrary, singularities are the very things around which *the social* revolves in late modernity.

To dissect the social logic of particularities without mystifying uniqueness is not, however, the same thing as denying the reality of singularities and revealing them to be mere appearances or ideological constructs. Such efforts at *exposure* can often be found masquerading as cultural critique. The critic will gleefully set out to demonstrate that the apparent particularities of others are in fact just further examples of general types, examples of popular tastes or of the eternal cycle of circulating of goods: Apple products, the films by the Coen brothers, and gifted children are not *really* extraordinary, and behind all purported originality there in fact lurks nothing more than conformist, average types. My analysis of the social logic of singularities will go out of its way to avoid such reductionism. As I mentioned above, it is not surprising that, as Kant proposed, everything particular can be interpreted from a different perspective as an example of something general. What appears to be particular can *always* be typecast. However, the fact that singularities are socially fabricated does not mean that their social reality should be denied. In this case, it might be best to recall the famous "Thomas theorem": "If men define situations as real, they are real in their consequences."[7] In our context, this means the following: in that the social world is increasingly oriented toward people, objects, images, groups, places, and events that are felt and understood to be singular – and is in part aimed at creating them as such – the social logic of singularities unfurls for its participants a reality with significant, and even dire, consequences.

The critique that denies individual singularities the value of the particular can itself be interpreted – and must be interpreted – in sociological terms. It is a characteristic *component* of the evaluative discourses of the society of singularities. These discourses derive their dynamics and unpredictability from the fact that the special value of goods, images, people, works of art, religious beliefs, cities, or events is often disputed and caught up in debates about what society considers valuable or not.[8] In general, the social assessments of something as particular or as an example of the general are extremely volatile and have preoccupied late modernity to an enormous extent. Indeed, one could say that late-modern society has become a veritable *society of valorization*. That which is regarded as exceptional today can be devalued as early as tomorrow and reclassified as something conformist and typical. And whereas, despite all efforts, so many people and things never achieve the status of the extraordinary, others are catapulted into the sphere of singularity by one evaluation process or another. In such a way, a valuable piece of vintage furniture can be dragged out of a garbage heap, and a social misfit can become an accepted nerd. This is to say that, in the society of singularities, processes of singularization and *de-singularization* go hand in hand. Both processes, however, confirm what is valuable: not the general but the particular.

It must be clearly stated: the social logic of singularity, whose proliferation has been observable since the 1970s or 1980s, fully contradicts that which had constituted the core of modern society for more than 200 years. The society of classical modernity, which crystallized in eighteenth-century Western Europe and reached its zenith as *industrial modernity* in the United States and Soviet Union during the middle of the twentieth century, was organized in a fundamentally different way. What prevailed then was a *social logic of the general*, and this prevalence was so radical and drastic as to have been unprecedented in world history. As Max Weber aptly observed, the classical modernity of industrial society was fundamentally a process of profound formal rationalization.[9] And, as I would like to add, every manifestation of this formal rationalization – whether in science and technology, economic–industrial production, the state, or the law – promoted and supported the dominance of the general. The focus everywhere was on standardization and formalization, on making sure that the elements produced in the world were equal, homogeneous, and also equally justified: on the assembly lines in industrial factories and in the rows of buildings in the International Style, in the social and constitutional state, in the military, in the "schooling" of children, in ideologies, and in technology.

As long as one remains attached to this old image of modernity, which is shaped by industrial society, it is easy to dismiss the emergence of singularities and singularizations as a mere marginal or superficial phenomenon. The logic of singularities, however, is not in the periphery but is in fact operating at the center of late-modern society. What are the causes of this profound transformation? My first answer to this question, which I will elaborate over the course of this book, is as follows: during the 1970s and 1980s, the two most powerful social engines that had been propelling the standardization of industrial modernity were converted into engines of social singularization: the economy and technology. In late modernity, the economy and technology have become, for the first time in history, large-scale *generators of singularization*. They have become paradoxical agents of large-scale particularity, and we are the first to experience and understand the whole scope of this process and its social, psychological, and political consequences.

Between industrial modernity and late modernity there thus occurred a twofold *structural breach*. The first originated in the structural shift from the old industrial economy to *cultural capitalism* and the *economy of singularities*, with the creative economy as its main branch. The capitalism of the knowledge and culture economy is that of a post-industrial economy. Its goods are essentially cultural goods, and they are "singularity goods" – that is, things, services, events, or media formats whose success with consumers depends on them being recognized as unique. With this transformation of goods, the structure of markets and employment has fundamentally changed as well. Following the example of classic works such as Karl Marx's *Capital* and Georg Simmel's *The Philosophy of Money*, social theory has to engage with the most advanced form of the economy if it wants to understand the most advanced form of modernity. The second structural breach is being brought about by the digital revolution, which marks a technological shift away from standardization toward singularization – from the data tracking of profiles and the personalization of digital networks to the use of 3D printers. Like nothing before it, the dominant technology of the digital revolution has the character of a "culture machine" in which primarily cultural elements – images, narratives, and games – are both produced and received.

If one considers just the economy and technology – that is, cultural capitalism and the culture machine – it becomes clear that the society of singularities has afforded a central position to something that the former industrial society had tended to marginalize: *culture*. For the way that late modernity is structured, culture plays an unusual role. Through its massive preference for rational processes and formal norms – and much to the chagrin of cultural critics – industrial modernity went out of its way to devalue cultural practices and objects. Today, on the contrary, unique objects, places, times, subjects, and collectives are no longer simply perceived as means to an end; in that they are assigned a value of their own – be it aesthetic or ethical – they are now strongly regarded as culture itself. Later, I will go into greater detail about what constitutes culture and how it circulates, but for now it is possible to state that culture always exists wherever *value* has been assigned to something – that is, wherever processes of *valorization* are taking place. It is important to understand that practices of valorization and practices of singularization go hand in hand. When people, things, places, or collectives appear to be unique, they are attributed value and seem to be socially valuable. Significantly, however, the inverse is also true: if they appear to lack any unique qualities, they are *worthless*. In short, the society of singularities is engaged in *culturalizing the social*, and profoundly so. It is busy playing a grand social game of valorization and singularization (on the one hand) and devaluation and de-singularization (on the other), and it invests objects and practices with a value beyond their functionality. In late modernity, moreover, the sphere of culture has adopted a specific form: no longer a clearly delineated subsystem, it has rather transformed into a global *hyperculture* in which potentially everything – from

Zen meditation to industrial footstools, from Montessori schools to YouTube videos – can be regarded as culture and can become elements of the highly mobile markets of valorization, which entice the participation of subjects with the promise of self-actualization.

We have thus come to another central feature of the society of singularities: the extreme relevance of affects. With its logic of the general and its drive toward rationalization, industrial modernity systematically reduced the role of affect in society. When people, things, events, places, or collectives are singularized and culturalized, however, they then operate by *attracting* (or repulsing) others. Indeed, it is only by affecting others that they can be regarded as singular at all. Late-modern society is a society of affect in a way that classical modernity never could have been. To a great extent, its components operate in an affective manner, and its subjects long to be affected and to affect others in order to be considered attractive and authentic themselves. In short, whereas the logic of the general is associated with processes of social rationalization and reification, the logic of the singular is related to processes of social culturalization and the intensification of affect.

Thus far, I have focused on the fact that late modernity has undergone a historically unprecedented structural transformation that revolves around singularization and culturalization. Yet are these processes really entirely novel? And, inversely, has the old logic of the general been completely supplanted by the new logic of the singular? The answer to both of these questions has to be no, and this fact complicates the larger picture considerably. First, it is necessary to revise our image of *modernity* altogether. If we understand late modernity – our present time – as that version of modernity which has replaced industrial society, then we are obliged to discuss the notion of modernity in general. However, the sociological discourse about modernity has frequently been one-dimensional in that it often conflates modernization with the processes of formal rationalization and reification. In my view, however, modernity should not be understood as a one-dimensional process in this sense, for, from its very beginning, it has been composed of two divergently organized dimensions: the rationalistic dimension of standardization, and the cultural dimension that involves the attribution of value, the intensification of affect, and singularization. The encyclopedic thinkers of the nineteenth century – Friedrich Nietzsche and Georg Simmel, for example, but also Max Weber – had a sense for this dual structure.[10]

The main impulse behind this second dimension – the dimension of non-rationalistic modernity – can be traced all the way back to the artistic movement of Romanticism around the year 1800, which may seem to have been marginal at first glance. It was the Romantics who first "discovered" and sought to promote singularities on all levels: the originality of works of art and hand-crafted objects; the diversity and poetry of nature; the particular features of picturesque locations; the beauty of a single moment; unique people, cultural circles, and nations; and, of course, the emphatic individuality and self-development of the subject. These themes did not die out during the nineteenth and twentieth centuries; rather, they pervaded all of modernity – for instance, in the field of art, in religion, and also in certain versions of the political. The Romantic tradition, which gives primacy to the singular, exerted a decisive influence over any number of aesthetic and cultural-revolutionary movements opposed to rationalistic modernity, the most recent large-scale example of which was the counterculture of the 1960s and 1970s. It was this tradition, too, that also instigated the new middle class's post-materialistic shift in values, which revolved around the idea of self-actualization and thus became a crucial precondition for late modernity's culture of particularity. In fact, I think it is possible to explain the rise of widespread singularization and culturalization as a convergence of three mutually enhancing structural moments: the emergence of cultural capitalism, the triumph of digital media technologies, and the new middle class's post-Romantic, revolutionary yearning for authenticity. All three of these developments will be examined in the present book.

Upon closer inspection, then, it becomes clear that modernity has been influenced from the beginning by standardization *and* singularization, rationalization *and* culturalization, reification *and* the intensification of affect. Without a doubt, modernity is modern in that it radicalizes and pushes rationalization to the extreme. Yet it is also and no less modern for having developed singularities in an extreme fashion. If, however, modernity is two-faced in this way and an age of extremes,[11] what is the precise novelty of late modernity? To what extent is it really a genuinely different and new form of modernity? As I hope to show over the course of this book, these questions can be answered by taking a close look at how the *relation* between the social logic of the general and the social logic of the particular has changed over the last 40 years. Of course, this process has *not* caused formal rationalization to vanish entirely. Instead, it has changed its *status*. This much can be said in advance: whereas, in industrial modernity, these two logics formed an asymmetrical dualism, in late modernity they have transformed into a foreground structure and a background structure.

Strangely enough, the mechanisms of formal rationality have been restructured in such a way that they are now "in the background" and function as general *infrastructures* for the systematic production of particularities.[12] Now, essentially instrumentally rational technologies are systematically able to produce unique objects. A prominent example of this is genetic research, which promotes a medical

Introduction: The Proliferation of the Particular

perspective that no longer classifies human beings according to types of illness or standard values but rather identifies them as being irreducibly particular.[13] A second prominent example is the act of data tracking by search engines and internet companies, which use anonymous algorithms to register the unique movements of users in order to determine their specific consumer preferences or political opinions and thus to "personalize" the internet for them. Instrumentally rational infrastructures for creating uniqueness can also be found in complex valorization technologies that, by means of ratings and rankings, make it possible to compare the particular features of restaurants, universities, coaches, or potential spouses. In short, late modernity also has its share of standardization techniques, but they are often part of complex background structures that help to keep the processes of singularization running smoothly.

In order to understand the society of singularities, it is necessary to examine its forms, consequences, and contradictions in various areas. Its basic structure can be seen in the Western societies of Europe and North America. It is in these traditional regions of bygone industrial modernity that the transition to post-industrial society has most clearly taken place. This book is thus about more than just Germany or the national "container" of German society. Rather, I have had to adopt an international perspective from the beginning. National differences notwithstanding, the economic, social, and political patterns of the society of singularities can be found in the United States as well as in France, Germany, Great Britain, Italy, Scandinavia, or Australia. Besides, it would be shortsighted to reduce this configuration to the West alone. The process of globalization has made the clear geographical boundaries between the global North and the global South porous, so that the formats of cultural capitalism, digitalization, cultural and knowledge-based labor, singularistic lifestyles, creative cities, liberal politics, and cultural essentialism now circulate throughout the entire globe and can thus be seen in certain areas of Latin America, Asia, or Africa as well.[14] In many places, the societies of the former global South have thus also begun to orient themselves toward the society of singularities. In all likelihood, they will determine our global future.

How does the late-modern present and future look? Will it be easy or difficult? For now, present-day society seems profoundly contradictory. On the one hand, there is a "brave new world" of design objects and international vacations with home exchanges, YouTube hits, the creative California lifestyle, events, projects, and aestheticized city districts from Shanghai to Copenhagen; on the other hand, there are also higher levels of stress, the social marginalization of a new underclass, and various sorts of nationalism, fundamentalism, and populism. In recent years, public commentary on late modernity has thus been extremely volatile, even nervous at times. Euphoric hopes for a knowledge society lacking the toil of industrialization, for an experiential society of multiple aesthetic pleasures, and not least for a digital society that profits from the opportunities of computer networks can be heard alongside pessimistic prognostications that foresee a dramatic rise in social inequality, excessive psychological stress, and global culture wars.

This book will take a step back from these frequently alarmist commentaries in order to make the more comprehensive panorama of modernity recognizable and, within this framework, to take a closer look at the specific structures of late modernity. And this is precisely what should be expected of sociology: that it should not fall prey to the ever-shifting trends of media debates, with their tug-of-war sort of emotional communication, but rather that it should analyze the *longue durée* of social development in terms of its structures and processes, which can be measured in decades (or even in centuries). With this perspective on (late) modernity in mind, it will be difficult to dismiss the idea that the opportunities and promises of today's society have the *same* structural cause as its problems and dilemmas: they are both based on industrial society's logic of the general losing its primacy to late-modern society's logic of the particular.

Without a doubt, the society of singularities has led to considerable increases in autonomy and satisfaction, particularly within the new, highly qualified, and mobile middle class. It has a fundamentally libertarian streak, which tends to tear down social barriers to opportunity, and it enables the self-development of individuals to an extent unimaginable during classical modernity. At the same time, however, it has also become clear that the problems burdening late modernity stem from the erosion of classical modernity's logic of the general and the rise of the structures of the society of singularities, and that it is only within the latter's framework that they can be understood at all. Thus, first, the high value that late-modern culture places on uniqueness and self-development represents a systematic generator of disappointment that does much to explain today's high levels of psychological disorder. Second, the post-industrial economy of singularities is responsible for the blatant divide between the forms of work that characterize the highly qualified knowledge and culture economies, on the one hand, and the deindustrialized service economy on the other, which has given rise to new social and cultural polarization, class inequality, and grossly divergent lifestyles. Third, and at the same time, it is the culturalization and singularization of collectives, with their current preference for particular identities, that has prompted the rise of

Introduction: The Proliferation of the Particular 13

late-modern nationalism, fundamentalism, and populism, with their aggressive antagonism between the valuable and valueless.

No simple assessments or short-term solutions should be expected from any sociological analysis of the society of singularities, and this is because the causes of the opportunities and the causes of the problems in today's society cannot be neatly separated. On the contrary, they are identical. In themselves, processes of singularization are neither good nor bad. It is therefore no more appropriate to join a romantic celebration of singularities or the uncritical choir of hopeful optimists than it is to reserve a luxury suite at the "Grand Hotel Abyss" – that is, to offer a sweeping cultural-critical condemnation of late modernity as a refuge for irrational and calamitous affect against the general. This does not mean, however, that sociology should make itself too comfortable on the high seat of the distanced observer. In my understanding, it should rather be engaged in a *critical analysis* of the present and its genesis. For me, however, critical analysis does not mean normative theory. Rather, it entails developing a sensibility for the configurations of the social and its historicity in order to recognize how it engenders structures of domination and hegemony whose participants might only be hazily aware of them. In such a way, it is possible to identify significant fields of tension, unintended consequences, and new mechanisms of exclusion.[15] Without imposing any conclusions itself, this book aims to consider the personal and political implications that can be drawn from the social constellation at the beginning of the twenty-first century.

Part I provides fundamental theoretical explanations of the social logic of singularities, how it differs from the social logic of the general, and how it is associated with culture, culturalization, and valorization. With this background, it will then be possible to distinguish historical phases of social development from the standpoint of singularization. The part concludes with a brief summary of the specific structure of late modernity, which will serve as a guide for the following chapters. An examination of the transformation of the economy and (media) technologies forms the core of the book. In Part II, I discuss the structural shift from industrial society to the economy of singularities and its cultural capitalism. The first chapter is concerned with what it means to singularize goods, while the second chapter concentrates on the transformation of markets into markets of singularity, with their specific configurations of attention, visibility, and valorization. Part III focuses on the transformation of the working world and demonstrates how it is now characterized by singularistic criteria such as creativity, talent, profiles, and performance (which have bright and dark sides). Part IV is devoted to the key technology of late modernity – to the complex of algorithms, digitality, and the internet – and it investigates how it promotes both cultural and automated aspects of singularization.

Having described the economic and technological foundations of the society of singularities, I then turn in Part V to the question of how it has affected lifestyles and the structure of society. Here it is shown that the contradictory basic formula of a singularistic lifestyle is that of "successful self-actualization" and that its most significant proponents are the members of the new, highly educated middle class. A central aspect of the social structure of late modernity is not only social, but also cultural, polarization between this new middle class and new underclass, a divide that involves aspects of the culturalization of inequality. Part VI is concerned with the singularization and culturalization of the political – with the politics of the particular. Here it is shown that late modernity is characterized by political antagonism between liberal hyperculture, which is the basis of both economic and social liberalism today, and communitarian cultural essentialism of various sorts. In my conclusion, I offer an outlook in response to the main socio-political question raised by the society of singularities: is there a crisis of the general?

In a fundamental way, this study is connected to my previous book, which dealt with processes of social aestheticization.[16] Thus, certain structural features, which I referred to there as the "creativity *dispositif*," can also be found in the economy of singularities, its cultural capitalism, as well as in the digital culture machine and on the level of lifestyles. Now, however, my focus has shifted. Whereas *The Invention of Creativity* was chiefly concerned with historical genealogy, *The Society of Singularities* has at its heart a social-theoretical claim. On the one hand, it is more theoretically oriented, while on the other hand it is more strongly focused on the present. For this reason, I have also sought to address certain traditional issues of sociological analysis – labor, technology, class, and politics, for instance – in light of how the transformation to the society of singularities has affected such matters. My impression is that this shift of analytic focus from the guiding concept of creativity to that of singularity or singularization – and the concomitant shift from aestheticization to culturalization – has enabled me both to expand and to sharpen my perspective.[17]

In any case, this is not a book about other books, a theory about other theories. The social theory that I have practiced here is actually curious about social reality. As I see it, theory and empirical research are inextricably intertwined and mutually nourishing. This book has been fed by the many empirical studies from various social and cultural-theoretical disciplines that I have had occasion to cite throughout its pages. At the same time, it is theory above all that lends a cogent structure to the multiple facets of sociology. While writing, I was often surprised how a conceptual heuristic adjustment – looking at things through the lens of singularization and valorization – could make empirical circumstances appear in a different light, so much so that the ostensibly isolated elements of late modernity began to fit together like puzzle pieces to form a coherent image. This is not to say that all the work has been done. This book is not a monolithic creation but rather just a nodal point in an open network. It hopes to contribute heuristics to a sociological research program for analyzing modernity that might stimulate further work and be taken in new and perhaps unforeseen directions. One matter, however, seems crucial to me, and this is that social scientists and cultural theorists will have to take seriously the social logic of singularities and processes of culturalization.

I
Modernity Between the Social Logic of the General and the Social Logic of the Particular

Throughout modernity, a social logic of the general and a social logic of the particular have competed with one another. This basic assumption is the starting point from which this book proceeds. The logic of the general is associated with the social process of formal rationalization, while the logic of singularities is related to a process of culturalization. Whereas, during classical – and, above all, industrial – modernity, processes of singularization and culturalization represented antipodes to the dominance of the general and were structurally subordinate to it, in late modernity they have become guiding and formative forces for the whole of society. At the same time, rationalization has changed its form and largely become a background structure for processes of singularization. In order to make a case for this thesis, I will first have to explain certain concepts and my historical schematic. My first goal in this part is to delineate the social logic of the general in classical modernity and its practice of formal rationalization (1). The next section will describe the concept of singularities, the features of the social logic of the particular, and its practices (2). This will be followed by a discussion of the connection between singularization and culturalization, and remarks will also be made about the revision of a strong concept of culture that revolves around processes of valorization and the question of "value" (3). With this background, it will then be possible to turn to the historical and social development from premodern societies to late modernity in order to identify phases of cultural transformation in which the social relation between the general and the particular has changed (4).

1
The Social Logic of the General

Modernity and Generality

What is modernity? What are the central features of modern society in its classical form? In my view, the answer is clear: the structural core of classical modernity, since its beginnings in eighteenth-century Western Europe, is a social logic of the general that encouraged the standardization, formalization, and generalization of all entities of society. Modernity fundamentally reformulated the world of traditional societies by thoroughly and relentlessly imposing new forms of the general on their practices, discourses, and institutional complexes. As an overarching praxis, it could be said that modernity "enacted generality" in the world.

Such an understanding of classical modernity can be associated with a particular sociological theory, but it elevates this theory to a more abstract level as well: modernity should be understood first and foremost as a process of formal rationalization. For its part, formal rationalization means that modernity transformed society in such a way that traditional customs were replaced by large-scale complexes of predictable rules, which in turn entailed technically or normatively regulated manners of behavior. Formal rationalization can be derived from the telos of optimization, whose ultimate aims are the efficient processing of nature and the transparent ordering of society. This understanding of modernity as an elementary process of rationalization is not, however, self-evident. In fact, if one were to ask sociologists about the central features of classical modernity, one would receive a great variety of answers. Often enough, and especially in Germany, modernity is equated with a process of functional differentiation. What is meant by this is, accordingly, the differentiation of specialized and functional subsystems (the economy, law, politics, mass media, education, etc.), each of which follows its own self-imposed logic and structure. Although it was Niklas Luhmann who formulated this approach most systematically, its basic ideas extend back to theories about the division of labor. On the international stage, however, another interpretation has been more influential. Going back to Karl Marx, this interpretation treats capitalism as the central organ of modernity in the form of an economic and technological formation that is oriented toward the uninterrupted accumulation of capital and leads to its vastly unequal distribution. It goes without saying that each of these approaches has identified important characteristics of modernity. Neither, however, is sufficient. From my perspective, the structure of modernity will only become comprehensible if one begins with the process of rationalization,[1] as Max Weber argued most convincingly.[2] Authors as varied as Georg Simmel, Martin Heidegger, Theodor W. Adorno, Hans Blumenberg, Michel Foucault, and Zygmunt Bauman would go on to espouse this idea as well, though each in his own way.[3]

The understanding of modernity as a process of rationalization can and must, however, be understood in a more abstract and fundamental way than has previously been the case, for what lurks behind rationalization is the social logic of the general. By rationalizing the social world, modern practices attempt to impose their general forms and configure the world according to them. In praxeological terms, the social logic of the general – with its "generalization," and by means of "doing generality" – encompasses four interconnected complexes of social practices that have an empirically open relationship to one another: practices of observation, evaluation, production, and appropriation. Whenever a society is subjected to rationalization and generalization, these four sets of practices are always at work.

Here, practices of *observing* the world (in science, the economy, the state, etc.) are unambiguously and unilaterally oriented toward the general – that is, systems of general concepts and schemata have been developed and applied in order to make it possible to register, measure, and differentiate every element of the world (people, nature, things, etc.) as a particular example of general patterns. In the case of practices of *evaluating* (for instance, in law or in school), those elements of the world that fit into the schema of the general are clearly treated positively and given preference for seeming "correct" or "normal."[4] Practices of *producing* (for instance in industry or education) are here at their heart oriented toward systematically creating elements of the world (things, subjects, spaces, etc.) that correspond to the schemata of the general and, in extreme cases, are even identical and fully interchangeable with one another. Finally, practices of *appropriating* the world now typically take the form of objectively dealing with things, subjects, etc., that are regarded as standardized and interchangeable entities – for instance, by treating objects as functional and useful, or subjects as having a certain role or function.

I Modernity Between the General and the Particular 21

That said, it would be a misperception to identify modernity entirely with the social logic of the general and its formal rationalization. To do so would be to fall victim to the totalization of the general that characterizes the rationalistic discourse of modernity (in philosophy and sociology, above all) and to formulate no more than a partial understanding of it. Even classical modernity cannot entirely be understood in terms of the logic of the general, and late modernity even less so. At this point, however, we will have to deal with the features of the general and its dominance in an "artificially" pure and rationalistic form before moving on to the next step, which will be to distinguish it from the social logic of singularities.

Typifications and Rationalizations

Historically speaking, it would of course be short-sighted to claim that a social logic of the general did not exist until the beginnings of modernity in the late eighteenth century or that there had not been any formats of formal rationality until 250 years ago. In a certain respect, both already existed in premodern societies – in the archaic (preliterate and nomadic) and in the traditional (high-cultural) societies as well. However, it is necessary to distinguish two different modes of the social logic of the general: typification and rationalization.

The practices that constitute the social world are always based on typification – that is, on making the individual elements of the world comprehensible and manageable in such a way that they can be categorized as particular examples of general sorts or types: people, animals, things, gods, and so on. If it is true that the "life-world of everyday life" is largely based on custom and repetition, this implies that, in the semantics of natural language and in implicit knowledge, typifying classifications are regularly performed, and thus that the particular, with which everyone is constantly confronted, is regularly subsumed under the general.[5] Here the particular is, so to speak, the *general-particular*. Such a logic of typification prevailed to a great extent in archaic "cold societies" (in Claude Lévi-Strauss's terms) of illiterate premodernity, which were relatively resistant to change, but it of course also features in (late) modern societies as well. As typifications, however, socially relevant generalities are usually not the object of rationalization; they are not, that is, subjected to systematic control and reflection. In the mode of typification, accordingly, it is not to be expected that general concepts are necessarily distinguished from one another in a sharp manner. As semantic prototypes, they rather represent zones of *similarities*.[6]

In premodern societies, too, there were also specific complexes of behavior that were instrumentally or normatively rational and formed something like insular complexes of rationalization. These distinguished themselves through the targeted systematization of behavior according to explicit rules and principles. The *techne* of these societies, for instance, was instrumentally rational and based more on practical than on theoretical knowledge. It is thus indicative of a systematic activity for processing nature, an activity that enabled these societies to domesticate and distance themselves from the world. Later, with the creation of high-cultural empires and their administrative and legal practices, normative practices also began to be systematized, and this led not only to the codification of social rules but also to the intellectual systematization of (especially religious) views of the world, not least through the medium of writing.[7]

The historically early forms of a rationalistic logic of the general have the same cause as the more sophisticated forms that came later: they can all be interpreted as a social response to *scarcity* and *disorder*. Society's relation to nature is defined first and foremost by scarcity and imminent shortages. With instrumentally rational practices, societies attempt to counteract scarcity by conserving means, labor, time, and energy. Instrumentally rational practices follow a *rule of thrift* in order to reduce scarcity and, at best, to fulfill all of society's demands. In addition, however, there is also a basic problem of order that, though also relevant to society's relation to external nature, concerns above all the relation between its subjects. This problem became especially acute at the moment when tribal and nomadic social forms were displaced by social systems under the conditions of sedentariness and elementary divisions of labor, which applied to people regardless of their physical presence. Normative rationalizations were thus attempts – by means of legal systems, for instance – to guarantee social coordination and control on a permanent basis.

Modern society went beyond the isolated instrumentally rational and normative-rational practices of traditional societies. Western modernity, which originated in early-modern Europe and began to flourish toward the end of the eighteenth century with the rise of industrialization, science, market economies, urbanization, and democratization, is essentially synonymous with the expansive institutionalization of entire systems of social practices that involved the systematic and lasting rationalization of behavior, production, things, subjects, and knowledge by means of a social logic of the general. Thus, modernity is both an extensive and an intensive *generalization machine*. Now, the social logic of the general no longer involved the mere typification of similarities, though this practice continued to take place on the margins; rather, its essential feature was that of an expansive systematization of the world in the form of standardization, formalization, and generalization. Conversely, one

I Modernity Between the General and the Particular   23

could say that what we refer to as "modern society" is nothing more than the expansion of this social generalization machine. Its precondition was modernity's awareness of contingency, which gradually encompassed all social practices and turned them into an object of targeted transformation that more or less led in only one direction: toward the general.[8]

From a praxeological perspective, the process of "rationalization" operates on both the macro and the micro levels. It is not the case that, at a particular point in time, a structure of formal rationality is put in place once and for all and remains fixed from that moment on. Rather, individual elements of the social – objects, subjects, collectives, spaces, times – are each made the object of rationalization through particular practices. They are repeatedly "made rational" through the practices of observation, evaluation, production, and appropriation.[9] It is the interplay of many local acts of rationalization that gives rise to the large-scale formal rationalization of society as a whole. Within the framework of the modern project of rationalization, this profound transformation of the social world and its relation to nature pursues the goal of optimization (that is, systematic improvement), which has often culminated in the semantics of progress.[10] The modern pursuit of progress was likewise a response to the basic problems of scarcity in nature and the preservation of social order, but to some extent the social response was far more aggressive than defensive. No longer was it enough simply to avoid shortages and anarchy; over the course of systematically rationalizing all realms of society, modernity sought to overcome the problems of scarcity and social disorder once and for all.

Standardization, Formalization, Generalization

Since the eighteenth century, the pervasive formal rationalization of modern society has taken place in three areas and approaches. What I have in mind is *technical* rationalization, *cognitive* rationalization, and *normative* rationalization, each of which involves specific practices and different variants of "doing generality."

Technical rationalization is mainly found in the fields of production, natural processing (industrial agriculture, the extraction of raw materials), the industrial manufacturing of capital and consumer goods, as well as in urban development and the transportation sector.[11] It entails reconfiguring behavior and implementing technology in order to increase the efficiency of the production and distribution of goods (as well as that of the behavioral coordination needed to do both). Here the practice of the general is one of *standardization*: to increase efficiency, it is necessary to standardize, homogenize, and identically reproduce the optimal types of behavior within the human–machine configuration in order to coordinate them according to a predictable pattern. At the same time, these human–machine configurations enable the production of standardized entities, especially identical goods in a seemingly unlimited number.

The locus of cognitive rationalization is the sciences – particularly the natural sciences, but the behavioral sciences as well. Here the practice of the general is one of *generalizing* knowledge, and its goal is to produce general, empirically tested theories with which to provide generally valid descriptions and explanations of reality, the ultimate aim being to subject reality to technological control. This general knowledge can then be conveyed to subjects within the framework of education. The intention of both technical and cognitive rationalization is to quantify and measure the general entities that they require and produce. For this reason, standardization and generalization are related to the modern ideal of quantification, according to which seemingly everything has to be measured, be it in terms of correlations, growth, or quantities.[12]

Finally, the normative rationalization of modernity involves the targeted regulation of intersubjective orders, characteristic of which is modern law with its origins in discursive arenas and its use in government administration. In a strict sense, it can have a normative or normalistic form.[13] Here the practice of the general is one of *formalization*. In law, the most general possible rules are established, and entirely deducible systems of rules are put in place in order to guide (and, if necessary, correct) individual acts of social behavior. On the one hand, the intention of modern law is to make activity predictable and transparent; on the other hand, however, it is also meant to convey the conviction of a regulated order in which equal things are treated equally and unequal things are treated unequally. Law, and with it the entire normative rationalization of modernity, which also encompasses non-judicial areas of civilian interaction and moral behavior, is intended to make social interactions predictable and reciprocal. Law and normative rationalization require fundamental legal equality, but they also require the psychological uniformity of subjects, who are expected to be self-responsible and follow norms.

As the three forms in which the rationalistic logic of the general operates and enacts generality, standardization, formalization, and generalization have been interconnected with one another since the end of the eighteenth century, and they have *made* the modern world what it is. Together they have had several consequences: they have lent relatively high levels of predictability, order, and transparency to the social, thus making it seemingly easier to foresee and plan. This logic goes hand in hand with the interchangeability of subjects, who are the primary bearers of functional roles, so that the

I Modernity Between the General and the Particular

functionality of subject positions can be independent of personalities, membership in a given family, or group affiliations. Moreover, the social logic of the general reduces the level of emotional intensity that is integral to the social. It leaves no room for participating in a given practice for its own sake, but rather only as a means to a (further) end – for instance to achieve greater efficiency, establish dominion over nature, or coordinate behavior in a more transparent manner. The reification that arises from the generality of these rules is thus associated with controlling and reducing affect. Here, the mode of social practice is not emotional engagement but rather the emotionally distant following of rules. Even moral rules are to be abided by out of duty and not out of inclination.[14] In modernity, the social logic of the general ultimately tends toward the ideal of the universal, toward that which is valid for everyone at all times. Even if this *universalism* is not achieved everywhere – on account of the restrictions of national states, for instance – it remains the ultimate goal of generalization.[15]

Objects, Subjects, Spaces, Times, and Collectives in the Social Logic of the General

The social logic of the general, which goes hand in hand with formal rationalization, affects all aspects of the social. The term "social logic" is thus related to a comprehensive way of structuring things that encompasses the practices of observation, evaluation, production, and appropriation discussed above, and also includes every social entity. In an analogous way, this will also be true of the social logic of singularities. The credibility of a given social theory generally depends on its ability to make statements about all elements or entities of society.[16] From my perspective, it is possible to distinguish (at least) five entities of the social that are formatted in a particular way by a social logic: objects, subjects, spaces, temporalities, and collectives. In other words, the social world consists of social practices in which subjects and objects participate, from which collectives are formed, and which structure time and place in a particular way. And in the classical version of modern society, all five entities are the object of "enacted generality."

For *objects* (including *things*), this means that they are produced to be identical (that is, as unending replicas of the same) or "more of the same" (that is, as variations of the same thing).[17] They are interchangeable. The prime example of this is the industrially manufactured product, which customers use or consume in a standardized way. If there are any differences between the objects, this is a matter of gradual differences in usefulness, performance, or suitability that nevertheless satisfy general and objective standards.

In this regard, even semiotic objects such as texts and images can be regarded as contributions to the general – namely, to general information. Here the objects remain stable even when they circulate: they are always the same (they do not have any cultural biography), and at most they will show no more than a few signs of wear over time. They are rational artifacts that have instrumental relevance in the manner of a tool; they are a means to an end that vanishes as soon as its purpose has been fulfilled or the means itself is no longer suitable. Beside the commodity, accordingly, the second main example of general objects is the machine. A machine is not only *produced* in identical copies; it also *produces* identical copies of goods. As an object type, the machine is a general piece of infrastructure for fabricating the general.

We now come to *subjects*, who are produced within the framework of classical modernity "doing generality" and also form themselves in this context. They are all trained to have the same competencies and to exhibit identical, or at least similar, manners of behavior. The competencies and activities of subjects here contribute to formal rationality. One model for such a general subject is a type of character driven from within by a sense of morality or utilitarianism – a character that accordingly follows a set of principle or acts according to cost–benefit analyses. Another model is the "socially adjusted person," who strives to meet intersubjective expectations and to be "normal" or "average" (in the non-pejorative sense).[18] The first model implies a static and stable sort of uniformity, while the second entails a dynamic sort of uniformity that is always readjusting to new social demands. In both cases, the subject becomes an object of social discipline. Any deviation from the standard is thus sanctioned for seeming abnormal.

Within the framework of classical modernity, of course, there are also subjects with special characteristics. Such cases are not examples of singularities in the strict sense, however; they are rather instances of the general-particular – that is, they represent differential positions within the framework of a general order.[19] This was typically a matter of either differences in specialization or gradual differences in performance. Subjects are encouraged to develop specialized competencies and roles. Above all, within a given set of professional qualifications, these activities are standardized and aligned to suit different sorts of jobs. While engaged in professional (or educational) activities, subjects in classical modernity are in turn evaluated according to what is called their achievement. The latter involves systematic differences that can be measured against a general and "objective" standard, either according to a qualitative scale of better or worse (the classic example being grades in school) or according to a quantitative scale of more or less (the classic example being production targets). In other words, the social logic

I Modernity Between the General and the Particular

of the general also allows for "individualism," but it is defined by every subject having the same rights and obligations, behaving in the same self-responsible manner, and fulfilling his or her duties and requirements in the same way. In the social logic of the general, "individualization" thus presents itself as individual differences in achievement along prescribed scales of evaluation.[20]

Within the rationalistic logic of the general, the *spatiality* of the social involves the replication of identical or similar spaces.[21] In this case, space is extensive and serial to the extent that it allows identical structures – series of the same thing – to extend beyond local contexts. What is more, rationalistic spatiality integrates a sort of container model into social reality by clearly assigning particular types of spaces to particular activities. Industrial cities, for instance, are characteristic of seriality and its container-like nature. In the sense of "serial construction," their components are in part even identical, so that they can literally be exchanged with one another.[22] Here, spatiality is functional and oriented toward the directive of technical (and normative) rationality. It accordingly entails a rigid spatial separation of individual activities (work, habitation, leisure, etc.).

The social logic of the general functions in an analogous way on the level of *temporality*. In classical modernity, time was rationalized, and this involved the standardization of comparable synchronized intervals.[23] Here it is characteristic that social praxis comes to be structured according to repetitive acts in time (the paradigmatic example of this is at the workplace) and that spaces of time are filled up in equal ways (thus the working week standardizes working conditions). The mode that shapes time in such a way is thus not the event but rather the routine; it is not a matter of occupying a given moment but rather one of reducing time's emotional qualities. It should also be noted that this sort of time is future-oriented: the present is only instrumentally interesting as a contribution toward achieving a future goal, whereas the past is closed off and seems obsolete. Time thus becomes the central object of future planning, which is understood in terms of progress, improvement, or growth. On the level of the lives of subjects, this corresponds to the model of linear biography.

What sort of *collectives* are produced by the rationalistic logic of the general? More revealing, perhaps, is the sort of past collectives that this logic is oriented against: traditional *communities* based on personal connections. These were replaced by the *organization* – that is, by an objectifying and impersonal collective formed to achieve a given purpose (the organization is thus an expression of the general principles of formal rationality).[24] At their heart, classical organizations are based on clear technical-normative rules and hierarchized responsibilities, on membership and qualifications, and on predictable decision-making. The bureaucratic state is thus just as paradigmatic of modern organization as are capitalist and socialist firms. Within the framework of the social logic of the general, organizations are typically structured in the same way regardless of their respective purposes, and they are thus experienced by subjects as similarly designed entities (as organizations, hospitals are more or less the same as schools, government agencies, corporations, etc.).

Finally, the rationalistic logic of the general and its formal rationality also manifest themselves in the overall form of social praxis in which subjects, objects, spaces, temporalities, and collectives participate. Here there is an overarching *mode of praxis*. In the latter, all practices tendentially take the form of instrumentally rational or normative-rational activity, so that they are explicitly oriented toward pursuing objectives or following social rules. The instrumentally rational treatment of objects and normatively regulated interactions (between those present or absent) are paradigmatic of this, and the conceptual pair "labor and interaction" can thus be said to designate the rationalistic mode of praxis as a whole.[25] The result is that, for the most part, activity here is no longer habitual but is rather routinized; in other words, it is now based on the sedimentation of explicitly and consciously refined, optimized, or perfected rules.

Industrial Modernity as a Prototype

Generally speaking, the history of Western modernity can be divided into three phases: bourgeois modernity, organized modernity, and late modernity.[26] Over the course of the eighteenth and nineteenth centuries in Europe and North America, bourgeois modernity gradually ousted the traditional feudal and aristocratic society. During this stage, a social logic of the general came to prominence in various sectors of society on account of early industrialization, the philosophy of the Enlightenment,[27] the rise of science, the emergence of transregional commodity markets and capitalist structures of production, the gradual establishment of democracy and the rule of law, urbanization, and the formation of the bourgeoisie (with its proclaimed self-discipline, morality, and productivity) as the leading cultural class. Technical, cognitive, and normative rationalization came to assert itself everywhere. That said, this first version of modernity was still relatively exclusive, and the social stratum from which it takes its name – the bourgeoisie – was still relatively small.

At the beginning of the twentieth century, formal rationalization underwent a qualitative and quantitative shift. Bourgeois modernity

I Modernity Between the General and the Particular

was then replaced by the second iteration of (classical) modernity: organized or industrial modernity. If one wants to understand the social logic of the general in its prototypical form and in all of its historical and empirical plasticity, it is necessary to look first of all at the organized or industrial modernity that reached its zenith between the 1950s and the 1970s.[28] During these years, this logic became a tremendous force that comprehensively and radically reconfigured the social, and readjusted the relation between humans and nature. It would be beneficial to examine the structural features of industrial modernity more closely, because they are antipodal to those of the late-modern society of singularities and because they continue to influence the sociological and political understanding of modernity today.

The impulse centers of post-bourgeois modernity were the United States of America and the Soviet Union. As I see it, the capitalism of the West and the socialism of the Eastern Bloc were not structural alternatives but were rather two varieties of radicalized rationalistic modernity. With its total social planning and determined de-singularization, moreover, state socialism in fact represented the purer form of industrial modernity and its logic of the general. That said, the Western capitalist version, as embodied by the culture of "Fordism" or "Americanism," turned out to be more influential over the long term and was ultimately able to transform itself into late modernity.[29] The framework of industrial capitalism gave rise to the type of collective order that was generally typical of the age of rationalization: the organization as an instrumentally rational association. Large corporations – hierarchically structured matrix organizations with clear divisions of labor – thus began to be formed around the beginning of the twentieth century. Labor in this context was, in the sense of scientific management, a system of coordinated and highly specialized activities, and the organization of labor was based on a system of jobs with unambiguous qualification requirements and routines. In both its capitalist and socialist varieties, the economic ideal of organized modernity was the industrial activity of standardized mass production.[30]

Organized modernity is thus that which sociologists call "industrial society,"[31] and therefore it is possible to speak more basically of industrial modernity. It was a technical culture in a strict sense, one that not only backed the establishment of mass production but also impressed upon all of society its engineering-based and mechanistic model, according to which the social world appeared as a system of optimally coordinated elements. The technology of machines and the technology of the social thus went hand in hand, their common telos being efficient order and the elimination of waste and redundancy. In such a technology-oriented society, the model subjects were technicians and engineers.[32]

In this Fordistic society, mass production was coupled with mass consumption. Instead of antagonism between the bourgeoisie and the proletariat, what appeared was the so-called "levelled middle-class society" of employees and skilled workers, who all participated in the consumption of standardized goods. This society promised a high standard of living for all. Especially during the *trente glorieuses* – the years 1945 to 1975 – this "affluent society" provided the imaginary backdrop of organized modernity. On the political level, this economic and technological formation was flanked by a socially regulating state, by a welfare state with a Keynesian and social-democratic or socialist plan to ensure social inclusion. The society formed along these lines was characterized by the expansive legal codification of social life and by political representation, which took place chiefly through people's parties with their massive support and their promises to fight for the common good.[33] On the spatial level, the functional city was the place where organized modernity crystallized. Both in the suburbs and in high-density public housing, the industrial city was based, as mentioned above, on functionalistic serial architecture and the spatial separation of work and domestic life.[34]

Whether in the economic, technological, political, or spatial sphere, organized modernity was guided by the semantics of the social, understood as the regulated collective.[35] The collectivized social – whether in the form of a crowd, group, political party, workforce, or even the nuclear family – now took on an independent and superior existence, to which the individual was subordinate. Quite fittingly, then, William Whyte and David Riesman referred to the post-bourgeois subject as an "organization man." This was a subject who developed an extreme sensitivity to the social expectations of his peers, to which he adapted accordingly. Orienting oneself toward the social standards of normality went hand in hand with a radical disciplining of emotions. As noted above, organized modernity was essentially a society of equals, of equality before the law, and of social uniformity. This culture of equality correlated with the uniformity of subjects: individuals were compelled to shape their lives to fit a "normal biography" with clear stages and with the aim of achieving life goals.[36] In Simmel's terms, the subjects of organized modernity were thus representative of an "individualism of equality."

All of this suggests that the social logic of the general – in the forms of standardization, generalization, and formalization, which industrial modernity enforced throughout the first two-thirds of the twentieth century – has some obvious downsides. These include social inhibition and repression on a large scale and the elimination of genuinely unique characteristics in a radical, systemic, and historically unprecedented way. These downsides affected all social

I Modernity Between the General and the Particular

entities: things, people, collectives, spaces, and times. In organized modernity, the particular or the unique was tendentially regarded as the insignificant, undesirable, or even repulsive "other" that had to be overcome (with violence, if necessary) because it did not fit into the generally valid functional order of society. Such things were treated as vestiges of the premodern, retrograde, and decadent past or – at best – as unintended and riskily peculiar marginal phenomena of modernity.

The social struggle against this "other" and against anything apparently non-rational was waged above all against ostensibly abnormal or asocial subjects, who were classified by the psycho-social complex as exhibitors of deviant behavior.[37] This struggle also led to a distaste for things and objects produced outside of industrial mass production, and encouraged the neglect or destruction of local and historical spaces – and the unique culture associated with them – in favor of the functional city. With its practices, industrial modernity thus enforced the de-singularization of the social. In the practices of observation, a vast system of general concepts and scales was developed for differentiating the general-particular, and this came at the expense of a now marginalized conceptual and perceptive sensitivity to the complexity of singularities. In the practices of evaluation, the result was to discriminate against or pathologize anything that could not be made to fit into the achievement differences determined by the logic of the general. In the practices of production, unique things were either created by mistake or were relics of premodern niche practices. In their practices of appropriation, subjects thus became successively accustomed to adopting objectifying approaches to things and in large part "unlearned," so to speak, how to deal with singularities.[38]

The rationalistic logic of the general achieved its zenith in organized, industrial modernity. It was during this time that society endeavored once and for all to triumph over the fundamental problems of scarcity and disorder mentioned above. Although many structural decisions made during this phase would remain influential in late modernity, organized modernity as an all-encompassing formation has since become history. Its social logic of the general would go on to serve as a negative example for late modernity, which would distance itself from it with its own social logic of singularities. As we will see, however, matters are somewhat more complicated. Industrial modernity was not organized in an entirely rationalistic manner, and it was not completely de-singularized. For its part, moreover, late modernity has developed its own version of rationalization, which now serves as an enabling form of infrastructure.

2

The Social Logic of the Particular

At first glance, the idea of a social logic of singularities may seem oxymoronic. Is not the social, after all, the natural counterpart of the particular? Is it not the *déformation professionnelle* of sociology to focus exclusively on crowds and collectives, rules and schemata? At its heart, that is, is sociology not a science devoted to the social logic of the general?[1] It is certainly no coincidence that sociology emerged as a discipline during the age of industrial modernity, and it still carries around a great deal of conceptual baggage from that time. Therefore, it might not seem well equipped to analyze processes of singularization – a problematic shortcoming if the goal is to understand late-modern society, which is organized around these very processes. In order to investigate the latter in a sociological and yet appropriate manner, it is necessary from the beginning to set aside the idea that sociality and singularity are fundamentally incompatible with one another. In fact, I would like to oppose this idea in decisive terms. In the case of singularities, it is not a matter of individual "vestiges" that remain behind after the social has withdrawn, or some sort of antithesis that battles against the social. Rather, if we remain open and curious about the inter-relations and entities that assemble "the social," it will be possible to view and analyze the logic of singularities, too, as a genuinely *social* logic.

What do I mean by singularities? In the history of concepts, the term "singularity" is relatively unladen; indeed, it is almost a neologism.[2] Yet it seems necessary to employ a little-used term in order to focus on the realm of phenomena that it designates without introducing any false presumptions. It encompasses a broad semantic field of related concepts: the particular and the special, the unusual and the extraordinary, individuality and the individual, the "other" and the peculiar, the unique and idiosyncratic, originality and the original, the exceptional and the exclusive. My concern here is not to relate a detailed conceptual

I Modernity Between the General and the Particular   33

history but rather to focus on the matter itself: the social logic of the particular, which has been central to the existence of late-modern societies.

The General-Particular, Idiosyncrasies, Singularities

In order to understand singularities, it is first necessary to draw a precise distinction between three different forms of the particular: the *general-particular*, the *idiosyncratic*, and the *singular*.

Here it is apt to begin with Kant's epistemological distinction between the general and the particular.[3] In relating to the world, one invariably deals with general concepts. Even before the rise of formal rationalization, a social logic of the general existed in the form of implicit types. At the same time, however, we always take notice of particularities: the individual person, the individual thing, the individual place. Seen in this way, the particular is nothing special, and indeed ubiquitous. This raises the question of the relation between the general and the particular, and it is easy to conclude that practices in the typifying mode classify the particular with the help of the general and categorize it as an example of a general concept. *This* chair is a *chair*, *this* person is a *mailman*, and so on. In this context, the particular is thus nothing more than a concrete example of something general. Or one could also say that it is the *general-particular*. As the general-particular, the particular implies concrete exemplars that exist within the social logic of the general; it implies variations and versions of what is essentially the same – things, that is, of the same *type*.

The general-particular is not only an object in the observed world (as it is according to Kant); it is also an object of social production, appropriation, and evaluation of the world. From a sociological perspective, the general-particular is especially interesting when complex social orders of the general are formed in which fixed or variable positions are created for particular cases and differences, so that the particular is made to fit into the general. As we have already seen, precisely such an approach is characteristic of the processes of formal rationalization. Examples include universal legal systems, which make it possible to subsume individual legal cases under predetermined categories, and the classification of achievement in the form of school grades. In this sense, a society dominated by formal rationalization also generates particularities to a considerable extent. Yet here it is always a matter of the general-particular, which is always created and understood within the framework of the processes of standardization, generalization, and formalization discussed above. The general-particular thus exists in unambiguous *rankings* of *qualitative* differences (school grades, for instance) and in *scales* of *quantitative* differences (quantitative measurements of various sorts).

The general-particular should not be confused with what I would like to call *idiosyncrasies*. Here one can begin again with the difference between the general and the particular and maintain that idiosyncrasies are aspects of entities that cannot be made to fit into the concepts or schemata of the general: residual, idiosyncratic characteristics. This could be a feature of a given chair that goes beyond the idea of chairs as a general type – for instance, the specific wear and tear that it has suffered in a particular household over the years, or the memory that one's grandmother once used to sit in it. Viewed in this way, idiosyncrasies are *peculiar features* that not only do not fit into the general but also oppose the orders of the general-particular.

Such a defensive understanding of idiosyncrasies, which presumes the primacy of the general, can be converted into a bold understanding. In bolder terms, one could say that all of the world's entities exist initially as idiosyncrasies.[4] They *are* special; they are unique to the extent that, in principle, they remain incommensurable with other entities. Nothing is identical with anything else; no entity can be converted into another without losing some quality. In this sense, every person is idiosyncratic, as is every plant, animal, or element of inorganic nature, not to mention every house or tool, every image and text, every location, every memory, every collective, and every belief. Thus understood, peculiarities are not the result of intentional design or the object of conscious appreciation or rejection; rather, as multiplicities, they are simply *there* – either independent of the existence of human beings (stones, animals, the cosmos, etc.) or as unintended side-effects of human activity (that is, as side-effects of the social). Regardless of whether idiosyncrasies are interpreted defensively or boldly, what is crucial is that they are unique features existing outside of the orders of the general that are not perceived as anything special by the social sphere itself. As unique features "in themselves," they are marginal cases both for the social world and for the (social) sciences. Though ubiquitous, they are nearly invisible.

What I mean by the social logic of singularities is neither the system of the general-particular nor idiosyncrasies. In a certain way, singularities exist between the two. Whereas, in the general-particular, the relatively particular reproduces the order of the general, and whereas idiosyncrasies operate beyond and before all forms of socio-cultural communicability, singularities function *within* the socio-cultural order and yet are *not* limited to reproducing the logic of the general. In the case of singularities, we are dealing with entities that are perceived, evaluated, fabricated, and treated as unique within social practices. Singularities are the result

I Modernity Between the General and the Particular

of socio-cultural processes of *singularization*. They come into their own within a social logic of the particular. In such a logic, objects, subjects, spaces, temporalities, and collectives are turned into singularities through practices of observation, evaluation, production, and appropriation. Singularity, in other words, is *enacted*.[5]

Within a social logic of singularities, particularities cannot be reduced to a general schema; rather, they appear unique and are certified as such. Whereas the general-particular designates variations of the same and idiosyncrasy designates pre-social peculiarity, singularity denotes socio-culturally fabricated uniqueness. To begin with, it is possible to define these unique entities in negative terms: as non-generalizable, non-interchangeable, and incomparable. Singular objects, subjects, places, events, and collectives are not merely exemplars of a general order. Stanley Kubrick's film *A Clockwork Orange* may admittedly belong to the genre of science fiction, but – in the complexity of its imagery and narration and in its unique tension between fascination and disgust – it cannot be reduced to this or any other type. Cineastes view and experience it as unique. Moreover, a singularity cannot be exchanged for or replaced by a different but functionally identical entity, as readily happens to functional objects and people within the framework of the logic of the general. For those who participated in it, the subculture of mods during the 1960s could not simply be exchanged for another subculture – the rockers, say – but rather developed a subcultural universe of its own with specific practices, symbols, affects, and identities. Finally, a singularity cannot be compared to other entities with any clear parameters, because no overarching standard exists along which it might be possible to measure their differences. To believers, for instance, it would make no sense to compare Shinto's Ise Grand Shrine to the Church of the Holy Sepulcher in Jerusalem.

On what basis are objects, subjects, places, events, and collectives now fabricated as unique in the social world? The basis is that, over the course of their singularization, these social entities are understood as *inherent complexities* with *inner density*. In the logic of singularization – to put this another way – the singular object (be it a work of art or design), the singular subject (a person perceived as unique), the singular place, or the singular collective becomes a "world of its own." Inherent complexity and inner density are nothing mystical. Complexity, as is well known, denotes a series of elements or nodal points between which there are relations, interconnections, and reciprocal effects. Whenever such a nexus of interrelations exists, one speaks of *complexity*, whose defining quality can be called *density*.[6] Of course, the type of elements and relations that form a given complexity and determine its density depends on the social entity at hand. An object (such as a painting), a theory, a culinary meal, or a smartphone differs in its composition from a human subject (that entity composed of body and mind), while a physical place (a living-room, a landscape, or a city) consists of elements and relations quite different from those of a temporal entity (such as an event) or a collective (such as a scene, a project, or a nation). Nevertheless, this material variation does nothing to change what singularization means for every social entity: they are constituted as inherent complexities with inner density.

Complexity and density are characteristics of the *internal* structure of singularities, and this is why I have used the terms *inherent* complexity and *inner* density. Singular entities, however, also have a specific relation to the *outside*. Yet it would be insufficient to claim that there are simply certain differences between them (between the urban logic of Rome and San Francisco, for instance). Of course, difference theory has taught us that, in the socio-cultural realm, it would be impossible to identify any entities at all without the existence of differences, because every entity is constituted in the first place by being different from others.[7] Despite its general appeal to cultural theorists, however, it would be a mistake to embrace difference theory fully, for it would bring two serious disadvantages to the analysis of singularities. First, the social relevance of the inherent complexity of entities would be marginalized in favor of the ostensibly ubiquitous "play of differences." Second, it would raise the risk of losing the capacity to distinguish between the multiplicities of differences that exist in the social world.

It must be stressed that, in the social logic of singularities, differences are certainly identified, but the *main* issue involves the production and appropriation of inherent complexities. What this means can best be illustrated with an example, for instance American literature. In this case, there are countless ways to identify a difference between the novels of Edith Wharton, John Dos Passos, John Steinbeck, or F. Scott Fitzgerald. Now, if we take the novels of Thomas Pynchon, they are not only unlike the latter; they not only "differentiate themselves" *ex negativo* from all of them. Rather, in their semantics, syntax, plot structure, characterizations, etc., they develop their own irreducible inner density *ex positivo*. This inherent complexity stands at the center of singularization in the minds of readers, critics – and the author himself. In contrast to the difference-theoretical primacy of difference over identity, the logic of singularities favors the primacy of inherent complexity over the outward identification of differences.

Within the social logic of singularization, of course, entities *also* gain their uniqueness by way of their differences, but these have a special form. Whereas, according to difference theory, all cats (differences) are gray at night, the issue now is to distinguish between forms of difference, and to do so according to a social logic. In the social logic of the general, which also identifies differences between

I Modernity Between the General and the Particular 37

its socially relevant entities (objects, subjects, etc.), its focus is on *gradual* differences of a qualitative or quantitative sort, as I already described above. In an order of singularities, in contrast, differences are always absolutely and without exception qualitative. What prevails here is not rankings but rather a qualitative *otherness*, which has the character of *incommensurability*. Incommensurability means that the entities in question lack a common measure; they are not understood as two variants of the same, but rather appear to be *incomparable* in the strict sense of the word.[8] Rome is incommensurable with San Francisco, as is Russia with China, or David Bowie with Van Morrison. The logic of singularization is thus concerned with identifying *strong differences*.

What happens, however, when the entities of social singularization are compared to one another? As a social practice, the act of comparison did not simply cease with the advent of singularities, and later we will see how, to a considerable extent, the expansion of the social logic of the singular in late modernity led to the creation of new technologies of comparison.[9] Comparisons between singularities, which are always inherent complexities, now do exactly what might be expected: they *reduce* the complexity at hand. In practices of comparison, general parameters are used in order to classify the singularities themselves according to a qualitative or even quantitative standpoint. This means seeing in them only that which fits into the given set of comparative parameters, whereas everything else falls out of view. Notre-Dame Cathedral in Paris and the Doge's Palace in Venice are thus two examples of Gothic architecture; Christianity and Islam are two monotheistic religions; the album *Sgt. Pepper's Lonely Hearts Club Band* sold more copies than the album *Blonde on Blonde*; and so on. The schemata of the general therefore reduce the complexities of singularities to a few chosen characteristics that make it possible to draw a comparison between them. Thus, comparisons made within the framework of the social logic of the general differ in a fundamental way from those made within the framework of the social logic of the particular, even if they resemble one another on the surface. A comparison made between entities in the social logic of the general (with various quantifiers or school grades, for instance) serves to represent these entities exhaustively, whereas comparisons made in the social logic of the particular reduce complexity, which does not then disappear but rather – and this is decisive – goes on to function in a *structurally formative* way (by affecting its recipients, for instance).[10]

What should we think about the relation between the three aforementioned configurations of the particular – again, the general-particular, idiosyncrasies, and singularities? It can be maintained first of all that the distinction between them should lead to more than just a classification – it can also help to analyze their interrelations. In all three cases, at any rate, we are dealing with real configurations in the social world. The social logic of singularities *exists*, as does the social logic of the general (with its production of the general-particular) as well as the population of idiosyncrasies, which may not be part of any social logic but exist nevertheless (in the manner of "things in themselves"). What is interesting is that these three spheres are not closed off from one another but rather share a dynamic *relationship* of translation and exchange, especially in late modernity.[11]

Idiosyncrasies can thus transform into singularities when previously unrecognized unique features are socially recognized for their uniqueness – when, for instance, a computer specialist with all his quirkiness is elevated to a nerd, or a formerly unacknowledged and seemingly worthless object is suddenly regarded as a work of art. Every idiosyncrasy has the potential to become a singularity. Conversely, as already mentioned, singularities can (if only temporarily) become part of the register of the general-particular at the moment when someone attempts to make their presumably incomparable qualities comparable or even gradable (for instance, in analyses of art or religion, in the quality rankings of films, etc.). Beyond that, it is possible for previously merely functional goods from the register of the general to be singularized (the mass-produced plastic chair, for example, advanced to become the singular Eames design) if a degree of inherent complexity is discovered in something that otherwise bears general features, as a result, for instance, of heightened cultural sensitivity or the development of more discerning tastes. Finally, singularities can lose their character as valuable entities, become *de-singularized*, and sink to the status of unnoticed idiosyncrasies (as when religions cease to be practiced or works of art cease to be recognized as such). As we will see more clearly later on, the rising significance of the social logic of singularities in late modernity owes a great deal to the fact that idiosyncrasies – but also examples of the general-particular – can transform into singularities. At the same time, the transformation of general-particular parameters into singularities has also gained significance, with the result that a broad spectrum of singularities has been cultivated by society and allowed to flourish.

It should have become clear from the foregoing discussion that a sociological analysis of singularities requires a sophisticated heuristic. Although I have already pointed out that the familar semantic complex of individualism, the individual, individualization, and individuality – to which sociology used to refer – is not especially helpful to this sort of analysis, I should at least explain why this is so.[12] One central problem is the widely variable meaning of these concepts and thus their unclear reference to the sphere of phenomena associated with the particular. Depending on who is

I Modernity Between the General and the Particular 39

using them, the terms individualism and individuality can designate extra-social idiosyncrasies *or* socially certified uniqueness *or* the particular within the framework of a general order. Sometimes the concept of individuality is used to denote idiosyncrasies. In other cases, these concepts refer to various facets of the individualism of equality, which was characteristic of classical modernity: to the equal rights that people have, to the equal worth that each person is ascribed, to the self-responsible and self-interested nature of certain activity – to every particular thing in the same way. Georg Simmel thus spoke of a modern and rationalistic individualism of the equal and general and juxtaposed it to the Romantic tradition's individualism of the particular.[13] Because we are concerned with the distinction between the social logic of singularities and that of the general, any concept that can unabashedly refer to both is, of course, out of the question.

That was the first problem with the concept of individualism: it is too broad and ambiguous. The second problem is that in other respects it is too narrow, and this is because it typically refers to human subjects alone. As I have already stressed on several occasions, however, it is paramount to keep in mind that the social fabrication of singularities is not restricted to subjects but rather encompasses all the other entities of the social named above: objects, spaces, temporalities, and collectives. A society of singularities cannot be understood if one remains fixated on the subject.[14]

Objects, Subjects, Spaces, Times, and Collectives in the Social Logic of Singularities

It cannot be repeated enough that all five entities of the social, which I discussed above in connection with the social logic of the general, can become the object of processes of singularization, too: objects and things, human subjects, collectives, spaces, and temporalities. One important feature of the intersectional term "singularity" is that it makes it possible to describe and relate socio-cultural particularities from every social entity. This can be illustrated in brief with a few examples of characteristic forms of singularization from the past and the present.

All forms of society have regarded a select number of entities as singularized *objects* with their own complexity and density (surprisingly, this social tendency to singularize entities from the world of objects and things has received less scholarly attention than one might suppose).[15] Paradigmatic examples of singular objects are material objects such as relics, other cult objects, and works of art such as paintings and sculptures, which only exist in one exemplar and to which Walter Benjamin famously ascribed an "aura."[16]

Buildings, furniture, and items of clothing can likewise be perceived, produced, and valued as singular. To exist in just a single exemplar, however, is not a necessary precondition for singularity in the sense intended here. Even objects that have a variable or technically reproducible material basis can be singularized. This is true, for instance, of religious, literary, or philosophical texts, which are frequently certified as original by being attributed to an author, and it is also true of music, photographs, films, and political symbols. Theories, narratives, and images are singularities that circulate in a variety of media formats.[17]

A specific example is the collection of various different objects under one identifiable *brand*, which is associated with the promise of uniqueness within the realm of cultural capitalism or with a particular aesthetic *style*.[18] Entities of organic nature can also be singularized: house pets, gardens, or the desert and the Alps as particular places of biodiversity, for example.[19] In every case, singularized things and objects are more than functional instruments; they either offer something in addition to that or they are exclusively cultural, affectively operating entities. As such, they are not stable throughout time but rather have their own object biographies. Generally, the elements and relations that constitute the inherent complexity and inner density of singular objects are highly diverse, and this is the case for obvious reasons. In this regard, materials, forms, and colors can play just as much a role as semantics, syntax, and the narrative, harmonic, melodic, or argumentative structures of texts, music, or theories.[20]

As mentioned above, the fashioning of singular *human subjects* has traditionally been treated under the misleading rubric of individuality. Subjects are singularized when their uniqueness is socially recognized and valued and when they actively engage in and cultivate certain techniques that invite this recognition.[21] In such cases, singularization means subjectification: the subject achieves an acknowledged degree of inherent complexity that defies typification (though this was and remains a possibility).[22] Singularized subjects cannot be reduced to functional roles or hereditary groups. Magi, prophets, and rulers, to whom Max Weber ascribed the attribute of charisma, have traditionally been subjects who could claim to be inimitable.[23] In modernity, artists and other creative people were the first to form milieus in which originality was both desired and demanded.[24]

Any number of a subject's characteristics and activities can be regarded as singular: his or her behavior, cultural products, appearance, bodily features, and biography. However, these things have to be *performed* in some way so as not to be mere idiosyncrasies but to be recognized as unique. The singularization of the subject is a process in which self-modeling and self-singularization go hand in hand with the control and singularization enacted by others. In late modernity, techniques for singularizing subjects have become ubiquitous, both in the professional world, where extraordinary performance is desired, and the private sphere. Typically, then, subjectification and objectification (the social fabrication of objects) – that is, the singularization of people and the singularization of things – are closely connected to one another: subjects make themselves distinct through the uniqueness of their objects (through their internet profiles, for instance, or through the way in which their apartments are decorated).[25] All of this makes it clear that the idea of indivisibility, which the old concept of the individual of course entails, is inapplicable to techniques of singularization, because here uniqueness is in fact *composed* of a variety of components or modules.[26]

When spaces are singularized, they are elevated to what theorists of space have come to call *places*.[27] The difference between space and place is the same as the difference between spaces in the social logic of the general and spaces in the social logic of singularization. Places are singular spaces in which material objects are arranged, endowed with meaning, and offered to be perceived in such a way that they are experienced as inherent complexities with specially composed spatial densities – as spaces unconfined by the standardization to which spaces are subjected in the social logic of the general. Such places are not simply used and passed through; rather, they seem valuable and emotionally attractive to those participating in them. Charming cities such as Venice and Paris – with their layouts and atmospheres, but also with the cultural associations and memories associated with them – are historical prototypes for "intrinsically logical" places.[28] Yet places of worship, palaces, sacred buildings, exceptional landscapes, monuments, and even apartments and atmospherically rich office landscapes in the creative branches can also be special places in this sense. Whereas, in the logic of the general, all spaces are meant to fulfill a particular function in the same way, the logic of the particular turns spaces into places of identification. Here, to some extent, space is not extensive but rather intensive. Here it is the *locality* of the space that interests people. Only a space that has been condensed into a place can become a locus of memory and a setting with *atmosphere*.[29]

Temporalities are singularized when they do not take on the form of a typified custom or rationalized routine but are rather oriented around a unique *point* in time with its own density. Its duration can vary, ranging from a very brief moment in the here and now to a longer episode with a clear beginning and end. Singularized time thus has the form of an *event* that is actively and intensively experienced. Uniqueness *can* indeed mean that something happens only once, but this does not necessarily have to be the case. Despite its repetitive character, for instance, a ritual (such as a yearly celebration) can be experienced as unique, and in fact celebrations and rituals are the traditional prototypes of singular temporalities. In late modernity, however, there has been an increasing proliferation of one-off events. From festivals and sporting events to TED conferences, *events* can be experienced as singular just as much as professional or political *projects*.

In this case, time is not something that is habitually or routinely filled in order to achieve certain objectives beyond the present. For its participants, on the contrary, it has an intrinsic value of its own; it is experienced in the moment of its seemingly overwhelming complexity – in the presence of its presentness, so to speak.[30] Whereas, in the mode of the general, temporality is desensitized to the present moment of activity and instrumentally oriented toward the future, in the mode of the particular it is present-oriented. However, such experiences might also involve references to the past: the memory of a previous event or the establishment of historical connections can serve to enrich the present. For this reason, historical narratives – which cultivate our "historical memory" of past events, moments, places, or people to the point of nostalgia – are likewise variations of temporality within the social logic of the particular.[31]

Singular *collectives* are not general, instrumentally rational associations or (idiosyncratic) "given" social milieus; rather, they are collectives that have a unique cultural value for their participants. According to one theory of modernization, they might be referred to as "particular groups," yet in this case the semantics of the particular is meant to devalue them as insignificant elements with limited scope as compared to the vast and general organizations of modern society. In reality, however, these collectives are more than just a *part* of something grander; from the perspective of their members, they are, rather, complete cultural universes of their own with high degrees of communicative, narrative, and affective complexity and significance. This was already true of any family genealogy with its own collective consciousness, but also of early-modern guilds and corporations whenever they were more than just instrumentally rational institutions. In (late) modernity, the singularization of collectives might also occur, for instance, in cultural and aesthetic subcultures, in self-chosen religious collectives, as well as in nations or regional communities (though in a somewhat different way).

In general, the old distinction between community and society applies only under certain conditions to the difference between collectives in the mode of the particular and collectives in the mode of the general. Unlike traditional communities, into which one is simply born, modern "neo-communities" (as they have come

I Modernity Between the General and the Particular   43

to be called) are *chosen*. Singular collectives are thus, in general, intensively affective socialities that share not only practices but also narratives and imaginations. Unlike collectives in the mode of the general, which appear identical from the outside, the unique nature of singular collectives can appear utterly alien to outsiders and even evoke aggressive contempt. It is especially on the level of collectives that singularities become the object of culture wars.[32]

The kaleidoscope of singularized entities that I have presented here perhaps raises a question: can *every* given object, subject, collective, spatiality, and temporality be singularized? Is inherent complexity entirely a matter of social construction? This question is of little importance to sociological analysis, for here the crucial issues are *that* and *how* singularization has taken place. That said, I am inclined to adopt a social-constructivist instead of a radical-constructivist position. On the one hand, what counts or does not count as unique depends on the practices of observation, evaluation, production, and appropriation discussed above. Nevertheless, one can assume that certain entities are somewhat easier to singularize than others: objects, subjects, etc., contain varying degrees of "affordance," which means that they can differ in what they offer.[33] They contain in themselves and offer varying levels of inherent complexity, which are more or less suitable to social singularization. Hieronymus Bosch's *Garden of Earthly Delights* is easier to recognize as being inherently complex than a brick, James Joyce's *Ulysses* is easier to recognize as such than a novel by Rosamunde Pilcher, and the singer Madonna is easier to see as such than "the Lithuanian assistant film director in the gray coat."[34] But, of course, there is no automatic way of knowing. Under certain circumstances, even stones (as relics, for instance), cheap novels, or gray coats can become cult objects, and renowned works of art and world-famous pop stars can fall into oblivion. In any case, it is clearly insufficient to speak of singularization in sweeping terms; rather, it is necessary to examine the specific practices through which this process occurs.

Practices of Singularization I: Observation and Evaluation

The social logic of singularities encompasses not only the five aforementioned social entities but also the four practices of singularization that I have already discussed at some length: the practices, that is, of observation, evaluation, production, and appropriation. Because singularities are *enacted* in these ways, they are never fixed once and for all; rather, they are continuously being fabricated.

These four sorts of practices are only separated here for heuristic reasons, for at times they can be intertwined or even combined with one another (as when something is produced and received through the same practice). They can also be highly specialized and differentiated from one another, sometimes even coalescing into entire institutional complexes of their own. In general, it can be said that practices of singularization have existed in all types of society and at all times, though in late modernity their institutional scope has broadened considerably while processes of singularization (and the parallel processes of de-singularization) have become contentious and controversial to a large extent. Here, I will look specifically at these four types of practices and describe how they operate within the logic of singularities.

First, *observation*.[35] Within a social logic of singularities, something can be interpreted, for instance, as non-interchangeable and unique. As such, it first has to be *recognized* or *discovered*. For this to happen, it is fundamentally necessary for there to have developed, in the form of practices of observation, a cultural *sensitivity* to the inherent complexity and density of the particular. Whereas the logic of the general requires the knowledge and competence for classifying, subsuming, and abstracting things, the ascertainment of singular objects, subjects, spaces, etc., requires a level of cultural sensitivity that has both a cognitive and a sensory dimension. Typically, someone not only has explicit knowledge about singularities but is, rather, able to understand or "get," in an instant, the density and inherent complexity of, say, a piece of music, a person, a city, or a belief.[36]

A sense for the inherent complexity of singularities is not something that people are simply born with; instead, it is learned and cultivated (or neglected) in social environments.[37] Without any *competence* for recognizing singularity – regardless of whether the specific competence in question pertains to religion or art, everyday aesthetics or architecture – the social logic of singularities cannot exist. Practices of observing singularities can be passed on through processes of imitating and associating with certain social groups (to gain a sense for classical music, a youth subculture, a religious belief, a specific world of objects, etc.), and they can also be professionalized in institutions (as is the case, for instance, with architects and scholars of art). Under certain conditions, the socio-cultural processes of attribution in which something is understood to be a singularity can be clear and uncontroversial (think of the relics in traditional society), whereas, under other conditions, understanding what is singular can be highly contentious and the object of heated debate (the classic example in modernity is the question of what counts as a work of art). Furthermore, what is recognized by participants in one socio-cultural context as having inherent complexity may be regarded by outsiders as no more than an example of a general type, or might even seem entirely unintelligible. For the uninitiated who lack the necessary observational competence, it

I Modernity Between the General and the Particular   45

will be difficult to identify the unique qualities of Duke Ellington's music, Michel Serres' texts, or the natural beauty of Loch Lomond.

Second, *evaluation*.[38] Although observation and evaluation are two different sets of practices, they are often interconnected. Evaluations do not result in a neutral understanding of the matter being evaluated; rather, the latter is understood in a positive or negative light. In the social world, things are of course constantly being evaluated; in the social logic of singularities, however, the process of (e)valuation differs from that in the social logic of the general. In the latter, as I have already discussed, the goal of evaluation is to determine whether something corresponds or not to the desired standard – that is, to determine whether something can be regarded as normal and acceptable. There, singularities are negatively sanctioned, and the act of evaluation involves *sorting* things into dualisms, rankings, and scales.

In the logic of singularities, on the contrary, evaluation means *ascribing value* in a strict sense. It designates a praxis of valorization in whose context a singular entity acquires the status of being valuable (or not). Here, to evaluate is to *certify*. In general, the criteria defining what is desirable are inverted: now, the singular is valuable, while mere examples of the general seem *profane* and are devalued. Whereas rationalism is based on the distinction between the correct/normal (general) and the abnormal (particular), the main distinction of singularism is between the sacred (particular) and the profane (general), in which case the sacred should not be associated too closely with religious holiness but rather implies that something has been regarded as intrinsically valuable.[39] Of course, even formal rationalization ascribes value to things in the *broadest* sense, but it is concerned with functional or instrumental value – that is, with something's *utility* or *function* according to a given order, ranking, or scale (and therefore I will avoid the term "value" in this context). In contrast, the logic of singularities valorizes entities in a strong sense by endowing them with a seemingly intrinsic worth, so that they appear to be valuable, good, and meaningful in their own right.

The central task of practices of valorization is now to determine *which* individual entities – things, people, places, etc. – should be recognized as singular. To this end, entire discursive universes and valorization techniques have been developed (think of the field of art criticism). Practices of valorization identify differences, and strong differences at that. On the one hand, they identify *asymmetrical differences* between the singular and the profane; on the other hand, they identify *absolute* (that is, non-gradual) *qualitative differences* between various singularities, each of which seems distinct from all others. As already mentioned, however, it is characteristic of late modernity for attempts to be made to reduce such complexity and to translate the absolute difference of singularities into the gradual differences of the general-particular (in the form of rankings, for instance), so that the sphere of valorization has taken on a multi-faceted form.

What is relevant is this: practices of valorization not only singularize but also *de-singularize*. Not only do they ascribe value, they devalue as well. It is of the utmost importance to underscore that singularization is not a one-dimensional process and that it involves aspects of dominance. Practices of valorization elevate and reject things; they distinguish things while ensuring that others remain invisible. Processes of singularization regularly operate in tandem with processes of de-singularization. Entities that were once valorized as singular can lose this status later on. Moreover, it can happen (and it often does) that entities that strive for singularity, or whose singular nature is doubted, never achieve this status and vanish in the sea of the profane (or, under certain circumstances, are singularized as something negative). In societies in which the social logic of the particular was no more than a niche phenomenon, this was less consequential than it is in the late-modern society of singularities, where de-singularization generally means *devaluation* (if not uselessness as well). It is little surprise, then, that processes of valorization can tend to be enormously controversial.

Practices of Singularization II: Production and Appropriation

Regarding *production*, singularities are an object of design and fabrication, of labor and creation, of representation and performance. In an immediate sense, they are socially engendered, manufactured, and produced. This social production – this *labor of singularization* – can take very different forms depending on whether objects/things, subjects, places, events, or collectives are being created as singular.

Fundamentally, it is possible to distinguish the situation in which an idiosyncrasy (or an example of the general-particular) already exists and is singularized through a process of reframing – a sort of secondary production – from those situations in which an entity is intentionally produced from the beginning and from the ground up as singular. The reframing of idiosyncrasies takes place, for instance, when a previously ignored object is discovered to be a relic, a work of art, or a valuable antique, when a reclusive person is found out to be an "original" artist, or when an overlooked geographical region is reinterpreted as a valuable site of biodiversity. In these cases, the practices of production hardly differ from those of observation and evaluation.[40] On the other hand, there are intentional acts of singularization that aim to produce brand new creations of unique things, subjects, places, events, or communities. This can involve such practices as hand-crafting an object, cultivating one's own

I Modernity Between the General and the Particular 47

uniqueness (by adopting certain interests or updating a Facebook account, for example), painstakingly reenacting a complicated ritual, putting on a live concert, writing, composing, or preparing a meal.

Are these manners of producing singular entities structured in a fundamentally different way from the production of general elements? Without a doubt, the fabrication of singularities also involves instrumentally rational and normative-rational practices. The production of a film, for example, requires the coordination of a number of highly specialized activities within the framework of the movie industry. In the case of the labor of singularity, however, these activities are typically associated with practices of a specific sort: *arrangements*. Arrangement entails compiling heterogeneous objects, texts, images, individuals (etc.) into a whole that is as coherent as possible. The labor of singularity is thus often (and especially in late modernity) a matter of managing heterogeneity. In addition to functional components, arrangements can also include narrative and hermeneutic, aesthetic (visual, for instance), and ludic elements. Despite their necessary material aspects, the narrative and aesthetic features of arrangements mean that they are essentially a form of "immaterial labor," though in a broad sense of the term.[41] Historically, the arrangement of singularities is *not* necessarily connected to the aim of creating something new.[42] This has normally been the case in modernity, however, so that here it is a matter of arranging novelties within the framework of what could be called a "creativity *dispositif*." Yet even the production of novel singularities is not without preconditions, given that it depends on already existing elements – often on idiosyncrasies or standardized elements, but also on networks of narratives and symbols. Whereas standardized productions rely on *immanent* criteria of utility, practicality, and functionality (and thus do not really have to take their public function into account), the production of singularity *must* incorporate the real or imagined perspective of the public in the creation of its entities.

Regarding *appropriation*,[43] an element of the social is only singular if it has been singularized in the situation of its use. Unlike instrumentally rational utility and routinized social interaction, which characterize the logic of the general, the appropriation of the particular has the structure of *lived experience*.[44] A singular object or thing, a singular subject, a singular place, a singular event, a singular collective – they are all experienced, which can only happen if they are truly experienced as unique and have a unique social reality. Experience is a mental but also physical process of appropriating the world in which objects of attention are perceived by the senses. As lived experience, sensory perception goes beyond the function of gathering information, which is the typical and essential function of perception within the framework of instrumentally rational activity. Lived experience is perception for its own sake – a sort of self-referential perception. Whereas, in the social logic of the general, appropriation involves manipulating the world in order to achieve a specific goal, lived experience is a matter of *processing* and *receiving* the world.

What is central to practices of experience – whether attending an opera or meditating, base flying or visiting a city, going to the opening match of the World Cup or simply hearing the national anthem on the radio – is that the singular entities in question *affect* their recipients.[45] It is the affective nature of the logic of singularities that structures, in a specific way, appropriation as experience. Whenever singular objects, subjects, places, events, or collectives are appropriated, intensive (positive or ambivalent) emotions are often at play: passion and admiration; affection and inspiration; shock and desire; fear and disgust; feelings of elation, pride, or beautiful harmony. And even when the intensity of these emotions is relatively weak – if someone is merely stimulated by something interesting, cool, or exciting – they remain at the heart of the matter. In that singular entities affect people, their appropriation incites a degree of emotional intensity. The latter, however, should not be understood as a behaviorist stimulus-and-response sequence but rather as an interpretive praxis: only those who interpret nature in a certain way, for instance, are able to "experience" it.[46]

Lived experience can take on a wide variety of forms. It can have an intersubjective character (when a group or audience is present), or it can involve a private act of engaging with an object. It can be of a primarily mental nature, with little or no bodily involvement, or it can expressly involve an active physical practice. In many cases, too, production and experience can go hand in hand (when people play a game together, for instance). Fundamentally, however, it must be said that subjective experience is not self-contained but is rather itself a component of social praxis – of the practices of appropriation that give it shape in a specific way. Compared to the appropriation of social elements in the mode of the general, which is relatively stable, the appropriation of singularities is riskier and more unpredictable on account of its psycho-physical aspect. It can fail altogether, it is not something that can be forced, and it may not result in any real experience at all.

Performativity as a Mode of Praxis and Automated Singularization

Regarding the social logic of the general, I discussed above a general structure of social praxis – a *mode of praxis* – that more or less applies to all four of the practices of observation, evaluation,

I Modernity Between the General and the Particular 49

production, and appropriation: the mode of instrumentally rational and socially coordinated activity. The social praxis of the general is thus essentially one of *labor* and *interaction*. How, in this regard, do things look in the social logic of singularities? What is its overarching mode of praxis? Basically, the social praxis of the particular has the structure of a *performance*, so that *performativity* is its central characteristic. In the mode of the singular, the social manifests itself in the situation of one or more people performing something for an audience that is meant to have cultural value. Singular entities are not primarily used in an instrumental way (like instrumentally rational activity) or treated normatively (like normative activity); rather, they are *presented* in the mode of performativity. Singular subjects, places, and objects are presented; as events, singular temporalities have a performative character; and singular collectives live off of this collective performativity. Singularities thus exist as *performances of singularity* before a social audience.[47]

Performances of singularity operate affectively. This is what fundamentally distinguishes the mode of praxis of the particular from that of the rationalized general, where affect is kept to a minimum. Things are quite different with the performance of singularity, in which, as we have already seen, the intensity of affect plays a decisive role. It should be noted that affects are not the internal emotions or feelings of subjects; rather, they should be thought about in terms of the processes and relations of *affecting*. This means that singular objects, subjects, places, events, and collectives are characterized by the fact that they address social participants affectively.[48] The social entities of the singular mobilize affective intensities primarily in the form of the positive affects of desire and interest, but also in ambivalent mixtures of these with fear or anger. The phenomenon of being affected in such ways is especially clear to see in the *appropriation* and *experience* of singularities, but it is also part of the practices of production, interpretive observation, and valorization. The process of affecting others characterizes the overall mode of praxis of the logic of singularities. In short, without affecting others, there are no singularities, and without singularities, people are not (or only minimally) affected.

Especially in late modernity, however, one encounters a form of singularization that fundamentally differs from such affecting performances and might best be called *automated singularization*. Although I will discuss this phenomenon in greater detail later on, it makes sense to mention it here in brief. This form of singularization has been present in various areas of life since the 1990s, and it is primarily an effect of digitalization. One example of mechanically fabricated uniqueness is the algorithmically generated profiles of internet users, which depend on data tracking. Noteworthy, too, is genome analysis, which makes it possible to examine the unique genetic composition of individuals. Further examples can be found in the field of human resources, which is concerned with systematically determining the talents and potential of employees. Automated singularization, however, not only is interesting with respect to subjects but also is applied in ways related to collectives, as in the case of marketing (which focuses on social niches with particular tastes and opinions) or in the case of political campaigns (which target particular groups of voters).

At first glance, one might be tempted to think that such cases are illustrative of the logic of the general and its instrumentally rational practices, and indeed they do involve instrumentally rational techniques. However, the techniques in question are *not* applied within the framework of the social logic of the general. Whereas the rationalistic technologies of industrial modernity produced standardized things and people, the technologies of late modernity have largely been transformed into *infrastructures of the particular*. That is, there is now an intrinsic technological and institutional interest in, and capacity for, making singularities visible and fabricating them automatically. Unlike rationalism and its inclination to generalize, this institutional and technological interest is not oriented toward treating unique entities as exemplars of general types but rather toward reconstructing individual entities in their uniqueness. Whereas the traditional medical perspective, for instance, evaluated individual patients in terms of general symptoms or health standards, the aim of genome analysis is to ascertain the incommensurability of every individual's genetic composition.

Even these automated singularities can be analyzed as the results of a fabrication process involving the practices of observation, evaluation, production, and appropriation. Here, however, these practices are internal mechanical *techniques*; they are conducted automatically by the technologies in question. Even more significant is the fact that automated singularities do not necessarily exist as performances before an audience that experiences them and is affected by them. Often, singularities produced in such a way are themselves the *object* of instrumentally rational practices, such as a type of medical treatment based on genome analysis or a consumer decision steered by an automatically tailored profile on an online shopping platform. Here the singularity is not *experienced* but rather *used*. In other cases, however, automated singularities can indeed put on an (automatically generated) performance, for instance by arranging images and texts on someone's social media platform in a tailored fashion that the user finds interesting, stimulating, and exciting.

All in all, late modernity's systems of automated singularization are highly remarkable. Intelligent technologies no longer simply standardize, as was the case during the period of industrial rationalization; they singularize as well. They have thus contributed to a transformation away from instrumentally rational practices toward a greater sensitivity to uniqueness and toward the establishment of a comprehensive technical infrastructure for the performance of the singular.

3
Culture and Culturalization

The social logic of singularities is closely linked to the dimension of the social that has traditionally been referred to as *culture*. Indeed, one could maintain that, if we proceed from the distinction between the logic of the general and that of singularities, it will be possible to shed new and informative light on "culture" – an ambiguous academic and political concept that is now encrusted in a layer of patina – and the cultural dimension of society. Conversely, recourse to the concept of culture makes it possible to anchor our analysis of singularities in social theory. The crucial point is this: at its core, culture is composed of singularities. The cultural sphere of a society is formed from social entities that are recognized to be unique – singular objects, subjects, places, events, and collectives – together with the affiliated practices of observation, evaluation, production, and appropriation. The logic of the particular is related to culture just as the logic of the general is related to formal rationality. Whereas the social logic of the general is expressed through a social process of rationalization, the social logic of singularities is expressed through a social process of culturalization. Rationalization and culturalization are the two opposing forms of socialization.

Culture as a Sphere of Valorization and De-valorization

The concept of culturalization may seem alien at first. Haven't we learned that everything is culture, that all things social are formed and coded by contexts of meaning that lend them direction and significance? How, then, can one speak of cultural*ization*? Such a concept of enhancement and intensification ultimately seems to require certain precultural elements that are then abandoned in a second step toward a specific cultural formation.

Culture is one of the most dazzling concepts of the human sciences; at the same time, it has also been central to the self-perception of

I Modernity Between the General and the Particular   53

modernity from its very beginning.¹ In the nineteenth century, culture was at first understood as a select, "cultivated" (that is, normatively desirable) form of life that strives for harmonious perfection (the normative concept of culture). Over time, the concept was then restricted to a social subsystem that essentially encompassed the artistic and intellectual spheres (the differentiation-theoretical concept of culture). Conversely, the concept of culture would also be radically opened up and applied to all ways of life in all of their diversity (the holistic concept of culture) and ultimately – in a more theoretically challenging turn – related to the symbolic and meaningful dimension of the social (the meaning-oriented concept of culture). In this case, culture designates the orders of knowledge and systems of classification against the backdrop of which social practices first become conceivable.²

For our context, however, none of these four concepts of culture is really suitable. They are either too broad or too narrow. From the perspective of the holistic and meaning-oriented concepts of culture, every social phenomenon can be understood as cultural, whereas the normative and differentiation-theoretical concepts of culture restrict what counts as culture to the bourgeois high culture of modernity and its products. What are the alternatives? I propose drawing a distinction between two levels: a weak or *broad concept of culture*, which denotes the cultural as a whole, and a strong or *specific concept of culture*, which pertains to objects or other entities to which society attributes particular *qualities*. What is meant by culture in the broad sense is thus all social and cultural practices and their orders of knowledge. In the specific sense, however, culture encompasses only those social entities (objects, subjects, spaces, temporalities, collectives) that have a particular feature: society ascribes to them not (or not only) utility or a function, but rather *value*. In addition to this character of value, the cultural entities in question also have a second significant feature: to a considerable extent, they produce (positive) affects. These cultural entities thus form a *cultural sphere* in which social processes of valorization and affecting take place.

According to the broad or weak concept of culture, the cultural designates the level of socially relevant contexts of meaning as a whole.³ All social practices contain implicit orders of knowledge, which classify the phenomena of the world in a particular way and therefore assign a specific meaning to them. They regulate how the world is represented and which practices appear possible, urgent, and sensible in it. In this sense, the social is always cultural; social practices are always cultural practices. From the perspective of this broad understanding of culture, moreover, social rationalization and the social logic of the general can also be regarded as cultural. Technical, cognitive, and normative rationalization depends on culturally specific criteria such as efficiency, equality, or truth. This involves a cultural process of *enacting rationality*, which constantly distinguishes the rational from the non-rational.

In the sea of the cultural in this broad sense, culture in the strong and specific sense forms distinct islands. It denotes a specific realm of the socio-cultural world, namely the cultural sphere in which objects and other entities of particular quality circulate. By asking what this qualification consists of, we can now draw a connection to our thoughts about the social logic of singularities and simultaneously build a bridge to the traditional concept of culture. This bridge can be erected on the level of the concept of *value*. My assumption is this: precisely those social entities (that is, those objects, subjects, spaces, temporalities, and collectives) that are socially singularized attain the qualities necessary for becoming entities of culture in this social context. Singular social entities become *cultural entities*, and the process of their singularization is also a process of their *culturalization*. Cultural entities are fabricated within the framework of all four practices of singularization discussed above: the practices of observation, evaluation/valorization, production, and appropriation/experience. From the perspective of cultural quality, however, one of these practices has a leading role: valorization, which is the fundamental process of assigning or denying value and thus certifies what *counts* as unique and as a cultural entity in general (and also what does not count and thus exists outside of the singular and outside of culture).

We have already seen the extent to which the specific practices of valorization, which are typical of the social logic of singularities, differ from the classifying and ranking forms of evaluation that characterize rationalism and the social logic of the general. Whereas, in the latter, the entities of the social are classified according to their utility and function, in the former they are attributed value in the strict sense – an intrinsic value that does not derive from anything else. It is a matter of things, objects, people, places, events, and collectives being recognized as *valuable*, and it is their acknowledged inherent complexity that makes them seem to be such. As bearers of value, they are not a means to an end; in a sense, they are ends in themselves.[4] Together, cultural entities thus form a sphere of the valuable in which, conversely, that which lacks value is rejected. The cultural sphere is therefore the sphere in which these values *circulate*.

It may come as a surprise that, in the wake of the social-constructivist turn and its radical expansion of the cultural, I would venture to advocate such a limited concept of culture, and one based on values at that. Wouldn't this be equivalent to turning back the clock to a restricted and normative concept of culture? I am of the opinion that the expansion of the cultural by theorists since the 1970s has undoubtedly been beneficial, for it means that more

I Modernity Between the General and the Particular 55

and more phenomena have been recognized as being culturally constituted and subjected to cultural-theoretical analysis. At the same time, however, this has left a noticeable gap, for it involved sacrificing the classical understanding of culture, according to which culture denotes specific *qualities* of the social. When the conceptual differentiation between culture and non-culture is abandoned, this has problematic consequences for a theory of modernity. I would go as far as to say that identifying modernity with a process of formal rationalization – and thus accepting a one-dimensional image of modernity as the large-scale machinery of the social logic of the general – requires losing the distinction between culture and non-culture, between the *sphere of value (and affect)* and the *system of utility and function*. By failing to distinguish between these two dimensions, one also fails to see modernity's dual structure, which consists of both rationalization and culturalization.

The concept of value can be salvaged from the legacy of the classical concept of culture and allow us to think against the grain. Today, its restricted applications to the bourgeois high culture of the nineteenth century and later to the limited subsystem of "art and culture" are rightly regarded as narrow-minded. The classical, normative concept of culture had associated value with particular high-cultural practices of the bourgeoisie – with the practices of education and art appreciation – and presupposed that cultural critique could only be undertaken from this perspective.[5] Its truly interesting legacy only comes to light, however, when one thinks about it abstractly and reconsiders the concept of value from a fresh cultural-theoretical perspective. Then it is possible to recognize that the value of cultural entities does not consist in the fact that a *cultural critic* finds them remarkable and has established their "objective value" but rather in the fact that these entities are valuable in the social world of *the participants* themselves. Culture exists wherever value is socially assigned.

The value-oriented concept of culture thus allows there to be a distinction, in an abstract form, between two different ways in which social entities are formatted by society: either as a cultural quality to which value is attributed, or as functional, standardized, and generalized entities of the social that are of instrumental use. Cultural entities are considered ends in themselves; they are regarded as having an intrinsic value of their own. In contrast, functional entities (functional objects, subjects, spaces, temporalities, and collectives) seem to be means to an end, and to this extent they have an extrinsic or instrumental structure. As to which specific entities are valorized and which are not, this is now an open question of social dynamics. Paintings, noteworthy places, or subcultures can become cultural entities just as baseball games, urinals (as in Duchamp's example), religious relics, or nations can. The social logic of singularities determines what counts as *particular* and *therefore* as "culturally valuable." Accordingly, there are also things in society that exist outside of culture – namely, those social entities that are regarded as valueless.

From what I have said so far, it is clear that the concept of culture is not the only thing that needs to be renewed. It is also necessary to dust off the concept of value if it is to become a matter of interest to contemporary sociology and cultural theory. Value should not be understood as a neo-Kantian value system that precedes praxis and motivationally guides it. This is not a matter of individual people or a society *having* certain values. Rather, the concept of value has to be understood in praxeological terms, so that the practices of *valorizing* individual objects become visible.[6] Values have to be interpreted as part of the social dynamics of circulation. These are open-ended and often controversial; it is here where culture wars take place, which are essentially conflicts about valorization. In processes of valorization, entities of the social are singularized and de-singularized; they are assigned or denied inherent complexities. Here, elements of idiosyncrasies or the general-particular are transformed into singularities, but they can also lose this value in turn.

If the praxis of culture is roughly understood as a praxis of valorization and de-valorization, it will also become clear that the conservative connotations of the old concept of culture can be stripped away and that it is possible to develop a value-theoretical and heuristically fruitful perspective on the mechanisms of power and domination that are inherent to culture. In social processes of valorization, value is assigned and value is *denied*. In these processes of *de-valorization* or *devaluation*, which are also processes of de-singularization, it becomes clear that more or less subtle mechanisms of exclusion are at work in the cultural sphere.[7] Whereas some social entities are recognized as valuable and unique, others remain invisible, are dismissed as general-particular, or are negatively singularized. In short: works of art, attractive cities, and remarkable people are not the only things that circulate in the sphere of culture; it also produces rubbish, flyover country, and white trash. De-valorization is a sort of devaluation that affects not only things/ objects, places, and events but also subjects and collectives. Under modern conditions, it is no surprise that these cycles of valorization and devaluation do not form a monolithic block but rather always entail counter-valorizations and readjustments to the criteria of evaluation.

Accordingly, the cultural sphere creates not only (positive) singularities *qua* valorization but also, under certain circumstances, *negative singularities*. Of course, most social entities that never achieve singularization – the things that do not seem unique or the people who lack originality, for instance – remain invisible in

I Modernity Between the General and the Particular   57

the cultural sphere. This is not a matter of negativity but rather of *indifference*.[8] Negativity, in fact, was a defining feature of normative rationalization and the logic of the general. Under that logic, people distanced themselves from that which did not follow the general pattern – from the particular and abnormal (which was in turn classified as a type). Beyond indifference, however, instances of strong devaluation can occasionally occur in the cultural sphere, so that something will be regarded as worthless or as a sort of "non-value" and thus be seen as problematic, threatening, or inferior. What is crucial here is that the "other" from which people keep their distance is in fact a singularity with inherent complexity, yet it has been endowed with a decidedly negative valence.

When they appear, *negative singularities* are met with considerable cultural, and above all narrative and aesthetic, interest. In the case of subjects, for instances, negative singularities have included serial killers, mass murderers, and terrorists, who tend to capture modernity's cultural imagination. A less drastic example would be a troublemaker politician who attracts attention and negative recognition. Other subjects can become stigmatized singularities, which are more than mere abnormal types.[9] It is also possible for places, events, and things to be negatively singularized: certain "no-go areas" in cities or entire problematic regions (West Virginia, for example, as the stronghold of hillbilly culture), repulsive and disgusting objects, violent rituals, or horrific historical events (such as the Holocaust). Finally, collectives can mutually perceive one another as negative singularities (fundamentalist communities versus liberal metropolitan culture). In the form of devaluation, de-valorization often involves a complicated dynamic. Here, in Julia Kristeva's terms, the "other," or the negative singularity, becomes something "abject" – an abject singularity and the object of condemnation.[10] Negative singularities are closely associated with negative affects, but even more often with ambivalent – or even fascinating – horror.

With this we have come to yet another element that, in addition to the concept of value, has to be salvaged from the legacy of the traditional concept of culture in order to develop a contemporary conception of culture and culturalization: the affective character of culture. In the traditional understanding, which is familiar from the comparison between culture and civilization or society,[11] culture was identified as a counterforce to formal rationality – as a non-rational or even irrational force that generates strong emotions and cannot be tamed by the rational and moderating rules of civilization. Although the opposition between culture and civilization may be obsolete today, the association of culture with the non-rational, the emotional, and its unpredictable possibilities can still be used analytically. As I have already noted, culturally endowed objects, subjects, places, events, and collectives function in a thoroughly affective manner; they exude a considerable affective intensity.[12] Here, too, we can draw a connection to our analysis of the social logic of singularities: a central feature of singularized objects, subjects, etc., is their ability to affect people, whereas the entities in the realm of the logic of the general produce little if any emotions and are treated in an almost affect-neutral manner.

To summarize: in the cultural sphere in the strong sense, singularities are endowed with value and have affective qualities. We are moved or touched by them, fascinated or disgusted in a compelling way; we experience a sense of horror or comfort in their presence. Positive singularities affect people in an intensely positive way, negative singularities in an intensely negative way. These affective processes are not, however, irrational. They have a sociologically comprehensible logic of their own. Valorizing objects, subjects, events, and collectives as unique and being affected by them are inextricably linked to one another. They are both formational components of the culture's sphere of circulation and its logic of singularities. That which seems to be valuable and unique operates in an affective manner *because* it is valuable and unique. And that which produces considerable emotions seems to be valuable and unique *because* it operates in such a strongly affective manner.

Culturalization versus Rationalization

In its valorizing and affective structure, culture in the strong sense always has the form of something non-rational or extra-rational, beyond any productive or intersubjective utility. In the history of cultural theory, such an understanding of culture was suggested in the context of the Collège de Sociologie by authors such as Georges Bataille and Roger Caillois.[13] From this perspective, culture does not appear as the totality of human ways of life or as the world of meanings but rather as a counterpart to rationalism, and so it has been from archaic societies to the society of the present day. Rationalism is always oriented toward production and accumulation, toward conserving and reinvesting social energies, toward efficiency and regulation. Culture, on the contrary, is to some extent unproductive. Its practices are *unconditional*, which means that they are without a purpose or function. They have value; they are strongly affective practices of *overspending*. Whereas rationalism is based on labor and dominating nature, culture is grounded in sovereignty – in going beyond instrumental praxis by distancing oneself from necessities. In contrast to the tranquil and *cold* complex of formal rationalization, the cultural sphere is *hot*.

The idea that a contrary logic of rationality and culture forms the basic structure of all societies is instructive. This tension cannot

I Modernity Between the General and the Particular

really be understood, however, unless one is aware of the existence of the oppositional social logics of the singular and the general. In this light, rationalization and culturalization can be systematically and ideal-typically compared as two structuring principles of society that format the social in two different directions. We have already seen that formal rationalization standardizes, generalizes, and formalizes social entities according to the specifications of the social logic of the general. The culturalization of the social, however, is precisely that social process in which objects, subjects, spaces, temporalities, and collectives are singularized in the sense described above. The cultural*ization* of the social means this: more and more of such singularized (that is, valorized and affectively operating) objects, subjects, places, events, and collectives are being fabricated, and the applied practices of observing, evaluating, producing, and appropriating them are becoming more and more extensive. This quantitative shift has a qualitative and structurally formational effect on society.

Culturalization can thus influence the macro-level of societies, but its effectiveness depends on the micro-level of the individual social entity. Food or a meal, for instance, can become the object of culturalization when it is valorized beyond its nutritional utility as a bearer of value ("healthy," "original," "holy," etc.) and when it functions affectively ("uplifting," "tasteful," "extraordinary"). Culturalization is simultaneously singularization, and vice versa. The meal is elevated out of the general catalogue of nutritional means; it develops its own inherent complexity and inner density (through its particular preparation and spatial atmosphere, by being part of a religious practice, etc.). Food that had previously served the rationalistic aim of eating can thus be transformed by the logic of singularities and enter the cultural sphere, with its valorizing and affecting dynamics.

In that affective entities of this sort are fabricated with value, what takes place in the process of culturalization could be called "doing culture."[14] The process of rationalization is always concerned with reducing complexity, with confining social entities to just a few parameters and therefore making them predictable and cooperative. Here, complexity is regarded as disruptive. Culturalization, in contrast, allows select objects, subjects, places, events, and collectives to develop inherent complexity and inner density, whereby they are singularized. Here, inherent complexity and inner density are the very appeal; they are the whole point.

Why in society are there not only processes of formal rationalization but processes of culturalization as well? Above, I explained that the rationalization of social praxis can be interpreted as a response to the problems of scarcity and disorder in society. In this respect, rationalization provides efficiency and stability. The culturalization of the social, in contrast, can be seen as a response to the social problem of *meaning and motivation*. Here the issue is why life should be lived in a certain way. Cultural practices – from telling mythical stories and engaging in collective rituals to traveling abroad and playing computer games – are answers to the question of to what end (collective or individual) life should be lived when privation and disorder have been averted. Whereas rationalization is a response to the question of *how*, culturalization answers the question of *why*. Essentially, cultural praxis and the cultural sphere make it possible for people to distance themselves from the necessities of the life-world and formal rationalization, and they do so not by reducing complexity along formal parameters but rather by allowing it to unfold. Above all, they promise to provide value and affect.

Cultural and social theorists have been fully aware of the existence of the problem of meaning and motivation, and they have written extensively about its role in archaic and traditional societies, with their magic, myths, religions, images, rites, games, and celebrations. To some extent, however, the prevailing interpretation of modernity as a process of formal rationalization implies that culturalization defines traditional societies just as rationalization defines modernity. This makes it seem as though the "irrational" culturalization of older societies was supplanted by the culturally neutral rationalization of modernity.[15] Put simply, older societies were concerned with meaning, while modernity has been concerned exclusively with efficiency. This interpretation, however, leaves us with just a one-dimensional image of things. Apart from the fact that premodern societies had their own formats of rationalization and were far more rational than modern thinkers would like to believe, modern societies have also developed their own forms of culturalization, their own social logic of singularities. Shrewd proponents of the rationalization narrative – Max Weber among them – have at least identified a problem in modernity's presumed replacement of culture by rationality, a problem that has been subjected to all sorts of cultural critique under the rubrics of disenchantment and the loss of meaning.[16] In reality, culture – with its valorizing and affecting nature and its preference for the unique – has not disappeared from modernity at all, and certainly not from late modernity, where it has experienced a historically unprecedented surge and structural transformation. The problem of meaning and motivation, to which culturalization is a response, is in general just as present as the problem of efficiency and order – and as soon as problems of efficiency and order became less pressing, it even took center stage. The truly interesting question, then, is not whether processes of culturalization simply represent a sort of problem of excess or luxury, but, rather, which form the cultural sphere has adopted and

I Modernity Between the General and the Particular   61

what exact relationship has developed between culturalization and rationalization in individual forms of society.

Qualities of Cultural Praxis: Between Sense and Sensibility

In what respects can social entities acquire a cultural quality? To answer this question, it will be necessary again to fall back on cultural theory and its sensitivity to cultural singularities, which I would like to apply to my sociological analysis of the social processes of culturalization. It is possible to distinguish five features or *qualities* that *qualify* objects, subjects, places, events, and collectives as valuable and affecting cultural entities: the aesthetic, the narrative-hermeneutic, the ethical, the creative, and the ludic quality. These pertain to all singularized entities. Objects, for example, can develop an aesthetic quality; they can be attributed an ethical quality; their primary content can be narrative and hermeneutic; they can be creative objects, or the objects of play. They can possess just one of these qualities or combine several of them together. The same is true of singularized places and events, subjects and collectives. These qualities are assigned or denied through practices of valorization, and they manifest themselves affectively. It is possible to provide some structure to this sequence of five qualities if we proceed from the assumption that, as far as cultural praxis is concerned, we are always dealing with two dimensions: with *sense* (or meaning) and *sensibility* (or sensuousness). On the one hand, cultural entities have a meaningful aspect: they describe, narrate, explain, and justify. On the other hand, they possess a peculiar sensuous dimension to the extent that they address our sensory perception in a particular way. Many cultural theories have foregrounded either the one or the other quality of culture and have therefore understood it either hermeneutically or aesthetically. It would be best, however, to think about them together.

The meaningful quality of culture has frequently been associated with myths, religious beliefs, or world views. On a more fundamental level, this is really a matter of the *narrative-hermeneutic quality* that objects, places, events, subjects, and collectives can acquire. The sensuous aspect of culture can in turn be described as its *aesthetic quality*. With their narrative-hermeneutic quality, cultural entities provide narratives about the world of nature and society, about the past and the future, about people, things, and gods. At issue here is understanding the context of the world and the place of the subject within this context.[17] With their aesthetic quality, cultural entities present themselves as objects of intensified sensory perception. The aesthetic can be associated with the imaginary – that is, with the capacity to imagine alternative worlds or things beyond what can be perceived by the senses.[18] When singularities happen to be performative, it is usually in these two ways. The singularized objects, places, events, collectives, and subjects that I have discussed above and that will continue to concern us throughout this book are always aestheticized and/or hermeneuticized in a variable manner. This is just as true of travel destinations and religious communities as it is of food, internet profiles, bodies, events, cities, nations, and media products. The inherent complexity and inner density that such things develop may be structured on a stronger aesthetic basis or on a stronger hermeneutic basis, or both aspects can be defining to the same extent.

Both in its narrative-hermeneutic and its aesthetic-imaginative quality, the praxis of the cultural sphere reconfigures the structures of everyday practices and (especially) instrumentally rational practices in a fundamental way. This applies equally to the status of representations of the world and to the status of sensory perceptions. In the pragmatic world of everyday life (and all the more so after the formal rationalization of activity), both representations and perceptions possess the (instrumental) character of *information* claiming to depict reality. Over the course of their rationalization, representations and perceptions acquire a sort of *cognitive* structure and serve the thrift-driven understanding of reality with the goal of making the natural or social world as efficient and orderly as possible. The praxis of culture does not provide any information of this sort but rather creates interpretive contexts (that is, *stories*) that are meant to depict the world (individual biographies, political history, cosmological structures, etc.) in all its complexity. Such stories can be told by places but also by events, communities, and objects – from works of art to consumer products. Something analogous is also true of sensory perceptions. The praxis of culture is not concerned with producing neutral perceptions of an informational nature; the aim here is rather intensive perception in all sensory dimensions and for its own sake. Any social entity can be the object of such aesthetic perception. In general, it can be said that information requires utility and a function, while narratives and aesthetic perceptions require value. Information is emotionally impoverished and objective; narratives and aesthetic perceptions mobilize affects.

In addition to these two basic qualities – the narrative-hermeneutic and the aesthetic – there are three further cultural qualities that, though related to the first two,[19] nevertheless have their own independent character: the ethical, the creative, and the ludic. All three can in turn apply to all entities – that is, to objects, subjects, places, events, and collectives. That these can acquire an *ethical* quality may at first come as a surprise. After all, is the ethical not a dimension of normative rationalization? The answer is no, and this

I Modernity Between the General and the Particular 63

has to do with the distinction between morals and ethics. In short, it comes down to the fact that the index of morals belongs to the logic of (normative) rationality, whereas the index of the ethical belongs to the logic of culture.[20] Morality is part of the social logic of the general to the extent that its principles and imperatives have a generally valid and universal character and can (therefore) serve as the basis of a normative system. It is strictly anti-affective and its principles can be followed without any ifs, ands, or buts – unemotionally and, if necessary, even reluctantly. The ethical, on the contrary, is part of the social logic of the particular and is related to ways of life as a web of practices that are regarded as intrinsically good by their participants. The ethical does not apply to everyone but rather occurs as a dimension of singularization in the form of individual ethics and particular-group ethics. In extreme cases, it can sanctify the good and, unlike morality, it is typically imbued with a narrative or aesthetic quality. In this sense, not only can subjects and collectives acquire an ethical quality – objects, events, or places can become ethically charged bearers of the good as well.

Let us turn now to the quality of *creativity*. Above, I maintained that production represents an essential bundle of practices within the social logic of singularities. This does not only create unique entities, however, but can itself be regarded as singular – that is, as something that has its own intrinsic value and as something that affects participants. This intrinsic value belongs to the *creative* process as such.[21] In this sense, if it has an intrinsic structure, this is not a matter of mere "production" but rather a praxis of creation in which elements are arranged in a way that results in innovatively or artistically perfected forms. The contemporary term "design" covers at least one aspect of this creative practice. The second is that it involves dealing with materialities (that is, materials and media of various sorts) and dealing with idealities (with symbols or narratives, for instance). Under certain circumstances, such practice can be interpreted as *expressive*, as the expression of the subject (or also a collective) in an object, but it can also be dramatized in a singular creative act or have the character of a subtle and quotidian reproduction.[22]

Finally, there is the quality of the *ludic* – of play and the playful. In the medium of play, non-ordinary worlds are realized that follow their own self-imposed sets of rules and open up their own realms of possibility. The spectrum of ludic practices ranges from strictly regulated rituals and competitions to the openly playful and purely exploratory. Every cultural entity creates a world of its own, but those with a pronounced ludic quality involve a world in which a co-player can actively enter and be *engaged* in events from moment to moment. Games possess an open logic of activity and experimentation that generates a unique sort of tension. They are not burdened by the pragmatics of daily life or rationalized processes. In short, play is the praxis *par excellence* in which culture demonstrates its ostensibly useless excess in opposition to the rational world.[23] It ranges from the individual game object to the playful event and the ludic collective.

Narrative, aesthetic, ethical, creative, and ludic qualities are not inherent to objects, subjects, places, times, and collectives; the latter only gain these qualities within the social logic of singularities, with its valorizations and de-valorizations. Individual entities are *instilled* with these qualities – or not. On the macro-level, the culturalization of the social thus includes more specific processes for turning social entities into narratives, aestheticizing them, and making them ethical, creative, or ludic.[24]

4
The Transformation of the Cultural Sphere

The development of society has frequently been described as a unilinear process of formal rationalization. Accordingly, it is thought to advance toward an increasingly comprehensive logic of the general in the form of more technology, science, and universalization, whereas singularities, valorizations, and affects are what humanity has left behind. What would it mean, then, if we were to change our perspective and examine the transformation of society in terms of the development of singularizing and culturalizing processes? How has the social logic of singularity and its cultural sphere transformed from premodern societies to late modernity?

I believe that the starting point of social theory should be the *dual structure of the social*. Society entails both rationalization *and* culturalization. This means that processes of rationalization cannot be analyzed in isolation from culturalization, because the two always accompany one another. Likewise, the cultural sphere cannot be artificially separated from the processes of rationalization. The social logic of the general and that of the particular should therefore be analyzed in parallel and in relation to one another. In the historical sequence of societies, modernity possesses a specific status, for it is here that both rationalization and culturalization advanced to become an actively pursued and structurally formational project. Modernity *radicalized* both rationalization and culturalization and developed, since its beginning at the end of the eighteenth century, a social logic of the general *and* a social logic of the particular with a historically extraordinary intensity that transformed the world of everyday life. However, the phases of bourgeois modernity, organized modernity, and late modernity model the relationship between the two in different ways. The culture of the particular, which was a secondary feature of classical (that is, bourgeois and organized) modernity, has advanced to become a primary form of structuring society in late modernity.

Premodern Societies: The Fixation and Repetition of the Singular

Premodern societies include both archaic (that is, preliterate) tribal societies and traditional (that is, high-cultural) societies. In archaic societies, the relation between the logic of the general and that of the particular can be described as one of *types* and *idiosyncrasies* that is defined by the pronounced difference between the *profane* and the *sacred*.[1] Archaic societies, which are distinguished by the great stability of their social structures, are essentially identical with a life-world defined by customs and complex typifications that form the basis for a social logic of the general. In part, the practices of these societies were already instrumentally rationalized in the sense of *techne*. Everyday typifications, however, left some room for similarities and a lack of clarity – and thus for idiosyncratic subjects, objects, and collectives. Yet it would be an anachronistic misunderstanding to regard these premodern idiosyncrasies as valued or even as systematically produced singularities. It is rather the case that archaic societies – perhaps more than any other social form – created space for people to view idiosyncrasies with outright *indifference*.[2]

At the same time, however, and in the background of this *profane* and quotidian life-world, *sacred* cultural practices were also developed that have fascinated cultural anthropologists from Émile Durkheim to Michel Leiris and Victor Turner:[3] highly affective and valued rituals in which the narrative-mythical and aesthetic-ludic dimensions overlap. In the context of these collective rituals, archaic societies singularized individual artifacts and instilled them with extreme hermeneutic and aesthetic qualities (as in the case of totemism, for instance). Here, too, places could be distinguished as holy; rituals could crystallize into singular performative practices; and, in rare cases, subjects (such as magi) could be experienced as singular as well. The cultural sphere that formed around these ritualized cultural practices was a relatively stable and socially inclusive sacred sphere: the sacred was socially fixed.

The transformation from archaic to (in the strict sense) traditional societies was initiated by the Neolithic revolution. This gave rise to agrarian societies with trans-locally governing central authorities and legal systems. Beyond the rural population, a ruling noble class was gradually formed that developed its own lifestyle. In time, mythical and magical world views were replaced by more strictly regulated religions, which were sustained by an institutionalized Church and clergy that required the medium of writing. To some extent, then, traditional societies involved a process of formal rationalization. At the same time, however, these isolated examples

I Modernity Between the General and the Particular

of rationalization rested on the extensive and intact traditions of the everyday life-world.

The culturalization of these traditional societies took place within a *triadic cultural sphere*, which was composed of segments from religion / the Church, courtly culture / high culture, and folk culture, as in the example of the European Middle Ages. The gradual differentiation between the Church and courtly society involved the institutional division of the hermeneutic-narrative and aesthetic dimensions of culture. Whereas the religious practices of world religions developed complex ontologies and cosmologies, spirituality, and formalized collective rituals, practices of courtly culture were institutionalized that combined sophisticated civility with excessive aesthetic opulence. In the case of both religious and aristocratic culture, culture stood under the directive of the state; it was central and hierarchically organized. Folk culture, however, maintained a degree of independence from both. Especially in urban contexts, singularities overlapped with one another in a complex manner on the level of collectives (in the case of guilds, for instance). In traditional societies, individual places and rural communities could also develop into singularities that – seen from the outside – clearly stand out from others and leave the impression of cultural heterogeneity.

There have been repeated attempts to assign the essence of the traditional cultural sphere to just one of these three segments: for Max Weber, it was religion; for Norbert Elias, it was courtly culture; for Mikhail Bakhtin, it was folk culture – although it seems that the coexistence of all three segments was in fact characteristic of the traditional cultural sphere.[4] It was characterized by a combination of *singularization* and *repetition*. In this form of society, it is clear that singularity did not entail innovation or creativity. The traditional cultural sphere was oriented toward cultural elements that were not novel but, rather, treasured objects of repetition. This was true, for example, of the canonical texts and rites of religion, of the classicizing art and architecture of codified courtly culture, and of the celebrations and festivals of folk culture.

In traditional societies, as in the case of archaic societies, processes of singularization seem to have been more present on the level of things than on that of subjects. Only rarely were subjects acknowledged to be singular (religious prophets or certain rulers, for instance).[5] The singularization of things took place, above all, in the realms of the Church and courtly culture. With the rise of representational buildings, architecture achieved a special status in the production of singularity.[6] Singular things therefore acquired a fixed place, where they could develop an "aura" (in Walter Benjamin's sense). In addition, media-technological developments (writing, image techniques) led to the fact that singular objects were increasingly produced on the level of texts and images. In general, the following can be said about all segments of the traditional cultural sphere: the value of singular entities – religious texts, royal palaces, religious or secular art, festivals – was socially codified and seldom controversial.

Bourgeois Modernity: The Romantic Revolution of the Unique

The break between traditional society and modernity – in its early bourgeois form, which emerged at the end of the eighteenth century and lasted until the beginning of the twentieth – was dramatic. I have already discussed the technical, cognitive, and normative processes of rationalization that were initiated at this time.[7] The large-scale phenomenon of "doing generality," which propelled early modernity toward industrial revolution, capitalization, socialization, the nation state, and globalization, is well known. However, the structural transformation of culturalization was no less significant. It gave rise to the lifestyle of the bourgeoisie, the bourgeois conception of art, and the radical aesthetic movement of Romanticism. Even in its early phase, modernity was thus distinguished not only by a radical social logic of the general but also by a historically unprecedented social logic of the particular, though the latter was admittedly a subordinate *counter-tendency*.

The bourgeois lifestyle was characterized by the *ambivalence* between its claim of cultural *generality* and its orientation toward the *singular* (understood as the individual). The bourgeois way of life laid claim to the concept of culture, and it did so emphatically.[8] In this lifestyle, aesthetic practices (engaging with art, experiencing nature, etc.) went hand in hand with hermeneutic-narrative practices (education through engaging with texts). The bourgeoisie thus lived off of the idea of the *general* validity of whatever might be recognized as culturally valuable. The *education* of the subject – of his or her character and general virtue – became a matter of enculturation in the strict sense. The aim of this lifestyle was to create a sphere of aimlessness, "disinterested pleasure" (as Kant called it), and education for its own sake. The bourgeois lifestyle thus found support in educational institutions as well as in the renewed field of the arts (literature, visual art, the theater, and music).

The modern field of art, which began to form around the year 1800, was the social field of modernity, which was systematically oriented toward the fabrication of unique entities. Its works of art appeared with a claim to singularity, which came to be expressed in the semantics of originality and artistic genius.[9] Modern art is, in fact, fundamentally different from premodern art: no longer interested in perfecting known forms according to a rule-based

I Modernity Between the General and the Particular 69

aesthetics, it is rather concerned with breaking rules and creating ever-new singularities. Singularity became linked to a regime of aesthetic novelty. In this context, artists too became matters of fascination on account of their radical singularity – their "individuality." They sought to actualize themselves *expressively* in their work. The bourgeois field of art was thus the first to institutionalize an attention market for cultural singularity goods. At the same time, however, bourgeois culture also endeavored to restrict uniqueness by tying it to normative and general principles, particularly by coupling aesthetics with the aforementioned ideal of education.[10] It was hoped that works of art would express a sort of normative generality and even universality (humanity, reason, etc.), and that education would involve appropriating a canon of individual works from that past that were generally recognized as valuable.

This complex synthesis of the particular and the general, which characterized bourgeois culture, was made dynamic by the revolutionary *singularism* that developed with the counter-cultural movement of Romanticism. The significance of Romanticism for modernity's culture of singularities cannot be overstated.[11] This was the first radically singularistic cultural movement in history, and it closely associated uniqueness with the ideal of authenticity. The immediate significance of Romanticism lies in the fact that it radically oriented the human subject toward singularity, which was treated in the semantics of "individuality." This then served the comprehensive project of singularizing *all* elements of the world. Here, too, the experience of art played an important role, and there also developed a radically in-the-moment, aesthetic awareness of time. But the experience of nature (not understood as a mechanical natural space but as an ensemble of singular landscapes), the experience of picturesque places, the experience of other subjects in the form of friendship and love, the singular formation of the material world (in the case of hand-crafted objects, for instance), a sensitivity to history as a venue for narratives and memories, the experiential sphere of religion, and identifying with the singularities of peoples and nations were all areas in which Romanticism subjected the world to a comprehensive process of singularization.

It has often been maintained that Romanticism was an attempt to re-enchant or re-mystify the world. It would be more accurate, however, to describe this process as a culturalization of the world that made it possible to transfer potentially *everything* from the side of the profane to that of the sacred. In the end, even a pair of shoes or a lover's birthmark could be of cultural value. This Romantic valorization of the world was enabled by its comprehensive tendency to singularize. The world was rediscovered as a realm of fascinating inherent complexities and was reconfigured as such. The fundamental postulate was this: any subject who wished to be authentic must have authentic experiences by engaging with the singularities of the world. In Romanticism, the explicit struggle against the modernity of the general – from Enlightenment philosophy to industrialization – was the constant downside to the comprehensive singularization of the world. From its beginning, this Romantic culture of singularity had entirely unpredictable effects on the calculated balance of bourgeois culture.

Ultimately, the nationalist movements of the nineteenth century concentrated on just *one* aspect of Romantic singularization and culturalization: that of collectives, which now meant the nation. With the "imagined communities" of nations, collectives were aggressively understood as singularities. Of course, the idiosyncrasies of social collectives – from tribes and clans to villages and principalities – also existed in traditional societies. Yet it was modernity, with its politicization of collectives, that first not only enforced the general existence of collectives in "freedom and equality," but also imposed an understanding of collective and historical singularities.[12] This development took place not only in Europe but also in the global anti-colonial nationalist movements (in India, China, the Near East) that arose at the end of the nineteenth century. Nationalisms frequently give rise to a genuine sort of *culturalism* that essentially identifies societies with a homogeneous and incommensurable culture.

In retrospect, it becomes clear to what extent early, bourgeois modernity had laid significant groundwork for the modern culture of singularities that has remained formative to the present day. In this regard, it could be said that the following factors were equally influential: the Romantic culture of authenticity and its comprehensive project of singularization, the idea of modeling art according to a regime of aesthetic originality, the cultural orientation of the bourgeois lifestyle, and the politicization of authenticity along nationalistic lines.

Organized Modernity: Mass Culture

Organized, industrial modernity, which extended from around 1920 to the middle or end of the 1970s, represents a breach within modernity itself. In its socialist instantiation, it was aggressively anti-bourgeois and anti-Romantic. Its lasting influence, however, derives from its Western version, which was largely propelled by the United States and its combination of Fordism and Americanism. As we have already seen, industrial modernity represents the zenith of the modern process of formal rationalization, with its expansive social logic of the general. It would be one-sided, however, to reduce it to that alone, for it also caused its own shift with respect to culturalization, especially in the fields of consumption and audiovisual

I Modernity Between the General and the Particular 71

media. Bourgeois-Romantic culture did not vanish entirely; instead, it was fundamentally subordinated to the social logic of the general in such a way that, from the perspective of bourgeois cultural traditions, little seemed to remain beyond anti-individualistic mass society.

Fordism was based on mass production and mass consumption alike. In the 1920s, the world of consumption began to develop into a new cultural sphere. In short, a consumption revolution took place.[13] Goods, which had previously served instrumental purposes above all, were now increasingly subjected to culturalization – that is, they started to become narrative, aesthetic, expressive, or ludic ends in themselves. Consumption drastically broadened the scope of culture and its processes of valorization beyond the confines of bourgeois art and education. The central point is this: in that goods were now currying the favor of consumers within a commercial market constellation, culture was no longer tied to the state but rather to the economy. Here, in individual segments, it is already possible to observe mechanisms of cultural innovation and differentiation that resemble something like a "fashion cycle."[14] That said, organized modernity posed two limitations. On the one hand, the culturalization of the world of goods was quite limited in comparison to the situation to come in late modernity. Most goods primarily served instrumentally rational purposes or the social function of preserving status. On the other hand, the value of these objects as singular entities was often limited. Given the influence of Fordism, they were mostly standardized, and in this sense we are dealing here with a *mass culture*.[15] Even the consuming subject in organized modernity was not concerned with being distinct but rather with demonstrating his or her general normality: the ideal model was that of "keeping up with the Joneses."[16]

Within the framework of this post-bourgeois culture, audio-visual media acquired a specific status. This was especially true of movies, which became the center of what came to be called the culture industry.[17] In the case of films, the new field of consumption intertwined with the old field of art. Films are clearly culturalized goods with both narrative-hermeneutic and aesthetic qualities. At the same time, every film promises something non-interchangeable and different, so that a system of valorization formed around them to gauge their value and appeal. In the cinematic sphere, the regime of aesthetic novelty, which constantly demands new originality and surprises, is even more prevalent than it is in bourgeois art. The social field of the film was pioneering to the extent that, as of the 1920s, it established a broad and hypercompetitive market around a cultural good whose respective value is uncertain and contentious.

To a certain degree, the culture industry also promoted the singularization of subjects, and especially in the form of "stars" (it would not take long, however, for such people to be denounced for their "prefabricated" nature, which did not meet the standards of bourgeois culture).[18] All typecasting aside, it remains true that if a star wanted to have any power of attraction, he or she would have to be regarded as unique. In a sense, the star thus inherited the role of the artistic subject. Both cases involve the social recognition and glorification of subjective singularity, though now it was not a matter of a unique work of art but rather the performance and glamor of subjects themselves. Throughout organized modernity, the star remained an exclusive and inimitable figure who stood outside of the reality of the leveled middle-class society.

Organized modernity thus carried out its own shift in the nature of culturalization. Whereas the culturalization of bourgeois society was one of *intensifying* culture through the bourgeois and Romantic practices of art and education, the culturalization of organized modernity entailed the *extension* of culture – that is, its large-scale dissemination through consumption and mass media. Whereas bourgeois intensification was related above all to the aesthetic-hermeneutic inner world of subjects, the Fordistic extension of culture was primarily directed toward the visual surfaces of subjects and objects.

Late Modernity: Competitive Singularities, Hyperculture, and Polarization

In various constellations, processes of culturalization and singularization have thus existed throughout all of social history. In late modernity, however, they have acquired a new quantity and quality. To visualize this proliferation of the particular, look no further than NASA's satellite images of Earth's city lights, which show the continents at night and thus underscore the bright illumination of the world's large cities. In a similar way, it is possible to imagine all of today's acknowledged singularities – all of the unique objects, subjects, places, events, and collectives, which are spread across the globe in a sea of social practices and which stand out, on account of their affective heat, like brightly shining points and paths. If one were to look at similar pictures taken from the years 0, 1200, 1800, 1900, 1950, 1980, and 2000, there would certainly be a few bright points and paths to see – the old rites and magi, the churches and courtly societies, the Romantic communities and bourgeois theaters, the cinemas and the stars – but as of 1980 one would notice an explosion of brightness. Of course, not everything has been illuminated, because the logic of the general still exists in the background. But what was once the exception is now the rule: ours is a society of singularities.

I Modernity Between the General and the Particular   73

In late modernity, the social logic of singularization, which is also the logic of culturalization and the intensification of affect, has become structurally formational for all of society. Since the 1970s or 1980s, the culture of the particular, which has been present since the beginning of modernity but was subordinate to the logic of the general, has itself become structurally formational on a large scale. Both the status and form of formal rationalization and its logic of the general have accordingly changed. As I have already said on several occasions, they have increasingly become a background structure – a general infrastructure for singularities. Especially in the propagation of global markets and technologies, the phenomenon of "doing generality" in globalized late modernity is obvious, but upon closer inspection it functions in many respects as a condition of possibility for the processes and arenas of singularization.

What are the *causes* that have led to the primacy of the logic of singularities? The transformation from organized modernity to late modernity has been due to a historical *coincidence of three factors*, each of which has been gaining strength since the 1970s. The three factors are the following: the socio-cultural revolution of authenticity, sustained by the lifestyle of the new middle class; the transformation of the economy into a post-industrial economy of singularities; and the technical revolution of digitalization. Their context warrants a more detailed examination.

Since the 1970s, a fundamental structural transformation has taken place in formerly industrial societies, and this has been a transformation of culture and values as well. At its heart stands the *new middle class*, which owes its existence to the expansion of educational opportunities and is characterized by its high cultural capital.[19] In this sense, the new middle class is an educated middle class that has been active primarily in the knowledge and culture economy of post-industrial society and has been the latter's most important standard bearer. This socio-structural transformation was accompanied by a transformation of values, over the course of which the values of materialism, duty, and acceptance, which were characteristic of industrial modernity, were replaced by a post-materialistic orientation toward self-development and actualization.[20] The leading measures by which people orient their lifestyles have thus changed from those of the general and functional to those of culture and the particular. The old, rationalistic measure of one's *standard* of living has been superseded by the measure of one's *quality* of life. The authenticity of the self has thus gained an enormous amount of significance. One's self should now develop into its uniqueness, and the pursuit of correspondingly authentic experiences (at work, at leisure, and in one's private life) has become a leitmotif. All of this has added up to an *authenticity revolution*. This transformation of values is linked to modernity's tradition of cultural and aesthetic counter-movements, which began with Romanticism and has ranged from the life-reform movement to the counterculture of the 1960s and 1970s. The counterculture, which is rather superficially understood with the label "1968," represents a historical link between the cultural counter-movement of Romanticism and the new middle class. Romanticism's comprehensive program of culturalization and singularization, which was historically no more than a subcultural phenomenon, became for the first time the central force behind the lifestyle of society's most influential population.

Parallel to and interwoven with the rise of this new, authenticity-oriented middle class, a structural transformation of the capitalist economy has also been taking place since the 1970s. Essentially, the latter has transformed from an industrial economy into a knowledge and culture economy – an economy of singularities with the creative economy at its center. At the same time, the related technological revolution of digitalization has also taken place. This has given rise to a historically unprecedented infrastructure for the systematic and expansive fabrication of singularities and culture. Together, the economy and technology have formed a global *cultural-creative complex*. Whereas the economy and technology of classical modernity were elementary engines of rationalization and standardization, the tides have now turned: the practices of production, observation, and evaluation have become engines for manufacturing cultural singularities. Cultural capitalism and computer networks are the driving force behind the expansive culturalization of the economy and technology. They have created an institutional structure that actively *fulfills* the formerly Romantic but now middle-class desire for the singularization and culturalization of the world. It goes without saying that this new structure has not left subjects and lifestyles unchanged.

Although the three factors that brought about the transition from industrial modernity to late modernity are each characterized by their own dynamics and relative autonomy, they have also influenced and enhanced one another. The genesis of the new middle class and its shift in values can be traced back to the unique educational dynamics of the twentieth century, as well as to the intrinsic logic of the cultural movements and lifestyles that have been going on since bourgeois modernity and Romanticism. At first, the rise of the post-industrial and post-Fordistic economy also followed an internal economic logic and can be understood as a reaction to the market saturation of standardized goods at the beginning of the 1970s, as well as a reaction to the automation of industrial production and the fundamental crisis of the Fordistic logic of acquisition and accumulation.[21] The digital revolution ultimately began along the inherently technical (and military-sponsored) path toward developing the computer and digital networks.[22]

I Modernity Between the General and the Particular 75

All three factors, however, are interlocked with one another. The new middle class has found professional employment in the knowledge and culture economy and, to satisfy its desire for authenticity, has acquired the broadest variety of cultural singularity goods. Cultural capitalism has not only responded to this demand but has further intensified it, thereby expanding the pool of singular goods and discourses of valorization (which now concern such things as education, cities, and religion). Finally, digitalization has been used and further developed in a specific way to satisfy the desires for communication, presentation, and consumption that characterize the late-modern subject and cultural capitalism. These new technological means simultaneously promote the singularization and culturalization of subjects and goods alike.

By mutually supporting each other in this way, the three factors in question have also changed their shape. The economy of singularities, the digital culture machine, and the new middle class (with its lifestyle of successful self-actualization) have each acquired their characteristic form from this constellation. Their coincidence is thus not without historical irony. After all, the Romantic image of culture and its singularities had implied that the latter could only exist outside of and in opposition to the economy and technology, which were regarded as large-scale equalizers and agents of utility. In late modernity, the Romantic orientation toward singularization may have become socially dominant for the first time, but this was only able to happen on account of the development of expansive economic and media-technological structures. Over the course of this process, however, post-materialism was also transformed.

Together, cultural capitalism and digital computer networks have institutionalized singularities within a highly specific constellation – namely, as *cultural singularity markets*. On these markets, objects, subjects, places, events, and (at least in part) collectives compete to be recognized and acknowledged as goods of unique cultural value. Singularities are thus divided into a structure of *competitive singularities*. This is a matter of markets that do not operate according to the criteria of industrial society and its standard markets. Now, performances seek attention and visibility; they aspire to affect their audience and to be evaluated as singular in processes of valorization. At their heart, these are thus markets of *attention, visibility*, and *affect*. They encourage a fundamental and genuine *cultural economization of the social*, in which not only commercial enterprise and the digital network participate but also most social spheres (media, education, cities, religion, relationships, etc.). As we will see in greater detail, these are *attractiveness markets* on which a specific form of *singularity capital* is accumulated. Here, both objects and subjects – but also cities, schools, religious communities, etc. – strive to create their unique *profile*, which has become one of the central forms of culture in late modernity.

Cultural singularity markets are not the only version of the social in which singularities operate in late modernity. As I will discuss later on, two other – and differently constructed – forms of the social have likewise developed a singularistic structure: *heterogeneous collaborations* and *neo-communities*. Heterogeneous collaborations do not arrange singularities in the form of public markets but rather as a *plurality of singular participants* (mostly subjects, but occasionally objects as well), whose diversity allows them to forge productive alliances and collaborations. Such is the case, for instance, in the many projects and networks that represent genuinely late-modern versions of the social. In neo-communities, on the contrary, the collective as a whole becomes a singularity – it is formed, that is, into a relatively homogeneous and unique entity. Such is the case in religious, political, or ethnic communities. Singularity markets, heterogeneous collaborations, and neo-communities all derive from historically traditional forms of the social – standard markets, communities, and also networks – but they have further developed these forms in such a way that they now represent three genuinely *singularistic forms of the social* populated by late-modern subjects. They can conflict with one another, but they can also combine and work together in surprising ways.

As I have already mentioned, the singularistic lifestyle, which is so dominant in late-modern culture, is primarily sustained by the new middle class. Its basic formula, by which it distinguished itself from the seemingly conformist and leveled middle-class society of organized modernity, is that of *successful self-actualization*. Here, the post-materialistic value of the actualized self is tied to the motive of social success and prestige. The resulting comprehensive singularization and culturalization of all aspects of life – living, eating, traveling, fitness, education, etc. – thus goes hand in hand with investing in one's own singularity capital for the sake of status, and with representing one's own *unique* life to others. To some extent, the model here is the "norm of deviance" or, in more positive terms, the norm of performative authenticity – of socially performing one's own uninterchangeable uniqueness.[23]

For the new middle class, culture has come to acquire the form of *hyperculture*, which is altogether characteristic of late modernity. In the case of hyperculture, potentially *everything* past or present can flexibly be valorized as culture. Be it high or low culture, local or global, contemporary or historical – all potential elements of culture are essentially on equal footing and are regarded as potential sources for enriching one's lifestyle. Hyperculture is distinguished by its cultural cosmopolitanism, within whose framework the elements of culture can be combined in seemingly endless ways. Uniqueness

I Modernity Between the General and the Particular 77

thus tends to derive from the model of *compositional singularity*: it is forever being arranged and curated from a diverse set of new and ever-changing elements. In fact, it is this compositional logic that enables late-modern culture to fabricate singularities on a mass scale.

The society of singularities has systematically created a series of new *social and cultural polarizations*, and these will be discussed at length in the following Part. It is important to keep in mind that these polarizations are not ancillary or accidental features but rather a direct consequence of the logic of singularization leaving behind social niches and becoming structurally formational for all of society. They are the result of society evaluating *what* counts as valuable and unique. It is here where processes of valorization and devaluation occur that are definitive of late-modernity. Five different levels can be distinguished:

The basic level is that of the *polarization of goods* on the markets of singularity, which is the precondition for all other polarizations. As markets of attention and valorization, singularity markets tend to form radically asymmetrical patterns. They are winner-take-all markets in which a few goods attract extreme amounts of attention, visibility, and value, while most goods achieve nothing of the sort. Cultural singularity markets are thus inclined to award things in excess and disregard other things entirely.

This is reflected on a second level: the *polarization of working conditions*, which has two aspects. Essentially, a dualism now exists between the highly qualified activities of the knowledge and culture economy on the one hand, and the simple or standardized activities of the service sector on the other. In late modernity, the professions that produce cultural singularity goods can claim legitimacy, status, and resources, whereas functional and "profane" labor cannot. What is more, tendencies toward polarization exist *within* the field of highly qualified professions. This field itself has adopted the features of a cultural singularity market on which performances, profiles, talent, and their recognition circulate, and this leads in its own way to the asymmetry of a winner-take-the-most market.

Third, all of this has given rise to a *polarization of classes and lifestyles*. The latter applies in particular to the relationship between the culturally ascendant new middle class on the one hand, and the culturally declining new underclass on the other. Whereas the new middle class can be understood as the cosmopolitan basis of culturalization and singularization processes, the new underclass has been socially and culturally devalued. Beyond the leveled middle-class society, this has thus resulted in more or less subtle cultural conflicts and tendencies toward segregation that affect such things as education, living conditions, and health.

Fourth, the polarization of goods, labor, and lifestyles has led to a *polarization of social spaces*. Regional, national, and global markets of spatial attractiveness have formed, and these have led to diverging developments in "attractive" places and regions that are said to have been "left behind." Whereas the former house the creative economy and the new middle class, the latter face the threat of being devalued altogether.

Finally, a *political polarization* has taken place in late modernity that can be interpreted as a reaction to the other levels of polarization. On the one hand, there is an "apertistic" (opening) and differential (difference-promoting) liberalism that is based on a combination of competition and cultural diversity. On the other hand, there is a slew of anti-liberal, (sub)political forms of cultural essentialism and communitarianism (ethnicity, nationality, religious fundamentalism, right-wing populism) that have mobilized collective identities against the hyperculture and its markets. Of course, these identity movements operate *within* the logic of the society of singularities. They, too, are based on a culture of singularity; however, theirs does not function on global markets but is rather situated within particular collectives (religious, national, ethnic, etc.). As a result of this polarization, the society of singularities is characterized throughout by cultural conflicts.

II
The Post-Industrial Economy of Singularities

Beyond Industrial Society

Since the 1980s, the Western economy has been changing from the mass production of standardized commodities to an economy of singularities. This singularization also entails a culturalization of the economy, at the heart of which there is a structural shift away from functional goods toward ones that have primarily cultural value and cultural qualities for consumers. The creative economy has thus become a driving force. The singularization and culturalization of goods have gone hand in hand with the singularization and culturalization of markets, forms of labor, and consumption. The structural features of the industrial economy and of industrial modernity in general, which defined Western societies for almost a hundred years, from the end of the nineteenth century until the 1970s, have thus been replaced by those of a genuinely post-industrial economy.

Sociologists have frequently associated the great transition from classical industrial society to post-industrial society with the transformation of the labor market: with the rapid decline in the number of industrial workers and the significant growth of service professions.[1] This change is indeed an important indicator of the end of classical industrial society. To conclude from this, however, that post-industrial society is essentially a society of service providers is only to scratch the surface. What is truly *post-industrial* about the late-modern economy is the fact that the *form of goods* (including services) and *therefore* also forms of labor, circulation, and consumption have widely been transformed.[2] The structural differences between the industrial economy and the post-industrial economy of culture and singularity can be seen on four different levels: first, the form of goods themselves; second, their manner of production, and thus also forms of labor and organization; third, the form of consumption; and fourth, the markets in which these goods circulate.

In light of these four levels, we can make the following claims about the economy of industrial modernity.[3] First, it was oriented toward standardized and functional mass-produced goods. This was an "economy of mass production" (in Piore and Sabel's terms) that was centered around material goods. Second, its production took place primarily in hierarchically structured matrix organizations with clear divisions of labor. In large part, this labor involved technical work with things, and repetitive routine tasks. Employees and workers distinguished themselves through their standardized formal qualifications, and the location where production took place was largely irrelevant and thus interchangeable. Third, industrial modernity was characterized by a normatively regulated and extensively standardized consumption of prefabricated utility goods (and also status goods). This practice was sustained by a middle class that was relatively homogeneous, both culturally and financially. Fourth, the markets in which industrial goods (as well as workers and employees) circulated and competed were so-called standard markets. These markets were relatively stable and not very risky; their processes were in part predictable and plannable.

The crucial matter is that, on all four levels, the economy of industrial modernity followed – or one could even say epitomized – the social logic of the general. Since the 1970s, however, the primacy of the *economy of the industrial general* has more and more been replaced by the primacy of the *economy of the cultural particular* and, as already mentioned, this has taken place on all four levels.

First, the post-industrial economy is centered around goods that, from the perspective of consumers, possess primarily cultural qualities and value. At the same time, they also make a claim to being unique (authentic, original, etc.).[4] To this extent, the post-industrial economy is thus an economy of singularities governed by *cultural capitalism*. Goods of this sort can have the character of things and objects, but they tend more and more to be events, media formats, or tailored services. They are *affect goods* that live off of their emotional effects and the possibility that people might identify with them.

Second, the production of cultural and singular goods requires forms of organization and labor that revolve around *creative work* – that is, around the creation of more and more new and non-interchangeable cultural products. The issue here is *cultural production*. The economy of singularities is based on flexible specialization, which is enabled by digital technologies (among other things). For work of this sort, matrix organizations are less suitable than project teams, whose social composition, emotional density, and limited time together make them *singular* social forms. In addition, cultural production is highly sensitive to the matter of location; it needs to be anchored in a specific place, above all in an urban environment. Accordingly, working subjects are now singularized as well. Beyond their standardized formal qualifications, they are evaluated according to the extraordinary nature of their performance and the uniqueness of their *profiles, competencies, talents*, and *personalities*.

Third, the consumption of cultural goods has also acquired a singularistic structure. With their consumption practices, late-modern subjects aim to achieve a lifestyle that is felt and staged to be authentic and unique. Mass consumption has been replaced by the pluralization of consumption patterns. Here, consumption is essentially *cultural consumption* – that is, the consumption of cultural things, services, and events. Consumers are co-creators who no longer *use* goods as much as they arrange and "curate" them in their own specific way.

II The Post-Industrial Economy of Singularities 83

Fourth, the standard markets for functional mass-produced goods have been replaced by singularity markets. They are characterized by the overproduction of ever more new cultural goods and thus by their *hyper-competitive* nature – that is, by a pronounced and unpredictable competition among unique goods for attention and esteem. Underpinned by a high degree of affect, these markets are not so much price or performance markets as they are *attractiveness markets* that feed off attracting attention and cultural valorization. They are speculative and lead to radical asymmetries according to a winner-take-all model.[5]

Unleashing the Creative Economy

At the institutional core of the singularization and culturalization of the late-modern economy, we find what has variously been called the creative industries, the cultural economy, or the creative economy.[6] The creative economy is the driving force behind the post-industrial economy. These concepts can be applied to certain economic branches which, historically, developed at the periphery of industrial mass production but whose value creation and employment numbers have been growing significantly since the 1980s, both in absolute terms and in terms of their share of the overall economy.[7] According to a narrow definition that is often used in official statistics, the creative economy includes architecture, advertising, the arts, crafts, music, film and video, design, fashion, computer games, software development and computer services, and finally media of all sorts, from print and radio to television and online. According to a somewhat broader definition, the creative economy also includes tourism and sports (spectator sports and individual sports), and thus it overlaps to some degree with the so-called experience economy.[8]

For the creative economy in either sense, it is possible to sketch an alternative economic history of modernity that does not proceed from the centers of heavy industrialization but rather from the creative niches of cultural production.[9] Here it is possible to identify several influential regional hotbeds of cultural production: the design-oriented craft industry of northern and central Italy ("Terza Italia"), whose local networks of cultural businesses have experienced a surprising renaissance since the 1970s; the London fashion scene of the 1960s and 1970s as the birthplace of youth-oriented cultural capitalism; the start-up scene in California, which has been developing at a breathtaking pace since the 1980s, especially in the field of information technology.[10] The late-modern creative industries, however, outgrew these local incubation centers long ago and have become established economic branches supported by global production networks. Whereas cultural and creative production is now concentrated in a network of cities and metropolitan regions in America, Europe, Asia, and Australia, the consumption of their cultural goods is global. In addition to a number of small and mid-sized companies, the creative economy also includes large international corporations such as Apple, Google, TUI, Nike, Disney, Time Warner, Bertelsmann, Nintendo, LVMH (Louis Vuitton, etc.), and Kering (Gucci, Yves Saint Laurent, etc.).[11]

It important to stress, however, that late-modern cultural capitalism goes *far* beyond the limited set of economic branches between software design and the film industry. In fact, the culturalization and singularization of the economy have entailed that even economic sectors that, during the period of organized modernity, were devoted to producing utility goods or traditional services have now been reconfigured to produce singular cultural goods. In other words, the *overall* production of goods and services in the Western economy has become increasingly *post-industrialized* and has adopted features of the creative economy. The economy of culture and singularity thus encompasses more than just culturally specific branches. Even the agricultural sector, the automobile and construction industries, the production of functional goods such as clocks or running shoes, and traditional services such as gastronomy or medical treatment have been shedding the old logic of mass-produced functional goods in favor of the post-industrial logic of singular cultural goods. More and more, their profiles consist of such things as organic products with claims to authenticity, car brands with experiential qualities, watches or athletic shoes as design objects, unique architecture, gastronomic originality, or individually tailored healthcare plans.[12]

As John Howkins has rightly pointed out, one indicator of the expansion of the creative economy and the growing international significance of its products is the increasing relevance of intellectual property law.[13] The goods of the singularity economy typically have identifiable originators; they have (individual or collective) creators who have introduced the novelty and uniqueness of goods to the world, and this has given rise to complicated (and controversial) legal claims, whether in the form of copyrights, patents, brands, or designs. Regarding the goods of the creative economy, the traditional economic triangle of producer, product, and consumer has transformed into a triad of author, work, and recipient/audience, which is familiar from the field of art.[14] Works of art have always been goods associated with a creator and recognized for their originality, uniqueness, and cultural value, and the goods of the creative economy are increasingly being treated in the same way. This applies to the creations of a top chef as well as to a given

II The Post-Industrial Economy of Singularities 85

designer's furniture, a football team's style of play, or a unique piece of architecture.

The establishment of the post-industrial economy is closely associated with the expansion of what sociologists have often referred to as the *knowledge economy*. Whereas economic theorists speak of cognitive capitalism, theorists of modernity accordingly speak of the knowledge society.[15] Without a doubt, the model that has succeeded industrial society is characterized by the need for more and more employees to have higher formal qualifications, by the increased relevance of expertise, and by the fact that knowledge (and especially the creation of new knowledge) and "human capital" have become key productive forces. From my perspective, however, what is central is that the specific structures of the post-industrial economy only become clear when one examines the form of its *goods*. These are of an entirely new sort: they are singularized and culturalized. At its heart, the knowledge economy is thus a culture economy and an economy of singularities.[16] Accordingly, it is no longer appropriate to describe it with the concepts of cognitive capitalism, which are too closely associated with industrial society's social logic of the general and its model of technological and scientific growth. What is produced and consumed in the post-industrial economy is not primarily functional knowledge and cognitive information but rather cultural goods (with their unique narratives, meanings, identities, and affects), aesthetic experiences, ethical goods, games, and designs.

In many respects, the social field of the *arts*, which receives, if anything, no more than a footnote in traditional sociological studies of labor and economics, has become the model for the economy of singularities. Indeed, the cultural capitalism of the early twenty-first century is defined by the structural features of the art world. In order to recognize the model-like character of art, however, it is first necessary to overcome its idealization (this is not only an inclination of philosophical aesthetics).[17] Art is particularly suitable as a model because of its specific characteristic as a social field: its extreme orientation toward the new and surprising, which is associated with a systematic overproduction of works, most of which turn out to be flops while just a few manage to break through. It is also a fitting model because of the intrinsic motivation of artists, which is oriented around the ideal of creativity, and because of the mercilessly competitive nature of the art world. Finally, and above all, if there is one social realm in modern society that is devoted to the singularization of objects, to the evaluation of inherent complexities, and to the logic of valorization and de-valorization, this is the field of art.

Has the entire late-modern economy become an economy of singularities? Of course not. The latter may represent the expansive center of the late-modern economy and late-modern society, but it coexists with old and new branches that follow an industrial logic and produce standardized goods and services. On the one hand, and despite deindustrialization, there still exists a traditional industrial sector devoted to producing capital goods (machines, etc.) and raw materials. On the other hand, there also exists an old, but newly routinized, set of services, which includes such things as cleaning, transportation, and public safety.[18] On the level of goods, labor, markets, and consumption, both sectors essentially follow the logic of industrial modernity. The relationship between the culture economy and industrial production or functional services is a complementary relationship between an *economy of the particular* and an *economy of the standardized*. To an extent, the economy of the standardized provides the necessary background infrastructure so that cultural capitalism, with its singular goods, can flourish in the foreground.[19]

1
Unique Goods in Cultural Capitalism

The Culturalization of Goods

In late-modern society, consumers show an increased demand for cultural and singular goods. The singularistic lifestyle, moreover, acquires its structure, its excitement, and its meaning by appropriating such goods. Accordingly, the economic sector strives to offer this type of good in the broadest possible variety and to fuel the desire for them even further. Here, the singularization of economic *objects* (in the broadest sense) goes hand in hand with the singularization of *subjects*. Whoever expects objects to be unique expects the same of subjects (including oneself), and whoever claims to be a unique subject will look for objects with which to express and further cultivate this uniqueness.

What is a good? What makes it a cultural good? And what makes it singular? In the most general terms, goods are distinguished by the fact that they are offered on markets and acquired by consumers. First of all, goods can be *things* that one uses or exhibits (food, drills, paintings, houses, etc.). Second, they include *services* (haircuts, therapy sessions, financial consulting, etc.). Third, they can have the form of *events* in which activities take place (vacations, live concerts, visits to a restaurant). Fourth, they can be *media formats*, which may admittedly have a material or digitalized basis, but this is forced into the background by textual, visual, or musical content (journalistic texts, novels, works of nonfiction, films, songs). Whereas the concept of the *commodity* stresses the exchange value – and thus also the price – of economic phenomena, the concept of the *good* emphasizes use value. "A good," according to George Shackle, "is an object or an organization that *promises* performance."[1] Or better: a good is already itself a performance. To this it can be added that, for consumers, goods contain a specific *good* in that they fulfill a purpose or have value. In the industrial economy of interchangeable mass products, it was easy to foreground the quantifiable exchange value of commodities and, accordingly, to push the aspect of use into the background. Yet because the late-modern economy has developed a highly complex manner of evaluating and experiencing the quality of goods, it is fitting now to focus, with the concept of the good, on the performance and value character of commodities.[2]

In order to understand what makes a good a cultural good, it is necessary to draw a distinction between *functional* and *cultural* goods. The difference between the two has nothing to do with the objective features of the good itself but rather depends on the viewer or the user. A good is functional when it serves a practical use; it thus follows an instrumentally rational logic. In contrast, a good becomes a cultural good when the consumer attributes an independent value to it and it thus acquires a cultural quality. In this case, the consumer becomes a recipient, and the good an object of valorization. Whereas the utility of a good is not an emotional matter, the value of a good is usually emotionally charged. Cultural goods affect subjects or, to be more precise, they promise to affect them *positively* (by providing pleasure, excitement, self-enrichment, the feeling of having done something meaningful, etc.). In short, cultural goods are *affect goods*. In addition to functional utility or cultural value, goods often promise something else: social prestige. Because both functional goods and cultural goods can create prestige, it is important not to treat cultural value and social prestige as one and the same.[3] Consumers experience the cultural quality (as well as the functional utility) of a good through the utilization of the good itself, whereas social prestige involves a third party.

Cultural goods have narrative–hermeneutic, aesthetic, design, ethical, and/or ludic characteristics, and thus they possess the qualities of cultural praxis that I discussed above. Each of these characteristics warrants a few words.

Cultural goods frequently have a *narrative and hermeneutic* quality in that they take the form of narratives that are meaningful to their recipients. That is, cultural goods often tell stories – and this cannot be stressed enough.[4] A narrative can become a good directly – in the form of a novel, a film, or a journalistic article. Or a complex web of storytelling can be spun around a good (whether driven by marketing or not): the story of design style or a designer associated with a certain object, or the multifaceted story of a city that can be experienced during a visit to it. A good can also become representative of a particular meaningful style, be it cool and contemporary or classical.[5] Cultural goods can also represent *ethical* value – that is, they can appear to be representatives of something good. In the realm of nutrition, for instance, this can be true of halal food, which is prepared in accordance with a religious code, or of organic products. Goods can follow an ethos of healthiness; they can be associated with ecological value; or they can be regarded as socially conscious (regional products, clothing not made in sweatshops, etc.).[6]

Cultural goods have an *aesthetic-sensuous* quality when they stimulate sensory perception in a satisfying or interesting way.[7] This can take place by means of the visual, auditory, tactile, and olfactory features of an individual thing, from a classic car or a symphony on a CD to wine or a movie. It can also pertain, however, to the aesthetic quality of an event, such as a live concert, a festival, a vacation, or a visit to a restaurant. Cultural goods can have a *design* dimension when they provide their recipients with a framework for creatively arranging materialities and meanings within their lifestyles.[8] They then take on an activating character. Creative design of this sort can be conveyed, for instance, through courses or therapies in which abilities are acquired or emotional structures are transformed. It can be a matter of designing one's leisure time or apartment or readjusting one's entire situation in life. Cultural goods frequently have a *ludic* quality. In this sense, games themselves can be a cultural good, and this is true both of those in which recipients participate (a computer game, using an app on a smartphone, a team or extreme sport, a fantasy game) and of those that they simply watch (a spectator sport, for example). It is also possible for events or services to contain playful elements – that is, to have the character of play without the fixed rules of a game (such as an activity-based vacation).[9]

The structural transformation of goods from industrial to post-industrial modernity certainly does not represent an absolute break but rather a shift in emphasis. Cultural goods circulated in organized (and bourgeois) modernity as well, and in late modernity there still exist certain goods with a primarily functional character. In the late-modern economy, however, the scope of cultural goods has increased enormously (and not only in a quantitative sense), and they have come to define economic production across the board. What is of central importance is that the social evaluation of types of goods has also been inverted. The distinction between the profane and the sacred, which applies in general to all processes of culturalization,[10] is now relevant in the case of goods. In late-modern society, functional goods are merely *profane*. They are no more than useful and basically disposable goods and services. This is most obvious in the case of routine services. Cultural goods, in contrast, appear to be *sacred* in that they are laden with value and affect. Whereas, in bourgeois and organized modernity, there was a tendency to discredit cultural goods as decadent and "useless" luxuries,[11] this way of evaluating things has been inverted in late modernity. Now, functional goods are regarded as profane, while cultural goods fascinate people and are valued.

Culturalization affects all four types of goods mentioned above: things, media formats, services, and events. So as not to suggest that we are dealing with an entirely immaterial economy of services and events, it must be stressed that the production and consumption of *material* goods has remained central in late modernity.[12] Cultural goods often have a material character, as in the expansive realms of fashion, interior design, and entertainment electronics. In this case, the tool paradigm of the material world has been superseded by a fetish or cult paradigm. For this reason, the *design* of things has become central, and this has gone beyond the design of attractive surfaces to include the construction of objects as a whole.[13] This has meant that the three-dimensional arrangement of things in and as *space(s)* has also gained relevance. In cultural spaces of this sort, their function is subordinate to their *atmospheres*.[14] In the late-modern economy, the utilization or staging of spatial atmospheres – be it in a library or one's own apartment, in a store or restaurant, or at a vacation spot – has become a conspicuous cultural good of particular complexity.

At the same time, the three other types of goods have become enormously more relevant. The rising significance of *services* in late modernity has frequently been underscored.[15] It is often the case, however, that this is a matter of functional and profane ("simple") services, which, as already mentioned, provide the structural background and thus enable cultural consumption. At the heart of culturalization, however, are highly qualified services that constitute what Shoshana Zuboff and James Maxmin have called the "support economy."[16] Essentially, these services create and convey stories, images, competencies, and feelings. Think of the broad fields of psychology and education, but also of aesthetically oriented consulting services whose goal is to change their clients' lives. In addition, there are services oriented toward the body, and these revolve around aesthetic attractiveness and physical fitness.

There has been a large-scale proliferation of *media formats* in the late-modern economy, not least because the digital revolution has made their production and distribution considerably easier. This is true of books, television programs, films, videos, and songs, but it also relates to the large bandwidth of text formats, audio formats, and image formats that circulate on the internet (both commercially and non-commercially).[17] The quantitative increase of media formats has gone hand in hand with an expansive culturalization of media. Admittedly, media content can also have the character of a functional good, which it in fact often was in the past. The difference between functional and cultural content depends on whether the media formats in question primarily provide *information* or *stories* – that is, on whether they are cognitively or narratively (and aesthetically) oriented. Essentially, the late-modern proliferation of media formats has been to the benefit of narrative and aesthetic media content. This pertains to fictional (or musical) formats but also to works of nonfiction, blogs, talk shows, and even news programs, which are now less often information media than they are *affect media*.

Events are extraordinarily significant in cultural capitalism.[18] For example, they include sporting events (the World Cup, the Olympics, etc.), which are attended by trans-local audiences and whose excitement derives from their singular nature and uncertain outcomes. No less noteworthy are artistic events, which may involve a live audience experience – concerts and festivals of popular or classical music, theater or film festivals with celebrities at hand – or they might take place for just a limited time, such as temporary exhibits in museums. This category can also be said to include small-scale private or official events, such as weddings or graduation ceremonies. Above all, however, the global tourism industry survives by providing travelers with short-term, emotionally satisfying events. By definition, as it were, events are not functional but, rather, cultural goods. They are not sought out by consumers to be *used* but, instead, to be *enjoyed* in the moment. Events are cultural affect goods *par excellence*.

Singular Goods: Originality and Rarity

The *cultural* goods that are fabricated and acquired in late modernity are predominantly *singular* goods. Of course, mass-produced and standardized cultural goods existed throughout modernity, and they still do. Yet they are now in decline and have sunk to the level of profanity.[19] What, however, makes a cultural good singular? How is it singularized in the economy of the particular? In order for a good to become unique, two factors come into play, and these cannot be reduced to one another: *originality* and *rarity*. In contrast, the standardized good, which is denied any singular status, is characterized by unoriginality and abundance.

First, *originality*. In order for a good to be regarded as unique, it has to seem original. This involves two characteristics that are already familiar to us. In a fundamental and qualitative way (and not just slightly), the good in question has to be different from other goods, and it also has to possess its own internal structure. That is, something becomes original by *inwardly* developing its own inherent complexity and cultural (narrative, aesthetic, ludic, ethical, design-based) density and by being *outwardly* characterized by its qualitative otherness. Originality always involves both: inherently complex density and "absolute" qualitative difference. It is no surprise that the concept of originality was first developed in the context of art theory around the end of the eighteenth century.[20] Modern works of art are singularities *par excellence*, and they provide the structural model for all other singular goods. Ultimately, the modern work of art – a novel or a painting, a play or a piece of music – always claims to be *different* from all other works. Here, otherness is not understood as an arbitrary or fine difference but rather as one that is absolute and qualitative. The purpose of this type of difference is to ensure that the work arouses a feeling of surprise when it first appears. The modern work of art is also paradigmatic with respect to the inherent complexity that is necessary for originality. Metaphorically speaking, it succeeds in creating a world of its own. A work of art is a system of unique density; it is a singular ensemble of plot and narrative style, melody, harmony, and rhythm, gestures, intonation, stage sets, etc. And the denser this inner structure is, the more likely it is to create an impression of uniqueness. By means of its inherent complexity, the cultural good appears to be irreducible and incommensurable. While the otherness of a cultural good causes *surprise*, its inner density and inherent complexity make it *interesting*.

Whereas originality represents a qualitative feature, *rarity* is, strictly speaking, a quantitative criterion that is nevertheless qualitatively charged. Here, to some extent, quantity is turned into quality. On this second level, a cultural good becomes unique by being *rare* or (in extreme cases) *non-recurring*, either by existing in a single exemplar or by occurring as a single event that has never happened before and will never take place again. Accordingly, the uniqueness of objects, places, and people differs from the unique, one-time nature of events.[21] Beyond the extreme form of rarity as a one-time event, there are of course different degrees of rarity. Something can exist in just a few exemplars or for just a limited amount of time, or it might only be accessible to a limited circle of recipients. In the latter case, that which is rare happens to be *exclusive*. At this point, we see the specific way in which singularity and exclusivity can be interrelated. A good becomes exclusive when it is reserved for a limited social circle that satisfies certain preconditions (social status, wealth, networks, education, street credibility, and so on).

What is the relationship between originality and rarity? I have already said that they are independent of one another, like two axes in a system of coordinates. Yet I should add that they do not have the same status. In my view, originality is a necessary condition for singularity, whereas rarity is a factor that can come into play but does not have to be involved. If a good is not perceived and experienced as original, it cannot become unique. Conversely, rarity is a variable that may influence uniqueness, but a singular good does not necessarily have to be seldom- or non-recurring. The best example of this comes from the culture industry and its "works of art in the age of their technological reproducibility." Films, novels, and songs

II The Post-Industrial Economy of Singularities   93

circulate in thousands or even millions of copies and exemplars, and many individuals enjoy them over and over again at different points in time. This does nothing to change the fact that originality has been attributed to them, thereby securing their singularity. However, because modern society as a whole has made it possible to reproduce original entities *en masse*, the second criterion of rarity can exert considerable influence over what is regarded as singular in late modernity.[22]

Things as Singular Goods

The singularization of cultural goods along the criteria of originality and rarity applies to all types of goods: things, services, media formats, and events. In these four areas, however, originality and rarity take on different forms. Let us first turn our attention to things.

The greatest challenge faced by the process of singularization is the modern material world. For, ultimately, the modern logic of the general manifests itself obtrusively in the mass reproduction and standardization of things. It is against the backdrop of the profane and mass-produced goods of industrial society that the late-modern singularization of the material world stands out most vividly.[23] Now, things can become original (in the sense described above) by being aesthetically designed in a particular way or by being embedded in a narrative. Traditionally, fashion and design have been the two branches that have worked most intensively to give an original shape to the perceptible objects of the material world.[24] Alongside art, fashion and design are thus structurally formational forces in the post-industrial culture economy.

There are four possible ways for a thing to become singular. The originality of an *individual* object can lie in its *aesthetic* appearance: the Vespa scooter, the Barcelona chair, the Chanel outfit, Yves Klein's *Blue Monochrome*. In this case, the original object can be reproducible; it does not, in other words, have to be non-recurring. Alternatively (or at the same time), originality can also take the form of an original aesthetic *style* that pervades various different objects.[25] An individual style is often associated with the *name* of its creator, as in the case of Rem Koolhaas's buildings or Jan Kath's carpets. For its part, a collective style can be associated with a group or milieu: Art Deco, the Young British Artists, the sneaker street style. Collective styles are often represented by a *brand*. In fact, the creation of cultural brands and their unique profiles should be regarded as one of the most effective forms of late-modern singularization. The design of a brand such as Apple, Hugo Boss, or Ligne Roset encompasses not only the aesthetic style of consumable things but also that of flagship stores, websites, and forms of consumer contact. Each brand stands for its own narrative and aesthetic world or identity in which consumers can participate through such things as an iPad, suit, or sofa.

As important as the aesthetic design of things may be with respect to their singularization, it is only by being situated in an infinitely expandable *narrative* context – with stories about historical or local origins, sophisticated production techniques, prominent users, and associations with other artifacts and styles – that goods with relatively limited sensual appeal (such as watches, wine, or home electronics) are transformed into singular goods. For example, it was only by being associated with the biography and design concept of Charles and Ray Eames, with the history of postwar modern design, and indeed with the cultural history of the United States as a whole that a banal plastic chair was able to become the legendary Eames Chair, whose characteristic silhouette now adorns so many open kitchens of the global educated class between Seattle, Amsterdam, and Melbourne.[26]

Inherent complexity can also involve an *ethical* dimension. To a considerable extent, the singularization of the material world in the late-modern economy has taken place in the form of so-called ethical consumption, which is clearest to see in the case of food. A type of food, however, can only become an ethical model by being embedded in a meaningful context, above all through the story told about its origins, processing, and transportation to consumers (about the appropriate treatment of animals, natural cultivation, fair-trade processing, local production, etc.). Often, therefore, cultural things acquire singularity through the specific details of their *biographies*.[27] Whereas functional things are simply used after their anonymous fabrication, cultural things have entire stories of their own. Fritz Hansen lamps and halal products are singular on account of their biographies.

In addition to making things original, making them rare can also contribute to the creation of singularities. As we have already seen, the extreme instantiation of the rare thing is the *unique specimen* in the strict sense, for which a work of art such as a painting or sculpture is paradigmatic. The international expansion of the art market since the 1990s is indicative of the pronounced late-modern interest in such specimens (at least among people who can afford them).[28] This is a matter of individual pieces produced for a potentially anonymous audience. Another possibility for singularizing things via rarity is customized production (of clothing or furniture, for instance), which has its roots in preindustrial craftwork.[29]

Things can also be rarified through two different types of scarcity: *temporal* and *topographical*. After a certain age, of course, goods that were produced in the past only remain available in a limited number (a fact that leads to forgeries and imitations). This is the case with antiques in the broadest sense: old furniture and artwork, classic cars, vintage sunglasses and clothing, and especially old homes and apartment buildings built in a given historical style. Of course, the good in question has to possess a degree of originality to begin with in order to be regarded as valuable (this is what distinguishes antiques from garbage), but the natural scarcity of antiques adds to their allure. A good can also be rarified though limitations of space. Since the 1990s, this has especially been the case with the hot real-estate markets in metropolitan areas. Homes with an ocean view in San Francisco are just as naturally rare as apartments on the Place Vendôme in Paris, which promise all the benefits of urban-nostalgic life.[30] Finally, there is the artificial rarefaction of goods, particularly by means of hand-made processes or limited editions. If goods are produced by hand and in a particular local context – hand-woven rugs from a particular shop in Nepal, for instance – their quantity will remain relatively limited (the same can be said of personalized goods). Accordingly, design companies have started the trend of producing just a limited number of certain goods (or offering them for just one season or only for a limited time in certain stores). In the end, the most trivial (but always effective) way to rarify a material good is through its price: only a few people can afford to buy *luxury goods*.

Services, Media Formats, and Events as Singular Goods

On account of their originality and rarity, services, media formats, and events can also become the object of singularization. In this regard, however, their starting point is different. Whereas the late-modern singularization of things stands in stark contrast to industrial modernity's excessive standardization of commodities, the services, media formats, and events that flourish in cultural capitalism are, instead, part of a historical continuum of singularizing practices.

It goes without saying that *services* can also be standardized, especially when they are executed anonymously and are purely functional. However, as soon as a personal relationship is implied between a service provider and a customer – the sort of relationship that in fact turns the customer into a client – the service begins to take on an element of the particular.[31] The relationship between service providers and clients can also have an emotional aspect, so that services are the prototype of what Arlie Hochschild has called "emotional labor."[32]

In the late-modern economy, cultural service relationships exist above all in the services of consulting, education, and those related to the body; roughly speaking, they can become singular in three respects. The first concerns the *style* of the service provider, who also has to have a specific competency profile. A therapist, for example, can be original for having developed a particular style of therapy, a hairdresser for having a particular aesthetic style. This is again a matter of originality as inherent complexity and otherness. The second respect results from the service provider developing a particular *sensitivity* to the special needs of a client. This is then an example of tailored, personalized service, which necessarily requires the ability to empathize. Third, the *relationship* between a service provider and a customer can itself become personal, non-interchangeable, and even unique in the strict sense. In the late-modern economy, as I have already mentioned, there is a sharp asymmetrical divide between cultural, highly qualified services and those that are functional and simple. The latter, however, can be culturalized and singularized in the ways discussed above and thus move from the side of the merely useful (and cheap) to the side of the valuable (where a service is "worth its price").[33]

Notwithstanding the opinion of certain interwar theorists, who believed that media content could never be singular on account of its technological reproducibility and ostensible conventionality,[34] *media formats* are indeed capable of being singularized. Exactly this has been taking place on an immense scale in late-modern cultural capitalism. This is plain to see in works of fictional literature, films, and music. But also computer games, software, and apps can create unique worlds, and the same can be said of talk-show moderators, comedians, bloggers, Instagram photos, journalistic texts, and television series. All of these cases involve the performance of singularity; from the perspective of their fans or users, they are all non-interchangeable goods. Furthermore, media formats make it clear that rarity is not a necessary condition for singularity, given that media content is the opposite of rare: it is *mass* produced, *widely* disseminated, and incredibly *cheap* (sometimes even free). The singular status of media formats (assuming that this status is achieved) derives entirely from their originality.[35]

It is therefore no surprise that these types of goods have a special relationship with the world of art. Media goods that are recognized as *works* with their own complexity and are attributed to an *author* or *creator* (novels, works of nonfiction, films, blogs, YouTube videos) thus constitute an important subset of media formats. Media formats can also base their claim to uniqueness on an individual style, which is not associated with one particular good but rather with several. Such is the case, for instance, with the music by Adele or Tocotronic, the films by Woody Allen or Angela Schanelec, the newspaper columns by Maureen Dowd, the movies starring Cary Grant or Tilda Swinton, the late-night shows hosted by

II The Post-Industrial Economy of Singularities 97

Stephen Colbert, or the YouTube videos by one person or another. Identifiable individual styles can lead to the creation of stars.

They overlap with what one could call *serial singularities*, which have been on the rise especially since the turn of the century.[36] This may sound contradictory. Are not *series*, in which the same cast and settings are repeated over and over, the exact opposite of singularities? The answer is no. Rather, television series such as *The Wire* or *Downton Abbey* are experienced and appreciated as unique worlds of considerable narrative–aesthetic complexity. Their uniqueness is simply spread over a longer period of time, which in fact makes it easier for people to identify with them. An additional source of singularization for media formats is the interactive participation of media users, who either can or must intervene over the course of certain media processes. Computer games are a typical example of such *interactive singularities*.[37] For its player, *Assassin's Creed* is a unique and highly complex narrative–aesthetic world *par excellence* that, in addition, offers different and unpredictable lived experiences every time it is entered. With their combination of narrative, aesthetic, ludic, and design qualities, computer games are perhaps the paradigmatic cultural good among late modernity's many media formats.

Of all singular goods, those from the realm of media formats incite the most controversy with respect to their uniqueness. This is an area in which adamant fans, who experience something as unique and inherently complex, stand opposed to detractors who regard the same object as cheap and repetitive fluff.[38] For fans of *Breaking Bad*, the Beatles, or Simon Beckett, who are fascinated by this filmic, musical, or textual material, the goods in question are indubitably original, whereas others might consider them predictable, uninspiring, and shoddy. The struggle over defining whether this or that is singular or standardized is a constitutive *element* of the economy of the particular, and debates about media content are a paradigmatic example of this.

We come at last to *events*, to those cultural goods that are predestined for singularization. What is decisive here is the factor of rarity, which is nowhere near as dominant in the case of other cultural goods. Whether we are talking about a football match or a vacation, events are distinguished by their uniqueness – indeed, by their non-recurring nature. Whereas, with things, there can be different levels of uniqueness, with the extreme case being the genuinely unique specimen, and whereas the originality of services arises indirectly from the individual relationship between service providers and their clients, non-recurring uniqueness is a constitutive feature of events and their temporal structure: the Olympic Games in Brazil or the screening of Antonioni's films at the C/O Berlin will never happen again, and neither will a tour of Israel that someone took five years ago or the elaborate wedding of one's friends H. and G. Here, too, there are different forms of temporal uniqueness. Examples include collective public events (sporting events, exhibitions) that are experienced by me and many anonymous others in a similar way,[39] collective private events attended by a unique group of people (weddings), and personal private events that take place at particular times and locations (vacations).

The fact that something occurs only once, however, is not enough to make it singular. Without the quality of originality described above, no good can be regarded as unique. For an event to be evaluated as unique, it must be perceived as such; it has to evoke impressions and meanings with particular density. That said, events are structured in such a way as to be predisposed to originality. The attention that they attract is unlimited and total; they are experienced with all the senses; in light of their spatial atmospheres, they are to some extent total works of art. Because events engage our sensory perception in its entirety, it is far easier for us to recognize their inherent complexity. Our complete focus allows us to perceive and associate so many interconnected elements and relations that the internal complexity of an event becomes readily apparent. For the traveler or the fan, the abundance and diversity of perceptions and feelings associated with a specific trip to Israel or a specific Simon and Garfunkel concert make these irreplaceable experiences. Events involve what Hans Ulrich Gumbrecht has called an "aesthetics of presence."[40] They appear to be valuable (or not) *in the moment*. Moreover, the event has a specific temporal structure: because it is a purely present good in the *here and now*, it can only be preserved *afterwards* in the medium of memory (which can, of course, distort things considerably). As cultural goods, events therefore have more than just ephemeral, present value; beyond that, they can occasionally also have remarkably stable value as memories, and this is what gives them their long-lasting effect.

Features of Singular Goods I: The Performance of Authenticity

Whereas consumers of functional goods expect them to fulfill a use, consumers of cultural–singular goods expect them to be *authentic*. Vacation destinations should be authentic, as should politicians, yoga courses, music, or food. Accordingly, the process of singularizing goods is always and at the same time a process of *authentication* – that is, a process of observing, evaluating, producing, or appropriating something as authentic. The late-modern economy is an economy of *authentic goods*.

II The Post-Industrial Economy of Singularities

Now, authenticity is a polysemous concept, and it is no coincidence that it derives from the semantic wellspring of Romanticism.⁴¹ Already in this historical and cultural context, uniqueness and authenticity were closely associated with one another, and Jean-Jacques Rousseau formulated a concept of the authentic that basically remains valid today: the authentic appears to be the opposite of the artificial; it is esteemed and felt to be *genuine* (and, in Rousseau's case, *natural* as well), whereas the inauthentic is merely *fake* or *pretend*. As far as the topic of this book is concerned, one could say that if a social entity – be it a person, a group, a place, or a thing – possesses a *particular* unique structure, then it is authentic in the eyes of its beholder, whereas if it only abides by the *general* rules of uniformity, then it is not. The concept of authenticity is related to affect and experience: something is immediately experienced and felt as authentic – it affects people and appears to be *genuine*. The impression of authenticity often has a spontaneous nature, but behind this lies an entity's inherent complexity, density, and otherness.

As a phenomenon of genuineness, the authentic is thus wide open to interpretation, so much so that in late modernity it has become a sort of "empty signifier"⁴² – that is, a nearly hollowed-out (and yet widely influential) symbol without any agreed-upon meaning.⁴³ From a sociological perspective, authenticity is thus based on a paradox, for, in the realm of the social, everything is *constructed* and *fake* in the strict sense – nothing, in other words, is natural. This applies just as well to the world of economic goods: they are all fabricated and they all typically circulate on markets. In the social world (and especially in the economic world), authenticity is therefore always a performance of authenticity, and it should be analyzed as such: it is not simply there by nature but is, rather, presented and performed. In this sense, for instance, Richard Peterson has demonstrated how rock and country bands *authenticate* themselves – through their musical style, their clothing, their performance venues, etc. – and are *authenticated* by their listeners. This "authenticity work," as he calls it, surrounds all the goods of the culture economy.⁴⁴ The authentic has both aesthetic and ethical connotations, and these are interrelated. From an aesthetic perspective, authenticity can be described as immanent coherence and, at the same time, as coherence between an entity and its context. From an ethical perspective, it is a matter of trustworthiness and credibility. In general, it is possible to understand the singularization of goods as a process of authentication. *If* a good manages to be evaluated and experienced as singular, it *then* appears to be authentic. Conversely, if a good is not accepted into the circle of singularities, it is regarded as inauthentic.

In this sense, for example, a certain city can prove to be an inauthentic travel destination if it lacks an anticipated degree of uniqueness and seems to have the same types of stores and streets as everywhere else. Or a new band can appear to be inauthentic because its songs lack a "certain something" and seem to be recycled. A coach, too, can be inauthentic because he lacks trustworthiness, is short on empathy, or seems to use only stock phrases. In a broader sense, authenticity can also include any self-conscious demonstration of one's own "constructedness." Post-modern pop musicians can ironically deconstruct their genuineness on the stage (as in the anti-rockism of the 1980s) and, if successful, achieve a sort of authenticity that one could call *meta-authenticity*.[45]

Here again, we have to pay special attention to cultural goods from the realm of art. Although, as we have already seen, they have served as models for the economy of singularities, the question remains whether works of art can still be fundamentally distinguished from other cultural goods in the age of all-encompassing singularization. Has the expansion of cultural capitalism perhaps led to a "de-artification of art" (the phrase is Adorno's) in the sense that the claims to originality associated with art can now be made for other goods in the same way? Can't every object potentially be not only culturalized but also "artified?" In light of the fact that the features of inherent complexity, inner density, and otherness can now be found in artistic and non-artistic goods alike, one could answer yes to this question. I would hesitate to do so, however, because of the ambivalent way that art can affect people. There are many indications that the valorization and appropriation of artwork in late modernity differ from those of other goods. Every cultural good affects its recipient, but in cultural capitalism they typically create positive emotions. The sorts of emotion incited by works of art, in contrast, can be contradictory, for they can *also* be negative.

It is clear that works of art are not perfectly compatible with late modernity's positive culture of affects. Rather, they can evoke discomfort and doubt; they can be disturbing, puzzling, awkward, or off-putting. This is not to say that they are negative singularities – they are indeed (positively) valued – but rather that they are *contradictory singularities*.[46] This might not obviously be the case with respect to the art of bourgeois culture, which tends to be harmonious and beautiful. Yet in late modernity's radically culturalized world of goods and consumption, artistic objects certainly stand apart by the fact that an installation, film, performance, or piece of music can be *disturbing*. Late-modern (or postmodern) art is therefore meta-authentic; instead of being unambiguous and homogeneous, it is ambiguous and does not fit into a single mold. It goes without saying that the reception and valorization of such artwork can be highly contentious.

II The Post-Industrial Economy of Singularities 101

Features of Singular Goods II: Moment and Duration

Singular goods have a specific temporal structure that fundamentally differs from that of functional goods. The latter are used until they are worn out, and thus their use value gradually diminishes. This is true of things, information, and services: electronic devices break at some point, information grows old, and the apartment that was cleaned yesterday will have to be scrubbed again next week. The temporal structure of singular cultural goods is completely different: they have an extremely *short-term* orientation toward experiencing the moment and an extremely *long-term* orientation toward maintaining lasting cultural value. In general, this temporal *dual structure of moment and duration* is characteristic of the world of culture. Whereas the world of instrumental rationality and functional goods is more or less one of medium-term temporality in which goods are expected to last for a while but will eventually break or become technologically obsolete, the cultural sphere is based on the fleeting moment *and* on long-lasting value.

Structurally, this combination of the short and the long term is based first of all on the difference between practices of *experience* and practices of *valorization*, both of which, as we have seen, are characteristic of the fabrication of singular cultural objects. By definition, experience is a bodily and mental act in the fleeting moment of the present. In that every cultural good is experienced, its appropriation has a *momentary* structure. This is most clearly the case with affect goods that have the character of events, as in the experience of a concert, a baseball game, or a vacation.[47] At the same time, however, because cultural goods are valorized, they are also defined by their pronounced *long-term nature*. Once assigned, their value does not simply wear out like the utility of a functional good; under some circumstances, it can in fact be retained and renewed for years or decades. This is what gives something the status of a *classic*.[48] Simply on account of their durability, material goods are especially apt to become classics, but of course media formats/content, furniture designs, old apartment buildings, cities, and entire brands can achieve this status as well.

At this point, however, a certain complication comes into play. On the one hand, the experience of cultural goods can acquire a long-term nature of the second order via individual and collective *memory*. On the other hand, the process of valorization can be extremely brief and volatile, as in the case of *fashions*. In this regard, too, there is also a difference between cultural and functional goods: functional goods are free from memories or fashions.

The essential matter is that cultural goods, because they are not only used but also experienced, are memorable. In the end, no one remembers the routine use of an object – people only remember affective experiences. Frequently, in fact, memory constitutes a large part of a singular event's perceived value and allows the event in question to have lasting and even formational effects. Often enough, the memory of an event can even be more complex than the original experience. In extreme cases of public and highly affective events – the Woodstock concert in 1969 or the World Cup in Germany in 2006 – the events can enter the collective memory and to some extent be experienced after the fact by people who did not even witness them in person.[49]

Conversely, valorization does not guarantee that a cultural good will be around for the long term and become a classic. Rather, the system of cultural goods is oriented first and foremost around the demand for ever *new* and *different* singular goods. In this respect, the late-modern economy participates in the creativity *dispositif*, which is a system of novelties, engaged in producing a never-ending sequence of new and unique goods.[50] To the extent that these goods are, in fact, experienced and evaluated as singular, this ascription of value might not last very long. In a relatively short amount of time, a good can lose all its value as soon as something new and exciting comes around to capture everyone's attention: the novel or theater event of the season, the latest pop song, but also the new vacation destination that is suddenly in vogue. This is precisely what characterizes fashion cycles, which apply to more than just clothing.[51] Out of this context of short-lived valuable goods, only a select few manage to become classics. This also means, however, that (nearly) every classic was once a seasonal hit that managed to acquire long-term cultural value on the basis of its initial short-term surprise. Today's classics were at one point revolutionary.

Features of Singular Goods III: Circulation and Hyperculture

Where do all of the cultural and singular goods come from that circulate in the late-modern economy and influence our lifestyles? Of course, the creative economy is systematically oriented toward the production of new cultural goods. Nevertheless, it would be naïve to think that this creative activity happens out of the blue. How, then, does the culture economy *relate* its singular goods to their narrative, aesthetic, ethical, ludic, and design qualities? There are two answers to this question, and both have something to do with the social *circulation* of singularities. On the one hand, singularities typically arise from the translation of idiosyncrasies or elements of the general-particular into the register of the singular. On the other hand, they are drawn from pre-economic cultural practices with local and historical associations. This

II The Post-Industrial Economy of Singularities 103

implies that the cultural goods of late modernity circulate in a global hyperculture.

We have already seen that three populations of the particular coexist in society: the general-particular, idiosyncrasies, and singularities. These are not isolated from one another – rather, there is constant traffic between them, not least in the case of idiosyncrasies or instances of the general-particular becoming singularities. The reservoir of socially circulating singularities is constantly being replenished from these two sources, which provide culture with material for the production of "fresh" unique entities.

The process by which goods are transformed from a general order into singularities is synonymous with the culturalization of formerly functional goods, which were available *en masse* in the age of industrial modernity. With the help of a narrative–aesthetic twist, motor scooters, wristwatches, or buildings in the International Style can be singularized. A good example of this is the history of the Vespa, an Italian motor scooter that first came on the market in 1946 and managed to be singularized during the 1990s through its nostalgic integration into the historical narrative of *italianità*.[52] Even buildings in the rather tasteless International Style, which are in fact examples of the rigid standardization of architecture, can experience a narrative reframing and be regarded as singularities of great complexity by architectural connoisseurs and tourists.

The singularization of idiosyncrasies is widespread. Here, valueless and overlooked unique entities are transformed into valuable singularities. In extreme cases, as I have already mentioned, what was once no more than quirky or a worthless trinket can suddenly be regarded as a work of art. There are plenty of examples of this in the fields of visual art, music, and literature (look no further than *art brut*).[53] However, the best and most economically influential example of the transformation of idiosyncrasies into singularities is probably the reevaluation of old homes and apartment buildings that has been taking place in Western cities since the 1970s (and has brought the real-estate market to a boil). Homes and apartments from the Victorian era, which were considered unmodern and obsolete during the postwar period and were therefore often neglected, are now widely regarded as original and valuable.

From the realms of the instrumentally rational general-particular and previously overlooked idiosyncrasies, the late-modern economy's sphere of singular cultural goods thus receives constant replenishment. Many singularities, however, do not take this path; rather, they stem from the sphere of culture itself, though from its pre-economic and non-market-based form. Here there is no need for culturalization to take place; instead, the transformation concerns the social framework in which certain cultural objects exist. To be precise, these are cultural singularities that were once exclusively embedded in particular local and historical practices and were then removed from this context to become globally circulating cultural goods that now compete with other goods and are acquired by discriminating consumers in multiple contexts.[54] This has given rise to late modernity's characteristic form of culture, which I prefer to call *hyperculture*. In today's hyperculture, potentially everything – from high or low culture, from today or the past, or from any place whatsoever – can acquire the value of culture. In hyperculture, any good can be freed from its original context and circulate from place to place around the globe; any good can be regarded as singular on account of its difference from other goods and be reappropriated in different contexts.

This is true of many goods in the late-modern economy. For example, the "world food" served in the many Italian, Chinese, Mexican, and African restaurants across the globe was at first the everyday food of people living in specific regions. The "world music" of singers and bands from Mozambique, Brazil, or Cuba was at first a locally specific type of music played by particular youth cultures. Initially, these cultural objects and practices were thus entirely independent of cultural capitalism. Without a doubt, their economization and transformation into mercantile goods entails a degree of commercialization: family food and music played by young people for one another are converted into commodities with exchange value (into restaurant cuisine, CDs, concerts). Yet it also means that cultural objects from diverse backgrounds are indiscriminately made available for consumption: we can choose between them, accept or reject them, and combine them with one another to suit our own lifestyles. It is precisely this attitude of choice that is typical of late-modern hyperculture.

What is decisive is that this has changed the form of what constitutes culture. In hyperculture, cultural objects and practices have experienced a radical *decontextualization*. It is only because they have been removed from their original local and historical contexts and injected into trans-local and trans-historical circulation that their recipients are now able to recognize their qualitative *difference* from other cultural objects and practices. Creole food, which was just an unavoidable part of everyday life in the Caribbean, has become one culinary specialty among others; only now is it possible to see how its unique features differ from those of, say, southern European food. What this means is that the global decontextualization of cultural objects has made us sensitive to comparative possibilities and has therefore *converted* the objects in question into singularities, singularities whose already existing inherent complexity – the complexity of flavor and history, in the case of food – is now recognized and appreciated on account of our newly established awareness of their otherness.[55] From the perspective of a global hypercultural economy,

II The Post-Industrial Economy of Singularities

literally the entire world – past and present, including all ways of life that have ever existed – has therefore become a *cultural resource*: a resource for the generation of singular goods.

Overall, the fact that the post-industrial economy has shifted away from functional mass-produced goods toward singular cultural goods is more than just an economic matter; rather, this shift has affected the way that late-modern subjects relate to the world and has thus altered the culture of late modernity as a whole. In the society of singularities, subjects are constantly surrounded by an abundance of things, spaces, events, media formats, and services that, with their narrative–aesthetic or ludic qualities and their affective appeal, can claim to be singular. Subjects have thus come to learn that this must be society's normal state of affairs: nothing matters in the world unless it is interesting and valuable – that is, unless it is singular, affective, and seemingly authentic. As a consequence, late-modern subjects now expect this uniqueness of other subjects – and of themselves.

2
Cultural Singularity Markets

Attractiveness Markets as Markets of Attention and Valorization

Over the course of the transformation from industrial modernity's economy of the general to the economy of singularities, there has also been a profound structural change in the markets on which goods circulate. More and more, standard markets have been replaced by *cultural markets*, in which goods compete to be recognized as singular. On these *singularity markets*, in other words, goods compete to attract attention. They are *attractiveness markets*.

The relationship between the economy and markets is generally more complex than it might at first seem. We have to rid ourselves of the idea that *the* economy and *the* market are timeless entities with immutable structures that will always follow something like a universal logic of exchange or labor. Rather, the economy and the market are historical and socio-cultural phenomena through and through. "The economic" is a transformative praxis: activities, things, people, temporalities, and spaces can *be economized* (just as they can also be culturalized, aestheticized, politicized, etc.). Economization, moreover, does not necessarily have to mean marketization. In certain historical contexts, as Fabian Muniesa has rightly shown, economization was associated above all with practices such as calculating, standardizing, evaluating, and investing.[1] In late modernity, however, which is dominated by cultural capitalism, the economic has acquired a particular structure. Now, the core of the economy is in fact the social form of the market, but in a *highly specific* form whose name has already been mentioned: that of attractiveness markets within the framework of the economy of singularities. These have the structure of incessant, affect-based competitions for the *attention* and *recognition* of cultural goods. Not until late modernity did the elements of this structure come together

II The Post-Industrial Economy of Singularities 107

in what is now its widespread instantiation, which I would like to call *cultural economization*.[2]

In light of his theory of formal rationalization, in contrast, it is no surprise that Max Weber believed that the most prevalent structural feature of the market was the act of exchange: the standardized, bivalent relationship between buyers and sellers governed by their rational and calculable financial interests. In Weber's opinion, the market was impersonal and ephemeral – it operated, that is, only in the brief moment of exchange.[3] This was an appropriate understanding of the standard markets of functional goods that were dominant throughout industrial modernity. Late modernity's competition for attention, however, is based on a trivalent relationship: at least two competitors compete for the favor of a third party, which has the status of an audience.[4] This *ménage à trois* has changed everything. Unlike the model of the market as a rational *exchange*, what defines the market today is in fact a constellation of *competition* among multiple goods.

This is, however, a very specific type of competition. For what, in the end, are all of these goods competing? As I have already suggested, the answer to this question is *attention* and *recognition* on the part of the public. In the case of cultural markets, narrative, aesthetic, design, ethical, and ludic goods are in competition to become visible and attract public attention. At the same time, they also compete to be recognized as valuable goods with unique characteristics. Many goods fail to achieve this; instead of being regarded as unique, they are considered repetitions of the same. The winners are those goods that succeed in establishing themselves as singular. In short, singularity markets are attractiveness markets, and these have the dual structure of *attention markets*, which center on the problem of visibility, and *valorization markets*, which revolve around the problem of evaluating the quality of unique cultural entities. Attraction competitions thus have a strongly performative nature, so much so that one could say that the economy of singularities is a *performative economy*,[5] an economy in which goods put on enticing performances before an audience.[6]

In cultural markets, the role of consumers is that of an *audience*.[7] The latter constitutes a public sphere of viewers or observers who either grant or deny their attention and recognition. Here, consumers are *recipients* who choose among competing singular goods, and their choices are based on the cultural criteria of experience and value. These markets are not (or at least not primarily) characterized by the emotionally neutral cost calculations that Weber attributed to standard markets. Rather, they revolve around emotionally charged performances. Here, the relationship between goods and the public is defined by more or less intensive forms of affecting (pleasure, tension, adventure, enjoyment, self-education, moral satisfaction, security) that culminate in attraction or attractiveness – and thus my use of the terms *attraction competitions* and *attractiveness markets*. Colloquially, *attraction* often designates a short-lived source of appeal, whereas *attractiveness* usually denotes a physical force of attraction. In our context, however, attraction refers more fundamentally to the positive affective nature of goods, and attractiveness refers to the specific attractive *force* of these goods – to their ability to affect and attract people. Attractiveness markets are thus markets on which goods distinguish themselves and are judged according to their attractiveness.[8]

The Cultural Economization of the Economy and Society

As already mentioned, the late-modern economy has undergone a specific structural transformation, which I referred to above as cultural economization. Upon closer inspection, however, it must be stated that this transformation has not been limited to the economic sector alone. In fact, two parallel yet interrelated processes have been taking place at the same time: one in the *economic sphere* in the strict sense, the other in *society* as a whole.

If the modern economic sphere is understood as an ensemble of the monetarized production, circulation, and consumption of goods, then its structural transformation toward attractiveness markets has had two significant effects. On the one hand, a comprehensive *marketization of the economy* has taken place – that is, there has been an expansion of market-based structures within the economy. On the other hand, the form of the market has transformed. What this means is that, in late modernity, marketization has essentially been driven and defined *by* cultural markets. This assertion may seem irritating at first, for is it not the case that the modern (or at least capitalist) economy necessarily has the form of markets? From a historical perspective, however, one could object by pointing out that the modern economy has not always been based on a radical market logic. Although it is true that there were market-based structures for the circulation of goods during industrial modernity, these existed alongside the alternative influential logic of normative regulation, which was *shielded* from markets.[9] For the functional goods of organized modernity, the markets were frequently regulated; there were oligopolies, monopolies, or direct state control.[10] This sort of regulation went hand in hand with a bureaucratic organization of labor, which was epitomized by state institutions. This relative detachment of the internal structure of Fordistic production from market logic, which reached its peak in state socialism, was possible because the organizations in question could proceed on the assumption that the markets for functional

II The Post-Industrial Economy of Singularities

mass-produced goods would be predictable and regulated. By the form of their goods and by their very structure, standard markets for functional goods are less competitive than markets for singular goods.[11]

Since the 1980s, however, market constellations in the circulation, production, and consumption of goods have become *ubiquitous*. Market situations no longer take place only in brief moments of exchange – instead, they are almost constantly present for producers and consumers. This is clearest to see in the deregulation of markets themselves, for instance in the marketization of mass media or housing (both of which – not coincidentally – are driving forces of global cultural capitalism). In general, it can be stated that, in late modernity, a marketization of the economy has taken place, a sort of economization of the economic. Its driving force, however, is its culturalization – which is to say, its cultural economization. The markets for singular cultural goods have developed an extreme structure of hyper-competitiveness that could not have existed in this form for organized modernity's markets for functional goods. Against this backdrop, the demands for versatile markets for singular goods have pushed organizations to adopt an "entrepreneurial" attitude: they are constantly forced to reorient themselves for market success by permanently producing innovative goods and forms of labor and by permanently observing the market itself.[12] As we will see later on, the radical marketization *qua* culturalization of the economy affects the position of both consumers and working subjects alike: the former are now in the position of permanently having to make choices between the goods available on attractiveness markets, while the latter are in the position of constantly having to update their professional profiles.[13]

Alongside the cultural economization of the economy, however, a *cultural economization of the social* and of society as a whole has also taken place. The highly specific structure of singularity markets as competitions for the visibility and recognition of cultural goods not only defines the economic sphere but has also had structurally formational effects on more and more segments of late-modern society. A good example of this tendency can be seen in the area of *education*: kindergartens, primary schools, and secondary schools have become (or hope to become) singular cultural goods, and they now operate on local, trans-regional, or even international attractiveness markets. In this case, the education market is no longer simply a matter of the government assigning seats within the framework of a regulated educational system. Since the turn of the century, the act of finding a romantic *partner* on a digital dating platform has also taken on the structure of a trans-regional singularity market: in a primarily physical but increasingly more general sense, this has become a competition between personalities wrestling to be seen and recognized as valuable and unique.[14]

Beyond this, the structure of competing singular goods has also come to define the booming local and international market for *religions*, in which religious beliefs, spiritual practices, and communities of believers have been competing with one another since at least the 1970s, when the connection between one's religion and one's place of origin first began to weaken in Western societies. A similar structure can also be found in the regional, national, and global singularity competitions among *cities* and regions and residents and employers, which have only become more intense on account of the mobility of the new middle class. Finally, the realm of *politics* has also increasingly transformed into a market of political goods *as* cultural goods (parties, candidates, social movements) that compete for visibility and valorization and endeavor to identify with voters in a narrative–hermeneutic, ethical, and aesthetic manner (in Europe, this has especially been the case since 1990, when the party landscape splintered). This transformation was initiated by the fact that the normative connections that parties once had to particular places (as communities of shared interest), which characterized them throughout organized modernity, have since eroded.[15]

I should stress once again that it would be superficial to describe the structural transformation of all these spheres (including that of the economy itself) as a general "economization of the social," despite the tendency of so many commentators to do so. The economization of late modernity has, rather, taken the form of a highly specific marketization in the sense of the attraction competition among cultural and singular goods discussed above. Its form, to repeat, is that of cultural economization. *None* of these goods, which circulate outside (as well as within) the economic sector in the strict sense, is a functional mass good; rather, *all* of them are cultural singularity goods. This is as true of education as it is of romantic partners, religious communities, places of residence, and – not least – of political parties and their candidates.

It is also impossible to reduce the cultural economization of the economy and society to neoliberal politics alone.[16] While it would be accurate to say that, from 1979 to 2008, neoliberalism *contributed* to the economization of the economy and society by deregulating markets (the media, the financial sector), dismantling the standards of the welfare state, and stimulating competition (in education and culture in general), neoliberalism alone is insufficient to describe or explain the particular radical form of marketization that has swept over late modernity. This can only be achieved by recognizing the fact that, in late modernity, we are dealing with a highly specific version of market logic whose chief component is the widespread institutionalization of the attention and valorization markets that surround singular goods. The central forces of cultural economization are emotionally charged markets for visibility and recognition on the part of an audience that can be affected (or not) by goods and assign them value (or not). It was a commonplace of modernity to think of the economy and culture as antipodes – commerce versus value, efficiency versus feelings, the bourgeoisie versus artistic bohemianism. In the late-modern economy of singularities, however, culturalization and economization are no longer opposites but have instead come together to form a powerful synthesis. In its dominant form, culturalization is tightly intertwined with a specific form of marketization, and processes of marketization contain processes of culturalization.[17] Cultural economization has thus given rise to a constellation of *competitive singularities*.

Overproduction and Winner-Take-All Competitions

Singularity markets are different. They differ from the standard markets for functional goods. Here again, art provides the structural model – first for the creative industries, then for the creative economy in the broadest sense, and finally for the attractiveness markets that influence the entire late-modern society. The argument that the field of art has become the structural blueprint of the late-modern economy may at first cause economists, sociologists, and art theorists to shake their heads. For a long time, economics and the sociology of organization and labor could dismiss art and the culture industry itself as exotic marginalia that have nothing to do with the hard realities of the industrial markets and production at the heart of modern capitalism. This assumption was certainly correct in the case of classical industrial society, but the image has been flipped with the culturalization and singularization of the late-modern economy. Because the fields of economics and sociology are closely linked to the rise of industrial modernity, it has not been easy for them to change their perspective and to realize that the structural features of narrative–aesthetic goods, including their markets and forms of production, are based on the field of art in the economy of singularities.[18]

I expect that art theorists are shaking their heads even more vigorously. For, since the time of German Idealism, their prevailing system of thought has treated the work of art, and art in general, as "the other" of modernity – as a counterforce to the capitalist economy. From a sociological approach, however, this perspective seems like no more than a mystification of art.[19] In reality, the exact opposite is true. If there has been one area of society that adopted the structural features of an economy of singularities very early on – namely, at the end of the eighteenth century – then this is the field of the arts. The economization of art was not a later development brought about by the rising culture industry of the 1920s or the expansion of the global art market since the 1990s; from the very start, it has been drastically marketized (that is, culturally economized) like no other sphere of modern society.[20]

Be it in art, the creative industries, the general creative economy, or in non-economic spheres, cultural markets are distinguished first and foremost by one characteristic that fundamentally sets them apart from standard markets: the *overproduction of goods*.[21] Regardless of the type of good in question – novels or smartphone apps, movies or travel destinations, scientific theories, fashion lines, or spiritual practices – overproduction means this: there will always be many more new cultural goods on the market than will ever capture the interest of the public and be recognized as unique. The majority of newly produced goods will never obtain singularity status, either because they seem uninteresting, conventional, and insignificant or because they simply fail to be noticed. Quite the opposite of the traditional economy, cultural markets are not faced with the problem of scarcity, at least not on the level of goods themselves. Cultural markets are characterized not by shortages but, rather, by *excess*. For singularity markets, therefore, *waste* is not pathological but, instead, constitutive.[22]

Overproduction is closely related to the pronounced social regime of the new – to the *dispositif* of creativity that prevails in the economy of singularities.[23] It is a systemic feature of cultural markets that they constantly produce, in an incomparably radical way, more and more *novel* goods. This does not mean that older goods necessarily disappear – in the case of valued classics, they can even stick around for a long time. Fundamentally, however, what prevails is the radical and anti-traditionalist imperative of cultural novelties, so that the singularity of cultural goods is associated in advance with their novelty. The cultural good claims to be *singular* in a *new* way and thus to be a unique entity without precedent.

Why, however, is so much effort spent on bringing such an excess of cultural goods into the world when, in the end, the majority of them will fail to earn any recognition at all? The answer is that new singular goods have the remarkable feature that their recognition is fundamentally unpredictable. In this respect, they are highly risky. If it were possible to know exactly which apps, movies, restaurants, or therapies will resonate and be recognized as singular, then perhaps only these things would be developed. But it is impossible to know: singularity goods are essentially *uncertain* goods, and cultural goods circulate on "nobody-knows-anything" markets.[24]

The reason for this uncertainty lies above all in the radicalized regime of the new. First, and fundamentally, a new good has to find people who are interested in it. In this regard, markets based

II The Post-Industrial Economy of Singularities 113

on traditional goods, which have a reliable customer base, are far more predictable than novelty markets. With respect to the novelty of a good, however, it makes a big difference whether the good in question is standardized or singular. New functional goods can come about as technical and objective *innovations*. Because they promise a generally valid form of technological progress, they are less risky in terms of their market success. Cultural creations, on the contrary, do not play in the key of the general but in that of the particular. Their promise is one of narrative, aesthetic, design, and/or ludic originality, which affects recipients emotionally and is recognized by them as valuable. They have to be *surprising*. It is fundamentally uncertain, however, whether the inherent value of new singularities will be recognized or whether they will have any affective force – by definition, they cannot derive from previously existing cultural schemata, valorizations, or affect cultures. Who can reliably predict which novel will take the world by storm and which will be set aside as boring, which computer game will move people and which will leave them cold? The late-modern economy is a *surprise economy*.

What is more, the sheer abundance of new cultural goods in the late-modern economy is extremely high, and it is made even more so by digital technologies. This quantitative state of affairs only enhances the problem of which goods will capture the public's limited attention. After all, that which is overlooked has no chance at all to affect people and become valuable. The sheer amount of variety thus has a considerable influence on the system of attention. In general, singularity markets have to be understood as *attention markets*, as social spaces in which the uncertain mobilization of public attention represents a structural challenge.[25] And because perception is necessarily selective, social practices and orders always function as attention regimes – that is, as forms of steering, intensifying, and filtering attention. What characterizes today's singularity markets is the historically unprecedented dynamization and dispersion of attention, whose exact distribution is unpredictable on a case-by-case basis. In this case, the attention of the public has become a scarce resource. In general, if there is any sort of scarcity in late modernity, this is no longer a scarcity of goods but rather a scarcity of attention (and appreciation).

In principle, it would be possible to conceive of a situation in which each of the large number of cultural goods would attract the attention of a small audience, so that the attention captured by each would be weak but equally distributed. This sort of perceptive egalitarianism, however, does not correspond to reality. Singularity markets are, instead, defined by a peculiar circumstance: given the existence, on the one hand, of an excess of new (and old) cultural goods – movies and vacation destinations, furniture and haircuts – and that of a local, national, or even global audience on the other, it may be uncertain precisely *which* new film (etc.) will win the attention of the public, but it is likely that this attention will ultimately be distributed in a highly unequal and radically *asymmetrical* manner. These hyper-competitive markets operate in an extremely polarizing way.[26] Whereas a few new goods will attract an enormous amount of attention, the vast majority of them will largely be ignored. Of all the movies that are filmed in a given year, for instance, only a few of them will make it to the cinema, and even fewer will be shown for multiple weeks and go on to win a prestigious prize. Most will turn out to be flops that are quickly forgotten. Quantitative empirical studies have shown again and again that, regardless of the type of singular good, the result will be a *Pareto distribution*: 20 percent of the goods on offer will attract 80 percent of the public's demand,[27] while the remaining 80 percent of goods will attract just 20 percent of total demand (and many of these goods will attract none at all).[28]

Because of this extreme asymmetry, the attention markets of the economy of singularities are excellent examples of what Robert Frank and Philipp Cook have called *winner-take-all markets* (or at least "winner-take-the-most"): polarizing markets with an asymmetry between just a few successful winners and the large glut of other competitors with little success.[29] In this case, one could also speak of a *superstar economy*. It follows the pattern of the *starification* of the economy of late-modern culture at large, which was familiar early on from the art world and then later from the culture industry and professional sports.[30] Not only subjects but also other sorts of cultural goods – things, services, media formats, or events – can acquire the nature of a star by attracting a phenomenal amount of attention. Individual YouTube clips can become stars, as can a trendy restaurant or a smartphone made by a certain company. In a second step, an entire brand or institution, such as a world-famous museum or a prominent football club, can develop star quality, and so can the person who came up with the idea for such developments: certain star architects, star authors, star chefs, and so on. Starification is a constitutive aspect of the economy of singularities.

Buzz Effects and the Struggle for Visibility

Cultural markets are fundamentally characterized by extremely high *risks* and by the necessity of *speculation*. Regarding the matter of risks, it would be too crude to trace them back in general to modern marketization. Rather, their pronounced structure of unavoidable uncertainty is clearly due to *cultural* markets, with their highly special goods, and to the post-industrial capitalism of singularities, which

II The Post-Industrial Economy of Singularities

differs from the more predictable capitalism of industrial modernity. Attractiveness markets are fundamentally risky markets because they offer singular *uncertainty goods* – with all the implications that this has not only for goods and economic enterprises but also for employees and the structure of late-modern labor. Whereas industrial society, by restraining markets and standardizing functional goods and forms of labor in the economic sphere, managed to create a relatively high degree of certainty, predictability, and risk-aversion, late modernity has become a risk society precisely through the culturalization and singularization of product markets.[31] Spans of attention, moments of surprise, and the appreciation of originality defy planning and control, and this is why strategies for managing risk have become so important.

This risk structure of cultural markets lends them a decidedly *speculative* structure. As a strategy of action that plays with uncertainty and places bets on what might or might not succeed, speculation is familiar from a select few sectors of the economy, such as financial markets and stock markets.[32] In the case of singularity markets, however, speculation defines their general structure. Every new piece of music, every new restaurant, and every new app is a speculative gamble on the future – a wager that something surprising and different will be recognized and appreciated as such by the public. At the same time, the risk is high that these bets will not pay off. That is, speculation is no longer just a matter of a few clever (stock-market) traders bucking the trend; rather, it has become a defining element of late-modern singularity markets, so much so that *everything* on offer as an attractive and surprising good now has a speculative aspect to it.

There are many sides to the process by which a cultural good succeeds or fails on the market of singularities. The high degree of uncertainty, both on the part of producers (as regards prospective success) and on the part of consumers (with respect to which goods deserve attention), has resulted in the formation of specific cultural patterns: consumers allow their attention to be steered this way and that, while producers attempt to minimize risk. A central aspect to all of this is that singular goods always have to pass through *two* filters, which are interrelated but only loosely connected to one another: the filter of *attention* and the filter of *valorization*. Of course, it is obvious that, if something fails to attract any attention, it will not be positively valorized. However, a successful effort to attract attention does not automatically result in positive valorization, and certainly not for the *long term*.

Because of their overproduction and because of the fact that their attractiveness is uncertain, new cultural goods are fundamentally at a disadvantage compared to traditional and functional goods. In a certain respect, however, this disadvantage is offset by the fact that, on attention markets, affect goods can become "contagious," so to speak. When a certain good – a film, a restaurant, a band, a travel destination, a comedy show – happens to evoke enthusiasm among a few recipients, then this fact alone can make it seem appealing and attract further interest, at least to the extent that there are enough social and media-technological channels to broaden this enthusiasm. This is the *attractiveness of the attractive* or the so-called *buzz effect* that only singularities can unleash.[33] And it is this buzz that also explains the asymmetrical distribution of attention. It is often the case that the few cultural goods that manage to become visible and affect people will soon attract even more and more attention. This can lead to an exponential increase in positive reception – to a sort of mass attraction, or at least to a short-term *Matthew effect*. Whoever is already receiving attention will almost invariably receive more attention. If a YouTube clip attracts 500,000 clicks off the bat, the next 500,000 are child's play.

This also explains why the initial phase of a singular good can be so crucial – the phase, that is, right after its first appearance on the market. At this stage, it is normally a matter of being "all in." The cultural good in question is engaged in an extreme *struggle for visibility*, whereby visibility (not just in the strictly visual sense, of course) has in general become a central category of the society of singularities. A singular good (an object, collective, event, etc.) is visible when it succeeds in attracting attention to itself. Whoever or whatever fails to find an audience will remain invisible, which means social death.[34] The initial phase of a novelty is about accumulating as much incipient attention as possible; it is a matter of *initial singularization*. This can concern an individual good but also the organization that produced it (the classic example is start-up companies) or, as in the art world and other branches of the creative economy, the *name* of the newcomer who created the good: the author, director, or designer. During this initial stage, goods, organizations, and names are blank slates. Everything seems possible. At the same time, this phase is typically characterized by a remarkable sort of irreversibility when it comes to attracting attention. Depending on the field, its length of time can vary, but it is only during this limited timeframe that a new good or new name has the opportunity to draw attention to itself. Afterward, there is either a (possibly meteoric) rise caused by the buzz effect, or the opportunity is irretrievably lost.[35]

The reason for the irreversibility of initial grabs for attention lies in the structural features of the creativity *dispositif*. Essentially, the latter directs the interest of the public toward novelties, which means that nothing can be less interesting than the goods left over from last season. Yesterday's unbought goods almost never have a second chance to produce a buzz effect. In the case of individual cultural

II The Post-Industrial Economy of Singularities

goods, this might not be ruinous: everyone knows that the name of the game is "better luck next time!" As regards entire organizations, however, this situation can be more difficult to overcome, for, without an initial boost, their success on the market might be severely jeopardized. Yet this irreversibility is even more crucial in the case of names – that is, in the case of goods that are associated by their nature with an author function. The failure of a debut novel, for instance, can be a lifelong stain on a writer's career. Yesterday's unsuccessful up-and-coming talents either have to give up entirely or accept the precarious destiny of artists who missed their big chance.

Conversely, however, the extreme uncertainty of this initial phase also means that if it *does* lead to a brisk accumulation of attention, then the cultural good, start-up company, or name can experience an extraordinary ascent (which itself could be called singular). Accordingly, the initial phase of a cultural good has become the topic of a familiar myth in the society of singularities: its well-known elements include the garage band or the garage company, the shooting star, the moment of discovery, or the breakthrough moment. This might at first glance seem to be just a minor variant of bourgeois society's "self-made man" – the proverbial dishwasher who becomes a millionaire ("rags to riches") – but there are major differences.[36] Whereas the narrative of the self-made man is based on the idea that success can be achieved through hard work and perseverance, the myth of the shooting star is based on the audiences that govern the attractiveness market. Here, a sudden breakthrough can happen on account of a *single* hit – one great stage appearance, one YouTube video, or one enthusiastically received collection of stories. This means that the rise to success is not slow and gradual but, instead, discontinuous and abrupt. What is crucial is not any objective achievement or long-term devotion to one's work but, rather, sudden success on the attractiveness market.

In many respects, it can be a matter of pure *coincidence* whether a cultural good manages to attract attention and generate buzz during its initial phase. That said, there are structures and authorities that attempt to influence visibility. They differ depending on the type of cultural good in question and the type of audience that they focus on – local, national, or global; a specialized audience, a broad crowd, or a combination of the two. Without a doubt, media technologies – and especially digital media technologies – play a decisive role in structuring and influencing attention; access to the appropriate media can considerably influence the initial attention received by a cultural good. Social networks – professional, private, or both – are just as significant in this regard. Singularity markets are "social-network markets."[37] Cultural goods are spread via word-of-mouth propaganda, both as recommendations from friends and colleagues and through the media. In all of this, the influence of gatekeepers should not be underestimated, be it in the mass media or be it of a professional sort. In the case of goods that rely in advance on institutional mediating authorities – record companies in the case of songs, galleries in the case of paintings, publishing houses in the case of books, but also to some extent theaters and agents in the case of stage actors – the reputation of these mediating authorities, which in turn smooths the path to the mass media, can also increase a good's visibility.[38]

Valorization Techniques and Reputation

The mechanisms for focusing attention and those for valorizing singular goods are often closely interrelated.[39] Even during the initial stage of accumulating attention, the visibility of a good is not value-neutral. In the case of a new film or a new museum, for instance, attention is mobilized through online and printed reviews, which make the novelty in question visible *and* evaluate its quality at the same time. High levels of attention typically go together with high levels of affect (mostly of a positive sort, as in the case of a good that is generating buzz), so that something will become a "must-see" or a "must-have." It is also possible, however, for an overwhelming amount of attention to be drawn to something that has been negatively evaluated, degraded, and scandalized.

Even if the initial attention that a good receives is associated with positivity, in the case of many cultural goods it is necessary to distinguish between long-term and short-term valorization. In this respect, it is possible to differentiate three types of goods. First, there are those whose markets are short-term-oriented to begin with – such is the case, for instance, with newspaper articles and online news reports, with YouTube clips, and also with television programs that are broadcast only once. In general, the internet favors short-term attention. Second, there are goods that are on their way to entering the market, in which case both the short term and the long term play a role; this is true of movies and fashion lines, for instance. At first, the markets for such goods are oriented toward short-term success, such as the opening week of a film or a seasonal shift in the fashion world. At the same time, it is possible for such goods to earn lasting recognition, as happens to select films, directors, actors, or designers. Third and finally, there are goods whose markets are strongly oriented toward the long term, so that their short-term success is of subordinate importance; such is the case with buildings, scientific publications, restaurants, museums, and therapies – not to mention entire cities.[40]

It is in the distinction between short-term and long-term valuation that the specific temporal structure of cultural markets manifests

II The Post-Industrial Economy of Singularities 119

itself, a structure that we have already encountered in the difference between goods that are merely trendy and those that are classics. In the case of singular goods, there are always two possibilities: either they are a *short-term* attraction or they develop a *long-term* appeal, which is then capable of generating additional new attractions. In an economy of singularities, both modes of attention and value exist side by side. Within this cultural framework, however, long-term appeal is the more valuable, because its attention-grabbing success is lasting. Long-term appeal means that a good has achieved a (positive) *cultural reputation* over time; it has acquired a sort of cultural capital – *singularity capital*, which accumulates over the long term and can be redeemed again and again, so that it procures the status of a *classic*, a recognized *name*, or a *brand*. Reputation means that the quality of a cultural good has been regarded as valuable for a long time and that the good itself has long been recognized as unique. Compared to evaluating functional goods, the valorization of singular goods is *elaborate*. So it was at the beginning in the world of art, and so it has remained with the expansion of the economy of singularities and the parallel expansion of digital media, which place new platforms and instruments for such valorization at our disposal.[41]

Whereas the utility of a standard good is relatively easy to measure with quantitative (more/less) and qualitative (better/worse) criteria, the evaluation of a singular good depends on complex, qualifying discourses and techniques of valorization.[42] In the art world, art criticism and the related field of art history were traditional loci where such valorizations took place. Now, the goods produced by the economy of singularities are far more varied than those produced by the field of art alone, and thus the forms of valorization are more varied as well. Finally, the traditional genre of the *review*, including its generalized and popularized forms, has remained at the fore – indeed, it has become one of the key media formats of the economy of singularities. It is no longer the case that only books or opera performances are reviewed; restaurants and hotels, cities, apps and computers, travel providers, and dentists are reviewed as well.[43] In a sense, the economy of singularities operates in a *mode of ongoing review*. Whereas the traditional art review was the domain of just a few specialists, who had exclusive access to prominent media platforms, digital media have made it possible for more and more people to evaluate cultural goods. Depending on one's perspective, valorization has either been democratized or vulgarized.

This proliferation of reviewers, however, has given rise to a second-order problem with respect to evaluation and attention: which evaluating authorities are reliable and worthy of attention? Here, too, there are those with a higher or lower reputation, and those who attract more or less attention. The traditional distinction between *experts* and *laypeople* is still relevant when it comes to distinguishing between different types of evaluators in the economy of singularities, but in a new form, since the layperson is no longer someone who lacks knowledge and expertise. The difference between the layperson and the expert now lies in their respective approaches to the singularity of the cultural good under evaluation, and this is related to the fact that singularities, as we have already seen, are both experienced and valorized. Lay and expert evaluations diverge in the amount of weight they give to these two elements.

The layman evaluates the inherent complexity of a good primarily on the basis of his own experience. Consequently, his valorizations tend to focus on how he *experienced* a cultural good and was *affected* by it. The tendency of the expert is completely different: experts maintain a degree of distance from experiential components (even though they are never fully detached emotionally) and they adopt an analytical approach to the individual elements and relations that constitute the otherness of a good. Frequently, they do so by means of comparison: the special aspect of *this* music, *this* theater production, or *this* location can only really be appreciated if one is familiar with other music, theater productions, and locations. The art of qualitative comparison consists in preserving and not (excessively) reducing the inherent complexity of singularities. This intellectualization of evaluation is characteristic of expert reviews of cultural goods beyond the traditional realm of high culture. Thus, experts are no longer exclusive to traditional media outlets or academic institutions but can be found on digital media as well. Status aside, one now becomes an expert by earning a high degree of trust from one's audience.

Singularity Capital

As soon as cultural goods become the object of lay and (especially) expert discourses of valorization, the possibility exists that they will be assigned cultural value, which can extend beyond the initial phase of successfully attracting attention. This value can become established and, thus, always guarantee new attention. The process of long-term singularization unfolds as follows: a valorized good accumulates singularity capital, which it preserves for as long as possible. Only a few select goods manage to achieve this, whereas most others will soon be forgotten after their brief and initial encounter with fame (if this happens at all). As a result of long-term singularization, goods can become modern *classics*, *brands*, and *names*.[44] This can happen to designer furniture and clothing, houses and apartments in a particular style or location,

II The Post-Industrial Economy of Singularities   121

travel destinations, as well as to media formats such as novels, works of nonfiction, and pieces of music (whether classical or popular), or films. Festivals, recurring sporting events, universities, and museums can also become "classics," and the same is true of various sorts of brands as well.[45]

The formerly clear separation between popular and high culture, which Pierre Bourdieu discussed in the case of nineteenth-century literature, for instance, no longer seems to apply for the economy of singularities.[46] In today's cultural capitalism, there is a highly dynamic interplay between widespread attention and expert opinion, which are no longer mutually exclusive but, in fact, often enhance one another. In the cultural sphere of late modernity, it can be said that the great variety of goods and the great variety of evaluation mechanisms (expert opinions here, popularity there) have made the divide between high and popular culture porous.

This dedifferentiation has come from both sides: it is a result of both the *popularization of high culture* and the simultaneous *intellectualization of the popular*. Since the 1990s, objects and events of traditional high culture – think of museums, classical music concerts, or art exhibits – have been "eventified" and "festivalized" to the point that they now have certain popular qualities: their affect value and authenticity value have been pushed into the foreground. Conversely, objects of ostensibly popular culture have become the topic of expert and quasi-intellectual valorization. Blockbusters such as *The Lord of the Rings* or *Harry Potter* and the latest developments in pop music, comics, and computer games are now dissected and discussed by cultural theorists. The sphere of cultural goods *as a whole* has therefore become the object of both popular attention dynamics (characterized by short-term valorizations) *and* expert evaluations, which tend to have long-term effects. Thus, the popular and the expert/high-cultural no longer designate two separate classes of goods but have, rather, transformed into two distinct forms of evaluation, which are both used to assess the majority of goods and thus overlap with one another.

In this case, one can speak of a *spill-over effect of attention and evaluation*, which is characteristic of late-modern culture: a rise in popular attention accorded to a cultural good will stimulate expert valorizations. Of course, popular attention does not *necessarily* translate into a positive expert assessment, but it usually means that experts will be unable to resist engaging with the "phenomenon" in question and setting their valorization machinery in motion. Art critics, for instance, simply cannot ignore the popular (that is, interesting to the mass media and thus also expensive) works of artists such as Damien Hirst or Jeff Koons. This is true of every cultural good that stems from popular culture – such as television series, for instance – and is now the object of expert valorizations.

Conversely, however, the positive valorizations of experts can also shift popular attention. This is especially true of competitions and award ceremonies, which are often staged by the mass media and thus have a considerable influence over public opinion.[47] The latter can be understood as *valorization spectacles*, at the end of which a jury of experts awards the winners. Paradigmatic examples of this are prestigious film awards (the Oscars, Golden Globes, Berlinale, etc.), whose ceremonies are celebrated as global media events. Here, valorization itself becomes an event. Award ceremonies can not only increase the reputation of established singularities; they can also lend extraordinary visibility to newcomers on the scene. This, of course, increases the possibility that something attractive to experts will translate into a popular attraction.[48] Interestingly, the category of the "controversial" can promote this process. Within the economy of singularities, it is not necessary for a cultural good to receive unanimous praise from experts. On the contrary, in many respects it can be more advantageous to be a source of controversy, because the controversial nature of a good is evidence of its inherent complexity and makes it more interesting. Controversy is advantageous because it heats up the valorization discourse and leads to even more attention.[49]

In sum, the *cultural capitalization* of both attention and reputation is characteristic of the attractiveness markets of cultural goods.[50] In this way, *singularity capital* arises and becomes a matter of fundamental significance. Cultural capitalism is capitalism in a very elementary sense. Before the question of commercialization and financial profit is even raised, uniqueness itself can be capitalized – that is, it can become an accumulable form of capital that yields gains without any additional labor. On these markets, singularity becomes capital on the condition that, beyond being just a temporary attraction, the good in question acquires the characteristic of lasting attractiveness. As a *combination of attention capital and reputation capital*, singularity capital is the cultural capital of that which is regarded as unique. Cultural capitalism is *singularity capitalism* in that the singularity of a good becomes its capital.

Attention capital means that a good has received so much attention that, for this reason alone, it attracts even more attention to itself. Because a good has become famous on account of its uniqueness, people take an interest in it, and this makes the good even more famous. This is also helped by the fact that consumers, who exist in a constellation of dispersed attention, are inclined to stick to what is well known. Attention can thus, as it were, be accumulated. Here, there is not only a short-term, but also a long-term, Matthew effect. Like all forms of capital, attention capital also guarantees effortless income and can ideally be realized (that is, converted into profit) at any time. The singular good does not have to do anything more; it

II The Post-Industrial Economy of Singularities 123

is sufficient that it simply exists in its famous uniqueness. This alone generates further attention for it, possibly even in excess.

Reputation capital means that a good has acquired so much reputation through (expert) valorizations that this alone causes it to garner an even greater reputation. Singularity capital can thus also be accumulated in the form of reputation capital. For example, if an architect, actor, designer, musician, or intellectual happens to receive an award, it is highly likely that he or she will receive further distinctions. Even though the public at large might not have an accurate understanding of a work in all its complexity, the simple fact that critics consider it uniquely significant can be enough to lead to its further appreciation. On the level of reputation, there is also therefore a long-term Matthew effect.[51] And here, too, it is the case that reputation capital can become a source of effortless income. Former fame can live on, and sometimes it merely has to be managed (however, it can also fade away if it is believed that someone's "best days are behind him" or if an artist is regarded as a "has-been").

For the most part, reputation capital is realized in the form of ongoing renewed attention from recipients. Especially successful are *living legends*, because they usually continue to produce new cultural goods and thus continue to operate within the creativity *dispositif*. Living legends thus remain a presence on account of their past goods *and* their current goods. On the attraction market, their new works thus have a rather large initial advantage because, in the field of the new, recipients typically direct their attention toward novelties produced by *well-known* and recognized names and brands (including, and especially, controversial ones) – the new film by the famous director X, the new product by the famous brand Y, the new museum in the famous city Z.

With their reputation capital, living legends can thus turn this into a *double* advantage. On the one hand, the cultural goods that they produced in the past already absorb a more or less considerable share of attention and recognition within the present cultural sphere.[52] On the other hand, living legends also have the aforementioned initial advantage of being well-known and recognized when it comes to their new goods, because their reputation can reduce the possibility of disappointment that is structurally associated with singularities. By their very nature, living legends promise quality, and for this reason they are guaranteed attention and valorization *in advance*. Under the conditions of singularity capitalism, as I have already mentioned, the two forms of singularity capital – attention capital and reputation capital – are usually *combined* with one another. Consider the example of names. Whereas the bourgeois art world was only able to offer popularity during an artist's lifetime *or* glory in an artist's old age (or posthumously), the winners in the economy of singularities combine fame *and* glory in the here and now. This is true of star authors and star architects, star designers and star actors, star artists and star chefs, and so on and so forth, and thus it applies to the whole upper crust of the creative economy.[53]

Quantifying the Unique

As a process of singularization, the valorization of cultural goods is one of *qualification* – that is, it is a process of determining and appreciating quality. This does not mean, however, that *quantification* has ceased to be a structurally formational force in the economy and society. Quite the contrary. Paradoxically, in fact, attractiveness markets and their ostensibly incomparable singular goods have brought about extensive *quantification techniques*. Since the 1990s, and especially in the wake of the digital revolution, quantitative comparative indexes and measuring procedures have clearly been on the rise, and these typically take the form of rankings or ratings.[54]

Of course, quantitative social technologies have been a central instrument of formal rationalization and its logic of the general since the second half of the nineteenth century. State institutions work with statistics in order to gather information about the population, and economic organizations practice accounting in order to monitor their internal processes. In light of this nexus between rationalization and quantification, it may at first seem surprising that the economy of singularities has given a new boost to quantitative measuring methods. What is decisive now, however, is that these new methods are not used to quantify general features and their distribution – rather, they are *quantitative techniques for representing singularities*. Here too, as in the society of singularities in general, we can see that instrumental rationality has undergone a structural transformation: it has become a general infrastructure for singularities.

How and why is this possible? The quantification of unique entities can be understood as a rationalistic response to the problem of *comparing* singularities.[55] Strictly speaking, singularities cannot be compared. *Nevertheless*, within the economy of singularities, there is a pragmatic need to compare them, both from the perspective of producers and from that of consumers. Both sides have an interest in gathering comparative information about the attention that goods are attracting and about the value that has been attributed to them. As producers or consumers, we would like to know which goods are really singular without having to spend the time and money to test them out ourselves on a case-by-case basis. For the late-modern economy of singularities, making comparisons between ostensibly incomparable cultural goods has become a central task, though one

II The Post-Industrial Economy of Singularities 125

that is not exactly easy to manage. Comparing the incomparable means that the inherent complexity of singularities can no longer be treated as such, but rather has to be examined according to a select set of comparative parameters. In other words, the inherent complexity of singularities has to be *reduced*.

On a qualitative and non-competitive level, comparisons between incomparable cultural goods are as old as singularity markets themselves. This is precisely what art critics were doing at the end of the eighteenth century when they ventured to compare different artistic styles to one another. *Qualitative-relational* comparisons of this sort, however, placed the matters being compared on an equal level and did not hierarchize them. The aim was to reach a better understanding of something unique in light of something different and, as much as possible, to maintain the inherent complexity and otherness of both. This approach is to be distinguished from the *qualitative-competitive* method of measurement, which results in rankings, or winners and losers. Significant examples of this method are the aforementioned competitions and award ceremonies that have developed on the market of cultural goods.

Within the framework of singularity competitions, the process of comparison involves a fundamental reinterpretation of the status of unique entities. Here, singularities are converted into examples of the general-particular. I have already mentioned that, under the conditions of (late) modernity, the three possible social forms of particularity – singularities, idiosyncrasies, and the general-particular – circulate among one another to a considerable extent.[56] When being compared, the singularity of a good is temporarily suspended, as it were, and transferred into the register of the general-particular. Under these circumstances, the value of individual cultural goods is no longer something to be viewed in isolation; according to certain criteria, one good will instead seem to be *more valuable* than another, which leads to a ranking of qualities (higher/lower) and the use of comparative adjectives in general. Something can now seem to be more original, more complex, or more groundbreaking than something else. The aim of these valorizations is not only to determine and understand quality but also to place it on a comparative scale.

In a subsequent step, the *qualitative* scales that result from competitions can be *quantified*, and exactly this has widely been taking place since the 1990s in the form of rankings. A pioneering form of quantifying a qualitative scale was the introduction of Michelin stars in 1926, which have been used since then to rank the world's top restaurants. The qualitative differences between restaurants were not only identified but also differentiated according to points (stars). This schematization made it easier both to compare restaurants and to categorize them into qualitative groups.[57] Whereas

Michelin stars represent a highly reputable form of evaluation, and the stars themselves are assigned by experts, the next step was to combine rankings of this sort with frequency counts. The result is then *quantitatively weighted rankings*. The latter are frequently used in the evaluations made by laypeople in order to balance out extreme assessments. This combination of rankings and frequency distribution characterizes the evaluation of cultural goods on many digital platforms.[58] Here, average point values and thus average ratings are calculated for each product.

In addition to rankings as quantitative conversions of qualitative *valorizations*, there are other, simpler, quantifying methods for measuring the *attention distribution* of cultural goods. Whereas it can be difficult to translate valorization from quality into quantity, the quantification of attention is relatively easy, because attention can be measured according to simple parameters. Typically, however, what is measured is not the actual attention of recipients but rather some external indicator of it. The simplest method here is to measure a cultural good's demand on the market: the number of books sold, the number of people who went to see a certain movie, the number of people who watch certain television programs, and so on. By means of digitalization, the quantification of attention has been automated, and it is now ubiquitous. Now, automatic tallies are made of the number of clicks attracted by an online news article, a YouTube video, a Facebook or Instagram page, or a Wikipedia entry, not to mention the measurements of *all* online content related to the name of a given star (or to a business or an individual cultural good) and the number of times any of this content has been viewed by users.[59]

The effect, however, of these quantitative techniques for representing singularities is that they *exacerbate* the already extreme disparities in the amount of attention that different cultural goods attract. By making this unequal distribution of attention *visible* – whether through lists or other visualizations – they make it easier for consumers to pay even more attention to whatever has already attracted a large audience, thereby setting a Matthew effect in motion. We read the book on top of the bestseller list, listen to the number 1 song on the Hit Parade, and view the online articles and clips that have already been seen the most (especially among our "friends"). The valorization techniques that result in scaled rankings have a similarly self-reinforcing effect. We go to the restaurant that has been awarded two stars and we see the movies that have won awards in Cannes or Berlin. Ultimately, the market of cultural goods is an uncertainty market not only from the perspective of producers[60] – it is also an uncertainty market from the perspective of consumers, who can never be sure whether a new song or restaurant will affect them positively and be qualitatively valuable. Comparative,

II The Post-Industrial Economy of Singularities 127

quantifying valorizations and visible, quantitative distributions of attention are therefore more effective means of facilitating the decision-making of recipients than any single evaluation. Attention measurements and quality rankings have thus transformed into instruments that further encourage the capitalization of attention and reputation. Paradoxically, quantitative-comparative representations of the particular, which function by means of *gradualization*, have therefore contributed to deepening the *absolute* differences between stars (later classics) and the sea of barely noticed goods. This has involved something like a double conversion: first, quantitative-comparative methods such as rankings and ratings transform the *absolute* qualitative differences between unique singular goods into *gradual* qualitative or quantitative differences. Yet, because this gradualization takes place on extremely polarized attractiveness markets and encourages the accumulation of attention capital and reputation capital, it transforms these gradual differences back into *absolute* differences, though on a different level. For, in the end, what emerges is the actual absolute difference between extremely visible and quasi-invisible goods – the difference, that is, between the few stars or classics and the many goods that never achieve the status of singularity and are quickly forgotten.

All in all, it is decisive that the process of singularizing and valorizing goods is not a purely immanent aspect of these economic markets or of other spheres that are now structured in a similar way, such as the competition among educational institutions, cities, or political parties. Because mobilizations of attention, routine valorizations (whether in the form of reviews or of a quantified sort), and valorization spectacles are conveyed through the media and visible to the public, their influence affects the habitus of subjects and late-modern society as a whole. The cultural markets for singular goods, in which the subject constantly participates at least as a consumer (if not also as a producer), teach us that this is the normal state of society under present conditions: objects and subjects are valuable and singular if they succeed in generating visibility and producing positive emotions in the never-ending competition for attention and valorization. The fact that consumers prefer singular cultural *goods* for the arrangement of their lifestyles certainly has a strong influence on late-modern culture, but the influence of the singularity *competitions* organized around these goods is just as profound, if not even more so.

III
The Singularization of the Working World

The Cultural Economization of Labor and Its Polarization

Over the course of the structural transformation of goods and markets in the late-modern economy, the working world has transformed as well. This has affected the practice of labor itself, the ways in which organizations are structured, as well as the competencies, desires, and requirements of working subjects. On all of these levels, forms of labor have undergone culturalization and singularization to the extent that they are no longer tied to industrial modernity's structures of standardized labor.

Over the past 20 years, sociologists have employed a variety of concepts to discuss the erosion of the industrial logic of the working world. The concept of *immaterial labor* indicates that labor is now more deeply involved with communication, symbols, and affects than it is with material goods. The talk of *flexible specialization* stresses the extent to which production processes have moved away from mass production. The diagnosis of the *subjectification of labor* underscores the relevance of an employee's non-formalized and subjective traits, so that, as work has begun to *extend beyond the workplace*, the dividing line between labor and the private sphere has become fragile. The special status of the *project* in knowledge-based types of work has also been discussed at length. Finally, it has been pointed out that the late-modern *entrepreneurial employee* (or "intrepreneur") and the *entrepreneurial self* are now in a permanent state of competition and have accordingly learned to fine-tune their employability.[1] In my view, all of these analyses of post-Fordistic forms of labor are accurate on their own, but I would like to refine and consolidate them by interpreting the overarching structural transformation that has taken place in terms of the singularization of the working world: a restructuring of working conditions through which the professional world has come to be defined by its extraordinary orientation toward singularities. This singularization has coincided with a culturalization or, to be more precise, with a cultural economization of labor forms. This means that the working world has adopted more and more features of the creative economy, which produces singular goods for cultural markets, and that the workforce itself has become a singular good on a cultural (labor) market.

The singularization of labor in the knowledge and culture economy encompasses a variety of aspects. In that the practices of labor are no longer oriented toward standardized goods and services but rather revolve around producing more and more new (or old) singular attractive goods, labor has essentially become *creative labor* engaged in *cultural production*. In this case, the singularization of labor means working *on* singularities. Even on the organizational level, there are signs that the logic of the particular is supplanting the logic of the general, given that hierarchical matrix organizations are being superseded by project structures and networks. Finally, working *subjects* have become a prominent object of singularization – both by themselves and by others. The need to acquire general formal qualifications has been supplanted by the need to develop unique *profiles* of competencies and potential. The late-modern working subject wants and is expected to be unique: a bundle of capabilities and talents whose performance is not interchangeable but, instead, as exceptional as possible. Singularization has thus instilled the ostensibly unemotional working world of modernity with enormous amounts of culture and affectivity.

Of course, singularization and culturalization have not influenced all working conditions since the beginning of the twenty-first century. In the knowledge and culture economy, immaterial or creative work is primarily performed by people with high formal educations who are engaged in highly qualified activities. This educated class makes up about a third of the labor force, and its numbers are growing. Maurizio Lazzarato has rightly pointed out the "mass intellectuality" that has resulted from the expansion of education since the 1970s and now constitutes the core workforce of the creative economy.[2] However, the knowledge and culture economy has obviously continued to coexist with the industrial production of capital goods and raw materials as well as with (though now to a greater extent) simple and routine services. At the same time, not even all the activities *within* the cultural economy involve such singularized labor, for the cultural economy also has a need for industrial production (even if this has become more and more automated) and supporting services. Despite the great expectations that Daniel Bell and others once had for the knowledge society of the future,[3] the transition from industrial to post-industrial society has consequently not meant that all working conditions have uniformly developed in the direction of qualified, knowledge-based labor. Rather, the post-industrial economy and its working conditions are highly heterogeneous, with a clear tendency toward the working world becoming *polarized* between the knowledge-based and cultural labor of highly qualified people on the one hand and the routinized services performed by the so-called service class on the other.[4] As the economists Maarten Goos and Alan Manning put it, the post-industrial economy has created "lovely jobs" and "lousy jobs" with hardly anything in between.[5]

It has to be stressed that this is not a matter of merely gradual distinctions between different levels of education. Rather, late-modern society has come to be characterized by the antagonism that exists between two forms and assessments of labor. Ultimately, however, this polarization of *labor forms* reflects the dualism

III The Singularization of the Working World 133

between culturally singular and functionally standardized *goods*. We have already seen that, in the economy of singularities, the difference between these two types of goods is expressed as a difference in value. Singular goods (including services and events) appear to have value and quality, whereas standardized goods (and services) seem to be merely profane goods that are useful but nothing more. What is decisive is that the polarity between these two types of goods extends to the forms of labor associated with them. The production of unique cultural goods requires a different type of labor: *creative* work that is oriented toward novelty and culture, is usually undertaken in the form of projects, and requires strong intrinsic motivation and the *entire personality* of the person engaged in it. In contrast, simple services and industrial labor have an entirely different structure. They usually involve repetitive, standardized, and functional activities that require little intrinsic motivation and no personality. At their heart, simple services are a form of *normalization labor*, which means that their goal is to preserve the status quo and ideally remain invisible.[6] Creative labor, on the contrary, is emphatically oriented toward being visible and *making a difference*.

This structural polarity between forms of labor is reflected in their contrary social and subjective evaluation: both in the eyes of late-modern society at large and in the self-perception of its working subjects, highly qualified, creative, and singular labor has the nimbus of socially valuable and subjectively satisfying activity, whereas standardized and routinized activity is seen as profane work that offers little satisfaction. In this now common hierarchical division, "highly qualified" and "low-qualified" people stand on opposite sides.[7] Accordingly, creative "valuable" work and repetitive "useful" jobs come with opposing levels of social prestige and feelings of self-worth. The sociologist Stephan Voswinkel has shown that the earlier way of earning recognition in industrial labor, which was based on appreciation for effort and achievement, is gradually being replaced by an entirely different type of recognition in which the only sort of labor that earns "admiration" is that which distinguishes itself through extraordinary performance.[8] This difference corresponds to the antagonism between routinized, merely useful labor and creative, value-enhancing labor. In short, labor is profane when the employee is replaceable (and also perceives himself in that way), and it is singular when this is not the case. This irreplaceability manifests itself most clearly at the top of the labor hierarchy, which is occupied by creative stars. With his position that the industrial workforce was the true source of social productivity and (economic) value, Karl Marx had formulated an understanding of industrial society that the economy of singularities has inverted. Now, singular goods seem to be the true locus of (cultural) value, and the "creative class" of highly qualified people – a concept that, not coincidentally, contains an element of self-glorification – is its productive basis.

The expansive field of knowledge-based and cultural labor in the creative economy is itself, however, characterized by a considerable degree of heterogeneity. Looking just at the creative industries in the strict sense, one is often reminded of their "hourglass structure."[9] On one side, there are the few, large, and often multinational corporations (from Google to Bertelsmann) that hire full-time employees at relatively high salaries; on the other side, there are the many small companies and start-ups with few employees, as well as numerous self-employed people and freelancers.

The culturalization and singularization of the economy, however, extends beyond the creative industries and includes the entire spectrum of labor performed by highly qualified "symbolic analysts," as Robert Reich called them.[10] From this broader perspective, the diagnosis changes somewhat. Not only are there additional large corporations to take into account but also a considerable number of mid-level companies with permanent employees (only a few of which properly belong to the creative industries). As a whole, then, the knowledge and culture economy is not so much a dualism as it is a triadic structure: first, the large corporations, which are often multinational; second, the mid-level organizations, which are mostly regional; and third, the small companies and freelancers. In the creative economy, extremely successful and prestigious types of employment thus exist alongside both mid-level jobs that perpetuate the normal working conditions of highly educated people, and low-paying and precarious types of work. This is to say that the late-modern working world is stratified even *within* the highly qualified labor force.

1
Practices of Labor and Organization in the Creative Economy

Cultural Production as Creative Labor

Modern labor is an instrumentally rational process that typically (but not always, as evidenced by the self-employed) takes place within the framework of organizations. This is also true of the labor involved in producing singular cultural goods in the creative economy. It, too, is based on formal rationalization; it is the goal-oriented, systematic form in which singular goods are produced, and it is governed by the same imperative of optimization that characterized classical modernity. The logic of the general, which continues to exist, forms the background for the creation of singular cultural goods. Over the course of the transformation of industrial production into what I would like to call *cultural production*, however, labor has changed its form. What has emerged is creative labor.[1]

Late-modern working subjects themselves regard the concept of *creative* labor as positive and normative: to be creative and to be able to develop creatively in one's work is seen as an ideal post-industrial professional culture, and this view has been influenced by the post-materialistic shift in values.[2] Unlike the "uncreative" labor of seemingly low-value routine activities, creative labor has an inherent value to those who perform it. In most cases, it is intrinsically motivated, even though it is *also* undertaken as a way to earn income. The highly qualified workforce of late modernity expects more from their labor than merely "earning a living." Creative labor has thus become a cultural practice according to the strong concept of culture.[3] That is, it may have hermeneutic or narrative meaning for those doing it (meaningful or interesting activity); it may have aesthetic qualities (experiencing the flow of production, for instance); it may have ludic qualities or ethical value ("being able to change things"); or it may involve producing novel entities through acts of design.

To work creatively is to work on cultural novelties and singular things, media formats, service relationships, or events. However, cultural production is not exclusively a matter of fabricating novelties; it can also involve tending to familiar classics and brands over the long term. Nevertheless, *permanent innovation* is its central objective. Despite what the term *innovation* suggests, the creative economy is not primarily concerned with what is technically or objectively new (for this might be of a general sort) but rather with cultural novelties as unique entities. The basic problem of creative labor is this: how is novelty brought into the world? How can something original and surprising be created that simultaneously appeals to recipients? In a word, cultural production is *bifocal*: on the one hand, it focuses on goods (things, texts/images/sounds, services, events) as open structures to be shaped; on the other hand, it also focuses on the public, which might potentially engage with these goods and be influenced by them. In the broadest sense, creative labor is thus *design work*, and indeed the concept of design refers precisely to the context of singularizing objects and events, which are open and yet materially bound, in light of their potential recipients.[4]

On account of this structure, creative activity differs significantly from the standardized activity of industrial society. In a sense, the objects of creative labor – things, media, services, events – are "epistemic objects."[5] They are not stable entities like standardized things and services but are rather open and designable cultural entities that are singularized by means of labor. The introduction of new singularities into the world – whether a television program or course of study, a meditation technique or a desk lamp, a party event or a novel, a type of personality coaching or a museum – requires an experimental practice in which new possibilities are discovered and tested. It also entails producing prototypes and testing their viability.[6] A central feature of creative labor is that it depends on having a rich abundance of knowledge about the cultural world, from which to derive inspiration for the production of unique goods. After all, the latter are not created *ex nihilo*. As I pointed out in the previous chapter, new singular goods are often reinterpretations of idiosyncrasies and standardized goods or the result of appropriating non-market-based cultural objects or practices from specific regional or historical contexts. Creative teams thus depend on having direct or indirect access to these cultural worlds. As cultural labor, creative labor therefore always has the nature of research in a broad sense. It is a matter of discovering novelties, exposing traditions, understanding particular contexts, or ascertaining needs.

In certain cases – the classic examples being authors, painters, or composers – singular labor involves only one person working on a project. The majority of labor in the creative economy,

III The Singularization of the Working World 137

however, is performed by creative teams, which have a different interactional and emotional structure from those of traditional industrial employment. Rob Austin and Lee Devin have outlined how teams engaged in cultural production attempt to institutionalize the practice of exploring. This is done by combining allotted slots of creative free time with a form of collaboration in which team members do not critique one another counterproductively but rather collaborate to inspire further ideas. The result is a synergistic collective ensemble with playful elements to it.[7]

The creative team is thus not a system of interchangeable role players with general qualifications, which is familiar from industrial matrix organizations, but rather forms a sort of *plurality of singularities*. What is required of team members is *diversity*,[8] which means that they can each contribute a wide array of cultural resources (from various disciplines, backgrounds, etc.) and personal attributes, which productively supplement and enhance one another. Diversity increases the chances that the collaboration will give rise to new ideas. The subjects working on a team therefore have to be singular themselves, and the hope is that they can collaborate without sacrificing what makes them special. Accordingly, the ideal role of management in this situation is no longer to set the pace and lead a hierarchically divided organization but rather to assemble the most diverse and creative team possible and then take care of its needs.[9]

The development of unique cultural goods by creative teams would be unthinkable without technology. Thus, it would be misguided to perpetuate the long tradition of antagonism between culture and technology, which goes back to the nineteenth century,[10] and claim that cultural production has replaced industrial society's technological orientation toward innovation with a purely immaterial form of fabricating meanings, narratives, and experiences. On the contrary, creative labor depends to a great extent on technologies, and especially on digital media and computer technologies.[11] Computer scientists, engineers, and other technical specialists are also participants in creative working practices, and in some branches they are, indeed, the most important contributors. In cultural production, technologies are not used to establish prescribed parameters; rather, they function as artifact systems that open up *spaces of possibility*, as in the case of computer technology. Beyond that, they can demonstrate the limits within which certain ideas can be realized (in the case of architecture, for instance), but these limits are always renegotiated. Design, which always has to be considered in discussions of culture and materiality, seems to serve as the model for cultural production as a whole.

The exploration and development of new and unique objects and events form just *one* side of singular labor; the *other* involves dealing with and addressing recipients and consumers: the public. Because no good will be regarded as singular until it affects people and is valorized by them (whether by experts or laypeople), cultural production has to anticipate the perspective of the public in a way that was not at all necessary in the case of traditional industrial production. By necessity, then, creative teams are also cultural entrepreneurs ("culturepreneurs"), and a considerable part of cultural production involves studying and mobilizing the public.[12] This is not just a matter of managing existing attention; potential recipients are already on the radar of creative teams during the process of developing goods, either via trend scouts or from other sources of information.[13] In principle, there are three possible strategies for relating to the public: it can be followed, anticipated, or cooperated with. The *trend strategy* of following the public involves tracking the particular desires and ideas of consumers – either through big data or with trend scouts – and transforming these desires and ideas into popular, customer-oriented goods. The *avant-garde strategy* of anticipating recipients consists in creating a unique vision in order to provoke the (perhaps initially skeptical) public to move in a certain direction, and thus either failing or succeeding wildly in doing so. Finally, the *collaboration strategy* of cooperating with the public means that creatives and customers work together to develop a tailored good. In this case, the recipient is thus a *co-creative*. The trend strategy, the avant-garde strategy, and the collaboration strategy are three ways of getting around the uncertainty of singularity markets.

Projects as Heterogeneous Collaborations

In the knowledge and culture economy, labor usually takes place in projects. These are undertaken by individual creative people, but above all by creative teams. In the wake of Luc Boltanski and Ève Chiapello's analysis of project-oriented sociality, which they considered characteristic of the late-modern spirit of capitalism, and a wealth of sociological studies on project-based labor in the knowledge and culture economy, there is now an awareness of the features and challenges of this social form, which has been on the rise not only in the economy of singularities but also in other areas (political projects, social projects, educational projects, personal relationships as projects, etc.).[14] If hierarchical matrix organizations – with their rigid positions, roles, responsibilities, and specialized routines – were the central locus of classical industrial society, then projects are now the emblematic social locus where the economy – and, indeed, the entire society of singularities – is realized on the organizational level.

III The Singularization of the Working World 139

Depending on the type of work and organization, the exact status of projects can vary considerably. A self-employed person can work on one or more projects of her own or can participate in one or more (collective) projects undertaken by one or more organizations. A small company can be fully devoted to just a single project. At large corporations, in contrast, there are usually many different (and often interrelated) projects going on at once, and thus in addition to project structures there is also a more traditional formal (though relatively less hierarchical) organizational structure. Projects can be launched in already existing organizations, but they can also be initiated in entirely new contexts, as in the case of newly formed companies. It is characteristic of the creative economy in general that it is always, and widely, generating new start-ups.

In terms of organizational sociology, Richard A. Goodman and Lawrence P. Goodman defined a project as "a set of diversely skilled people working together on a complex task over a limited period of time."[15] From our perspective, it can be said that projects represent a *singularistic* form of the social *par excellence* and that they have ousted the bureaucratic structure of matrix organizations, with their social logic of the general. This singularism pertains to the levels of time, subjects, and the collective itself, and all three of these levels warrant a closer look.

Whereas traditional organizations are oriented toward long-term durability and reproduction, the most prominent feature of projects is their *time limits*. Projects are episodes with a beginning and an end, and thus they have the character of an *event* in a broad sense of the term. In addition, projects are highly open to the new and unexpected (including the reality that certain ideas might be dead ends), and they form a narrative arc. A project begins with an exploratory initial phase, moves into a phase of research and testing with feedback loops, and ends with an especially intense final phase. This is followed by a feeling of collective relief, the presentation of the project's results, and possibly by a euphoric and exhausting post-production phase.[16] Often, the participants in the project consciously experience each of these phases in their respective *presentness*. Despite all the routine tasks that of course come up in any project, every project nevertheless unfolds differently and is perceived as being inherently complex to a high degree. From the perspective of its participants, the specific narrative structure of beginning, middle, and end thus lends it affective density. Although the glorification of enthusiasm is certainly something that distinguishes project work from the monotony of routine tasks, there is more to it than that. Here, the affectivity can be contradictory: projects can undoubtedly involve phases of collective or individual enthusiasm, but they are also venues of social drama, subtle or obvious competition, and feelings of failure and inadequacy.

The singularistic structure of projects extends to the level of subjects and the collective. As mentioned above, projects are ensembles of "diversely skilled people" who, as a creative team, form a plurality of singularities. Counter to the logic of the division of labor, project teams work "hand in hand" on a complex task. Projects thus rely on an ensemble of different personalities with diverse cultural and mental resources, who either supplement one another or create a sort of productive tension. That the subjects working on a project do not act as functional role players but as singularities is also due to the fact that, in addition to their formal qualifications, this context depends on their *entire personalities*, complete with their cultural, social, and emotional competencies and experiences. The plurality of singularities is not a mere aggregation of subjective individual traits; it is a cooperative or (even better) a *collaborative plurality*. The collaborators pursue a common objective. Projects are thus an example of a social form that I would like to call *heterogeneous collaboration*.[17] This is significant in late-modern culture as a whole. The concept of collaboration implies a common praxis that is both goal-oriented *and* imbued with inherent cultural value and affective density. Understood as a praxis of *working together*, collaboration is thus a stronger and more specific concept than interaction, communication, or cooperation, each of which has a rich history of its own in sociology.[18] On the one hand, projects are temporary purposive associations that typically work toward a single goal. For their participants, on the other hand, they have inherent value in themselves while they are being worked on: they represent a cultural praxis in the strong sense, with narrative, design, ethical, ludic, and even aesthetic qualities. As a form of *heterogeneous* collaboration, however, the project depends on the heterogeneity of its individual members – on the plurality of singularities. To an extent, heterogeneous collaborations play around with the uniqueness and diversity of their temporary members.

The project is also singularistically structured by the fact that it *itself* becomes singular as a *collective* unit. It is decidedly more than the sum of its parts, which means that it is more than just the aggregation of the people (and things) participating in it. This collective singularity can perhaps best be described with a concept borrowed from the theater: the *ensemble*.[19] An ensemble is composed of highly different personalities, and at the same time it is that which these people are working on: the unique achievement of their specific collaboration. Collaboration gives rise to a third, emergent level of the social in the form of praxis, which is itself just as singular as the interplay between *these* individuals at *this* point in time. To some degree, the project is an ensemble achievement with an ensemble experience.[20] Of course, projects are always in danger of

III The Singularization of the Working World 141

not satisfying the criteria of the social logic of the particular. As in the case of objects, people, or places, the threat of de-singularization always looms. When they no longer seem to be singular, they lose their value; they are de-valorized and can at best be thought of as useful. At that point, however, they are no longer projects but rather just formal and rational collectives with a purpose. A de-singularization of this sort can happen on all three levels: from the fact that the temporal structure of the project has become routine and monotone; from the fact that its subjects were too similar and prone to conformist groupthink to begin with; or, finally, from the fact that the level of the collective has unintentionally devolved into a general organizational structure with rigid hierarchies and divisions of labor.

Organizational Cultures and Networks

With the analysis of projects as heterogeneous collaborations, we have reached an important point in our study of the economic sphere. For, fundamentally, the question arises of which form *the social* takes in a society that singularizes itself. Singularity markets provided us with one answer to this question, and projects a second. We have seen that public markets of attention and valorization can be interpreted as genuine social platforms for singularities. And we have seen that projects represent a second, though differently structured, form of social singularity, namely that of heterogeneous collaborations. Heterogeneous collaborations are likewise platforms for singularities, but the latter operate here in a different way: not in the mode of competing for attention but rather in the mode of working together. Unlike the case of anonymous markets, moreover, projects as heterogeneous collaborations can themselves become singular social units. They are not only platforms *for* singularities but are *themselves* singularities to the extent that, as ensembles, they form something unique and, as such, possess cultural and affective value.[21]

Both within the economic sector and outside it, attraction markets and heterogeneous collaborations thus represent two alternative singularistic forms of the social. They are not necessarily in conflict with one another – rather, in the economic sphere (and elsewhere, for instance in the realm of politics) they are interlinked. After all, the singular goods that arise from projects often find themselves on attraction markets. Usually, projects have an ambivalent relationship to markets: internally, on account of their structure of affective collaboration, they are relatively autonomous from markets; as part of organizations for which they produce singular goods, however, they present these cultural goods on markets, where the goods in question will compete for attention and valorization. At the same time, the members of a project are drawn from labor markets, which themselves have the character of profile competitions. As already mentioned, the proliferation of heterogeneous collaborations has not changed the fact that, even in the late-modern knowledge and culture economy, they are typically embedded within the framework of organizations. However, the status of the bureaucratic structures of organizations has changed. Now they rather form an institutional background structure that places financial means, space, and personnel at the disposal of project teams; provides them with external contacts; and offers them administrative support. Here, the institutional logic of the general is a condition that enables the logic of the particular to flourish.[22]

Along with cultural singularity markets and projects, it is possible to identify two additional singularistic forms of the social that have spread in the late-modern economy. First, a *culturalization of organizations* themselves has taken place, and this has affected both their organizational culture in the strong sense and their dependence on specific locations. Second, in addition to projects, there is another subtype of heterogeneous collaborations that deserves special attention: *networks*.

In late modernity, organizations have attempted to culturalize and singularize *themselves*, and they have attempted to do so not only externally (that is, by tending to their brands) but also internally (that is, in their own practices and for their employees). What they have developed is *organizational culture*, a concept that has been circulating in the management discourse since the 1980s.[23] Even if "organizational culture" is often just a trite slogan, it is important not to overlook the actual ways in which late-modern organizations have attempted to model themselves as singular and specifically identifiable ensembles. In order to be regarded as having intrinsic value, organizations put on a show of uniqueness for their employees by developing common rituals and holding extraordinary events; by cultivating a cultural memory and a corresponding storyline about the company, its outstanding figures, and its history; by designing their facilities in an aesthetically pleasing manner; by coaching and further developing the skills of their staff; by maintaining a diverse workforce; by allowing employees to take time off to pursue their own creative endeavors, etc.[24]

Beyond this, ties to specific *locations* have had a singularizing effect on late-modern organizational culture. Whereas large industrial companies were not bound to specific places or meaningfully attached to them, organizations in the knowledge and culture economy are much more firmly anchored to specific locations. The irreplaceability of a given area is related to the unique nature of its creative cluster and to the features of the city or region itself: its

III The Singularization of the Working World

scenes and milieus, its facilities (education, cultural institutions), and its geographical location.[25] Creative clusters are location-specific contexts of communication for cultural enterprises and also represent strategic spaces in which different offices can collaborate with one another, have access to gatekeepers, and continue to make profitable contacts. Ultimately, the creative potential of the knowledge and culture economy is highly dependent on tapping into the relevant cultural currents that are circulating in society, and these currents are consolidated in particular metropolitan regions. The singularity of a location is thus a crucial component of the identity of the creative economy and its mode of operation.

Along with creative clusters, there is an additional social form that has become central to the economy and society of singularities: *networks*. Various sociological analyses have shown that networks should be treated as an independent form of sociality that is fundamentally distinct from the market and from forms of bureaucratic hierarchy and has acquired enormous significance in late-modern society, not least within the framework of the post-Fordistic economy.[26] As mentioned above, networks can be interpreted as a further variant of heterogeneous collaborations, but their emphasis differs from that of projects. In the economy of singularities, networks play a role on two levels in particular: as networks of organizations and as networks of working subjects. It has often been claimed that the organizations and projects of late-modernity are not isolated but are rather integrated in corporate or institutional networks that cooperate with one another in various ways.[27] In addition, social networks are just as important for self-employed people and creative businesses as they are for any employee with changing aspirations. They are networks of relationships based on familiarity and mutual appreciation that can potentially be mobilized when it comes to finding work on new projects.[28] Projects profit both from the networks of the organization as a whole and from the networks of their individual members. As a social form, networks thus have a variety of specific features: they are cooperative relationships between various entities (subjects, organizations) that are characterized by their potential. They *can* be used to one's benefit, but they do not have to be. What prevails here is the famous "strength of weak ties," which means that casual connections can be enormously effective.[29] Networks are dynamic and open-ended: they can easily change by gaining new participants (or as others become less important) and they can potentially be transformed into actual collaborations. The relationships are non-exclusive, and the relations between a network's nodal points are in principle cooperative and non-hierarchical.

Networks are thus a form of the social that is singularistically structured in two respects. On the one hand, they are a form of heterogeneous collaboration, and on the other hand they are a background structure for singularities. The significance of social networks lies in the fact that their interconnected elements are not examples of a general structure but are, instead, unique, and it is for this reason alone that they are interesting network partners. Therefore, social networks are essentially based on the diversity of their participants. Moreover, every organization and every working subject creates a network of their own, so no two are alike. For this reason, too, networks qualify as a variety of heterogeneous collaboration, for each of their elements – as in the case of projects – cooperates with others in a unique way. They are likewise a combination of instrumental rationality and inherent cultural value. Networks differ from projects, however, because they are comparatively less affective and because they attract less attention. This has an important consequence. Whereas, on the collective level, projects are *themselves* singularities and are experienced as such by their participants, networks typically lack the collective identity needed to become a collective singularity. Instead, they are *background structures for the development of singularities*,[30] which means that they are infrastructures for particular projects, subjects, or goods.

2
The Singularization and Self-Singularization of Working Subjects

Beyond the Formalization of Labor

With the project-based labor of the knowledge and culture economy, a fundamental structural shift has taken place in the ways that working subjects shape themselves and are shaped by others.[1] One important aspect has already been mentioned: today, labor is associated with strong intrinsic motivation. What is more, the subject is *expected* to develop such motivation. From the perspective of subjects, the (highly qualified) labor in late modernity is, to a considerable extent, something to be identified with: expecting more than just to earn a living, people are looking for a specific quality of work.[2] Intrinsic motivation is not, however, just a private matter for individual employees – rather, it is a built-in requirement of culturalized labor. It has superseded industrial society's extrinsic motivation for working as a means to an end: income, security, status – though this latter motivation, of course, still exists.[3] In addition to this shift in the motivational structure of work, there has also been a fundamental transformation in the system of subjectification. With respect to working subjects, industrial society's *system of formalization* is increasingly being replaced by a *system of singularization*. In short, whereas the industrial labor system was based on qualifications, achievement, and positions / functional roles, the post-industrial labor system is based on the criteria of competence/ potential, profiles, and performance.

The formal rationalization of the working world, which prevailed from the beginning of the twentieth century into the 1970s, was characterized by the basic structures of what constituted a working subject in classical modernity. This was a matter of a comprehensive system of formalized and standardized labor. *Formal qualifications* were central to the hiring practices of industrial organizations. Diplomas, degrees, or certificates from various sorts of educational institutions (and the grades that one earned there) formed the basis of job applications and job placement. Employees thus had to pass through a crucial filter before entering the workforce: the *examination*, which verified their qualifications.

Within these organizations, working subjects then occupied permanent *positions*, for which their education made them formally qualified. These positions usually involved clear and well-defined tasks. Here, the employee took on a *functional role*, which could essentially be fulfilled by any other person with the same formal qualifications (in principle, that is, any employee could easily be replaced). Expected *achievements* were unrelated to the unique characteristics of employees and were understood as objective work results (products, services, etc.). In the classical "achievement society," the evaluation of accomplishments and higher compensation occurred gradually: higher qualifications, better achievement, and greater output were honored accordingly. In this light, professional biographies had the temporal structure of a relatively predictable *career path*. After one's education – and often regardless of one's later achievements – what took place was a more or less steady and typically formalized rise through the ranks.

The system of standardized and formalized labor could be seen as the epitome of modernity's social logic of the general. Within this framework, working subjects fulfilled the general requirements of their qualifications and positions. It could essentially be assumed that people with the same qualifications and the same professional objectives would achieve the same results at work. Within this system, the differences between working subjects were of a gradual nature. Of course, the system of standardized labor implemented by the "achievement society" is an ideal type. Even at the height of Fordism in the West and state socialism in the East, the reality in organizations was more complicated.[4] Nevertheless, one can safely say that this system of labor represented one of classical modernity's basic frameworks. In the leveled middle-class society, it was the basis of professional achievement and pride on *every* level, and it also served to balance out inequalities.

As it has been increasingly implemented since the 1980s in the knowledge and culture economy, and thus in the entire field of highly qualified work, late modernity's system of singularized labor represents something entirely different. In this new system of evaluation, working subjects are recognized for their singularity; they present themselves as unique and are shaped as such by organizations and networks. The employee has become a *collaborator* whose particular personality is valorized and utilized. Uniqueness is no longer a source of disruption or a condition treated with indifference – rather, it is systematically *cultivated*. Instead of the fulfillment of duties and average productivity, what is now expected is extraordinary performances that "make a difference." On the one

III The Singularization of the Working World   147

hand, this singularization proceeds from organizations, projects, networks, and markets. An entire catalogue of social requirements insists that we all become singular collaborators who accomplish extraordinary feats. On the other hand, the singularization of late-modern working subjects is often desired and fueled by the subjects themselves: they no longer want to be bureaucratic pencil-pushers or mere workers but, instead, creative individuals who live up to their potential. Self-singularization and external forces of singularization are therefore interrelated.

The Profile Subject: Competencies and Talents

In the system of singularized labor, formal qualifications have become subordinate to what is often referred to as *competencies*.[5] Of course, formal qualifications continue to play a role, and some of them (high-school diplomas, university degrees) are still expected for many activities in the knowledge and culture economy. However, they are now just a necessary *precondition* for an initial selection process. They are not enough in themselves, for what really sets candidates apart for employment, status, and success is the uniqueness of their *informal competencies*. For project work, it is fundamentally assumed that what is *truly* necessary are capabilities that go beyond any formally verifiable qualifications. These include, for instance, social and emotional competence, the ability to work in a group and be enthusiastic about new things, entrepreneurial competence (which means having a sense for favorable opportunities and being willing to take chances), and creative competence. Beyond all the general "key competencies," working subjects are expected to possess a level of competence that is somehow special. This has to be a unique *set of competencies* that combines diverse and valuable abilities in a particular way. In other words, the working subject has to develop a visible and non-interchangeable *profile*.[6]

In general, the format of the profile is fundamental to the subjectification of the late-modern self.[7] In the economy of singularities as well (and especially so), subjects are *profile subjects*. The "profile" is a metaphor from physiognomy: whoever has a profile is as clearly and sharply contoured as the silhouette of his or her face viewed from the side. In its transferred meaning, the profile thus designates the unique combination of an individual's various attributes, which at the same time create an identifiable whole. This is to say that, inwardly, the profile has a high degree of inherent complexity, and that, outwardly, it showcases someone's otherness and distinctness: it contains features of the singular. The profile is thus always a product of social ascription – both ascription by others and self-ascription. In order to be recognized as singular, competencies have to possess two contradictory characteristics: *well-roundedness* and *coherence*. Conversely, this means that a profile in the late-modern working world runs the risk of being de-singularized if it is either too one-sided or incoherent.

Well-roundedness is a central requirement of the competencies of working subjects. In light of post-materialistic values, which contain traces of the idealistic holistic personality, it is also something that is appreciated and sought after. To some extent, well-roundedness relates to the requirement of diversity, which enhances organizational culture, and to the inner structure of the subject. Such well-roundedness cannot exist unless the subject goes beyond formal qualifications and acquires a breadth of informal competencies. Conversely, it is disadvantageous for a co-worker to seem one-dimensional or appear to have a "flat character." Though such a one-dimensional employee would have thrived in an industrial organization, today he or she would flounder and strike people as a formally qualified but uninspired one-track specialist.

A cluster of competencies, in contrast, ideally combines multiple facets of cognitive, social, creative, entrepreneurial, and cultural competence into a unique form. Even a particular sort of cognitive expertise – knowledge of Japanese, a vast familiarity with art history, or a certain form of subcultural expertise, for instance – can develop significance within the framework of an overall profile, namely as an additional and highly *unusual* component of someone's set of competencies. Working subjects usually do not acquire such abilities through their formal education but rather through a particular praxis and real-life experiences, whether outside or inside of work ("on-the-job training"). In order to build an attractive profile, it is thus essential to have a variety of skills and a whole palette of interesting or intensive professional and non-professional experiences. In late-modern working culture, such things are always showcased on the CVs of high-potential employees; to expert job applicants, they lend something unusual and serve as a "distinguishing feature." In this sense, profiles can be enhanced by one's experience on various projects in various professional contexts as well as by internships abroad, social or political engagement, or special hobbies. All of these activities and the experiences associated with them contribute to rounding out the personality of the working subject. Although they were of little if any significance to the "organization man" of industrial society, they are indispensable to working subjects in the society of singularities.

On its own, however, well-roundedness is insufficient. In order for a profile to be recognized as singular, it also has to have a perceptible degree of *coherence*. Otherwise, you might be dealing with a subject who is easily distracted, erratic, or arbitrary – with someone who is difficult to figure out and perhaps lacks determination. If a

III The Singularization of the Working World 149

heterogeneous set of competencies forms a coherent whole, however, then the profile will be identifiable as such right away; it may appear to suit the needs of an organization and even prove to be the decisive factor in hiring decisions. In other words, the profiles of singular working subjects need to have a recognizable "common thread," which could take the form of a personal vision, a life theme, or an ultimate goal.

In the late-modern culture of highly qualified labor, there is not only a competition involving competencies but also one involving *talents*. Their demonstrable abilities aside, subjects can become singular through the *potential* that others see in them. The concept of "talent" was at first confined primarily to the field of art. In the economy of singularities, however, it has developed into a general category with which subjects are assessed not only according to their present capabilities but also according to their potential to accomplish something extraordinary in the future. In many respects, the late-modern economy of highly skilled labor is thus a *talent economy*.[8] Whereas the notions of talent and potential must have seemed eccentric to the professional world of industrial society, the economy of singularities is imbued with more than just the rhetoric of talent – think of Tom Peters and Robert Waterman's often-cited discussion of the "war of talents"[9] – and the rhetoric of potential ("high potential"). This discourse goes hand in hand with a potential-oriented practice of subjectification that is consistent with an economy that, faced with an open future, produces more and more new and surprising singular goods, is reliant on more and more new creative teams, and is always recruiting more and more young personnel.

The development of profiles and that of potential are therefore both based on a dual structure of self-singularization and external singularization. On the labor market and in the networks and projects of cultural capitalism, working subjects *develop* a profile because they see this as their only chance to be perceived as unique and (therefore) employable. Instilled with a post-materialistic work ethic, however, they often also do this because they wish to have experiences and to acquire skills that will allow them to actualize themselves as unique personalities. On the other side, the organizations of the knowledge and culture economy *expect* such profiles and potential from their collaborators. Depending on the case at hand, the type of profile expected by an organization can be more open-ended (someone who can provide a creative spark at work, though he or she must be "brilliant") or more specific (someone who convincingly combines exactly these three skills...). There is thus a competition between various profiles as well as over whose profile best suits an organization's complex needs. Highly qualified working subjects thus have no choice but to accumulate *singularity capital* if they want to have success on the job market.[10]

Labor as Performance

In the singularistic working culture, profiles, sets of competencies, potential, and talent are tied to the expectation that they will translate into performance. Whereas, in the logic of formalization, employees in permanent positions were measured according to their objective *achievements*, the success of working subjects in the logic of singularity depends on their unique *performance*. The semantics of performance is ubiquitous in the late-modern economy: markets, companies, projects, and not least working subjects are all spoken about in terms of their performance.[11] At least for highly qualified individuals in the knowledge and culture economy, the praxis of late-modern working culture has been reorienting itself more and more toward the format of performance and away from objective achievement. In the model of achievement, the results of one's labor could be classified according to criteria of ostensibly objective correctness, quantity, or quality, and no public audience played any role in this whatsoever. There was a direct connection between the result of labor and the process of its completion – for instance in the form of hours worked, a method of necessary steps, or particular amounts of physical or mental exertion – and this correlation made it easily possible to compare the work of different employees. Achievement belonged to the logic of the general.

The model of labor as performance is quite different.[12] It is not measured according to the standard of objective correctness but is, instead, evaluated according to its success. It belongs to the social logic of the particular. As we have already seen in the case of singular goods, what makes a successful performance is its positive valorization by an audience. This applies similarly to the specific good of labor. In the broadest sense, performances involve showcasing something to an audience; the latter does not classify anything but rather allows itself to be affected and assigns value (or not). In this sense, a performance is *successful* if its audience regards it as singular. Whereas an achievement can be good or even above average, a performance can seem unique and thus extraordinary. The flipside of valorizing only unique and extraordinary performances is the utter devaluation of that which is merely average.

An audience is just as unpredictable in its evaluations of one's performance at work as it is in evaluating (different) singular goods. It is a not a neutral authority; its attention is divided asymmetrically; it often valorizes unique entities on the basis of implicit criteria; and, not least, it *experiences* performance as a sensuous

III The Singularization of the Working World 151

and affective event. In terms of ideal types, it is possible to distinguish two different constellations. In the first, the economic good is identical with the singular performance of working subjects. In this sense, actors, singers, therapists, authors, and architects are *performance workers* – essentially, their labor amounts to putting on a performance for their audience, which is its immediate demander and consumer. In the other extreme case, the performance remains internal to an organization. Here the audience consists of colleagues who are not just members of an audience but are also, to some extent, fellow performers on the same stage. Everyone is performing for and with one another. In this case, the audience of the performance is not necessarily the consumer, but this does not make the matter any easier. As Christiane Funken, Jan-Christoph Rogge, and Sinje Hörlin have shown, those working on projects within organizations are faced with considerably high expectations to perform.[13] The collaborators on these projects have to demonstrate which competencies they truly possess, what sort of potential they really have, and what they can actually contribute to the group as a whole.

Essentially, performances make manifest all the competencies and potential that a given working subject might have. In order for performances to succeed, however, they also need another attribute that, as we have already seen, is likewise important in the case of singular goods: authenticity. In late modernity, working subjects have to convey the image of authentic personality; they have to leave the impression that they are genuine and thus "being themselves." In order for a performance to succeed, it has to be experienced as a *natural* singularity. Even though every performance is staged, it has to seem as though this is not the case. As in the case of profiles, performances suffer if they are one-sided or incoherent. By this point, at least, it has become clear that the professional performances of working subjects also involve a number of their personal characteristics, though of course only those features that are generally considered positive: charm and wit, physical attractiveness, hospitality and the ability to listen, a pleasant personality, tolerance and enthusiasm, etc. In the late-modern working world, character traits have become professional assets.[14]

In an organization's hiring process, a candidate's performance takes on a fateful significance. This is the *constellation of casting* that is ubiquitous in late-modern culture.[15] This concept, which originally stems from the film industry, is far better suited to describe the selection process in today's knowledge and culture economy than the traditional examination. Whereas examinations prove someone's knowledge, casting involves a sort of test performance under conditions of extreme competition. Potential collaborators (and therefore competitors) are now "on the runway" of an organization, where they have to demonstrate their unique qualities. Whereas the results of an examination can be determined more or less objectively, the judgement of a performance depends much more strongly on implied and subjective criteria – and to a great extent on the "gut feeling" of the jury (that is, on intuitive and emotionally colored knowledge). A candidate either has "that certain something" or "doesn't have it." Casting involves more than just one person presenting his or her personality; what is decisive is the personal way that the decision-makers *experience* a job candidate's presentation.[16]

Objective achievement was tied to a professional position with defined activities and tasks, regular working hours, and a fixed workplace. In the creative economy, such positions have been replaced by performances. Organizations no longer want people to fill clearly defined positions but rather to produce convincing and extraordinary results. This is not a matter of checking items off of a set list of activities – rather, working subjects are themselves responsible for figuring out how best to proceed. The traditional format of the *profession* is being replaced by highly general, variable, and results-oriented job descriptions. Traditional working hours have also lost their function: when, where, and how long someone works was once a central issue of the old logic of achievement. In the case of a successful performance, on the contrary, it is essentially irrelevant whether someone works at night or while on a vacation, or whether someone works extremely long hours or with unbelievable efficiency.

Because late modernity's working culture is oriented toward performance, it is, as Sighard Neckel has rightly pointed out, less and less a culture of "achievement" and increasingly a culture of "success."[17] From our perspective, however, what is decisive is that this shift from criteria of achievement to criteria of success is essentially a result of the cultural economization of the working world and its remodeling into an economy of singularities. In general, *success* means that something has simply been valued on the market – for whatever reasons and regardless of objective achievement. In the context of cultural economization, success means that an audience (whether within an organization or outside one) has appreciated one's performance as singular.

It is no surprise that the transition from the achievement society to the success economy has also been accompanied by a transformation of the labor market – a transformation that unfolded much like the structural shift from functional to singular goods described above. In industrial modernity, the hiring of employees often took place bureaucratically on the basis of formal qualifications. Within such organizations, the fulfillment of tasks *by* every individual employee was typically detached from any competitive logic *between* them. The subsequent differentiation of a seemingly endless number of individual profiles, however, has gradually given

III The Singularization of the Working World

rise to a hypercompetitive struggle for visibility and appreciation, and this has affected the labor market as well. It is impossible to predict which profile will be positively valorized and successful, and any commitment to a particular profile – both on the part of the working subject *and* on the part of organizations – contains an element of speculation. The question of whether a certain profession, skill set, or profile "has a future," which would have been atypical in industrial society, is characteristic of the economy of singularities.[18] At the same time, the orientation of working subjects toward performance *within* organizations means that workplaces, too, are characterized by a constant state of competition. Employees can no longer simply rest on their laurels when their future performance is always expected to be unique. This uncertainty is reduced considerably, however, for those who have already made a *name* for themselves. What is true of the performance of cultural goods applies just as well to the performance of working subjects: past performance can cause someone (or something) to build a reputation and a name. If someone already has a big name on account of a previous outstanding performance, this is suggestive of his or her *irreplaceability*.

The Singularization Techniques of Labor

Late-modern working culture has developed specific singularization techniques in an attempt to provide a practical answer to two of its fundamental problems. First, on what basis should the quality of working subjects be evaluated? Second, in what ways can the valued singularity of working subjects be further perfected? Let us look at the social practices and structures that have been developed to address these two issues.

In this regard, an important role is played by the aforementioned *social networks*, which themselves function as a form of singularization technology.[19] The notorious problem of uncertainty, which characterizes the competencies and potential of possible collaborators, can be overcome by organizations and projects if they can count on the personal recommendations available on networks regarding the abilities of a given job candidate. Networks provide knowledge about the unique skills of potential employees, at least so long as the latter are well networked. Working subjects can singularize themselves on social networks by building a reputation, and project leaders and organizations tend to hire collaborators whose reliability has already been demonstrated in other contexts. Since the 1980s, a striking normative shift has taken place in the way that social networks function in the professional world. In the working culture of late modernity, networking is no longer a matter of "back-room politics" but has become an essential factor in overcoming the problem of uncertainty when it comes to hiring decisions. In fact, networking itself has become an indispensable skill for late-modern working subjects, who rely on it to cultivate their visibility and reputation.

Another important role in today's singularistic working culture is played by a similarly informal factor, and one that could not differ more blatantly from the traditional logic of achievement: *embodied cultural capital*.[20] If, aside from their formal qualifications, the success of late-modern working subjects depends on their authentic and yet multifaceted personality, then this raises two questions: under what conditions do they *acquire* the personal characteristics that predestine them for singularity? And at what point do they *qualify* as being suitably profiled and authentic in the eyes of organizations and project leaders? The first question has long been central to the field of educational sociology, which has attempted to determine the extent to which cultural backgrounds play a role in the acquisition of formal educational qualifications.[21] Yet the issue of background is even more relevant when it comes to the personality traits that make people seem singular and are required of highly qualified workers in the knowledge and culture economy – characteristics such as emotional competence, originality, wide-ranging interests, cosmopolitanism, and an entrepreneurial spirit. In large part, these key competencies derive from what Pierre Bourdieu referred to as "embodied cultural capital," which is acquired primarily through one's background, family, and (adolescent and post-adolescent) peer groups.[22]

This sort of cultural capital, which features above all in educated milieus,[23] encourages people to develop multifaceted personalities (with experience abroad, social engagement, interests in pop culture) and helps to create the fragile balance between concentration and nonchalance that the creative economy appreciates and requires in so many branches. In other words, it fosters the refined mixture of confidence and self-questioning – a fondness for experimentation and a subtle interest in profiling – that the performance economy expects. Endowed with the proper amount of embodied cultural capital, a working subject can operate in the knowledge and culture economy with the sort of self-confidence and self-understanding that is appealing to organizations and projects. Positive valorization and the experience of authenticity are more likely when people share the same cultural background and experiences: they will have the "right chemistry." One may appreciate the singularity of a co-worker, but it has to be an *acceptable* and seemingly valuable form of uniqueness – the sort that is compatible with the context of a museum, an advertising agency, a university, a tech company, a top-ranked restaurant, and so on.

III The Singularization of the Working World 155

In addition to these informal singularization techniques, the working culture of late modernity also makes use of highly rationalized and reflexive methods of singularization. As I have already pointed out, late-modern organizations are and remain objects and agents of decidedly formal rationalization, which means that they aim to optimize processes and competencies. Organizations direct this optimization toward themselves, toward their employees, and toward their processes, but working subjects also strive for optimization – namely to optimize themselves. In this case too, however, the rationality of means to an end has changed its form. It no longer serves to create uniform working subjects but has rather become a general infrastructure for promoting and identifying singular employees and job candidates. A good example of this is the format of human resource management (HRM). This management technique, which is based on the idea of human capital, focuses on both current and potential collaborators.[24] It involves using a combination of qualitative and quantitative methods for continuously assessing and promoting the competencies and potential of every individual (and for controlling their further development). HRM is a singularization technique to the extent that it combines two forms of problematization with one another. On the one hand, it is concerned with strategically and technically promoting employees as unique clusters of competencies and talents. On the other hand, it transfers the register of singularities into the register of the general-particular: clusters of competencies are broken apart into discrete and prescribed abilities (entrepreneurial activity, social-communicative capabilities, etc.), which can then be differentiated according to the criteria of "more" or "less."

A second reflexive technique of singularization concerns the self-guidance of working subjects in the form of *personality-oriented coaching*.[25] This is no longer just a matter of providing general recipes for self-management; rather, it involves analyzing the complex capabilities and desires of individual personalities in order to discover untapped potential, to refine and develop personal visions, and to figure out alternatives, opportunities, and risks with the aim of developing career strategies. With its goal of empowerment, personality-oriented coaching is thus always suspended in a field of tension between promoting personal growth (a concept strongly influenced by humanistic psychology) and strategically planning for success. In general, predictable and gradual professional tracks have been replaced in late-modern working culture by the *career* – in the sense of "forging a career" out of a jagged sequence of interruptions and detours. A decisive quality of late-modern careers is the unique and incomparable path that everyone takes from one step to the next – a sort of professional development that was previously familiar from the fields of art and showbusiness. Careers are the result of a contingent patchwork of profiles, potential, decisions, market circumstances, networking, performance, and coincidence.[26] Individuals turn to coaching in an effort to find strategies for planning the unplannable.

Fields of Tension in Highly Qualified Labor: Between the Artist's Dilemma and the Superstar Economy

The singularistic working culture, which has defined highly qualified labor since the beginning of the twenty-first century, has resulted in a number of paradoxes, contradictions, and tensions. Foremost among these is the tension between creative labor's aspiration for intrinsic value and the entrenchment of this aspiration in hyper-competitive market structures.[27] In that the late-modern working world has undergone the process of cultural economization described above, it is now at a place where historically unprecedented culturalization happens to intersect with an intense and equally unusual process of marketization. Without the economy of singularities, a post-materialistic work ethic never could have established itself as a culture of self-actualization, and creative labor never would have been possible to such a great extent. We have also seen, however, that the working subjects who attempt to enter the knowledge and culture economy, or simply preserve their positions there, are met with highly unpredictable markets and audiences.

The labor and the profiles of subjects are therefore caught in a double bind: work is supposed to have intrinsic value and create satisfaction as autonomous activity, but at the same time it is only successful when it satisfies the fickle demands of markets and the fluctuating expectations of the public. For the working subject, the acquisition of competencies and potential is supposed to be a matter of personal development, and yet at the same time it is necessary to develop a profile with unique features in order to score points in organizations and on the market. Accordingly, the relation of working subjects to one another is characterized by a tension between collaboration and competition: on the one hand, social networks and the team culture of projects promote a culture of intensive collaboration and cooperation; at the same time, however, working subjects are constantly engaged in a merciless profile competition with one another.

Ultimately, the late-modern knowledge and culture economy is thus characterized by an updated version of the *artist's dilemma* that first emerged in the nineteenth-century art world.[28] The rise of the modern, autonomous artist and the formation of an anonymous public took place at the same time. Artistic subjects thus developed two conflicting orientations: toward their work in itself, and toward

III The Singularization of the Working World 157

its evaluation on the market. Moreover, the relationship among artists was defined from the beginning by both mutual inspiration and fierce competition. The working culture of the creative economy has now elevated this dilemma to a more general level. This often results in a paradox: the competencies that are dearest to a subject's heart might not be suitable for a marketable profile and, conversely, the development of such a profile might indeed guarantee status and success, but doubts might remain about whether one's true potential has been reached. Regarding the relationship between working subjects, if the collaboration is too unselfish, then profile-building will suffer, but if the profile-building is too aggressive, then the collaboration and the entire project will suffer.[29] It is an open question whether this tension necessarily has to be perceived as such by working subjects or whether the working culture of the twenty-first century has developed hybrid formats that can accommodate both self-worth and the demands of the market. It is conceivable that social networks and projects can be fields of both collaboration *and* competition, and thus that they can represent a practice of *coopetition* that goes beyond the traditional opposition between cooperation and competition.[30] Moreover, the fact that goods address consumers does not necessarily mean that autonomous expression is taken out of the equation. At its heart, *design work* is based on a model of *bound creativity*, which involves cooperating with recipients and users.

Unintended consequences and open questions result not only from the relationship between culturalization and marketization, but also from the internal logic of both of these processes. The culturalization of labor, which has turned work into one of the main sources of a meaningful life, not only increases our satisfaction on the job but also tends to encourage *self-exploitation* in a typically late-modern way.[31] This is reflected in the qualitative and quantitative temporal expansion of work into private lives. This, too, is a blatant difference from traditional normal working conditions, whose emphasis on the extrinsic motivation of status and income may seem culturally and emotionally lacking in retrospect, but which had the advantage of limited working hours and allowed employees to create distance between their lives at home and at the office. The intrinsic satisfaction of work contains the risk that the work itself will no longer have any limits and that working subjects will have nowhere to retreat on account of the disappearing distance between professional self-actualization and personal identity.

Yet the logic of radical competition, which characterizes the performance economy, is also full of tension. It leads to the extremely asymmetrical distribution of prestige and income between highly qualified working subjects. I have already discussed the logic of winner-take-all competitions as it relates to the market for singular cultural goods. The corresponding competitive logic of a *superstar economy* also exists in relation to working subjects, and its form can be more or less drastic depending on the creative branch in question. This leads to radical asymmetries between a few highly successful individuals (in the extreme case: stars) and the many largely replaceable people who either have a mid-level position in an organization or work precariously from one contract to the next.[32] The superstar economy is clearest to see in the arts, in showbusiness, and in professional sports – that is, in small but highly visible fields. However, the asymmetries of the singularity economy are not limited to the publicly visible performances of individuals (football players, film directors, and so on) but can also be found in the polarization between *organizations* – with global corporations and elite institutions at the top – as well as in the differences in performance and status that exist between similarly qualified employees *within* organizations, with their asymmetries between "high potentials" and "water boys."[33]

From the perspective of the industrial society's norms of justice, the superstar economy and its excessive rewards for singular performances seem irritating or even scandalous, and this is for three reasons that I have already mentioned in part. First, it is now the case that different individuals with the same formal qualifications and the same type of job (lawyers, computer scientists, journalists, architects, artists, etc.) can have drastically different levels of success on the market. This leads to inconsistent levels of status, with some people earning a great deal and others very little. Second, professional success has been decoupled from work effort (hours worked, job commitment, etc.). In only slightly exaggerated terms, whoever has talent (phenomenal potential and competence) and luck (the right market niche) can easily outstrip many others who are working just as hard. Third, and finally, to a neutral observer of the singularity economy, it will appear as though slight and subtle differences in performance somehow translate into an absolute, qualitative polarity between winners and losers.

However, the orientation of the economy of singularities toward successful performance is entirely consistent with its internal logic.[34] Unlike achievement, performance hinges on the response of an audience, and this is a crucial difference. *For the audience*, the slight differences between A and B detected by a neutral observer are *not* slight at all, but rather determine the value and affective quality of the performance as a whole. For the audience, the singularity of a performance is the only thing that is interesting; from this perspective, formal qualifications and work effort are merely incidental. This logic of assessment can be illustrated quite clearly with the extreme example of the art world. According to the rationalistic logic of achievement, the works of highly esteemed artists such as Wolfgang

III The Singularization of the Working World

Amadeus Mozart, Gustave Flaubert, Michelangelo Antonioni, Neo Rauch, or Jonathan Franzen may seem to differ only slightly from the works of many other composers, novelists, filmmakers, and painters who never became superstars. From the perspective of the logic of singularities, however, the fascinating and affective originality of the superstar works is so fundamentally *different* from and superior to the other works that the extremely unequal distribution of public attention and recognition seems *just*. The logic of attention and valorization thus shatters any sense of justice when it comes to qualifications or effort.[35]

The superstar economy has consequences for the structure of emotions and affects. Admittedly, it is right to underscore the positive affectivity of the singularistic working culture – that is, its promotion of enthusiasm and self-actualization through creative work and intense projects. However, the unpredictability of the performance economy and its tendency to create asymmetrical distributions also strengthens certain negative or ambivalent emotions that were not as prevalent in the traditional achievement economy: vanity on account of one's own success, envy because of the success of others, low self-esteem, and the feeling of not receiving sufficient attention or of failing completely.[36] In the late-modern working world, the potential to experience disappointment is increased by the fact that the traditional demands of achievement have not entirely gone away. As a requirement for singularization, working on one's own competencies, profile, and potential is thus in itself a highly complex *achievement* that is expected of working subjects in the sense of self-optimization. The suggestion is that whoever has perfected his or her own uniqueness can be counted on to achieve recognition. There is no guarantee of this in the performance economy, however, and even less so as more and more working subjects continue to fine-tune their professional singularity and make the performance competition even harder than it already is.

A final area of tension in the late-modern working world arises from the *informal, personal*, and *coincidental* nature of the criteria on whose basis opportunities are distributed and recognition is awarded. Although the educational system continues to function on the basis of formal qualifications and thus perpetuates traditional ideas about achievement in society, success in the performance economy is largely dependent on other factors – factors that would have been regarded as *informal, personal*, and *coincidental* in the world of industrial modernity. I have already discussed a number of these factors at length: the growing significance of social networks for success, the high relevance of cultural capital derived from one's background, the need for performances to be evaluated by fickle audiences, and finally the dependence of success on the unpredictable trends of the attention and valorization markets for singular goods. In light of all this, the ability to make shrewd speculations about future opportunities – of a profile, a good, or an entire economic sector – has become a fundamental skill in the culture of late-modern labor. Such predictions, however, do not always pan out.

Of course, whether, or to what extent, the singularistic working culture is perceived as problematic depends on the cultural criteria that are in place for evaluating the distribution of recognition and status.[37] What the former achievement society dismissed as irrational appears entirely consistent within the logic of the performance economy. In this context, informalization and personalization are comprehensible mechanisms for enabling successful creative work, and the unpredictability of singularity markets does not look like something that can be eliminated. Without a doubt, the informalization and cultural economization of late-modern working culture have created new opportunities for those who are virtuosos at playing the informal, personal, and speculative game. Yet this has meant giving up the well-intended neutrality toward the personal and informal that industrial modernity, with its preference for formal qualifications and impersonality, did so much to cultivate. The economy of singularities massively *desires* the uniqueness of working personalities. The industrial achievement society, in contrast, was indifferent to idiosyncrasies. One could say that it *tolerated* them. As long as people simply did their jobs, industrial society thus allowed for the recognition of certain particular qualities that late modernity tends to reject because they are out of sync with the market or because they fail to conform to certain performance expectations – the qualities of people who are socially awkward, bad at networking, introverted, irascible, lacking in charm, and provincial.

IV
Digitalization as Singularization: The Rise of the Culture Machine

From Industrial Technics to Digital Technology

How people act, feel, produce, govern, communicate, and imagine in a society is decisively influenced by the technologies at their disposal. Of course, technology does not determine social structures in a strict sense. Rather, technical artifacts are always linked to social practices, which appropriate them in a specific way. Artifacts and systems of artifacts – from the wheel to writing and printing, from simple tools to industrial production, from biotechnology to computer software – represent material *affordances* that can be applied in multiple (but not arbitrary) ways.[1]

When compared to other societies throughout history, modern society has rightly been regarded as a genuinely "technical culture."[2] It is no surprise that contemporary thinkers – whether during the Enlightenment, the bourgeois nineteenth century, or the era of state socialism – frequently equated the "modernity" of modern society with its advanced technology. On the one hand, this sweeping technologization of the social was rooted in industrialization, but it also involved the *technical rationality* of the instrumentally rational systems that were implemented to coordinate activity throughout society as a whole. Since the 1980s, however, the technological structure of society has been changing in a fundamental way not seen since the age of industrialization. At its heart is a complex that arose from the interplay of algorithmic processes, the digitalization of media forms, and the communication network of the internet. Taken together, these three components can be discussed as *technologies of the digital computer network*, or simply as technologies of the digital network. The transformation from industrial modernity to the society of singularities is based not only on the economic shift to an economy of singularities (which we looked at in detail in the previous chapters) but also on the structural reorientation of technological systems toward digitalization, computerization, and networking. Although both processes have their own internal dynamics, they are interrelated.

What, however, is specifically new and different about the key technologies of late modernity? It is difficult to answer this question because we are still in an ongoing process of radical change. Nevertheless, there has been no shortage of exaggerated utopian or dystopian interpretations of digitalization, such as talk of a "new global democracy" and "ambient intelligence," or of "surveillance technologies" and a "disastrous collapse of attention spans."[3] In order to understand the social transformation that it has brought about, however, more is needed than such sweeping narratives of progress or decline. If we take a step back and examine the phenomenon by way of a historical comparison, we will see that there has been a fundamental break between the old technics of industrialization and the new technology of the digital computer network. This shift can be described as follows: whereas industrial technics only made it possible to mechanize and standardize the world, digital technology enforces the singularization of subjects, objects, and the social in general. Whereas industrial technics were an engine of functional rationalization and objectification, the digital network is a generator of social culturalization and the intensification of affect.

Although the early computers of the 1970s and 1980s could still easily be perceived in the traditional cybernetic sense as instruments for perfecting the logic of control, since the beginning of the twenty-first century it has been possible to see a structure that contradicts this first impression: the technological complex of computers, digitality, and the internet enables and forces the ongoing fabrication of subjects, objects, and collectives as *unique*. What might at first seem like distinct characteristics of digital culture can in fact, upon closer inspection, be interpreted as manifestations of *technologically instigated singularization*. This ranges from the social-media profiles that are competing for originality and visibility to the data tracking of our "digital footprints," which allows the internet to be personalized, to the particular online communities (digital "tribes") that each have their own self-contained world views.

The technologically instigated singularization of the social goes hand in hand with a *culturalization of the technological*, which determines what culture means under digital conditions. Compared to the old technics of industrial society, which in many respects seemed oppositional to the cultural sphere, digitality and the internet compel the culturalization of the social. What this means is that the leading technologies of late modernity are no longer used to produce machines, energy sources, and functional goods but are, rather, engaged in the expansive and pervasive fabrication of cultural formats with narrative, aesthetic, design, ludic, or ethical qualities: texts and images, videos and films, phatic speech acts, and games. For the first time, modern technology has essentially become a *culture machine*.

Late modernity has thus changed the orientation of what technology means. Gilbert Simondon illustrated this difference by juxtaposing the "closed machines" of old, industrial *technics* with the cybernetic, "open machines" of high-modern *technology*.[4] Or, to put this in our terms, industrial-mechanical technics, which dominated modernity from the second half of the eighteenth to the middle of the twentieth century, was the engine of the social logic of the general and the instrumental logic of functionality. Such was the case for all the socially relevant technical paradigms since 1780: for the industrial revolution in the narrower sense, for the paradigm of

IV Digitalization as Singularization

steam engines and railroads, and for that of steel, electricity, heavy industry, oil, automobiles, and the mass production of consumer goods.[5] Each of these examples involved industrial technics of mechanization, the efficient division of labor, energy production, and standardization. They were accordingly accompanied by a socially defining technical habitus: a predictable and future-oriented type of behavior with reduced affects whose emblematic social figure was the engineer.

Since the end of the twentieth century, however, the most advanced technology of the age has to some extent switched sides and has transformed from a conveyer belt of rationalization into one of culturalization – from an engine of standardization into a generator of singularities. In a special way, technology is now a promoter of what it had previously sought to eliminate: unique entities and culture. A fundamental technological conversion has taken place: from the *technical culture* of industrial modernity to the *culture machine* of late modernity. The technological paradigm of information and communication, which has been in place since around 1980, will therefore be grossly misunderstood if it is seen as merely an extension or perpetuation of the old industrial paradigm. As I have said, we are dealing with a fundamental break from the past. For the first time in history, the leading technological complex in society is one that is centered on the production, circulation, and reception of cultural formats. At the same time, we are also dealing with the first key technology in the history of modernity that enables, instigates, and even enforces the singularization of objects and subjects. Like the old industrial technics, the new digital technology also breeds a habitus and emblematic social figure corresponding to it: the mobile users of computer screens, who are always at the same time an audience being affected by the latest texts and images that are (secretly) selected for their attention and who are themselves relentlessly feeding their own creations and self-representations into this digital cultural universe.

1
The Technology of Culturalization

Algorithms, Digitality, and the Internet as Infrastructures

It can be difficult, however, to gain insight into this structural transition. On the one hand, we have been accustomed since early modernity to think about technology in terms of the industrial-mechanical paradigm of standardization and thus also in terms of discipline and control. On the other hand, and at least on *one* level, the digital computer network has in fact reinforced and even radicalized the paradigm of the general – of predictability, uniformity, and universality. However, the very fact that digital algorithms have radicalized the logic of the general is what paradoxically enables the singularization of subjects, objects, and collectives. In order to make this connection clear, I will have to revisit the concept of infrastructure.[1] Digital technologies have taken on the status of a *general infrastructure for the fabrication of singularities*. In other words, the heart of the technological system is (also) governed by processes and formats of standardization and universalization, but these form the background structure for the fabrication of singularities. As infrastructure, the logic of the general has thus acquired an instrumental status. It is now a function of (automated and cultural) singularization and of the establishment of a global culture machine.

To what extent do the new technologies reinforce a social and technical logic of the general? In order to answer this question, it will first be necessary to take a closer look at the three central processes that constitute the new technological complex. As I have already mentioned, these are the algorithms of computing, the digitalization of media formats, and the development of a global communication network: the internet.[2] Each of these processes is engaged in "doing generality," and this is the case in the three relevant respects of instrumental rationality, formalization, and universal generalization.

Let us begin with *computing*, whose processes are those of a universal calculating machine (as imagined by Charles Babbage

IV Digitalization as Singularization 167

in the nineteenth century, realized by Alan Turing in 1937, and perfected by John von Neumann in the form of a universal Turing machine). With late modernity's portable computers and mobile smartphones, these calculating machines have acquired extraordinary capacities. They also, however, possess the same structure of "computericity" that characterized the Turing machine: they are symbol-processing machines that execute algorithms. Algorithms are simply computable technical instructions. By way of an algorithm, input is translated into output through a finite number of steps. The instructions are formalized and unambiguous. Over time, more and more dynamic self-learning and self-perfecting algorithms have been developed, and these enable the automation of operations.[3] The computerized processing of algorithms certainly represents a high point of formal rationalization in the sense of instrumentally rational computability. In their mathematical and automated form, the calculating machine and its instructions are general procedures. At the same time, however, it is also clear that here the *social* logic of the general is contained within the machine itself; to this extent, it is a *technical* logic in the strict sense, given that it is not engaged in coordinating the activities of human subjects but, rather, in computing automated operations within the internal structure of artifact systems.

Following Lev Manovich, one can say that computer technology arose from the convergence of two processes that were developed independently: computing and its algorithms on the one hand, and the *digitalization of media formats* on the other.[4] Computing meets media. As is well known, digitalization means that certain media formats are composed of *digital* signals (with discrete times and values), which in practice typically have two states: 0 and 1. Rather than being continuous, they are numerical, discontinuous representations. This binary logic, which Boole developed in the middle of the nineteenth century, could be applied by the Turing machine to all media formats. Since 1940, the universal Turing machine has itself been universalized to some extent, for it is able to accept texts or images as the input of its algorithms and, conversely, to generate such texts or images as the output of its algorithms. The convergence of media technologies and computing machines has therefore made it possible to control the configuration, reconfiguration, reproduction, and transferability of all media formats by means of programs. This, too, has had the consequence that the digitalization of media formats is now "doing generality" in its own sort of way and has even led to a pronounced form of de-singularization that has occasionally been lamented by cultural critics. The images, texts, and sounds of predigital culture possessed their own fully independent and non-translatable materiality and quality. Now, at least from a technical perspective, all media have the same uniform structure. Again, this formalization is not one that subjects impress upon objects or ideas – rather, it is a matter of automated formalizations *within* the technological system.

Algorithms and digitalization are linked to a third, originally autonomous, factor that has since transformed the first two: that of *communicative networking* between computers (and other apparatuses). At its heart lies the internet, but it also includes communication between different devices within the framework of the "internet of things."[5] Whereas computers were at first autistic machines, unlimited data transfers and thus communicative networking have been possible since the 1960s. The establishment of the general and open IP protocol in 1973 provided the foundation for a *single* comprehensive *network*. This internet not only connected computers to one another but also presented itself as a "world wide web" – as a gigantic platform of interconnected websites that combines various media formats (texts, images, sounds) with one another.[6] The internet, too, thus enforces its own sort of generality, and it does so particularly on the level of global connectivity. It depends on algorithms and digitality as generalizing processes, but, with the help of general protocols (TCP/IP or HTTP), it goes beyond them by enabling *universal* and essentially unlimited communication and cooperation among its users. The generalization of the network thus has the form of universalized communication, which has meanwhile come to include non-human participants within the framework of the internet of things. This communicative network has established both a global, general audience and a global arena of participants.

But enough of this first level, on which computers, algorithms, the digitalization of media, and the general protocols of the internet enforce a socio-technical logic of the general. At this point it is important to point out the *locus* of these generalizing procedures: they operate *within* the technologies of the digital computer network. Essentially, this act of "doing generality" takes place in interactions between machines.[7] However, these new technologies are not only automated systems; they are embedded in the social practices in which human subjects engage with them. It is only through this engagement that they have become socially significant. In order to understand the extent to which their internal enforcement of generality has made them true technologies of singularization, we first have to determine the extent to which they have contributed to the culturalization of the social.

The Digital Culture Machine and the Ubiquity of Culture

To what extent do digital technologies, which increasingly influence the everyday practices of late-modern subjects (their professional

IV Digitalization as Singularization

activity and their private communication; the ways in which they consume, travel, find partners, and entertain themselves), instigate the culturalization of technology and society? How does this change what "culture" means in late modernity? It goes without saying that late-modern culture is not identical with digital culture. A great deal of social activity is structured in an analog way – and sometimes aggressively so, as a counter-reaction to digitalization. However, even these analog practices are often tied to and influenced by digital media and apparatuses – from the selection of consumer goods on websites to the digital photographs that document events and vacations and are fed back into social media. Without saying that the digital world is all-encompassing, one can still maintain that it has contributed to the transformation of the cultural sphere in a decisive way.

Why is it even necessary to talk about culture here? The first and most basic feature of new technologies is so elementary that it is easy to overlook and misinterpret: with the rise of digital computer networks, data and information have become ubiquitous, but cultural objects and cultural formats have become ubiquitous as well (and here I mean culture in the strong sense of the term). The digital computer network is a *culture machine*, which means that its technologies are focused on the production, circulation, and reception of narrative, aesthetic, ludic, or design-based formats of culture. We are all familiar with the thesis that the computer and the internet have brought about an information or knowledge society and have led to a proliferation of information and data.[8] This argument, however, is still too deeply rooted in industrial society's tradition of thought and its culture of instrumental rationality. It fails to see the most influential aspect of the computer revolution, which is the fact that it has impelled the omnipresence of culture and affectivity.

A clear distinction has to be drawn between data, information, and cultural formats. We encounter all three in digital media. *Data* can be understood as systems of distinctions that exist within automated processes (binary codes, algorithms) and are thus independent of the knowledge of subjects.[9] Unlike data, information and cultural formats form contexts of meaning with which human subjects engage. Whereas *information* has an instrumental function, *cultural* formats have inherent value from the perspective of participants. Information has a cognitive status; it is useful knowledge for achieving certain ends. In contrast, cultural formats are intrinsically motivated for their participants *because* they affect them: as I have already mentioned several times, they have a narrative, aesthetic, ludic, ethical, or design quality. The line between information and culture is not always an easy one to draw, not least because texts and images are both bearers of information and cultural formats.

Nevertheless, the following difference usually sets them apart: a crucial indicator of the cultural character of texts and images is that they are charged with *affects*, whereas information is essentially free of emotion.

To a considerable extent, the internet is an *affect machine*. Its circulating elements excite, entertain, cheer up, relax, arouse, and generally affect people. In light of all the arguments about our supposed knowledge society, it can be easy to overlook the fact that, in large part, the digital objects that captivate recipients and producers are not cognitive in nature but rather possess a narrative, aesthetic, design, or ludic character.[10] This is true of images, films, texts, sounds, and games.

Especially in the form of photographs and videos, *images* are one of the primary types of media that are created, circulated, and viewed on the internet. To a great extent, digital culture is a culture of visuality.[11] This is clear not only from platforms such as YouTube and Instagram but also from the fact that other social media, such as Facebook and Twitter, have increasingly reoriented themselves around images. Images dominate the news about politics, sports, and entertainment; pornographic images are circulated in greater and greater numbers; and the streaming of television shows and films can be mentioned here as well. The information value of these images is only secondary; primarily, they have an affective character – that is, an aesthetic or narrative form. In particular, the influence of digital photography on the aestheticization of internet culture has been massive.[12] Ever-present cameras have transformed entirely humdrum aspects of daily life into "scenes" that are viewed for their own sake and without regard for their original context.

Surpassed in importance by this omnipresent visuality, written *texts* now occupy second place on the internet. Yet, even in the case of texts, one can see a tendency to reduce information and increase *emotion*. More and more texts are produced for their affective content. Even everyday practical texts now have certain affective qualities. Texts posted on social media primarily have the character of phatic communication.[13] Their informational function has faded into the background in favor of communication for the sake of communication, the point of which is to create a feeling of community. Even a micro-blogging platform like Twitter is not entirely characterized by the informational content of its short messages but also by the fact that these posts generate excitement about things that are happening at the moment. For their readers, blogs or entire news portals have an overarching narrative value and, at the same time, the potential to arouse feelings of morality: their texts weave together a socio-political "grand narrative" that appeals to their audience. Late-modern journalism on the internet does

IV Digitalization as Singularization

more than just convey information; it is also a narrative machine with considerable emotional effects.[14]

In addition to images and texts, *sounds* also circulate in the digital world in a prominent way, above all in the form of music.[15] Digitalization has made music ubiquitous. By definition, it is not a form of information but rather an aesthetic object with affective intensity. Finally, ludic practices are also highly relevant online, especially in the form of *computer games*.[16] To some extent, these represent interactive total works of art, given that they create artificial spatial atmospheres and simultaneously have the nature of events. Here, participants are themselves active in design and strategy. In genres such as science fiction, history, horror, or adventure, computer games are comprehensive spaces of aesthetic and narrative immersion. Once inside them, people act in a way that transcends the boundaries between strategy and aesthetics. The most important feature of this activity is that it is experienced by the player in an affective manner. What is more, the abundance of digital ludic practices beyond computer games, which are often discussed in terms of "gamification," further contributes to the aestheticization of computer-based practices.[17]

On the level of images, texts, sounds, and games – wherever you look, the internet is a culture machine. Here, too, the praxis of culture has the form that I outlined above: its structure is one of performativity and experience. Digital images, texts, and sounds are all *performed*, and this before an audience in the broad sense that itself can play along. Inundated with digital performances, this audience finds itself in a state of *permanent lived experience*. The culturalization enforced by digital technologies has now become *ubiquitous*. The omnipresence of this culturalization can be precisely defined: there are *more* cultural elements, (nearly) *all* cultural elements are affected by it, they are present *constantly* and *everywhere*, and they are distinguished by social *transgressions*.

It is well known that the digital revolution has led to extreme growth in the total number of texts, images, sound sequences, and game formats. In this case, culturalization has simply resulted in a massive quantitative increase of cultural formats. Whereas former media technologies each specialized in a particular format and the production of new things was typically a separate task from the preservation of old things, the digital culture machine has integrated all formats together. Here, nearly the entire corpus of created images, texts, and sounds has been collected, stored, and made available. On the extreme end, this culture machine preserves everything that anyone has produced as a cultural format. Moreover, mobile devices have essentially made everything available at any place and time.[18] Whereas the old media were typically consumed in particular contexts – books in libraries, films in movie theaters – late-modern subjects are permanently accompanied by texts, images, sounds, and games via their smartphones or other portable devices. Less and less a tool, technology has increasingly become a technological environment in which subjects operate. At its core, this environment is a *cultural environment* that affects subjects on an ongoing basis.[19]

The culturalization of digital technology ultimately derives its intensity from its social transgressions. These pertain to the boundaries between the public and the private as well as to those between the mediated and the real. Roughly speaking, the new media have transformed the personal and private into something public or at least semi-public. At the same time, more and more elements of daily life are now available for observation on digital media. This concerns not least the reality of the human body, people's appearances, their voices, and the way in which they move. By means of mobile cameras and microphones, the physical aspects of everyday pragmatic reality have become an object of observation that is viewed in various narrative-semiotic and aesthetic perspectives. The basic acts of the human body have therefore transformed – whether willingly or unwillingly – into a performance for an audience's viewing experience.

Culture Between Overproduction and Recombination

The digital culture machine is characterized by five important features that distinguish it from bourgeois high culture and the mass culture of organized modernity. It thus adds an additional dimension to what I referred to above as the "hyperculture" of late modernity.

First, the culture machine generally creates a structural asymmetry between the *extreme overproduction of cultural goods* (and information) and the *scarcity of recipients' attention*. On the one hand, an enormous number of images and texts are brought into the world and made public on the internet, and more and more new and different images and texts are constantly being added without the older images and texts disappearing. On the other hand, the attention of recipients cannot be increased at will. The culture machine thus produces culture in excess. Whereas industrial technics centered on the problem of scarcity, digital technology is a *technology of excess*. We are thus dealing with a constellation that is already familiar to us from the situation of cultural goods in the economy. Just as the economy of singularities is extremely wasteful to the extent that it introduces far more goods into the world than can possibly attract attention and be appreciated, the internet also instigates an overproduction of cultural elements that compete for

IV Digitalization as Singularization 173

the attention of users. Here, too, what prevails is an extreme *struggle for visibility*.

In the case of the economy of singularities and digital media technology, it is important to point out that we are dealing with two *independent* structures of cultural overproduction. However, these two structures have mutually *reinforced* one another over the course of the widespread implementation of visibility and attractiveness competitions among singularities. By this point, it has become clear *why* digital media did not stick to the circulation of information but rather shifted their orientation toward the circulation of cultural formats. Culture has a decisive advantage over information on the market of attention and valorization: it mobilizes affect. Any battle for attention will sooner be won by affecting (entertaining, shocking, fascinating, etc.) texts, images, and games than it will by unemotional information. Moreover, what is experienced in the short term and valued in the long term is not utility but rather the formats of culture. The combination of overproduction and scarce attention has thus set a dynamic in motion that has increasingly turned the digital world into a culture and affect machine (beyond the information machine that it, of course, still is).

Second, the dualism between cultural producers and their public audience has weakened. What has taken place is a *generalization of the role of cultural producers* as well as a *generalization of the role of the audience*. Both bourgeois high culture and the mass culture of industrial modernity were based on the model of *few* producers making things for *many* recipients. This situation has fundamentally changed in digital late modernity, for every recipient can now become a producer, be it only on a small scale (by posting vacation pictures on the internet or reviewing books on one platform or another).[20] This leveling out of cultural production is partly responsible for the extreme overproduction of digital cultural elements. Interestingly, however, it has not brought about the "end of audiences."[21] On the contrary, the role of the audience has been generalized. This has happened by means of screens, which function as an interface to the world and – especially since they have become mobile – ensure that the subject is constantly in the position of an audience member. Via screens, the late-modern subject has become a more extensive viewer and reader than ever before.[22]

Third, the culture machine has led to the *de-hierarchization of cultural formats*. Whereas classical modernity recognized and cultivated a clear hierarchy between high culture and popular or mass culture as well as between public and private culture, these hierarchies have crumbled in the digital world of late modernity. All cultural elements are now available in the *same* way and are subject to the same mechanisms of attention and valorization markets. In the digital world, cultural formats are *all on one level*, which is highly pluralistic; only a few clicks are needed to lead recipients or users from their private vacation photos to classic films, from their friends' messages to a report issued by a government body, from pornography to Shakespeare's *The Tempest* or to pictures of luxury suites in a glamorous Parisian hotel.[23] At the same time, these cultural formats also compete with one another on the same level: there is a competition for visibility and recognition, and it comes down to the number of clicks, links, and likes that establish rankings on search engines. In this competition, private vacation photos are on the same footing as Shakespeare's sonnets, Parisian hotels, parliamentary reports, and tweets. Of course, de-hierarchization does not mean that everything is of equal value. On the contrary, cultural formats differ drastically from one another with respect to their prestige and perceived quality. Just a few highly visible elements happen to stand out in a massive crowd of nearly invisible elements. Like the economy of singularities, the internet is also characterized by a pronounced asymmetry of visibility, and these two asymmetries – the economic and the media-technological – are interrelated.

Fourth, a radical *temporalization of cultural formats* has taken place. On the internet, instantaneity, novelty, and up-to-date material rule the day.[24] The cultural formats on the internet thus possess a temporality of their own. Unlike books or films in the old media culture, they are not stable but, rather, *processual* objects – that is, they are performances that are constantly changing over time (at least to some extent). Moreover, an unfathomable number of digital performances – news sites, blogs, Facebook profiles, tweets, television streaming services, etc. – are always taking place at the same time. For the user, there are now no limits to lived experiences, which had been restricted to particular formats during the age of traditional television culture. Because the digital cultural sphere processes everything in real time, its effect is one of ongoing currency. The cultural environment is only as it is for a single moment; in the next moment, it will already be something different.

The internet is therefore governed by a social regime of novelty. On the one hand, new texts, images, etc., are always being posted. To a great extent, these supplant the old texts, images, etc., and at least make the basic claim of being original and interesting. On the other hand, many digital objects are internally structured to be mutable – such is the case, for instance, with blogs and Facebook profiles.[25] On this level, the regime of novelty takes the form of updating. Instantaneity, an orientation toward novelty, and constant updating have had the effect that the relation of recipients (and producers) has become *moment-based*. Culture has acquired a fleeting character and is *experienced* in the moment. References to the past or to the future have dwindled, for all that matters is what is new and current in the present moment.

Fifth, the internet encourages a culture of *recombination*. Because of the digital availability of texts, images, etc., it is easy to appropriate and manipulate them.[26] This has led to the fact that, today, novelties are often remixes of previously existing things. What counts as new is thus no longer what has never been – that which marks a clean break from the past in the manner of the avant-garde. Rather, a category of *relative* novelty has arisen as a result of the techniques of recombination and recontextualization (think of "mashups"). As a consequence, the bar for novelty has been lowered, and the contrast between *originals* and *copies* has become blurry. The ability to create links has also contributed to the recombinative form of culture. The culture machine has thus turned culture into a system of *cultural resources*.

All five features of the culture machine discussed above have a common effect: they contribute to the dissolution of cultural generality that existed in classical modernity. The idea that culture possessed general qualities was characteristic of bourgeois high culture and education. Then, what counted as culture counted for everyone in the same way (at least within the bourgeoisie). Bourgeois culture's clear differentiation between producers and recipients of culture, its orientation toward "classical" cultural objects and their hierarchization, its restriction of cultural practices to specific contexts (theaters, concert halls, reading rooms, etc.), and its clear division between the old and the new – all of this contributed to the establishment of a generally valid canon that was slow to expand. In comparison to this, the mass culture of organized modernity – the dominant culture of film, radio, and television that prevailed into the 1980s – was governed far more radically by a regime of novelties, fashions, and hits. Yet it, too, enabled and enforced cultural generality, though a sort that affected not only high culture but popular culture as well. As before, there were just a few cultural producers creating things for a large public audience; as before, cultural practices were contextualized (movie theaters, living-rooms), cultural objects were stable (the individual film, for instance), and the difference between new and old remained intact and influential. Things are now entirely different in late-modern digital culture, which, on account of the features outlined above, has created a cultural space that is "over-abundant," pluralistic, and in a constant state of change. In doing so, it has thus shattered the structural model of generally valid culture and replaced it with diverse forms of singularization.

2
Cultural and Automated Processes of Singularization

It is amazing to see how so many apparently distinct aspects of digital technology can all be interpreted, upon closer inspection, as processes in which singularities are systematically created and prized. As I noted above, the basic technical components of the digital network – algorithms, digitality, and the universality of the internet – constitute an infrastructure that compels the singularization of subjects, objects, and collectives.[1] In this case, it is necessary to distinguish between *cultural* and *automated* singularization.

On the one hand, there are *cultural* (and affective) processes of singularization, which result from interactions between subjects and machines or between subjects using machines. Examples include profiles on social media, which compete to be original; singular images, texts, and things, which are made possible by software and 3D printers; and communities of like-minded people, which come together on internet platforms. Here, the uniqueness of subjects, objects, or collectives is negotiated in the social practices of visibility markets, valorization processes, community building, and networks.

On the other hand, there are *automated* processes of singularization, which take place purely on the level of machine–machine interactions and run their course in such a way that subjects are unaware of their existence, or unable to interpret them. My assertion above that computer technology is engaged in "doing general" is thus not the whole truth, for in fact singularities also arise from machine–machine interactions; indeed, digital technology has become increasingly oriented toward systematically noticing singularities and processing them automatically. A paradigmatic example of automated singularity is the widespread use of data tracking, which helps to create consumer profiles and keep them up to date. By processing immense volumes of big data, *general* algorithms are thus able to create *particular* profiles of individual people and, presumably, a unique profile for every individual. As regards the relation between the socio-technological logic of the general and

IV Digitalization as Singularization 177

that of the particular, digital technologies are thus characterized by three levels: (1) the cultural singularization of subjects, objects, and collectives through the social practices of using computers; (2) the automated singularization of subjects and objects; and (3) the technical enactment of generality by means of algorithms, digitality, and the transmission of data, which provide the infrastructure for the first two levels.

The Digital Subject: Performative Authenticity and Visibility

Digital technologies have transformed what it means to be a subject.[2] They submit the late-modern self to a specific form of singularization, which, at the same time, could not exist without our own participation. Now it is the case that subjects cultivate themselves into something unique and are viewed by others as potentially singular. The digital singularization of subjects exists in two distinct forms: the cultural singularization of their public representations, which are certified by an audience, and the automated singularization of subjects, which takes place, as it were, "behind their backs." In both procedures, subjects are fabricated as unique, and in particular as *modular* or *compositional* singularities that arise from the assembly of different individual elements or modules. It is this composition of individual modules that produces the profile of a subject. Below we will see in greater detail the extent to which digital technologies have turned the late-modern subject into a *profile subject*.

First, however, I should discuss the public singularization of subjects on the internet and how they endeavor to ensure the visibility of their unique qualities. It is a peculiar feature of the internet that potentially everyone can be present there *themselves* – not as mere types or averages but as individuals with their own names, faces, and personal characteristics. Unrestricted by the confines of class and status, all late-modern subjects have the historically unprecedented privilege (though this has increasingly become more of a necessity) of representing themselves in the culture machine and constantly working on their self-presentation. Social media can be regarded as the most significant locus of such self-presentation; in fact, it is even possible to speak of a "Facebook paradigm," which is characterized by the fact that deliberate profiles are posted and cultivated there.[3]

In general, this (self-)formation of digital subjects takes place on the same cultural-economic basis that is characteristic of late-modern culture as a whole: in the form of competitions for visibility and valorization – that is, on the attractiveness markets of singularities. Digital media are largely responsible for the fact that this cultural economization pertains not only to *objects* in the economy of singularities, as I described above, but also to the relation that *subjects* have to one another. In addition to the labor market of the knowledge and culture economy, the singularization of profile subjects on the internet is thus the second important institutional foundation of the social singularization of subjects in late modernity. People now learn from an early age that it is only possible to craft a valuable existence by cultivating a visible and unique profile, which in turn competes with others for attention and valorization. The late-modern self is thus a *dramaturgical* self, and subjectification takes place primarily through one's successful self-representation *to others*. Increasingly, the late-modern subject has become identical with his or her performance before an *audience*, and the internet is its central arena.

Yet what is the structure of such performances? This can be illustrated with a comparison. In his study of organized modernity in the 1940s and 1950s, David Riesman identified a type of subject who was likewise always concerned with representing himself to others. The goal of this "other-directed character" was to put on – as an employee at work, as a young person in a peer group, or as a neighbor in the suburbs – a successful performance for others.[4] So far, this sounds quite familiar. However, the crucial and instructive difference comes into play when one examines the structure of these performances. Whereas Riesman's other-directed character sought to be socially *inconspicuous*, to have *no* eccentric individuality, and to fit the standards of normal and *adjusted* people, the goal of the profile subject's performance is to achieve precisely the opposite: to stand out as unique in the digital competition for attention. Now, it is insufficient and subjectively unsatisfying merely to be an inconspicuous member of a group. Rather, late-modern subjects want and are expected to present their lives as *non-interchangeable*. Their concern, as I have repeatedly stressed, is to *be themselves* in an authentic way.

We have already seen the great value of the authentic in late-modern culture and the connection between authenticity and singularity in the case of goods on cultural markets. The pursuit of authenticity, however, also characterizes the self-design of digital subjects, and it has the paradoxical form of *performative authenticity*. It is paradoxical because, according to the very meaning of *authenticity*, the authenticity of a subject should concern no more than how one relates to oneself: a subject is authentic when he or she feels "genuine" and not artificial, which means following one's own wishes and ideals and, if necessary, doing so against the opposition of others. This is what the late-modern subject *wants* to do. At the same time, however, this subject lives in a culture in which authenticity has become a central social expectation. The subject is thus *expected* to be authentic, and being yourself is not quite the

IV Digitalization as Singularization 179

same thing as knowing that you had better be yourself. We have already seen the extent to which social recognition in the society of singularities depends on being perceived as uniquely authentic, and therefore subjects are forced to present themselves *as* singular and authentic. The self-production of the digital subject is nothing but the fabrication of such performative authenticity.

When it comes to competing for attention, online performances of authenticity take place under the intense conditions of having to fight with other profiles, blogs, etc., for visibility and appreciation – conditions that we have already seen in our discussion of the economic sphere. It is only by being *visible* – by being perceived as unique in an authentic and interesting way – that a subject can survive this struggle and accumulate enough singularity capital to secure lasting recognition and social status. Visibility and appreciation are dependent on the attention of an audience, and this attention is scarce in the culture machine for the reasons outlined above: the extreme overproduction and constant updating of cultural formats by an enormous number of users. In bold and simple terms, visibility alone leads to social recognition, while invisibility means digital death. That this is a basic principle of the society of singularities is in large part a consequence of its media technologies.

Compositional Singularity and the Form of the Profile

I have already pointed out that the format of the profile is fundamental to the digital singularization of subjects.[5] By means of profiles, which are a combination of textual and visual elements, the digital subject attempts to demonstrate his or her irreplaceability and unique personality. In some cases, profiles are formalized by having to fit into prescribed and standardized rubrics,[6] but in other cases users are free to create profiles however they like. We have already examined the profile as a leading format for working subjects in the knowledge and culture economy. It is also, however, a key format of digital media, in which it serves to represent "entire personalities" and has thus become a locus and means for the production of identity. To singularize oneself by means of a profile, moreover, is now an ongoing task for subjects; it is a relentless activity undertaken on one's own behalf.

In the culture machine, the criteria for successful profiling are the same as those in the economy of singularities, and the two institutional complexes reinforce one another. A personality that is recognized as singular is distinguished by its originality and distinctness; in an unusual and complex way, the profile of such a personality is the personality itself, which means that it has an inner density that makes the subject seem *interesting*. At the same time, it has to look different from other profiles, so that it contains an element of *surprise*. With their digital profiles, subjects cultivate their singularity by combining the two conflicting criteria of versatility and coherence. On the one hand, they try to demonstrate the heterogeneity of their interests and the diversity of their experiences; on the other hand, these heterogeneous elements are supposed to form an identifiable and appealing whole.

In digital profiles, both the subjective desire and the social expectation for versatility are managed in the form of a *modularized tableau*. By "tableau," I mean that people make use of two-dimensional space in order to represent their personalities as a collage of material elements (texts, images, links, etc.). For its part, "modularized" means that there are individual components that are visible as such and function on the basis of prescribed formats. The representation of subjects via modularized tableaus replaces the unfamiliar and often mysterious features of "individuality" – which in the predigital age could only be ascertained (if ever) after a long period of friendship or acquaintance – with a visible collage of various singular components that, in one look, is immediately comprehensible and legible as a "composition" – somewhat like an open book. Interest in a certain type of music, for instance, which is not only stated but demonstrated with links to upcoming concerts and entire audio files; interest in particular political topics; passion for certain countries, cities, or landscapes; the connection that someone has to where he or she lives or used to live; or enthusiasm for a local sports team or for a certain type of cooking – all of these disparate elements of someone's personality are brought together in a digital tableau and are thus, in principle, equally visible. None of the individual features of a profile is very interesting on its own; it is rather the *combination* of all these elements that gives rise to an individual personality and its unique "cosmos." In short, profiles construct uniqueness in the form of *compositional singularity*.

Far from being static, however, profiles are characterized by their ongoing performance of novelty. From the beginning, the logic of blogging has been defined by the necessity of keeping up to date, and the need to maintain a dynamic profile has been fueled all the more by Facebook's introduction of the "timeline." Accordingly, the profile subject has to demonstrate his or her originality and versatility over and over again by constantly putting on a new performance. It is not enough to announce at one point that you love Colombia, Baroque opera, and your children; instead, you have to demonstrate these passions and interests to the public on an ongoing basis by posting pictures, comments, and links about your recent trip to Colombia, about your recent experience at a Baroque music festival, or at least about something halfway remarkable that

IV Digitalization as Singularization 181

you are doing *right now* with your children. The permanent act of performing novelty has transferred the internet's general orientation toward the present moment to the level of fabricating subjects. In this case, singularization means that someone's multifaceted activities always involve something new and that the features of one's profile have to be kept up to date to reflect what is happening in the here and now.

The preferred form in which profile subjects constantly fabricate themselves as unique is the *visually represented lived experience*.[7] The chronicle of the self now tends to foreground photographs and films whose visual realism suggests immediacy and eventfulness. The activities best suited for photographic or filmic documentation are events, trips, and even small quotidian episodes in which something new or unusual happens. The self is always included in this documentation (not least in the form of a "selfie"). Yet external activities are not the only things that are visually documented, for profile subjects are also concerned with showcasing their subjective *experiences* to the public. The crucial point is that late-modern subjects present themselves not only as people who do interesting things but also as people who have interesting experiences. That is, they also portray themselves as unique in the special way that they perceive and feel uniqueness itself. Here, too, the idea of authenticity comes into play. Subjects will seem authentic if, in addition to presenting themselves in a given situation, they also depict themselves as being satisfied or "fulfilled" in this situation. But how is it possible to visualize for others the opaque and fleeting psycho-physical process of experience? The implied purpose of digital photos is to make one's own experiences vicariously comprehensible. They are often far from perfect, but all of these seemingly authentic snapshots and short films, which are taken "in the moment" (in the middle of a rock concert, for instance), are meant to provide their viewers with a real-time look into what the subject is experiencing (or pretending to) in the here and now.[8]

Links and likes also contribute to self-singularization. Compared to activities and experiences, they are a less intensive way to represent oneself as unique. To provide a link, of course, means that the subject has rummaged through the vast array of current texts and images in the culture machine and picked out a few that are worthy of attention. Following Georg Simmel, who believed that individuality is formed at the intersection of social circles,[9] one could say that, to a considerable extent, the singularity of digital subjects arises from the fact that they are the nodal points of their links. On the basis of my links, you can see who I am. The versatility and inherent complexity of the linking subject are manifested in the diversity and originality of his or her references to the texts and images of others. Likes, such as those on Facebook, function in a similar but more schematic way: I am not only my links but also my likes, which means that I am composed of the things that appeal to me. With their links, subjects demonstrate their (digital) cosmopolitanism; with their likes, they demonstrate their specific affectivity. Finally, a special form of links and likes consists of the profiles of other people to whom one is connected: one's "friends." Linking to other subjects with similarly interesting profiles makes social circles (in Simmel's sense of the term) visible in the digital world: subjects demonstrate their own versatility and uniqueness through the versatility and uniqueness of their online and visible acquaintances.

Profiles institutionalize an *affectively positive culture* around the digital subject for the simple reason that the emotions that they involve almost always have a positive valence. Visually documented experiences typically capture positive moments, from family celebrations and vacations to eating at a restaurant. Together, the features represented in a profile demonstrate a world of passions, interests, and the activities associated with them, and most of these things are culturally uncontroversial (such as traveling, music, or family life). Studies of the perception of profiles in the Facebook paradigm have shown that they often seem so "polished" as to appear enviable or even glamorous.[10] A constant concern is to demonstrate one's personal attractiveness, which does not mean being perfect in a conventional way (which would be unoriginal and inauthentic) but rather in seeming extraordinary in light of the interesting nature of one's everyday experiences. However, the fact that profiles tend to be positive does not mean that they leave no room for flaws. In fact, the demonstration of imperfections can make someone seem more "personal" and thus more authentic.[11] That said, these "minor inadequacies" have to be framed in such a way as to contribute something to the image of an overall attractive personality.

In this case, too, it is ultimately the audience that, by means of its attention and appreciation, singularizes a profile – or not. As I have already said, digital subjects participate in a media-based *attractiveness market*; to some extent, they *themselves* have become cultural goods that fight for attention and valorization. However, whereas goods and their consumers (their audience) are mostly separate from one another in cultural capitalism, the positions of producers and recipients are interchangeable on the digital attractiveness market of the culture machine: profiles are mutually observed and evaluated by one another. Of course, the circle of recipients toward which digital profile subjects are directed is highly variable and can range from a potentially unlimited audience (in the case of bloggers or people posting videos on YouTube, for instance) to a circumscribed and only semi-public group of friends on social media. However, the problem of attention and valorization is the same throughout: regardless of the situation, the goal is to gain

IV Digitalization as Singularization 183

visibility and attract attention. The universal aim, in other words, is to win over the "jury" of people who happen to be looking for something interesting.

In this regard, the internet provides specific quantification techniques with which subjects can measure how much attention and valorization their profiles have received. By means of the number of clicks on or links to a site (attention) and the number of likes or "friends" (valorization), it is possible to determine one's own *singularity status*.[12] Here, too, the laws of the attention economy likewise apply: whoever has already attracted attention has a good chance of attracting even more. Moreover, algorithms such as those used to create Facebook's news feed make sure to post things that have already received a high number of clicks and likes. In this way, the digital infrastructure fuels the Matthew effect of unequal attention even further and helps to create winner-take-all markets online. In the digital world, as in the world of cultural goods, there are thus a few stars with outsized visibility, who benefit from the recognition of friends and anonymous admirers, and the many other people whose profiles receive only scant attention.

Big Data and the Observation of Profiles

Parallel to the public singularization of mutually observing online subjects, however, another type of singularization happens to be taking place "behind their backs." It is purely automated and is the result of subjects being observed *by* the digital computer network. The latter has thus become an algorithmic observation system that attempts to "understand" subjects in all their uniqueness. Here, observation does not primarily mean surveillance but rather, more generally, that systems observe their environment in order to identify and classify the phenomena occurring there.[13] The digital methods that are implemented here – from the data analytics used by Facebook or Google to the self-tracking devices that people wear on their bodies – are not mental or communicative systems of observation but rather *material apparatuses of observation.* They do not process information or contexts of meaning but rather data, and lots of it: big data. Algorithm-based observation, which collects and evaluates volumes of data, can be made to focus on various types of phenomena – on specific places or trends, for instance – but it is especially significant that it can be used to monitor the activities of subjects.[14] The crucial point is that, from this automated and algorithmic perspective, subjects are not perceived as mere types but rather as singularities.[15]

The digital computer network has been used to develop a type of technology that does not standardize subjects but rather singularizes them over the course of their observation, and this represents a new rift in the history of modern technology. Traditionally, when modernity addressed its subjects as *general* or *particular*, it cultivated a division of labor between the public and private spheres. In the world of personal and private relationships, people were of course sensitive to individuality, but economic, governmental, and scientific institutions, which were closely connected to industrial technologies, regarded subjects as bearers of general features. In these contexts, if a particular feature became visible, it was usually pathologized as a form of deviance, criminality, insanity, or perversity. It is telling and somewhat ironic that the format of the profile, which has become the leading format of singularization in late modernity, first came to prominence at the end of the nineteenth century in the context of institutionally negative singularization: the *criminal profile* developed by the police. In order to find and arrest a criminal, it seemed necessary to identify the unique characteristics of his mental outlook and the peculiar features of his personality.[16]

This distinction between the personal (private) and the systemic (general) has collapsed in late modernity, and not least because of digital technologies. The uniqueness of the subject has left the confines of the private sphere and, with the help of digital infrastructure, has entered a public sphere with a potentially global audience. At the same time, economic, political, and scientific institutions have developed an *interest* in observing subjects in their uniqueness, and technologies now have the *capability* to do so. This singularity is no longer pathologized by institutions but rather regarded as valuable knowledge. Companies now use algorithms to create an image of the specific tastes of consumers; political parties use them to profile individual voters; and the medical industry uses them to customize healthcare. Automated observation is characterized by the fact that it never monitors the subject as a whole but only in part – that is, as a modular entity composed of *discrete elements*. The modules that constitute the singularity of subjects might be, among other examples, the traces that they leave behind on the internet, their various bodily processes, or the specifics of their sensory perception.

The most familiar and widespread versions of *tracking* are the network protocols and analytic methods of so-called "people analytics," which are employed by platforms such as Facebook and search engines such as Google.[17] Here, profiles are successively created out of the myriad of individual traces that users leave online – out of what sites they visit, what sites they link to, what "friends" they have, and which groups they belong to on the internet. By means of these traces, it is possible for algorithms to fabricate a profile of someone's interests. Unlike the public profiles of users, these automated subject profiles do not have to be coherent; it is

IV Digitalization as Singularization 185

sufficient for them to compile ensembles of heterogeneous preferences related to a subject's taste in music, politics, or clothing. In the case of algorithmic observation, the subject is treated as a sort of *multiple self* whose *individual* elements form patterns that are also displayed by other users (a certain taste in music, for example). Here, too, the uniqueness of a given profile emerges from the *combination* of these modules. It goes without saying that the goal of this sort of automated singularization is to reveal the tendencies of individual subjects in order to make predictions about their future behavior. This type of uniqueness is thus not the same as what was once called the "individual factor," which lent a degree of unpredictability to every social rule. On the contrary, the uniqueness of digital subjects becomes predictable as soon as their various individual preferences become transparent.

The profiles created by means of automated singularization are thus not representational profiles (as in the case of social media) but rather *observational profiles* that monitor the activities of subjects in order to understand their internal structures from a particular perspective. In this sense, automated profiles can claim to understand individual subjects better than they understand themselves.[18] Contrary to the opinion of techno-critical skeptics, it has to be stated that this is not just a matter of new processes of generalization and typecasting. The algorithms of people analytics are used to observe the *uniqueness* of individual profile subjects (their unique tastes, for instance). Here, the "social norm" is too crude and uninteresting. In this respect, digital systems of observation are fundamentally different from the observation techniques of industrial modernity. Then, too, there were consumers and voters, but the small data sampling used at the time made it impossible to treat anyone as a singular subject. In fact, this did not even seem to be necessary. Frequency and correlation statistics were very well suited for identifying large groups of consumers and voters with similar preferences, but the big data available to digital instruments of observation have since made it possible to identify and track singular profiles, which can then be addressed as such.[19]

In addition to tracking online footprints, the automated singularization of subjects has also taken on another form: *tracking bodies*.[20] Think of the devices that constantly measure and evaluate bodily functions, or of the cameras and microphones that people wear to record their movements or sensory perceptions. On an *organic* level, this involves the observation of unique profiles in order to come up with customized forms of therapy. Here, the modularization of uniqueness is related to individual organic functions. The individual body no longer seems like a mere exemplar of the type *Homo sapiens*, which accordingly suffers from general types of illnesses, but is rather comprehensible as an irreducible singularity that can benefit from personalized forms of healthcare.[21] By being aware of the activities of their own bodies, subjects themselves can now reflexively observe them in all their uniqueness.[22]

A similar phenomenon is so-called "lifelogging," which involves creating a digital protocol of one's life with a portable camera (among other devices).[23] What is recorded here is primarily someone's singular visual perspective on the world as it appears throughout his or her waking hours. Lifelogging makes it possible to process perceptive data in an interpretive and reflexive manner. Because lifeloggers record moments of their daily lives that might in retrospect seem meaningful, influential, or problematic, such visual sequences can be reconfigured into a sort of personal encyclopedia for interested others, or simply for biographical self-reflection. This reflexive turn in the observation of subjects creates a link between automated singularization and subjective self-singularization: whereas automated profiles created by data tracking are not available to subjects, the mobile recording of sensory perceptions can lead subjects to reflect about themselves, their lifestyles, and where their lives are going.

The Personalized Internet and Softwarization

In addition to subjects, objects and things are also singularized on the digital computer network, and this happens in two ways: by means of automated algorithms, and by means of subjects using digital instruments. The most important example of the first way is what has often been referred to as the "personalization of the internet."[24] The second way is primarily an effect of managing software – of the "softwarization" of objects. The former case concerns the internet as a whole, as it is presented to users, while the latter case concerns individual digital objects (texts, images, etc.) as well as material things.

Because search engines and platforms such as Google and Facebook create observational profiles of users, they are able to influence, via feedback, how the internet is arranged and presented to individuals. In this sense, the internet is personalized – that is, singularized – by means of algorithms. Subjects thus encounter a tailored cultural world that attempts to suit their current wishes and desires as accurately as possible. At the moment, the two most prominent forms of this singularization are the news feeds on Facebook and the way that Google presents search results. When users are logged on to their Facebook pages, they are confronted with the current cultural environment of the internet in the form of a news feed that is tailored just for them.[25] Depending on who their friends are and what groups they associate with, as well as on the institutions and

IV Digitalization as Singularization 187

news portals that they are connected to, users are presented with a series of current posts and links that is *just for them*. On the basis of the vast number of texts, images, and links that have been posted by these friends, groups, institutions, and news portals, algorithms are able to generate a selection that suits the individual interests of users. For many people, the Facebook news feed functions as a sort of window into their digital environment – or into their cultural world as a whole. What they see through this window, however, is a personally tailored cultural universe.

Google's search engine operates in a similar way. From its perspective, the digital world basically has the status of a database.[26] Like all databases, this one is never visible to its users as a whole; instead, information is provided on the basis of their specific search requests. When users search for information on Google, the list of websites that appears is not only arranged according to their page rank, which is the frequency with which sites are linked to and thus corresponds to their "objective" popularity. In addition, the order in which the sites are listed also depends indirectly on the specific observational profile of the individual user (which Google has determined by way of data tracking). Consequently, his or her previous preferences influence how the internet is presented to the user via Google. Here, the search profiles of users – and thus everything that they are shown – attempt to match their (previous) interests as closely as possible.

In an automated and algorithmic manner, portals such as Facebook and Google thus transform the essentially *universal* cultural *world* of the internet into countless singularized *environments* that are designed to suit individual subjects, who receive only these environments to see. And, moreover, the internet only exists in theory as a general or universal entity, for the only thing that is accessible to users is their personally tailored excerpt of the world. This way of singularizing the digital world can be interpreted as a response to the problem of attention that arises from the sheer volume of online texts and images. These require a drastic culling, and this is what has brought about personalized access portals. In this case, singularization does not mean that something unique has been created *ex nihilo* but rather that algorithms have selected a few digital objects out of the abundance that already exist and have arranged them in a specific way. This singularization of the world of objects is subject-oriented in advance: it takes place according to the particular interests and desires of subjects. Conversely, this means that the algorithmic customization of the digital environment tends to make subjectively unsettling or disturbing objects invisible.

In addition to this, the culture machine also enables users to singularize "their own" digital objects actively and intentionally, primarily with the help of computer software. Lev Manovich has rightly pointed out that our relation to the technical world fundamentally changed when industrial mechanization was replaced by the "softwarization" of objects.[27] Software has turned the everyday user into a cultural producer and has thus made creative production an everyday activity. Every layperson is now in a position to create new and unique cultural objects: texts, images, graphics, three-dimensional environments, etc.[28] This form of singularization is likewise based on modularization. The main operations of software are selection and composition. Software enables and requires choices to be made between alternatives, and combinations to be made out of the elements that have been selected: cut and paste.

Software thus fragments the process of creating new and original things into individual, comprehensible steps, and it forces people to engage with already existing objects and design alternatives. Here, too, what already exists is *not* unique but rather standardized (modular) or the same for everyone. Uniqueness rather results from the combination of individual decisions, and thus software creates a space for mashups and experimental further developments. In this light, it is possible to speak of software-supported *bound creativity* whose methods are reminiscent of the classical montage. However, objects made with the help of software are not viewed in terms of their combinatory process of creation: in the end, the text, image, graphic, or game simply appears as though it fell out of a mold. Finally, this has been taken a step further by 3D printers, which were originally used by the maker movement and the do-it-yourself culture in collectively shared "makerspaces" and "fab labs." They make it possible to translate digitally singularized objects into a material form – into three-dimensional things that are unique pieces or tailored objects.[29]

Digital Neo-Communities and the Sociality of the Internet

Theorists of digitalization have provided a variety of answers to the question of how the internet has affected society and politics. At first, the prevailing hope was that it would institutionalize a new, general, and global public sphere in which everyone could participate. What has happened, however, is the complete opposite: the internet has in fact assisted in the creation of a multitude of particular collectives. These communities can be described as digital *neo-communities*, and they are distinguished by the fact that they singularize themselves *as collectives*. These unique interpretive communities, which exist alongside one another, are highly valued by their participants and are associated with intense affectivity.

Such particular communities have emerged in various contexts; it is typical for them to form around emotionally charged cultural objects, on whose basis they develop a collective identity.[30] These can be groups of passionate fans that come together around a television series, travel destination, or leisure activity. They can be political communities that share a certain ideological orientation, groups concerned with the issues of discriminated minorities, but also the diverse communities that come together on the dark web. In general, it can be said that trans-regional networking has made it possible for relatively small communities with highly specialized interests to form for the long term, and that these groups would have struggled to come together during the predigital era on account of the physical distance between their few adherents. Paradoxically, the *universality* of global interconnectivity has facilitated the formation of *particular* communities.[31]

In debates about online culture, there is a tendency to treat all forms of sociality under the umbrella term of "social networking."[32] This makes sense, for the concept of the "internet" implies that, from a sociological perspective, this communication platform has the form of a network. In my opinion, however, this view of things is too undifferentiated. It disguises the fact that there is not *one* prevailing social form in the digital world but rather *three* forms that exist side by side: heterogeneous collaborations (including networks), singularity markets, and neo-communities. Though each has its own distinct configuration, they are all singularistic forms of the social, and they are all characteristic of the society of singularities as a whole (that is, beyond the digital world).

Of course, the digital computer network is *also* populated by social networks in a sociologically precise sense. Such networks are a version of the social form that I referred to earlier as heterogeneous collaborations in my discussion of post-industrial working culture. To repeat, social networks should be understood as an ensemble of relationships between entities (such as subjects) that does not have any external limits but is rather dynamic and open-ended. Here, the relationships between entities are not exclusive and they can be combined at will. They are defined by their potential nature: they *can* result in real collaborations, but they do not have to. In a network, participants work together, but they also maintain their heterogeneity within the framework of their collaboration. A social network is a platform for singularities to the extent that people collaborate on it. Various specific forms of social networks are now formed on the internet. These include *collaborative networks*, in which people work together to achieve a common objective with no deadline (Wikipedia or open-access programs come to mind),[33] as well as *communicative associations*, in which the goal is not to accomplish something in common but rather to engage in phatic communication (as in the example of social media platforms).

In addition to social networks, however, markets – or, to be more precise, cultural singularity markets, which are also attractiveness markets – form a second and ultimately dominating form of the social that is structured by digital practices. We have already examined in detail the structurally formational relevance of digital singularity markets in the context of the singularization of profile subjects and their visibility markets. These markets share structural similarities and are interconnected with the markets of the late-modern economy. To a great extent, the internet has the form of just such a market; the overproduction of cultural elements – from YouTube videos to blogs – leads to a competition for public attention and appreciation. We have also already seen that these digital attractiveness markets function in their own way as a social platform for singularities. They form an ensemble of social practices through which singularities – both subjects (such as bloggers) or objects (such as video clips) – profile themselves.

Neo-communities, which are the third variant of singularistic sociality, have a different form altogether. They have neither the structure of singularity markets nor that of open networks. Neo-communities operate within the framework of digital practices, but they also exist outside of this framework, for instance in the political sphere. In general, they are a formative feature of the society of singularities. From the perspective of their members and external observers, neo-communities have the characteristic of singularity *as a whole*. Their uniqueness does not derive from individuals or objects (images, texts) but rather from the collective in its totality. The fact that an entire collective can be built on the notion of uniqueness is, of course, characteristic of a very traditional social format: communities. Yet, like other late-modern communities, such as those in the religious or political realm, digital communities have less to do with communities in the traditional sense. Rather, as I have already said, they are *neo-communities*. The crucial difference lies in the status of membership. Whereas someone can be born into a traditional community, neo-communities are voluntary communities that individuals choose to join. By joining a (digital) neo-community, subjects give up their own claim to uniqueness (at least for a while) and in a sense transfer this claim to the collective.

The communities of Trekkies (fans of the *Star Trek* series), Breitbart devotees, Ayurveda fans, conspiracy theorists, ISIS members, or fans of a particular style of music all seem to be singular from the perspective of their participants. Inwardly, such collectives possess a (higher or lower) degree of narrative or aesthetic inherent complexity; outwardly, they draw a (more or less) sharp line between themselves and others (the "non-believers"). Unlike the neo-communities in the offline world, digital neo-communities essentially consist of textual and visual communication among people who are not physically present to one another. They are thus genuine communicative communities that function as interpretive communities and collective attention filters. They form what Eli Pariser has called "filter bubbles," which, in various communities, can lead to the development of distinct world views, and even to genuinely parallel, media-based societies.[34]

Communication within digital communities is not structured by the asymmetry between a producer (who seeks attention) and an audience (which grants attention) but is rather based on the egalitarian structure of their members, who are encouraged to participate actively. Whereas the subjects and goods on the dynamic digital attractiveness market fight for valorization (and often lose this fight), the members of digital communities earn value by participating in something that is regarded as valuable by everyone involved, be it an aesthetic practice, a cult object, or a political narrative. In such communities, subjects may have a derivative sort of value, but this value is secure. Here, communication is of a highly affective nature. Unlike the positivity culture of the Facebook paradigm, in digital neo-communities there are often intensive affects of both types: positive *and* negative, welcoming *and* distancing. This internal communication, which gives shape to a group's identity, also enforces a high degree of *homogenization*. Heated debates can take place within such communities, but they are so controversial *because* the (homogeneous) collective identity of the group is the very basis of the communication in question. This is the decisive difference that distinguishes neo-communities from networks and singularity markets: whereas the latter two form a platform for the heterogeneity of subjects and objects, neo-communities work together as a whole social unit to cultivate their uniqueness and homogeneous particularity.[35]

Fields of Tension in Online Culture:
From the Pressure to Create Profiles to Extreme Affect Culture

With its tendency to singularize the world, the digital computer network has given rise to a number of tensions and paradoxes. Behind the infinite possibilities of the internet and its liberation from the constraints of mass culture, there now lurks a new set of constraints and dilemmas. I would like to discuss five of these before bringing this part to an end.

First, the culture of the internet has obviously given subjects the opportunity to present themselves as people with multifaceted and even eccentric interests, and to network with those who share similar interests. The unique qualities of subjects no longer seem threatening but, rather, legitimate. Certain attributes that would have been marginalized or pathologized in organized modernity – think of ethnic minorities or members of the LGBTQ community – have acquired a recognized place within the framework of cultural pluralization that the internet endorses. However, the singularization of the subject does not mean that everything is possible. Rather, the act of being socially adjusted (both online and offline) has shifted to a more abstract level: to the *social expectation of being unique*, though in an *acceptable* way. This form of social adjustment is subtler than that which David Riesman observed in the "other-directed character" of postwar society.[36] Whereas, in that context, the aim was to behave as normally as possible and be an Everyman, now we are all expected to fine-tune our originality, interests, and activities in order to present to the world ever new and surprising details and experiences from our own lives. Now there is a prevailing *pressure* to create profiles, which, at the same time, is a pressure to be original, creative, and open to experiences. In the case of subjects, too, the valorization of originality is an unpredictable and volatile affair. As in the case of cultural goods on economic markets, singularization and valorization go hand in hand with de-singularization and de-valorization in the case of subjects on the digital market of visibility and evaluation.

The demanding expectations faced by late-modern subjects – both online and offline – have led to new mechanisms of exclusion, and these can be found on three different levels. The first consists of those problematic subjects whose performance of singularity has failed on account of seeming *conformist*. They are then regarded as "flat characters" – as passive and conventional people who seem to lack creativity, activism, and passion for the world. Whereas, in the previous culture of conformism, nonconformists were treated with disdain, in the new culture of nonconformism, it is conformism that seems pitiful. Yet, even though every individual is idiosyncratic, late-modern culture allows only a select few to become valuable and attractive singularities.

A second level of exclusion involves *unacceptable peculiarities*. In mild cases, these are idiosyncrasies that are not pathological in the strict sense but are still too "awkward" to be received as valuable. They run the risk of causing embarrassment. In fact, there are many indications that in late modernity, which has supposedly left behind the traditional bourgeois culture of guilt and the superego, there has been a strong revival of shame culture, and that this has been promoted, above all, by (digital) media. The feeling of shame arises from the awareness that one does not, in one given instance or in general, meet the demanding requirements of attractive and singular subjectivity. Being ashamed of one's own self corresponds to a feeling of embarrassment on the part of an audience, and this

IV Digitalization as Singularization

feeling can be aroused by a certain type of situational behavior, by someone's outward appearance, or by his or her overall personality.[37] More blatant cases of unacceptable peculiarity are indeed regarded as *pathological*. These can be illegal activities, extreme political positions, violent tendencies, but also addictions or harmful sexual proclivities such as pedophilia. The late-modern plurality of subjectivities is thus no stranger to the distinction between the normal and the abnormal. However, there is a tendency in late-modern media culture to (negatively) singularize even pathological cases of uniqueness – that is, to make an intensive theme of criminals in all of their disturbing otherness and inherent complexity.[38] It should also be stressed, moreover, that the grounds for determining whether something is original (on the one hand) or conformist, awkward, or even pathological (on the other) have become highly dynamic. Devaluations can quickly be converted into positive valorizations, and discriminated groups can create online forums overnight. The nerd can become a hipster, the outcast can become a genius, and disparaged groups (such as overweight, asexual, or depressed people) can work together to shed their pathological image.

Second, despite the diversification of the subject that the internet culture has allowed, a digital *cementation of the individual* has also taken place there. To the theorists of early online culture, such things as multi-use chat rooms still seemed like promising arenas for experimenting with identities,[39] and this sort of experimentalism has not fully disappeared, especially not from the internet's anonymous spaces. However, several factors have led to the fact that users are now increasingly compelled to establish a stable online identity, whether they want to or not. The algorithmic construction of user profiles and the corresponding fabrication of customized digital environments, which I discussed above, have meant that individuals are confronted less and less with things that are completely different, surprising, or random – irritating encounters that, in the past, would often incite users to alter their online identity. The "filter bubbles" of networks and neo-communities have had a similar effect. Moreover, the fact that online and offline identities are interlinked – the digital subject is no longer anonymous but usually has a name and a face – has also inhibited the inclination to experiment. This inclination is further inhibited by the fact that the internet does not forget: when the sins of the past live on forever, the temptation to "try things out" might have long-lasting negative effects.

Third, a compulsory social orientation toward the particular can lead to the erosion of the general. This tendency is clear to see, for example, in the digital public sphere. Here, what has taken place is the *devitalization of the general public sphere*. In one respect, of course, the internet is the medium of radically democratic pluralism, and it plays host to extremely intensive public discussion.

This, however, is related to the establishment of a multitude of parallel public spheres. The pluralism on the internet is not about a single shared space; it is rather about the parallel existence of different and generally incompatible spaces. When everyone treats his or her individually tailored news feed as a window to the world, the result is such a broad diversification of perspectives that, in extreme cases, different subjects no longer share a common basis for debate. The same is true of collective entities: the cultural environment outside one's network of friends and communities (neo-communities) can seem strange or even incommensurable.[40] Here, the phatic communication that takes place within groups corresponds to an indifferent or even inimical attitude toward those on the outside.

Fourth, the internet is oriented toward the actuality of the present moment. In order to capture the attention of users, the latest texts, images, and links thus have to be associated with affective excitement: interesting or shocking, exhilarating or bizarre. What prevails online is thus a radicalized digital regime of the new – a *regime of affective actualism* in which things that have just happened are often quickly forgotten. The flipside of this is that topics and ideas of long-term significance tend to be ignored. When scrolling through profiles on social media, nobody is interested in long-winded biographical narratives or prolix discourses about the world at large. What people want to see are the latest short posts. Affective actualism is clearest to see in the news coverage of political and social issues and events. News sites, which depend on repeatedly attracting the attention of readers, therefore tend to post new and exciting items with minimal lasting interest or to focus on topics that incite negative feelings such as outrage, fear, or envy and thus absorb the attention of users.[41] Short, one-time, up-to-date narratives thus alternate with themes that remain topical for several days or even weeks, only to disappear abruptly as soon as they have lost their interest. The less surprising flipside to the online regime of affective actualism is that it marginalizes whatever happens to be uneventful and affectively neutral or ambivalent.[42]

Fifth, the internet is home to a *digital affect culture of extremes*. On one side, there is a sort of *positivity culture*, so that the internet can seem like a "feel-good" medium. Profile subjects present themselves as attractive; communication among "friends" is overwhelmingly phatic; and algorithms can tell the desires and interests of subjects from the look in their eyes, so to speak. At this extreme, the internet has become an echo chamber of desire that fulfills wishes before they are even articulated. In this positive culture, negative affects (from irritation to repulsion) and experiences (disappointments, failures, serious illnesses, life crises) are suppressed, avoided, or excluded.[43] Likewise, the phatic communication among digital friends leaves

IV Digitalization as Singularization

little room for personal or political differences or disputes. It is basically reserved for mutual affirmation.

Standing opposite to this positive culture of attractiveness is, of course, the digital eruption of decidedly negative affects. At this extreme, we find aggressive cyber-bullying, untethered Schadenfreude, and the malicious derision of people in embarrassing situations – all the formats, that is, in which people can be the object of communicative aggression, shaming, and contempt. The comment sections on news sites deserve special mention here. Whereas subjects participating in the positivity culture are usually known by name, the subjects who engage in this culture of negativity typically hide behind the protective veil of anonymity. This is an indication of the illegitimacy of negativity, but the latter has still managed to find plenty of space for itself. Although the causes of these negative affects may in part derive from the offline social world, in many respects they can be interpreted as a product of frustrations created by digital culture itself. Because the latter, via its ongoing competition to seem attractive, crowns relatively few digital winners (both on the large scale of the internet as a whole and on the smaller scale of social media), who attract a high degree of visibility and achieve prominence, it also creates innumerable "digital losers," who fail to attract attention and remain invisible bystanders – primarily of the ostensibly fulfilled, acknowledged, and singular lives of others.[44]

V
The Singularistic Life: Lifestyles, Classes, Subject Forms

The Late-Modern Self Beyond the Leveled Middle-Class Society

The establishment of the post-industrial economy of singularities and the rise of the digital culture machine form the structural backbone of the late-modern society of singularities. Over the course of the last three parts, we have traced this structural transformation in detail. In this chapter, I would like to examine what this process has meant for the way that late-modern subjects shape themselves and their lives, how such things are shaped by external factors, and how this transformation has influenced the overall social tableau of lifestyles and class structures.

Since the 1980s, the assumption that the late-modern self is fundamentally different from the social character that dominated the classical modernity of industrial society has instigated a number of prominent sociological analyses. Examples include Ulrich Beck's studies of reflexive modernization and the risk society, Anthony Giddens's discussions of the high-modern self as a project, Zygmunt Bauman's thesis of "fluid" and consumption-oriented identities, Richard Sennett's work on the flexible nature of late-modern life, and Manuel Castells's theories about the network society.[1] I am of the opinion, however, that the question of the late-modern lifestyle has to be approached yet again with fresh eyes. Despite what is often suggested, it is not sensible to separate the question of *the* late-modern lifestyle from that of its representative *social groups*. In its most advanced form, the late-modern subject does not exist in a vacuum but rather operates in a clearly definable socio-cultural milieu, or, to put this in more precise terms, in a socio-cultural class: the *new middle class*.[2] This is the milieu of (mostly) highly educated people who possess a high degree of cultural capital and work in the knowledge and culture economy – a milieu that we have already examined in previous chapters.[3] In this sense, the new middle class is a milieu of educated individuals; it is an *educated* middle class or, in short: the educated class.[4]

By using the term "representative group," I do not mean to suggest that only certain elements and milieus of society are affected by culturalization and singularization. As general processes of the economy, technology, and shifting values, they influence society as a whole and all of its subjects in every milieu. Their influence may be stronger or weaker here or there, but no one can avoid it entirely. Its purest form, however, can be found in the *singularistic lifestyle* of the new middle class. Within this class, the "creative milieu" functions as a cultural incubator, and this is the relatively small but culturally influential milieu of those who are active in the professions associated with the creative industries in the strict sense (computers and the internet, media, art, design, marketing, etc.). In late modernity, it is the educated middle class that, spurred on in large part by this creative milieu, endeavors to singularize and culturalize its lifestyle in a fundamental and trend-setting manner by prioritizing "culture" and appreciating the value and experience of uniqueness. Authenticity, self-actualization, cultural openness, diversity, quality of life, and creativity are the parameters of this lifestyle, which has now achieved prominence beyond the borders of its primary representative group and become a hegemonic force. Since the 1980s, the milieu of university graduates and highly qualified professionals has not just been home to a small elite; rather, in Western societies, it constitutes around a third of the population, and its numbers are rising. It *is* the new middle class.[5]

Beyond the new middle class, however, it has to be made clear that this revolution in the structure of lifestyles has influenced the society of singularities as a whole. In late modernity, we are dealing (yet again) with a class society. However, this does not only exist in a strict material sense – rather, it is also, and even more importantly, a matter of cultural classes. In addition to being distinguished by the unequal distribution of material resources (income, assets), today's classes also fundamentally differ from one another with respect to their lifestyles and their cultural capital. The socio-structural transformation that Western societies have been experiencing since the 1980s can be described as a transition from a *leveled middle-class society* to a *cultural class society*. This diagnosis may seem surprising at first in light of the basic assumptions that (especially German) sociologists have been making during this same timeframe. Ulrich Beck, who has been particularly influential in this regard, maintains that post-industrial society has replaced the former large-scale social and political classes with processes of individualization. In their studies of postmodernity, cultural sociologists have accordingly detected a pluralization of equally valued lifestyles.[6] From today's perspective, however, this idea of free-floating and hierarchy-free lifestyles and individuals has proven to be an optical illusion. By now, we have gradually come to realize that the culturalization and singularization of late-modern society have brought about not the *end*, but rather the *beginning*, of a new class society.

In retrospect, one could in fact say that it was industrial modernity that came closest to developing a classless society. This was true not only of its socialist version but also of its Western version, whose social structure, according to Helmut Schelsky's apt description, was that of a "levelled middle-class society."[7] This structure was epitomized by the *trente glorieuses* from the 1950s to the 1970s, during which the model of an all-encompassing middle class was realized above all in the United States, West Germany, and Scandinavian countries. The leveled middle-class society correlated with industrial society at large, with mass culture (with its mass media and mass consumption), and with the "social-democratic consensus" in politics. In light of the distinction made here between the social logic of the general and the social logic of the particular, one could say that, in addition to the rationalism of industrial society, the leveled middle-class society was also defined through and through by the logic of the general, by a logic of standardized resources, and by the *normalization of ways of life*. Here, the term "middle" did not simply designate a socio-statistical average around which more than 90 percent of the population hovered; it was also a proud cultural expression that denoted an average lifestyle: normal working conditions, a normal family, a normal and reasonable amount of consumption, etc. As we have already seen, the main objective of the leveled middle-class way of life was to cultivate a *standard* of living – furnished with similar resources and similar comforts for all.

The Cultural Class Divide and the "Paternoster-Elevator Effect"

Along with industrial society in general, this leveled middle-class society has been eroding since the 1980s, and what has appeared in its place is a new, conspicuous, and culturally based class divide. Within Western societies, this transition is clearest to see in the United States, but it has been nearly as drastic in Great Britain, France, and Germany.[8] The changes that this has brought about have affected the upper segment of society as well as the lower. The former middle has eroded, and what remains is a polarity between one class with high cultural capital (as well as medium to high economic capital) and another class with low cultural and economic capital: the new middle class on the one hand, and the new underclass on the other.

Robert Putnam has identified the most important features of this transition from a middle-class to a polarized society, and although his analysis is concerned with the United States, his findings are representative of the West as a whole.[9] In sum, what characterized the leveled middle-class society was relatively minimal inequality with respect to income, and widespread prosperity, which could also be enjoyed by blue-collar workers and low-level employees. There was a degree of educational mobility, but formal education was not a necessary precondition for achieving the middle-class standard of living. Residential areas were thus relatively mixed and homogeneous at the same time: there was a mixture of different professional groups, who all lived essentially the same middle-class life. Personal relationships (including marriages) also frequently cut across the boundaries between different professions and levels of qualification.

These parameters have fundamentally changed since the 1980s, and it is already possible to identify, with formal precision, the two representative groups of this new socio-cultural polarization: the new middle class, which is mostly university educated, is opposed by a new underclass, which has minimal (if any) formal educational qualifications.[10] The old, non-educated middle class exists between these two poles. Since the turn of the millennium, several eye-catching studies have been published about the intensification of social inequality, and these works tend to focus on the small segment of the "super rich" – the 1 percent of the population that has accumulated an exorbitant amount of capital.[11] However, what is more relevant and consequential regarding the transformation of the structure of society, lifestyles, and culture as a whole is the formation of the new (and far larger) educated middle class, which encompasses around a third of the population. Its expansion has been facilitated by two interrelated social processes, both of which have been taking place since the 1970s: first, the shift, described above, of the economy's structure toward post-industrialism, which has led to the expansion of qualified professions in the knowledge and culture economy; second, the expansion of education, which has allowed the proportion of highly qualified people (typically with university degrees) to swell into a significant segment of society.

The inverse image of the rise of this new educated class is the formation of a *new underclass*. Gøsta Esping-Andersen was one of the first scholars to identify the expansion of simple service jobs and concomitant rise of a new, low-qualified service class as an equally important feature of post-industrial society.[12] Altogether, the new underclass is a thoroughly heterogeneous group of simple service providers, semi-qualified industrial laborers, part-time employees, unemployed people, and social welfare recipients (as well as socially excluded people in the strict sense) who likewise constitute about a third of today's Western population. With respect to their income, assets, and social status, this group exists on a level that is clearly below that of the old middle-class society. The social causes behind its creation are the inverse of those that engendered the new middle class: the transition to the post-industrial society has entailed a rapid erosion of traditional industrial jobs (as well as that of highly routinized jobs) and, at the same time, a rapid expansion in the sector of simple services, which has been stimulated directly or indirectly by the new knowledge and culture economy and by the needs of the new middle class. Paradoxically, the expansion of education has also contributed to the creation of the new underclass: those untouched by it now form a new group of under-educated people whose minimal qualifications fetter them to the economic and cultural service class. The late-modern polarization of living conditions affects material and cultural factors at the same time.[13] On the material level, the relatively egalitarian model of income distribution has been replaced by a diverging development. Particularly consequential is the historical loss of prosperity suffered by the new underclass, which has fallen below the middle-class living standard and whose employment is often precarious. In terms of material well-being, the development in the educated class has been more varied: for the fraction in the upper middle class, who have profited from the global "war of talents" in the knowledge economy, economic capital has grown considerably, whereas income has remained stable (in comparison with that of the old middle class) for the vast majority and, for some (especially young employees), economic stability is far from certain.[14] Nevertheless, it is fundamentally the case that the income gap in the West between those with and those without a college degree has clearly widened since the 1980s.[15] The polarization that has taken place is therefore *also* of a material sort.

However, the truly unifying bond of the educated class – the aspect that enables its common lifestyle – is its high *cultural* capital. In general, polarization on the level of education and cultural capital is *the* central feature that defines the social structure of late-modern society. Whereas, in the leveled middle-class society, the type of school or university degree that one held was hardly a decisive factor in achieving a middle-class lifestyle, the opposition between the high-qualified and the low-qualified has become a formational aspect of late modernity. It is now the "education factor" that largely determines the standard of living and lifestyle that individuals can achieve. This overwhelming significance of education to social stratification pertains to both formal academic degrees and informal cultural capital. The segregation of educational attainment is thus linked to a reduction of educational mobility. Moreover, the polarization of classes is also reflected in living conditions. Especially in cities, the formerly mixed residential areas of middle-class society have been replaced by the spatial segregation between the "attractive areas" of the educated class and the "rough areas" occupied by the underclass. A comparable situation is the spatial polarization that now exists between economically successful regions and regions that are thought to have been "left behind." It is no wonder, then, that personal relationships across classes (even within one's extended family) and partnerships between individuals from different milieus have been in steep decline since the 1990s.[16]

Aside from the drastic polarity between the new educated middle class and the new underclass, there are two other relevant classes in late modernity that should be mentioned here (I will return to them at the end of this Part): the upper class and the "old" middle class (that is, the middle class without college degrees). They complete our picture of socio-structural polarization. With its enormous accumulation of assets, the *(new) upper class* is a genuine result of the winner-take-all processes of the economy of singularities (in the financial sector, professional sports, management, etc.), and it differs from the new middle class less drastically through its cultural capital than it does through its economic (and social) capital. This capital enables luxurious lifestyles that are not dependent on employment income.[17]

Finally, the *old* middle class (without college degrees) is the immediate descendant of the formerly dominant lifestyle of the leveled middle-class society. Here, a moderate amount of cultural and economic capital is thought to be enough to secure a moderate standard of living and to lead a presumably "normal" lifestyle. If the new middle class constitutes the upper third (with the tiny upper class on top) and the new underclass constitutes the lower third of the late-modern class structure, then the old middle class forms its (generally shrinking) middle third. Late-modern society is thus a *three-thirds society*.[18] In material, but especially in cultural, terms, the old middle class has been waning since the 1980s. It is no longer the dominant and trend-setting middle of society, as it was from the 1950s to the 1970s, but is now wedged between the new educated class and the new underclass, to which it is also losing members. The allegedly normal lifestyle of the middle class is no longer generally valid. Instead of being something to aspire to, it is simply *mediocre*, while the singularistic lifestyle of the educated class is flourishing on its one side, and the new underclass faces the threat of being socially "left behind" on its other side.[19]

An examination of this social structure as a whole leads to the following conclusion: in contrast to the "elevator effect," which characterized industrial modernity and promised increased prosperity for all strata of society,[20] the social structure of late modernity is characterized by what I would like to call the *paternoster-elevator effect*. In the leveled middle-class society, everyone was more or less on a comparable (but not equal) material level and led a similar cultural lifestyle, so that both compartments of the "social paternoster elevator" were still around the same floor. Since the 1980s, however, the compartment containing one social segment – the new, educated class (including the new upper class) – has gone up, while the compartment containing the other segment – the new underclass (and part of the old middle class) – has gone down. This effect is easy to overlook if one remains fixated on the distribution of income and assets. Of course, this ascent and descent *also* have a material component. Far more important, however, is the fact that the culturalization of the social, which we have already seen in other areas of society, has wielded a strong influence over today's lifestyles and classes as well. The paternoster-elevator effect therefore pertains also – and especially – to the *cultural rise* and *cultural decline* of the respective social groups.

The cultural rise of the new middle class and the cultural decline of the underclass (and part of the old middle class) involve three different levels. The *first* level, which I have already mentioned, is that of cultural capital. In a society in which formal education and informal cultural capital have become central resources for attaining social status, opportunities to shape one's lifestyle, and feelings of self-worth, the highly qualified members of the new middle class have become the "climbers," while everyone else, and particularly those with minimal formal and informal educational capital, have essentially been handicapped. Whereas, in the leveled middle-class society, low levels of education could lead to opportunities and were regarded as "normal" and "average," people with such qualifications today are now considered "low-qualified" and have extremely limited possibilities.[21]

The *second* level concerns the self-culturalization of one's lifestyle. This is the hallmark of the new middle class. The relationship of its members to the world and to themselves is distinguished by a particular cosmopolitan relation to culture and by the comprehensive aestheticization and ethicization of everyday life, all in the pursuit of self-actualization and authenticity. Beyond seeking a certain standard of living, this singularistic lifestyle is directed toward cultural value: toward a quality of life (the "good life"). It is this quality of life that furnishes the new middle class with prestige. This is in contrast to the minimal opportunities for culturalizing one's life in the precarious underclass, which is predominantly oriented toward maintaining normality and satisfying basic needs. What prevails here is the logic of "muddling through," which is necessarily focused on managing the difficulties of everyday life. Relative to the way of life of the leveled middle-class society, which cultivated security and a certain standard of living, the culturalized lifestyle of the new middle class is thus more advanced and ambitious (rise), whereas the way of life of the underclass no longer fulfills the former expectations of middle-class society (decline).

The *third* level involves the distinctive processes of valorization and devaluation between the classes. If culture in the strong sense entails drawing distinctions between the valuable and the valueless, then such processes of valorization and devaluation are fundamental to the late-modern class structure. The lifestyle of the new middle class as such is now socially prized as a *valuable way of life*, and its representative subjects are regarded as *valuable subjects* with valuable qualities (creativity, openness, a sense of style, an entrepreneurial spirit, a capacity for empathy, cosmopolitanism, etc.). The subjects of the new middle class can thus be understood as representatives of a forward-looking way of life that has become the social standard of successful life in general. Conversely, the way of life of the new underclass (and that of the old middle class, in more subtle ways) seems valueless and deficient – both in the self-perception of subjects and in its social representations. It is an object of *negative culturalization* and *devaluation*. As its name suggests, the *under*class is perceived by outsiders and by most of its own members as occupying a lower rung in the social hierarchy – as a culture of "losers" who have been "left behind."[22] Here, what has taken place is the *culturalization of inequality*.[23] This means that, in social representations and in the self-perception of subjects, inequality is no longer just a matter of material disparities but also one of cultural differences in the competencies, ethos, everyday aesthetics, and overall acknowledged value or worthlessness of lifestyles.

In sum, the paternoster-elevator effect of the late-modern social structure has arisen from the rise of the well-resourced and valorized lifestyle of the satisfied and successful new middle class and the countervailing decline of the underfunded and devalued lifestyle of the new underclass, which is struggling to get by. Whereas the leveled middle-class society was able to promise a comfortable lifestyle for most people, late modernity's singularistic lifestyle serves as an attractive model for all of society, but it is not something that everyone can attain.

1
The Lifestyle of the New Middle Class: Successful Self-Actualization

Now it seems appropriate to take a closer look at the singularistic lifestyle of late modernity as it appears in its purest form – that is, as it is practiced by the new educated middle class. The best way to do so will be to examine the individual everyday practices of which this lifestyle is composed: the role that food and nutrition play in it; the relationship between work and leisure; the way that subjects relate to their own bodies and move through the world; where they live and how they furnish their homes; the significance of travel and stays abroad; and, finally, the ways in which the members of this class raise their children and value schools and education in general. I will go into greater detail about each of these elements in the second chapter in this Part. First, however, it will be necessary to discuss the abstract logic behind the lifestyle of the new middle class.

Romanticism and Bourgeois Culture: The New Symbiosis

In order to understand the principle of the singularistic lifestyle, it first has to be contextualized within the *longue durée* of lifestyles and subject forms that have existed throughout the 200-year history of Western modernity. Only then will it become clear that the new middle class has synthesized two cultural models that were at first antipodal: the lifestyle of Romanticism and that of the bourgeoisie. Our cultural-historical lens will thus have to focus on the period *before* the leveled middle-class society of industrial modernity – that is, on the period of early bourgeois modernity.

It cannot be repeated enough that the configuration of the singularistic lifestyle has been shaped by a modern cultural tradition that was only of marginal and subcultural relevance until 1970: the tradition of Romanticism, with its notions of the emphatic originality of the subject, which had to be developed and actualized.[1] Proceeding from the model of the self-actualization and self-development of the subject, the Romantic movement endeavored to culturalize and singularize the world in a comprehensive manner. The overall objective was to move beyond an instrumentally rational and unemotional relationship to the world and to treat objects, subjects, places, events, and collectives as aesthetic, hermeneutic, ethical, and ludic entities in order to gain affective satisfaction from them. This culturalization went hand in hand with de-standardization and singularization: the Romantics concentrated their attention on the *particular* person as an individual, the *particular* thing (a handcrafted object, work of art), the *particular* place, the *particular* event. Only in this very special context was it possible for authenticity to be valued just as highly as creativity; it was only by being unique and singular that a place or an individual (for instance) could seem authentic, and such things were expected to be the object of creative design.

The Romantic movement, which began around the year 1800, marks the starting point of a lineage of artistic and aesthetic countercultures, which ranges from the bohemianism of the nineteenth century to the life-reform and avant-garde movements around 1900 and all the way up to the counterculture of the 1970s. For nearly two centuries, these anti-mainstream subcultures were of limited influence. The counterculture of the 1970s – which often goes by the convenient label "1968" and whose influential epicenter was the "California lifestyle"[2] – represented the next historical turning point. On account of the expansion of education, many of this movement's ideas were shared by a critical mass of the population (the ascendant new middle class), and this enabled a "silent revolution" to take place that caused a shift away from the values of obligation, acceptance, and status toward the post-materialistic value of self-actualization.[3] In order for the post-Romantic authenticity revolution to establish itself after 1968, it obviously needed the support of certain institutional and systemic structures during the following decades, and this support came in the following forms: the rise of the economy of singularities (discussed at length in Parts II and III) with its attendant forms of labor and consumption, which met and further encouraged the needs of self-actualization; the rise of a psychological and pedagogical complex based on the "positive psychology" of self-growth and human potential; and, finally, the breakthrough of socially liberal political reforms, which established the right to individual self-determination, emancipated women, and provided equal rights to children, adolescents, and same-sex couples.[4]

However, the post-Romantic complex of self-actualization, authenticity, and creativity was not alone in influencing the singularistic lifestyle of the educated class. It would be absurd to maintain that late-modern subjects are no more than modernized Romantics or post-68ers. Rather, their lifestyle also draws much from that of the bourgeoisie – that is, from Romanticism's historical antipode. Since the beginning of the eighteenth century, the bourgeoisie created the first genuinely modern form of lifestyle that can be said to have been dominant.[5] Its central concern was the successful maintenance of status, which meant that the *cultivation* of status was a necessary undertaking. Education across generations was one of the important pillars of this bourgeois status investment. To a great extent, the bourgeoisie acquired its identity from its work ethic, an ethos of self-responsibility and achievement that required an entrepreneurial attitude and a deft understanding of market processes. It adhered to the ideal of an independent self who could exhibit distanced sovereignty and connoisseurship when dealing with the world at large and, not least, with culture.

Bourgeois culture went into decline during the period of the leveled middle-class society (even though – or perhaps because – the *petit*-bourgeois model was so influential at that time), but certain elements of it have experienced a revival since the 1980s. At issue here is not a superficial "renaissance of bourgeois values" but rather the *institutional* promotion of bourgeois cultural patterns in an abstract sense. Today's orientations toward entrepreneurship, market savviness, and self-responsibility for our own decisions, which have been encouraged by post-industrial cultural capitalism and political neoliberalism, ultimately derive from bourgeois dispositions. The traditional bourgeois interest in investing in status and education is likewise reflected in the increasing significance of educational processes and institutions to one's chances of achieving success in post-industrial society. Finally, the high value of culture in the late-modern lifestyle can be related to the bourgeois habitus of sovereign cultural expertise in worldly things (even though such things are no longer restricted to the realm of bourgeois high culture).

For nearly 200 years, as I have already mentioned, Romanticism and the bourgeoisie had an antagonistic relationship with one another,[6] and this long tradition of antagonism has been refashioned into an unusual symbiosis by late modernity's new, educated middle class. When we look back to the beginning of late modernity in the year 1968, what we see is a cultural revolution against the conformism of a leveled middle-class society, which the counter-culture regarded as an expression of alienation and repression. Afterwards, however, the attractive project of self-actualization became a core part of the new establishment. The translation of this authenticity project into a lasting lifestyle obviously required skillful and appropriate ways of dealing with the post-industrial social world. In large part, the late-modern subjects of the new middle class have drawn upon the bourgeois habitus and its expertise in dealing with markets, work, education, and cultural goods. The bourgeois orientation toward status thus converged with the Romantic ideal of self-actualization. The formula that has enabled the educated middle class to cohere between Romanticism and bourgeois values is paradoxical: *successful self-actualization*.

Self-Actualization and the Valorization of Everyday Life

The lifestyle of late-modern subjects in the new middle class is shaped by the ideal of self-actualization in possibly all of its everyday practices. This is not, however, a sort of self-actualization that is enacted in opposition to the modern world; rather, it is supposed to unfold *in* this world and to do so in a socially successful and recognized manner. This lifestyle therefore follows the contradictory model of *successful self-actualization*. Whereas traditional bourgeois subjects, who were fixated on social status and success, often had to subordinate their own desires in favor of obligations and conventions, and whereas Romantic subjects experimented with their lives at the cost of being outcast to the margins of society, late-modern subjects want to have both: self-actualization *and* social success and recognition.[7]

Self-actualization has become a polysemous concept that one encounters more and more in the everyday world. I would therefore first like to remind readers that the idea of a self who legitimately strives to realize his or her "own" or "innermost" thoughts and desires – that is, to *express* them in acts and deeds – was a peculiar semantic invention of Romanticism and *Sturm und Drang*. In the 1950s and 1960s, this idea was lent a scientific basis by the psychology of self-actualization and self-growth.[8] In this context, it seemed possible to distinguish two diametrically opposed relations to the self and to the world: on the one hand, an instrumentally rational or normative relation, which is concerned with pursuing ends in order to satisfy primary needs and material interests or to align oneself with the externally motivated norms of society; on the other hand, a world relation of self-actualization, the aim of which is to experience the self for its own sake (through creative activity, love, religion, nature, art, etc.). The self-actualizing subject does not want to "have" or to "appear" but, rather, in his or her practices and at any given moment, to "be" and ideally to enjoy "peak experiences" (in Maslow's terms).

The ideas formulated by the psychology of self-actualization, which have been disseminated through psychological practices, parenting guidebooks, marriage counselors, and pedagogical concepts, have in fact contributed a great deal to the formation of the structure of the late-modern subject. Put bluntly, it could be said that, since 1968, the thought of self-actualization has been *the* "sunken cultural good" of late-modern culture and its new middle class. Here, subjects presuppose that they are *capable* of and *entitled* to self-actualization; they see themselves as sources of potential and claim to have a sort of moral right to develop their unique selves however they see fit. Accordingly, this attitude of entitlement is linked to strong feelings of self-worth: late-modern subjects attribute value to themselves as individuals, and this attribution is based on the presumption that the freedom to develop oneself as one pleases is unquestionably legitimate and even natural.[9]

In social terms, the self can be actualized or realized in one of two ways, the first of which derives from the counterculture of the 1970s, whereas the other way has become dominant in the new middle class. The *world-averse self-actualization* of counter-cultures took place in subcultural niches and was directed against the "system" of the majority of society and its alienated, "square" practices. In this context, the self was often understood as an object of extensive self-exploration, over the course of which one's true and authentic desires could be discovered. To some extent, world-averse self-actualization was an "inward journey" in a dual sense.[10] *World-embracing self-actualization*, which has been dominant since the 1980s, is a different matter entirely. In this case, the pursuit of experiences is not restricted to subcultures but is rather oriented toward the heterogeneous cultural offerings of the entire world.[11] It goes without saying that this self is not retreating on an inward journey *against* the world but can only be actualized by dealing *with* the world: what I truly am and really want to be will only come to light through my everyday practices, which I will test out for myself and undertake with pleasure or passion. This world-embracing self-actualization is based on the presupposition that the world is equipped for such an attitude. And, in fact, late modernity – with its rich offerings from the global and digital economy of singularities (between yoga retreats, ethnic food, creative work, Facebook, and singing lessons) but also with its liberal parenting styles and emancipated gender relations – does indeed accommodate and encourage this subjective pursuit of self-actualization. The habitus suits its context.

The world-embracing self-actualization of late modernity is thus, at the same time, a self-oriented world-actualization. It is associated with everyday processes of culturalizing and singularizing the world. Yet what is it, precisely, that makes the late-modern lifestyle *singularistic*? The answer is that culturalization and singularization are not only macro-processes of cultural capitalism and the digital media; in addition, the subjects of the new middle class are themselves constantly engaged in micro-practices of culturalization and singularization by which they intend to actualize themselves. Through the process of culturalization, the broadest possible aspects of the everyday world have been reconfigured into practices that are not only undertaken for instrumental reasons or to conform with society but also because they seem intrinsically valuable and worth pursuing for their own sake. Such practices are associated with affective satisfaction and experiences.[12] What occurs here is the *valorization* and *culturalization of everyday practices*. This can take the form of aestheticization, but it can also involve instilling practices with ethical importance or turning them into games, narratives, or objects of creative design. The aestheticization of life, in which everyday things and practices become objects of sensory pleasure – from design and cultural events to raising children – should be stressed in particular, but the "ethicization" of life, which means designing practices according to the standard of what seems ethically good – from food culture, healthcare, and being mindful of one's own body and mind to an ethical approach to politics (activism, humanitarianism) – is just as characteristic of the lifestyle of the new middle class.

Self-actualizing subjects attempt to culturalize as many elements of their lives as possible, and thus to make them *valuable* in a strict sense. Work is no longer just about earning money but should rather be intrinsically motivated and meaningful; partnerships and marriages are not entered and families are not made simply to fulfill social obligations but rather with the expectation that such things will lead to further individual development, satisfying free time, and "new experiences" (with one's children, for instance); one no longer eats simply to be satiated but rather to ingest what is ethical, good, and healthy; and because we want to see and experience unique things, we no longer take vacations advertised in generic brochures but, instead, travel, etc., etc. Over the course of this thorough culturalization of everyday life, a pattern is formed that could be called *lifestyle as culture* – a lifestyle whose every element is cultural and thus intrinsically valuable. At the same time, this culturalization of everyday life is also a *labor of singularization*: one pursues the unique, or is driven to create something singular (that is, something inherently complex), through one's own design. This is just as true of work as it is of partnerships, food, and travel. The tastefulness of food, the multifaceted nature of a travel destination, the uniqueness of one's children and their gifts, the aesthetic design of one's apartment – everything is a matter of being original, interesting, multifaceted, and different.

The singularization and valorization of the everyday world are also projects aimed at making life *authentic*. When dealing with the world, the late-modern subject generally strives for authentic experiences. In short, if something is good, it has to be authentic, and if something is authentic, it is good. As we have already seen, the value of authenticity also stems from the cultural tradition

V The Singularistic Life 213

of Romanticism and is based on the criterion of "genuineness," whereas inauthenticity applies to things that are artificial, fake, commercialized, and standardized. Something is experienced and evaluated as authentic, however, when it is recognized to be singular and when its inherent complexity is comprehendible and perceptible: when food is not mass-produced fast food but rather an expression of a particular local or ethnic tradition; when a vacation does not follow the "beaten path" of tourists but rather involves traveling somewhere "different," and so on.

By this point, it is clear that late-modern subjects culturalize and singularize *themselves* through the process of culturalizing and singularizing everyday life. They thereby make themselves valuable. However, it would be too simplistic to say that their immediate goal is for themselves to become unique and original. Rather, self-actualizing subjects wish to populate their lives with practices in which *objects, events, collectives,* and *other subjects* can be appreciated and enjoyed as unique in their singularity. The singular subject is the *result* of engaging with the world in such a way. Subjects become original and valuable through the unique composition of their various everyday practices and through the uniqueness of these practices. One could say: it is *through* my t'ai chi and my friends (who are unique on their own and unique as a group), *through* my expert knowledge of French cinema and my passion for Latin America, *through* my relationship with my boyfriend (who himself has a cultural background different from mine), and *through* my work as an author and teacher that I myself become "wide-ranging," acquire a complexity of my own, and am thus regarded as unique. It is this *compositional singularity* that lends value to the late-modern self: "I am large ... I contain multitudes."[13]

The late-modern subject in the educated class is a person with grand ambitions. When Abraham Maslow explained self-actualization as a worthwhile ideal, he famously assigned it a particular place within the hierarchy of psychological needs. Maslow observed that subjects strive at first for security, wealth, and status, but at some point these aims are no longer sufficient, so that they eventually prescribe to "higher," non-material values, and above all to that of self-development.[14] Although it is easy to dismiss the automatism toward which Maslow's hierarchy of needs is inclined, it remains true that the singularistic lifestyle and its promotion of authentic self-actualization has brought about a shift in values away from a *standard* of living toward a *quality* of life – toward the so-called *good life*. The singularistic lifestyle of the new middle class is designed in such a way as to lend quality to life. Daily life is no longer expected to be a mere means to an end; in as many of its aspects as possible, it is rather expected to be *good*, which is to say valuable, authentic, and satisfying.[15]

The Curated Life

Late-modern subjects, and especially those in the new middle class, find themselves in the position of having to curate their world and their lives: they live *curated* lives. The curator originated in the world of art and has been a leading figure there since the 1970s. Curators make choices, acquire disparate works of art from various traditions, and arrange them for exhibitions according to a sophisticated and convincing concept. Essentially, curating involves putting things together.[16] By now, the practice of curation has spread beyond the art world and become a common element of the late-modern lifestyle as a whole.

As is well known, the aesthetic movements of modernity taught us to treat our lives like a work of art and, thus, in some sense, to act as artists. In light of the late-modern lifestyle, however, it seems more accurate to say that subjects behave less like artists than they do like curators of their own lives. The traditional notion of aesthetic genius proceeded from the assumption that artists express themselves in their own independently created work. The work itself seemed like a demiurgical act, as though the artist had brought it into the world *ex nihilo*. The late-modern subject, on the contrary, never starts "from scratch" but is rather situated within an enormous, heterogeneous, global, and transhistorical hypercultural network of already existing and circulating practices and objects: from Qigong to Cuba as a vacation spot, from working as an author to enjoying art deco, from veganism to the gender codes of mothers and "tough women" – all of this already *exists* in our culture. This is the exact situation of curators: for them, too, works of art, everyday objects, theories, photographs, etc., are already present; they never introduce entirely new objects into the world. Their art lies in the clever way that they select, appropriate, transform, and embed disparate things into a harmonious whole that nevertheless preserves its heterogeneity.

The attitude of the curator has left its mark on just about every aspect of the late-modern lifestyle. Be it once or on an ongoing basis, the subjects of the new middle class curate both their individual activities – meals, trips, apartments, and even marriages – and their lives *as a whole*. Against the backdrop of all the cultural practices and objects that circulate and exist, the goal is to bring together those that might enrich the quality of one's own life and make it exciting. In curating one's life, exploration and routinization go hand in hand. At first one has to have an *exploratory* attitude, for it is necessary to try out different things in order to find what is both suitable and affective. After this discovery has been made, the selected items and activities can be made a long-lasting and *routine*

V The Singularistic Life

part of one's life (at some point, of course, such things can in turn be abandoned for others). To some extent, the curated life is thus itself composed of modules; it applies the logic of the *plurality of singularities*, which we discussed above, to the level of lifestyles: the integrated practices, things, and other people form, for the subject, a heterogeneous collaboration of its own sort, in which the individual elements also maintain their independence and unique meaning.[17] The intersectional practice of curation clarifies what makes the singularistic lifestyle a *creative* lifestyle.[18] Creativity is not only a value with which late-modern subjects identify; beyond that, the opportunity and pressure to configure things creatively are systematically built in to their lifestyle. Here, specifically, creativity means *reconfiguring* the realities at one's disposal in light of a late-modern culture in which, as we have seen, cultural practices and objects exist in excess. Therefore, what is new in the *creative lifestyle* is typically not new in the strict sense of something that has never existed before – rather, it is *relatively* new.

The intersectional practice of curation has replaced the intersectional practice of consumption, and absorbed it at the same time. In relation to the objects vying for their favor, subjects find themselves in the position of having to make selections. In late modernity, this choice is typically no longer (only) made on the basis of instrumentally rational criteria but rather (and often primarily) according to cultural criteria:[19] Zen Buddhism or German Protestantism? Pasta or sushi? Opera or hip-hop? Preparatory school or Montessori school? iPhone or Galaxy? Friedrichshain or Kreuzberg? The cultural objects and practices of late-modern consumption do not seem prescribed or compulsorily normative; instead, they are *possibilities* that, in principle, exist on equal footing and are equally available.

Regarding the creative lifestyle of the new middle class and its practice of consumption, however, this is not the full story, for there is another decisive factor at play. Creative subjects, who are busy curating their lives, no longer relate to cultural objects simply in terms of *choice*. On top of the practice of simple consumption (selection and use) is added the practice of *appropriation*, by means of which individual objects are reconfigured and combined with other objects.[20] For its part, this appropriation can have the character of *cultural labor* or of working on oneself, given that the curated life has become an overall source of a subject's self-worth: I feel valuable and special when I experience a multitude of authentic and unique things in my life and when I can compile such things for myself in a masterly way. Within the framework of the singularistic lifestyle, mere consumption has basically been devalued as a *deficient* activity, so that the curated life can be both things at once: radically consumeristic and fundamentally anti-consumeristic. And, in fact, even though nearly every element of new middle-class life is based on a consumeristic attitude – that is, on choosing between options in the name of self-actualization – the new middle class often perceives itself as being highly skeptical of consumerism. Members of the new middle class often speak out against rampant consumerism and vile commerce,[21] and they often do so with a disdainful attitude toward "vulgar" consumers, by which they explicitly or subtly mean people in the underclass. What makes this derision possible is the difference between *simple* consumer choice and *sophisticated* curatorial appropriation, between *passive* consumption and *active* praxis. This *cultural activism* has become central to the lifestyle of the creative subjects in the new middle class. Whether in the case of sports or travel, cultural events or restaurants, the lifestyle of the educated middle class is highly active.

Culture as a Resource and Cultural Cosmopolitanism

We have already seen that the singularistic lifestyle of the new middle class treats all of world culture – all places, times, and social heritages – as available resources for the fulfillment of self-actualization. From this perspective, culture is not something that is reproduced within one's own social group, as was traditionally the case, but has rather transformed into a resource in the form of a heterogeneous sphere of possible appropriations. Within this *hyperculture*, potentially everything can become culture – that is, potentially everything can become an object or a practice that is available for aesthetic, ethical, narrative-semiotic, ludic, or design-based appropriation. Because the elements of this hyperculture circulate globally and trans-historically, they are practically unlimited. On the one hand, the objects and practices circulating within it are all different and singular, but, on the other hand, and as far as their recognized difference is concerned, they are essentially on the same level. In other words, hyperculture does not have any preconceived preferences; it simply makes things available. This *de jure* equality of cultural elements means that the traditional *boundaries* of perceived cultural value have *dissolved*, and particularly the boundaries between the contemporary and the historical, between high and popular culture, and between one's own culture and that of others.

In the model of "culture as a resource," people can help themselves to cultural objects from the present just as easily as they can to objects from the past. In late modernity, the past is thus conspicuously present, and this has expanded the possibilities of cultural appropriation immensely. This is indeed something new, for the culture of industrial modernity clearly preferred contemporary and future-oriented objects and practices as an expression of the superiority of modernity over the backward and obsolete past. In late-modern hyperculture, on the contrary, cultural elements from the past are regarded as a welcome enrichment of the here and now. With respect to singularity value, moreover, historical things are especially appealing because they often involve complex and different narratives and layers of meaning, which give them a good chance of seeming authentic.[22] The late-modern renaissance of the historical is particularly clear to see in the case of urban development; here, it manifests itself in the appreciation of old city centers, where the new middle class now prefers to live. It can also be seen, however, in the case of travel, with the renewed interest in cultural tourism and "cultural heritage,"[23] as well as in the revived curiosity about very old spiritual and religious traditions.[24] Incidentally, the renaissance of the historical should not be confused with a crude form of historicism, for it is not the case that the present day and modernity have been devalued in comparison with some imaginary classical era.[25] It is, rather, the case that hyperculture has dissolved the value boundary between the present and the past and has replaced it with undifferentiated access to *both* spheres.

A second boundary that hyperculture has dissolved is that between high culture and popular culture. All empirical studies have shown that traditional high culture – classical music, literature, visual art, etc., which featured so prominently in the bourgeois lifestyle – has lost, for the new educated class, its privileged status as an expression of legitimate taste. Rather, members of that class now turn without prejudice to sources of culture that once belonged exclusively to the popular sphere: they attend pop concerts, go to see Hollywood blockbusters, and cheer at football stadiums. Richard Peterson and other cultural sociologists have therefore concluded that the postmodern consumer has become an "omnivore."[26] This diagnosis needs to be refined, however, for this broadening of cultural taste did not come from just anywhere. What is new is the decisive point that, now, *potentially* everything is fit to contribute to a lifestyle driven by authenticity and self-actualization. Even pop-cultural objects and events *can* be interesting and attractive – on the condition that they can be experienced as authentic. This is analogous to the dissolution of the first boundary: traditional high-cultural and bourgeois objects have not at all lost their relevance but have, rather, experienced a renaissance, as is clear from the rising popularity of museums and concert halls since the 1990s, which are of course subject to the same condition of authenticity. High culture, too, will be dismissed if it is experienced as ingenuine, boring, and stiff, just as popular culture will be renounced if it seems too cheap, commercial, primitive, or artificial.

Finally, hyperculture has broken down the rigid boundary between one's "own" culture and the culture of "others" – the boundary between cultural spheres, nations, and regions. As far as the singularistic lifestyle is concerned, there is no longer any reason to prefer the objects and practices of one's own culture over those that come from other cultures. The reason for this is not political or moral but is, rather, based on the pursuit of self-actualization and its constant search for different experiences. To be culturally ethnocentric would simply be to limit the possibilities of experience and valorization that world culture has to offer. That which was once "foreign" has now become a potential source of self-enrichment, and thus the new middle class tends to regard the "colorful mix" of cultures in metropolises as more exciting than the bleak monoculture of the old industrial city. Here, too, the situation is not one of "either-or" but, instead, one of "both-and." It is not necessary to decide between this or that culture; without any problem at all, it is, rather, possible to combine various cultural elements from, say, Indian spirituality, Italian childcare, Latin American "body culture," and the German sense of orderliness. In this way, it is possible to create a sort of feedback loop between foreign elements and one's own local or national culture. These comparative possibilities, in other words, enable one to view one's own culture – Swabian cooking, the North Sea coast, or Franz Schubert – through a foreign lens, and this can enrich things in unexpected ways.

This attitude of "both-and," which plays a role in the dissolution of all three of these boundaries, indicates that the subjects of the new middle class have become competent in trans-historical and intercultural "switching." They are not arbitrary "omnivores" but are, rather, effortlessly able to skip back and forth between the contemporary and the historical, between popular and high culture, and between their own culture and those of others – always in pursuit of the singular and authentic. This ability, in fact, constitutes what might be called the *cultural connoisseurship* of the new middle class.[27] In relation to valorized cultural objects, people often develop a high level of expertise, and this expertise, by bringing to light the intricate complexity of objects, further intensifies the experience of singularity. This connoisseurship, which is familiar from traditional high culture (literati) as well as from segments of the bourgeois lifestyle (oenophiles), has now extended to other objects and activities (often from popular culture) that people integrate into their lifestyles: to computer games or sophisticated cooking techniques, to music bands or travel destinations in southern France, to vintage furniture, racing bicycles, and making marmalade, or to the works of Gilles Deleuze and the ins and outs of sneaker culture.

In sum, the subjects of the new middle class are characterized by their *cultural cosmopolitanism*.[28] To them, culture is a global reservoir overflowing with diverse elements, each of which has its own legitimacy and value and can become the object of appropriation by

V The Singularistic Life 219

those seeking authenticity. Here, there is no longer any claim to ownership on the part of one community or another; rather, every cultural element can – at least potentially – be combined with any other.[29] In a sense, cultural cosmopolitanism is a form of globalism that lives off the value of local diversity. It does not prize those global objects and practices that are the same everywhere but, rather, local particularities: authentic singularities that nevertheless have to circulate globally in order to be available in the first place. And it is also based emphatically on *openness*, which, in addition to creativity, has become a leading value of late-modern hyperculture. Cultural cosmopolitanism presupposes an apparently unquestioned feeling of *entitlement* when it comes to appropriating any facet of world culture for the sake of enriching one's own lifestyle.[30] The subjects of the new middle class claim the right to appropriate cultural elements – which means making them their *own* – and such elements can come from countercultures, from working-class culture, or from other traditions that are originally *not* their own.

With respect to value, cultural cosmopolitanism thus creates a boundary of its own: against the *provincial*, which is thought to lack diversity, cultural sovereignty, and connoisseurship. The provincial seems to be immured within a closed set of walls. From the perspective of the cosmopolitan educated class, the social locus of provincialism can be found above all in the underclass (at least in its local and sedentary faction) and in the old middle class, with its "petit-bourgeois" way of life. The cosmopolitanism/ provincialism binary has become a central symbolic struggle in late modernity. In this regard, the new middle class is a *global class* both in its general features and in the details of its lifestyle. In a similar way, it sets the tone not only in the United States, Germany, France, Sweden, Italy, etc., but also in rapidly modernizing countries such as China, and its cultural patterns are similar across national borders.[31]

Status Investment and the Prestige of the Unique

Above, I maintained that the subjects of the new middle class hope to achieve *successful* self-actualization, which means personal satisfaction within the framework of recognized social status. In this sense, they rely on strategies and competencies of the modern bourgeoisie, whose legacy has been perpetuated by the educated class in many respects. Here, the permanent investment in social status provides the background for the culturalization and singularization of lifestyles. The combination of striving for both authenticity and success characterizes the lifestyle of the new middle class on multiple levels. In a rather traditional way, the basis of this dual pursuit is esteemed professional activity, which, in the West, now takes place in the highly qualified knowledge and culture economy. As we have already seen, the work of highly qualified people is characterized by its dual structure: on the one hand, it forms identities, is undertaken with intrinsic motivation, and is supposed to be interesting and satisfying; on the other hand, it is supposed to provide social recognition and sufficient resources for a cosmopolitan lifestyle. It would thus be naïve to claim that the value structure of the new middle class is entirely post-materialistic. Rather, its post-materialism is *materialistically based*: the "good life" possesses a quality of life that goes beyond a mere standard of living, but at the same time it requires (economic, cultural, and social) capital, whose acquisition and reproduction are permanent tasks.

Uwe Schimank, Steffen Mau, and Olaf Groh-Samberg have demonstrated that the act of investing in status is a characteristic strategy of the middle-class lifestyle.[32] In the educated middle class, where *high* cultural capital is expected, this investment in status takes on an especially demanding form. Sufficient status is no longer provided by the normal working conditions of the leveled middle-class society; rather, it has to be cultivated on risky markets. In general, this requires a self-entrepreneurial spirit and a sensitive awareness of market shifts. Creative subjects also have to be entrepreneurial selves who constantly observe cultural markets, notice what is being valued there, and position themselves accordingly; they have to take clever chances and risks and thus avoid being wildly speculative. This is especially true of the dynamics of the labor market, but it also applies to the markets for romantic partners, real estate, investments, education, and finally to the diverse consumer markets and their trends. To the extent that the middle-class lifestyle is increasingly defined by the structures of cultural markets, on which the subject is both a supplier and a consumer, this lifestyle *itself* is subject to cultural economization.

The self-entrepreneurial investment in status, which has become a central objective of the educated middle class, involves all relevant forms of capital.[33] One's high *cultural capital* always has to be continuously developed and kept up to date. Moreover, it is also necessary to initiate an appropriate and forward-looking educational path for one's children, and this will involve providing them with international experience and opportunities to develop competencies beyond those provided by standardized degrees. Income, assets, and other forms of *economic capital* have to be developed on the labor market, the real-estate market, and the financial market, each of which is volatile. A significant amount of effort also has to be devoted to accumulating *social capital*: the new educated class is distinguished by its highly differentiated cultivation of *network capital*, both of the sort that can be professionally valuable and of the sort that can provide general advice (about healthcare, legal matters, or education) or is relevant for designing one's leisure time (the use of vacation homes, international housing swaps, local recommendations, etc.).[34]

Finally, it has become increasingly necessary under late-modern conditions to cultivate an additional sort of resource: *psychophysical subject capital*. What I mean by this is the need for subjects to work on their physical and mental states in order to create a stable foundation both for professional success and for a successful lifestyle. This is a matter of pursuing self-optimization. Central in this regard is status investment in health and fitness, though it can also be important to work on one's own mental stability (keyword: resilience) and psychological development (keyword: therapy). Under the unpredictable conditions of competitive cultural markets, one's physical attractiveness might also be an important asset, and so it can never hurt to exercise and seek style advice.

Despite all the importance of accumulating capital, it is nevertheless the case that, in the ideal-typical model of "lifestyle-as-culture," investing in status is not an end in itself but, rather, a means to the end of developing a singularistic lifestyle. One could say that investing in status is an *ancillary* undertaking – although it *accompanies* many activities, it is not the life *goal* of the new middle class, which, as I have already mentioned, is more interested in achieving a high quality of life than a mere standard of living. It differs in this respect from the old middle class, which strove (and continues to strive) somewhat overeagerly for income, assets, and status (symbols) without really "understanding how to live."

However, the creative lifestyle is not entirely self-oriented, for it is also concerned with social prestige. It thus has the paradoxical structure of *performative self-actualization*, which involves presenting one's self-actualization before an audience in order to be recognized as having an "attractive life." The educated class further embodies a symbiosis of Romanticism and bourgeois culture to the extent that it combines the conflicting orientations of being inward-looking (self-actualization) and outward-looking (prestige): the singular life has prestige value.[35] Even though, on one level, the singularistic lifestyle can only be understood in light of the desire of subjects for self-actualization, the curated life nevertheless creates social prestige to the extent that it is performatively staged (intentionally or in an apparently nonchalant manner) for others to see. Whereas social status could once be enjoyed simply by achieving the standard of living that was typical of the leveled middle-class society (house, car, high income), the most important criterion for earning social recognition today is to demonstrate one's (ostensibly) successful self-development, individual uniqueness, authenticity, and multifaceted nature.[36]

Although you may find it personally interesting and challenging to hike through Latin America for four weeks, this is also a source of social recognition as a demonstration of your interesting experiences and cosmopolitan personality. Free climbing may be fun, but it also impresses others ("Is there anything you can't do?!"). Making animated movies might be personally satisfying, but it also comes with the prestige of being a creative person who would never be content with a humdrum office job. All of this illustrates how, in today's social game, singularity has transformed into *singularity prestige*. Self-actualization and authenticity are thus not only negotiated in the relationship that subjects have to themselves but also through their *representation* of self-actualization and authenticity to others: to their circle of friends and family, to their "friends" on broader social networks (where experiences can be demonstrated with posted photos), to their colleagues, and finally to the public at large.

All of the elements of the singularistic lifestyle, which I will examine more closely in the next chapter, lend themselves to social demonstrations of self-actualization: travel and cultural events, which are captured in photographs that are sent around in posts; food, which is celebrated before others regardless of whether it is enjoyed at a restaurant or prepared by oneself; healthy and active bodies, which are put on public display while jogging or participating in extreme sports; houses and apartments, which have presentation value; and finally, "well-raised" children young and grown, whose strong personalities and success are showcased. In regard to their singularity prestige, subjects thus find themselves in a more or less subtle competition for distinction. Recognized singularity can itself become a form of capital: *singularity capital*. Having a high degree of singularity prestige, which means being perceived as having an interesting, multifaceted, and open personality, can create advantages on a diverse range of markets – on the professional market of the creative economy above all, but also on the market for romantic partners. If one's self-actualization is socially successful, this success will be visible to others in the form of an *attractive life*.[37]

To summarize: in the singularistic lifestyle of the educated middle class, a *valorization of subjects* occurs by way of the valorization of goods and the accumulation of singularity capital, and this affects one's feelings of *self*-worth as well as the prestige that one has in the eyes of *others*. By appropriating valuable goods from around the world – by traveling to them and living in them, by living with them (partners, children) and attending them (cultural events, elite universities), or by making them one's own in any other way (as a type of physical exercise or spiritual practice, for instance) – subjects gain value and valorize themselves. The valorization of goods and practices has been socially transposed to the level of valorizing subjects. In short, what has taken place is a *valorization transfer*. Late-modern subjects are therefore not valuable because of their general competencies and special achievements or even on account of their basic humanity; rather, they can only become valuable, both in their own eyes and in the eyes of others, through processes of appropriation by which acknowledged singular goods and practices are integrated into their lifestyles or function as capital.

2
Elements of the Singularistic Lifestyle

The singularistic lifestyle of the new middle class revolves around certain sets of trend-setting practices. These involve food and nutrition, houses and apartments, travel, physical fitness and attractiveness, and finally the upbringing and education of children. These are the practices to which people typically devote intensive interest, and from which they derive identity and affective satisfaction. Despite their great variety, all of these areas have become preferred objects of culturalization and curatorial singularization: under the model of "lifestyle-as-culture," they have been reconfigured into cultural practices that, beyond their mere functional utility, have acquired *value* of their own, and such value is now expected of them. As objects of culturalization (aestheticization, "ethicization," creative design, etc.), they have become focal points of disputes about value (and worthlessness) with accordingly complex dynamics of (collective and personal) valorization and de-valorization.

In conjunction with this, the new middle class has also turned food, homes, travel, bodies, and the upbringing of children into objects of singularization. The members of this class now desire and expect a *unique* eating experience, a *unique* neighborhood, a *unique* physical experience, and *unique* children who attend *unique* schools. This, too, has given rise to conflicting dynamics of singularization and standardization. All of these areas have become preferred sources of authentic experiences. It is no surprise, incidentally, that some of the activities named above seem rather *profane* from the perspective of traditional bourgeois culture. Unlike that of the educated bourgeoisie, the emphasis of late modernity's educated class is no longer focused on traditional high culture (though, as we have already seen, this has in no way disappeared) but rather on certain formerly profane areas that have surprisingly been re-valorized and even *sacralized*. Owing to a culture of authenticity, the activities involving food, homes, travel, bodies, and children have been upgraded, and this is because of their immediacy and meaningfulness in everyday life. In the singularistic lifestyle, however, these rather "elementary" practices have also become an object of considerable intellectualization and have developed subtle aesthetic and ethical meanings of their own.

Food

Since the 1980s, it is remarkable how significant food has become to the lifestyle of the new middle class – its nutritional value, its origins and quality, meals, drinks, culinary cultures, chefs, kitchens, communal eating, and dining in restaurants (not to mention food tourism).[1] In an extensive manner, food has become an object of care, enjoyment, experience, knowledge, competencies, performance, and social prestige, and it has the power to shape our identities: we are what we eat. Authenticity, which is one of the guiding values of the singularistic lifestyle, has perhaps found its clearest expression in the culture of food.

Of course, eating has never been just a biological activity undertaken for the sole purpose of nutritional sustenance. Ethnologists such as Claude Lévi-Strauss and Mary Douglas have pointed out the symbolic and socially integrative significance that food already possessed in early societies.[2] Nevertheless, one can say that nutrition was generally functionalized in industrial society, and that this did much to rob food of its cultural significance (in the strong sense of culture). Food was industrialized with the aim of feeding the masses, and this entailed standardized food products and meals.[3] Industrial modernity's much-bemoaned tendency to de-sensualize things resulted not least in a dietary and culinary de-sensualization. In the leveled middle-class society, eating was largely a satiating means to an end; it was meant to sustain one's ability to work. The renaissance of culinary culture owes much to the counterculture of the 1970s and 1980s, which was also a culinary counterculture. Against the commercialism of standardized food products, an ideal of "authentic" eating was established, which involved healthy and "organic" food, local ingredients, the cultivation of local culinary traditions, and the art of cooking from scratch. The two most important historical incubators of this ideal were the Californian counter-cuisine, which took shape in Berkeley's "gourmet district," and the slow food movement from Northern and Central Italy.[4]

Since the beginning of the twenty-first century, the culinary culture of the late-modern educated class has been supported by a broad network of global institutions, discourses, and objects. The ever-expanding and highly differentiated types of cuisine now available (especially in large cities), the flourishing of local agricultural production (often of organic quality), and the diffusion of culinary knowledge through various media outlets have placed food and gastronomy among the most important branches of the creative economy. Within the framework of the late-modern lifestyle, the identity-formational power of food always has two sides: in the context of gastronomy and eating at restaurants, the activity is receptive; in the context of cooking at home, the activity is creative. It should be noted that this valorized and singularized food distinguishes itself from the sorts of food that still follow the functional logic of the general. In explicit contrast to the aesthetically and ethically impoverished standardization of industrialized food (as exemplified by fast food chains such as McDonald's, ready-to-eat processed meals, or traditional cafeteria food, which largely belong to the eating practices of the underclass), *culinary singularization* has been taking place in several dimensions.

The *first* and perhaps most important dimension has been the spread of local and regional culinary cultures, which has mainly been caused by migration.[5] Local cuisines – Vietnamese and Italian, South African and Caribbean, Near Eastern and French, etc. – singularize food; they are unique on account of the specific inherent complexity of their ingredients, manners of preparation, dishes, presentation, and the way that they are eaten. Local cuisines each have their own characteristic aesthetic style with respect to the way that they taste, look, and smell. This style is further enriched by the historical narratives that accompany every culinary culture. Globalization has thus encouraged the heterogenization of food: the global presence of culturally diverse local culinary traditions. It is only because of the fact that they exist side by side in large cities that we are able to experience their uniqueness. In such places, "foodies" can enter an incomparable culinary universe at any time and further refine their sense of aesthetics. In short, the globalization of food is the most glaring example of how originally local traditions have transformed into hypercultural resources that reveal contrasts and thus make it possible to view (and taste) cultural goods *as* singular.

Second, the singularization of food has taken place through the bold experimentalism of late-modern cooking.[6] Whether in restaurants, cookbooks, cooking shows, or the family kitchen, cooking has become a creative practice intent on producing new and surprising dishes. The goal is to create a unique, and thus unprecedented, eating experience. To some extent, cooking itself has become a curatorial art of bringing heterogeneous things together. On a basic level, of course, this creative cooking starts with ostensibly simple ingredients and dishes. The expectation here is to transform something profane into something extraordinary.[7] As in the traditional example of wine, apparently simple and standardized dishes and drinks can be aestheticized and thus singularized by varying the origin of their ingredients and the method of their preparation and by developing a sensitivity to subtle distinctions in taste, as has happened in the case of coffee (with its various types of beans, roasting techniques, and preparations), beer (craft beer), tea, bread, and chocolate. In this way, even common meals such as steak frites can be rehabilitated as classics. Aside from the singularization of the profane, culinary experimentalism also and especially involves making new combinations of ingredients and local cooking traditions ("crossover cuisine"), with the ideal result of creating something that has never been eaten before. The combination of seemingly incompatible ingredients leads to surprising and original gustatory experiences that can depend on the tiniest details. It is therefore no wonder that chefs have become recognized creative stars.

Third, the aesthetic culturalization of food has been accompanied by – and partially connected to – its strong association with ethics.[8] The educated middle class appreciates food not only on account of its flavor but also on account of its intrinsic *virtue*. The key term here is "ethical consumption."[9] One main criterion for the ethical value of food is the way in which it is produced: ecologically, locally, sustainably, humanely. Entire eating styles have formed around ethical orientations, and hence the boom in vegetarianism and veganism. An additional ethical aspect of food that is just as important is the extent to which it seems "healthy." In general, the ethos of healthy living pervades the entire lifestyle of the new middle class and manifests itself especially clearly in its eating habits.[10] On the basis of individual ingredients and the presumed effects on animals, ethically virtuous and healthy products are distinguished from "bad" or unhealthy products, good fat is distinguished from bad fats, self-prepared food from fast food, etc.

Fourth, aesthetic and ethical value has also been attributed to the *practices* of eating and cooking, which have morphed into unique and extraordinary events.[11] Among the urban middle class, going out to eat is popular and no longer reserved for "special occasions." Accordingly, the singularity of restaurants themselves derives not only from the food that they serve but also from their carefully designed atmospheres. Gastronomy has become a nodal point of the urban creative scene, and cooking often has a performative quality, especially when it takes place in open kitchens before an audience. No less important is the recent lionization of home cooking as a cultural practice, which not a few members of the new middle class undertake with passion. Since the 1990s, kitchens have thus moved from the periphery of apartments and houses to the center, where they often dominate the living space in an open form. In the act of cooking, the otherwise "cerebral" members of the late-modern educated class can experience themselves as hands-on, creative subjects who engage directly, carefully, and expertly with natural objects. Cooking fosters new sensitivities to organic material and its preparation, and for some people it even has meditative qualities. Finally, not only is cooking something valuable in itself, but so is the emotionally satisfying ritual of eating together with friends and family.

Homes

In addition to food, another central interest of the new middle class is the location and appearance of houses and apartments. You are what you eat, but you are also where and how you reside. In our homes, we design the spatial and atmospheric environment in which we spend much of our days, and so it is no surprise that their location and design have become an important source of late-modern identity.[12]

In industrial society, housing was primarily a problem of social engineering,[13] and the solution was standardized residences for the masses, whether in multi-family homes or in series of single-family homes in the suburbs. Neighborhoods were roughly interchangeable, and this is why residential areas said relatively little about those who lived there in the leveled middle-class society. In this context, home furnishing was primarily functional, but it was also part of standardized mass consumption, so that complete sets of furniture could be bought "off the rack" (so to speak).[14] In this regard, a historical turning point was once again provided by the counterculture of the 1970s, which treated the question of where and how one lived as a political issue of privacy. People began to move to neglected old parts of town and inner cities in order to experience urban life and escape from standardized homes. The way that apartments were used and decorated also became more open and experimental (no more quaint dining areas and walls full of boring wardrobes). With the rise of alternative subcultures, whose members happened to be the unwitting pioneers of urban gentrification, the value of authenticity made its way into the domestic world.[15]

As I have already mentioned, there are two aspects to the new middle class's infatuation with its living situation: *location* and *design*. In both respects, residences have been culturalized and singularized. Where one lives has become a matter of particular cultural value and social prestige, and the design of one's living space has become an object of everyday creative curation. Furniture, architecture, and interior design have accordingly become pillars of the creative economy.

Instead of being interchangeable, neighborhoods are now either assigned or denied social value, and this has become a decisive factor in the global, national, regional, and local geography of late modernity. Locations have become an object of the social dynamics of valorization. Many neighborhoods thus have their own image and are associated with specific characteristics, and it feels different to live in one as opposed to another. In Berlin, for instance, living in Wilmersdorf is "entirely different" from living in Neukölln-Nord. This game of qualitative differences extends to fine distinctions between cities and regions (Hamburg or Berlin? Boston or Portland?).[16] The flipside of this valorization is, of course, the devaluation of other neighborhoods, cities, and even entire regions. The cultural polarization of late-modern classes manifests itself in and is intensified by these evaluations and segregations of space.

For the new middle class, choosing where to live therefore represents a difficult and consequential decision, especially because of the cultural-economic pressure created by the scarcity of "attractive locations." In addition to social prestige, the criterion of authenticity also plays a major role in this decision: the experience of urbanity – the liveliness of "mixed-use" neighborhoods that Jane Jacobs extolled as the ideal of European city life[17] – seems to be a central characteristic of the areas thought to be authentic by the educated class. Often, preference is therefore given to old neighborhoods near the center of cities, which have experienced a striking reappraisal since the 1970s: whereas, according to industrial modernity's logic of utility, they seemed outdated and dilapidated, the logic of culturalization has turned them into symbols of urbanity and aesthetic grandeur. In the new and city-oriented middle class, the single-family house has generally lost its status as the uncontested ideal home, and urban living has come to seem all the more attractive.

As soon as the right place has been acquired in the right neighborhood, designing and decorating it becomes an ongoing task. The careful arrangement and interior design of apartments represents one of the most important activities in the late-modern subjects' efforts to aestheticize their lifestyle. Self-actualizing subjects adopt a highly specific perspective toward their living space: their apartments are staged both *for themselves* and *for others*. At the same time, it is in their apartments where they can really "be themselves," and thus they hope to create a self-satisfying atmosphere that is as relaxing as it is stimulating. Apartments are three-dimensional extensions of the ego and places that express identity; at the same time, their spatial qualities also affect the attitudes and emotions of the people living there. These are two reasons, then, for designing them carefully.

In this light, the standardized interior design practiced by the leveled middle-class society can only seem like an expression of bland conformism and an utter lack of style. In contrast to this, the new middle class has developed a complex aesthetic taste for living spaces, so that apartments have become the object of creative curation and expressions of individual style. *Curated living* means arranging diverse and interesting heterogeneous things into a clever and harmonious whole. Together, this composition of singular objects is supposed to create a unique space with considerable inherent complexity: a *place of the self*.[18] The creative milieu of cultural producers (in the strict sense) functions as a model for curated living.[19] Examining the apartments of the educated class between Vancouver, Amsterdam, and Melbourne, one will find the same overarching aesthetic pattern of culturally cosmopolitan interior design, which consists of a delicate balance between two spatial qualities: clarity, tranquility, and simple elegance on the one hand; interesting objects and cultural diversity on the other. Obviously, an apartment will seem authentic if it combines both – when it has both a classic *and* unusual look. The atmosphere of an apartment should be unique and thus reflect the uniqueness of its residents without, of course, overtaxing the senses with extreme variation and arbitrariness. Regarding interior design, this is a matter of three elementary layers: the general qualities of the space itself, furniture, and decorative accessories.

As far as general *spatial qualities* are concerned, late-modern subjects expect their apartments to have the quality of a stage: a stage for the objects that are placed in it, and a stage for the people who live there. In comparison to the standardized multi-room apartments in large-scale housing projects, there has thus been a clear tendency to increase the size of rooms and let them blend into each other (as in a combined living and dining space). The loft style is the leading model. Ideally, the physical layout of an apartment should lend itself to individually tailored types of use and should offer aesthetically pleasing viewing angles both on the inside and to the outdoors. Large windows and high ceilings can also enhance the inviting feel of a space. It is therefore no surprise that the *fin-de-siècle* buildings and industrial warehouse spaces are so appealing to the urban educated class. The walls and floors of apartments are usually designed in such a way as to provide a clear and neutral background (white walls, monochrome floors) but also to appear as authentic as possible (painted instead of wallpapered, exposed brick or concrete, parquet flooring, steel beams, molding, and so on).

The *furniture* in these living spaces follows the pattern of de-standardization as well as a style that could be called "soft modernism."[20] One no longer finds premade matching sets of furniture (seating arrangement plus armoire, etc.) but, rather, sophisticated combinations of *individual* pieces arranged according to a curatorial logic (a large wooden dining-room table with several *different* chairs). However, these arrangements are not arbitrary: "soft modernism" means that, when it comes to furnishings, the clear lines of the Bauhaus style or of Scandinavian design are preferred, but these are supplemented by individual pieces that are made of natural materials and come from various places (antiques, flea-market finds, industrial designs, original pieces by young designers, etc.). The cool aesthetic of modernism, which is the neoclassicism of the late-modern educated class, is softened by the warm and tactile crafts aesthetic and thereby made more interesting and authentic. The result is a carefully arranged stylistic break from what Deleuze and Guattari referred to as "smooth and striated space."[21]

In the case of the third level of interior design, *accessories*, curatorial talent is put on full display.[22] Because they lend a personal flair to apartments, accessories are chosen and arranged especially carefully. These can be functional objects – from chopping boards to electrical socket covers – that are singularized as hand-made or aesthetically original items. Even more important, however, are genuinely unique pieces, which are common in the apartments of the educated class and include such things as paintings, sculptures, works of graphic design, artistic photographs, and concept art. Typical and widespread, too, are strategically placed pieces of travel memorabilia, which are not commercial souvenirs but rather have the character of found objects taken here and there from global culture: an old football from Dakar, a piece of driftwood from a beach on the Pacific, a movie poster from Mumbai, a heat shield from the Apollo 13 spacecraft, a decorative fringe from a Vietnamese mountain tribe, or metal model cars from wherever. Many people focus on highly specialized and often unusual sets of objects, in which they have developed a degree of expertise: skateboards, Nollywood film posters, bizarre penguin figurines, and so on. Personal and memorable items from one's past can also be used as accessories: a deceased grandmother's handbag or the jute beanbag received as a gift on one's sixteenth birthday. All in all, the apartments of the new middle class are thus populated with carefully selected *objets trouvés* that resemble art objects but have highly personal and biographical associations. In that they combine various regional styles, works of art, and memorabilia from around the world, apartments have thus become places for presenting and experiencing global hyperculture.

The aesthetically curated apartment is therefore a locus of performative self-actualization: on the one hand, it has a subjective atmospheric quality that satisfies its inhabitants; on the other hand, it is a staged venue for visitors, and aesthetic singularity can be a source of social prestige. Neighborhoods and apartments have become objects of cultural valorization; more than mere matters of functionality, they are investments in status. Just as individual objects of interior design are valued for more than their functional utility – from the cool cheese grater and the vintage dresser to the artwork hanging on the wall – the carefully curated and often elaborately restored total ensemble of an apartment and its particular location are laden with value as a whole. Ideally, this social value should be of a lasting and personally fitting sort, so that the rooms, things, and residents of an apartment age well together. In the late-modern educated class, the valorization of subjects and their lifestyles goes hand in hand with the valorization of their living spaces.

Travel

Travel is a central and identity-forming activity for the subjects of the new middle class. It is more than a matter of taking a "vacation" in order to have a relaxing break from work. Rather, travel is also, and increasingly, understood as an activity that involves getting to know unfamiliar places. What has taken place is a *dedifferentiation of travel*, which is no longer restricted to vacation days. On the one hand, the professional activity of many people in the knowledge and culture economy involves traveling throughout the year, so that it is possible to combine work and leisure time. Moreover, many careers and educational paths involve extensive stays abroad that catapult subjects into foreign cultural contexts.[23] On the other hand, it is also possible to act as a tourist in one's *own* neighborhood and to treat it and the surrounding areas as places where there is "always something new to discover." That is, one can be at home and "on the road" at the same time. In short, travel is a key practice in the lifestyle of the educated class, and it does much to shape the cosmopolitan consciousness of its members. It is institutionally supported and promoted by the elaborate infrastructure of the tourism industry, which is one of the largest and most expansive branches of the creative economy.[24]

Late-modern travel has become a thoroughly culturalizing and singularizing activity. It is a matter of taking actively curated trips in search of unique and authentic places and moments.[25] Ideally, it is nothing like the mass tourism that characterized industrial modernity. To a degree, the latter was a sort of industrial tourism with standardized vacation packages and one clear purpose: relaxation away from work. In contrast to this, the travel of the late-modern educated class, even though it relies extensively on the global infrastructure for tourism, is often expressly anti-touristic: travelers do *not* want to be tourists who passively consume their vacations. Instead, they actively pursue what is different, exciting, interesting, and challenging. In terms of cultural history, the late-modern traveler is thus carrying on the legacy of the "tourist gaze," which, according to John Urry, originated among the bourgeoisie around 1800.[26] Here, travel presupposes a certain attitude toward seeing things that goes beyond the instrumental rationality of everyday life. The Romantic tourist gaze was that of a traveler who found aesthetic pleasure in exploring foreign places, nature, architecture,

V The Singularistic Life 233

and ways of life (a classic example being a tour of Italy). He or she sought – much like the urban *flâneur* later on – new experiences in foreign environments. Although mass tourism suspended this tourist gaze for some time, it was revived by the 1970s counterculture and its alternative tourism. The counterculture was a global movement of travelers and globetrotters who set out on their own to discover foreign cultures "off the beaten track" (visiting India was a must) and who also had an active interest in exploring nature (often in physically challenging ways).

The travel of late-modern subjects is an object of active design and skillful curation: it takes its own *unique* course through *unique* places with *unique* experiences, which are all entirely different from the familiar aspects of everyday life. The singularization achieved by late-modern travel is thus, at its heart, a singularization of *space* and *time*: familiar spaces are left behind for unique places, and routines are set aside for unique moments. The new middle class has cultivated highly diverse types of travel, and it is common to switch between them: short city trips or longer stays; nature excursions in one's surrounding area or more active nature adventures (cycling through the Alps or hiking through southern China); tours of entire regions (14 days with a rental car through northern Spain or on a train through Argentina); travel involving on-site activities (a yoga retreat in India) or specific educational or health-related interests. Travel can be improvised on the fly (which is typical of young people), or it can be extremely luxurious and exclusive.[27] The overarching feature of all these travel concepts, however, is that they involve seeking "authentic experiences" beyond those of everyday life.

Members of the new middle class typically travel to places that are regarded as singular – to destinations with the sort of inherent spatial complexity that makes them interesting and surprisingly different, so that, rather than having an emotionally neutral reaction toward them, one is instead taken under their spell, intellectually stimulated, or even irritated by them.[28] Singular density and otherness can be encountered in the urban buzz of large cities or in picturesque villages, in spectacular natural landscapes or in depressing slums, in the daily life of a small Mexican town or in a religious ceremony in Varanasi. The fact that places such as Paris or Tuscany have become classic travel destinations is due to the spectacular uniqueness of their spatial structures. Even more interesting, of course, are "secret tips" (about a particular neighborhood in Chicago or a particular region in Myanmar) that further enhance the singularity of a location by revealing special features that have yet to be discovered by many other travelers. The search for the unique aspects of a location extends to individual micro-situations as well: travelers wind through particular streets in pursuit of particular restaurants or museums, and choose particular hotels on account of their specific atmospheres. Of course, late-modern travel includes traditional sightseeing and aspects of high culture, but it is especially interested in experiencing the authenticity of "foreign everyday life."[29] In general, the uniqueness of a place lies in the eyes of its beholder, and travelers thus attempt to "keep an open mind" to whatever they might encounter (this is even true of the irritating slum tourism in South Africa).[30]

In late-modern travel, the singularization of places goes hand in hand with the singularization of temporal moments. Travelers are always on the hunt for extraordinary moments, and travel should ideally consist of a sequence of them. Such memorable moments can occur at random or while someone is experiencing particular architectural or natural highlights, attending particular events (a religious ceremony, a concert, etc.), or participating in certain activities: surfing in the Pacific, hiking in the Pyrenees, eating and drinking at a picturesque restaurant in Umbria or at a food stand made of sheet metal in São Paulo, where one happens to strike up a conversation with locals. In order to have moments that are unique, stir emotions, and create life-changing "experiences," it is necessary to travel in a way that is as actively curated and non-standardized as possible. Although unique experiences cannot really be planned, their likelihood can be increased by doing such things as renting a room in someone's home (through Airbnb, for instance) instead of staying in a hotel, or exchanging apartments with someone for several weeks in order to "live like a local" and "properly" get to know a given country or city. Curated travel is always a combination of planning and coincidence: certain parameters are put in place to ensure that no highlights will be missed but also to leave enough leeway for the unexpected to happen.

In its unconstrained form, travel is a field of activity that lends itself perfectly to the world-embracing form of self-actualization that the educated class cultivates. While gallivanting around the world and taking in its cultural and natural abundance and diversity, subjects enrich themselves with experiences. Thus, it is typical for late-modern subjects to have individual *travel biographies*, with certain trips marking important and often consequential stages in their lives. Travel is another prime example of the hypercultural understanding of culture as a resource: in all of its facets, globality is now a resource for the development of the ego. This is true not only of short trips but also of long-term stays abroad (during one's school and university years or during one's professional career as well), which the educated class tends to promote from one's teenage years on. This, too, requires the rather entitled presumption that one is competent enough (and permitted) to appropriate the world and the cultures of others for the sake of expanding one's own personal horizons.

In this regard, the travel of the new middle class not only expands horizons; it is also an investment in status (the acquisition of cultural capital through spending time abroad, for instance) and an example of performative self-actualization: the cosmopolitanism of travel – not least when it is documented on social media – enhances social prestige and increases one's singularity capital. It is also important to note, however, that late-modern travel takes place in a nearly irresolvable field of tension between standardization and singularization. Although everyone is looking for authentic experiences, it is nevertheless almost impossible to avoid the standardized offers of the tourism industry. We exist in an extremely "touristified" global society in which, whether we like it or not, we are constantly forced to be part of one collective of tourists or another. Finally, travel destinations are also subject to the unpredictable dynamics of valorization and devaluation.[31] The pursuit of the authentic, which defines late-modern travel, is therefore highly susceptible to disappointment. This has given rise to the semi-ironic attitude of "post-tourists," who are aware of the fact that, by doing such things as visiting the Taj Mahal, they are imitating what millions of people have already done before them, but they do so anyway in order to enjoy their own personal aesthetic experience.[32]

Bodies

The body, too, has become an object of the singularistic lifestyle in late modernity. Whereas the bourgeoisie and the old middle class were modest about bodies in general, the new middle class has made them an object of conscious design, activity, and experience. The body is now set in motion, and late-modern identity is shaped by body-related practices to a considerable extent.[33] Moreover, bodies are now subjected to relentless processes of cultural valorization: healthy and fit bodies stand opposed to those that are unhealthy, overweight, and inactive.

In large part, industrial modernity functionalized the body. It was either a means to the end of gainful employment, or silently ignored by those who had white-collar jobs. The twentieth century was the age of popular sports; on the one hand, athletic bodies competed with one another in spectator sports, while on the other hand there were (and are) opportunities for non-professionals to compete in club sports. In the case of bodies, too, the counterculture of the 1970s and 1980s effected a transformation by ennobling bodily experiences. This gave rise to a growing interest in Asiatic cultures of human motion as well as in the playful sportiness of the California lifestyle, which introduced new types of athletic activity such as windsurfing and roller skating.

In an intense way, the body has become an object of everyday concern in late-modern culture, and especially among the educated middle class. This involves not only mechanisms of singularization and culturalization but also a combination of three ways of "governing" the body.[34] First, the body is now part of comprehensive efforts toward self-optimization. It has become an object of training in order to ensure and enhance physical fitness and health.[35] Whereas, for the old bourgeois class, corpulence was a sign of stateliness, seriousness, and prosperity, today's thin and fit members of the creative and managerial class exhibit their tenacity and self-discipline by running marathons. In this case of physical self-optimization, which can be measured according to *general* and objective parameters, the body has in fact become extremely standardized and therefore rationalized. In a sense, fitness training equips late-modern subjects with the general corporeal material (infrastructure) that is supposed to enable the unique aspects of their lifestyles both at work and during their leisure time.

Second, in late-modern culture, working on one's physical appearance and the attractiveness of one's body has become important in a strict sense. Whereas, in the early stages of modern culture, this activity was undertaken almost exclusively by women, in late-modern culture it is expected of everyone.[36] Physical attractiveness is seemingly a foundation for the feeling of self-worth, and it is also a factor of social prestige: it has become "subject capital." Sophisticated techniques for creating an attractive body have gained increasing significance (fitness training, fashion, cosmetics and hairstyling, body accessories and cosmetic surgery – all the way to personal style advice and voice coaching). Cultivating an attractive body is a practice of aestheticization in a very direct sense – it is a practice of creating "beauty" – and its relation to singularization is ambiguous. On the one hand, the aesthetics of faces and bodies seems to be one of the few things in society for which there are generally accepted criteria (symmetry, appealing color combinations, slenderness). On the other hand, there are also tendencies here toward singularization: the standardization of beautiful bodies is often regarded as anemic and artificial. In this case, too, the value of authenticity is relevant: personality and look have to fit together to form a sort of charismatic attractiveness.

Third – and most importantly for the culturalization and singularization of the body – is the fact that, since the 1980s, a broad range of *body cultures* has been differentiated, and these now constitute an important element of the new middle class's lifestyle.[37] Such cultures include activities from the realm of sports, but they mostly no longer have the form of competitive club sports or passive spectator sports. What has gained prominence are active individual sports such as running, cycling, freeclimbing, and rafting. In this sense, sports are less interesting in terms of competition and passive spectatorship; the focus here is rather on one's own bodily activity, which provides a physical outlet for the typically "cerebral" creative subject. Practices of movement outside of sports in the strict sense have also gained significance, such as dancing (think of the international tango craze) or certain techniques of physical exercise (yoga, martial arts) that train both the body *and* the mind. In part, late-modern practices of movement are also conducted as a means to an end – for the sake of improving one's physical fitness, for instance – but it is more important that they have the character of "technologies of the self" that, for subjects, become ends in themselves: pushing one's body to its physical and mental limits can have an aesthetic and ludic value, whether in relation to oneself or while engaging with nature or another subject. In this regard, there are five noteworthy ways that singularization can take place.

First, many body cultures that are now popular around the globe have a very specific local and historical cultural background: t'ai chi and qigong, hatha yoga and aikido, tango and salsa, etc. These traditional cultural contexts lend these activities a sort of density and inherent complexity that is not only physical but also narrative and hermeneutic. By practicing these techniques, people immerse themselves to some extent in a foreign cultural universe in which they can become capable experts. The local body cultures circulating around the globe thus form a hyperculture that consists of both "exotic" and historical resources that can be appropriated.[38]

Second, some late-modern practices of movement promise extraordinary or even ecstatic experiences that can push people to their physical and mental limits.[39] These are extreme practices, as in the extreme sports that allow subjects to test the outermost capabilities of their bodies: freeclimbing, acro paragliding, freediving, BASE jumping, and so forth.

Third, whereas the forms of movement in traditional competitive sports are often relatively regulated and standardized, many of the late-modern body cultures allow people to develop individual body styles and to experiment in an improvisational manner with their own physical abilities. This is true of sports like surfing or inline skating or the extreme sports mentioned above, but it is also true of the international tango movement.[40]

Fourth, whereas many traditional club sports take place in gymnasiums or on playing fields, the body practices of late modernity take place out in the open. Jogging, hiking, or cycling may be repetitive activities, but they are distinguished by the specific experience of moving through urban or natural landscapes. What seems to make these genuinely outdoor activities exciting is the holistic experience of passing through places. The often-discussed experience of "flow" while running results from the fact that the space around the runner (the path, the environment, noises, the wind) is "felt" in a particular way.[41]

The *fifth* and final variant of singularization concerns the form of the subject engaged in a given practice of movement. It is not uncommon now for subjects to be in a position of having to undertake a heroic struggle against themselves.[42] The heroization of athletes has been part of modern competitive and spectator sports from the beginning. Under the conditions of the society of singularities, which constantly produces winners and losers through its extensive cultural economization of the social, spectator sports have functioned like a universal educational program for training people to regard competition as a natural form of sociality.[43] More important in this context, however, is the heroization of the active (lay) athlete. Running a marathon, doing a triathlon, or participating in other endurance sports or extreme sports is no longer about competing against others but is rather about the experience of struggling against oneself. The singular subject is here a *heroic* subject intent on conquering herself and nature.

Parenting and Early Education

Since the 1990s, the amount of engagement that families in the educated middle class have devoted to the parenting and education of their children has been immense. The everyday commitment to raising children, fostering their talents, and supporting them at school has become remarkably intense. Nowhere are the two most important motivations of the educated class's lifestyle – the desire for self-actualization and social prestige – more closely connected than in the upbringing and education of children.

In industrial modernity, school represented a prominent social arena of formal rationalization and standardization. The defining social logic was that of the general and the same: mass education was (and still is) a form of "industrial" education in which the entire population is divided according to age groups and "trained" in elementary and certain higher cognitive skills. Here, ideally, all pupils learn the same thing at the same pace and in the same way. The ideal of general education in a society of identical people goes hand in hand with standardized schooling.[44] Admittedly, the way that people raise their children at home has followed its own historical path, which is not identical with the developments in institutional education. However, there is much to support the claim that the prevailing parenting style during the phase of the leveled middle-class society was in agreement with the ideal of equality promoted by standardized schooling. Since the 1930s, and especially in the United States, the middle class implemented the ideal of the "socially adjusted child."⁴⁵ The basic idea was that, because people are always in groups (families, peer groups at school, and finally groups of professional colleagues), modern children should be raised to be socially competent and rule-abiding. Individual unconventionality, emotionality, introversion, and eccentricity were thus treated with suspicion.

Since the 1980s, parenting and education have undergone a multifaceted social transformation that is not easy to reduce to a common denominator. As in the case of the late-modern lifestyle, it makes little sense to speak of a unilinear transformation when it comes to parenting and education. Although a single overriding pattern might have applied to the leveled middle-class society, it loses meaning in a society defined by class differences. In fact, parenting and schooling form one of the most significant and revealing areas in which socio-structural and cultural polarization manifests itself in late modernity. Whereas the educated middle class has intensified and refined its efforts in the sphere of child-rearing and education, members of the underclass, whose children often attend "problem schools," have largely been "left behind" by education.

The field of educational sociology has shown that, since the 1980s, the new middle class has developed a demanding parenting style that can be described as "intensive parenthood." Despite the fact that these are often dual-income families, they have become child-centric to a historically unprecedented extent. The idea is that the uniqueness of individual children should be promoted as much as possible. Beyond fostering their children's emotional, social, linguistic, and cognitive-argumentative competencies, parents in the new middle class are also expected to provide them with a number of diverse inspirations. Annette Lareau has referred to this educational strategy as "concerted cultivation."⁴⁶ We read to our children, take them to museums, go on faraway trips with them, teach them how to interact in socially "appropriate" ways, and introduce them to art, music, foreign languages, and nature.

Since the 1980s, the parenting strategies of the new middle class have been based on neuro-physiological findings about the plasticity of children's brains, which allegedly have to be "nourished." In many respects, the late-modern parenting style is thus opposed to the practice of raising socially adjusted children that was dominant among the old middle class. Although social competence remains relevant just as before, the ideal is not to raise adjusted children but rather to bring up autonomous and self-motivated children with strong feelings of self-worth and multifaceted interests, and to foster their unique qualities. One could say that the late-modern practice of parenting is a *program for singularizing children*. According to this conviction, every child is different and special – and is expected to be so. Every child is now regarded as an entirely unique ensemble of gifts, potential, and attributes, the development of which is to be encouraged. Now, conformist children without unique interests are treated with skepticism.

In the parenting practice of the new middle class, the two central orientations of the singularistic lifestyle therefore converge: world-embracing self-actualization and investing in status. Behind the ideal of the intensively encouraged child lies the idea that even children should develop and "grow" their selves.[47] According to this idea, child self-development takes place within the framework of an open and positive practice of embracing the world and requires a type of parenting that playfully brings children into contact with the diverse aspects of the world "in all its richness": music, sports, travel, nature, etc. However, this parenting style is also governed by a second requirement: on the one hand, self-actualization is valuable in itself, but on the other hand it is about acquiring competencies that are supposed to guarantee educational and professional success. Children have therefore become prominent objects of post-bourgeois status investment. In order for them to achieve status in the society of singularities, formal education is, of course, a necessary and indispensable condition. At the same time, as we have already seen, it is not enough in itself to guarantee success in the volatile knowledge and culture economy, so that informal cultural capital has become essential as well. The latter is conveyed above all through one's family background, and thus it follows that early-childhood personal development has become such a crucial asset in today's portfolios of human capital.[48]

In the educated middle class, parenting and early education have been interlocked for some time. Since the 1990s, however, the development of schools has seemed – at least at first glance – to contradict this tendency to singularize children. The old industrial system of education has not only been rebuilt, it has also been expanded. As is especially apparent from the widespread use of national and international examinations to test the cognitive skills of pupils (such as PISA and TIMSS), today's school systems are hardly averse to the standardized dissemination of knowledge and the establishment of general educational standards. At least on this level, schools have succumbed to a quasi-industrial imperative of standardization and have thus had a retarding effect within the society of singularities.[49]

It is necessary, however, to take a closer look. Since the turn of the millennium, the ultimate goal of standardized tests has not been to treat everyone as equals but rather to maintain a minimum standard of education *at the low end*. The issue that they address is the fact that, in problem schools and bad neighborhoods, basic competencies are not (or no longer) being learned. In our terms, the social logic of the general, which manifests itself in the promotion of educational standards, is being applied to families of low-qualified people with the aim of maintaining a minimum standard. At the same time, however, it is also easy to see the rise of an educational logic of the particular, which, in Western societies, is oriented toward the families of the new middle class. For, just as the working conditions, lifestyles, and neighborhoods have been polarized in the society of singularities, schools have been polarized as well.[50] Even within the framework of a non-differentiated school system, there is now an entire network of public and private schools whose ambition is to create eye-catching profiles that showcase their unique culture and particular educational opportunities.[51]

Since the 1990s, the singularization of *ambitious schools* has turned this segment of the school system into a complex cultural market, especially in big cities. Early education has now itself emerged as a cultural good with promises of singularity, and its excessively critical and selective consumers are the families of the new middle class. Ambitious schools *want* to stand out on account of their educational quality and they are *expected* to be singular because this is what parents and pupils desire from them and because, in the end, they themselves are in competition with other schools to be recognized as "excellent" educational institutions.

The singularization of schools affects their organization and collective culture. In industrial modernity, schools were ultimately subordinate administrative authorities whose objective was to convey the prescribed content of standardized curricula. Accordingly, the enrollment of a pupil in a particular school was an administrative act: people typically attended the school closest to their house. Late-modern schools now have greater leeway to create individual profiles; at the same time, their self-perception has changed, so that they now consider themselves to be representative of a particular *school culture* of learners, teachers, and parents. They claim to have their own atmospheres, with a specific climate of togetherness, as well as their own histories and traditions. Ambitious schools distinguish themselves from one another not only through their educational programs but also in light of what might be called their "hidden curricula," and they develop profiles that emphasize a wide range of extra-curricular activities, which are meant to serve the personal development of their pupils.

Ambitious schools perceive themselves as cultures for developing the talents and potential of their pupils. Ideally, the singularization of a school should correspond to the singularization of its educational methods, which might involve such things as project learning and mentoring.[52] The fact that pupils are no longer addressed as passive consumers of learning material but rather as active subjects who are eager to learn and hungry for experience requires that they possess a sufficient degree of self-organization, motivation, and other informal cultural capital – requirements that the educated middle class assiduously endeavors to fulfill. For parents in the new middle class, the decision of which primary and secondary schools their children should attend has become an expensive investment in status, and it is not made without taking many qualitative parameters into consideration (the educational profile of the school, the backgrounds of its other pupils, the quality of its teachers, its reputation, etc.).

Ultimately, ambitious schools have to combine two different goals: the pedagogical goal of developing the potential of individual pupils, and the institutional goal of becoming an effective springboard to life and career opportunities. Singular schools thus participate in a market of schools for which being average does not suffice; they have to be excellent and, as "creative schools," offer unique and tailored opportunities.[53] The demanding requirements of the post-industrial economy, for which formal education is necessary but personality is essential, and the challenging life goals of the educated middle class, which is intent on successful self-actualization, are likewise imposed upon late-modern schools to a point that seems excessive.

Work–Life Balance, Urbanity, Juvenilization, Degendering, and New Liberalism

Every modern form of life has to respond to certain fundamental conditions regarding its own reproduction and its relation to the social world. Such conditions concern the status of work and leisure, the perception of social space, the understanding of youth and old age, the treatment of gender differences, and the exigencies of politics. Where does the new middle class stand in these respects?

Work–life balance: Industrial modernity's way of life was based on the dualism of gainful employment and family/leisure time, which stood opposed to one another as two spheres governed by contrary types of logic. The sphere of (typically male) gainful employment was thoroughly rationalized, unemotional, and instrumentally oriented. The purpose of gainful employment was to create the economic foundation for family and leisure time. This latter sphere followed a different set of rules; it was dominated by relaxing free time and the emotional and communicative bond with one's family. Even if things were never so simple, the leveled middle class generally maintained a clear "division of labor" between these two spheres. In the new middle class, in contrast, it is possible to observe a *structural alignment of work and the private sphere*, and this change has proceeded from both sides.[54] On the one hand, as we have already seen, the highly qualified forms of labor in the knowledge and culture economy themselves require communicative, interpretive, and also creative competencies and practices; moreover, work is now associated with high levels of emotional engagement and a strong sense of personal identification, so that it is often more than just a means to an end. On the other hand, this culturalization of the working world is mirrored by the cultural economization and curatorial treatment of leisure and the private sphere. Late-modern subjects are compelled to be active and productive in their free time as well, where they develop an entrepreneurial feel for cultural resources and participate in various sorts of cultural markets (including the market for romantic partners, which has become challenging).[55] Over the course of these concurrent developments, the spheres of work and leisure have become more and more similar: both promise identity and satisfaction, and both are devoted to productive activity. On account of this structural alignment, work–life balance between these two psychologically demanding spheres has become a paradigmatic problem of the new middle class.

Urbanity: The question of how the new middle class is situated in social space is quite easy to answer. The singularistic lifestyle is an emphatically *urban* lifestyle. Studies of social geography have clearly shown that the new middle class is clustered in large cities and metropolitan regions (and their surrounding areas), and that certain especially attractive cities and regions are preferred.[56] Whereas the distinction between urban and rural areas was not an important criterion during the era of industrial and leveled middle-class society, which was equally distributed in geographical terms as well, late-modern society has trended toward a high degree of socio-spatial polarization between post-industrial large cities as centers where the new middle class is concentrated and other residential areas (former industrial cities, small towns, villages) as peripheries. For years, highly qualified people have accordingly been migrating to large cities. The reasons for this are obvious enough: urban environments offer educational and professional opportunities (universities, jobs in the knowledge and culture economy), and they also have much to offer for those living an active lifestyle (high culture and events, natural spaces, restaurants, shopping, a good selection of schools, private networks of people, etc.). The educated class is distinguished by its high degree of geographical mobility (including, in part, international mobility as well): for subjects of the new middle class, it is typical to leave the place where one grew up (often to go to university) and then intentionally choose new places to live.[57]

Juvenilization: The demographic development of late-modern societies is well known: life expectancy is increasing and all societies are growing older. At the same time, however, a process of *juvenilization* has been taking place on the cultural level, which means that youthfulness has become a dominant and attractive cultural model for all age groups. For its part, the singularistic lifestyle of the new middle class contains an inherent affinity for youthfulness. A cultural model of (moderate) youthfulness defines most of this lifestyle's undertakings, which aim for self-actualization and "openness," strive for new experiences at work and at leisure, are urban, and often involve considerable physical activity.[58] In juvenilized late modernity, the opposite of youthfulness is no longer adult maturity but rather elderliness. As a consequence, "active aging" has been adopted as an ideal by senior citizens – or at least by those in the educated middle class, who have access to the necessary cultural, medical, and economic resources.[59] The effect of this hegemonic juvenility on young and post-adolescent people themselves has been remarkable: the era since the 1990s seems to be the first phase in modern cultural history that has not produced any genuine youth movements. The very thing that youth cultures used to fight for against the conformist establishment has itself become the hegemon: freedom to self-actualize.[60] In the milieu of the educated middle class, generational conflicts have accordingly lost their relevance. Here, parents and children instead seem like allies engaged in a common lifestyle of materialistically based post-materialism.[61]

Degendering: Has the late-modern culture of the new middle class also singularized genders? The situation here is more complicated than that of the general features discussed above. First it has to be stated that it was the patriarchal, dualistic gender culture, which prevailed from the eighteenth century to well into the twentieth, that separated men and women into two "human types" (essentially singularizing them *as collectives*) and that understood the seemingly natural and yet elaborately staged concepts of "authentic femininity" and "authentic masculinity" as unique and clearly distinct worlds. In contrast to this, what is happening on one level in late modernity's new middle class is a process of *degendering*.[62] In light of the long history of women in the workforce, their inclusion in the expansion of education, and the unprecedented number of women among people with college degrees, the same competencies are now expected of both sexes. Degendering thus means that the most relevant professional skills (an entrepreneurial spirit, social competence, or intelligence, for instance) are now assumed to be gender-neutral. The same is true of lifestyles and their general goals of subjective self-actualization and social prestige.[63]

Gender differences have not, however, dissolved in late-modern culture; rather, they have acquired a different status.[64] The new middle class in particular avails itself of a broad repertoire of gender models (of both femininity and masculinity), out of which its members each compose their own gender *profile*. It is no longer

V The Singularistic Life 245

the case that the entire collective is singularized; instead, individual subjects are singularized as *unique* representatives of their gender roles. The late-modern gender culture has thus made a whole portfolio of gender accessories available, including the models of the "empathetic woman" or the "tough woman," the "new man" (also: "new fathers") or also the masculine man. There is, therefore, a repertoire for any combination of appropriate gender roles, though, in our hegemonic culture, there are still limits to what is socially acceptable (the "vulgar woman" and the "effeminate man," for instance, have not been fully accepted).[65]

New liberalism: Where does the new middle class stand politically? In terms of party politics, it consists of a broad spectrum of voters who range from supporting center-left parties (Social Democrats, Social Liberals, Greens) to center-right parties (Conservatives, Economic Liberals) but hardly ever support the populist right. The educated class seems to lack a homogeneous political class consciousness. Nevertheless, there are several indications that it shares a common and quasi-sub-political world view that is closely connected to its lifestyle. This world view, which can be called new liberalism,[66] contains three components: meritocratism, quality of life, and cosmopolitanism.

The new middle class, whose entire self-relation and relation to the world is based on its high educational and professional qualifications, has a deeply rooted meritocratic consciousness, according to which success in life should stem from professional achievement (which, in turn, requires education).[67] The political consequences of meritocratism can vary considerably: it can lead to a decidedly market-oriented social politics, to special efforts to renovate the educational system, or to left-wing skepticism toward unearned wealth. The ethos of achievement has always been a feature of the modern middle class; what is characteristic now, however, is the fact that it is decidedly linked to the prerequisite of education.

Because the late-modern educated class favors enjoying a high quality of life over achieving a mere standard of living, it is no surprise that it tends to support *post-materialistic* political agendas. Since the 1980s, this tendency has especially elevated the role of ecology, healthcare, cultural politics, and citizen-friendly urban development. In this regard, the new-liberal political understanding distances itself from the classical bread-and-butter themes of industrial modernity. Finally, the cultural cosmopolitanism of the new middle class translates into political cosmopolitanism and globalism. The latter manifests itself in support for such things as free trade, globalization, and international cooperation, in openness toward the influences of migration and multicultural societies, but also in tolerance for and the equal treatment of previously discriminated groups (women, gays and lesbians, disabled people), and in an understanding of foreign policy as a global humanitarian project (foreign aid, human rights, humanitarian interventions).[68]

As already mentioned, meritocratism, post-materialism, and cosmopolitanism contain both economic and socio-political liberal ideas. On an individual basis, the new liberalism of the new middle class can accordingly lean more toward the left or more toward the market-oriented side. Fundamentally, however, the three components form a unit in which the new middle class's understanding of *progress* comes to light, and this understanding favors the globalization of markets, post-industrialism, the expansion of education, ecology, sustainable policies, and cosmopolitan equal rights.[69]

Fields of Tension in the Lifestyle of the New Middle Class: The Inadequacy of Self-Actualization

There is no question that the singularistic lifestyle of late modernity provides enormous opportunities for the subjects of the new middle class (in particular) to lead fulfilling lives. This has been made possible above all by the steady culturalization and singularization of everyday life, processes that promise emotional satisfaction and recognized social value. At the same time, this way of life contains certain pragmatic aspects on account of the inherent necessity of investing in status. The ideal of late-modern subjects is a modernized synthesis of Romanticism and bourgeois culture that incorporates the advantages of both lifestyles (self-actualization and status) and avoids their disadvantages (economic uncertainty and repression). It can hardly come as a surprise, then, that this lifestyle of lofty expectations has also created new tensions, dilemmas, and pressures.[70]

The dual structure of world-embracing self-actualization (on the one hand) and investing concurrently in social status (on the other) is fundamentally fraught with tension. Here, two conflicting orientations toward life are brought into a delicate balance. Thus, there is always the risk that the lifestyle scales will tip too far in one or the other direction – too far toward Romanticism or too far toward the bourgeois obsession with status, each side with its own disadvantages. In a sense, the new middle class is caught in a *Romanticism–status dilemma*. If someone focuses too strongly on self-actualization and neglects to invest in status – for instance by choosing a course of study, profession, or partner on hedonistic principles alone, by slacking off too much, or by being sentimentally attached to a place that lacks opportunities – this can come at the cost of relatively insecure social status. Conversely, if someone concentrates mainly on investing in status – for instance by choosing a course of study, profession, or partner on careerist grounds, by overworking, or by moving around excessively for better and better jobs – he or she will certainly accumulate capital but will also run the risk of neglecting the goal of self-actualization. In the latter case, investing in status is in danger of becoming that person's primary activity.[71] From the perspective of the singularistic lifestyle, publicly visible subjects who seem to have solved the Romanticism–status dilemma are especially admired: the creative stars and successful artists, designers, and entrepreneurs who have managed to achieve high social status as well as great success in self-actualization.

The orientation toward self-actualization, however, has a fundamental problem of its own: in its post-Romantic and decidedly world-embracing form, it is not self-sufficient but is rather defined by a typically modern structure of intensification.[72] As we have seen, self-actualization is no longer a matter of unfolding one's natural inner being according to its own intrinsic logic – rather, subjects self-actualize through the world's wealth of practices and objects, which are presented to them in excess. This, however, has given rise to an *imperative of the unlimited self*: late-modern subjects derive enormous satisfaction not from being settled once and for all but, rather, from being able to discover more and more new and different activities and possibilities for themselves – new travel destinations, new types of sports, a different partner, a different place to live, etc. The goal is to mobilize as much of one's potential as possible and help it unfold. The standard of this lifestyle is to enjoy life's abundance to the *fullest possible extent*.

The flipside of the unlimited self is the overstrained self. The *opportunity* to have and do new and different things can become a *self-compulsion* to have and do new and different things – a self-transformation for its own sake – that no longer provides any satisfaction but rather involves constantly shuffling through different objects of experience and valorization. Ideally, everything desirable should be actualized at the same time: career *and* family, being settled *and* traveling around the world, adventure *and* steadiness, etc. To renounce any of these possibilities seems to have fundamentally negative connotations; the late-modern imperative of self-actualization contains a built-in *aversion to abstention*. Accordingly, someone's ability to self-transform can also become a sort of performance requirement when he or she is judged by others (whether in a professional or private context). Whoever appears to be content with what he or she has already discovered in life will soon be regarded as narrow-minded and insufficiently open. It has thus become clear yet again that the value assigned to the uniqueness of subjects in late-modern culture is in no way unconditional. Although the singularistic subject culture may tolerate and encourage a number of different interests, talents, and ways of life, the radius of possibilities is nevertheless limited by what is regarded as *valuably singular*.[73] The *immobile subject* in particular, who is understood as someone whose personality structure is lacking in "openness," represents here a negatively valued foil to the creative subject.

For systematic reasons, the new middle class's demanding lifestyle of self-actualization is *prone to disappointment*. Disappointment generally means that subjective expectations remain unfulfilled, and this results in negative emotions (from self-reproach to anger). Broadly speaking, one could say that classical industrial modernity tended to minimize subjective disappointment through the systemic predictability of its institutions. In that economic and government processes (not to mention private lives) were made to be plannable, subjective expectations were typically fulfilled. During the *trente glorieuses*, this may in fact have been the case – at least in terms of standard of living. In this respect, classical modernity's promise of progress was a disappointment-avoidance program. The culture of late modernity, in contrast, has proven to be a *structural generator of disappointment* – and this also pertains to the educated class, notwithstanding its ongoing efforts to create planning security by investing in status.[74] This social production of disappointment has two systematic causes: first, the cultural economization of broad areas of the social; second, the high status that "lived experience" has acquired in the culture of self-actualization.

We have already seen in detail that late modernity has subjected broad areas of the social to cultural economization, which means that it has transformed them into markets for cultural singularity goods characterized by overproduction, a winner-take-all (or the-most) logic, and structures of risk and speculation.[75] This is especially true in the case of the goods that are relevant to the educated middle class. In the knowledge and culture economy, the labor market in particular has become far more unpredictable than it was in the industrial economy. Established professions can suddenly lose value, while new types of activity suddenly open up unforeseen possibilities. Nationally and regionally, the labor markets for highly qualified people have become differentiated in a significant way. There is now a large gap between the extremely successful and the less successful even within the *same* area of activity (journalists, artists, IT experts, designers, lawyers, doctors, scientists, etc.). The role that coincidence plays in this can hardly be overestimated. Education, too, has become a risky market good: the inflation of high academic degrees has led to processes of devaluation, so that choosing the right school for one's children and the right university and course of study for oneself has become enormously important, and wrong decisions can have considerable consequences. For the new middle class, the highly speculative nature of the real-estate market also has unsettling effects: the attractive locations in large cities have become unaffordable, but buying a home in the suburbs can be risky in the long term. On top of all this, the heightened "cultural economization" of the market for romantic partners has led to a greater number of break-ups, and thus to a greater number of people seeking new relationships, so that even this area of the private sphere now has a higher share of both opportunities and risks.[76]

Thus, for the new middle class (and for the other classes as well), the cultural economization of the social has created – in addition to the many opportunities that it has provided – a number of potential and systemic disappointments that were unknown to industrial modernity. The experience of disappointment has been enhanced by the fact that it typically affects subjects as isolated individuals, and by the fact that *successful* professionals, degree holders, owners of real estate, or married couples are largely *visible*. In late modernity, the *visibility of other people's success* – in representations of prominent people by the mass media, in posts about private vacations and events on social media, in the conspicuous consumption that takes place in big cities and vacation spots, in the polarization of urban real-estate markets, etc. – generally amplifies the experience of disappointment by making people feel as though they cannot "keep up," or as though they have irretrievably "missed out on something."

As a central touchstone of a fulfilled life, moreover, self-actualization has paradoxically proven to be a generator not only of opportunities but of disappointments as well. Subjects consider themselves to be actualized when they have authentic experiences and perceive their lives as a whole to be authentic. Compared to earlier measures of a successful life – simple survival, moral principles, social respect within one's community, or a high standard of living – the new standard of self-actualization is in fact far more volatile, subjective, emotional, and thus fragile. Ultimately, it is the *lived experience* of subjects – their perceptions and emotions – that determines what is authentic or inauthentic. However, it is impossible to predict with certainty whether something will be experienced as conducive to self-actualization. This only becomes clear after the fact. Moreover, this impression and emotional state can change over time.

This is already the case on the micro-level: whereas the success of a functional good or status good was easy to anticipate – in the leveled middle-class society, a new house or new car "automatically" brought prestige – it is impossible to predict whether the experience of a singular cultural good will be successful. There is a fine line between a novel experience and a disaster.[77] Even more profound are the consequences of long-term biographical decisions: over time, a career choice or marriage can turn out to be unsatisfying and no longer feel "authentic," and this might be because one's preferences and desires have simply changed. Of course, this can only become a problem *if* one expects self-development and a specific quality of life from one's profession and marriage (which was not typically the case in classical modernity).[78] In this case, too, the extent to which subjects compare their success in life to that of others has been intensified by digital media and the size of large social networks. The real or presumed personal fulfillment of others can make one's own lack of fulfillment even more painful.

Despite its structure as a generator of disappointment, late-modern culture offers few resources for tolerating or managing it.[79] This is also true of disappointments caused by existential "inevitabilities."[80] These include, first of all, death and sickness – which, despite the late-modern obsession with healthiness, cannot be overcome – as well as accidents and catastrophes. Despite all efforts, certain psychological conditions cannot be changed at will, nor can the (social and geographical) family background into which someone is born or, to a large extent, the way one's own children develop.

By implementing certain control mechanisms – from medicine to insurance – classical modernity attempted to make such inevitabilities manageable, but such efforts have taken on an entirely different quality within the framework of the singularistic lifestyle. Now, and to an extreme extent, subjects attempt to form their own lives, which means that the task of risk management has been delegated away from social systems to individuals. In cases where such efforts at self-formation fail, this project of subjective self-liberation and optimization hits a wall, and the culture of successful self-actualization seems to be ill equipped to process these experiences of disappointment. In late modernity, equanimity and even humility seem to be obsolete cultural models; instead, the tendency is for personal failure to fall squarely on the shoulders of individuals. Often, psychological therapy promises nothing more than increased self-transformation ("more authenticity," "stronger resonance," "learning from failure"). At its heart, late modernity is a culture of positive affects that makes little legitimate room for negative or even ambivalent experiences.[81]

With reference to the work of Alain Ehrenberg, it has often been stated that depression is the characteristic illness of late-modern culture – and particularly (though not exclusively) of its new middle class.[82] Of course, one should exercise extreme caution when correlating certain illnesses with certain types of society. That said, there are many indications that this assumption is correct, and now we can see why: with its model of successful self-actualization, the singularistic lifestyle not only provides new opportunities for high satisfaction but also many opportunities for disappointment, and there are hardly any cultural means for managing the latter. In short,

V The Singularistic Life 251

late-modern culture has made it possible for subjects to climb very high with respect to their success in life – higher than they ever could in the leveled middle-class society – but also to fall very low (or, in other words, to "fail").

Disappointments are not purely cognitive acts; they arouse negative emotions such as self-reproach, (directed and undirected) anger, or sadness (about missed opportunities). In this sense, depression can be interpreted as an illness caused by unmanageable (over)reactions to individual or recurring experiences of disappointment. The accumulation of failure gives rise to intense self-focused emotions and is converted into a psychological symptom that short-circuits subjects, leaving them in a passive and emotionless condition in which they are unable to feel and act. It is only fitting that depression has become a characteristic illness in a form of society that promises so much and yet, at the same time, increases the risk of disappointment without providing any resources for processing this negative experience. If the late-modern subject suffers from anything, it is no longer from having an overly strong superego – as was the case in Sigmund Freud's bourgeois society – but rather from having strong feelings of subjective inadequacy in response to disappointments with which he or she is unequipped to cope.[83]

3
The Culturalization of Inequality

The Underclass's Way of Life: Muddling Through

Oriented toward the model of successful self-actualization, the lifestyle of the new middle class in late-modern society is diametrically opposed to the new underclass's way of life. The latter class includes heterogeneous groups of employees in the simple service industry, people who are precariously employed or have to hold several jobs, industrial workers who do not enjoy the normal working conditions of traditional blue-collar employment, as well as unemployed people and recipients of social welfare. Despite their differences, all of these groups share a similar life situation. If, in comparison with the old middle-class society, the educated middle class is socially and culturally "on the rise," then the new underclass can be said to consist of groups that are "in decline."

As I have already said, the polarization between the new middle class and the new underclass pertains to more than just the social inequality of material resources; it is also an opposition defined by the different types of *cultural logic* behind their respective lifestyles.[1] The classes are not disconnected; rather, they perceive each other and view themselves in relation to one another. In contrast to the new middle class and its self-perception as the group that represents *the* advanced lifestyle in the society of singularities – a perception that is also broadly supported by institutions (in politics, education, healthcare, etc.) – the new underclass has become an object of negative culturalization. This concerns the minimal amount of (formal and informal) cultural capital possessed by its members, their limited opportunities to (legitimately) culturalize their own lives in an ethical and aesthetic manner, and the devaluation of their entire lifestyle as one that is deficient and lacking in quality, recognition, and perspective – a devaluation that comes from the outside but also, in the form of self-devaluation, from within.

V The Singularistic Life 253

It has often been asserted that the new underclass consists of people whom modernization has left behind.[2] This is undoubtedly true to the extent that, since the 1970s, modernization has meant the transition to post-industrial society – with the rise of the knowledge and culture economy, which requires highly qualified personnel, and the simultaneous decline of industrial labor and its workforce. The "losers" in modernization are often disadvantaged on *all* the ubiquitous and competitive social markets that have formed over the past few decades: on the post-industrial labor markets first of all but also – and mostly as a result of this first disadvantage – on the markets for homes, education, and (not infrequently) romantic partners as well. In our context, however, it is important that they are also *losers in the process of culturalization* – that is, they are "losers" in the process according to which cultural capital determines social prestige, and according to which the singularistic lifestyle of the new middle class is the only lifestyle that is considered truly contemporary and valuable.

Whereas the lifestyle of the new middle class, which strives for self-development and is oriented toward investing in status, is ambitious, the prospects of the new underclass have been strongly reduced. Its way of life is one that is structured by the *everyday logic of muddling through*: day by day and year by year, one somehow has to pull through, scrape by, and persevere. The daily life of the individuals in the new underclass is thus defined by two elements: dealing with permanent difficulties, and the consequent inability to look or plan far ahead. Regarding the so-called service-sector proletariat, Heinz Bude, Friederike Bahl, and others have shown how, on account of a number of adversities, this way of life is organized around the humble goal of survival, keeping afloat, and carrying on both at work (assuming one is employed) and at home.[3] This type of daily life is dominated by the "difficulties" that one wants to avoid and overcome, but that nevertheless keep appearing. Viewed from the outside, these might seem like minor difficulties, but they can in fact quickly become debilitating: illnesses that keep people away from work, accidents, lay-offs, bankruptcy, trouble paying rent, trouble with one's children at school, etc. From this minimalistic perspective, the desired but unrealistic aim is to achieve a life free of existentially threatening incidents. In this situation of reduced prospects, long-term projects of self-actualization and the idea of valorizing all aspects of life seem unthinkable and even extravagant. One instead proceeds from problem to problem, and long-term planning does not take place. This is a life of short-term *ad hoc* reactions, and it leaves little if any room for making status investments in cultural, economic, social, and subject capital, which is a typical activity of the (old and new) middle class. Members of the new underclass lack the means and foresight to invest in assets and education, and their social network is also limited. In a sense, their lives are often on the edge of being overstrained. A central role in mastering this type of life is not played by self-actualization or investments in status but rather by *self-discipline* – a cultural legacy of the old middle class and its industrial workforce that, though perpetuated by the new underclass, is no longer a point of pride. Self-discipline is no longer relied on to achieve a decent standard of living or perhaps even to "rise through the ranks." It is now simply necessary to manage everyday life and to avoid falling any further down.

In comparison to the new middle class, the new underclass thus has a fundamentally different orientation toward work. Whereas members of the new middle class expect their jobs to provide satisfaction and identity alongside secure social status and sufficient income for their elaborate lifestyle, the new underclass's relationship to work is purely instrumental: work serves the exclusive purpose of maintaining subsistence. In the traditional workforce, this instrumental attitude was associated with an ethos of "hard work," which, though difficult, was often a source of pride that allowed people to lead their lives with "dignity."[4] As Friederike Bahl has shown, however, what now prevails among the members of today's service-sector proletariat is a decidedly scornful attitude to their own jobs.[5] The background for this scorn is the end of the *"instrumentality deal" of labor*, which had been kept in place throughout industrial modernity: then, effort could be exchanged for status. In industrial modernity, an instrumental relation to labor was the norm that applied to nearly every worker, but it also reliably guaranteed a moderate standard of living via long-term employment under normal working conditions.

For those in the post-Fordistic service economy and for many blue-collar workers, this "deal" no longer holds; rather, the labor of the underclass now seems to be *doubly handicapped*. With the rise of the new middle class, society's ideal of labor has shifted toward "attractive work," which requires effort but also promises satisfaction, so that routine jobs now seem all the more unattractive. At the same time, both the income and the social status that can be earned from doing "simple routine jobs" have drastically decreased. Whereas, at least ideally, the professions of the new middle class provide material *and* subjective satisfaction, the jobs of the underclass usually meet *neither* of these two conditions. This can thus be seen as a twofold devaluation.[6]

Accordingly, the life of those in the new underclass outside of work is largely defined by the practice of dealing with shortages in an effort to make up for the limited compensation earned from their jobs. Their consumption is thus characterized by its strict thriftiness, and, instead of being active and public, their free time tends to be oriented toward family and their immediate environment.[7] The consumption practices of the new underclass generally correspond to what Pierre Bourdieu referred to as a "taste for necessity": a taste for what is feasible and necessary, with little to no consideration paid to aesthetic or ethical matters.[8] For the underclass as a whole, leading a merely conventional lifestyle is already an achievement that has to be wrested from difficult circumstances. This is also true of family life. Fostering a good family life was of high and even central value to the traditional middle class, which included industrial workers, and while this is still often the case in the new underclass, it has become an increasingly more difficult task to manage.

The new underclass is not, however, homogeneous. Although it is generally defined by the everyday logic of muddling through, the socially inconspicuous act of *staying afloat* coexists alongside a more aggressive life practice of *toughing it out* (not to mention the more passive practice of *letting oneself go*). In terms of cultural history, both forms of logic can be found in the petit-bourgeois proletariat as well as in the sub-proletariat.[9] Since the 1990s, this more aggressive, demonstrative, and often state-dependent variant of the underclass has attracted a great deal of media attention in Germany, Great Britain, France, and the United States, and this "underclass discourse" has contributed immensely to the negative culturalization of this group in the public eye.[10] The media have tended to focus on factions of the underclass that practice conspicuous consumption, cultivate verbal and nonverbal aggressiveness (particularly among men), and in which family structures have dissolved or the ethos of self-discipline and hard work has weakened. What is important, however, is that the difference between the two versions of the underclass also affects self-perceptions within the class itself: the "respectable" underclass, which attempts to keep a grip on everyday life and abide by the ideas of order and discipline, often looks down upon those who have become complete social outcasts, misfits, or criminals, and indeed the sub-proletariat now seems to be regarded as a threat to itself (or to its own children).[11] From the perspective of the "respectable" underclass, which in this regard perpetuates the ethos of the old middle class, the sub-proletarian underclass represents a locus of both anomie and recklessness. It has become a new *classe dangereuse*.

Cultural Devaluations

In all facets of late-modern culture, the new underclass has become an object of negative culturalization and de-valorization; it is marked as being *valueless* with respect to all the components that I discussed in relation to the lifestyle of the new middle class. In a sense, the new underclass has become the new middle class's negative foil. Just as, in the new middle class, the social valorization of appropriated goods and practices is converted into the valorization of subjects, the social *de*-valuation of the goods and practices used by the new underclass translates into the *de*-valorization of subjects. In this process, the everyday socio-cultural praxis of the underclass is interconnected with a specific interpretation of this praxis by institutions such as the media, academia, and politics, which generally express and corroborate the standards of the new middle class.[12]

In addition to the central area of work and the expiration there of the "instrumentality-deal," which I discussed above, there are three additional prominent and public cultural areas in which the de-valorization of the underclass takes place: food and nutrition, the body, and parenting and education. Although food and nutrition were once an apolitical and almost trivial matter, they have become, as we have seen, a cultural proving ground in late modernity.[13] Whereas the model of middle-class eating habits is to eat healthy and "good" food, which is ascribed ethical value, the underclass has become a milieu of "poor nutrition": unbalanced meals, excessive meat and sugar, irregular meal times, with a preference for fast food. In other words, the eating habits of the underclass, which often involve plenty of snacks, are associated with unhealthiness, malnutrition, harmful substances, obesity, and thus also with the susceptibility to illness. Things are similar with the body: whereas fit, healthy, and active bodies are the model for the middle class – bodies that are looked after, exercised in a health-conscious manner, have cultivated aesthetic value, and are engaged in a variety of activities – the bodies of underclass subjects are often problematic. Either they seem unhealthy, inactive, and overweight, and are thus, from the perspective of subjects, a burden or blemish that becomes increasingly prone to illness as one ages, or they are regarded as being "over-styled," as in the case of excessive weightlifting by men (bodybuilding) or, in the case of women, being excessively "done up," so that the bodies in question seem threatening or vulgar.[14]

Regarding parenting and early education, which are central to the valorization of late-modern lifestyles, studies of the underclass's parenting style have shown that it is in many ways the opposite of that of the new middle class.[15] Members of the "respectable" underclass resort to strict discipline in order to prevent their children from falling in with a "bad crowd." Here, having an open personality and embracing the world are certainly not ideals; rather, constraints are put in place in order to impose order on how children develop. Family interactions are often characterized by a high level of constant stress, which makes it challenging to manage everyday life. This type of parenting is about "not letting oneself go" and "being hard on oneself and others." The main achievement, which has to be wrested from reality, consists in leading a "respectable life." Here, creating a degree of normality is already hard work in itself. The intensive and child-centric "positive parenting" of the new middle class is thus in opposition to the sort of "negative parenting" practiced by the underclass – a preventative type of parenting that concentrates on establishing boundaries and avoiding the worst (but also leaves children with a considerable amount of leeway). The ideal of underclass parenting is thus the disciplined and rule-abiding child, and the opposite of this ideal comes from the sub-proletarian variant of the underclass itself: children and adolescents who "cause trouble." The definitive parenting ideal of the underclass is to raise children who do not slip into delinquency.

In the case of parenting, the paternoster-elevator effect of late-modern cultural classes operates particularly clearly. The "normality ideal" of the leveled middle-class society no longer meets the advanced parenting standards of the new middle class, while the new underclass is struggling to maintain the old standards of normality in the face of adverse conditions. This polarity between parenting styles is institutionally bolstered on the level of schools. Parents in the educated middle class, who carefully select their children's schools and remain actively engaged in their children's education, stand opposite to the "uneducated" parents of the underclass, who are not experts in the school system, and ambitious schools with high status stand opposite to "problem schools," in which it is an institutional achievement simply to maintain discipline and widen the perspectives of a few pupils.[16] Their best outcome is often just to equip pupils with basic skills. In the end, with the increase in higher academic degrees, "lower" qualifications, which were once the norm, are generally devalued.

The other components that we have identified as typical of the new middle class's singularistic lifestyle are also diametrically opposed to corresponding aspects of the underclass's way of life, and in these cases, too, mechanisms of de-valorization/devaluation are at work. Not only do the realities of life experienced by these two classes differ – what is decisive, again, is the fact that the cultural conceptions of what can and should be achieved form contrary universes of evaluation. This is especially clear in the case of living situations: since the 1980s, as I have mentioned more than once, the "attractive" residential areas of the educated middle class have gradually been segregated from the "precarious" neighborhoods of the underclass. Whereas, for the new middle class, one's residence is an investment in status with aesthetic criteria, the most urgent problem (aside from affordability) that housing poses for the underclass is the safety of the area. This adds further poignancy to the urban/rural divide: the concentration of the new middle class in metropolises and university towns has led to shrinking populations in rural areas and small cities, where a large portion of underclass (and of the old middle class) is concentrated and remains immobile. The urban/rural divide has become a difference between the center and the periphery, and thus also a difference between *central* and *peripheral lifestyles*.[17]

The question of aging is also problematic for the underclass, as is its relation to youth. On the one hand, growing old as a member of this class is often economically, psychologically, and physically taxing on account of unstable employment and minimal pension entitlements. Given these circumstances, the juvenilization of the new middle class seems unrealistic. At the same time (and in contrast to the middle class), young members of the underclass are highly conspicuous, though not in the sense of a progressive youth movement but, rather, as a group of unruly "hooligans." With respect to the role of gender, too, the attitude of the underclass stands opposite to the model of degendering and flexible gender repertoires that characterizes the new middle class: in the underclass, gender roles are more clearly differentiated from one another, whether because of the stronger distinction between men's and women's jobs or because of this class's more aggressive performance of allegedly authentic masculinity and femininity.[18]

This cultural polarization is just as clear in the area of politics. The postulates of the new liberalism espoused by the educated middle class – meritocracy, quality of life, cosmopolitanism – and its political representatives are typically rejected by the new underclass. Here, as many empirical studies have shown, what prevails instead is a generally fatalistic political world view in which people consider themselves to be excluded from the political process and society as a whole, or at best to be "losers" in this process who have been "left behind."[19] In this light, the political developments that have been taking place in many Western societies since the year 2000 are hardly surprising. Whereas the new educated middle class often votes for the center-left, the new (white) underclass still tends to vote in part for the left but also – more and more frequently and as an act of protest – for the right, which is now associated with a new form of populism that is anti-globalism and critical of the elite.[20] From the perspective of the liberal-cosmopolitan new middle class and the institutions supported by it, the political articulations of the underclass have therefore also become an object of negative culturalization: they are regarded as being ethically "wrong."

Singularistic Counter-Strategies of the Underclass

In late modernity as a whole, the underclass seems like a locus of "bad" culture that has no value but is instead problematic or even threatening, on account of its lack of education and cultural

V The Singularistic Life 259

competencies; its bad eating habits and health; its bad parenting, neighborhoods, and schools; its difficult youth; its backward notions of masculinity and femininity; and, finally, its problematic political views.[21] Culturalization means, above all, aestheticization and ethicization, and although the negative culturalization of the underclass certainly takes place in an aesthetic register (in the sense that the tastes of the underclass are perceived as insignificant or vulgar), it occurs all the more prominently on the level of ethics: seemingly lacking the features of a *good* life, the underclass's way of life is regarded as a composite of *bad* characteristics, from its eating habits and parenting style to its politics. Studies have shown that this devaluation from the outside corresponds to self-devaluation within this class and a decidedly negative self-image. The perception or anticipation of outside opinions, which in Western societies are the opinions of the (new) middle class and society's leading institutions, translates into a corresponding self-perception: members of the underclass often see themselves as part of the "bottom" of society, as part of a group of people who have not "made it" and who have been "left behind." This can give rise to feelings of stigmatization and shame, or it can result in anger.[22]

Here, a comparison with the traditional working class is revealing: although the latter considered itself socially subordinate to bourgeois society, it was also defined by a positive class consciousness, by its class pride in doing socially necessary work, which was in part associated with a culture of heroic and "hard-working" manliness. Supported by socialist parties and labor unions, the working class could also regard itself as politically avant-garde: as the "class of the future." The "affluent worker" was an essentially integrated component of the leveled middle-class society. Post-industrial society, in contrast, has witnessed the development of a *negative class consciousness*. The new underclass perceives itself as a group of people going nowhere, who have not achieved, and never will achieve, the publicly visible "attractive lifestyle" of the new middle class. The legitimation of industrial society's values, which were shaped above all by blue-collar work – manual labor as "hard, honest work" and a symbiosis of self-discipline and hedonism – has eroded, and today's underclass often envisions its social and political future in merely fatalistic terms.

Within the new underclass, however, one can also see that certain counter-reactions and defensive strategies have been developed in response to these devaluations. One traditional counter-strategy, which was in fact typical in classical modernity, is to climb gradually upward in society over the course of generations via education and the accumulation of cultural capital. In contrast to the situation in the leveled middle-class society, however, such *education-driven upward mobility* – particularly the ambition to rise from the underclass to the educated class – is not only more difficult in polarized late modernity; in addition, it often requires cutting all ties with one's background.[23]

It is noteworthy, however, that three additional counter-strategies from the milieu of the underclass are themselves based on singularity and authenticity, though in a way opposed to the educated middle class. Certain members of the underclass now partake in the late-modern game of singularization and authentication, but they do so by defining them in a specific way. The first strategy that should be mentioned here involves imagining *a singular ascent via talent*. This is not uncommon among young members of the underclass who are unable (or do not want) to go down the traditional educational path but, instead, hope to take their chances with the winner-take-all logic of the creative economy. Encouraged by popular talent shows, the hope is to be "discovered" by cultural capitalism and quickly "rise to the top,"[24] which means being elevated out of the masses as an extraordinary individual through the culture economy's mechanisms of attention and valorization. The model for this comes from areas in which success does not depend so strongly on established cultural capital – popular culture and professional sports being the most obvious examples.

Beyond such a "fairy tale" rise from nobody to stardom, the milieu of the underclass also offers other paths to singularization. Although "muddling through" may at first seem like a uniform way of life, those individuals who are especially adept at managing their everyday struggles stand out and are recognized as singular in their communities. Walter Miller pointed out some time ago that, in underclass culture (and especially its sub-proletarian version), individuals distinguish themselves according to a different set of values.[25] Instead of education or achievement, the underclass values cleverness, and it favors "being lucky" over investing in status, and appreciates people who act autonomously against the social order instead of fitting into it. Illegal activity (from black-market employment and aggressive youth gangs to organized crime) also plays a role here. Some individuals excel at such things and can achieve an extraordinary amount of success that, though regarded as *illegitimate singularity* by society at large, can lead to high recognition and respect within their own milieu.

A final version of underclass singularization relies more on the collective as a whole than on the individual. Particularly in youthful milieus (but also in certain adult milieus), self-conscious attempts are often made to cultivate authenticity as a *classe populaire* – a sort of *plebian authenticity* with its own culture of honor, manliness, pride, or vulgarity. Underclass youth cultures, which are often associated with certain branches of pop culture, are based on such things as a "cool" immigrant or black identity (as in the case of gangster rap),

V The Singularistic Life   261

which can then be appropriated by white adolescents in a different way (as in the example of hip-hop culture).[26] The youth cultures of the underclass are often characterized by an aggressive and physical form of masculinity that demands "respect." This is a sort of street authenticity in which the pitiful social conditions of a collective are converted into self-confidence.

In general, examples of singularistic underclass identity survive from the self-confident traditions of British working-class culture and American "redneck culture." Such identities can have an ethical dimension (the "decency" of "simple people"), and they can be translated into a political register that promotes anti-elite populism. In such cases, one sees the underclass's approaches to a culture war – "the bottom against the top," "the people against the establishment" – in which the culture of the new middle class, who now appear to be the elite, is made to seem "contrived," "dishonest," and lacking in authenticity. It thus becomes clear that the contest of valorization and singularization between the new middle class and the underclass is not as rigged as it might initially seem. Rather, attempts are being made to turn the tables and – by citing criteria such as natural bodies, gender norms, "honest work," local roots, and historical traditions – to attribute an authenticity to the underclass that the "elite" new middle class is denied. With this interpretation, members of the underclass no longer perceive themselves as the "bottom" but as the "simple people" who constitute society's foundation. It is telling, however, that this plebian authenticity relies on the *same* structural criteria of value, uniqueness, and authenticity that define the society of singularities as a whole. It simply fulfills these criteria in a different way.[27]

The Tableau of Late-Modern Classes and Their Relations

We have seen the extent to which the new middle class, with its singularistic lifestyle, has become the dominant carrier group of post-industrial late modernity. In a sense, it is the socio-structural correlate to the economic, technological, and cultural forms of the society of singularities. However, the social structure of late modernity is not exhausted by the polarity between this new middle class and the underclass. In order to appreciate the broader social dynamics and relations between these two large social groups, it is necessary, if only briefly, to bring the two other classes into the discussion: the upper class and the "old" middle class.

Formally, the upper class – the extremely small upper 1 percent of society – can be defined by its exorbitantly high economic capital (income and assets). But how does this affect its lifestyle, and what relevance does it have for the remaining 99 percent of society?

Beyond pointing to statistics about income and assets, sociology has difficulties defining the upper class.[28] As far as lifestyle is concerned, however, one can presume that, as in the middle class, there is now a differentiation in the upper class between *old* and *new*. Whereas, like the old middle class, the *old* upper class ("old" in a cultural sense) continues to exercise demonstrative restraint in maintaining its orientation toward a certain standard of living, and whereas the *nouveaux riches* (which likewise have a long tradition) convert this orientation into an interest in demonstrative luxury and excess, the new upper class generally adheres to the cultural model of an advanced creative lifestyle, as is already familiar to us from the new middle class. On the one hand, the *new* upper class includes the professions of the global functional elite (in the areas of finance, law, management, etc.); on the other hand, it also consists of creative stars, that is, publicly visible stars from sectors of the culture economy – design, journalism, sports, IT branches, etc. In both cases, we are dealing with people who belong to a decidedly global and international class.

There is much in favor of the hypothesis that, in principle, the new upper class has *not* developed a unique lifestyle of its own but rather shares the curated lifestyle of the educated middle class, thus confirming that the latter serves as the dominant cultural model. Also, with respect to cultural capital, which is high in both cases, the new upper class is only slightly different from the new middle class. The new upper class can, however, intensify the singularistic lifestyle on account of its greater wealth.[29] Moreover, the members of the new upper class are often no longer dependent on the strategy of investing in status, an activity that characterizes the middle class as a whole. With respect to the grandness of their lifestyles, their future planning, and their private and professional "experiments," members of the new upper class are free to "play around" to an extent that is unimaginable to the middle class. Especially among the group of upper-class professionals, who have access to greater economic resources, the lifestyle can become one of stylish luxury, whereas, in the case of the creative stars, who painstakingly cultivate a curated lifestyle and who also act as trendsetters, there is the added factor that their social capital is also extremely high on account of their fame.[30]

Creative stars thus provide a publicly influential window not only into the lives of the upper class but ultimately into the singularistic–creative lifestyle in its "most attractive" form. The relationship of the educated middle class to the upper class seems ambivalent. On the level of lifestyle, the new upper class appears attractive to the middle class in many respects: the two classes share the same cultural criteria and values, but the upper class is able to translate these into practice on a far grander scale. At the same time, however,

V The Singularistic Life 263

members of the new middle class must concede that, regarding the upper class's economic and social capital and thus the perceived casualness of its lifestyle, they could never keep up with those "at the very top." Despite their own high cultural capital, they are nevertheless aware that, in relation to the upper class, they are still "only" *middle* class. Proud of their education and achievements, members of the educated class will often take a critical stance against the presumably "unearned" (by any standard of achievement) volumes of capital held by the new and old upper class.[31]

Regarding the overall tableau of the post-industrial social structure, the upper class is far less important (quantitatively) than the social group that lies between the new middle class and the new underclass: the old, non-college-educated middle class, which forms the middle segment of the three-thirds society. With respect to its lifestyle and resources, this is the group that is familiar from the milieu of the leveled middle-class society, and consists of employees with secure positions and self-employed people who generally possess a mid-range-level economic and cultural capital.[32] In late modernity, this group finds itself in a situation that, for it, is new: since the 1980s, it has lost its position as the hegemonic socio-cultural middle ground. In a process of shrinking, it is now squeezed between the expanding and rising new middle class on one side and the declining but likewise expanding new underclass on its other side.

In terms of culture, even today's old middle class is not identical with the middle class of the 1950s to the 1970s, for it, too, is influenced by processes of culturalization and singularization. Nevertheless, it is still governed by the guiding factors that distinguished the old middle class – by the dual formula of *status investment and self-discipline*. On the one hand, the subjects of the traditional middle class work to maintain a comfortable standard of living, which requires them to invest in various sorts of capital; at the same time, they place a high value on order and stability – on "orderly conditions." In this context, work is mostly an instrumental means to an end, but the "instrumentality deal" of industrial modernity (still) functions here, which means that effort and income are in a state of balance. To a great extent, family life is a foundational aspect of this group's identity, and traditional gender roles (with respect to divisions of labor) remain common. In general, the old middle class is distinguished by its relatively high level of *sedentariness*, which is to say that its members are anchored to particular places and regions – usually their places of origin, because their personal connections (both family and friends) are mostly tied to these places as well. The majority of the old middle class lives in rural or small-town areas.[33]

Since the 1960s, the old middle class has been losing members in two directions: those who profited from the expansion of higher education have risen to the educated middle class (and typically moved to cities), and those who, over the course of de-industrialization, "stayed behind" in non-urban areas have partially fallen into the underclass. In a sense, the old middle class is thus a transitional space on the socio-structural paternoster elevator. For now, at the beginning of the twenty-first century, it finds itself in an ambivalent situation. Whereas part of the old middle class may be able to reproduce and maintain its stable position "in the middle" (especially in prosperous small cities),[34] a second fraction has loftier cultural goals and has set its eyes on earning further qualifications and emulating the singularistic lifestyle of the educated class.[35] This is no surprise. When members of the old middle class invest in sufficient status and have enough educational success, they eventually join the ranks of the new middle class.

A third fraction perceives itself as being stuck in a sort of sandwich position, with anxieties about falling into the underclass and with resentment toward those both above *and* below. This defensive portion of the old middle class has seen from the underclass what it means to decline and fail. At the same time, the new middle class – with its college degrees, professions in the knowledge and culture economy, and its creative-singularistic lifestyle – has made it clear to this group that it is in historical decline and has lost its gold status as the "backbone" of society. Within the defensive fraction of the old middle class, the goal of investing in status seems less and less realistic, so that the borders between it and the new underclass (that is, its respectable and self-disciplined fraction) have become fluid.

The traditional middle class has also become an object of cultural devaluation, although, compared to the de-valorization of the new underclass, this process has taken place with more subtlety. Its effects can be seen on several levels. Clearest of all is the value lost by previously respected mid-tier educational qualifications (vocational training in Germany, for instance, or a high-school diploma in the United States) over the course of the general expansion of higher education and the increase in college or university degrees. In its social representations, an intermediate level of education is made to seem below average, and it is proving less and less able to provide the basis for a middle-class standard of living. The traditional work ethic of the old middle class is also on the defensive: here (and unlike in the case of the underclass), work continues to be a source of social status, but the intrinsic motivation of "attractive work," which is a defining feature of highly qualified professions, seems less realistic in the traditional and routinized white-collar (or blue-collar) professions of the old middle class. Whereas the new middle class has tended to embrace a culture of degendering (and a more open set of gender repertoires), the old middle class is more

V The Singularistic Life   265

strongly inclined to preserve traditional gender-based divisions of labor (including marriages with housewives), which, culturally, are likewise on the defensive.

On the level of culturalization and singularization, the difference between the lifestyles of the old and new middle class is especially clear to see in the discrepancy between the cosmopolitanism of the new middle class and the sedentariness of the old. From the perspective of the urban, highly mobile, and international educated class, the tendency of the old middle class to remain tied to specific places seems inflexible and provincial. Finally, there is a general discrepancy between the new middle class's culture of self-actualization, which cultivates singularity and strives for an aesthetic and ethical *quality* of life, and the implicit aspiration of the old middle class to live "just like everyone else" (even though this old hegemony no longer exists) and to maintain a certain *standard* of living. From this perspective, the old middle class – with its dual formula of "status investment and self-discipline" – seems rather like a locus of mere generality, standardization, conventionality, and conformity. Although it may still be well situated in material terms, the old middle class can thus perceive itself as being on the *cultural defensive*. In part, these disappointments are also expressed politically in attitudes of anti-elitism and anti-globalism, so that it is possible for the old middle class to form temporary alliances with portions of the underclass, which it otherwise views with a critical eye.[36]

Before bringing this chapter to a close, I would like to take another quick look at the ways in which the new underclass relates to the entire tableau of classes. These reciprocal relationships are more complex than they might at first seem. For the "respectable" underclass, the old middle class symbolizes a place of longing where it is possible to enjoy an orderly way of life. In contrast, the underclass differentiates itself clearly from the new educated middle class, except in cases when the latter is seen as a goal to be achieved via an ambitious educational climb. The distinctive educational and cultural capital of the educated class – not to mention its meritocratic consciousness – demonstrates to the underclass its inferiority, and the negative ethical culturalization from "above" is regarded as arrogant by those on the social "bottom." Accordingly, this can give rise to pronounced feelings of resentment against "the elite." Of course, elements of the underclass can in turn, from the perspective of the educated middle class and cultural capitalism, become interesting as cultural set pieces of "plebian authenticity." In light of the educated class's appreciation of cultural diversity, select aspects of underclass culture, such as elements from working-class culture or from black and immigrant cultures, can develop a certain appeal.[37] For some factions of the underclass, certain members of the genuine upper class – certain professional athletes and pop musicians, for instance, who consciously break the rules of the middle class, or certain "boorish" *nouveaux riches* – can in turn become projection screens for fantasies of a "fairy tale" rise to wealth and fame. In such cases, anti-elite resentment is suspended.[38]

VI
Differential Liberalism and Cultural Essentialism: The Transformation of the Political

The Politics of the Particular

How have the culturalization and singularization of the social affected the political sphere? And to what extent, in turn, has politics influenced them? These are the guiding questions of the present Part, which will conclude my study of the structural transformation of modernity. It is not a matter of debate that, since the 1980s, there has been not only an economic, technological, and socio-cultural transformation but also a paradigm shift in national politics. The politics of late modernity is fundamentally different from the politics of organized modernity. This paradigm shift is often attributed to the rise of a neoliberal form of politics that is intent on strengthening and spreading market and competitive structures in all areas of society.[1] The relevance of neoliberalism is beyond doubt, but, when examined from a somewhat greater distance, the transformation of the political proves to be clearly more complex and contradictory. To put it succinctly: in late modernity, the *politics of the general* is being replaced more and more by the *politics of the particular*. The politics of the particular appears in two versions, and culture plays a significant role in both of them. Beyond the traditional realm of "cultural policy," a *culturalization of politics* has been taking place in two respects.

First, in Western Europe and North America, a form of government has been developed that is oriented toward both competitive structures and cultural diversity (and therefore includes neoliberalism). This is the politics of *apertistic* and *differential* liberalism. It is apertistic because its ongoing concern is to open up and transgress economic, social, and cultural boundaries; it is differential because it emphasizes and promotes social and cultural differences. From the 1980s to the present, apertistic–differential liberalism has been the dominant political paradigm and, as such, it encompasses the entire political spectrum from the center-left to the center-right. Whether it will remain the dominant paradigm remains to be seen. *Second*, on the global level, one sees political tendencies that, despite their heterogeneity, can be encapsulated with the terms "cultural essentialism" or "cultural communitarianism." These tendencies are positioned against apertistic–differential liberalism. I will examine some of these tendencies more closely below, but for now I can state that the instances that they invoke are particular cultural communities and collective identities.

Two contrary political forms of structuring culture thus stand in opposition to one another. In apertistic–differential liberalism, culture is treated as a cosmopolitan and diverse resource for increasing people's quality of life and enhancing their capacity to compete. From the perspective of cultural essentialism, in contrast, culture is seen as the basis of historical or ethnic communities, and often as a criterion for demarcating such communities from the outside. Whereas the former insists on *culturally oriented governmentality*, the latter revolves around *identity politics*. Whereas apertistic–differential liberalism actively promotes not only economic but also cultural globalization, cultural essentialism mostly opposes the hybridizing effect of globalization, which weakens the borders between national cultures. *Both* cases involve a form of politics that is based on the particular instead of the general: on the *differences* of performance and the *diversity* of culture in the case of apertistic–differential liberalism and, in the case of cultural essentialism, on the *particularity* of cultural communities.

Although political paradigm shifts are of a long-term and fundamental nature, they tend to crystalize in prominent events. Such events can trigger structural developments and thus come to acquire historical symbolic value. Regarding the political paradigm shifts from organized modernity to late modernity and the rise of the "politics of the particular," it is possible to name several key years: 1968, 1979, 1990, and 2001.

Of course, 1968 was the year of student and protest movements. As an expression of a "cultural-revolutionary" counterculture, they provided a decisive impulse for the post-materialistic shift away from the values of duty and acceptance toward the values of self-actualization, and thus they also stimulated the social liberalism of the subsequent decades, which promoted quality of life, individual self-determination, and cultural diversity. It was in 1979 when Margaret Thatcher began, as the British Prime Minister, to implement a political neoliberalism that subjected economic and social policy to a radical, deregulated market and competitive structure. This was the initial impetus behind the global spread of a policy that enforces the innovation-oriented competition state. It was also in 1979, however, that the Islamic Revolution took place in Iran, and this can be regarded as the first eventful escalation in the rise of religious-fundamentalist movements.

The events of 1990 have a similar symbolic effect. The implosion of state socialism in the Soviet Union and Eastern Europe marked the end of a 70-year social experiment: a system based on the comprehensive regulation of all social processes in the name of an ideal of equality. This extreme version of a "politics of the general" was replaced by the global deregulation of economic and cultural processes. At the same time, the dissolution of the multinational Soviet Union into a series of independent nations can be interpreted as a symbol of the rise of political and cultural movements based on national identity. Finally, 2001 was the year of the terrorist attack on the World Trade Center in New York. The events of 9/11 consolidated the violent radicalization of religious-Islamist

VI Differential Liberalism and Cultural Essentialism 271

fundamentalism – and the positioning of the West against it, which has partially taken place in terms of a "war between cultures."

The years 1968, 1979, and 1990 stand for the gradual erosion of the politics of organized modernity and the rise of apertistic–differential liberalism. The years 1979, 1990, and 2001 symbolize the rise of cultural essentialism.

1
Apertistic–Differential Liberalism and the Politics of the Local

From the Social-Democratic Consensus to New Liberalism

From the 1940s into the 1970s – that is, during the golden age of organized modernity – politics was defined by a social-democratic and corporatist consensus, as exemplified by Franklin D. Roosevelt's "New Deal" and the social democracies of Scandinavia.¹ This corporatist/social-democratic paradigm enforced an unambiguous politics of generality and equality, and it did so as a reaction to the revolutions and upheavals – in the United States, the New Deal was a response to the global economic crisis of the 1930s – of a rapidly industrializing and urbanizing late-bourgeois society. In order to achieve the goal of aligning the living conditions of all strata of the population and the goal of comprehensive inclusion, emphasis was placed on the government regulation of society and of the (capitalist) economy – or, to be more precise, emphasis was placed on the Keynesian, national regulation of economic processes, as well as on the establishment of social welfare standards to minimize individual risks and reduce social inequality.² The (national) state appeared as the legitimate locus of social generality, and it was modeled as the central planning and governing authority of national society. This politics of the general required a national society that was minimally differentiated in social terms and comparatively homogeneous in cultural terms, and it promoted this form of society at the same time. Its most pointed political-cultural expression was the Swedish concept of the "people's home" (*folkhemmet*).

In the late 1970s, the corporatist/social-democratic consensus eroded and was gradually replaced by apertistic–differential liberalism,³ which admittedly includes neoliberalism but is *not* identical with it (this is important to keep in mind). Rather, apertistic–differential liberalism has two dimensions: one that is primarily concerned with socio-economic policy and is situated on the center-right of the political spectrum, *and* one that is primarily concerned

VI Differential Liberalism and Cultural Essentialism 273

with social policy and is located on the center-left. From a broader perspective, however, it becomes clear that these two components combine to form a political paradigm of comprehensive liberalization.[4]

The central imperative that characterizes this *apertistic–differential* liberalism of late modernity is that of opening up and deregulating the social. In terms of both economic *and* social policy, it is opposed to what is now perceived as the "over-regulation" that governments practiced during organized modernity. With respect to economic policy, this means that market structures have been universally implemented with the overriding goal of creating and securing global competition. This has been accompanied by the determined promotion of innovation and by a pronounced culture of entrepreneurship. With respect to social policy, liberal openness has meant that personal rights have been demanded and instituted and that the diversity of people, cultural communities, and lifestyles is now valued. Legal reforms pertaining to gender relations, family life, and migration have been central activities of socio-political liberalization.

Whereas the neoliberal strand of new liberalism was at first supported by the conservative spectrum, and socio-political liberalization was defended by the left, the two strands have been interlinked since the 1990s (under the governments of Clinton, Blair, and Schröder, for example). In this process, apertistic–differential liberalism developed into a comprehensive form of governance that attempts to steer not only state institutions but also all of society in the direction of innovation, competition, personal rights, and diversity.

This political paradigm shift has been *flanked* by the elements of overall social transformation that, as described in my previous chapters, led from organized modernity to late modernity. At the same time, politics has *forced* this structural change. The erosion of the economic-technological structure of industrial society and its transformation into a post-industrial society with a knowledge, culture, and service economy have undermined the basic assumptions of the corporatist/social-democratic consensus, which was oriented toward industrial society. In contrast, the competition-oriented and entrepreneurial politics of new liberalism is aligned with and further propels the global deregulation of markets, post-industrial forms of labor, and permanent innovation. The post-materialistic shift in values (that is, toward values of self-actualization) and the increased cultural heterogeneity of Western societies (which, since the 1970s, has been caused by larger and larger migration movements) have made the classical social-democratic "people's home" look antiquated and have led to socio-cultural pluralization and openness, which the new liberalism further promotes. In short, economic and cultural globalization, post-industrialism, and post-materialism have made societies more socially differentiated and more culturally heterogeneous – a tendency that apertistic–differential liberalism strengthens.

The Competition State and Diversity: The Two Sides of New Liberalism

The neoliberal political orientation toward a comprehensive marketization of the social, which has been formational since the 1980s (and still remains intact even after the 2008 financial crisis), has been described and discussed at length. In our context, what is decisive is that neoliberalism has contributed to the singularization of the social. Instead of the broad concept of neoliberalism that is commonly used today, however, I prefer, for the sake of analyzing the market-oriented form of the political at issue here, the more precise Schumpeterian understanding of the term, according to which it denotes an innovation-oriented competition state.[5] In contrast to the nationally oriented economic governance of organized modernity, the late-modern competition state positions itself within the global context of border-crossing goods, production processes, ideas, and workers. As already mentioned, its central goal is to strengthen competition in a constellation of deregulated markets, this being seen as a condition for prosperity. The presupposition is that the market represents the most efficient system of incentives and sanctions and is thus fundamentally superior to government and bureaucratic regulation. As a consequence, the marketization of production and the circulation of goods are central aims, but so are the marketization of education, labor markets, cultural institutions, social security provisions, and public administration.

In particular, the late-modern competition state is concerned with promoting innovation, and not only in the strict technological sense (which is prominent in the field of IT) but, rather, in all areas of society. The regime of the new, whose flipside is the degradation of old and "uncompetitive" sectors, is now regarded as a central precondition for growth and employment. This has been accompanied by a transformation of the type of subject that the state addresses: in the place of organized modernity's national and social citizens have appeared self-entrepreneurs and consumers, for whom the state wishes to provide optimal conditions.[6] Today's social model now seems to be the culture of (self-)entrepreneurship, which entails the constant development of human capital, and the constant development of new and initially risky and speculative solutions.[7]

In one respect, the innovation-oriented competition state has thus replaced an old system of the general (the regulatory welfare state) with a new system of the general, the purpose of which is to generalize market structures. Every sphere of the social is now, without exception, subjected to the structures of competition. With this background in place, however, the politics of the competition state enforces a political logic of the particular; here, too, the general ultimately functions as an "infrastructure" for the promotion of singularities. In other words, the general structures of the market do *not* favor the standardized and customary but, rather, that which is different and new. In the foreground of today's politics, too, is thus the promotion of entrepreneurial performances that bring something new into the world, something that is demanded on one market or another and claims to have a *unique selling point*. Now universally expected, unique selling points are significant factors in the context of local, regional, and national economic development; in the context of developing schools and universities; and in the context of developing cultural institutions and human capital.

Instead of government regulations of the Keynesian sort, in which welfare states institute general rules that evenly allocate the general achievements of society, the innovation-oriented competition state promotes performances that, in the context of markets, *make a difference*. This is the *differential* side of the new (economic) liberalism: it encourages *differences* – that is, any sort of undertaking that *deviates* from what has come before and is therefore successful on the markets. In the end, this differential orientation toward governance applies not only to state institutions but, indeed, to all structures of governance, including those of commercial or non-commercial organizations. In this light, it is no surprise that the creative industries – from IT to design – have received especially intensive government support since the 1990s, for they promise permanent innovation and creation.[8] Finally, new liberalism's most important area of activity is not on the national level but, instead, on the regional and urban level, for it is the politics of cities in particular that contributes to the specific cultural economization of the social that I discussed in Part II. However, in order to understand the culturally oriented governmentality at work in late-modern politics, it is also necessary to take into account the second aspect of apertistic–differential liberalism: the socially liberal promotion of cultural diversity.

As I have already said, it would be misleading to identify the new liberalism of late modernity with the competition state alone. The liberalization that has been taking place in Western societies since the last quarter of the twentieth century also includes a "socially liberal" side. In contrast to organized modernity's precondition, and political "cultivation," of cultural homogeneity, late-modern liberalism is fervently concerned with respecting and promoting personal and group-specific rights and values in all their diversity. This has given rise to a heterogeneous range of policies that revolve around the issues of nondiscrimination and quality of life. In this regard, new liberalism has installed a comprehensive system of the general: the system of human rights. Since the end of the 1970s, but especially after the fall of the Berlin Wall, human rights have become an influential structure of political legitimation that provides the general background for national and international politics to protect the uniqueness and particular identities of individuals and entire cultural groups.[9]

An important aspect of this socially liberal politics is the strengthening of the personal rights of individuals, particularly the rights of people who were discriminated against in organized modernity: women, gays, lesbians, transgender people, disabled people, people leading alternative lifestyles, etc. The key term here is nondiscrimination.[10] In addition to this, a politics concerned with quality of life was developed, and its main concentrations have been ecology and environmental protection.[11] Finally, what is particularly interesting for our context is the strand of new liberalism in which culture itself has become an immediate theme; here, the focus is on promoting cultural diversity and cultural resources. Like the competition state, *cultural diversity* has become a socio-political imaginary of late modernity whose influence extends far beyond the activity of state institutions and forms of government.[12] According to the model of cultural diversity, the respective uniqueness of cultures and their practices, objects, identities, and communities is expected to be valued and encouraged. Here, diversity designates the richness of singularities in the plural.

One historical source of the political value of diversity was the North American civil rights movement of the 1970s, particularly the demand of ethnic minorities (especially African Americans) for their identities to be recognized and for equal rights in society. This broader movement included the multiculturalism movement. The political thematization of cultural diversity has been gaining traction since the 1980s, and its meaning has since changed. Independent of the specific rights of individual groups, cultural diversity has come to be regarded as a *value in itself* not only on the national level but increasingly on regional, local, organizational, and supra-national levels as well. Throughout this process, cultural diversity has often been thought about in terms of biodiversity: just as the diversity and heterogeneity of nature should be cultivated and monocultures should be avoided, the diversity of cultures – from the global to the local level – should also be considered intrinsically valuable.[13]

One expression of diversity politics has been the instatement of international, national, and regional policies for protecting and preserving cultural heritage – historical traditions of various sorts, from architecture and museums to cultural practices (including languages).[14] The politics of cultural heritage emphasizes the inherent value of historical traditions, which can also be linked to the cultural rights of minorities (as in the case of minority language communities). In part, cultural heritage is also a means to an end: by providing unique selling points for certain regions, they can become economically lucrative for the tourist industry or they can serve as a springboard for solving socio-political problems. A wide variety of social phenomena can be culturalized by the politics of diversity and interpreted as "cultural resources," so that they are regarded as valuable and worthy of preservation: local rap music or rural dances, cooking traditions, architectural and design traditions, the communal living of immigrants, or classical high culture.[15]

In a symbiosis of inherent value and instrumental rationality, cultural diversity is also subject to *diversity management*, which is enforced by government and economic institutions and likewise has historic roots in the civil rights movements after 1968.[16] It began with programs for the promotion of women but has since expanded to include the promotion of various cultural identities, not least the ethnic-cultural identities whose heterogeneity has characterized Western societies since the 1980s on account of the expansion and diversification of migration movements. In businesses, government administrations, schools, and urban development, cultural diversity is considered to be intrinsically *good* and a source of enrichment. Deviating from the norm is no longer a shortcoming – it is, rather, an *asset*. In this case, diversity is closely connected to the late-modern ideal of being open to otherness and novelty, and diversity management can be interpreted as a modernized form of the "politics of difference," in which differences are no longer seen as divisive but, rather, as desirable opportunities to cooperate across various boundaries. In this context, moreover, the feature of diversity no longer applies to collectives but, instead, to individual people, who are regarded as having particular cultural characteristics. At the same time, diversity is also viewed as something useful to organizations or institutions – as something, for instance, that can enhance their organizational culture and creative capabilities.

To repeat, the politics of the competition state and the politics of cultural diversity are the two faces of late modernity's new, aperistic–differential liberalism. They are synthesized in an exemplary manner in the late-modern politics of cities, a form of urban governance that can be described as culturally oriented governmentality. It will be beneficial to take a closer look at this type of politics, because cities now form a politically supported cultural singularity market *par excellence*.

The Politics of Cities I:
New Urbanism and the Global Attractiveness Competition

Since the 1980s, the large cities and metropolitan regions in Europe and North America (and meanwhile, too, those in the emerging countries of the global South) have represented hotspots of late-modern liberal politics, which is oriented toward profiling cultural uniqueness.[17] The global urban landscape – from Amsterdam to Vancouver, from Philadelphia to Marseille, from Cape Town or Brisbane to Shanghai – manifests the post-industrial transformation of the political, the social, and the cultural in a spatially compressed form. Whereas the politics of organized modernity's regulatory welfare state was closely linked to nations, the waning significance of state regulation in late modernity is connected not only to the rise of supra-national regulatory authorities (such as the European Union) but also to the rising significance of political authorities *beneath* the national level – that is, to the increased significance of regional and municipal governments. While it is indisputable that the processes of globalization have been weakening the functions of the nation state since the 1980s, it is also true that they have paradoxically bestowed increased political influence upon the sub-national, *local* level.[18] In some respects, large cities are now more similar to one another than they are to the rural regions of their respective countries. Urban centers have thus become nodal points of *glocalization* (that is, the convergence of global currents on the local level).[19]

Large cities and metropolitan areas are not only centers of *local governance*; they are also actively engaged in urban *sub-politics* – that is, in quasi-political design initiatives undertaken beneath the national level on the part of other social authorities, especially businesses and organizations in the creative economy as well as social groups (mostly from the new middle class). It is generally characteristic of late modernity that unconditional and quasi-mechanical "social planning" no longer takes place on the national level; rather, national politics tends to focus on developing strategies for understanding and anticipating the dynamic and unpredictable processes of the economy and the socio-cultural milieu and, on this basis, to influence these processes with positive and negative stimuli. It is precisely this sort of indirect control – a second-order control over social processes, which are acknowledged to have their own unpredictable inherent dynamics – that lies at the heart of new liberalism's *governmentality*.[20]

In the globally interconnected urban centers, the singularized and culturalized society of late modernity is densely concentrated, for it is here where the post-industrial creative economy, the politics of apertistic–differential liberalism, and the polarized social structure of the new middle class and the underclass all mix together.[21] As a consequence, the structures of social space have fundamentally changed since the end of industrial modernity. Of course, industrial modernity was also an urbanized society, but what set the trend here was the mass production and mass employment in industrial cities. These "functional cities" were venues of both social and spatial

VI Differential Liberalism and Cultural Essentialism

standardization.[22] They were all planned according to the same general model, whose leading feature was "serial buildings" (that is, architectural replications of the same). Industrial cities therefore did not represent unique, identifiable places (they were, as cultural critics would often lament, "featureless"); rather, they were interchangeable spaces of which nothing was expected (not value, not emotion) beyond functionality.

In this regard, the "urban renaissance" since the 1980s has effected a radical change.[23] In late modernity, large cities and metropolitan regions have increasingly become particular places that want, and are expected, to be attractive on account of their uniqueness. The singularization and culturalization of cities have received massive support from municipal politics. Beyond their functionality, cities now model themselves as bearers of unique value. They want people to identify with them, they are designed to be authentic places, and they have become objects of aesthetic valorization. As Martina Löw has convincingly shown, late-modern cities have developed an "intrinsic logic,"[24] which means that – in their material form (their architecture and layout), in their social practices, and in their cultural perceptions – they have developed a level of distinctiveness that is experienced as such by their citizens and visitors and, at the same time, is explicitly promoted by economic and political measures.

Of course, cities have been singularizing themselves from the beginning; the European cities of the Middle Ages, early modernity, and the bourgeois era were not designed to be replicable *spaces* but, rather, identifiable *places*.[25] In this light, the urban standardization that took place during the age of industrial modernity can be interpreted as structural interruption, or indeed as a dismantling of urban singularities.[26] It must be stressed, however, that, in order for national politics even to begin to develop cities into attractive "brands" with unique and citizen-friendly features, it was first necessary for urban spaces to be culturalized and singularized *from below* – that is, by the social milieus of the cities themselves. Here, too, it is the case that the singularization of cities cannot be reduced to neoliberal politics or to the economization of the social alone. Yet again, the new middle class proved to be central to this development and, yet again, the historical turning point took place in the 1970s. At this time, dissatisfaction with the "inhospitableness of our cities" (in Alexander Mitscherlich's words), with the monotony of suburban developments, and with the decay of urban life in city centers gave rise to a "back-to-the-city" counter-movement that was spearheaded by the artist scene and the counterculture. Later, large portions of the new middle class moved to urban areas, bringing the knowledge and cultural economy in tow.[27]

In light of the altered structure of urban populations, this process is often referred to as gentrification. At its base, however, lies an everyday *vernacular culturalization* of cities, and particularly their aestheticization by the new middle class, which, as I discussed above, is less interested in having a certain standard of living than it is in achieving a high quality of life – a sort of life that can best be experienced in urban environments. The decisive shift in perspective lies in the fact that the new middle class does not perceive cities, which cultural critics so long bemoaned as monotonous, as merely functional entities, but rather as spaces that possess (and are expected to possess) affectively attractive qualities: authenticity, distinctiveness, cultural openness, and liveliness. Such is the attitude of "new urbanism," which celebrates cities as places of culturally diverse activities and milieus.[28] Appreciating city centers and urban neighborhoods should be understood as a process of subtle valorizations – as a repositioning of urban space away from the functional sphere of utility into the cultural sphere of emotionally based attributions of value.

In the new urbanism, the praxis of culturalizing cities is simultaneously a praxis of singularizing urban space, which means converting the latter into an emotionally affecting *place* (quite unlike suburban developments and large-scale housing projects).[29] In part, this has been achieved through heterogeneous collaborations and projects such as citizen action groups, neighborhood revitalizations, or grassroots politics.[30] Cities are now expected to develop their own intrinsic logic as specific and non-interchangeable places, and they are expected to do so on three interrelated levels: their materiality (that is, their architecture and spatial structure), their social practices (jobs, street life, culture in the strong sense, etc.), and their representations in narratives, associations, and images. Especially for the new middle class, the city has become an object of authentication as a whole and in all its details: an object of lived experience, of evaluation as authentic or inauthentic (featureless, lacking inspiration, etc.), and partially, too, an object of intentional modifications that are meant to develop, enhance, or protect desirable qualities. A city will seem authentic when it has developed inherent complexity and distinctness on the three levels mentioned above.[31]

The vernacular culturalization and singularization of cities has taken place in conjunction with the cultural economization of the social. Since the 1980s, cities in Europe and North America have transformed, as it were, into spatial cultural singularity goods that compete with other cities for visibility, attention, and valorization. This competition for residents and visitors occurs on a regional and global attractiveness market. It must be stressed, however, that the creative economy and urban politics are complicit in and fuel this competition between cities by ensuring that, *for their part*, subjects and milieus have already begun in advance to view and compare residential areas in terms of their attractiveness or unattractiveness, thereby placing them in a competitive situation. Without the new middle class and its members' post-materialistic aspiration for successful self-actualization in their own lives, which is now also directed toward cities as living spaces, cities never would have found themselves in a state of competition to begin with. This is the social basis of urban competition: for the new middle class, which is distinguished by its high degree of spatial mobility, where one lives has become a matter of *choosing* between different possibilities.

Of course, people still have to consider certain functional aspects when choosing which city to live in (the availability of suitable jobs, for instance). However, the cultural and emotional aspect of a city's attractiveness – that is, the intrinsic logic of its atmosphere – has become an equally important selection criterion of its (future) residents.[32] This intrinsic logic can stem from a city's particular natural environment (with its many possible leisure activities), from a particular "city feel" in certain desirable neighborhoods (coolness, elegance, a colorful mix, etc.), from the presence of a particularly enriching milieu (creative scenes, youth culture, educated senior citizens), from the diversity of a city's particular cultural offerings, or from a characteristic architectural look. In addition to cities having to compete for *residents*, they also compete for touristic *visitors*, who are largely recruited from the same, globally disseminated, social group of the new middle class.[33] Finally, the intrinsic logic of a city – now in the sense of its opportunities for cooperation and inspiration – has also become a criterion in the choices made by *investors* (as they are seen from the perspective of city politics) – that is, by the companies and organizations of (primarily) the creative economy. Sooner or later, enticing job opportunities for highly qualified people eventually cluster in attractive cities.

The Politics of Cities II: Culturally Oriented Governmentality and Singularity Management

The vernacular culturalization of cities and the attractiveness competition between them, which are driven and intensified by the new middle class, thus provide the backdrop of urban politics on the national level. This is a matter of culturally oriented and competition-oriented governmentality, which seems to be paradigmatic of the way in which politics has been conducted since the 1980s. Late-modern city politics has been one of the most important pillars of the innovation-oriented competition state; *at the same time*, culture has here become, as a resource of diversity, an object of government control. The goal is to create a city with an attractive intrinsic logic that is appreciated by its (potential) residents and visitors, and that gives its urbanity an edge in the global competition among urban areas. At its heart, city politics is thus a sort of singularity management. Its constant concern is to produce or maintain a "profile" of urban uniqueness, the likes of which we have already seen in other contexts: inherent complexity, otherness, and, if possible, rarity as well.[34]

The attractive *inherent complexity* of a city results from its spatial and cultural density, which is to say the density of its materialities, its practices, and its representations. In general, there are two possible ways for a city to achieve this. It can be homogeneous and highly coordinated, as though it was created in a mold – the museum-like city. Or (and this is more widespread in late-modern conditions) it can be in its own specific way a heterogeneous, hybrid, diverse, and successful arrangement of contradictory elements – the metropolis. The crucial challenge of urban governmentality arises from the fact that the inherent logic of a city cannot be completely planned or created from scratch. Rather, city politics has to work with materialities, practices, and representations that already exist and have, in part, been developing over centuries: the morphology of the city in question, its natural environment, its zoning and architecture, its established practices (nightlife districts, scenes, high culture, traditional vocations), and its existing representations (such as its history and representations in the media). Unlike the purely future-oriented politics of industrial modernity's functional cities, the late-modern politics of culturalized cities is thus inevitably a politics of the historical as well. The historical inertia of existing architecture and urban design, the existence of well-established practices (types of work or gastronomic traditions, for instance), and traditional representations (Amsterdam as a trading city, Berlin as a city with a complicated past) continue to have an effect in the present and lend a degree of path dependency to urban cultural development.

The art of the urban politics of the particular lies in recognizing already existing unique qualities, cultivating and developing them further, and – if necessary – giving them a new and believable twist by adding new elements to them or assigning them a new cultural interpretation (as has been attempted, for instance, in Glasgow, Barcelona, and Marseille). Cities are thus expected to have a unique and credible *brand*, which is not only related to their public image but also to their material practices and architecture. As in all of late modernity's competitive constellations, the competition among cities for inherent logic and otherness also has potential winners and potential losers – those cities that have been historically favored on account of their *urban singularity capital*, and those that are disadvantaged. Cities with historically accumulated singularity capital – the traditional metropolises, trading cities, university cities, or those with old architectural substance – already possess

VI Differential Liberalism and Cultural Essentialism 283

recognized attractive assets, which they simply have to preserve and cleverly develop further. Traditional industrial cities, in contrast, have inherited just a small amount of singularity capital, and they are therefore always in danger of losing out in the attractiveness competition on account of their interchangeability and minimal cultural density. In metropolises and old industrial cities alike, however, one sees typical strategies of *urban singularity management* that, in their orientation toward cultural novelty, owe much to the creativity *dispositif*. In addition to renovating and aestheticizing old city centers, other strategies of singularity management include attracting branches of the creative industry, commissioning spectacular new works of architecture, increasing high-cultural offerings (concert halls, museums, literary festivals), promoting the local-scene culture (clubs), repurposing industrial architecture, "playing up" a city's location on a body of water ("a city on the sea"), and rediscovering and cultivating locally specific cultural practices ("Seville as the city of flamenco") or other aspects of a city's historical cultural heritage.[35]

Since the beginning of the twenty-first century, the attractiveness competition among cities, and the culturally oriented and competitive urban politics that attempts to create profiles of cities, have given rise to several areas of tension. One such area concerns the focus of city politics: should it concentrate on the global visibility market of visitors, investors, and potential residents *or* should it focus on the quality of life of the people who already live there? Culturally oriented governmentality attempts to do both at the same time, but it is easy for two spheres of valorization to develop apart from one another: the value criteria of external observers, which are closely connected to the issue of visibility and image, and the value criteria of internal observers, for which the quality of life of the people experiencing and using the city every day is the guiding factor. Conflicts between these two spheres of valorization – between the logic of outsiders and that of insiders – are characteristic of the late-modern city.

An additional area of tension concerns the relation between the singularization and the standardization of cities. Targeted efforts to singularize cities can fail if they rely on schemes that are too simple or already worn out. As a consequence, it is possible for attempts at singularization to be perceived by residents and visitors as acts of urban standardization, so that even post-industrial cities, despite their supposed distinctness, can seem interchangeable and featureless ("the same type of trendy neighborhood everywhere," "the same star architects everywhere"). Sharon Zukin has rightly pointed out that, in such a way, even thriving cities such as New York run the risk of losing authenticity in the eyes of their residents, and, ultimately, in the eyes of their visitors as well.[36] Do strategic singularization and urban globalization inevitably lead to the re-standardization of cities and to the de-authentication of their intrinsic logic? The answer is no, for here again we are dealing with a dynamic system of valorizations in which singularizations and authentications take place *in parallel with* devaluations and de-singularizations, so that individual cities (and even individual neighborhoods) can experience, with respect to their valorization, times of ascendancy or decline – periods of booms and busts, as it were. Much like "classics" in the creative economy, however, traditionally attractive cities with large amounts of singularity capital (often accrued over centuries) do not tend to lose visibility and appreciation. Contrary to the popular thesis that globalization leads to uniformity, the globalization of the competition among cities has, instead, led to the establishment of a dynamic sphere of evaluating and producing intrinsic urban logics, a sphere in which de-singularization and standardization take place as well.

As a whole, the national and global attractiveness competition among cities is characterized by a sort of tension that is already familiar to us from the creative economy: the tension created by the logic of a winner-take-all market. In late modernity's urban landscape, the few cities with high visibility and recognized attractiveness stand opposed to the many cities, towns, and regions that are lacking in both.[37] In the manner of the Matthew effect, popular cities typically become more and more popular. Conversely, whereas it was normal and unproblematic for the cities of industrial modernity to be indistinct and featureless, now cities with minimal singularization potential have not maintained their position but have, rather, lagged behind. The boom of teeming metropolises is thus correlated with the departure of social climbers from shrinking cities, which, in a sort of vicious circle, have lost much of their appeal (when it comes to quality of life) and become socially invisible.[38] Their low level of attractiveness thus puts them at risk of being devalued and of becoming negative singularities. The paternoster-elevator effect, which is characteristic of the post-industrial social structure, can therefore also be seen on the level of social spaces: in the polarity between thriving cities and the stagnating, "left-behind" peripheries that is just as apparent in Germany as it is in France, the United States, and Great Britain.

There are, however, certain processes and effects that go against these trends. In part, one can see that small and rural places have experienced a revalorization of sorts. For non-metropolises, the same way out exists that is familiar to us from the creative economy: winner-take-all structures can be relativized by the so-called "long tail" that they produce – that is, by the variation of many cultural niches that attract a small but stable group of supporters.[39] Accordingly, small cities in particular can develop their

VI Differential Liberalism and Cultural Essentialism 285

own intrinsic logic by focusing on a relatively homogeneous and sharply defined profile for which their milieu happens to be known: a small university town or a city that is especially amenable to senior citizens, for example.[40] The same can be said of the revalorization of rural regions, which, by reviving older traditions and emphasizing their cultural heritage and natural beauty, have now managed to develop a certain touristic appeal to the urban new middle class.[41]

Conversely, it is also possible for thriving cities to be devalued. The simple fact that attractive singular places are geographically limited gives rise to social consequences and paradoxical spatial effects. Limited space can lead to a situation of overpopulation, which can diminish or even destroy the authenticity of a city and its atmosphere for both its residents *and* its visitors. Such is the danger of the "touristification" of urban spaces. Moreover, a steady influx of new residents in popular cities can drive real-estate prices through the roof, and this can lead to upper-class monocultures that in turn cause urban authenticity and attractiveness to suffer. Such places are difficult for even the new middle class to afford, and they certainly push away the traditional middle class and the new underclass. These conditions can lead to what might be called "attractiveness overkill," in which case the very success of popular cities can be their downfall.[42] Urban politics is thus faced with the challenge of reacting to the unintended consequences of its liberal governmentality.

2
The Rise of Cultural Essentialism

Collective Identities and Particular Neo-Communities

We have seen that apertistic–differential liberalism has been the dominant form of politics in late modernity. Since the 1980s, however, a political counter-trend has been the development of a multifaceted and global sphere of cultural essentialism and cultural communitarianism within the Western societies of Europe and North America, as well as within (though in a different way) developing nations and the global South. Four forms of this can be observed: ethnic communities, whose politicization involves identity politics; tendencies of cultural nationalism; versions of religious fundamentalism, particularly of the Islamic and Christian sort; and, finally, forms of right-wing populism. Although the origins and structures of these four types are clearly distinct and need to be differentiated, they nevertheless share certain fundamental basic features in that they are all, in their own way, engaged in culturalizing and singularizing the social and the political.

From the perspective of the classical theory of modernization, these tendencies to cultivate *particular (neo-)communities*, which have been flourishing since the beginning of the twenty-first century, should not exist at all.[1] From this perspective, communities as a social form are a characteristic of traditional types of society that would sooner or later disappear with the rise of modernity. This may essentially have been true of organized modernity, but the idea has proven to be obsolete in the case of late modernity. As early as the 1980s, Michel Maffesoli diagnosed a new "time of the tribes," which he then identified primarily with aesthetic subcultures and lifestyle groups.[2] Since then, however, the true rise of neo-communities has taken place in the realm of the political and sub-political, with its ethnic, religious, and national identities.[3] Mind you, these political neo-communities are *not* anti-modern foreign bodies but should rather be understood as a subcomponent of the society of

VI Differential Liberalism and Cultural Essentialism 287

singularities, whose fundamental features they in fact share. They, too, operate in the medium of culture in the strong sense, with affectively charged valorizations, and they, too, practice a form of singularization: the singularization of cultural collectives as unique and non-interchangeable, with their particular history, with a particular ethics (in part), and with a particular space that they occupy.

Cultural essentialism practices its own regime of valorization. Both the objects and modes of this valorization differ from those of the creative economy's hyperculture, from those of apertistic– differential liberalism, and from those of the new middle class's cosmopolitan lifestyle. Regardless of whether we are dealing with an ethnic, religious, or national community, what bears value in cultural essentialism is now a collective, or, to be more precise, one's *own* collective as a cultural entity. In this sense, cultural essentialism is a form of communitarianism that ascribes primacy to the communality of one's own group.[4] Within this framework, the other pillars of the social – individuals, objects, spaces, and temporalities – only acquire significance in relation to the community. Especially consequential is the shift in the relationship between the individual and the collective.[5] Within the framework of cultural communitarianism, individuals are not addressed as particular entities who develop themselves by working on their own uniqueness but rather as members who have inserted themselves into the code of a given ethnic group, religious community, or nation. On the one hand, individuals therefore forfeit the possibilities of autonomous singularization; on the other hand, they gain the certainty of being recognized within the community. Because communities are not market-based, their members are freed from having to fight for visibility, personal value, achievement, and success.

Cultural communities are not rational associations with a given purpose; rather, their participants regard them as having an intrinsic value of their own. Within the cultural-essentialist framework, this value is not mobile but stable; it has to be (and is expected to be) *fixed* in an ongoing process of securing value and possibly creating distance from that which is valueless. It is therefore characteristic of the valorization of cultural communities that it does not take the form of dynamic and unpredictable valuations and devaluations within an expansive cultural sphere, as is familiar to us from the hyperculture of the creative economy, but is instead based on attempts to create permanent value. Cultural communities are appreciated as bearers of *authenticity*, and their core or origin (of a religion, nation, or ethnicity) appears to constitute their unquestionable *essence*. Central to the culturalization and singularization of communities is the boundary between the inside and the outside, which is also cemented on the level of ingroup ("we") and outgroup ("they").[6] Cultural communities thus always have two points of reference. On the one hand, they cultivate a particular *internal* social life and self-image, both through the social practices of community life and their performance and through discourses that thematize the community's characteristics. Community praxis requires clearly defined membership: one is either on the inside or on the outside – *tertium non datur*. In general, communities tend toward homogenization, and this homogeneity always has a cultural side and a social side, which means that it pertains to practices and discourses, which are intended to be free of contradictions and ambivalence, as well as to the relationship between individuals, who all follow the directives of the community in the same way (or according to a rigid hierarchy).

On the other hand, cultural communities always differentiate themselves from the *outside*, which means that they always pay attention to those beyond their own borders. There is a broad spectrum of ways in which they relate to the outside world: it ranges from communities that focus on cultivating their internal world and have relatively weak barriers to entry (as in the case of certain regional movements or linguistic minorities) to those that cultivate, by drawing aggressive friend–enemy distinctions, strong feelings of distaste for strangers outside of their "own." The inside–outside difference of cultural communities is associated with a sense of antagonism between the valuable and the valueless: from the perspective within a given community, the outside world seems at best value-neutral, but often it is perceived as having negative value or as an opponent to be fought. This cultural-essentialist form of valorization differs significantly from the valorization regime of hyperculture: there, goods recognized as valuable stand opposed to the broad background of other goods that have failed to attract attention and positive valorization. The attitude toward the latter is one of *indifference*, not negativity. Things are entirely different in the case of cultural essentialism, which is often characterized by an affect culture of *negativity*: the identity of the inside is extremely dependent on being sharply demarcated from the rejected, foreign, or even demonized outside (the unfaithful, the uncultivated, the enemies of the nation), which is constantly made visible and de-valorized.

On the inside, cultural communities share a collective identity, and this has positive emotional effects: individuals understand themselves to be part of a "we." For late-modern cultural communitarianism, three levels of identity-formation are especially significant: history, space, and ethics. First, as regards *history*, every community cultivates a collective memory and perceives itself as a locus of memorial culture engaged in creating narratives of its own past (it is only through narratives, of course, that the past is turned into

VI Differential Liberalism and Cultural Essentialism

"history"): the history, for instance, of a religious community from the time of its prophets, or the history of a nation with "roots" that connect the past to the present day.[7] Historical narratives are necessarily singular: it is the power of a particular and unique history – of Russia, of the Jewish people, of African Americans, etc. – that draws people to identify with certain communities. The temporal structure of cultural essentialism is therefore different from that of hyperculture. Whereas the latter is characterized by the *dispositif* of creativity, which in principle favors the novelty of the present over bygone things from the past, cultural communitarianism cultivates a *regime of the old* by constantly emphasizing the past and insisting that the present and future should be viewed in its light.

Second, collective identities are often based on *space*. Beyond individual places – religious sites and memorials, for instance – it is typically suggested that collectives are linked to a particular territory and its natural environment. Here, space is a specific and nonexchangeable locality. Finally, cultural-essentialist communities often make reference to a common *ethics*. They define themselves through a common good that is reflected in a particular normative code, as is most obviously the case with religious communities. This is not a matter of universal morality or aesthetic individual ethics but, rather, of the ethos of a particular group.

Cultural communities already existed in traditional society, but in late modernity we are dealing with neo-communities that, in their cultural essentialism and cultural communitarianism, have acquired a genuinely modern form.[8] What happens here is not merely recourse to pre-modernity but, rather, a reaction *to* the culture of modernity from *within* it. Historically, this reaction took place in two steps. The first was the Romanticism at the beginning of the nineteenth century, which "discovered" communities for modernity, for example in Johann Gottfried Herder's celebration of the uniqueness of peoples and nations. It was only against the backdrop of the formal rationalization and scientific and moral universalization of emerging modernity that communities could now appear as an *attractive way of life* that might compensate for, or overcome, modernity's shortcomings. The central difference is that traditional communities appeared as an implicit background for which there was no alternative, whereas modern, post-Romantic, and post-traditional neo-communities have to be created and institutionalized anew, and subjects decide to participate in them on account of their cultural and affective appeal. The institutionalization of neo-communities always involves the inherent paradox that they are social constructions in the sense of "imagined communities" (as Benedict Anderson called them), and yet they have to make their contingency invisible by implying that they are based on unquestionable foundations (of a nation, of a religion, of an origin, etc.).[9]

The first wave of post-Romantic cultural essentialism thus enveloped Europe in the nineteenth century, its most visible form being the national and nationalist movements.[10] Since the 1980s, however, we have witnessed a second and even more powerful wave of particular neo-communities within Western societies and beyond. The causes of their creation are various and depend on whether they happen to be ethnic, religious, or national communities. Two factors, however, have been of overarching importance. First, migration movements from regions of the global South into the Western societies of Europe and North America have been increasing considerably since the 1970s, so that the latter have become more culturally heterogeneous overall. Directly and indirectly, these migration movements have given rise to numerous contradictory forms of establishing, enacting, classifying, and also discriminating between "cultural communities." Second, cosmopolitan hyperculture, as an embedded element of the creative economy, the new middle class, and apertistic–differential liberalism, has incited various sorts of cultural essentialism to form as a *counter-movement*, which, in its own way, now calls for the *restriction* of culture and the re-establishment of collective identities. Paradoxically, however, cultural cosmopolitanism also *encourages* certain types of cultural communitarianism, especially in the form of multiculturalism.

As stated above, late-modern cultural essentialism and cultural communitarianism and their neo-communities have, in various respects, a genuinely (late-)*modern* form that distinguishes them from traditional communities. Several features are worth mentioning here.

First: often, culture is no longer merely the implicit background of everyday praxis but has instead become an object of discursification, thematization, or codification, both "inwardly" and "outwardly."

Second: culture and collective identity regularly become the object of politicization; they enter the political arena, where arguments are made for and against particular identities.

Third: the formation of communities often involves digital processes and forums and is thus closely associated with particular digital communities.

Fourth: although particular neo-communities typically de-singularize individuals, it is often the case in late modernity that individuals *decide* to join a given community and can thus regard this decision as part of their own personal biographies (a religious conversion, for instance).

Fifth: along with the global hyperculture, cultural essentialisms operate in a public sphere in which there is a struggle for attention and recognition. Therefore, they do not remain within inwardly turned subcultures but, rather, frequently endeavor to claim visibility in the public arena, where they can cultivate their attractiveness, experience rejection, and recruit adherents and opponents.

Sixth: in late modernity, cultural communities are the object of dialectical processes of self-culturalization and external culturalization. It is not only the case that these communities form themselves; often, they are formed by the outside – for instance, by the media, the state, or other authorities that, for their part, can now, as it were, performatively create cultural collectives ("the Muslims," "the blacks," "the separatists," "the populists," and so on).

Ethnic Communities Between Self-Culturalization and External Culturalization

Ethnic communities, whose renaissance in Western societies has been observable since the 1970s, form an important but non-uniform segment within the sphere of particularistic movements. These communities are ethnic in the sense that their members share a common *origin*. In light of a social-constructivist understanding of ethnicity, that which counts as a common origin depends on the collective practices and discourses that define this origin in a particular way.[11] The field of ethnic communities is complicated by the fact that, under late-modern conditions, they exist in three different types: communities *in themselves*, communities *in and for themselves*, and communities *for others*. The first exist in the practices of their *participants* alone; the second attain, in addition, an *outward* self-awareness; and the third are formed through views and classifications *from the outside*.

The renaissance of ethnic communities has been driven by two central impulses. The first was provided by the civil rights movements of the 1970s, especially in the United States. In this context, the pace was set by the movement of African Americans, who, in a paradigmatic way, combined an internal singular identity (their history and present as former slaves) with outward political representation (making themselves visible as an "invisible" group, anti-discrimination). The African American civil rights movement was thus the spearhead of the new identity politics, which is based on the existing cultural legacy and uniqueness of a common "historical situation" (in Cornel West's terms) and, at the same time, uses this situation to demand political and cultural participation. Here, in a sense, ethnicity is both a stigma and a resource. What is at stake is not only equal rights but also, in the sense of a politics of difference, the matter of respecting cultural otherness.[12]

Within the context of the so-called minority rights revolution, other ethnic communities throughout the West have similarly demanded identity, respect, and participation, and have come together in the spirit of cultural self-empowerment.[13] Examples of this identity politics include the movements of indigenous ethnic groups in the United States, Canada, Australia, and New Zealand, as well as those of other ethnic and linguistic minorities (such as the Danish and Sorbian minorities in Germany). It is often the case that ethnic and linguistic identities coincide. Ethnic movements, which share a common political desire for visibility and recognition, are all essentially engaged in self-culturalization, which frequently involves aesthetic forms as well (literature, film, etc.). Based to various degrees on common practices, historical narratives, and experiences, they actively form around the theme of their particular origin and situation. Accordingly, they typically relate to the outer world not by aggressively defining themselves *against* the outside but rather by representing themselves (culturally and politically) *to* the outside.[14]

The second impulse behind the renaissance of ethnic collectives since the 1970s has been the growing migration movements from the global South into Western societies (for instance, from Mexico to the United States, from North Africa to France and the Netherlands, from Turkey to Germany, from South Asia to Great Britain). The course of these migration movements has led to the creation of dispersed ethnic communities that, in the broadest sense, can be understood as diasporas: families that share a common origin and often a common language and religion, that are networked across regions to one another as well as to their homeland, and that preserve, to varying degrees, a clear cultural orientation toward their place of origin. Although the diaspora is a historically old structure, the conditions of late modernity, with its intensified migration and technical possibilities for social networking, have made it an astonishingly contemporary phenomenon.[15] The degree to which these migration collectives form intense and dense neo-communities is an empirically open question: there are communities whose identities are based on just a few historical memories or traditional everyday practices (eating habits and the like), and there are others that draw a strict line between the inner sphere and the outside world, thereby distinguishing themselves sharply from the majority culture of the West.[16] These are the much-discussed "parallel societies" that have formed in Western milieus. Even in the case of relatively closed migrant neo-communities, however, such societies are not inevitable givens but, rather, the object and result of essentially unpredictable cultural processes of negotiation in which, for example, certain elements of a group's "own" culture are attenuated and "forgotten" or intentionally reactivated and reinterpreted.[17] The supposed homogeneity of an ethnic culture is thus *not* a monolithic given but, rather, the product of *homogenizing processes* within the communities in question.[18] It would therefore be false to equate processes of migration with the creation of homogeneous migrant communities. What has emerged is, instead, complex *super-diversities* – that is, hybrid overlappings of various cultural and social affiliations and

VI Differential Liberalism and Cultural Essentialism 293

resources (origin, language, religion, education/profession, gender, access to networks) that can, *in certain cases*, consolidate into neo-communities.[19]

However, ethnic communities are not only culturalized from within; since the 1980s, they have also been culturalized by *others*. Political, governmental, scientific, and media authorities, institutions, and discourses have begun to classify and evaluate "cultural collectives" and treat them as an object of their interventions. Here, ethnic collectives (of migrants, indigenous groups, cultural minorities, etc.) are often viewed in terms of "culture" in an essentialist sense. They thus appear as homogeneous communities that, deep down, share a common cultural model. Like the culturalization of inequality discussed in Part V, a *culturalization of migration* is now taking place in late-modern society's political and media discourses about ethnicity.

This external culturalization of ethnic groups has taken two highly divergent paths. The first is that of multiculturalism, with its symbiosis of socially liberal diversity politics and the cultivation of particular communities.[20] Its aim is to perceive and recognize the diversity of ethnic communities as something that enriches society as a whole. In this light, society is imagined as a diverse ensemble of cultural groups with their own narratives, experiences, and practices. Multiculturalism is a form of politics that celebrates cultural singularities. At least in part, it ascribes collective cultural rights to individual communities (indigenous communities, local linguistic minorities, individual migrant groups, etc.), which in turn means that individuals are identified according to "their" community.

In different political and media discourses, multiculturalism and its positive connotations of external culturalization are opposed by the "negative" external culturalization of ethnic groups in the form of "neo-racism." In this perspective, all members of an ethnic collective are defined by a particular set of ostensibly immutable cultural characteristics that supposedly give rise to types of behavior that are viewed negatively (a tendency toward violence, minimal interest in education, a weak work ethic, etc.). In Étienne Baribar's terms, this is a matter of "racism without race," which, in other words, means that culture has ousted biology.[21] Whereas the classical racism of the nineteenth and early twentieth centuries was based on biological criteria, the neo-racism of late modernity treats the presumably historical cultural habitus of a collective as a differentiating feature – as a sort of "national character" that is thought to predetermine problematic manners of behavior. From the perspective of such *external cultural essentialism*, culture is viewed as an unchanging grammar from which individuals can never escape. Aware of such negative external culturalization through their everyday experiences of discrimination, subjects often retaliate by strengthening their own self-culturalization: it is, above all, the culturalizing and discriminating view of outsiders that causes individuals to perceive themselves as part of a discriminated group and to construct a corresponding identity.[22]

Cultural Nationalism

Besides ethnic (neo-)communities, the nation is a second orientation point of particular identities, and in this regard, too, there has been a renaissance since the 1980s. On the one hand, the new national and nationalist movements include groups of people seeking autonomy or national independence within Western societies (Quebec, Catalonia, Scotland, etc.); on the other hand, they pertain to the nationalisms of independent states, especially outside the traditional West (China, Russia, India, etc.). Although the lines between ethnicity and nationality as socio-cultural categories are generally fluid, the collective identities of nations go beyond ethnicities in two respects. First, they are typically associated with a fixed and circumscribed spatial territory; second, they *always* have a national-political reference point, either through their connection to a nation state or through their demand for self-governance within a state.

As a socio-cultural form, the nation has been a genuine product of modernity since 1800.[23] With the nation, universalistic modernity, which was committed to overcoming all types of local particularism, indeed managed to endow its inner structure with a form of particularity that seemed legitimate to it. Nations have thus always contained a dual structure of universalization and singularization. On the one hand, the nation is a universal "formula of inclusion" – within and according to its state, all national citizens are equal,[24] and to this extent national movements can also be democratic movements. On the other hand, the nation is a singular entity with its own unique history, territory, and national culture. Nations can lean more toward the universalizing pole and develop a republican self-understanding, so that they are relatively indifferent to the origin and ethnicity of their citizens. If, instead, they tilt more toward the singularizing type, then they often associate themselves with the common ethnic background of a people. As I stated at the beginning of this section, the new nationalism of late modernity proceeds, on the one hand, from regional entities *within* Western societies and, on the other hand, from nation states on the global level that often position themselves against "the West." In both cases, the construction of national identities is primarily based on the appreciation of a common particular culture; broadly speaking, the late-modern renaissance of the national has the form of *cultural nationalism*.

VI Differential Liberalism and Cultural Essentialism 295

Regarding regional nationalist movements, the paradigmatic example is that of Quebec in Canada.[25] This is a movement for political autonomy or independence whose basis is the cultural community of the French minority. The preservation of their own culture (especially the cultivation of their language) stands at the heart of Québécois cultural politics. This regionalist cultural nationalism thus resembles the identity politics of ethnic communities and, in part, it has been reacted to with a politics of multiculturalism, according to which the cultural traditions of different regions should be allowed to have a legitimate place within the state as a whole – in this case, Canada.[26] In addition to experiences of marginalization and other motives for seceding from the central state, the individuals involved in such movements clearly attribute a degree of cultural and emotional *attractiveness* to their respective collective identities. Since the 1970s, the national cultures of Quebec, Catalonia, or Scotland have functioned like a *cultural resource* of unique linguistic features and historical narratives. The latter serve to nurture subjective desires for authenticity and an interest in culturally enriching one's own way of life: they offer something exceptional. If the culture of the "regional-national" is interpreted as a cultural resource in this sense, it becomes clear that the latter either fills a cultural and identificatory hole in the late-modern subject – in which case, the regional-national becomes a primary identity – or it provides an *additional* interesting and subjectively satisfying aspect to the other cultural elements and identities of his or her curated lifestyle.[27] Thus, regional cultural nationalism can either adopt a position *against* liberal cultural cosmopolitanism or it can classify itself as one identity-related nodal point among others *within* cultural cosmopolitanism.[28]

In the case of the second variant of cultural nationalism, which is based on the nation state as a whole, there is also a broad spectrum between concentrating strongly on the cultivation of one's "own" culture and focusing on creating distance from what is "foreign" (sometimes aggressively so). In general, however, it is striking that the renaissance of this sort of nationalism is concentrated in states that are challenging the dominance of the Western model of society. Since the year 2000, regional powers such as China, Russia, and India have been claiming to offer a social alternative to the North Atlantic West. However, the discursive underpinning of this independent modernity typically involves reference to their own, normatively defined, national cultures. Analogous to the Eurocentrism of old, this can be interpreted as the "new cultural centrism of the global South."[29] The (Chinese, Russian, Indian, etc.) nation is presented as a bearer of its own "civilization," which is self-consciously distinguished from Western civilization. Explicitly or implicitly, this gesture often adheres to a theory of cultural spheres (*Kulturkreislehre*) in the style of Herder, Oswald Spengler, or Samuel Huntington. Cultural nationalisms develop in a broad field of human-scientific, political, and media discourses. Frequently, they provide the background for a corresponding form of national politics, which is reflected in foreign policy but especially in educational policy, religious policy, and media policy. In China and Russia, for example, native cultural sciences (or "culturologies") have acquired an important function in legitimating their own respective "cultural sphere," especially in terms of the politics of history. This therefore represents a reversal of the old ethnocentric discourse of culturalization: whereas, since the end of the nineteenth century, the "old Russia" or the "old China" had been culturalized as backward civilizations, both from the Western perspective and in the eyes of the native Westernized elite, what is happening now is the intentional self-culturalization of their own positive singularity.[30]

Such national efforts at self-culturalization typically operate with the essentialist notion of an authentic and homogeneous culture (with historical "roots") and, at the same time, with the notion of national *exceptionalism*. In cases where nations aggressively define themselves against the outside,[31] the West appears either as a valueless place of cultureless rationalism or as one of cosmopolitan hypermodernity with an excessive preference for individual self-actualization. Here, apertistic–differential liberalism is the opponent. Cultural nationalism of this sort thus portrays the West as a pillar of empty universalism, which is "in decline" and in opposition to the substance of one's own cultural tradition and communality.

Religious Fundamentalism

The late-modern renaissance of the religious has not escaped anyone's attention. Whereas organized modernity initiated a trend toward secularization (which in certain respects is still intact), religious practices and communities have gained renewed relevance and visibility since the 1980s, both within Western societies and on the global level. Here, the religious has a new form: it operates on a global market of religions in which particularly fundamentalist varieties, with their promise of radical religious authenticity, have become increasingly attractive.[32]

Cultural-historically, the realm of religions is one of two cultural spheres (the other being the aesthetic) in which social processes of valorization and de-valorization have their typical place, and this is because they both involve "sacred" cultural practices that promise meaningfulness and sensuousness. The rationalization and de-culturalization of Western modernity is therefore consistent with the process of secularization: here, religion has been made profane within the framework of official churches, so that the religious – when it has not disappeared entirely in agnosticism – is generally reduced to formal ecclesiastical acts and to a sort of private faith that is not in radical tension with everyday praxis but is more or less aligned with it.

The fact that the religious has gained appeal can be interpreted as part of the general culturalization of the social in late modernity, which is a response to the narrative-hermeneutic, ethical, and affective shortcomings of modernity in its thoroughly rationalized and organized form. Now, however, it is less the old official churches that are gaining followers; instead, new religious communities have formed in which believers are integrated into an affectively dense collective praxis. The central point is that, whereas it was traditional to be socialized into a religion from a young age and by way of an official church, the new religious communities are an object of choice, which often represents to the believer an existential event of "conversion" (into a Born-Again Christian, for instance). In a sense, religious communities thus circulate on the global level as cultural singularity goods of their own sort, and they are in competition with one another.[33] This is just as true of Zen Buddhism as it is of new-age communities, evangelical Christianity, or Salafism. Religious communities therefore present themselves as attractive objects of subjective appropriation that promise a collective cultural praxis and an intensive subjective experience. The new religions do not exhaust themselves in private faith and routine church activities – rather, they are constituted in collective, non-quotidian, and singularly experienced performances and events (from communal meditation to charismatic worship).

By no means can all of these late-modern religious options and communities be classified as "fundamentalist." Many of them serve as "spiritual" components within the framework of the singularistic lifestyle.[34] The fundamentalist communities, however, have a structure of their own and are powerful nodal points of cultural essentialism.[35] This is especially true of the evangelical communities in the United States, the Pentecostalists in Latin America, and the fundamentalist versions of Islam among migrants in Western Europe as well as in predominantly Muslim countries themselves (though in a different way). It is important not to overlook the fact that, paradoxically, the fundamentalist communities that profess the absoluteness of their faith also exist on a *market* of religions and thus within a cultural-economic constellation. Believers actively choose to join them; they are global religious "offers" that represent anything but the traditional and territorially bound characteristics of particular cultural spaces.[36]

Fundamentalist communities live off their basic claim to religious authenticity: the fundamentals of their faith appear to be given and beyond debate. This requires there to be historical continuity between a given religion's foundational event or foundational writings and the religious praxis of the present. Of all the forms of late-modern cultural essentialism, religious fundamentalisms draw the sharpest distinction between an ethically valuable inner world and an ethically rejected outer world. In Max Weber's terms, they are world-denying religions of salvation *par excellence*.[37] The modern everyday world – its economy, its private life, its politics (etc.) – is not merely regarded as profane (and, thus, at least tolerable) but rather as morally objectionable and in need of being overcome; it is the object of maximal devaluation. In fundamentalist communities, the levels of subjective religious experience and the narrative-hermeneutic meaning of religious narratives are typically subordinated to the religion's ethical and moral orientation: a strict ethical code is prescribed, behind which any individual desire for self-actualization has to recede.

Religious fundamentalisms can either withdraw, like a sort of subculture, into a separate counterculture or they can attempt to influence the outside with their (partially) aggressive political interests. Fundamentalists can thus be interpreted not only as part of a counter-movement against the rationalized culture of (organized) modernity but, even more, as part of a movement against the hyperculture of late modernity *itself*: be it as a means of resistance employed by members of social groups that have been marginalized or have fallen into cultural or social decline within post-industrial culture (the old middle class, the migrant underclass),[38] or be it as a critical response to the experiences of disappointment produced by the singularistic lifestyle and its relativization of ethical maxims.

Are fundamentalist religious communities engaged in singularizing the social, and do they form singular neo-communities? Across the world, as Olivier Roy has shown, late-modern fundamentalism makes use of standardized forms. Here, there is a general *postmodern religious format* that is characterized by three components: the spiritual quest of the individual, religion as an unambiguous and normative system, and the figure of the priest.[39] This is one side. On the other side, however, fundamentalist communities are contrasted with the seemingly "profane" everyday world and experienced by converts as a unique and inherently complex microcosm of like-minded people and specific practices, which, in addition, links them to a thousand-year-old tradition. Seen in this way, fundamentalist communities offer a counter-world that represents an attractive way of life to converts and provides them with a collective identity. They therefore cultivate their own *religious exceptionalism*: precisely because they are not (state-supported) official churches for one and all, but rather separate themselves from the outside and create a milieu of active believers, they can be understood by their members as extraordinary, identity-based communities. Here, religious subjects are not singular themselves (though their religious conversion may be experienced as such) but, instead, integrate themselves into the community and acquire singularity indirectly through their membership in an exceptional collective.[40]

Right-Wing Populism

Right-wing populist parties have been entrenched in the European party system since the 1990s.[41] They can be interpreted as an additional version of political cultural essentialism, which is in part interrelated to cultural nationalism, and they are characterized by their close connection to socio-cultural "identitarian" movements.[42] Right-wing populism is, therefore, not only a form of party politics; it is engaged in a politics of ideas, with the goal of cultural hegemony.

The rise of right-wing populism cannot be understood simply as an extension of traditional right-wing radicalism – rather, it is an expression of the restructuring of the Western party system. In organized modernity between 1945 and 1980, this system was defined by the dominance of people's parties (as "custodians of the general") and by the difference ("cleavage," as it is called) between the social-democratic center-left and the conservative center-right parties.[43] Since the 1980s, the party landscape of late modernity has been characterized by the diminished significance of people's parties and by the ascent of diverse smaller parties, giving rise to a market of self-profiling political groups striving for "authenticity."[44] As I have already discussed, there has been a paradigm shift from the corporatist/socio-democratic consensus to apertistic–differential liberalism, whereby the new cleavage now runs *within* this paradigm between neoliberalism and social liberalism. With the rise of right-wing populism, however, a new line of conflict has been drawn within the overall party system, and it is clearly a *reaction* to the established hegemony of new liberalism. Right-wing populism is a challenge to the paradigm of apertistic–differential liberalism both in its socially liberal *and* economically liberal types. This new, strong cleavage is based on the opposition between a "communitarian" and anti-pluralistic politics of the "people's" socio-cultural community, on the one hand, and a liberal and cosmopolitan politics of open markets and identities on the other: this is a cleavage between a politics of exclusion and a politics of openness.[45]

At its heart, however, right-wing populism is characterized not by its political content but, rather, by its fundamentally different political model.[46] Populism can be precisely defined as a political form: it claims to translate the will of the people *immediately* into political praxis; it presumes that it is possible and desirable for those governing to be *identical* with those being governed, and thus it operates, at least implicitly, with a democratic-theoretical model that does not proceed from the basis of plurality and representation. From this perspective, there is rather *one* collective interest of the people, which should be translated without any mediating authority directly into political action. This anti-pluralist approach to identity is more elementary than the anti-elitism that populism practices. At the basis of the critique of elites lies the understanding of a non-plural and allegedly "authentic" democracy in which "the people" appear as an unquestionable moral authority with natural interests and values – the "real Americans," the *classe populaire*, etc. In this sense, populists view themselves not as representatives but rather as part of the people, as the spearhead of a "movement": "*We* are the people," and "We *are* the people."

In the populist model of politics, the crux of the matter is thus that the "people," as the basis of democracy, are thought of as being *homogeneous*.[47] This can be on two different levels: the social (in the strict sense) or the cultural. The model of *social* homogeneity suggests that there is social uniformity in the life situation of "real" people, and thus in their interests as well. These are the "ordinary people" – the employees and wage-earners who "do the hard work and build this country," etc.[48] The model of *cultural* homogeneity suggests that there is a cultural uniformity of values and practices, a national culture in its collective identity, a natural sort of common sense, a generally accepted conception of morality upheld by "decent people," and so on. To a considerable extent, then, right-wing populism falls back on cultural essentialism, but in addition it also incorporates the idea of social homogeneity. It is an expression of cultural essentialism in that the political unity of the people is essentially understood in terms of national-cultural unity: as a collective identity of "authentic French people" (Austrian people, Dutch people, Hungarian people, etc.) with its own unique history, traditions, territory, and "national character." The culture of the people is believed to possess a natural ethos and "common decency."[49] "Real people" are often regarded as a social unit to the extent that they form the "silent majority" of "ordinary folk." Overall, this politics is directed toward the people as an alleged social *and* cultural community – as a *demos*, *populus*, and *ethnos* all in one – whose interests and values should be put into practice. At the same time, the intention of populist politics is to *preserve* this socio-cultural community as it is.

The populist version of cultural essentialism is also based on an antagonism between the inside and outside – on the notion of "us versus them."[50] To a considerable extent, it relies on polarizing valorizations and devaluations according to a sort of friend–enemy logic. Preferred targets of such devaluations include cosmopolitans

VI Differential Liberalism and Cultural Essentialism 301

and immigrants. Immigrants do not belong to the "authentic people," either because they do not share the national culture in question or because they lack the "right" background or religion. For their part, cosmopolitans are rejected because they do not represent the values and interests of the native local majority. This distaste is directed toward the global elite ("globalists"), toward members of the new middle class with cosmopolitan values, toward the typical inhabitants of metropolises, and toward supporters of progressive movements that are critical of traditional family values (feminism, the LGBTQ movement) or are internationally oriented. From the perspective of right-wing populism, the main representative group of the post-industrial society of singularities – the new middle class of the knowledge and culture economy, with its self-conscious adherence to an advanced contemporary lifestyle – is thus transformed into an enemy of the "real people," into a parasitic group on the outside. It is only against the backdrop of this general populist form of the political that the specific platforms of right-wing populist parties acquire their significance. They represent a communitarian alternative to apertistic–differential liberalism. Their opponents are neoliberalism (which promotes competition in society) and social liberalism (which promotes diversity), and thus the political goals of right-wing populist parties are to regulate national economic and social policy and to promote homogeneity through cultural and immigration policy.[51]

In its relation to the wider world, right-wing populism often promotes ethnopluralism.[52] It does not necessarily devalue other nations, which can instead be respected as equal but different. What is central, however, is that one's own nation is preserved in its distinctness, singularity, and authenticity. Anything that hybridizes culture is the enemy, as are any universalistic mechanisms that cut across nation states (the global economy, international organizations, etc.). The ideal situation for right-wing populists is to have coexisting "cultural spheres," each closed off from the outside. However, political ethnopluralism can also precipitate a clash between cultures, an exemplary case (within the right-wing populist context) being the cultural "war against Islam" that has been ongoing since the beginning of the twenty-first century.

Cultural Conflicts Between Essentialism, Hyperculture, and Liberalism

Where are the cultural-communitarian and essentialist tendencies positioned within the society of singularities, and what is their relation to the dominant politics of apertistic–differential liberalism? Things are more complicated here than they might at first seem. In short, cultural communitarianism exists *within* the global structure of the society of singularities, but it often (but not necessarily) *opposes* the latter's dominant hyperculture. This gives rise to cultural conflicts that take the form of conflicts *about* culture.

We have seen that late modernity is in opposition to formal rationalism's paucity of meaningfulness and sensuousness and that it promotes, in general and on various levels, elements with a strong cultural claim to value, uniqueness, affectivity, and authenticity. Cultural communitarianists in ethnic, religious, and national communities work to reinforce just such a structure. These cultural communities are therefore not anti-modern foreign bodies but rather a genuine and consistent element of the society of singularities. Indeed, we have seen that neo-communities, alongside singularity markets and heterogeneous collaborations, are a characteristic form of the social in late modernity. They create a singularistic type of sociality. What is more, cultural and essentialist communities also participate in large part on cultural markets. Identity politics, cultural nationalisms, right-wing populisms, and many forms of religious fundamentalism are anything but self-enclosed subcultures; rather, they compete with goods, commodities, and other political instances on the same visibility market that we examined at length in the context of the creative economy and digital media. They all compete to look attractive and find supporters on a global market of identities.

At the same time, the model of self-actualizing individuals combining and hybridizing cultural elements, which defines the lifestyle of the new middle class and for which the creative economy is tailor-made, represents the opposite of the cultural model espoused by essentialists: the homogeneous community, which the individual joins as a member of the whole.[53] As a synthesis of self-actualization and the market, hyperculture is thus the structural opponent of cultural communitarianism. The *singular individual* of hyperculture is opposed by the *singular community* of cultural essentialism, the mobility of valorization within an infinite space of cultural elements is opposed by the attempt to fix valorization through ingroup/outgroup antagonism, the creativity *dispositif* is opposed by the regime of the old, and the model of unlimited positive affectivities is opposed by an offensive-minded game with negative affectivities.

In general, cultural-essentialist movements can thus be interpreted as a critical reaction to hyperculture and as a counter-movement against the structure of competitive singularities, and this is true in two respects. First, they can be understood as a response to the systematic disappointing experiences of hyperculture, and thus as a practical *cultural critique* of its lifestyle. The subjective disappointments that can be caused by the culture of self-actualization, the hyper-competitiveness of singularity markets, and the creativity

VI Differential Liberalism and Cultural Essentialism 303

dispositif are being countered by a radical alternative model that is based on anti-individualistic communities, equality, and tradition. Cultural communitarianism promises "unassailable" collective identities that the mobile hyperculture is unable to offer. Under certain conditions, cultural communitarianism can, paradoxically, furnish the singular identity of an individual with an additional satisfying layer (Scottish, Latina, Baptist, Salafist, etc.).

Second, cultural essentialism can be interpreted as a means of *mobilizing the periphery* against the center. In the shape of ethnic communities of migrants or indigenous people and in the case of religious fundamentalists, right-wing populists, and (though in a different way) anti-Western cultural nationalisms, a multifarious and self-perceived social, political, and cultural periphery has formed on the global and national level against the center – against, that is, the economic, technological, social, and cultural structure that is the theme of this book. It is no surprise that, in Western societies, cultural essentialism and communitarianism have been supported above all by segments of the old middle class and the new underclass – by the very groups that late modernity has pushed into a socially and culturally defensive position. Cultural essentialism is thus wielded as a tool in the struggle against apertistic liberalism as a way to counteract the experiences of disparagement and disappointment that derive from it.

On the political level in the strict sense, the relationship between cultural communitarianism and apertistic–differential liberalism has hardly been straightforward. At first, there was even the possibility of a symbiosis between the two, which is the model of liberal multiculturalism. Given that social liberalism has been so insistently open to identities and cultural diversity, it has in fact encouraged the formation of particular, identity-based communities. Within this framework, regional-national movements and (in part) religious groups have come to expect not only tolerance but also active support, as entities that enrich the overall cultural heritage of society.[54] During its first phase, "identity politics" (such as that of African Americans or Canadian Québécois) did not have a confrontational relationship with differential liberalism but rather resided within its framework. Rather ambitiously, however, multiculturalism requires cultural communities to accept the general legal and cultural norms of liberal politics, within which they can then exist as respectful equals alongside one another.

This coexistence of liberalism and cultural communitarianism has certainly not disappeared, but since the turn of the millennium it has largely become antagonistic (and on an international scale at that). On the national and international level, cultural essentialists are now united in opposition to political liberalism, and often aggressively so. Such is the case with right-wing populism, cultural nationalism, and several versions of religious fundamentalism, and it is also true (though indirectly) of ethnic communities that are culturally closed off from the world. Each of these cases brings to light the fundamental antagonism between two different social and cultural models: subjective self-development and the market of cultural goods stand in opposition to the homogenization of communities, and the hybridization of culture is opposed by the requirement to maintain a strict difference between ingroups and outgroups. Moreover, this has also given rise to surprising alliances between various cultural essentialists who have joined forces against a common enemy, such as an international alliance of right-wing populists against liberal foreign policy or an alliance between different fundamentalist religious communities against liberal family policy. The relationship that cultural essentialists have with each other is thus often characterized by ethnopluralism. The enemy is not so much other nations or religious communities – rather, the common struggle is against the political structure that tends to make rigid cultural collectives more fluid: apertistic and differential liberalism.[55]

In the early twenty-first century, the question that thus remains open is how apertistic–differential liberalism will react to this cultural-essentialist opposition – whether it will go on the offensive, wage a war of resistance, disappear altogether, or transform itself in a new direction. The fact of the matter is that every political paradigm has time limits; every political paradigm responds to a particular set of problems, but after a while it exhausts its ability to resolve further problems when the situation in society has changed. Within apertistic liberalism, it is therefore no surprise that, in addition to unflinching resolve, it is now possible to see signs of self-critique, and this is true in both its socially liberal and economically liberal strands. The socially liberal goal of cultural diversity attracts criticism as soon as it becomes clear that cultural essentialists such as ethnic or religious communities are often more than just obedient particular communities within a culturally diverse landscape. Instead, some of them openly call into question the basic liberal structures of society. From within liberal politics, a critique has thus developed against the "ethno-cult" and against the "separatism of cultures."[56]

This raises the question of a renewed political model of culture that not only positions itself against the particularism of communities but also introduces a political alternative to the model of hyperculture, which has thus far defined the creative economy and the middle-class lifestyle. Debates about "cultural integration" and the perceived desideratum of a new politics oriented toward universal and group-transcending practices and values indicate that liberal reflections concerning a politically appropriate model of culture have not come to an end.[57] This is also a matter of ensuring that communality and collectivity, which are of course central to communitarianism as a cultural reference point, are not ceded to communitarianism alone but can, rather, also be appropriated by the heterogeneous national societies of late modernity in a way that preserves pluralism and yet goes beyond the model of hyperculture.[58]

At the same time, the neoliberal branch of apertistic–differential liberalism – the model of the innovation-oriented competition state – has obviously reached its limits as well.[59] Paradoxically, it is the rise of cultural communitarianism that makes this clear. The liberalism of deregulated markets lent additional force to the mechanisms of the post-industrial economy and thus further enhanced its tendency to create polarization between high- and low-qualified forms of labor, between socio-cultural winners and losers, and between thriving regions and shrinking regions. Within the context of this social and cultural polarization of classes and life perspectives, segments of the new underclass and old middle class, which have been subjected to experiences of devaluation and have been pushed to the periphery, have sought recourse in various forms of cultural essentialism. The rise of cultural essentialism can likewise be interpreted as a revolt of the periphery, which, in part, was indirectly and unintentionally created by the politics of apertistic–differential liberalism itself. The political challenge for liberalism, then, lies not only in how it will choose to engage in a political battle with the many varieties of cultural essentialism, but also in how it will respond to the social and cultural processes of devaluation that gave rise to such essentialism in the first place and continue to fuel it.[60]

The Politics of Violence:
Terrorism and Mass Shootings as Celebrations of the
Singular Act

To conclude this chapter, I would like to take a brief look at another way in which the political manifests itself in late modernity: terrorist acts and shooting sprees. Ever since al-Qaida crashed two airplanes into the World Trade Center in 2001, there have been more and more new terrorist attacks around the globe – committed above all by fundamentalist-Islamic networks such as IS, but also by right-wing radicals (as in the case of the Norwegian attack in the year 2011). A structurally related phenomenon is the numerous mass shootings (especially by young perpetrators) that have taken place internationally since the massacre at Columbine High School in 1999.[61] One token of late modernity, as these unsettling events imply, is the politics of violence.

As to how these acts are political, this may not be immediately apparent. In fact, they would not be political at all if politics were identified exclusively with state governance and the goal of shaping society. In an elementary sense, however, politics is also about dealing with physical violence and about the modern state as the sole authority that claims to have a monopoly on its legitimate use. Acts of terrorism and mass shootings make it clear to see, however, that this claim is baseless. Here, violence is not a means to an end (as in the case of robbery or murder); rather, the issue here is that of demonstrative violence. Whereas terrorist attacks are linked to a political motive in the strict sense, mass shootings remain primarily within the realm of personal motives. What is decisive in both cases, however, is not their intentions but their political *constellation*. And, in this respect, the society of singularities provides the structure: these are demonstrations of violence that, to the horror of the public, enact a social state of emergency.

Fundamentally, singular demonstrations of violence are related to the question of how violence is structured in modernity. In his theory of violence, Norbert Elias described modernity as a process in which the state and society increasingly regulate violence and civilize negative affects. However, it would be more accurate to say that modernity implements the structural violence of its institutions in order to suppress individual violence.[62] Late-modern society since the 1970s can be interpreted as the pinnacle of this process. The socially liberal branch of new liberalism – but also the related shift of the post-industrial working world toward projects and networks, as well as the shift in parenting toward the "concerted cultivation" of children – have increased our sensitivity to types of physical and psychological violence that simply would have been "shrugged off" during classical modernity. These types of violence, too, are now expected to be contained.[63]

From this perspective, late-modern culture seems to have reached the summit of social pacification. However, although today's practices of interaction are clearly more informal than they were during bourgeois and organized modernity, this deregulation of behavior has required subjects to internalize non-violence and non-aggression all the more strongly.[64] Against the backdrop of this late-modern ideal of non-violence, singular demonstrations of violence in terrorist acts and mass shootings appear even more disturbing. To put it bluntly, they reveal one of late modernity's trade secrets in an embarrassing way. Its hyperculture, its post-industrial knowledge and culture economy, its curated lifestyle, its gender equality, its markets and projects, its liberal politics – all of this silently *requires* a pacified society and individuals with extreme mental self-control in their daily lives. Terrorism and shooting sprees challenge this requirement in a spectacular fashion.

Upon closer inspection, it becomes clear that these demonstrations of violence exploit the mechanisms of the media-supported and culturally affective visibility market for singularities, and that they would be utterly unthinkable without this format.[65] Three sets of actors play a role in this: the perpetrators, the victims, and the public audience. Unlike trivial crimes, which are carried out in a clandestine manner, these are acts that take place before an audience: not a personally familiar audience but a potentially global anonymous audience that can be reached through the media (and today, especially, through digital media). The victims are not personally targeted for one reason or another; they are random. The public therefore identifies with the victims, who seem like surrogates: in principle, this could happen to anyone and, in principle, "anyone" is indeed the intended target. Terrorism and mass shootings can be understood as singular acts to the extent that they are unique and they disrupt the pacified order of the general. In a culture of non-violence (and structural violence), the publicly visible and intentional act of physical violence is, in the truest sense, *extraordinary*. At the same time, this is not just any given type of violent activity; the uniqueness of these acts derives from their excessive cruelty, from the excessive indignity associated with them, and from their breathtakingly malicious settings: the architectural landmark of capitalist modernity in the cultural melting pot *par excellence*, a social-democratic youth group on a vacation island, or an audience enjoying a pop concert in a trendy urban neighborhood.[66]

Here, as in the case of all visibility markets, it is ultimately the audience that singularizes things, and in this respect its main criterion is the intensity of affect. Demonstrations of violence fit neatly into just such a structure: their aim is to create visibility by affecting people – except now by producing *negative* affectivity to an extreme extent. The perpetrators of such atrocities thus implement the logic of late-modern visibility markets and pervert it at the same time: in this case, what attracts attention is not that which is amazingly, interestingly, or originally unique, but rather that which is horrifyingly and repulsively unique. Late modernity's culture of positive affectivity is thus disrupted by an act of obscene cruelty. It cannot be denied: in a culture of positive affects, nothing is more shocking than excessive negativity, and the public is virtually forced to certify the abhorrent grandiosity of the act. Demonstrations of violence through terrorism and mass shootings thereby become *negative singularities* and thus belong to a genre that we have already encountered – a genre which includes subjects, objects, and places that, as counter-examples to attractiveness, reside outside of hyperculture's acceptable realm of singularities and draw attention to themselves as objects of disparagement or pity.[67] Things are different, however, in the case of subjects who commit demonstrative acts of violence. They, after all, are *self-conscious* negative singularities who intentionally commit negatively evaluated acts.

They are by no means the object of anyone's pity. Pleased with what they have done, they celebrate their deviance.

Demonstrations of violence have a peculiar form because they are not conducted outside of, but instead within, the social processes of culturalization and valorization. It is typically the case that (physical) violence is a means to an end: it is used to achieve a particular goal (to take possession of someone else's property, to conquer a territory, etc.). The late-modern demonstrative violence of terrorism and mass shootings is different: here, the violent act is an end in itself and thus, in a disturbing way, a cultural praxis. In this case, what Walter Benjamin wrote about violence is true: "It is not a means but a manifestation."[68] As a cultural praxis, it has a narrative-hermeneutic dimension in that it tells a story of retribution (eliminating those who are ruining the West, the scornful triumph of those whom society has left behind, etc.); it has an "ethical" dimension in the sense of a particular retaliatory ethos (revenge against the West or against the institutions that never took the perpetrator seriously, for example); and it has an "aesthetic" and design dimension in the sense that it stages an event in a way that captures the sensory perception of the public in the most disturbing way possible. Demonstrations of violence do not, therefore, circulate within the sphere of utility and functionality, but rather in the sphere where value is attributed. If, however, there is one phenomenon to which late-modern culture assigns unambiguously *negative* value, that phenomenon is violence.[69] Terrorism and mass shootings are provocative because they accomplish the most atrocious thing possible in the eyes of civilized late modernity; such acts have irreversible consequences and – what is more – their perpetrators often remain unpunished (usually on account of suicide).

In this way, not only do such acts of violence acquire singularity status; their perpetrators do as well. By committing a spectacular act of this sort, the formerly marginalized mass shooter or terrorist manages to get his "fifteen minutes of fame," which, as Andy Warhol suggested, is a major motivation of the late-modern subject. This is a sort of *negative heroism*, which the perpetrator achieves by killing random victims as a demonstration of his omnipotence. Those who have been overlooked thereby force people to look at them. The result is recognition for having committed an act of such negative grandiosity (among the perpetrators' "sympathizers," however, the result is honor and admiration). As to why certain perpetrators become terrorists or mass shooters in the first place, the obvious answer lies in the structural conditions of the society of singularities. Perpetrators are recruited from the circle of this society's socio-cultural "losers." With respect to mass shooters, we are usually dealing with personally offended, Western middle-class young men who have flopped in their attempts to play the cultural

VI Differential Liberalism and Cultural Essentialism 309

game of "successful self-actualization." Regarding terrorists, these are usually people who, having experienced social and cultural degradation, identify with religious or politically radical cultural essentialism, in whose name they participate in a crusade against the hegemony of the West. For its perpetrators, violence can thus become an "attractive way of life,"[70] and this is because it promises to convert them from victims into negative heroes. If late modernity's hyperculture is a culture of attractiveness, then demonstrative violence acquires its own appeal for those in the shadows of attention and appreciation. By committing an act of this sort, perpetrators follow the rules of the society of singularity but, at least for a moment, overturn its order of violence.

Conclusion: The Crisis of the General?

Both sociologically and politically, the late-modern society of singularities is a challenge. By radically readjusting the social relation between the general and the particular, it is shaking the foundational structures and certainties of that which hitherto constituted modernity. This should be a provocation to sociology, which emerged as a scientific discipline during industrial modernity and has long derived its basic concepts from that framework. This will also be a test for the political discourse, which has long been driven by the "project of modernity" and its idea of general progress.

Since the last third of the twentieth century, as we have seen, the forms of the social have been reconfigured. The social logic of singularities has become a force that shapes structures of the economy, of technologies and the professional world, of lifestyles and everyday cultures, as well as of politics, whereas the social logic of the general that dominated classical modernity now plays the role of an enabling infrastructure. Processes of singularization have led to anything but the "liberation of the individual." In ways that can be analyzed quite precisely in praxeological terms, they rather involve the highly dynamic social fabrication of unique entities on the level of objects, subjects, events, places, and collectives. Far from being pre-social, singularities have given rise to complex singularistic forms of the social in which unique entities are produced and observed, valorized and appropriated. Instead of debunking the modern myth of the "individual," processes of singularization have rather demystified it – which has done nothing to detract from the mystifying effect of singularities in the social world. In the background, the society of singularities is still largely enabled by formal and unemotional rationalizations; in the foreground, of course, it is a society shaped by hyperculture, which is repeatedly challenged by cultural essentialism and is a generator of socially circulating affects. Cultural economization, with its attention and visibility markets for cultural singularity goods, is the dominant form of the social in late

Conclusion: The Crisis of the General? 311

modernity: here, things and services are singularity goods fighting for visibility and appreciation, and the same can be said of subjects (looking for jobs, partners, or general recognition), cities and regions, schools, religious communities, and even terrorist groups. Heterogeneous collaborations (such as projects and networks) and neo-communities of the religious, ethnic, and political sort are the two alternative forms that the social can take within the framework of a singularistic logic; they are partly a component of cultural economization, and partly its competitor.

It is worth asking whether the society of singularities is actually still a part of modernity or whether it is not on its way to becoming something entirely different – some sort of successor formation. In fact, it would be naïve and short-sighted to declare that Western modernity, which has been running its course since the late eighteenth century, leads to the "end of history," as Hegel, Kojève, and Fukuyama suggested.[1] After all, modernity is not monolithic or universal. Instead, it is itself a historical process with its own beginning and development. And, at some point, it will also enter the time of its disappearance and transformation into different and subsequent social formations.

For now, however, there are still good reasons to continue speaking of late *modernity*. In addition to certain institutional paths that Western society has been taking almost consistently over the last 250 years or so – the market, parliamentarianism, law, science, etc. – modernity as a whole is characterized by what I have discussed throughout this book: the relation between a social logic of the general and a social logic of the particular as *the* central problem of modern society. From its beginning, modernity has been a society of extremes, for it radicalizes and systematizes society's orientation toward the general and its orientation toward the singular in a historically unprecedented way. It is late modernity, which has been the focus of this book, that first began to elevate the previously secondary logic of singularization into an extensive and structurally formational force. The break from industrial modernity to the society of singularities has had one fundamental effect: it has unsettled what defined and accompanied classical modernity from the end of the eighteenth century into the 1970s, namely the normative ideal of social progress – the "project of modernity."[2] But to what extent?

First, in the society of singularities, the "grand narrative" of political progress has in many respects been replaced by the "minor narratives" of (private) success and of the (private) good life. Paradigmatic of this is the lifestyle model of the new middle class, which, as we have seen in detail, is oriented toward successful self-actualization – here, to some extent, normative ideals are realized on the level of the particular and not on that of the general. *Second*, the temporal structure of late-modern society, as regards both its social fields and its ways of life, is fundamentally oriented toward the present, so that systematic future processing, which is characteristic of progress-oriented societies, is no longer as prevalent. Late modernity is governed by a radical regime of novelty, which is concerned with the present moment; it is not oriented toward long-term innovation and revolution, but rather toward the affectivity of the here and now.[3]

Third, there is obviously no longer a clear answer to the question of whether late modernity has, when compared to industrial modernity, brought about social progress. Over the course of the transformation from industrial modernity to late modernity, gains and losses, progress and regression, and positive and negative valuations have been distributed unequally throughout various groups in Western societies – between the highly qualified and the low-qualified, between creative people and laborers, between men and women, between native residents and immigrants, between heterosexuals and homosexuals, between cosmopolitans and sedentary people, between city dwellers and people in the country, between extroverts and introverts, between those interested in a quality of life and those interested in a standard of living, between individuals with special talents and "generalists," between various age groups, etc., etc. In the many places where these categories overlap, the social shift over the last 40 years has given rise to two diverging lines, one rising and one falling. Within the framework of late modernity's dominant cultural order to date – which is composed of the interrelated models of successful self-actualization, hyperculture, the knowledge and culture economy, and apertistic–differential liberalism – it is admittedly possible to claim that progress has been made over industrial modernity, especially when it comes to increased autonomy and decreased levels of violence. As I hope to have shown during the course of this book, however, it is also possible at the beginning of the twenty-first century to detect late modernity's fundamental moments of crisis. In sum, three crises can be identified: a crisis of recognition, a crisis of self-actualization, and a crisis of the political.

The *crisis of recognition* is a result of the transformation from the industrial mass economy to the post-industrial economy of singularities.[4] As we have seen, the latter is characterized above all by two polarizations. With the end of industrial society, on the one hand, a systematic social divide opened up between the highly qualified people of the new and expanding knowledge and culture economy and people with minimal qualifications, who typically work in the simple service industries or are out of work altogether. On the other hand, there is also asymmetry within the segment of the advanced knowledge and culture economy between those who are more successful and those who are less successful on the market.

Because the post-industrial economy follows the model of the creative economy, with its winner-take-all or winner-take-the-most markets, the distribution of social recognition is highly unequal. The sparkling winners are those who contribute immediately to the design of complex singular goods or whose work seems like a precious singular achievement in itself; the losers are those with interchangeable routine jobs. This polarization betrays whatever promises were made about a post-industrial knowledge economy and its educational revolution, which suggested that there would be social ascendancy and increased qualifications for all. Instead, the society of singularities is based on a paradoxical combination of radical meritocracy and its destabilization. In a radically meritocratic manner, the highly qualified are distinguished from the low-qualified.[5] At the same time, however, the predictability of the criteria that define achievement and qualification is offset by the unpredictability of market success and of what constitutes a "successful performance," thereby disappointing any notions of justice that still linger from the industrial achievement society.

The polarization of working conditions corresponds not only to a social and material divide but also to a cultural polarization of lifestyles. We have seen how, in accordance with the paternoster-elevator effect, the educated middle class and the new underclass (and part of the old middle class) have been moving in opposite directions: culturally, one group is on the rise while the other is in decline. Not only can the new middle class count on professional recognition; it is also able to develop a culturally oriented, curated lifestyle that places a high (ethical and aesthetic) value on multiple factors – from health and cosmopolitanism to education, parenting, and neighborhoods – and, in fact, seems to be leading a valuable "good life." In contrast, the new underclass has experienced a devaluation of its work, and this has been accompanied by a devaluation of its entire lifestyle. As a result, a considerable segment of society seems to have been cut off from having any hope for progress.

The society of singularities is also characterized by a cultural *crisis of self-actualization*. Whereas the crisis of recognition affects parts of society that are on the social and cultural defensive, the crisis of self-actualization pertains to the culturally dominant center or, to be more precise, to the lifestyle of "successful self-actualization," which, as the focal point of late-modern culture, the new middle class (above all) aims to achieve. This lifestyle, which synthesizes the Romantic tradition with the bourgeois orientation toward status, has proven to be not only an engine of increased autonomy and fulfilling experiences but also a systematic generator of disappointment, which, in extreme cases, can lead to psychological repercussions such as depression (the emblematic illness of late modernity).[6] As we have seen, this generator of disappointment is driven by the fact that, in the lifestyle of self-actualization, personal fortune is tied to the volatility of subjective experience, on the one hand, and to the judgement of others on unpredictable cultural markets (job markets, partnership markets, friendship markets) on the other hand. Whereas, in bourgeois and industrial modernity, self-actualization seemed like a way to break free of the corset of social constraints, it has now become, as the dominant and socially expected lifestyle model, a source of frustration and disappointment. Together, the imperative to transform oneself, the fear of missing out on experiences, the expectation that one should always put on an attractive performance, the unpredictability of popularity, and the lack of cultural resources for dealing with disappointment and negative emotions have all contributed to the crisis plaguing the culture of self-actualization.

Finally, the society of singularities has reached a *crisis of the political*. Since the end of organized modernity, the political sphere has lost its ability to control society as a whole. Instead, primacy has been gained by the inherent dynamics of the economy, (media) technology, and the culture of lifestyles – and apertistic–differential liberalism has reinforced this process. The crisis of the political concerns the political public sphere and its cultural foundations, as well as the state. Political debate now takes place within autonomous and fragmented public spheres, and this is not least due to the rise of digital media. The diverse political tendencies of cultural essentialism – from religious fundamentalism and ethnic sub-politics to national populism – have also contributed to this fragmentation; cultural neo-communities withdraw their essentialism from political debate and simply declare themselves to be sacrosanct.[7] In addition, the paradigm shift from the regulatory state to the innovation-oriented competition state has led to the dismantling of basic government functions. Attuned to the consumer needs of its citizens, the late-modern state perceives itself as an institution for enabling private consumption; it is less interested in achieving goals that might improve society as a whole.[8]

Together, the social crisis of recognition, the cultural crisis of self-actualization, and the political crisis of the public sphere and the state can be interpreted as instantiations of a *crisis of the general* faced by a society that is radically oriented toward the particular. If we acknowledge that such a crisis exists, this will also shift our perspective on classical modernity – on industrial–organized modernity, but also on bourgeois modernity as well. Whereas, from the perspective of late modernity, classical modernity could at first seem like a sort of "repressive authority" that implemented the general at the expense of the particular, now it is also possible to see what was gained – and has since, in part, been lost – by the past's orientation toward the general. Looking back at the bygone

Conclusion: The Crisis of the General? 315

generality of industrial and bourgeois modernity thus always has the character of "nostalgic" hindsight.

Again, all of the crises mentioned above can be interpreted as instantiations of a crisis of the general. This is true, first, of the crisis of recognition. In retrospect, industrial society, which operated within the framework of a distributive tax state, represents a "society of equals" (in Rosanvallon's terms) with comprehensive social inclusion: a labor society in which specialized work of every sort was treated equally and in which contributions to social welfare were accepted necessities.[9] In the post-industrial economy of singularities, such an appreciation for an individual's special contribution to the general has been replaced by an appreciation for the economically successful (and perhaps also culturally admired) uniqueness of a given individual's or company's performance.

The crisis of self-actualization can also be seen as a consequence of the "loss of the general." In this case, what seems to have been lost is the generality of culture. The classical culture of the bourgeoisie provided a general system of enculturation in which subjects could perfect themselves by conforming with an already existing cultural structure – a system of morals, obligations, and education.[10] In the late-modern culture of self-actualization, in contrast, this system of culture has transformed into an ensemble of cultural resources that individuals draw upon flexibly for the sake of their own singularization. The reassuring (but limiting) act of committing oneself to a generally accepted fixed set of cultural singularities has been replaced by the need for individuals to engage in the mutable, and thus unpredictable, act of curating hyperculture.

Finally, the crisis of the public sphere and the state – and the rise of cultural particularism as well – can also be interpreted as a crisis of the general. In classical modernity's own understanding, the predominant role of politics was to promote and represent the general. The political system was expected to be a guiding force for the development of society as a whole, and the general public sphere had a socially integrative function in the mass media and the people's parties. The fragmentation of the political public sphere into diverse communities, the rise of the ethnic and religious particularism of cultural essentialism, and the partial retreat of the state can thus be interpreted as an expression of the disappearance of the general from politics.

The crisis of the general in the society of singularities does *not*, therefore, concern formal rationalization in its aforementioned dimensions of standardization, formalization, and generalization. As opposed to processes of singularization, formal rationalization may only have a facilitating and enabling function in late modernity, but it continues to operate, as we have seen, by providing the necessary and irreplaceable infrastructure for its hyperculture.

However, the crisis of the general on the levels of social recognition, culture, and politics is not about infrastructure but about what is socially, culturally, and politically *shared in common*: it is about mutual and reciprocal forms of recognition, common systems of cultural values, and the forms of communication and normative frameworks in society as a whole. As that which is socially shared, the general is neither a stable integrative consensus nor a previously existing normative foundation; even during classical modernity, it was always controversial and contested.

What status has been attributed to this crisis in the society of singularities? In response to this question, it should first be said that crises are nothing out of the ordinary in the history of modernity; indeed, modern society as such is in a perpetual state of crisis.[11] This is not the case because modernity is excessively pathological, but rather because it is always creating new discrepancies as the fast pace of social change clashes with the demanding normative standards of modern life. Thus, whatever else the crisis of the general may be about, the idea cannot be dismissed that it concerns a sort of cultural phantom pain: the normative criteria of classical modernity continue to operate in a rudimentary way, even though social reality left them behind long ago. This raises the question of whether the society of singularities could establish an entirely different and new set of normative standards, so that the nineteenth- and twentieth-century criteria of progress, justice, or happiness would not even seem to be applicable anymore.

The answer to this question remains open. At the same time, the door has certainly closed on the possibility of going back to industrial modernity, to its leveled middle-class society, its culturally homogeneous lifestyle, its industrial mass economy, its mass media, its socio-spatial uniformity, and its system of political planning – even though the possibility of taking such a path is presently being suggested by many populist movements. In light of the situation at the beginning of the twenty-first century, however, the crises of recognition, self-actualization, and politics are in fact focal points within the current political and cultural-critical complex of problems – indeed, it can be presumed that these crises will largely define the agenda of the ensuing phase of the society of singularities. In closing, I would thus like to outline how "doing generality" is currently problematizing matters *within* the society of singularities, and how this problematization might look in the future.[12]

The social crisis of recognition contains a significant amount of socially, psychologically, and politically explosive material. As I have already discussed at length, one of the unintended consequences of the transition to post-industrial society was the formation of certain socio-cultural polarizations, which were not anticipated by the utopian visions of a new knowledge and information society:

divisions created by the winner-take-the-most markets of highly qualified individuals, as well as by the general decline of activities and qualifications that do not require a university education. From a political perspective, this raises the question of whether the state can regulate the turbulent swings of winner-take-all markets and whether it can appropriately readjust the social status of low-skilled jobs, particularly those in the service sector, and establish high-quality workplaces that do not require a university education. Related to this is the challenge faced by municipal and regional planning to counteract socio-spatial polarization.[13]

However, because the crisis of recognition concerns not only social and material issues but also the cultural question of what is regarded as valuable, the problem ultimately runs even deeper: at stake is nothing less than our understanding of labor, the working world, dignity, recognition, and the social necessity of all types of work, regardless of whether they are more or less successful on singularity markets.[14] Yet, even though it is possible to debate and regulate what achievement, qualification, and work should mean, there is no way to regulate which type of work, working subject, lifestyle, or residential area will seem attractive. This is important, because so much of the polarization of post-industrial society is caused by the perceived cultural difference between "satisfying" and "unsatisfying" jobs, between "admirable" and "deplorable" subjects, between thriving cities and "struggling" regions. As is clear to see, an economy of singularities and a culture of attractiveness persistently undermine the standards of justice upheld by industrial and bourgeois modernity.

The cultural crisis of self-actualization is not so much a political matter as it is a matter of private ways of life; not without reason, it preoccupies cultural-critical debate and beckons psychological diagnoses and therapies. Here, too, one is confronted with disillusionment. Whereas, in the case of the crisis of recognition, the disillusionment concerns the inability of the knowledge society to live up to its utopian promise of "social advancement for everyone," here there is disillusionment about the utopian notion of achieving personal happiness through the ideal of self-actualization. The latter ideal had always depended on a system of compulsory cultural generalities (the norms of bourgeois or mass culture), but what happens when this system has gone away? At present, two divergent cultural strategies have developed in response to this crisis: a strategy of radicalized singularization and one of self-limitation.

The strategy of radicalized singularization is inspired by the experience that the society of singularities does not recognize every unique feature, but rather only those that are regarded as "attractive" and are thus acceptable. The prevailing model is indeed that of successful self-actualization, and success depends on the valorization of others, who adhere to the strict criteria of attractiveness. It thus makes perfect sense that the social movements of culturally marginalized people insist that their otherness and uniqueness should be recognized.[15] From this perspective, late modernity is not singularistic *enough*, and it is built around more or less subtle structures of discrimination. The strategy of self-limitation, which developed in the realm of psychological and life counseling as a reaction to the dominance of self-growth psychology, goes in a different direction. It does not urge individuals to extricate themselves entirely from their self-actualization spirals but, rather, to relativize the demands of self-development and learn how to cope with life's disappointments.[16] The aim here is to deflate the great importance that the post-materialistic lifestyle places on "the good life"; in a sense, the ideology of self-development is confronted by the psychological "limits to growth." Cultural critics, too, increasingly point out the dark sides of a subject culture that is based on a symbiosis of cultural attractiveness markets and the desire for self-development.[17] However, the strategy of self-limitation is up against a powerful and media-driven culture of attractiveness, success, and satisfaction in which not every success and failure is treated equally.

The crisis of the political in the strict sense has also provoked new debates and strategies. The fundamental issue is how it might be possible, at least provisionally, to "reconstitute the general" within a society of singularities. In this case, the general cannot simply be rediscovered; it has to be produced anew in a necessarily contested way. Various possible ways of reconnecting the body politic have been proposed. In light of the fragmentation of public attention via media, one popular issue concerns the question of how to reconstruct a general public sphere – be it on the local, national, or international level – in which subjects from different social classes and milieus are brought together. Noteworthy, too, are the efforts of new social movements to reconfigure how resources are shared in a way that goes beyond markets, the state, and neo-communities. The "commons" movement is perhaps the most prominent example in this regard, but others are also working on such things as promoting alternative economic forms and alternative forms of urban development.[18] Finally, the question of reconstituting the general also pertains to the complex of problems associated with "cultural integration," which involves far more than the consequences of migration processes. Insight into the dangers posed by cultural-essentialist tendencies and "parallel cultures" has made the problem of how to create common cultural norms across ethnic, religious, and class boundaries a focal point of political debate. Of course, the universality of a common culture does not rest firmly on a binding and unchanging foundation; rather, the endeavor of working toward universality, generally accepted cultural norms, and commonly shared goods is an ongoing task. What seems to be needed here is for politics to engage in "doing universality," which can provide a counterweight to late modernity's ubiquitous practice of "doing singularity."

All in all, there are increasing signs that the political paradigm of apertistic–differential liberalism, which ousted the exhausted social-democratic and corporatist paradigm and has so far defined late modernity, has meanwhile exhausted itself in its inability to respond to new sets of problems and is thus making way for the arrival of a new paradigm, which could be called regulatory liberalism.[19] The decisive challenge faced by the latter consists in regulating both the social, with the aim of addressing the issues of social inequality and the labor market, and the cultural, with the aim of securing general cultural goods and norms for all of society. The task of generalizing the social and the task of generalizing culture are thus the two sides of the political challenge of "doing universality." In both respects, incidentally, certain authorities that apertistic–differential liberalism tended to minimize could gain renewed significance within the framework of regulatory liberalism: the institutions of the state.

That said, political fantasies of comprehensively steering social and cultural processes – the sort of planning and control that characterized industrial modernity – will be frustrated by the society of singularities. The latter does not draw its dynamics from politics – which is, at most, an indirect influence, but never the only steering factor – but rather from the hypercultural triangle composed of the economy of singularities, the culture machine of digital technologies, and the singularistic lifestyle of the new middle class. And, unless I am mistaken, there is every reason to believe that the society of singularities will continue to gain momentum in the future, especially at the global level. The social asymmetries and cultural heterogeneities that it produces, its unpredictable dynamics of valorizations and devaluations, and its liberation of positive and negative affects will show notions of a rational order, an egalitarian society, homogeneous culture, and a balanced personality structure – ideas still nurtured by some – for what they are: pure nostalgia.

Notes

Introduction: The Proliferation of the Particular

1 On cultural capitalism, see Jeremy Rifkin, *The Age of Access: The New Culture of Hypercapitalism, Where All of Life is a Paid-for Experience* (New York: Putnam, 2000); and Pierre-Michel Menger, *The Economics of Creativity: Art and Achievement Under Uncertainty* (Cambridge, MA: Harvard University Press, 2014).
2 Although here I am using the terms "singular," "unique," and "particular" as synonyms, over the course of this book I will distinguish various social forms of the particular.
3 See David Riesman, *The Lonely Crowd: A Study of the Changing American Character* (New Haven: Yale University Press, 1950).
4 See Ulrich Beck, *Risk Society: Towards a New Modernity*, trans. Mark Ritter (London: Sage, 1992).
5 For a socio-economic discussion of this concept, see Lucien Karpik, *Valuing the Unique: The Economics of Singularities* (Princeton University Press, 2010). For a cultural-anthropological viewpoint, see Igor Kopytoff, "The Cultural Biography of Things: Commoditization as Process," in *The Social Life of Things: Commodities in Cultural Perspective*, ed. Arjun Appadurai (Cambridge University Press, 1986), pp. 64–91. Kopytoff and Karpik have been my two greatest sources of inspiration. My use of the concept of the singular or singularity differs from the way that it is used by artificial-intelligence researchers or by transhumanists such as Ray Kurzweil. See the latter's *The Singularity is Near: When Humans Transcend Biology* (New York: Penguin, 2005).
6 See Immanuel Kant, *Critique of Pure Reason*, trans. Paul Guyer and Allen W. Wood (Cambridge University Press, 1998), pp. 172–8; Kant, *Critique of the Power of Judgement*, trans. Paul Guyer and Eric Matthews (Cambridge University Press, 2000), pp. 271–84. For a brief overview of Kant's discussion, see Rainer Kuhlen, "Allgemeines/Besonderes," in *Historisches Wörterbuch der Philosophie*, vol. I, ed. Joachim Ritter et al. (Basel: Schwabe, 1971), pp. 181–3.
7 William I. Thomas and Dorothy S. Thomas, *The Child in America: Behavior Problems and Programs* (New York: Knopf, 1928), p. 571.
8 See Michael Thompson, *Rubbish Theory: The Creation and Destruction of Value* (New York: Oxford University Press, 1979); and Beverley Skeggs, *Class, Self, Culture* (London: Routledge, 2004).
9 See Max Weber, "Author's Introduction," in *The Protestant Ethic and the Spirit of Capitalism*, trans. Talcott Parsons (New York: Charles Scribner's Sons, 1930), pp. 13–31.
10 See David Frisby, *Fragments of Modernity: Theories of Modernity in the Work of Simmel, Kracauer, and Benjamin* (Cambridge: Polity, 1985); Sam Whimster, "The Secular Ethic and the Culture of Modernism," in *Max Weber, Rationality,*

and Modernity, ed. Sam Whimster and Scott Lash (London: Routledge, 1987), pp. 259–90; and Volker Gerhardt, *Pathos und Distanz: Studien zur Philosophie Friedrich Nietzsches* (Stuttgart: Reclam, 1988), pp. 12–45.
11 In a sense quite different from that proposed by Eric Hobsbawm in his book *The Age of Extremes: The Short Twentieth Century, 1914–1991* (London: Michael Joseph, 1994).
12 On the concept of infrastructure, see Susan Leigh Star, "The Ethnography of Infrastructure," *American Behavioral Scientist* 43 (1999), pp. 377–91.
13 See, for instance, Priya Hays, *Advancing Healthcare through Personalized Medicine* (Boca Raton, FL: CRC Press, 2017).
14 Of course, economic and cultural processes of transformation outside of Europe and North America have had a different form and a different rhythm. In no way is it possible to proceed from the assumption that these regions have simply copied Western patterns. Rather, it is necessary to take into account hybrid forms and "multiple modernities," which would require precise case studies for each individual region of global society.
15 For a similar understanding of the role of critique, see Michel Foucault, "What is Enlightenment?" in *The Foucault Reader*, ed. Paul Rabinow (New York: Pantheon Books, 1984), pp. 32–50.
16 Andreas Reckwitz, *The Invention of Creativity: Modern Society and the Culture of the New*, trans. Steven Black (Cambridge: Polity, 2017).
17 Under modern conditions, the social logic of singularities is often (if not always) associated with a regime of cultural novelty. The aestheticization of the social can be understood as an element of the culturalization of the social.

I Modernity Between the Social Logic of the General and the Social Logic of the Particular

1 The Social Logic of the General

1 Rather than being obsolete, the theory of functional differentiation and that of capitalism are still effective for analyzing *structural elements* of societies that are characterized by formal rationalization.
2 See Max Weber, *Economy and Society: An Outline of Interpretive Sociology*, trans. Guenther Roth and Claus Wittich (Berkeley: University of California Press, 1978); and Wolfgang Schluchter, *The Rise of Western Rationalism: Max Weber's Developmental History*, trans. Guenther Roth (Berkeley: University of California Press, 1981).
3 See, for instance, Georg Simmel, *The Philosophy of Money: Third Enlarged Edition*, trans. Tom Bottomore and David Frisby (London: Routledge, 2004); Martin Heidegger, "The Age of the World Picture," in *The Question Concerning Technology and Other Essays*, trans. William Lovitt (New York: Harper & Row, 1977), pp. 115–36; Theodor W. Adorno and Max Horkheimer, *Dialectic of Enlightenment*, trans. John Cumming (New York: Verso, 1979); Hans Blumenberg, *The Legitimacy of the Modern Age*, trans. Robert M. Wallace (Cambridge, MA: MIT Press, 1983); Michel Foucault, *Discipline and Punish: The Birth of the Prison*, trans. Alan Sheridan (New York: Vintage, 1977); and Zygmunt Bauman, *Modernity and Ambivalence* (Cambridge: Polity, 1991).
4 On normality and normalism, see Jürgen Link, *Versuch über den Normalismus: Wie Normalität produziert wird*, 5th edn. (Göttingen: Vandenhoeck & Ruprecht, 2013).
5 See Alfred Schütz and Thomas Luckmann, *The Structures of the Life-World*, 2 vols., trans. Richard M. Zaner et al. (Evanston, IL: Northwestern University Press, 1973–89).
6 Similarities thus operate outside of the dualistic logic of identity and difference. See Anil Bhatti et al., "Ähnlichkeit: Ein kulturtheoretisches Paradigma," *Internationales Archiv für Sozialgeschichte der Literatur* 36 (2011), pp. 261–75.

7 For such broad understanding of *techne*, see Hans Blumenberg, *Schriften zur Technik* (Berlin: Suhrkamp, 2015). On the traditional rationalization of religion and law, see the fifth and sixth chapters of Weber's *Economy and Society*.
8 On the awareness of contingency, see Michael Makropoulos, *Modernität und Kontingenz* (Munich: Fink, 1997).
9 See also John Law, *Organizing Modernity: Social Ordering and Social Theory* (Oxford: Blackwell, 1994).
10 On the notion of progress, see Reinhart Koselleck, *Futures Past: On the Semantics of Historical Time*, trans. Keith Tribe (New York: Columbia University Press, 2004).
11 On this complex, see David F. Noble, *America by Design: Science, Technology, and the Rise of Corporate Capitalism* (New York: Oxford University Press, 1979); and Yehouda Shenhav, *Manufacturing Rationality: The Engineering Foundations of the Managerial Revolution* (Oxford University Press, 1999).
12 See H. Floris Cohen, *Scientific Revolution: A Historiographical Inquiry* (University of Chicago Press, 1994); and Stephen Toulmin, *Cosmopolis: The Hidden Agenda of Modernity* (University of Chicago Press, 1990).
13 See Link, *Versuch über den Normalismus*.
14 The classic treatment of this subject is Norbert Elias, *The Civilizing Process: Sociogenetic and Psychogenetic Investigations*, rev. edn., trans. Edmund Jephcott (Oxford: Blackwell, 2000). Regarding organized modernity, see Peter N. Stearns, *American Cool: Constructing a Twentieth-Century Emotional Style* (New York University Press, 1994). Of course, the reduction of affect does not mean its absence. In fact, rational complexes often have an emotional aspect, for instance the desire to create an orderly bureaucracy or the aesthetic pleasure taken in the symmetry of architecture.
15 See Geert J. Somsen, "A History of Universalism: Conceptions of the Internationality of Science from the Enlightenment to the Cold War," *Minerva* 46 (2008), pp. 361–79.
16 I will keep the question open about which elements or entities in fact "assemble" the social. For further discussion of this issue, see Bruno Latour's *Reassembling the Social: An Introduction to Actor-Network-Theory* (Oxford University Press, 2005).
17 See Kopytoff, "The Cultural Biography of Things." The classical locus of criticism against the standardization of the world of objects has been the arts-and-crafts movement.
18 On both models, see Riesman, *The Lonely Crowd*.
19 I will treat this concept in greater detail in the next chapter.
20 This is the effect of individualization that, according to Foucault's *Discipline and Punish*, characterizes disciplinary societies. Notably, Simmel associated this sort of individualism with freedom and equality; see, for instance, Georg Simmel, *Sociology: Inquiries into the Construction of Social Forms*, trans. Anthony J. Blasi et al. (Leiden: Brill, 2009), pp. 637–8.
21 For a clear discussion of this phenomenon in the twentieth century, see Theo Hilpert, *Die funktionelle Stadt: Le Corbusiers Stadtvision – Bedingungen, Motive, Hintergründe* (Braunschweig: F. Vieweg und Sohn, 1979).
22 See Marc Augé, *Non-Places: Introduction to an Anthropology of Supermodernity*, trans. John Howe (New York: Verso, 1995). It could be said in short that, according to the social logic of the general, *all* spaces are non-places.
23 See Barbara Adam, *Time and Social Theory* (Cambridge: Polity, 1994), pp. 123–5.
24 See Weber, *Economy and Society*; and Niklas Luhmann, *Legitimität durch Verfahren* (Frankfurt am Main: Suhrkamp, 1969).
25 See Jürgen Habermas, "Labour and Interaction: Remarks on Hegel's Jena Philosophy of Mind," in *Theory and Practice*, trans. John Viertel (London: Heinemann, 1974), pp. 142–69.
26 I refer to the first two phases of modernity as classical modernity because the social logic of the general is dominant in both of them.

27 German Idealism, within whose framework the particular can only be the general-particular, represents the high point of the philosophical foundation of the logic of the general.
28 On this phase, see also Andreas Reckwitz, *Das hybride Subjekt: Eine Theorie der Subjektkulturen von der bürgerlichen Moderne zur Postmoderne* (Weilerwist: Velbrück Wissenschaften, 2006), pp. 336–439; Peter Wagner, *A Sociology of Modernity: Liberty and Discipline* (London: Routledge, 1994), pp. 73–122; and Scott Lash and John Urry, *The End of Organized Capitalism* (Cambridge: Polity, 1987), pp. 17–87. Here I use the terms "organized modernity" and "industrial modernity" synonymously.
29 On the concepts of Americanism and Fordism, see Antonio Gramsci, *Selections from the Prison Notebooks*, trans. Quentin Hoare and Geoffrey Nowell Smith (New York: International Publishers, 1971), pp. 277–318. On the concept of organized capitalism, see Rudolf Hilferding, *Organisierter Kapitalismus* (Kiel, 1927).
30 See Alfred D. Chandler, *The Visible Hand: The Managerial Revolution in American Business* (Cambridge, MA: Belknap Press, 1977); and Maury Klein, *The Flowering of the Third America: The Making of Organizational Society, 1850–1920* (Chicago, IL: Ivan R. Dee, 1993).
31 See Raymond Aron, *18 Lectures on Industrial Society*, trans. M. K. Bottomore (London: Weidenfeld & Nicholson, 1967).
32 See Cecelia Tichi, *Shifting Gears: Technology, Literature, Culture in Modernist America* (Chapel Hill: University of North Carolina Press, 1987); and Thomas P. Hughes, *American Genesis: A Century of Invention and Technological Enthusiasm, 1870–1970* (New York: Viking, 1989).
33 See John Kenneth Galbraith, *The Affluent Society*, 2nd edn. (London: Hamilton, 1969). Regarding the *trente glorieuses*, see Jean Fourastié, *Les trente glorieuses, ou la révolution invisible de 1946 à 1975* (Paris: Fayard, 1979).
34 On the state, see Pierre Rosanvallon, *The Society of Equals*, trans. Arthur Goldhammer (Cambridge, MA: Harvard University Press, 2013). On the city, see Hilpert, *Die funktionelle Stadt*.
35 On my discussion below, see William Graebner, *The Engineering of Consent: Democracy and Authority in Twentieth-Century America* (Madison: University of Wisconsin Press, 1987); William H. Whyte, *The Organization Man* (New York: Simon and Schuster, 1956); and Riesman, *The Lonely Crowd*.
36 See Martin Kohli, "Gesellschaftszeit und Lebenszeit: Der Lebenslauf im Strukturwandel," in *Die Moderne: Kontinuitäten und Zäsuren*, ed. Johannes Berger (Göttingen: Schwartz, 1986), pp. 183–204.
37 On the construction of abnormality, see Michel Foucault, *Abnormal: Lectures at the Collège de France, 1974–1975*, trans. Graham Burchell (New York: Verso, 2003); Howard Saul Becker, *Outsiders: Studies in the Sociology of Deviance* (New York: Free Press, 1963); and Bauman, *Modernity and Ambivalence*.
38 On the level of subjects, de-singularization is not the same thing as de-individualization. As an achievement society, organized modernity was based through and through on the post-traditional self-responsibility of subjects, which Georg Simmel referred to as the "individualism of freedom and responsibility." Thus, it cannot be said that organized modernity was characterized by de-individualization.

2 The Social Logic of the Particular

1 This *déformation professionnelle* is also a legacy from Western philosophy, whose thinking prioritizes the general (at least at its rational and theoretical core from Aristotle to Kant and Hegel). Philosophers who, in various ways, have focused instead on the singular or individual include Spinoza and Deleuze, and in some respects Kierkegaard and Stirner as well.
2 The term has appeared sporadically in scholarly literature, but never with a

consistent meaning. The way that I employ it here is inspired by Kopytoff and Karpic, though they apply it more narrowly and primarily to objects. See Kopytoff, "The Cultural Biography of Things"; and Karpik, *Valuing the Unique*. In *The Society of Equals* (pp. 360–6), Rosanvallon applies the term to subjects. On the earlier history of the concept, above all as it was used in late-medieval and early-modern philosophy (uses which are of no concern to me here), see Klaus Mainzer, "Singulär/Singularität," in *Historisches Wörterbuch der Philosophie*, vol. IX, ed. Joachim Ritter et al. (Basel: Schwabe, 1995), pp. 798–808. In a different, normatively laden, form, which I also do not draw upon, the concept has also been used by post-structuralist authors such as Jacques Derrida, Gilles Deleuze, Jean-Luc Nancy, and Antonio Negri.
3 Kant, *Critique of the Power of Judgement*, pp. 271–84.
4 This is the position to which Deleuze and Guattari are inclined. See Gilles Deleuze and Félix Guattari, *A Thousand Plateaus: Capitalism and Schizophrenia*, trans. Brian Massumi (Minneapolis: University of Minnesota Press, 1987). Here I have no interest in entering an ontological discussion about the stakes of idiosyncrasies, which would be of no use to the sociology of singularities.
5 As you have come to see, my analytical framework is fundamentally praxeological. On this approach, see Andreas Reckwitz, "Toward a Theory of Social Practices: A Development in Culturalist Theorizing," *European Journal of Social Theory* 5 (2002), pp. 243–63; the articles collected in Hilmar Schäfer, ed., *Praxistheorie: Ein soziologisches Forschungsprogramm* (Bielefeld: Transcript, 2016); and Theodore Schatzki, *Social Practices: A Wittgensteinian Approach to Human Activity and the Social* (Cambridge University Press, 2009).
6 On the concept of complexity, see, for instance, John Holland, *Hidden Order: How Adaption Builds Complexity* (Reading, MA: Basic Books, 1995); and, from a different angle, Niklas Luhmann, "Komplexität," in Luhmann, *Soziologische Aufklärung 2: Aufsätze zur Theorie der Gesellschaft* (Opladen: Westdeutscher Verlag, 1975), pp. 204–20. The concept features strongly in the tradition of systems theory, which I do not follow. The notion of density was developed by Nelson Goodman in his *Languages of Art: An Approach to a Theory of Symbols* (Indianapolis, IN: Bobbs-Merrill, 1968). Goodman, however, understood the concept in purely art-historical terms, whereas I use it more generally.
7 See Ferdinand de Saussure, *Course in General Linguistics*, trans. Roy Harris (London: Duckworth, 1990). This idea was the basis of all of semiotics and structuralism (up to Pierre Bourdieu's logic of distinction).
8 Within the context of the theory of science, the concept of incommensurability was established by Thomas Kuhn and Paul Feyerabend. See Thomas S. Kuhn, *The Structure of Scientific Revolution*, 4th edn. (University of Chicago Press, 2015); and Paul Feyerabend, *Against Method: Outline of an Anarchist Theory of Knowledge*, 4th edn. (London: Verso, 2010).
9 This topic will be addressed in Part II, chapter 2.
10 When this no longer happens to be the case, then the singularity in question simply joins the register of the general-particular. This is, of course, a possibility and, as I will describe later in greater detail, it implies devaluation. Over the course of this book, whenever I use the term "the particular" without comment, it is meant to denote singularities / unique entities. Whenever I am discussing idiosyncrasies or the general-particular, I use these terms explicitly.
11 Translational processes of this sort are discussed with different terminology in Michael Thompson's *Rubbish Theory*.
12 On this heterogeneous semantic field, see Flavia Kippele, *Was heißt Individualisierung? Die Antworten soziologischer Klassiker* (Opladen: Westdeutscher Verlag, 1998); Thomas Kron and Martin Horáček, *Individualisierung* (Bielefeld: Transcript, 2009); and, for its narrower and yet interdisciplinary approach, Manfred Frank and Anselm Haverkamp, eds., *Individualität* (Munich: Fink, 1988).
13 See Simmel, *Sociology*, pp. 621–66.

14 It should be noted that Simmel already relates the concept of the individual not only to subjects but also to their social circles (see ibid., p. 621).
15 Objects always have a material basis. The distinction between objects and things is contested; in general, the concept of the thing underscores the delineable materiality of an object. Yet for certain objects – such as novels, myths, or songs – it is characteristic that they are not associated with a single material bearer but can rather materialize in various forms. On this topic, see Gustav Roßler, *Der Anteil der Dinge an der Gesellschaft: Sozialität – Kognition – Netzwerke* (Bielefeld: Transcript, 2015).
16 See Walter Benjamin, "The Work of Art in the Age of Its Technological Reproducibility: Third Version," in *Selected Writings: Volume 4, 1938–1940*, ed. Howard Eiland and Michael W. Jennings (Cambridge, MA: Harvard University Press, 2003), pp. 251–83.
17 The objects of aesthetics, literary theory, music theory, or theology are thus to a large extent singularities in this sense. For a somewhat rhapsodizing historical look at the singularity of things, see Neil MacGregor, *A History of the World in 100 Objects* (New York: Penguin, 2013). For a more theoretically informed approach, see Sherry Turkle, *Evocative Objects: Things We Think With* (Cambridge, MA: MIT Press, 2011).
18 On the concept of style, see Hans Ulrich Gumbrecht and K. Ludwig Pfeiffer, eds., *Stil: Geschichten und Funktionen eines kulturwissenschaftlichen Diskurselements* (Frankfurt am Main: Suhrkamp, 1986); and Dick Hebdige, *Subculture: The Meaning of Style* (London: Routledge, 1979).
19 See Bruno Baur, *Biodiversität* (Bern: Haupt, 2010).
20 Regarding objects, this book will look extensively at cultural goods from the economic sphere and their appropriation for the sake of lifestyles (food or living situations, for instance).
21 In this regard, see the articles collected in Richard van Dülmen, ed., *Entdeckung des Ich: Die Geschichte der Individualisierung vom Mittelalter bis zur Gegenwart* (Cologne: Böhlau, 2001).
22 In Foucault's sense of the term, which I have borrowed here, subjectification should not be confused with singularization. In the social logic of the general, subjectification operates in a different direction.
23 See Weber, *Economy and Society*, pp. 241–5.
24 See Verena Krieger, *Was ist ein Künstler? Genie – Heilsbringer – Antikünstler: Eine Ideen- und Kunstgeschichte des Schöpferischen* (Cologne: Deubner, 2007); and Nathalie Heinich, *L'élite artiste: Excellence et singularité en régime démocratique* (Paris: Gallimard, 2005).
25 In this book, the singularization of subjects will be analyzed extensively as it relates to the lifestyle of the new middle class (Part V, Chapter 1), to the way that working subjects are profiled (Part III, Chapter 2), and to digitalization (Part IV).
26 Despite all my skepticism about the usefulness of the semantics of individualism, the question is whether it still has any analytic value. The answer is yes, but only when the concept of individualization is clearly related to the social logic of the general and is thus understood as a complementary concept to singularization. In late modernity, individualization and singularization are undoubtedly closely associated with one another, but this connection can only be investigated if both processes are treated as clearly distinct concepts.
27 On the distinction between space and place, see Yi-Fu Tuan, *Space and Place: The Perspective of Experience* (Minneapolis: University of Minnesota Press, 1977).
28 On the intrinsic logic of cities, see Martina Löw, *Soziologie der Städte* (Frankfurt am Main: Suhrkamp, 2008).
29 See Pierre Nora, *Realms of Memory*, 3 vols., trans. Arthur Goldhammer (New York: Columbia University Press, 1996–8); and Gernot Böhme, *The Aesthetics of Atmospheres*, ed. Jean-Paul Thibaud (London: Routledge, 2017). In this book, I will go into greater detail about the singularization of places as it relates

to the late-modern city, but also as it relates to lifestyles, travel, and living situations.
30 On the concept of presence, see Hans Ulrich Gumbrecht, *Production of Presence: What Meaning Cannot Say* (Stanford University Press, 2004).
31 On rituals, see Victor W. Turner, *The Ritual Process: Structure and Anti-Structure* (London: Routledge, 1969); on events, see Winfried Gebhardt, *Fest, Feier und Alltag: Über die gesellschaftliche Wirklichkeit des Menschen und ihre Deutung* (Frankfurt am Main: Peter Lang, 1987); on being oriented toward the present moment, see Karl Heinz Bohrer, *Der romantische Brief: Die Entstehung ästhetischer Subjektivität* (Frankfurt am Main: Suhrkamp, 1989); and, more generally, see John Urry, *Sociology Beyond Societies: Mobilities for the Twenty-First Century* (London: Routledge, 2000). Later, I will discuss the singularization of time as it relates to cultural goods, the economy, professional projects, and lifestyles.
32 On aesthetic communities, see Michel Maffesoli, *The Time of the Tribes: The Decline of Individualism in Mass Society*, trans. Don Smith (London: Sage, 1996); on the nation, see Bernhard Giesen, *Nationale und kulturelle Identität: Studien zur Entwicklung des kollektiven Bewußtseins in der Neuzeit* (Frankfurt am Main: Suhrkamp, 1991); and on recent identity movements, see Manuel Castells, *The Power of Identity*, 2nd edn. (Oxford: Blackwell, 1997). In this book I will revisit the topic of neo-communities at length in Part VI, Chapter 2 (which concerns their role in late-modern politics), and more briefly in Part IV (which addresses how they relate to digital communities).
33 See Latour, *Reassembling the Social*, p. 72. The concept of affordance was first formulated by James J. Gibson in his book *The Senses Considered as Perceptual Systems* (Boston, MA: Houghton Mifflin, 1966).
34 The phrase is from René Pollesch, "Lob des litauischen Regieassistenten im grauen Kittel," in *Kreation und Depression: Freiheit im gegenwärtigen Kapitalismus*, ed. Christoph Menke and Juliane Rebentisch (Berlin: Kadmos, 2016), pp. 243–9.
35 Here, observation is used as an overarching concept for the practices of representation and understanding.
36 This can require a tentative inclination toward interpretations that are not self-evident but rather have to be reached through a sort of open-ended inquiry (as in interpretations of works of art, people, and so on). On the concept of interpretation, see Umberto Eco, *The Open Work*, trans. Anna Cancogni (Cambridge, MA: Harvard University Press, 1989).
37 The same can be said of any orientation toward the general, which can also be systematically fostered or inhibited.
38 On processes of evaluation and the field of "valuation studies," see Michèle Lamont, "Toward a Comparative Sociology of Valuation and Evaluation," *Annual Review of Sociology* 38 (2012), pp. 201–21.
39 This distinction stems from Émile Durkheim's *The Elementary Forms of Religious Life*, trans. Joseph Ward Swain (London: G. Allen & Unwin, 1915), though I use it more generally here. See also Michael Thompson's *Rubbish Theory*, in which a distinction is drawn between goods of lasting value, goods that lose their value, and "rubbish."
40 In this regard, see also Boris Groys, *On the New*, trans. G. M. Goshgarian (London: Verso, 2014). It should be kept in mind, however, that the discovery and reframing of idiosyncrasies can itself become an independent and complex *production* process (the efforts of the music industry to find new local music is an example of this, as is the attempt to turn something into a classic design by reframing the narrative around it).
41 See Maurizio Lazzarato, "Immaterial Labor," in *Radical Thought in Italy: A Potential Politics*, ed. Paolo Virno and Michael Hardt (Minneapolis: University of Minnesota Press, 1996), pp. 133–48.
42 In archaic and traditional societies, for instance, the cultural sphere is not oriented toward innovation.

43 Appropriation is an umbrella term for the practices of dealing with objects, subjects, etc. Such practices include, for instance, utilization and reception.
44 For various approaches to the concept of lived experience, which has a rich tradition, see Georg Simmel, "Die historische Formung," in Simmel, *Aufsätze und Abhandlungen, 1909–1918* (Frankfurt am Main: Suhrkamp, 2000), pp. 321–69; Alfred Schütz, *The Phenomenology of the Social World*, trans. George Walsh and Frederick Lehnert (Evanston, IL: Northwestern University Press, 1967), pp. 215–17; and Gerhard Schulze, *Die Erlebnisgesellschaft: Kultursoziologie der Gegenwart* (Frankfurt am Main: Campus, 1992), pp. 34–88.
45 On this matter, see Brian Massumi, *Parables for the Virtual: Movement, Affect, Sensation* (Durham, NC: Duke University Press, 2007); and Michaela Ott, *Affizierung: Zu einer ästhetisch-epistemischen Figur* (Munich: Edition Text + Kritik, 2010). Under the concept of "resonance," Hartmut Rosa has discussed a specifically normative form of affecting; see his book *Resonance: A Sociology of Our Relationship to the World* (Cambridge: Polity, 2019).
46 Under certain conditions, practices of lived experience can acquire an especially intensive form. In an experience in the narrow sense, the subject structure of the participating individuals can be transformed, or emotions can be felt that had never been felt before. See, for instance, Victor Turner's discussion of liminal experiences in his book *The Ritual Process*.
47 On performativity, see Erika Fischer-Lichte, ed., *Performativität und Ereignis* (Tübingen: Francke, 2003); and Jörg Volbers, *Performative Kultur: Eine Einführung* (Wiesbaden: Springer, 2014).
48 On the affectivity of things, see Luc Ciompi, *Die emotionalen Grundlagen des Denkens: Entwurf einer fraktalen Affektlogik* (Göttingen: Vandenhoeck & Ruprecht, 1997); and Andreas Reckwitz, "Practices and Their Affects," in *The Nexus of Practices: Connections, Constellations, Practitioners*, ed. Allison Hui et al. (London: Routledge, 2017), pp. 114–25.

3 Culture and Culturalization

1 See Raymond Williams, *Culture and Society, 1780–1950* (London: Chatto & Windus, 1958).
2 For further discussion of these concepts of culture, see Andreas Reckwitz, *Die Transformation der Kulturtheorie: Zur Entwicklung eines Theorieprogramms* (Weilerwist: Velbrück Wissenschaft, 2000), pp. 64–89. There, however, I espoused the meaning-oriented concept of culture, which no longer seems sufficient to me.
3 In this regard, see Reckwitz, *Die Transformation der Kulturtheorie*; and Doris Bachmann-Medick, *Cultural Turns: New Orientations in the Study of Culture* (Berlin: De Gruyter, 2016). This understanding of the cultural is identical with the fourth concept of culture mentioned above, which relates culture to the symbolic and meaningful conditionality of ways of life.
4 The idea that culture exists for its own sake can be traced as far back as Aristotle (*praxis* versus *poiesis*). Later, it would be adopted by aesthetic theory and by ethics as well (though not in a different way).
5 This classical–normative concept of culture can be found, for instance, in the works of Matthew Arnold and Georg Simmel. See Arnold's *Culture and Anarchy: An Essay in Political and Social Criticism* (London: John Murray, 1949); and Simmel's "The Concept and Tragedy of Culture," in *Simmel on Culture: Selected Writings*, ed. David Frisby and Mike Featherstone (London: Sage, 1997), pp. 55–74. For further discussion of this topic, see also Clemens Albrecht, "Die Substantialität bürgerlicher Kultur," in *Bürgerlichkeit ohne Bürgertum: In welchem Land leben wir?* ed. Heinz Bude et al. (Munich: W. Fink, 2010), pp. 131–44.
6 For a praxeological understanding of value, see John Dewey, *Theory of Valuation* (Chicago: University of Illinois Press, 1939). For perspectives from today's "valuation studies," see Fabian Muniesa, "A Flank Movement in the

Understanding of Valuation," in *Measure and Value*, ed. Lisa Adkins and Celia Lury (Oxford: Wiley-Blackwell, 2012), pp. 24–38; and Michel Callon et al., "The Economy of Qualities," *Economy and Society* 31 (2002), pp. 194–217. For a cultural-anthropological perspective, see Thompson, *Rubbish Theory*. Interesting, too, in this regard, is Isabelle Graw, "The Value of the Art Commodity: Twelve Theses on Human Labor, Mimetic Desire, and Aliveness," *ARQ* 97 (2017), pp. 130–45.

7 On the ways in which valorization and de-valorization are related to domination and social class, see Skeggs, *Class, Self, Culture*.

8 This issue pertains to the attention economy, which I will discuss in greater detail in the next Part. Indifference means not paying attention.

9 Regarding serial killers, see David Schmid, *Natural Born Celebrities: Serial Killers in American Culture* (University of Chicago Press, 2008); on troublemakers, see Dieter Thomä, *Troublemakers: A Philosophy of Puer Robustus* (Cambridge: Polity, 2019); and, regarding stigma, see Erving Goffman, *Stigma: Notes on the Management of Spoiled Identity* (New York: Touchstone Press, 1986).

10 See Julia Kristeva, *Powers of Horror: An Essay on Abjection* (New York: Columbia University Press, 1982).

11 See Alfred Weber, *Fundamentals of Culture-Sociology: Social Process, Civilization Process, and Culture-Movement*, trans. G. H. Weltner and C. F. Hirshman (New York: Columbia University Press, 1939). Here and elsewhere (in Simmel's works, for instance), culture is openly associated with vitality, or also with spiritual matters.

12 Of course, this affectivity can be theorized in very different ways, be it psychoanalytically or vitalistically. See, for instance, Massumi's influential book *Parables for the Virtual*.

13 See Georges Bataille, *The Accursed Share: An Essay on General Economy*, trans. Robert Hurley (New York: Zone Books, 1988); and Roger Caillois, *Man, Play, and Games*, trans. Meyer Barash (Chicago: University of Illinois Press, 2001). In this regard, see also Stephan Moebius, *Die Zauberlehrlinge: Soziologiegeschichte des Collège de Sociologie* (Konstanz: UVK Verlagsgesellschaft, 2006). According to Rüdiger Safranski, the opposition between rationalization and culturalization was also influential in Nietzsche's work; see Rüdiger Safranski, *Nietzsche: A Philosophical Biography*, trans. Shelley Frisch (New York: W. W. Norton, 2002).

14 For a somewhat different understanding of this concept, see Karl H. Hörning, *Doing Culture: Neue Positionen zum Verhältnis von Kultur und sozialer Praxis* (Bielefeld: Transcript, 2004).

15 Niklas Luhmann's theory of functional differentiation in modernity, for instance, does not grant any systematic place to culture (a dimension that Talcott Parsons always recognized).

16 On this topic, see Helmut Brackert and Fritz Wefelmeyer, eds., *Kultur: Bestimmungen im 20. Jahrhundert* (Frankfurt am Main: Suhrkamp, 1990).

17 See Albrecht Koschorke, *Fact and Fiction: Elements of a General Theory of Narrative*, trans. Joel Golb (Berlin: De Gruyter, 2018); and Vera Nünning and Ansgar Nünning, eds., *Erzähltheorie transgenerisch, intermedial, interdisziplinär* (Trier: Wissenschaftlicher Verlag, 2002).

18 See Andreas Reckwitz et al., eds., *Ästhetik und Gesellschaft: Grundlagentexte aus Soziologie und Kulturwissenschaften* (Berlin: Suhrkamp, 2015); Andreas Reckwitz, "Ästhetik und Gesellschaft: Ein analytischer Bezugsrahmen," in *Ästhetik und Gesellschaft*, ed. Reckwitz et al., pp. 13–52; and Karlheinz Barck, ed., *Aisthesis: Wahrnehmung heute oder Perspektiven einer neuen Ästhetik* (Leipzig: Reclam, 1998).

19 To be precise, the ethical quality is related to the narrative quality, the ludic quality is related to the aesthetic quality, and the creative quality is related to both.

20 See Wilhelm Schmid, *Philosophie der Lebenskunst: Eine Grundlegung* (Frankfurt am Main: Suhrkamp, 2003), pp. 60–70; and Charles Taylor, *Sources of the Self:*

The Making of Modern Identity (Cambridge, MA: Harvard University Press, 1989), pp. 3–110.
21 This does not necessarily have to be the case. The practices of producing singularities can also be undertaken in such a way that no specific value is attributed to them *as* production practices.
22 "Design" is not a widespread term in cultural theory and the social sciences. See, however, Claudia Mareis, *Theorien des Designs zur Einführung* (Hamburg: Junius, 2014).
23 See Alfred Schäfer and Christiane Thompson, eds., *Spiel* (Paderborn: Schöningh, 2014). On the general cultural-theoretical significance of games, see also Michael Hutter, *The Rise of the Joyful Economy: Artistic Invention and Economic Growth from Brunelleschi to Murakami* (New York: Routledge, 2015).
24 As to which dimension happens to be stronger in a given case, this is an empirical question.

4 The Transformation of the Cultural Sphere

1 Social-theoretical interpretations of archaic societies are controversial. For antipodal views, see Deleuze and Guattari, *A Thousand Plateaus*, which stresses the aspect of idiosyncrasies, and the third chapter of Talcott Parsons's *Societies: Evolutionary and Comparative Perspectives* (Englewood Cliffs, NJ: Prentice Hall, 1966), which focuses primarily on collectivism.
2 Consider, for example, the openness with which transgender persons are treated in native American societies. See Sue-Ellen Jacobs et al., eds., *Two-Spirit People: Native American Gender Identity, Sexuality, and Spirituality* (Urbana: University of Illinois Press, 2005).
3 See Durkheim, *The Elementary Forms of Religious Life*; Michel Leiris, *Ethnologische Schriften I: Die eigene und die fremde Kultur*, ed. Hans-Jürgen Heinrichs (Frankfurt am Main: Suhrkamp, 1985); and Turner, *The Ritual Process*. On totemism, see also Claude Lévi-Strauss, *Totemism*, trans. Rodney Needham (London: Merlin Press, 1964).
4 On traditional religious systems, see Max Weber, *The Sociology of Religion*, trans. Ephraim Fischoff (Boston, MA: Beacon Press, 1999); and Helmut von Glasenapp, *Die fünf Weltreligionen* (Cologne: Diederichs, 1985). On courtly cultures, see Norbert Elias, *The Court Society*, trans. Edmund Jephcott and Stephen Mennell (New York: Pantheon, 1983). On folk culture, see Mikhail Bakhtin, *Rabelais and His World*, trans. Hélène Iswolsky (Bloomington: Indiana University Press, 1984).
5 This is a multifaceted topic. See, for instance, Jan A. Aersten and Andreas Speer, eds., *Individuum und Individualität im Mittelalter* (Berlin: De Gruyter, 1996).
6 See, for example, Gottfried Kerscher, *Architektur als Repräsentation: Spätmittelalterliche Palastbaukunst zwischen Pracht und zeremoniellen Voraussetzungen* (Tübingen: Wasmuth, 2000).
7 See Chapter 1 in this Part.
8 See Manfred Hettling, "Bürgerliche Kultur: Bürgerlichkeit als kulturelles System," in *Sozial- und Kulturgeschichte des Bürgertums*, ed. Peter Lundgreen (Göttingen: Vandenhoeck & Ruprecht, 2000), pp. 319–40; Thomas Nipperday, *Wie das Bürgertum die Moderne fand* (Stuttgart: Reclam, 1998); and Dieter Hein and Andreas Schulz, eds., *Bürgerkultur im 19. Jahrhundert: Bildung, Kunst und Lebenswelt* (Munich: Beck, 1996).
9 See the second chapter of Reckwitz, *The Invention of Creativity*, as well as Pierre Bourdieu, *The Rules of Art: Genesis and Structure of the Literary Field*, trans. Susan Emanuel (Stanford University Press, 1996); and Oskar Bätschmann, *Ausstellungskünstler: Kult und Karriere im modernen Kunstsystem* (Cologne: DuMont, 1997).
10 See Georg Bollenbeck, *Bildung und Kultur: Glanz und Elend eines deutschen Deutungsmuster* (Frankfurt am Main: Suhrkamp, 2001).

11 See Reckwitz, *Das hybride Subjekt*, pp. 204–30; Lothar Pikulik, *Romantik als Ungenügen an der Normalität: Am Beispiel Tiecks, Hoffmanns, Eichendorffs* (Frankfurt am Main: Suhrkamp, 1979); Gerald N. Izenberg, *Impossible Individuality: Romanticism, Revolution, and the Origins of Modern Selfhood, 1787–1802* (Princeton University Press, 2001); Isaiah Berlin, *The Roots of Romanticism*, ed. Henry Hardy (Princeton University Press, 2014); and Taylor, *Sources of the Self*, pp. 368–92.
12 See Eric Hobsbawm, *Nations and Nationalism since 1780: Program, Myth, Reality* (Cambridge University Press, 1992); and Benedict Anderson, *Imagined Communities: Reflections on the Origin and Spread of Nationalism*, 2nd edn. (London: Verso, 1991). Regarding Asia in particular, see Pankaj Mishra, *From the Ruins of Empire: The Revolt Against the West and the Remaking of Asia* (London: Penguin, 2012).
13 See T. J. Jackson Lears, *Fables of Abundance: A Cultural History of Advertising in America* (New York: Basic Books, 1993); and Janet Ward, *Weimar Surfaces: Urban Visual Culture in 1920s Germany* (Berkeley: University of California Press, 2001).
14 See Georg Simmel, "Fashion," *The American Journal of Sociology* 62 (1957), pp. 541–8.
15 See Michael Makropoulos, "Massenkultur als Kontingenzkultur," in *Lautloses irren – Ways of Worldmaking Too ...*, ed. Harm Lux (Berlin: Harm Lux, 2003), pp. 151–73.
16 For further discussion of this phenomenon, see Reckwitz, *Das hybride Subjekt*, pp. 409–40. On consumption and imitation, see Whyte, *The Organization Man*, pp. 312–14.
17 In their book *Dialectic of Enlightenment*, however, Adorno and Horkheimer reduced the cinematic film to a place in which the commercial logic of the general could operate.
18 See Edgar Morin, *The Stars* (Minneapolis: University of Minnesota Press, 2005).
19 The "new middle class" has been analyzed from a number of different theoretical perspectives. From the perspective of the knowledge society, see Daniel Bell, *The Coming of Post-Industrial Society: A Venture in Social Forecasting* (New York: Basic Books, 1973); or Peter Drucker, *Post-Capitalist Society* (New York: Harper Business, 1994). From the perspective of post-Fordism, see Lazzarato's essay "Immaterial Labor," and Yann Moulier Boutang, *Cognitive Capitalism*, trans. Ed Emery (Cambridge: Polity, 2011).
20 See Ronald Inglehart, *The Silent Revolution: Changing Values and Political Styles Among Western Publics* (Princeton University Press, 1977); Paul Leinberger and Bruce Tucker, *The New Individualists: The Generation After the Organization Man* (New York: Harper Collins, 1991); and Daniel Bell, *The Cultural Contradictions of Capitalism* (New York: Basic Books, 1976). Recently, the transformation of values that has taken place in Germany has been empirically confirmed yet again – see Jutta Allmendinger, *Das Land, in dem wir leben wollen: Wie die Deutschen sich ihre Zukunft vorstellen* (Munich: Pantheon, 2017).
21 See Michael Piore and Charles Sabel, *The Second Industrial Divide: Possibilities for Prosperity* (New York: Basic Books, 1984); and David Harvey, *The Condition of Postmodernity: An Enquiry into the Origins of Cultural Change* (Oxford: Blackwell, 1989); pp. 121–200.
22 See Paul E. Ceruzzi, *A History of Modern Computing* (Cambridge, MA: MIT Press, 2003).
23 See Marion von Osten, ed., *Norm der Abweichung* (Zurich: Edition Voldemeer, 2003).

II The Post-Industrial Economy of Singularities

1 See Bell, *The Coming of Post-Industrial Society*; and Hartmut Häußermann and Walter Siebel, *Diensleistungsgesellschaften* (Frankfurt am Main: Suhrkamp,

1995). From 1950 to 2013 in (West) Germany, the percentage of employees working in the industrial sector dropped from 43 to 25 percent, whereas the proportion working in the service sector rose from 32 to 74 percent. See Statistiche Bundesamt, "Arbeitsmarkt: Erwerbstätige im Inland nach Wirtschaftssektoren," online. Between 1952 and 2015 in the United States, the percentage of employees working in the industrial and agricultural sectors fell from 47 to 14 percent, while the proportion of those working in the service industry increased from 53 to 70 percent. See Richard Henderson, "Industry Employment and Output Projections to 2024," *Bureau of Labor Statistics: Monthly Labor Review* (December 2015), online.
2 Although they stress different factors, theories of post-industrialism and post-Fordism offer similar approaches. See Krishan Kumar, *Prophecy and Progress: The Sociology of Industrial and Post-Industrial Society* (New York: Penguin, 1978); Ash Amin, ed., *Post-Fordism: A Reader* (Oxford: Blackwell, 1996); and Andrea Fumagalli and Stefano Lucarelli, "A Model of Cognitive Capitalism: A Preliminary Analysis," *European Journal of Economic and Social Systems* 20 (2007), pp. 117–33.
3 On classical industrial society as organized capitalism, see Lash and Urry, *The End of Organized Capitalism*. On what succeeded it, see the same authors' *Economies of Signs and Space* (London: Sage, 1994).
4 It is in this strict sense, which is related exclusively to services, that Lucien Karpik uses the term "economy of singularities" in *Valuing the Unique: The Economics of Singularities*.
5 The transformation of goods and markets will be discussed in greater detail in this Part, while the transformation of forms of labor and organization will be treated in the next one. Within the broader framework of lifestyles, the transformation of consumption will be addressed in my fifth Part.
6 On this circle of topics, see Richard Caves, *Creative Industries: Contracts Between Art and Commerce* (Cambridge, MA: Harvard University Press, 2000); David Hesmondhalgh and Sarah Baker, *Creative Labour: Media Work in Three Cultural Industries* (London: Routledge, 2011); Terry Flew, *The Creative Industries: Culture and Policy* (London: Sage, 2012); Rosamund Davies and Gauti Sigthorsson, *Introducing the Creative Industries: From Theory to Practice* (Los Angeles: Sage, 2013); and John Howkins, *The Creative Economy: How People Make Money from Ideas* (London: Penguin, 2001).
7 See Davies and Sigthorsson, *Introducing the Creative Industries*, pp. 8–10.
8 See Flew, *The Creative Industries*, p. 18; and Jens Christensen, *Global Experience Industries: The Business of Experience Economy* (Aarhus University Press, 2009).
9 See Reckwitz, *The Invention of Creativity*, pp. 164–82.
10 On the Terza Italia region, see Sebastiano Brusco, "The Emilian Model: Productive Decentralisation and Social Integration," *Cambridge Journal of Economics* 6 (1982), pp. 167–82; on youth-oriented cultural capitalism, see Angela McRobbie, *British Fashion Design: Rag Trade or Image Industry?* (London: Routledge, 1998); and on the IT scene, see Paul Freiberger and Michael Swaine, *Fire in the Valley: The Making of the Personal Computer* (New York: McGraw-Hill, 1999).
11 On the global corporations of the cultural economy, see Christensen's book *Global Experience Industries*.
12 Regarding agriculture, see Klaus-Werner Brand, ed., *Die neue Dynamik des Bio-Markts* (Munich: Oekom Verlag, 2006). On the automobile industry, see Mimi Sheller, "Automotive Emotions," *Theory, Culture & Society* 21 (2004), pp. 221–42. On watches as design objects, see Del Coates, *Watches Tell More Than Time: Product Design, Information, and the Quest for Elegance* (New York: McGraw-Hill, 2003). Regarding athletic shoes, see Elizabeth Semmelhack et al., *Out of the Box: The Rise of Sneaker Culture* (New York: Skira Rizzoli, 2015).
13 See Howkins, *The Creative Economy*.
14 See Lazzarato's essay "Immaterial Labor."

15 On the knowledge economy, see Drucker, *Post-Capitalist Society*; and Nico Stehr and Richard Ericson, eds., *The Culture and Power of Knowledge: Inquiries into Contemporary Societies* (Berlin: De Gruyter, 1992). On cognitive capitalism, see Isabell Lorey and Klaus Neundlinger, eds., *Kognitiver Kapitalismus* (Vienna: Turia + Kant, 2012).
16 In what follows, I will therefore make frequent use of the overarching formula "knowledge and culture economy."
17 See Pierre-Michel Menger, *Portrait de l'artiste en travailleur: Métamorphoses du capitalisme* (Paris: Seuil, 2002).
18 For further discussion of such services, see Friederike Bahl, *Lebensmodelle in der Dienstleistungsgesellschaft* (Hamburger Edition, 2014).
19 On the one hand, the economy of the standardized perpetuates the industrial tradition of production. On the other hand, however, the economy of the particular has shifted it in a new direction with its increased demand for "simple" services. On this phenomenon, see Saskia Sassen, "Dienstleistungsökonomien und die Beschäftigung von MigrantInnen in Städten," in *Migration und Stadt: Entwicklungen, Defizite und Potentiale*, ed. Klaus Schmals (Wiesbaden: Verlag für Sozialwissenschaften, 2000), pp. 87–114.

1 Unique Goods in Cultural Capitalism

1 G. L. S. Shackle, *Epistemics and Economics: A Critique of Economic Doctrines* (London: Transaction Publishers, 1972), p. 178 (emphasis original). See also Jens Beckert and Patrik Aspers, *The Worth of Goods: Valuation and Pricing in the Economy* (Oxford University Press, 2011).
2 The concept of the good is applicable not only to the commercial, monetarized economy but also to the constellations of competition and consumption in which the goods in question are religions (with their spiritualities), scientific theories (with their truths), places of residence (with their lifestyles), political parties (with their promises to identify with people), or "cultural goods" such as those designated as world heritage sites by UNESCO.
3 For an example of this mistake, see Pierre Bourdieu, *Distinction: A Social Critique of the Judgement of Taste*, trans. Richard Nice (Cambridge, MA: Harvard University Press, 1984). For a correct understanding of the matter, see Jens Beckert, "The Transcending Power of Goods: Imaginative Value in the Economy," in *The Worth of Goods*, ed. Beckert and Aspers, pp. 106–30. The specific social prestige of authenticity goods will be discussed in Part V.
4 On this aspect, see Rolf Jensen, *The Dream Society: How the Coming Shift from Information to Imagination Will Transform Your Business* (New York: McGraw-Hill, 2001); Petra Sammer, *Storytelling: Die Zukunft von PR und Marketing* (Cologne: O'Reilly, 2014); and Mark Gottdiener, *The Theming of America: Dreams, Visions, and Commercial Spaces* (Boulder, CO: Westview Press, 2001). At this point, it becomes clear to what extent religions and political world views have also become cultural goods under late-modern conditions.
5 On the symbolic character of goods, see Jean Baudrillard's early and pioneering study *Symbolic Exchange and Death*, trans. Iain Hamilton Grand (London: Sage, 1976).
6 On the matter of ethical consumption, see James G. Carrier, ed., *Ethical Consumption: Social Value and Economic Practice* (New York: Berghahn Books, 2015); and Jonas Grauel, *Gesundheit, Genuss und gutes Gewissen: Über Lebensmittelkonsum und Alltagsmoral* (Bielefeld: Transcript, 2014).
7 This aspect has been discussed widely in terms of aestheticization. See Gilles Lipovetsky, *L'esthétisation du monde: Vivre à l'âge du capitalisme artiste* (Paris: Gallimard, 2016); and Joseph B. Pine and James Gilmore, *The Experience Economy: Work is Theatre and Every Business is a Stage* (Boston, MA: Harvard Business School Press, 2006).

8 See Tim Brown, *Change by Design: How Design Thinking Transforms Organizations and Inspires Innovation* (New York: Collins Business, 2009).
9 See Nora Stampfl, *Die verspielte Gesellschaft: Gamification oder Leben im Zeitalter des Computerspiels* (Hanover: Heise, 2012).
10 The functional and cultural natures of goods are not mutually exclusive but can rather be combined. In this regard, it is important to keep in mind the distinction between culture and the cultural. In a broad sense, the "cultural" also includes functional goods as well as the distinction between culture and functionality itself, and this is because the way that goods are used depends on culturally specific contexts that define how things are used in a functional manner. In a genuine and strict sense, cultural goods are those that, from the perspective of recipients, possess an independent value and one or more of the cultural qualities discussed above.
11 Then, cultural goods could be found among the aristocracy and (in a different way) in bohemian subcultures. This is not to suggest, however, that the bourgeoisie did not cultivate its own cultural goods (though these were mostly "imported" from the aristocracy).
12 On this matter, see Konrad Paul Liessmann, *Das Universum der Dinge: Zur Ästhetik des Alltäglichen* (Vienna: Paul Zsolnay Verlag, 2010).
13 See Guy Julier, *The Culture of Design* (London: Sage, 2000).
14 See Böhme, *The Aesthetics of Atmospheres*.
15 See Häußermann and Siebel, *Dienstleistungsgesellschaft*.
16 Shoshana Zuboff and James Maxmin, *The Support Economy: Why Corporations Are Failing Individuals and the Next Episode of Capitalism* (London: Penguin, 2004). See also Jacques de Bandt and Jean Gadrey, eds., *Relations de service, marchés de services* (Paris: CNRS, 1998).
17 This phenomenon has been referred to as "medialization" or "mediatization." See Andreas Hepp et al., eds., *Medienkultur im Wandel* (Konstanz: UVK Verlagsgesellschaft, 2010).
18 On event culture, see Winfried Gebhardt et al., eds., *Events: Soziologie des Außergewöhnlichen* (Opladen: Leske + Budrich, 2000).
19 Conversely, primarily functional goods can also become the object of tailored singularization or customized production. A good example of this particular shift is so-called "maker culture." See Chris Anderson, *Makers: The New Industrial Revolution* (New York: Crown Business, 2012).
20 See Jens Häseler, "Original/Originalität," in *Ästhetische Grundbegriffe*, vol. IV, ed. Karlheinz Barck (Stuttgart: Metzler, 2002), pp. 638–55. A foundational early study was Edward Young's *Conjectures on Original Composition* (London: A. Millar, 1759). As early as 1797, Friedrich Schlegel even formulated a critique of the orientation toward originality and the interesting; see his book *On the Study of Greek Poetry*, trans. Stuart Barnett (Albany: State University of New York Press, 2001).
21 It is thus no surprise that the concept of uniqueness has been such a hotly debated topic in the modern theory of art – a debate initiated by Walter Benjamin's essay "The Work of Art in the Age of Its Technological Reproducibility."
22 This is especially true of a new type of luxury goods whose value derives from their rare historicity and which, according to a recent analysis by Boltanski and Esquerre, are characteristic of post-industrial capitalism. See Luc Boltanski and Arnaud Esquerre, *Enrichissement: Une critique de la marchandise* (Paris: Gallimard, 2017).
23 On this topic, see Mario Pricken, *Die Aura des Wertvollen: Produkte entsehen im Unternehmen, Werte im Kopf – 80 Strategien* (Erlangen: Publicis, 2014).
24 See Bonnie English, *A Cultural History of Fashion in the Twentieth Century: From the Catwalk to the Sidewalk* (New York: Berg, 2007); and Peter Dormer, *Design since 1945* (London: Thames and Hudson, 1993).
25 On the concept of style, see Gumbrecht and Pfeiffer, *Stil*.
26 On this topic, it is sufficient to read Pat Kirkham's book *Charles and Ray Eames: Designers of the Twentieth Century* (Cambridge, MA: MIT Press, 1995).

27 See Kopytoff, "The Cultural Biography of Things."
28 See Wolfgang Ullrich, *Siegerkunst: Neuer Adel, teure Lust* (Berlin: Klaus Wagenbach, 2016).
29 The production of unique objects with 3D printers belongs to this category as well, even though it lacks a hand-crafted and personal touch (see Anderson, *Makers*).
30 Another type of natural scarcity that comes to mind is the use of limited raw materials or resources (from Tibetan wool to prosciutto from Parma).
31 See Bandt and Gadrey's book *Relations de service*.
32 Arlie Russell Hochschild, *The Managed Heart: Commercialization of Human Feeling* (Berkeley: University of California Press, 1983).
33 A good example of this is hairstyling. For a long time, this was just a standardized and functional service (and thus low-paying), and then certain individual hairdressers managed to develop their own styles and thus transformed the standard good of the haircut into a singular, cultural good. In doing so, of course, they also earned prestige and higher pay. At the same time, however, there are also countervailing processes of de-singularization, which are accordingly associated with the reduction of a given service's prestige. Think of air travel, for instance, which was once an exclusive (and expensive) pleasure and has now become a means of mass and inexpensive transportation.
34 See Adorno and Horkheimer, *Dialectic of Enlightenment*, pp. 120–67.
35 There is an exception to this, however. If the media format in question becomes a live event and thus switches over, in a sense, to that category of goods, then it can have the quality of being non-recurring as well.
36 On seriality and the format of the series, see Frank Kelleter, ed., *Populäre Serialität: Narration, Evolution, Distinktion* (Bielefeld: Transcript, 2012); and Olaf Knellessen et al., eds., *Serialität: Wissenschaft, Kunst, Medien* (Vienna: Turia + Kant, 2015).
37 See Claus Pias, *Computer Game Worlds*, trans. Valentine A. Pakis (Zurich: Diaphanes, 2017).
38 On the topic of the fan, see Mark Duffett, *Understanding Fandom: An Introduction to the Study of Media Fan Culture* (New York: Bloomsbury, 2013); and Cheryl Harris and Alison Alexander, eds., *Theorizing Fandom: Fans, Subculture, and Identity* (Cresskill, NJ: Hampton Press, 1998).
39 It should be mentioned here that the *spectacle* is a special type of event, namely a public collective event with a particular abundance of atmosphere and excitement.
40 See Hans Ulrich Gumbrecht, *Präsenz* (Berlin: Suhrkamp, 2012).
41 On the history of the concept of authenticity, see Lionel Trilling, *Sincerity and Authenticity* (Cambridge, MA: Harvard University Press, 1972); and Charles Taylor, *The Malaise of Modernity* (Toronto: CBC, 1991), pp. 25–30.
42 On this concept, see Ernesto Laclau, "Why Do Empty Signifiers Matter to Politics?" in Laclau, *Emancipation(s)* (London: Verso, 1996), pp. 36–46.
43 On authenticity in late modernity, see Phillip Vannini and Patrick J. Williams, eds., *Authenticity in Culture, Self, and Society* (London: Routledge, 2016); and James H. Gilmore and Joseph Pine, *Authenticity: What Consumers Really Want* (Boston, MA: Harvard Business Review Press, 2015).
44 Richard Peterson, "In Search of Authenticity," *Journal of Management Studies* 42 (2005), pp. 1083–98.
45 Diedrich Diederichsen has written a lucid study about these mechanisms and about authenticity in popular culture. See his book *Über Pop-Musik* (Cologne: Kiepenheuer & Witsch, 2014).
46 Rebentisch and Lepecki have applied the concept of singularity to art in a similar way. See Juliane Rebentisch, *Theorien der Gegenwartskunst zur Einführung* (Hamburg: Junius, 2013), pp. 106–16; and André Lepecki, *Singularities: Dance in the Age of Performance* (New York: Routledge, 2016). A comparable understanding of art can also be found in Jean-François Lyotard, "The Sublime and the Avant Garde," trans. Lisa Liebmann, *Artforum* 22/8 (1984), pp. 36–43. This

is not to exclude the possibility, however, that other goods in cultural capitalism might also have a disturbing nature (certain types of architecture or fashion, for example).
47 For a classic discussion of this topic, see Karl Heinz Bohrer, *Das absolute Präsens: Die Semantik ästhetischer Zeit* (Frankfurt am Main: Suhrkamp, 1994).
48 Although this topic has primarily been discussed by literary critics and art historians (see, for instance, Ulrich Schulz-Buschhaus, "Klassik zwischen Kanon und Typologie: Probleme um einen Zentralbegriff der Literaturwissenschaft," *Arcadia* 29 [1994], pp. 165–74), it is pertinent to sociology as well, and I will return to it in the second half of this Part.
49 See Aleida Assmann, *Mnemosyne: Formen und Funktionen kultureller Erinnerung* (Frankfurt am Main: Fischer, 1993). Memory-enhancing technologies such as private digital photography or public film recordings facilitate this phenomenon. In addition, service relationships – a therapy session, a workshop, a university course – can also have lasting effects by way of memory.
50 See Reckwitz, *The Invention of Creativity*.
51 See Roland Barthes, *The Language of Fashion*, trans. Andy Stafford (London: Bloomsbury, 2005); and Elena Esposito, *Die Verbindlichkeit des Vorübergehenden: Paradoxien der Mode* (Frankfurt am Main: Suhrkamp, 2004).
52 For further details, see Davide Ravasi et al., "Valuing Products as Cultural Symbols: A Conceptual Framework and Empirical Illustration," in *The Worth of Goods: Valuation and Pricing in the Economy*, ed. Jens Beckert and Patrik Aspers (Oxford University Press, 2011), pp. 297–318.
53 On *art brut*, see Michel Thévoz, *Art Brut*, trans. James Emmons (Geneva: Albert Skira, 1995). In his book *Rubbish Theory*, Michael Thompson describes in detail the process of culturally valorizing former idiosyncrasies, with examples from architecture and arts and crafts. For a different approach to these mechanisms, see Groys's book *On the New*.
54 On such contexts, see George Yúdice, *The Expediency of Culture: Uses of Culture in the Global Era* (Durham, NC: Duke University Press, 2003). On the global circulation of cultural goods in general, see Scott Lash and Celia Lury, *Global Culture Industry: The Mediation of Things* (Cambridge: Polity, 2011).
55 Byung-Chul Han has interpreted this phenomenon quite differently – namely, as a process of leveling things out and making everything equivalent. See his book *Hyperkulturalität: Kultur und Globalisierung* (Berlin: Merve, 2005).

2 Cultural Singularity Markets

1 Muniesa, "A Flank Movement in the Understanding of Valuation."
2 On the sociology of markets and competition in general, see Klaus Kraemer, *Der Markt der Gesellschaft: Zu einer soziologischen Theorie der Marktvergesellschaftlichung* (Opladen: Westdeutscher Verlag, 1997); Dietmar J. Wetzel, *Soziologie des Wettbewerbs: Eine kultur- und wirtschaftssoziologische Analyse* (Wiesbaden: Springer, 2013); Frank Nullmeier, "Wettbewerbskulturen," in *Der Sinn der Politik: Kulturwissenschaftliche Politikanalysen*, ed. Michael Müller et al. (Konstanz: UVK Verlag, 2002), pp. 157–76. The history of markets is a classic theme; see, for instance, Fernand Braudel, *Civilization and Capitalism, 15th–18th Century*, trans. Siân Reynolds (Princeton University Press, 2002). In more recent economic theory, the transformation of markets through the culturalization of goods has become an important issue; see Beckert and Aspers, *The Worth of Goods*.
3 Weber, *Economy and Society*, pp. 635–40.
4 See also Georg Simmel, "Sociology of Competition," trans. Horst J. Helle, *Canadian Journal of Sociology* 33 (2008), pp. 945–78.
5 For a strict definition of this concept, see Sighard Neckel, *Flucht nach vorn: Die Erfolgskultur der Marktgesellschaft* (Frankfurt am Main: Campus, 2008). The term has been used somewhat differently by Michel Callon and his research

group. See Michel Callon, ed., *The Laws of the Market* (Oxford: Blackwell, 1998).
6 In a very general sense, of course, all goods function in a performative manner, either by promising to perform in a particular way or by being performances themselves (as in services, for instance). On attractiveness markets, however, goods function as performances in a strong sense that preserves the theatrical and cultural connotations of the term.
7 On the concept of the audience from a systems-theoretical perspective, see Rudolf Stichweh, *Inklusion und Exklusion: Studien zur Gesellschaftstheorie* (Bielefeld: Transcript, 2005).
8 In scholarly literature, the term "attractiveness" has been used almost exclusively to refer to physical or erotic attraction; see Gillian Rhodes and Leslie Zebrowitz, eds., *Facial Attractiveness: Evolutionary, Cognitive, and Social Perspectives* (Westport, CT: Ablex, 2002). Interestingly, however, this has begun to change; see, for instance, James Valentine, *Attractiveness of New Communities to Industries and Workers* (Saarbrücken: Lap Lambert Academic Publishing, 2012).
9 See Lash and Urry, *The End of Organized Capitalism*; and Wagner, *A Sociology of Modernity*, pp. 73–88.
10 Such was the case in large economic sectors such as the energy supply and transportation, but it was also true of the mass media (the government broadcasting monopoly) and the housing supply (government-subsidized apartments).
11 This is also reflected in practices of consumption. Relatively speaking, the middle-class consumers in organized modernity were strongly influenced by the social norms of *proper* and *status-appropriate* consumption. They therefore seldom found themselves in market situations because such decisions were already made for them by the accepted standards of normality.
12 On the transformation of the economy into an economy of innovation, see Tom Burns and George M. Stalker, *The Management of Innovation* (Oxford University Press, 1994). On cultural innovation in the field of design management, see, for instance, Roberto Verganti, *Design-Driven Innovation: Changing the Rules of Competition by Radically Innovating What Things Mean* (Boston, MA: Harvard Business School Press, 2009).
13 These topics will be discussed in Parts V and III, respectively.
14 See Eva Illouz, *Why Love Hurts: A Sociological Explanation* (Cambridge: Polity, 2013).
15 On religion, see Hartmut Zinser, *Der Markt der Religionen* (Munich: Fink, 1997); on regions, see Richard Florida, *Cities and the Creative Class* (New York: Routledge, 2005); and on politics, see Franz Walter, *Im Herbst der Volksparteien? Eine kleine Geschichte von Aufstieg und Rückgang politischer Massenintegration* (Bielefeld: Transcript, 2009).
16 On this topic, it is sufficient to cite only Ulrich Bröckling et al., eds., *Gouvernementalität der Gegenwart: Studien zur Ökonomisierung des Sozialen* (Frankfurt am Main: Suhrkamp, 2000); Colin Crouch, *The Strange Non-Death of Neoliberalism* (Cambridge: Polity, 2011); and Michel Foucault's fundamental work *The Birth of Biopolitics: Lectures at the Collège de France, 1978–1979*, trans. Graham Burchell (New York: Palgrave Macmillan, 2011).
17 Conversely, this of course means that there are types of marketization that have little or nothing to do with culturalization and singularization. Consider, for example, the classical deregulations of industrial markets such as energy markets.
18 For works that have defied this trend, see Menger's pioneering books *Portrait de l'artiste en travailleur* and *The Economics of Creativity*. Boltanski and Chiapello have also made indirect references to the groundbreaking function of the art world: see Luk Boltanski and Ève Chiapello, *The New Spirit of Capitalism*, trans. Gregory Elliott (London: Verso, 2005).
19 The sociology of art has opposed this perspective from the beginning. In addition to Howard Saul Becker's book *Art Worlds* (Berkeley: University of

California Press, 1984), Bourdieu's *The Rules of Art* is also important in this regard.
20 See Reckwitz, *The Invention of Creativity*, pp. 33–56. The marketization of art, moreover, took place regardless of whether works of art were commercial commodities or government-regulated products, regardless of whether they were popular and entertaining or elite and serious, and regardless of whether they followed classical standards or were avant-garde. In this respect, see also Martha Woodmansee, *Author, Art, and Market: Rereading the History of Aesthetics* (New York: Columbia University Press, 1994); and Bätschmann, *Ausstellungskünstler*.
21 See Caves, *Creative Industries*.
22 Keep in mind that overproduction does not pertain here to the excessive production of identical goods (as in the case of the "butter mountains" and "milk lakes" of the 1970s) but rather to the excessive variety of new and unique goods.
23 See Reckwitz, *The Invention of Creativity*.
24 See Hesmondhalgh and Baker, *Creative Labour*; and Caves, *Creative Industries*. As it pertains to cultural markets, the phrase "nobody knows anything" is usually attributed to the American screenwriter William Goldman.
25 On the phenomenon of attention, see Jonathan Crary, *Suspensions of Perception: Attention, Spectacle, and Modern Culture* (Cambridge, MA: MIT Press, 2001); Georg Franck, *Ökonomie der Aufmerksamkeit: Ein Entwurf* (Munich: Hanser, 1998); and Markus Schroer, "Soziologie der Aufmerksamkeit: Grundlegende Überlegungen zu einem Theorieprogramm," *Kölner Zeitschrift für Soziologie und Sozialpsychologie* 66 (2014), pp. 193–218.
26 There is, however, an alternative to such radical asymmetry, which, in the context of the digitalization of the economy, Chris Anderson has referred to as the "long tail" (see his book *The Long Tail: Why the Future of Business is Selling Less of More* [New York: Hyperion, 2014]). Because of digital formats, even those goods that have failed to attract widespread attention and recognition can remain on the market for a long time, and at least some of them become niche products that are appreciated by small but stable groups of fans. This has given rise to a "long tail" of moderately successful niche products.
27 Measured in terms of items sold, scientific citations, or audience ratings.
28 See Menger, *The Economics of Creativity*, pp. 142–235. Studies of the success (and failure) of academic publications have revealed even greater asymmetries. In this case, what obtains is "Lotka's law," whereby just a tiny 3.2 percent of all academic publications are responsible for a whopping 50 percent of all academic citations. See Derek J. de Solla Price, *Little Science, Big Science* (New York: Columbia University Press, 1963).
29 See Robert Frank and Philipp Cook, *The Winner-Take-All Society: Why the Few on the Top Get So Much More than the Rest of Us* (New York: Penguin, 2010).
30 See Sherwin Rosen, "The Economics of Superstars," *American Economic Review* 71 (1981), pp. 845–58.
31 For a general discussion of risk, see Wolfgang Bonß, *Vom Risiko: Unsicherheit und Ungewißheit in der Moderne* (Hamburger Edition, 1995).
32 In this regard, see Urs Stäheli, *Spectacular Speculation: Thrills, the Economy, and Popular Discourse*, trans. Eric Savoth (Stanford University Press, 2013). It is probably for this reason that, during the 1990s, stock-market and financial speculation became a source of cultural fascination: such practices seem like a model for the late-modern economy as a whole.
33 See Emanuel Rosen, *The Anatomy of Buzz: How to Create Word-of-Mouth Marketing* (New York: Doubleday Currency, 2002).
34 On the concept of visibility, see Andrea Mubi Brighenti, *Visibility in Social Theory and Social Research* (Basingstoke: Palgrave Macmillan, 2010); and Markus Schroer, "Visual Culture and the Fight for Visibility," *Journal for the Theory of Social Behavior* 44 (2003), pp. 206–28.
35 See also Menger, *The Economics of Creativity*, pp. 179–87.

36 See, for instance, Horst H. Kruse, ed., *From Rags to Riches: Erfolgsmythos und Erfolgsrezepte in der amerikanischen Gesellschaft* (Munich: Goldmann, 1973).
37 See Jason Potts et al., "Social Network Markets: A New Definition of the Creative Industries," *Journal of Cultural Economics* 32/3 (2008), pp. 167–85.
38 See Alexandra Manske, "Zum ungleichen Wert von Sozialkapital: Netzwerke aus seiner Perspektive sozialer Praxis," in *Soziale Netzwerke und soziale Ungleichheit*, ed. Jörg Lüdicke and Martin Diewald (Wiesbaden: Verlag für Sozialwissenschaften, 2007), pp. 135–62; and Mark Lutter, "Soziale Strukturen des Erfolgs: Winner-take-all-Konzentrationen und ihre sozialen Entstehungskontexte auf flexiblen Arbeitsmärkten," *Kölner Zeitschrift für Soziologie und Sozialpsychologie* 65 (2013), pp. 597–622.
39 Regarding the processes of valorization on cultural markets, see in general Beckert and Aspers, *The Worth of Goods*; and Jens Beckert and Christine Musselin, eds., *Constructing Quality: The Classification of Goods in Markets* (Oxford University Press, 2013). Helpful in this respect, too, are works from the field of valuation studies, among them Fabian Muniesa and Claes-Fredrik Helgesson, "Valuation Studies and the Spectacle of Valuation," *Valuation Studies* 1/2 (2013), pp. 119–23. Of course, the fundamental book on this topic is Karpik's *Valuing the Unique*.
40 In the creative economy, the development and reproduction of brands and names is in general a way to secure long-term attention and appreciation. In such a way, certain creators (if they already have a name for themselves) can acquire long-term success even through digital news, television programs, or YouTube clips.
41 Regarding cultural goods and their ability to acquire a reputation, see Pierre Bourdieu, "The Market of Symbolic Goods," in *The Field of Cultural Production: Essays on Art and Literature*, trans. Rupert Swyer (New York: Columbia University Press, 1993), pp. 112–45; and Georg Franck, *Mentaler Kapitalismus: Eine politische Ökonomie des Geistes* (Munich: Hanser, 2005). Regarding the sciences in particular, the classic work is Robert K. Merton's *The Sociology of Science: Theoretical and Empirical Investigations* (University of Chicago Press, 1998). Regarding art, see Becker's book *Art Worlds*.
42 See Callon et al., "The Economy of Qualities."
43 For a thorough discussion of this phenomenon, see Karpik, *Valuing the Unique*.
44 In certain cases, the career of a singular good can unfold in a more complicated manner. On the one hand, it is possible for something that was once perceived as a classic to undergo a long-term period of devaluation. On the other hand, it is also possible for goods to be rediscovered and for something that was once overlooked or evaluated negatively to rise in appeal.
45 On the topic of brands, see Hanna Busemann, *Das Phänomen Marke: Betrachtung und Analyse aktueller markensoziologischer Ansätze* (Saarbrücken: VDM, 2007); and Jeannette Neustadt, *Ökonomische Ästhetik und Markenkult: Reflexionen über das Phänomen Marke in der Gegenwartskunst* (Bielefeld: Transcript, 2011).
46 See Bourdieu, *The Rules of Art*.
47 See Markus Tauschek, ed., *Kulturen des Wettbewerbs: Formationen kompetitiver Logiken* (Münster: Waxmann, 2012); and James F. English, *The Economy of Prestige: Prizes, Awards, and the Circulation of Cultural Value* (Cambridge, MA: Harvard University Press, 2005). Regarding the genealogy of competition as a spectacle of valorization, the first award ceremony of the Academy of Motion Picture Arts and Sciences (the "Oscars"), which was held in 1929, represents a milestone.
48 Of course, this is not always the case. There are, in addition, purely popular goods and purely valuable goods, but only on the extreme ends, whereas everything in between is a mixture of the two.
49 An example of this situation is the prominence of deconstructionist architecture since the 1990s, which Georg Franck discusses in great detail in his book

Mentaler Kapitalismus. The success of this type of architecture is closely related to the debates among experts about its value.
50 In this regard, Bourdieu's classic discussion of the cultural capital of subjects and its relation to cultural goods (including names) has to be taken further. For a recent and thorough effort to do so, see again Franck's *Mentaler Kapitalismus*.
51 Regarding the Matthew effect on the markets for cultural goods, and the sciences in particular, see Robert K. Merton's classic essay, "The Matthew Effect in Science," *Science* 158/3810 (1968), pp. 56–63.
52 Many music fans, for instance, listen exclusively to recognized pop music from the 1960s and 1970s, which was once considered to be valuable, and they do not even bother with new releases. Similarly, many restaurant patrons in Paris prefer their local, established eateries and never venture to try anything new.
53 On all of these types of stars, see Chris Rojek, *Celebrity* (London: Reaktion, 2001).
54 On this topic, see Jan-Hendrik Passoth and Josef Wehner, eds., *Quoten, Kurven und Profile: Zur Vermessung der sozialen Welt* (Wiesbaden: Springer, 2013); and Steffen Mau, *The Metric Society: On the Quantification of the Social*, trans. Sharon Howe (Cambridge: Polity, 2019).
55 On comparison as a social practice, see Bettina Heintz, "Numerische Differenz: Überlegungen zu einer Soziologie des (quantitativen) Vergleichs," *Zeitschrift für Soziologie* 39/3 (2010), pp. 162–81.
56 See Part I, Chapter 2.
57 See Beckert and Musselin, *Constructing Quality*.
58 Think of the rankings of books, songs, or films on Amazon.
59 Academic citation indexes are a special case in this regard. The latter are a combination of attention measurements and quality rankings. What they measure is how often other academics – not just any random readers – have referred to individual texts (and thus recognized them as valuable). See Merton, *The Sociology of Science*.
60 For producers, too, quantifications often lead to self-reinforcing effects. A topic that has received many hits on a news portal will probably be the topic of more articles in the future; a band or an author with initial success will be promoted even harder by record labels or publishers, etc.

III The Singularization of the Working World

1 See Lazzarato, "Immaterial Labor"; Manfred Moldaschl and Günter Voß, eds., *Subjektivierung von Arbeit* (Munich: R. Hampp, 2002); Boltanski and Chiapello, *The New Spirit of Capitalism*; Piore and Sabel, *The Second Industrial Divide*; Hans Pongratz and Günter Voß, *Arbeitskraftunternehmer: Erwerbsorientierungen in entgrenzten Arbeitsformen* (Berlin: Edition Sigma, 2003); Nick Kratzer, *Arbeitskraft in Entgrenzung: Grenzlose Anforderungen, erweiterte Spielräume, begrenzte Ressourcen* (Berlin: Edition Sigma, 2003); Peter Kalkowski and Otfried Mickler, *Antinomien des Projektmanagements: Eine Arbeitsform zwischen Direktive und Freiraum* (Berlin: Edition Sigma, 2009); and Ulrich Bröckling, *The Entrepreneurial Self: Fabricating a New Type of Subject*, trans. Steven Black (London: Sage, 2016).
2 Lazzarato, "Immaterial Labor," p. 133. On the expansion of education, see Paul Windolf, *Expansion and Structural Change: Higher Education in Germany, the United States, and Japan* (Boulder, CO: Westview Press, 1997).
3 See Bell, *The Coming of Post-Industrial Society*.
4 On this polarization, see David H. Autor et al., "The Polarization of the U.S. Labor Market," *American Economic Review* 96/2 (2006), pp. 189–94; Maarten Goos et al., "Job Polarization in Europe," *American Economic Review* 99/2 (2009), pp. 58–63. For discussion framed in terms of global social theory, see Allen Scott, *A World in Emergence: Cities and Regions in the 21st Century* (Cheltenham: Edward Elgar, 2012). See also Gøsta Esping-Anderson's fundamental book *Changing*

Classes: Stratification and Mobility in Post-Industrial Societies (London: Sage, 1993).
5 Maarten Goos and Alan Manning, "Lousy and Lovely Jobs: The Rising Polarization of Work in Britain," *Review of Economics and Statistics* 89 (2007), pp. 118–33.
6 On this concept, see Stephan Voswinkel, *Welche Kundenorientierung? Anerkennung in der Dienstleistungsarbeit* (Berlin: Edition Sigma, 2005). On the labor of the service class, see Bahl, *Lebensmodelle in der Dienstleistungsgesellschaft*. I will go into greater detail about the service class in Part V.
7 Since the 1990s, statistics that hierarchize subjects according to different levels of qualification (college degree, high school diploma, etc.), and thus imply that those with higher qualifications are better, have been ubiquitous (in the mass media, too). This fits with the fact that, on the political side of things, a rise in the number of university graduates (in the total population, in a city, or in a particular group such as immigrants) is regarded as a success in itself.
8 See Stephan Voswinkel, "Anerkennung der Arbeit im Wandel," in *Anerkennung und Arbeit*, ed. Ursula Holtgrewe et al. (Konstanz: UVK, 2000), pp. 39–61.
9 See David Hesmondhalgh, *The Cultural Industries* (London: Sage, 2002); and Andy Pratt, "Creative Cities: Cultural Industries and the Creative Class," *Geografiska Annaler: Series B – Human Geography* 90/2 (2008), pp. 107–17.
10 Robert Reich, *The Work of Nations: Preparing Ourselves for 21st-Century Capitalism* (New York: Vintage Books, 1991).

1 Practices of Labor and Organization in the Creative Economy

1 In recent years, numerous interesting studies have come out on the form of creative labor, and especially as this relates to the creative industries. Here it will be sufficient to cite Hesmondhalgh and Baker, *Creative Labor*; Mark Deuze, *Media Work* (Cambridge: Polity, 2007); Mark Banks, *The Politics of Cultural Work* (New York: Palgrave Macmillan, 2007); Angela McRobbie, *Be Creative: Making a Living in the New Culture Industries* (Cambridge: Polity, 2016); Hannes Krämer, *Die Praxis der Kreativität: Eine Ethnographie kreativer Arbeit* (Bielefeld: Transcript, 2014); and Alexandra Manske, *Kapitalistische Geister in der Kultur- und Kreativwirtschaft: Kreative zwischen wirtschaftlichem Zwang und künstlerischem Drang* (Bielefeld: Transcript, 2016).
2 This was already beginning to be the case in the early 1990s. See Martin Baethge, "Arbeit, Vergesellschaftung, Identität: Zur zunehmenden normativen Subjektivierung der Arbeit," *Soziale Welt* 42 (1991), pp. 6–19.
3 On the distinction between the broad and strong concepts of culture, see the discussion in Part I, Chapter 3.
4 On the broadening of the concept of design, see Julier, *The Culture of Design*. On design work, see Brown, *Change by Design*.
5 On this concept, see Hans-Jörg Rheinberger, *Experiment, Differenz, Schrift: Zur Geschichte epistemischer Dinge* (Marburg: Basilisken-Verlag, 1992).
6 For further discussion of this practice, see Rob Austin and Lee Devin, *Artful Making: What Managers Need to Know About How Artists Work* (Upper Saddle River, NJ: Prentice Hall, 2003); and Verganti, *Design-Driven Innovation*.
7 See Austin and Devin, *Artful Making*.
8 See Monika Salzbrunn, *Vielfalt/Diversität* (Bielefeld: Transcript, 2014).
9 See Chris Bilton, *Management and Creativity: From Creative Industries to Creative Management* (Malden, MA: Blackwell, 2006).
10 See, for instance, Matthew Arnold's book *Culture and Anarchy*.
11 See Verganti, *Design-Driven Innovation*; and Deuze, *Media Work*.
12 See Tom Kelley and Jonathan Littman, *The Art of Innovation: Lessons in Creativity from IDEO, America's Leading Design Firm* (London: HarperCollins, 2001).
13 It is no surprise that one of the directives of "design thinking" is to think about

every good from the perspective of the consumer and to ask whether the good in question will be experienced in a unique way. In this view, it is not the bicycle, for instance, that is a good, but rather the bicycle experience; not the hotel, but the hotel experience; not the museum, but the museum experience, and so on. See Brown, *Change by Design*.

14 See Boltanski and Chiapello, *The New Spirit of Capitalism*, pp. 103–64; Ricarda Wildförster and Sascha Wingen, *Projektmanagement und Probleme: Systematische Perspektiven auf Organisationsberatung und Begleitforschung* (Heidelberg: Verlag für systemische Forschung, 2001); Kalkowski and Mickler, *Antinomien des Projektmanagements*; and Christiane Funken et al., *Vertrackte Karrieren: Zum Wandel der Arbeitswelten in Wirtschaf und Wissenschaft* (Frankfurt am Main: Campus, 2015). For a more general discussion, see Markus Krajewski, ed., *Projektemacher: Zur Produktion von Wissen in der Vorform des Scheiterns* (Berlin: Kulturverlag Kadmos, 2004).

15 Richard A. Goodman and Lawrence P. Goodman, "Some Management Issues in Temporary Systems: A Study in Professional Development and Manpower – The Theater Case," *Administrative Science Quarterly* 21 (1976), pp. 494–501, at p. 494.

16 On these phases, see Davies and Sigthorsson, *Introducing the Creative Industries*, pp. 138–57.

17 The concept of collaboration and related terms for describing non-communal collectives have been used vaguely and inconsistently in contemporary theoretical discussions. My goal here is thus to refine matters theoretically. For one approach, see Richard Sennett, *Together: The Rituals, Pleasures, and Politics of Cooperation* (London: Allen Lane, 2012). Somewhat different are Bruno Latour's idea of the "connective" (in *Reassembling the Social*) and Jean-Luc Nancy's notion of community and communication in his book *The Inoperative Community*, trans. Peter Connor et al. (Minneapolis: University of Minnesota Press, 1991). For a more pragmatic approach to the subject, see Gesa Ziemer, *Komplizenschaft: Neue Perspektiven auf Kollektivität* (Bielefeld: Transcript, 2013).

18 Interaction and communication denote very general and neutral phenomena that are not necessarily goal-oriented. Cooperation is indeed goal-oriented, but it lacks the connotation of inherent cultural value.

19 See Austin and Devin, *Artful Making*.

20 In this regard, projects can certainly develop a collective identity – not, however, in the sense of a homogeneous community but rather in the sense of an identity as a collaborative plurality of singularities. As affective practices, moreover, projects can also remain valuable for a long time in the memory of their participants.

21 Only in particular interesting cases do markets become socially visible as a whole. Consider, for instance, valorization competitions such as casting shows, the European Song Contest, and also political campaigns. In this regard, sporting events are especially significant for the obvious reason that they dramatize and make it possible to experience the abstract constellation of competition that is ubiquitous in society. On this topic, see Alain Ehrenberg, *Le culte de la performance* (Paris: Calmann-Lévy, 1991). Another example of the representation of markets as a whole is the financial economy, which operates with visualizations on a screen. See Karin Knorr-Cetina and Urs Bruegger, "Traders' Engagement with Markets: A Postsocial Relationship," *Theory, Culture & Society* 19/5 (2002), pp. 161–85.

22 On the relationship between projects and late-modern organizations, see Gernot Grabher, "Ecologies of Creativity: The Village, the Group, and the Heterarchic Organisation of the British Advertising Industry," *Environmental Planning A: Economy and Space* 33 (2001), pp. 351–74; and Bilton, *Management and Creativity*.

23 See Martin Parker, *Organizational Culture and Identity: Unity and Division at Work* (London: Sage, 2000); and Julier, *The Culture of Design*, pp. 191–210.

24 On such practices, see Paul du Gay, *Consumption and Identity at Work* (London: Sage, 1996); and Nigel Thrift, *Knowing Capitalism* (London: Sage, 2005).
25 See Bas van Heur, *Creative Networks and the City: Towards a Cultural Political Economy of Aesthetic Production* (Bielefeld: Transcript, 2010); and, regarding New York in particular, Elizabeth Currid, *The Warhol Economy: How Fashion, Art, and Music Drive New York City* (Princeton University Press, 2007).
26 On networks in general, see Latour, *Reassembling the Social*. On networked organizations, see Walter W. Powell, "Neither Market nor Hierarchy: Network Forms of Organization," *Organizational Behaviour* 12 (1990), pp. 295–336. Regarding networks in late modernity, see Manuel Castells, *The Rise of the Network Society* (Cambridge, MA: Blackwell, 1996); and Henning Laux, *Soziologie im Zeitalter der Komposition: Koordinaten einer integrativen Netzwerktheorie* (Weilerwist: Velbrück, 2014).
27 See Arnold Picot et al., *Information, Organization, and Management* (Berlin: Springer, 2008); and Hartmut Berghoff and Jörg Sydow, eds., *Unternehmerische Netzwerke: Eine historische Organisationsform mit Zukunf?* (Stuttgart: Kohlhammer, 2007).
28 See Andrew Wittel, "Toward a Network Sociality," *Theory, Culture & Society* 18/6 (2001), pp. 51–76.
29 See Mark S. Granovetter, "The Strength of Weak Ties," *American Journal of Sociology* 78 (1973), pp. 1360–80.
30 In certain cases, networks too can be represented, and thus become visible as a whole. Think of the list of "friends" on a Facebook page.

2 The Singularization and Self-Singularization of Working Subjects

1 What I mean by "subject" here is not autonomous subjectivity but rather the way in which individuals are subjectivized by professional culture – that is, the way that they adopt specific social norms, forms of habitus, and mental dispositions, and make them their own.
2 In Part V, I will discuss how the working culture of highly qualified people is drastically different from that of low-qualified employees.
3 The post-materialistic work ethic is clearest to see in the creative industries. The latter are driven by the ego-ideal of creative people, which has traces of the (classical) modern ideal of the artist. See Cornelia Koppetsch, *Das Ethos der Kreativen: Eine Studie zum Wandel von Arbeit und Identität am Beispiel der Werbeberufe* (Konstanz: UVK, 2006).
4 Organizational sociologists have shown, for instance, that there was more to classical organizations than simply formal qualifications and achievement. They, too, had their share of micropolitics, trust management, impression management, and informal exit strategies.
5 See Marcelle Stroobants, *Savoir-faire et competénce au travail: Une sociologie de la fabrication des aptitudes* (Brussels: l'Université de Bruxelles, 1993); Menger, *Portrait de l'artiste en travailleur*, pp. 81–4; Menger, *The Economics of Creativity*, pp. 142–235; and Thomas Kurtz and Michaela Pfadenhauer, eds., *Soziologie der Kompetenz* (Wiesbaden: Verlag für Sozialwissenschaften, 2010).
6 See Davies and Sigthorsson, *Introducing the Creative Industries*, pp. 107–13. Similarly, Charles B. Handy wrote about the "portfolio life" in his book *The Age of Unreason* (Boston, MA: Harvard Business School Press, 1989). This trend is especially obvious in the field of consulting; see, for instance, Jürgen Salenbacher, *Creative Personal Branding* (Amsterdam: BIS Publishers, 2013).
7 I will return to the topic of the profile in my analysis of digitalization in Part IV.
8 See Nigel Thrift, "A Perfect Innovation Engine: The Rise of the Talent World," in *Cultural Political Economy*, ed. Jacqueline Best and Matthew Paterson (New York: Routledge, 2010), pp. 197–222; and, once again, Menger, *The Economics of Creativity*, pp. 142–235. On the significance of potential development in everyday project work, see Funken et al., *Vertrackte Karrieren*; and Uwe Vormbusch,

"Taxonomien des Flüchtigen: Das Portfolio als Wettbewerbstechnologie der Marktgesellschaft," in *Quoten, Kurven und Profile*, ed. Passoth and Wehner, pp. 47–68. In the field of economics, the concept of potential stems from Gary Becker's theory of human capital; in the field of psychology, it derives from the psychology of personal growth.
9 See Thomas J. Peters and Robert H. Waterman, *In Search of Excellence: Lessons from America's Best-Run Companies* (New York: Harper & Row, 1982).
10 This is analogous to the singularity capital of goods discussed in Part II.
11 See Aldo Legnaro, "Performanz," in *Glossar der Gegenwart*, ed. Ulrich Bröckling et al. (Frankfurt am Main: Suhrkamp, 2004), pp. 204–6. On the general concept of a performance economy, see Fabian Muniesa, *The Provoked Economy: Economic Reality and Performative Turn* (London: Routledge, 2014).
12 On this topic in general, see Neckel, *Flucht nach vorn*, pp. 80–99. Regarding the praxis of project work in particular, see Funken et al., *Vertrackte Karrieren*.
13 See Funken et al., *Vertrackte Karriere*.
14 See Davies and Sigthorsson, *Introducing the Creative Industries*, pp. 114–19. The relevance of such personal characteristics to professional success has also become a hot topic in the field of psychology. See, for instance, Angela Duckworth et al., "Grit: Perseverance and Passion for Long-Term Goals," *Journal of Personality and Social Psychology* 92 (2007), pp. 1087–1101.
15 See Bilton, *Management and Creativity*, pp. 28–30. On casting in general, see Bernhard Pörksen and Wolfgang Krischke, eds., *Die Casting-Gesellschaft: Die Sucht nach Aufmerksamkeit und das Tribunal der Medien* (Cologne: Halem, 2010); and André Pradtke, *Casting Shows als Märkte für Marktpotenziale* (Marburg: Metropolis, 2014).
16 This phenomenon is captured beautifully in Till Harms's documentary *Die Prüfung* (2016), which is about the audition and casting process at a German acting academy.
17 See Neckel, *Die Flucht nach vorn*. For similar insights, see also Rosanvallon, *The Society of Equals*.
18 On the matter of predicting which sort of work has future prospects and which does not, see Lynda Gratton, *The Shift: The Future of Work is Already Here* (London: Collins, 2011).
19 See Davies and Sigthorsson, *Introducing the Creative Industries*, pp. 104–13; and Wittel, "Toward a Network Sociality."
20 This is a topic that has only been cautiously touched upon in the scholarly literature; see, for instance, Davies and Sigthorsson, *Introducing the Creative Industries*, pp. 114–19.
21 See, as one example among many, Pierre Bourdieu and Jean-Claude Passeron, *The Inheritors: French Students and Their Relation to Culture*, trans. Richard Nice (University of Chicago Press, 1979).
22 Pierre Bourdieu, "The Forms of Capital," in *Handbook of Theory and Research for the Sociology of Education*, ed. John G. Richardson (Westport, CT: Greenwood Press, 1986), pp. 241–58.
23 In Part V, I will go into greater detail about the specific socio-cultural form of this new, educated middle class. In still another way, social background and "fit" are even more decisive at the top levels of management. See Michael Hartmann, *Der Mythos von den Leistungseliten: Spitzenkarrieren und soziale Herkunft in Wirtschaft, Politik, Justiz und Wissenschaft* (Frankfurt am Main: Campus, 2002).
24 For a comprehensive discussion of this technique, see Uwe Vormbusch, "Karrierepolitik: Zum biografischen Umgang mit ökonomischer Unsicherheit," *Zeitschrift für Soziologie* 38/4 (2009), pp. 282–99.
25 On this phenomenon, see Boris Traue, *Das Subjekt der Beratung: Zur Soziologie einer Psycho-Technik* (Bielefeld: Transcript, 2010).
26 Regarding careers in general, see Ronald Hitzler and Michaela Pfadenhauer, eds., *Karrierepolitik: Beiträge zur Rekonstruktion erfolgsorientierten Handels* (Opladen: Leske + Budrich, 2003). For discussions of the topic as it relates to

specific fields, see Joanna Grigg, *Portfolio Working: A Practical Guide to Thriving in the Changing Workplace* (London: Kogan Page, 1997); and Vormbusch, "Karrierepolitik."

27 See, for instance, Hesmondhalgh, *The Cultural Industries*; and the articles collected in the special issue of *Polar: Zeitschrift für politische Philosophie und Kultur* 4 (2008).

28 See Reckwitz, *The Invention of Creativity*, pp. 33–56.

29 The ideal late-modern working culture perfectly combines a sort of work that enables creativity and personal development with success on the market of attention and valorization. Successful artists (designers, architects, etc.) embody this ideal. See Sarah Thornton, *33 Artists in 3 Acts* (London: Granta, 2014). Angela McRobbie has analyzed the aspect of gender in this regard: the ideal of the creative person in late modernity applies not only to men but particularly to women (see *Be Creative*, pp. 87–114).

30 On the concept of "coopetition," see Stephan A. Jansen and Stephan Schleissing, eds., *Konkurrenz und Kooperation: Interdisziplinäre Zugänge zur Theorie der Co-opetition* (Marburg: Metropolis, 2000).

31 For various approaches to this topic, see Arlie Russell Hochschild, *The Time Bind: When Work Becomes Home and Home Becomes Work* (New York: Metropolitan Books, 1997); Diedrich Diederichsen, "Kreative Arbeit und Selbstverwirklichung," in *Kreation und Depression: Freiheit im gegenwärtigen Kapitalismus*, ed. Christoph Menke et al. (Berlin: Kadmos, 2010), pp. 118–28; and Svenja Flaßpöhler, *Wir Genussarbeiter: Über Freiheit und Zwang in der Leistungsgesellschaft* (Munich: Deutsche Verlags-Anstalt, 2011).

32 For further discussion of this labor structure, see Menger, *Portrait de l'artiste en travailleur*; and Jean-Paul Fitoussi and Pierre Rosanvallon, *Le nouvel âge des inégalités* (Paris: Seuil, 1996). On the concept of stars, see Rosen, "The Economics of Superstars."

33 This can be related to Stinchcombe's distinction between two types of labor logic. On the one side, there are star jobs in which fine distinctions in output create disproportionate differences in the overall performance, attention, valorization, and success of an organization, and are rewarded accordingly. On the other side, there are standardized activities in which such fine distinctions are largely inconsequential for the organization in question. See Arthur L. Stinchcombe, "Some Empirical Consequences of the Davis–Moore Theory of Stratification," *American Sociological Review* 28 (1963), pp. 805–8.

34 For a more detailed analysis of this phenomenon and a discussion of its various interpretations, see Menger, *The Economics of Creativity*, pp. 142–235; and Menger, *La différence, la concurrence et la disproportion: Sociologie du travail créateur* (Paris: Fayard, 2014). With reference to Franz Kafka's story "Josephine the Singer, or the Mouse Folk," Gerald Raunig has developed another interesting perspective on the question of the logic of uniqueness and its justice. See Gerald Raunig, *Fabriken des Wissens* (Zurich: Diaphanes, 2012), pp. 7–14.

35 This is also evident from the fact that even teachers, for instance, are now expected to make a difference through their "inspiring" teaching, and that only certain IT products manage to "strike a chord" despite the technological sophistication of their competitors.

36 A sociology of vanity has yet to be written. The closest thing to it might be studies of narcissism, though these tend to pathologize the matter. The classic work on the subject is Christopher Lasch's *The Culture of Narcissism: American Life in an Age of Diminishing Expectations* (New York: W. W. Norton, 1978). Oddly enough, the history of envy has also been neglected. See, however, Frank Nullmeier, *Politische Theorie des Sozialstaats* (Frankfurt am Main: Campus, 2000). On the topic of failure, see Matthias Junge and Götz Lechner, eds., *Scheitern: Aspekte eines sozialen Phänomens* (Wiesbaden: Verlag für Sozialwissenschaften, 2004).

37 I will avoid the temptation here to enter a normative discussion of justice. For such an approach, see Neckel, *Flucht nach vorn*, pp. 80–99.

IV Digitalization as Singularization: The Rise of the Culture Machine

1 Here I am using the term "affordance" in Bruno Latour's sense of the word (see *Reassembling the Social*, p. 83). On the concept of technology in general, see Don Ihde, *Technology and Lifeworld: From Garden to Earth* (Bloomington: Indiana University Press, 1996). For a praxeological understanding of artifacts, see Andreas Reckwitz, "The Status of the 'Material' in Theories of Culture: From 'Social Structure' to 'Artefacts,'" *Journal for the Theory of Social Behaviour* 32/2 (2002), pp. 195–217.
2 See Siegfried Giedion, *Mechanization Takes Command: A Contribution to Anonymous History* (Oxford University Press, 1948). The technical culture of modernity has been theorized in various ways by writers such as Hans Blumenberg, Martin Heidegger, and Günther Anders. On this topic, see also Jan-Hendrik Passoth, *Technik und Gesellschaft: Sozialwissenschaftliche Techniktheorien und die Transformation der Moderne* (Wiesbaden: Verlag für Sozialwissenschaften, 2008).
3 On the optimistic side, see Clay Shirky, *Here Comes Everybody: The Power of Organizing Without Organizations* (New York: Penguin, 2008); and Eric Schmidt and Jared Cohen, *The New Digital Age: Transforming Nations, Businesses, and Our Lives* (New York: Random House, 2013). Representative works of the critical discourse include Byung-Chul Han, *In the Swarm: Digital Prospects*, trans. Erik Butler (Cambridge, MA: MIT Press, 2017); and Frank Schirrmacher, ed., *Technologischer Totalitarismus: Eine Debatte* (Berlin: Suhrkamp, 2015).
4 See Gilbert Simondon, *On the Mode of Existence of Technical Objects*, trans. Cécile Malaspina (Minneapolis: University of Minnesota Press, 2017). Here I will combine Simondon's terminology with the distinction between technics and technology found in Serge Moscovici's *Essai sur l'histoire humaine de la nature* (Paris: Flammarion, 1968). On this complex of problems, see also Erich Hörl, "Die technologische Bedingung: Zur Einführung," in *Die technologische Bedingung: Beiträge zur Beschreibung der technischen Welt*, ed. Erich Hörl (Berlin: Suhrkamp, 2011), pp. 7–53.
5 See Carlota Perez, "Technological Revolutions and Techno-Economic Paradigms," *Cambridge Journal of Economics* 34 (2010), pp. 185–202.

1 The Technology of Culturalization

1 On this concept, see Star, "The Ethnography of Infrastructure"; and Brian Larkin, "The Politics and Poetics of Infrastructure," *Annual Review of Anthropology* 42 (2013), pp. 327–43.
2 In what follows, when I speak of digital technologies, the internet, computer culture, digital culture, etc., all three structural elements are meant: algorithms, digitality, and the internet. The only term that does justice to all three at once is the "digital computer network," which I have decided to use only sparingly because of its awkwardness.
3 On algorithms, see Felix Stalder, *The Digital Condition*, trans. Valentine A. Pakis (Cambridge: Polity, 2018), pp. 101–24.
4 See Lev Manovich, *The Language of New Media* (Cambridge, MA: MIT Press, 2001). Manovich's is still the soundest theory of computer media, though of course it does not take the internet into account.
5 On this topic, see Martin Warnke, *Theorien des Internet zur Einführung* (Hamburg: Junius, 2011).
6 See Theodore H. Nelson, *Literary Machines* (Sausalito, CA: Mindful Press, 1981).
7 In an instructive way, Luciano Floridi has distinguished technologies based on interactions between humans and nature or humans and machines from those in which machines automatically and somewhat independently interact with one another (machine–machine interactions). With digital technologies, we have

arrived at this last stage. See Luciano Floridi, *The Fourth Revolution: How the Infosphere is Reshaping Human Reality* (Oxford University Press, 2014).

8 See Manuel Castells, *The Internet Galaxy: Reflections on the Internet, Business, and Society* (Oxford University Press, 2001); and Darin Barney, *The Network Society* (Cambridge: Polity, 2004).

9 This is also true of organic processes, for instance on the level of DNA. In his book *Information: A Very Short Introduction* (Oxford University Press, 2010), Luciano Floridi regards such phenomena as information as well, though here I use the term "information" exclusively to refer to what Floridi calls "semantic information."

10 It should also be noted that the boundaries between "new" and "old" (print and audiovisual) media have become fluid. As a sort of hyper-medium, the new media have absorbed the old media or are networked with them. They also influence the ways in which old media are represented.

11 On this topic, see Nicholas Mirzoeff, *An Introduction to Visual Culture* (New York: Routledge, 1999); and Martin Lister et al., *New Media: A Critical Introduction* (New York: Routledge, 2009), pp. 97–163.

12 See Martin Hand, *Ubiquitous Photography* (Cambridge: Polity, 2012).

13 See Vincent Miller, *Understanding Digital Culture* (Los Angeles: Sage, 2011), pp. 203–4.

14 On this aspect, see Stefan Schulz, *Redaktionsschluss: Die Zeit nach der Zeitung* (Munich: Carl Hanser, 2016).

15 See, for instance, Michael Bull, *Sound Moves: iPod Culture and Urban Experience* (New York: Routledge, 2007).

16 See GamesCoop, *Theorien des Computerspiels zur Einführung* (Hamburg: Junius, 2012).

17 See Martin Fuchs et al., eds., *Rethinking Gamification* (Lüneburg: Meson Press, 2014).

18 See Jordan Frith, *Smartphones as Locative Media* (Cambridge: Polity, 2015).

19 On this concept of environment, see Mark Hansen, "Medien des 21. Jahrhunderts, technisches Empfinden und unsere originäre Umweltbedingung," in *Die technologische Bedingung: Beiträge zur Beschreibung der technischen Welt*, ed. Erich Hörl (Berlin: Suhrkamp, 2011), pp. 365–409. The terms "web-augmented reality," "ambient intelligence," and "online experience" have similar connotations.

20 This structural feature has been known for some time, and various terms have been devised for it ("produser," "prosumer," etc.). See Mark Poster, *The Second Media Age* (Cambridge: Polity, 1995); and Axel Bruns, *Blogs, Wikipedia, Second Life, and Beyond: From Production to Produsage* (New York: Peter Lang, 2008).

21 See Sonia Livingstone and Ranjana Das, "The End of Audiences? Theoretical Echoes of Reception Amidst the Uncertainties of Use," in *A Companion to New Media Dynamics*, ed. John Hartley et al. (Chichester: Wiley-Blackwell, 2013), pp. 104–21.

22 On the screen as an interface, see Manovich, *The Language of New Media*, pp. 94–110. With the advent of the touchscreen, moreover, it is now possible for subjects to "interact" with the screens in front of them.

23 The formal equalization of cultural elements has gone hand in hand with their decontextualization. Traditional cultural hierarchies were also stabilized by clear differentiations between contexts: books in the library, news on the television, classical music in the concert hall, private communication through letters or on the telephone. Now, however, all of these heterogeneous cultural formats are available through the "same channel."

24 In this respect, digital media provide a firm backing for late modernity's creativity *dispositif*.

25 See Dirk von Gehlen, *Eine neue Version ist verfügbar: Wie die Digitalisierung Kunst und Kultur verändert* (Berlin: Metrolit, 2013).

26 For an early collection of articles on this topic, see George P. Landow, ed., *Hyper/Text/Theory* (Baltimore, MD: Johns Hopkins University Press, 1994). For more recent discussions, see Dirk von Gehlen, *Mashup: Lob der Kopie* (Berlin:

Suhrkamp, 2011); Florian Mundhenke et al., eds., *Mashups: Neue Praktiken und Ästhetiken in populären Medienkulturen* (Wiesbaden: Springer, 2015); and Stalder, *The Digital Condition*, pp. 59–79.

2 Cultural and Automated Processes of Singularization

1 It should be added that temporalities and spaces can also be singularized by the digital network – for instance, by its ability to locate individual places.
2 On the topic of subjects and subjectification, see Andreas Reckwitz, *Subjekt* (Bielefeld: Transcript, 2013).
3 On various forms of social media, see José van Dijck, *The Culture of Connectivity: A Critical History of Social Media* (Oxford University Press, 2013); and Ramón Reichert, *Die Macht der Vielen: Über den neuen Kult der digitalen Vernetzung* (Bielefeld: Transcript, 2014). Regarding the Facebook paradigm in particular, see Roberto Simanowski, *Facebook Society: Losing Ourselves in Sharing Ourselves*, trans. Susan H. Gillespie (New York: Columbia University Press, 2018); Howard Gardner and Katie Davis, *The App Generation: How Today's Youth Navigate Identity, Intimacy, and Imagination in a Digital World* (New Haven, CT: Yale University Press, 2013); Clara Shih, *The Facebook Era* (New York: Prentice Hall, 2011); and Oliver Leistert and Theo Röhle, eds., *Generation Facebook: Über das Leben im Social Net* (Bielefeld: Transcript, 2011).
4 See Riesman, *The Lonely Crowd*. For further discussion of this type of subject, see Reckwitz, *Das hybride Subjekt*, pp. 409–11.
5 On the concept of the profile, see also Miller, *Understanding Digital Culture*, pp. 170–3.
6 In 2016, for instance, Facebook introduced the following profile rubrics, among others: "life events," "work and education," "places you've lived," "music," "movies," and "books." The German online dating platform Parship provides open-ended statements for the profiles on its site: "A perfect day for me is when …," "I wish I could have …," "Two things that I could never live without are …," and so on.
7 On this topic, see also Simanowski, *Facebook Society*.
8 In cultural critical terms, one could argue that photographs and films do not objectify experience but rather replace it.
9 See Simmel, *Sociology*, pp. 363–408.
10 See Gardner and Davis, *The App Generation*, pp. 60–91.
11 For a discussion of this phenomenon as it relates to YouTube videos, see Reichert, *Die Macht der Vielen*, pp. 82–93.
12 For a more detailed discussion of this procedure, see van Dijck, *The Culture of Connectivity*; and Passoth and Wehner, *Quoten, Kurven und Profile*. Here there is a connection to the quantification methods used in the economy of singularities, which I discussed above in Part II.
13 See Niklas Luhmann, *Die Wissenschaft der Gesellschaft* (Frankfurt am Main: Suhrkamp, 1992), pp. 68–121. Here, however, I do not associate the concept of observation with the concept of meaning.
14 See Viktor Mayer-Schönberger and Kenneth Cukier, *Big Data: A Revolution that Will Transform How We Live, Work, and Think* (London: John Murray, 2013).
15 Of course, this interest in subjects does not stem from the computers themselves but rather from human actors with their commercial, medical, or political intentions. Computers, however, are now able to serve these interests in a historically unprecedented way.
16 The same is true of the criminal profiling conducted today. On this complex, see David Canter, "Offender Profiling and Investigative Psychology," *Journal of Investigative Psychology and Offender Profiling* 1 (2003), pp. 1–15; and Andreas Bernard, *The Triumph of Profiling: The Self in Digital Culture*, trans. Valentine A. Pakis (Cambridge: Polity, 2019), pp. 1–26.

17 See Stalder, *The Digital Condition*, pp. 104–24; Ramón Reichert, "Facebooks Big Data: Die Medien- und Wissenstechniken kollektiver Verdatung," in *Big Data: Analysen zum digitalen Wandel von Wissen, Macht und Ökonomie*, ed. Ramón Reichert (Bielefeld: Transcript, 2014), pp. 437–52; Miller, *Understanding Digital Culture*, pp. 111–33; and Christoph Kucklick's popular and informative book *Die granulare Gesellschaft: Wie das Digitale unsere Wirklichkeit auflöst* (Berlin: Ullstein, 2014).
18 So far, the most important type of automated profile has been the consumer profile, but people analytics has also opened up possibilities in the political realm. On Barack Obama's election campaigns in 2008 and 2012, for instance, see Michael Scherer, "Inside the Secret World of Data Crunchers Who Helped Obama Win," *Time Magazine* (November 12, 2012), online.
19 See Mayer-Schönberger and Cukier, *Big Data*.
20 See Deborah Lupton, *The Quantified Self: A Sociology of Self-Tracking Cultures* (Cambridge: Polity, 2016); and Stefan Selke, *Lifelogging: Wie die digitale Selbstvermessung unsere Gesellschaft verändert* (Berlin: Ullstein, 2014).
21 See Hays, *Advancing Healthcare through Personalized Medicine*.
22 Of course, these particular bodily processes can also be measured according to the general criteria of optimal health. In this case, self-observation serves the end of self-optimization – a goal that has been promoted above all by the quantified-self movement.
23 See Selke, *Lifelogging*, pp. 149–54.
24 So-called radio-frequency identification (RFID) chips are a related phenomenon.
25 See Schulz, *Redaktionsschluss*, pp. 23–75.
26 See Felix Stalder and Christine Mayer, "Der zweite Index: Suchmaschinen, Personalisierung, Überwachung," in *Deep Search: Politik des Suchens jenseits von Google*, ed. Konrad Becker and Felix Stalder (Innsbruck: Studien Verlag, 2009), pp. 112–31. On the relevance of the database as a social form, see Manovich, *The Language of New Media*, pp. 218–20; and Marcus Burkhardt, *Digitale Datenbanken: Eine Medientheorie im Zeitalter von Big Data* (Bielefeld: Transcript, 2015).
27 See Lev Manovich, *Software Takes Command* (New York: Bloomsbury, 2013).
28 See Reichert, *Die Macht der Vielen*; and Jean Burgess and Joshua Green, *YouTube: Online Video and Participatory Culture* (Cambridge: Polity, 2009).
29 Here one sees a close connection to the sort of singularization that takes place in the creative economy (see Anderson's book *Makers: The New Industrial Revolution*). On the cooperation between designers and users that this technology enables, see Katharina Bredies, *Gebrauch als Design: Über eine unterschätzte Form der Gestaltung* (Bielefeld: Transcript, 2014).
30 See Miller, *Understanding Digital Culture*, pp. 184–206. A classic study of online communities is Howard Rheingold's *The Virtual Community: Homesteading on the Electronic Frontier* (Cambridge, MA: MIT Press, 2000). On the compartmentalization of the news, see Stephen Reese et al., "Mapping the Blogosphere: Professional and Citizen-Based Media in the Global News Arena," *Journalism* 8/3 (2007), pp. 235–61. Regarding fan groups, see Nancy Baym, "Interpersonal Life Online," in *The Handbook of New Media: Social Shaping and Consequences of ICTs*, ed. Leah Lievrouw and Sonia Livingstone (London: Sage, 2006), pp. 35–54.
31 Referring to a somewhat different context, Chris Anderson has described this phenomenon as the "long tail" (see his book of that title).
32 See, for instance, Barry Wellman, "Physical Place and Cyberspace: The Rise of Networked Individualism," in *Community Informatics: Shaping Computer-Mediated Social Relations*, ed. Leigh Keeble and Brian Loader (New York: Routledge, 2001), pp. 17–42; and Barney, *The Network Society*.
33 See Clay Shirky, *Cognitive Surplus: Creativity and Generosity in a Connected Age* (New York: Penguin, 2010). In a strict sense, online networks also include the marketplaces of the so-called "sharing economy." See Jeremy Rifkin, *The Zero Marginal Cost Society: The Internet of Things, the Collaborative Commons, and the Eclipse of Capitalism* (New York: Palgrave Macmillan, 2014).

34 See Eli Pariser, *The Filter Bubble: How the New Personalized Web is Changing What We Read and How We Think* (New York: Penguin, 2011).
35 Singularity markets, neo-communities, and heterogeneous collaborations are ideal types. In the reality of digital culture, they tend to overlap. Depending on their intentions, for instance, social media can be structured in a way that is strongly influenced by markets or by communicative associations. In the case of fan communities, their structure might resemble more closely that of an interpretive neo-community or that of a network.
36 See Riesman, *The Lonely Crowd*.
37 On the new culture of shame and embarrassment, see Andrea Köhler, *Scham: Vom Paradies zum Dschungelcamp* (Springe: Klampe Verlag, 2017); and Ulrich Greiner, *Schamverlust: Vom Wandel der Gefühlskultur* (Reinbek: Hamburg Rowohlt, 2014). With the rise of reality shows since the 1990s, television has in general been just as responsible as the internet for showcasing the shame and embarrassment of subjects. On this topic, see Susan Murray and Laurie Ouellette, eds., *Reality TV: Remaking Television Culture* (New York University Press, 2009).
38 Examples of this in German-speaking countries include the media's obsessive coverage of the so-called "dungeon of Amstetten" in 2008, the sexual-abuse scandal at the Odenwaldschule in 2011, and the crash of Germanwings Flight 9525 in 2015.
39 See, for instance, Sherry Turkle, *Life on the Screen: Identity in the Age of the Internet* (New York: Simon & Schuster, 1995).
40 In many countries, the polarization of television programming has had a similar effect (think of Fox News and MSNBC in the United States).
41 For a detailed discussion of this phenomenon, see Schulz, *Redaktionsschluss*.
42 The problem with anything that survives in this context for a long time is that it is only able to attract this ongoing attention by being laden with affect, as in the case of a polarizing public figure or a topic that evokes persistent outrage. However, certain counter-movements have begun to form against this trend, such as the subculture of "slow journalism" (see, for instance, the movement's journal *Delayed Gratification: The Slow Journalism Magazine*).
43 At best, such experiences can be spun in a positive light as something that has been overcome, or discussed in terms of a heroic battle ("against cancer," for instance), but never in their pure negativity.
44 Of course, there are also alternative formats on the internet that accommodate ambivalent affects as well. Examples include digital storytelling, in which individuals do not shy away from thematizing traumatic events, and machinima culture, which is based on irony. See Joe Lambert, *Digital Storytelling: Capturing Lives, Creating Community* (New York and Abingdon: Routledge, 2013); and Reichert, *Die Macht der Vielen*, pp. 94–109.

V The Singularistic Life: Lifestyles, Classes, Subject Forms

1 See Beck, *Risk Society*; Anthony Giddens, *Modernity and Self-Identity: Self and Society in the Late Modern Age* (Cambridge: Polity, 1991); Zygmunt Bauman, *Liquid Modernity* (Cambridge: Polity, 2000); Richard Sennett, *The Corrosion of Character: The Personal Consequences of Work in the New Capitalism* (New York: W. W. Norton, 1998); and Castells, *The Rise of the Network Society*.
2 By "class," I mean more than just a segment of society that fits into a certain range of social statistics (for which the term "stratum" is better suited). It is rather a social group that shares a common cultural model for leading one's life, a common social position (with access to socially relevant resources or capital), and a particular form of work.
3 From the beginning, the transition to the post-industrial society has been discussed in terms of its creation of a "new (middle) class" of highly qualified professionals. See, for instance, Bell, *The Coming of Post-Industrial Society*; and

Michael Young, *The Rise of Meritocracy, 1870–2033: The New Elite of Our Social Revolution* (London: Random House, 1959). It is crucial, however, to recognize the form of its lifestyle. In this regard, see Mike Featherstone's early study *Consumer Culture and Postmodernism* (London: Sage, 1991); and David Brooks's essayistic book *Bobos in Paradise: The New Upper Class and How They Got There* (New York: Simon & Schuster, 2000). Richard Florida has discussed the lifestyle of the educated middle class in his work on the "creative class"; see his book *The Rise of the Creative Class: And How It's Transforming Work, Leisure, Community, and Everyday Life* (New York: Basic Books, 2002). This concept should be used with caution, however, because the adjective "creative" has implications that can easily lead to a normative overestimation of this type of lifestyle.

4 Here I will use these three terms synonymously.

5 Data on the expansion of education in Western countries are not always easy to compare because of the differences in their respective educational systems. Nevertheless, there has been a clear and universal increase in the proportion of people earning high academic degrees. In the United States, for instance, the proportion of the total population with a college degree in 1950 was just 5%. By the year 2009, this number had steadily grown to 30%. See Camille Ryan and Julie Siebens, "Educational Attainment in the United States: 2009," *United States Census Bureau* (February 2012), online. In Germany, the number of newly enrolled university students per year increased from 6% of the population in 1960 to 37% in 2005. In 2012, university graduates constituted 41% of the British population and 31% of the population in France. See Mathias Brandt, "Bevölkerungsanteil mit Hochschulabschluss," *Statista: Das Statistik-Portal* (September 9, 2014), online.

6 See Ulrich Beck, "Jenseits von Stand und Klasse? Soziale Ungleichheiten, gesellschaftliche Individualisierungsprozesse und die Entstehung neuer sozialer Formationen und Identitäten," in *Soziale Ungleichheiten*, ed. Reinhard Kreckel (Göttingen: Schwartz, 1983), pp. 35–74; and Schulze, *Die Erlebnisgesellschaft*.

7 See Helmut Schelsky, "Die Bedeutung des Schichtungsbegriffs für die Analyse der gegenwärtigen deutschen Gesellschaft," in Schelsky, *Auf der Suche nach Wirklichkeit: Gesammelte Aufsätze* (Düsseldorf: E. Diederichs, 1965), pp. 331–6. For similar arguments made by Anglophone scholars, see Galbraith, *The Affluent Society*; Charles Wright Mills, *White Collar: The American Middle Class* (New York: Oxford University Press, 1951); Whyte, *The Organization Man*; and, with a somewhat different orientation, John Goldthorpe et al., *The Affluent Worker in the Class Structure* (Cambridge University Press, 1969).

8 This development has been especially acute in the United States and Germany. France and Great Britain, on the contrary, preserved more features of nineteenth-century working culture and the classical bourgeoisie (not to mention the aristocracy) during industrial modernity.

9 See Robert Putnam, *Our Kids: The American Dream in Crisis* (New York: Simon & Schuster, 2015). Putnam provides an abundance of quantitative evidence for this structural change. For evidence supporting the class polarity between high- and low-qualified people from a global perspective, see Scott, *A World in Emergence*. In parallel to this, representations of social inequality now tend to depict hierarchical instead of gradual differences. See Neckel, *Flucht nach vorn*, pp. 149–57.

10 In the United States, according to Putnam's study, this line is relatively easy to draw: between those with and those without a college degree. What counts as high cultural capital, however, itself depends on social processes of evaluation. The expansion of education has thus led to the fact that a college degree in itself may not be a source of high cultural capital, but rather only a degree from a prestigious university. Regarding the similar situation in Great Britain, see Mike Savage et al., *Social Class in the 21st Century* (London: Pelican, 2015), pp. 219–58.

11 See, for instance, Thomas Piketty, *Capital in the Twenty-First Century*, trans. Arthur Goldhammer (Cambridge, MA: Harvard University Press, 2014); and Branko Milanović, *Global Inequality: A New Approach for the Age of Globalization* (Cambridge, MA: Harvard University Press, 2016).
12 Esping-Andersen, *Changing Classes*. See, also, Heinz Bude, *Die Ausgeschlossenen: Das Ende vom Traum der gerechten Gesellschaft* (Munich: Hanser, 2008); and Oliver Nachtwey, *Germany's Hidden Crisis: Social Decline in the Heart of Europe*, trans. David Fernbach and Loren Balhorn (London: Verso, 2018). Nachtwey's book contains an abundance of statistical evidence for social decline.
13 See Putnam, *Our Kids*, pp. 36–7.
14 With respect to income and assets, the educated class thus includes a broad range between the upper middle class and those whose employment is precarious (mostly young people). My thesis, however, is that its lifestyle follows an overarching cultural pattern despite these differences in material resources.
15 See Putnam, *Our Kids*, p. 35.
16 For further discussion of these phenomena, see, again, ibid.
17 See Ralf Dahrendorf, "Die globale Klasse und die neue Ungleichheit," *Merkur* 54/11 (2000), pp. 1057–68.
18 The concept of the "three-thirds society" was first formulated in a working paper presented by the Friedrich-Ebert-Stiftung: "Gesellschaft im Reformprozess" (Berlin, 2006), online. This working paper prompted a full-length study by Rita Müller-Hilmer, "Gesellschaft im Reformprozess: Umfrage im Auftrag der Friedrich-Ebert-Stiftung," *TNS Infratest Sozialforschung* (2006), online.
19 Although my analysis of the late-modern social structure has in part been inspired by Pierre Bourdieu, my results are not identical with his. What I refer to as the educated class may consist of elements from Bourdieu's notion of the upper class as well as from the previous middle class, but it has a cultural structure that is entirely its own.
20 The concept of the "elevator effect" (*Fahrstuhleffekt*) was first formulated by Ulrich Beck in his article "Jenseits von Stand und Klasse?" On Beck's elevator, all social strata travel upward; differences remain between them, but they all reach a higher level. Ironically, Beck developed this concept to describe what he called "second modernity" (the period after classical modernity), though it has now become clear that it is in fact more applicable to his notion of "first modernity" (industrial modernity).
21 On this topic, see also Tanjev Schultz and Klaus Hurrelmann, eds., *Die Akademiker-Gesellschaft: Müssen in Zukunft alle studieren?* (Weinheim: Juventa Verlag, 2013).
22 "Underclass" is a difficult term; it goes without saying that I do not mean it pejoratively here.
23 On the culturalization of inequality and the underclass, see Beverley Skeggs's clear-sighted discussion in her book *Class, Self, Culture*. For a historical perspective, see Anne McClintock, *Imperial Leather: Race, Gender, and Sexuality in the Colonial Contest* (New York: Routledge, 1995).

1 The Lifestyle of the New Middle Class: Successful Self-Actualization

1 I discussed this tradition above in Part I, Chapter 4.
2 See Reckwitz, *Das hybride Subjekt*, pp. 452–5. On the California lifestyle, see especially Diedrich Diederichsen and Anselm Franke, eds., *The Whole Earth: Kalifornien und das Verschwinden des Außen* (Berlin: Sternberg Press, 2013).
3 See Ronald Inglehart, *Modernization and Postmodernization: Cultural, Economic, and Political Change in 43 Societies* (Princeton University Press, 1997); and Miguel E. Basáñez, *A World of Three Cultures: Honor, Achievement, Joy* (New York: Oxford University Press, 2016).
4 Regarding positive psychology, see Duane Schultz, *Growth Psychology: Models of the Healthy Personality* (New York: Van Nostrand Reinhold, 1977). On this

process as a whole, see Daniel Bell's lucid discussion in his book *The Cultural Contradictions of Capitalism*.
5   See Reckwitz, *Das hybride Subjekt*, pp. 97–108 and 242–7.
6   The front lines of these culture wars are well known. Countercultures fight against the rationalism, moral repression, educational rigidity, and commercialism of the bourgeoisie, whereas the latter endeavors to keep the aesthetic decadence, unworldliness, and subversive forces of the countercultures at bay. From the beginning, however, there has been a complex interplay between these two poles: the protagonists of aesthetic countercultures often come from the bourgeoisie and have been influenced by its interests in art and education. Conversely, the bourgeoisie is often fascinated with the expressive freedom of bohemians. On this topic, see Peter Gay, *Pleasure Wars: The Bourgeois Experience, Victoria to Freud* (New York: W. W. Norton, 1988).
7   Among the ten socio-cultural milieus identified and analyzed by the SINUS Institut in Heidelberg, four are representative of the overarching cultural model of the educated class: the milieu of so-called "expeditives" (the "creative milieu" in the strict sense), the "liberal-intellectual" milieu, the milieu of "performers," and the "socio-ecological" milieu. In quantitative terms, these four groups constitute approximately 30 percent of the population. See SINUS Markt- und Sozialforschung GmbH, "Information on Sinus-Milieus" (2018), online.
8   Here it is sufficient to cite Abraham H. Maslow, *Motivation and Personality* (New York: Harper & Row, 1954); and Maslow, *Toward a Psychology of Being*, 2nd edn. (New York: Van Nostrand Reinhold, 1968).
9   From a cultural-critical perspective, this attitude can be regarded as narcissistic. See Christopher Lasch's book *The Culture of Narcissism*.
10 For further discussion of this structure, see Leinberger and Tucker, *The New Individualists*, pp. 226–31.
11 A certain version of this outlook is discussed in Paul Ray and Ruth Anderson, *The Cultural Creatives: How 50 Million People Are Changing the World* (New York: Three Rivers Press, 2001).
12 This is a point of connection with Schulze's book *Die Erlebnisgesellschaft*.
13 Walt Whitman, "Leaves of Grass," in *Walt Whitman and Emily Dickinson: Selections from the Norton Anthology of American Literature*, 5th edn., ed. Hershel Parker (New York: W. W. Norton, 1998), pp. 21–64, at p. 64 (line 1314).
14 See Abraham H. Maslow, "A Theory of Human Motivation," *Psychological Review* 50 (1943), pp. 370–96.
15 The question of what constitutes the "good life" has been addressed in nearly every popular self-help manual since the year 2000. It has also, however, been a recent concern of philosophers. See, for instance, Schmid, *Philosophie der Lebenskunst*; and Luc Ferry, *Learning to Live: A User's Manual*, trans. Theo Cuffe (Edinburgh: Canongate, 2010).
16 See Beatrice von Bismarck, "Introduction," in *Cultures of the Curatorial*, ed. Jörn Schafaff et al. (Berlin: Sternberg Press, 2012), pp. 7–20; and Paul O'Neill, *The Culture of Curating and the Curating of Culture(s)* (Cambridge, MA: MIT Press, 2012).
17 The concept of a plurality of singularities is outlined in Part III, Chapter 1.
18 On this aspect, see Reckwitz, *The Invention of Creativity*, pp. 201–35.
19 See Don Slater, *Consumer Culture and Modernity* (Cambridge: Polity, 1997).
20 Consumption has thus become co-creation. On this topic, see Dirk Hohnsträter, ed., *Konsum und Kreativität* (Bielefeld: Transcript, 2016); and Wolfgang Ullrich, *Alles nur Konsum: Kritik der warenästhetischen Erziehung* (Berlin: Wagenbach, 2013). Ullrich speaks of "consumption as a cultural technique" and thus further develops the concept of the "prosumer" that Alvin Toffler had first formulated as early as the 1960s.
21 See Savage et al., *Social Class in the 21st Century*, pp. 121–6.
22 In this regard, it is not the "original" context of historical things that makes them exciting in late modernity but rather the resituating of old things in the present to achieve a retro style. See Fredric Jameson, *Postmodernism, or the*

Cultural Logic of Late Capitalism (Durham, NC: Duke University Press, 1991), pp. 16–25.
23 See, for instance, Michael Jager, "Class Definition and the Aesthetics of Gentrification: Victoriana in Melbourne," in *Gentrification of the City*, ed. Neil Smith and Peter Williams (London: Routledge, 1986), pp. 78–91; and Hyung Hu Park, "Heritage Tourism," *Annals of Tourism Research* 37 (2010), pp. 116–35.
24 A prominent example of this is the reception of Buddhism in the Western educated milieu; see Charles S. Prebish and Martin Baumann, eds., *Westward Dharma: Buddhism Beyond Asia* (Berkeley: University of California Press, 2002).
25 This is clear to see in how important it is for late-modern subjects to have the latest digital technology, but also in their desire to keep current with contemporary music, fashion, and art.
26 See Richard A. Peterson and Roger M. Kern, "Changing Highbrow Taste: From Snob to Omnivore," *American Sociological Review* 61 (1996), pp. 900–7. For a similar interpretation, see Bernard Lahire, *La culture des individus: Dissonances culturelles et distinction de soi* (Paris: La Découverte, 2004).
27 See Savage et al., *Social Class in the 21st Century*, pp. 114–17.
28 See Ulf Hannerz, "Two Faces of Cosmopolitanism: Culture and Politics," *Statvetenskaplig Tidskrift* 107/3 (2005), pp. 199–213.
29 These elements are thus objects of hybridization. In light of the cosmopolitanism of the new middle class, the postcolonial concept of hybridity, which was first used to refer to local mixed cultures, is something that has to be intuited as part of the combinatory nature of the curated lifestyle.
30 This point is rightly underscored in Skeggs, *Class, Self, Culture*, pp. 155–72.
31 This has been demonstrated in the studies conducted by the SINUS Institut in Heidelberg, which examined 44 different national societies and identified similar overarching "milieus" with concordant cultural profiles.
32 See Uwe Schimank et al., *Statusarbeit unter Druck? Zur Lebensführung der Mittelschichten* (Weinheim: Beltz Juventa, 2014).
33 My discussion here of different types of capital is loosely based on the distinctions drawn by Pierre Bourdieu in his essay "The Forms of Capital."
34 See Savage et al., *Social Class in the 21st Century*, pp. 127–62.
35 On this topic, Gerhard Schulze and Pierre Bourdieu offer complementary one-sided approaches that should be thought about together. According to Schulze, late modernity is exclusively a matter of self-referential lived experiences, and thus social prestige no longer seems to play much of a role. For Bourdieu, in contrast, distinction and prestige are everything, and intrinsic values only remain as an ideological pretence. The singularistic lifestyle, however, operates on both levels simultaneously – on that of subjective experience/value and that of social prestige – and thus it is somewhat careless to think about them in such neat oppositional terms.
36 This is in line with Jeremy Rifkin's thesis that, as a symbol of status, the possession of goods is now less significant than having access to goods. See his book *The Age of Access*.
37 The inclination to showcase attractive lives can also be seen in family celebrations of big occasions (weddings, milestone birthdays), which, since the 1990s, have acquired an outsized status that goes far beyond that of traditional celebratory rituals. Here, the uniqueness and success of individuals (and couples) is reflected in the frequently extravagant uniqueness of the events themselves, which are often fully choreographed and held at select locations. On this phenomenon, see Jennifer Wiebking, "Event-Gesellschaft: Der Moment ist das Geschenk," *Frankfurter Allgemeine Sonntagszeitung* 34 (August 23, 2015), p. 9.

2 Elements of the Singularistic Lifestyle

1 For general overviews of this topic, see Carol Counihan, ed., *Food and Culture: A Reader*, 2nd edn. (New York: Routledge, 2008); and Anne Murcott et al.,

eds., *The Handbook of Food Research* (London: Bloomsbury Academic, 2013). Regarding food and the educated class in particular, see Wendy Parkins and Geoffrey Craig, *Slow Living* (New York: Berg, 2006).

2 See Claude Lévi-Strauss, *The Raw and the Cooked*, trans. John Weightman and Doreen Weightman (University of Chicago Press, 1983); and Mary Douglas, *Food in the Social Order: Studies of Food and Festivities in Three American Communities* (New York: Russell Sage Foundation, 1984).

3 See Jack Goody, *Cooking, Cuisine and Class: A Study in Comparative Sociology* (Cambridge University Press, 1982), pp. 154–90.

4 See Warren J. Belasco, *Appetite for Change: How the Counterculture Took on the Food Industry* (New York: Pantheon Books, 1989). Other important contributions to this renaissance include experimental new developments from bourgeois and aristocratic cooking traditions (especially French food in the form of *nouvelle cuisine*) and so-called molecular cooking.

5 See Krishnendu Ray, *The Ethnic Restaurateur* (London: Bloomsbury Academic, 2016); and David Inglis and Debra L. Gimlin, eds., *The Globalization of Food* (London: Routledge, 2008).

6 For examples of such experimentation, see the discussion of restaurants in Sven Hausherr and Nina Trippel, eds., *Cee Cee Berlin*, 2 vols. (Berlin: Distanz Verlag, 2014); and the discussion of recipes in Meike Peters, *Eat in My Kitchen: To Cook, to Bake, to Eat, and to Treat* (Munich: Prestel, 2016).

7 By means of particularly high-quality ingredients or particular methods of preparation, for instance, basic components of a dish can be redefined as exciting and authentic ("tomatoes that actually taste like tomatoes," organic beef, etc.).

8 See Parkins and Craig, *Slow Living*; and Michaela DeSoucey and Isabelle Techoueyres, "Virtue and Valorization: 'Local Food' in the United States and France," in *The Globalization of Food*, ed. David Inglis and Debra L. Gimlin (London: Routledge, 2008), pp. 81–96.

9 See Rob Harrison et al., eds., *The Ethical Consumer* (London: Sage, 2005).

10 See Grauel, *Gesundheit, Genuss und gutes Gewissen*.

11 See Alison Pearlman, *Smart Casual: The Transformation of Gourmet Restaurant Style in America* (University of Chicago Press, 2013); and Michael Pollan, *Cooked: A Natural History of Transformation* (New York: Penguin, 2014).

12 Cultural-sociological studies of how and where people reside – beyond the social politics of urban living spaces – are few and far between. One work that comes to mind is Irene Nierhaus and Andreas Nierhaus, eds., *Wohnen-Zeigen: Modelle und Akteure des Wohnens in Architektur und visueller Kultur* (Bielefeld: Transcript, 2014).

13 See Hilpert's book *Die funktionelle Stadt*.

14 For contemporary documentation of this, see the photographs in Herlinde Koelbl et al., *Das deutsche Wohnzimmer* (Munich: C. J. Bucher, 1980). In contrast, the bourgeoisie was, of course, more aesthetically refined, and thus today's educated middle class still often relies on its sense of style.

15 See, for instance, Sharon Zukin, *Loft Living: Culture and Capital in Urban Change* (New Brunswick, NJ: Rutgers University Press, 1989); and Richard George Rogers, *Towards an Urban Renaissance* (London: E. & F. N. Spon, 1999).

16 For widely divergent perspectives on this phenomenon, see Richard Florida, *Who's Your City? How the Creative Economy is Making Where to Live the Most Important Decision of Your Life* (New York: Basic Books, 2008); and Andrej Holm, "Die Karawane zieht weiter: Stationen der Aufwertung in der Berliner Innenstadt," in *Intercity Istanbul–Berlin*, ed. Mario Pschera et al. (Berlin: Dağyeli, 2010), pp. 89–101.

17 See Jane Jacobs, *The Death and Life of Great American Cities: The Failure of Current Planning* (New York: Vintage Books, 1961).

18 On the new middle class's approach to designing apartments, see Zeynep Arsel and Jonathan Bean, "Taste Regimes and Market-Mediated Practices," *Journal of Consumer Research* 39 (2013), pp. 899–917.

19 As empirical evidence for this statement and the following remarks, see the texts and photographs in Frederik Frede et al., eds., *Freunde von Freunden: Berlin* (Berlin: Distanz, 2011), which is based on a blog from the creative scene. Incidentally, it should be noted that the economic capital of members of the new middle class is hardly reflected at all in the style of their apartments. In its basic structure, this style is basically the same for everyone, from the creative stars of the upper class to precariously employed artists. The only detectable differences are in the sizes of apartments and the costs of their decorations (from original classic designs to pieces bought at flea markets).
20 On this concept in the history of design, see David Gebhard, "William Wurster and His Californian Contemporaries: The Idea of Regionalism and Soft Modernism," in *An Everyday Modernism: The Houses of William Wurster*, ed. Marc Treib (San Francisco Museum of Art, 1995), pp. 164–83.
21 More than mere neutral background pieces, modernist furniture has also been singularized through a preference for classic designs. Finally, vintage furniture – used pieces from the flea market or inherited from relatives – has the double advantage of seeming singular, and often, at the same time, already being in the modernist style.
22 This is especially clear from their color schemes. Whereas rooms and the majority of furniture are typically in neutral or natural colors (brown, gray, white, black), accessories can be in any color in the crayon box.
23 Long stays abroad can also be privately motivated, and this has been facilitated by intercontinental markets for apartment swapping between big cities and vacation spots (often fueled by the trend of senior citizens spending the winter months in warmer climates).
24 See Christensen, *Global Experience Industries*, pp. 41–112.
25 See John Urry, *The Tourist Gaze: Leisure and Travel in Contemporary Societies* (London: Sage, 1990); Robert Schäfer, *Tourismus und Authentizität: Zur gesellschaftlichen Organisation von Außeralltäglichkeit* (Bielefeld: Transcript, 2015); and Dean MacCannell's classic study *The Tourist: A New Theory of the Leisure Class* (New York: Schocken Books, 1976).
26 See Urry, *The Tourist Gaze*.
27 As in the case of houses and apartments, so too with travel: economic capital, which varies considerably within the educated class, has no effect on the general cultural *pattern* followed by its members' traveling practices.
28 See Andreas Pott, *Orte des Tourismus: Eine raum- und gesellschaftstheoretische Untersuchung* (Bielefeld: Transcript, 2007); and Sophia Labadi, "World Heritage, Authenticity, and Post-Authenticity," in *Heritage and Globalization*, ed. Colin Long and Sophia Labadi (New York: Routledge, 2010), pp. 66–84.
29 Accordingly, travelers have to prepare in advance in order to know what to see: "One only sees what one knows" (as Goethe put it). In this respect, travel guides now do much more than point out traditional attractions. See, for instance, "Wallpaper City Guide" or the *Süddeutsche Zeitung*'s regular column "Ein perfektes Wochenende in …".
30 On the phenomenon of poverty tourism, see Malte Steinbrink and Andreas Pott, "Global Slumming: Zur Genese und Globalisierung des Armutstourismus," in *Tourismusräume: Zur soziokulturellen Konstruktion eines globalen Phänomens*, ed. Karlheinz Wöhler et al. (Bielefeld: Transcript, 2010), pp. 247–70.
31 Regarding the (de)authentication of so-called "trendy neighborhoods," see Jan Glatter and Daniela Weber, "Die mediale Konstruktion des Stereotyps Szeneviertel in Reiseführern," in *Tourismusräume: Zur soziokulturellen Konstruktion eines globalen Phänomens*, ed. Karlheinz Wöhler et al. (Bielefeld: Transcript, 2010), pp. 43–66.
32 See Maxine Feifer, *Going Places: The Ways of the Tourist from Imperial Rome to the Present Day* (London: Macmillan, 1985).
33 On this entire complex of topics, see Chris Shilling, *The Body in Technology, Culture, and Society* (London: Sage, 2005).
34 From an economic perspective, these three body regimes are in turn part of the

late-modern experience and creative economy (fitness, fashion, cosmetic surgery, athletic apparel, physically active vacations, etc.).
35 See Dierk Spreen, *Upgradekultur: Der Körper in der Enhancement-Gesellschaft* (Bielefeld: Transcript, 2015).
36 See Waltraud Posch, *Projekt Körper: Wie der Kult um die Schönheit unser Leben prägt* (Frankfurt am Main: Campus, 2009); and Cornelia Koppetsch, ed., *Körper und Status: Zur Soziologie der Attraktivität* (Konstanz: UVK, 2000).
37 On the following discussion, see Thomas Alkemeyer et al., eds., *Ordnung in Bewegung: Choreographien des Sozialen – Körper in Sport, Tanz, Arbeit und Bildung* (Bielefeld: Transcript, 2009); Thomas Alkemeyer et al., eds., *Aufs Spiel gesetzte Körper: Aufführungen des Sozialen in Sport und populärer Kultur* (Konstanz: UVK, 2003); and Belinda Wheaton, *The Cultural Politics of Lifestyle Sports* (London: Routledge, 2013).
38 This does not involve copying original practices but rather appropriating them through global processes of cultural translation. On the tango movement, for instance, see Gabriele Klein, ed., *Tango in Translation: Tanz zwischen Medien, Kulturen, Kunst und Politik* (Bielefeld: Transcript, 2009). Regarding yoga, see Suzanne Newcombe, "The Development of Modern Yoga: A Survey of the Field," *Religion Compass* 3 (2009), pp. 986–1002.
39 See Martin Stern, *Stil-Kulturen: Performative Konstellationen von Technik, Spiel und Risiko in neuen Sportpraktiken* (Bielefeld: Transcript, 2010).
40 See ibid. Although tango may at first sight seem like a highly regulated dance, today's dancers are in fact playfully testing its possibilities (in matters such as gender dualism, for instance).
41 See Ronald Lutz, *Laufen und Läuferleben: Zum Verhältnis von Körper, Bewegung und Identität* (Frankfurt am Main: Campus, 1989).
42 See Martin Stern, "Heldenfiguren im Wagnissport: Zur medialen Inszenierung wagnissportlicher Erlebnisräume," in *Aufs Spiel gesetzte Körper*, ed. Thomas Alkemeyer et al., pp. 37–54.
43 See Alain Ehrenberg's book *La culte de la performance*.
44 In the case of the United States, see Wayne J. Urban and Jennings L. Wagoner, *American Education: A History* (London: Routledge, 2008), pp. 185–292. The flipside of educational standardization is the consequent production of distinctions by means of grades, which are used to justify different professional career paths.
45 See Steven Mintz and Susan Kellogg, *Domestic Revolutions: A Social History of American Family Life* (New York: Free Press, 1988), pp. 107–32.
46 For detailed discussions of this phenomenon, see Annette Lareau, *Unequal Childhoods: Class, Race, and Family Life* (Berkeley: University of California Press, 2003); and Putnam, *Our Kids*, pp. 80–134.
47 The ideal of child self-actualization has been familiar to modern pedagogy from the life-reform movements since Rousseau's time. With its reformed pedagogy, the counterculture of the 1970s and 1980s also introduced an important stage of development. Whereas, there, the idea of child self-actualization (according to the Summerhill model, for instance) was *laissez-faire*, the "concerted cultivation" practiced by today's educated middle class entails intensive parenting.
48 On human capital, see Harry Hendrick, "Die sozialinvestive Kindheit," in *Kindheiten in der Moderne: Eine Geschichte der Sorge*, ed. Meike Sophia Baader et al. (Franfurt am Main: Campus, 2014), pp. 456–91. Regarding the current parenting discourse, see Gerald Hüther and Uli Hauser, *Jedes Kind ist hoch begabt: Die angeborenen Talente unserer Kinder und was wir daraus machen* (Munich: Btb Verlag, 2012).
49 See, for instance, Heinz-Elmar Tenorth, *Geschichte der Erziehung: Einführung in die Grundzüge ihrer neuzeitlichen Entwicklung* (Weinheim: Juventa, 2010), pp. 364–88.
50 In this regard, see also Heinz Bude, *Bildungspanik: Was unsere Gesellschaft spaltet* (Bonn: Bundeszentrale für politische Bildung, 2011).
51 Tenorth mentions this phenomenon only in passing (*Geschichte der Erziehung*,

p. 369). For a more comprehensive ethnographic discussion, see Putnam, *Our Kids*, pp. 135–90. From the perspective of parenting, see Agnès van Zanten, "A Good Match: Appraising Worth and Estimating Quality in School Choice," in *Constructing Quality: The Classification of Goods in Markets*, ed. Jens Beckert and Christine Musselin (Oxford University Press, 2013), pp. 77–99.

52 See Margret Rasfeld and Stephan Breidenbach, *Schulen im Aufbruch: Eine Anstiftung* (Munich: Kösel, 2014); and Ken Robinson and Lou Aronica, *Creative Schools: The Grassroots Revolution That's Transforming Education* (New York: Penguin, 2016). Accordingly, what is required of teachers has also changed. Rather than being standardized purveyors of knowledge, teachers are now expected to be charismatic personalities with leadership and mentorship qualities. Teachers themselves have thus become important figures in the creative economy. That said, the organization of teaching still seems to restrict the singularization of pupils and their educational development.

53 On the notion of excellence in education, see Urban and Wagoner, *American Education*, pp. 389–444.

54 For discussions of this topic with somewhat different emphases, see Hochschild, *The Time Bind*; and Flaßpöhler, *Wir Genussarbeiter*.

55 For further discussion of the structure of late-modern partnerships, the most important aspects of which are the project of self-actualization and the economics of choice, see Reckwitz, *Das hybride Subjekt*, pp. 527–54.

56 See Florida, *The Rise of the Creative Class*; and Florida, *Cities and the Creative Class*.

57 On mobility and its relation to social class, see David Goodhart, *The Road to Somewhere: The Populist Revolt and the Future of Politics* (London: Hurst & Company, 2017).

58 See Lutz Roth, *Die Erfindung des Jugendlichen* (Munich: Juventa, 1983); and Benno Hafeneger, *Jugendbilder: Zwischen Hoffnung, Kontrolle, Erziehung und Dialog* (Opladen: Leske + Budrich, 1995). Of course, excessive and transgressive elements of youth culture are mostly excluded from middle-class juvenility, which is strongly oriented toward healthiness.

59 On this topic, see Silke van Dyk and Stephan Lessenich, eds., *Die jungen Alten: Analysen einer neuen Sozialfigur* (Frankfurt am Main: Campus, 2009).

60 Even the aesthetic youth scenes since the 1990s never really stabilize as countercultures; instead, they are quickly sucked into the pool of interesting options for cultural consumers in the creative economy, which is based on the constant replenishment of cultural novelties.

61 See Klaus Hurrelmann and Erik Albrecht, *Die heimlichen Revolutionäre: Wie die Generation Y unsere Welt verändert* (Weinheim: Belzt, 2014), pp. 96–116.

62 See Michael Kimmel, *The Gendered Society* (New York: Oxford University Press, 2000), pp. 264–8.

63 Historically speaking, the women of the new middle class are thus the "gender climbers" of late-modern society, while the men of the underclass are its "gender losers." There is thus a gendered aspect to the paternoster-elevator effect. It would be amiss, however, to think about the question of gender independently from the issue of class. The claim in certain popular diagnoses that, regardless of any class distinctions, men in general have become historical "losers" is therefore off the mark. See, for instance, Susan Faludi, *Stiffed: The Betrayal of the American Man* (New York: William Morrow, 1999).

64 See Élisabeth Badinter, *Man/Woman: The One is the Other*, trans. Barbara Wright (London: Collins Harvill, 1999); and Susanne Schröter, *FeMale: Über Grenzverläufe zwischen Geschlechtern* (Frankfurt am Main: Fischer, 2002).

65 The wide acceptance of gay men and lesbian women in the new middle class can also be attributed to this diversification of gender roles. In this case, gender variation concerns sexual orientation. It remains to be seen whether this might be a sign of the general singularization of sexual orientations as well. A wider dissemination of bisexuality – in all its different varieties – or also of asexuality might also be an indicator of this. For now, the possible singularization

of so-called biological sex is also an open question (since the year 2010, an indication of this has been the rise in the number of people who identify as transgender).
66 As distinguished from the nineteenth-century classical liberalism of "possessive individualism" (in C. B. Macpherson's terms). The new middle class supports the politics of apertistic–differential liberalism, which I will discuss in Part VI.
67 On meritocracy, see Michael Young's classic study *The Rise of Meritocracy*. For a current analysis, see Thomas Frank, *Listen, Liberal: Or, What Ever Happened to the Party of the People?* (New York: Metropolitan Books, 2016). In light of the high levels of under-employment among young educated people after the 2008 financial crisis, the question remains whether meritocratism has been temporarily damaged or permanently eroded.
68 See Joachim Raschke, "Politik und Wertwandel in westlichen Demokratien," *Aus Politik und Zeitgeschichte* 36 (1980), pp. 23–45; and, for more recent developments, Ray and Anderson's book *Cultural Creatives*. Regarding the new political divide between globalization and isolationism, see Hanspeter Kriesi et al., "Globalization and the Transformation of National Political Space: Six European Countries Compared," *European Journal of Political Research* 45 (2006), pp. 921–56.
69 Since the 1980s, this new liberalism has transformed both of the two large people's parties that stem from industrial modernity: the Conservatives and the Social Democrats. This is clearest to see in the case of the Democratic Party in the United States, which, from 1970 to 2010, transformed from a working-class party to one supported by the educated class. New liberalism has also contributed to the creation of a series of new, socially liberal, parties (such as the Greens in Germany, the Green-Liberal Party in Switzerland, and the Neos Party in Austria).
70 I have already discussed, in the previous chapters, the tensions created by today's labor market and internet culture. Some of these issues will be revisited here.
71 The case is similar when the performative dimension of self-actualization takes the upper hand and the *staging* of experience becomes more important than the experience itself.
72 On the modern game of intensification, see Gerhard Schulze, *Die beste aller Welten: Wohin bewegt sich die Gesellschaft im 21. Jahrhundert?* (Munich: Hanser, 2004); and Hartmut Rosa, *Social Acceleration: A New Theory of Modernity*, trans. Jonathan Trejo-Mathys (New York: Columbia University Press, 2013).
73 At this point, it is possible to draw a connection to Jürgen Link's idea of "flexible normalism," which he formulated in his book *Versuch über den Normalism*. Consider, for instance, personality traits such as laziness, indiscipline, messiness, or social phobias, which, though undoubtedly idiosyncratic, are not perceived as having the value of the singular by those leading an attractive lifestyle.
74 One common reaction to this ineluctable disappointment has been to develop a more flexible coping strategy. In this regard, see Uwe Schimank, "Lebensplanung!? Biographische Entscheidungspraktiken irritierter Mittelschichten," *Berliner Journal für Soziologie* 25 (2015), pp. 7–31; and Heinz Bude, *Gesellschaft der Angst* (Hamburg: Hamburger Edition, 2016).
75 I discussed this phenomenon above in Part II, Chapter 2.
76 In light of all this, "crisis-proof" forms of capital have become all the more important to the educated middle class. A large inheritance, for example, can usually guarantee a certain amount of security, as can a degree from an elite American or British university.
77 On the concept of disappointing experiences, see Schulze, *Die Erlebnisgesellschaft*, pp. 53–7.
78 My intention here is not to ennoble this historical way of life but rather to point out the unintended consequences of the late-modern lifestyle.
79 The psychologist Rainer Funk stressed this point in his book *Der entgrenzte Mensch: Warum ein Leben ohne Grenzen nicht frei, sondern abhängig macht* (Gütersloh: Gütersloher Verlagshaus, 2011).

80 This concept should not be understood in a theological sense here. Late-modern art has made a theme of the *limits* of subjective self-formation. An example of this from literature is the protagonist of Hanya Yanagihara's novel *A Little Life* (New York: Doubleday, 2015).
81 On this aspect, see Elisabeth Mixa, "I Feel Good! Über Paradoxien des Wohlfüls-Imperativs im Wellness-Diskurs," in *Un-Wohl-Gefühle: Eine Kulturanalyse gegenwärtiger Befindlichkeiten*, ed. Sarah Miriam Pritz et al. (Bielefeld: Transcript, 2015), pp. 95–132. In an interesting way, David Brooks has highlighted the differences between the late-modern culture of self-actualization and the culture of organized modernity, which acknowledged self-limitations and weaknesses in "character." See his book *The Road to Character* (New York: Random House, 2015).
82 See Alain Ehrenberg, *The Weariness of the Self: Diagnosing the History of Depression in the Contemporary Age*, trans. Enrico Caouette et al. (Montreal: McGill-Queen's University Press, 2010). So-called "burnout" is also often regarded as a form of depression; see Sighard Neckel and Greta Wagner, eds., *Leistung und Erschöpfung: Burnout in der Wettbewerbsgesellschaft* (Berlin: Suhrkamp, 2014).
83 In addition to depression, a second contemporary reaction to accumulated experiences of disappointment is public violence, in which case emotions are not directed inwardly but rather outwardly. I will address this topic in Part VI.

3 The Culturalization of Inequality

1 On the general classification of the new underclass, see Esping-Andersen, *Changing Classes*; and Nachtwey, *Germany's Hidden Crisis*. The studies of social milieus published by the SINUS Institut in Heidelberg divide the underclass into three groups – "traditional," "precarious," and "hedonists" – that together constitute approximately 30 percent of the population.
2 On the concept of the "losers" in modernization, see Norbert Götz, "Modernisierungsverlierer oder Gegner der reflexiven Moderne," *Zeitschrift für Soziologie* 26/6 (1997), pp. 393–413.
3 For detailed studies of the underclass as a cultural way of life, see Joan Williams, *White Working Class: Overcoming Class Cluelessness in America* (Boston, MA: Harvard Business Review Press, 2017); Bahl, *Lebensmodelle in der Dienstleistungsgesellschaft*; Bude, *Die Ausgeschlossenen*; and Heinz Bude et al., eds., *ÜberLeben im Umbruch: Am Beispiel Wittenberge – Ansichten einer fragmentierten Gesellschaft* (Hamburg: Hamburger Edition, 2011). Regarding the younger segment of the underclass, see Stefan Wellgraf, *Hauptschüler: Zur gesellschaftlichen Produktion von Verachtung* (Bielefeld: Transcript, 2012); and Moritz Ege, *Ein Proll mit Klasse: Mode, Popkultur und soziale Ungleichheiten unter jungen Männern in Berlin* (Frankfurt am Main: Campus, 2013).
4 See Michèle Lamont, *The Dignity of Working Men: Morality and the Boundaries of Race, Class, and Immigration* (New York: Russell Sage Foundation, 2000).
5 See Bahl, *Lebensmodelle in der Dienstleistungsgesellschaft*.
6 Regarding the polarization of labor in late modernity, the sociologists Maarten Goos, Alan Manning, and Anna Salomons have compared what they call the "lousy jobs" held by the underclass with the "lovely jobs" that are typical of the new middle class. See Goos et al., "Job Polarization in Europe."
7 See Bude et al., *ÜberLeben im Umbruch*.
8 See Bourdieu, *Distinction*, pp. 374–85 (of course, Bourdieu's discussion here concerns the traditional working class). In this context, it should also be noted that the marriages and partnerships in the new underclass are usually not based on post-Romantic notions of self-actualization, as they often are in the new middle class (think of "power couples"), but are more often pragmatic unions maintained for the sake of subsistence.

9 See Skeggs, *Class, Self, Culture*, pp. 96–118. In the British context, this is the difference between the "rough" and the "respectable" working class.
10 In Germany, this discourse usually dwells on "lower-class culture," whereas in Great Britain it typically concerns "chavs." See Ege, *Ein Proll mit Klasse*; and Owen Jones, *Chavs: The Demonization of the Working Class* (London: Verso, 2016).
11 Joan Williams discusses this phenomenon at length in her book *White Working Class*.
12 Of course, this process of devaluation has a history of its own. See Richard Sennett and Jonathan Cobb, *The Hidden Injuries of Class* (New York: Vintage Books, 1972).
13 See Eva Barlösius et al., eds., *Ernährung in der Armut: Gesundheitliche, soziale und kulturelle Folgen in der Bundesrepublik Deutschland* (Berlin: Edition Sigma, 1995); and Richard Wilkinson, *Unhealthy Societies: The Afflictions of Inequality* (New York: Routledge, 1996).
14 See Skeggs, *Class, Self, Culture*, pp. 96–118. Regarding obesity, see Eva Barlösius, *Dicksein: Wenn der Körper das Verhältnis zur Gesellschaft bestimmt* (Frankfurt am Main: Campus, 2014).
15 See Putnam, *Our Kids*, pp. 46–134; and Lareau, *Unequal Childhoods*. Regarding the parenting style of underclass immigrants, see Didier Lapeyronnie, *Ghetto urbain: Ségrégation, violence, pauvreté en France aujourd'hui* (Paris: Robert Laffont, 2008).
16 See Putnam, *Our Kids*, pp. 135–90.
17 On cities in decline, see Karina M. Pallagst et al., eds., *Shrinking Cities: International Perspectives and Policy Implications* (New York: Routledge, 2015). At the same time, an additional and larger segment of the underclass (people with service jobs and the majority of immigrants) live side by side with the new middle class and the upper class in large cities.
18 See Skeggs, *Class, Self, Culture*, pp. 96–118.
19 See Philipp Staab, *Macht und Herrschaft in der Servicewelt* (Hamburg: Hamburger Edition, 2014); and Arlie Russell Hochschild, *Strangers in Their Own Land: Anger and Mourning on the American Right* (New York: The New Press, 2016). Writers have repeatedly thematized the racist, sexist, and homophobic tendencies of the underclass, as is clear from two recent and much-discussed autobiographies from France: Didier Eribon's *Returning to Reims*, trans. Michael Lucey (Cambridge, MA: MIT Press, 2013); and Édouard Louis's *The End of Eddy*, trans. Michael Lucey (New York: Farrar, Straus & Giroux, 2018).
20 See Ronald Inglehart and Pippa Norris, "Trump, Brexit, and the Rise of Populism: Economic Have-Nots and Cultural Backlash," *Harvard Kennedy School Faculty Working Paper Series* (August 2016), online. Regarding the political structure of right-wing populism, see my discussion below in Part VI, Chapter 2.
21 Historically, this is a revival of the nineteenth-century negative discourse about the underclass and the fear expressed then of the *classe dangereuse*. See Louis Chevalier, *Laboring Classes and Dangerous Classes in Paris During the First Half of the Nineteenth Century*, trans. Frank Jellinek (New York: Howard Fertig, 1973).
22 See Bahl, *Lebensmodelle in der Dienstleistungsgesellschaft*; Staab, *Macht und Herrschaft in der Servicewelt*; Wellgraf, *Hauptschüler*; Savage et al., *Social Class in the 21st Century*, pp. 331–58; and Hochschild, *Strangers in Their Own Land*. An extreme example is people referred to as "white trash," which is a cultural topos of its own. See John Hartigan, *Odd Tribes: Toward a Cultural Analysis of White People* (Durham, NC: Duke University Press, 2005); and Nancy Isenberg, *White Trash: The 400-Year Untold History of Class in America* (New York: Penguin, 2017). It is typical for people on the lower rungs of the class hierarchy to have (painful) perceptions of themselves as a class, whereas those on top of the hierarchy often have no sense of their place within the class structure: to the

(new) middle class, its lifestyle (including its politics) seems normal, "classless," and unquestionably valuable. Class blindness, in other words, is common among the privileged.

23 See Rolf Becker and Wolfgang Lauterbach, eds., *Bildung als Privileg: Erklärungen und Befunde zu den Ursachen der Bildungsgleichheit* (Wiesbaden: Springer, 2010). Both Eribon's *Returning to Reims* and Louis's *The End of Eddy* – the two autobiographical works cited above – derive much of their narrative force from the authors' descriptions of leaving behind their respective family and home town.

24 See, for instance, Dietrich Helms, ed., *Keiner wird gewinnen: Populäre Musik im Wettbewerb* (Bielefeld: Transcript, 2005).

25 See Walter Miller, "Lower Class Culture as a Generating Milieu of Gang Delinquency," *Journal of Social Issues* 14/3 (1958), pp. 5–20.

26 See Ege, *Proll mit Klasse*; Wellgraf, *Hauptschüler*; and Marc Dietrich and Martin Seeliger, eds., *Deutscher Gangsta-Rap: Sozial- und kulturwissenschaftliche Beiträge zu einem Pop-Phänomän* (Bielefeld: Transcript, 2012).

27 See, for instance, Bethany E. Bultman, *Redneck Heaven: Portrait of a Vanishing Culture* (New York: Bantam Books, 1996); and Hochschild, *Strangers in Their Own Land*. On the mobilization of an ethics of "simple people," in which the concept of "character" plays a significant role, see Williams, *White Working Class*, pp. 25–33.

28 See Olaf Groh-Samberg, "Sorgenfreier Reichtum: Jenseits von Konjunktur und Krise," *DIW Wochenbericht* 76/35 (2009), pp. 590–612; Chrystia Freeland, "The Rise of the New Global Elite," *The Atlantic* (January/February 2001), online; and Dahrendorf, "Die globale Klasse."

29 A good demonstration of the way in which members of the new upper class live and travel is the representation of their houses, apartments, and travel destinations in international magazines such as *Architectural Digest*, *Wallpaper*, or *Monocle*.

30 In some cases, creative stars will consciously break away from the self-controlled style of subjects in the educated middle class.

31 In some aspects of life, such as the real-estate markets in large cities, the upper class appears as an immediate and far stronger competitor, and this can evoke feelings of inferiority on the part of the new middle class.

32 In terms of the studies of social milieus published by the SINUS Institut in Heidelberg, this class includes the "adaptive-pragmatic milieu," the "new middle-class milieu," and at least parts of the "established conservative milieu," which together make up approximately 25 percent of the population. See SINUS Markt- und Sozialforschung GmbH, "Information on Sinus-Milieus."

33 For a discussion of many of the features of the old middle class, see Goodhart, *The Road to Somewhere*, pp. 19–48, 117–214. On the middle class in general, see Schimank, *Statusarbeit unter Druck?* On the tradition of petit-bourgeois culture, see Heinz Schilling, *Kleinbürger: Mentalität und Lebensstil* (Frankfurt am Main: Campus, 2013). Some of the interpretations presented in Joan Williams's book *White Working Class* also pertain to the old middle class.

34 Especially in Germany, which cultivates a system of vocational training that provides an alternative to college education, the traditional middle class is more stable than it is in the United States or Great Britain.

35 This group includes employees who work closely with the educated middle class, such as certain professionals in the fields of healthcare and education (physiotherapists, childcare providers, retail workers in fashionable stores, etc.), and who are still in the process of earning higher qualifications.

36 The popularity of the Front National in France, which has been growing since the 1990s, and the Brexit vote in Great Britain in 2016 can be attributed to just such an alliance between the new (white) underclass and the rural old middle class. In general, the much-discussed "crisis of the middle class" pertains to the old middle class. On this topic, see Steffen Mau, *Lebenschancen: Wohin driftet die Mittelschicht?* (Bonn: Bundeszentrale für politische Bildung, 2012).

37 This can be seen, for instance, in the forms of popular culture that are enjoyed by younger members of the educated class. On this matter, see Skeggs, *Class, Self, Culture*, pp. 105–18.
38 In 2016, this element seems to have played a role in the election of the billionaire Donald Trump as President of the United States.

VI Differential Liberalism and Cultural Essentialism: The Transformation of the Political

1 See David Harvey, *A Brief History of Neoliberalism* (New York: Oxford University Press, 2005).

1 Apertistic–Differential Liberalism and the Politics of the Local

1 The corporatist/social-democratic paradigm also had a conservative variant (in the politics of Konrad Adenauer and Charles de Gaulle, for instance), so that it formed the background of the entire left-to-right spectrum. Following Jan-Werner Müller, one could even say that the Christian-democratic conservative parties were even more influential in carrying out corporatist-driven policies after 1945. See Jan-Werner Müller, *Contesting Democracies: Political Ideas in Twentieth-Century Europe* (New Haven, CT: Yale University Press, 2011), pp. 124–70.
2 See Wagner, *A Sociology of Modernity*, pp. 73–122; Lash and Urry, *The End of Organized Capitalism*, pp. 17–83; Rosanvallon, *The Society of Equals*; and, regarding the particular example of Sweden, Thomas Etzemüller, *Die Romantik der Rationalität: Alva & Gunnar Myrdal – Social Engineering in Sweden* (Bielefeld: Transcript, 2010).
3 On this context, see Lash and Urry, *The End of Organized Capitalism*; and Wagner, *A Sociology of Modernity*.
4 This dual structure of late-modern liberalism is easy to overlook (or, within the framework of the left–right distinction, it is often misinterpreted as the "neoliberalization of social democracy" or the "socio-political liberalization of conservatism," for instance). It is probably no coincidence that the dual structure of new liberalism has been perceived most clearly (and usually judged negatively) by outsiders – that is, by proponents of the radical left or the radical right. See, for instance, Jean-Claude Michéa, *Realm of Lesser Evil: An Essay of Liberal Civilization*, trans. David Fernbach (Cambridge: Polity, 2009).
5 See Bob Jessop, *The Future of the Capitalist State* (Cambridge: Polity, 2002), pp. 95–139. For additional analysis of neoliberalism, see Thomas Biebricher, ed., *Der Staat des Neoliberalismus* (Baden-Baden: Nomos, 2016); and Gerhard Willke, *Neoliberalismus* (Frankfurt am Main: Campus, 2003).
6 See Nikolas S. Rose, *Governing the Soul: The Shaping of the Private Self*, 2nd edn. (London: Free Association Books, 1999).
7 At this point, it is important to keep in mind that the economization of the social in late modernity, which I discussed in detail in Part II, cannot be *reduced* to a mere result of state politics. As we have seen, it has already been taking place autonomously and with its own dynamics in the economic sphere as well as in other areas (such as in medial–digital interactions or religious markets). However, the competition state supports and *intensifies* this process of marketization in those areas that are accessible to it, either directly (education, social welfare, healthcare) or indirectly (the liberalization of product markets, tax law), and it undergirds this process on discursive levels.
8 See Terry Flew, *Global Creative Industries* (Cambridge: Polity, 2013), pp. 131–56. For a critical response to this development in the case of Great Britain, see Robert Hewison, *Cultural Capital: The Rise and Fall of Creative Britain* (London: Verso, 2014).

9 See Samuel Moyn, *The Last Utopia: Human Rights in History* (Cambridge, MA: Harvard University Press, 2010).
10 See, for instance, Shannon Harper and Barbara Reskin, "Affirmative Action at School and on the Job," *Annual Review of Sociology* 31 (2005), pp. 357–79; and Ulrike Hormel and Albert Scherr, eds., *Diskriminierung: Grundlagen und Forschungsergebnisse* (Wiesbaden: Verlag für Sozialwissenschaften, 2010).
11 See Alban Knecht, *Lebensqualität produzieren: Ressourcentheorie und Machtanalyse des Wohlfahrtsstaat* (Wiesbaden: Verlag für Sozialwissenschaften, 2010).
12 See Steven Vertovec, "'Diversity' and the Social Imaginary," *European Journal of Sociology* 53/3 (2012), pp. 287–312; and Salzbrunn, *Vielfalt/Diversität*.
13 See Baur, *Biodiversität*. On the international level, this development manifested itself most clearly in UNESCO's "Universal Declaration on Cultural Diversity" (2001), which champions the protection and promotion of the heterogeneity of cultural forms of expression and the heterogeneity of ethnic-cultural groups.
14 See Helmut K. Anheier and Yudhishthir Raj Isar, eds., *Heritage, Memory, and Identity* (London: Sage, 2011).
15 See Yúdice, *The Expediency of Culture*.
16 See Salzbrunn, *Vielfalt/Diversität*; Regine Bendl, *Diversität und Diversitätsmanagement* (Vienna: Facultas, 2012); and Günther Vedder et al., eds., *Fallstudien zum Diversity Management* (Munich: Rainer Hampp Verlag, 2011).
17 For a more detailed discussion of this process (with a somewhat different emphasis), see Reckwitz, *The Invention of Creativity*, pp. 173–200.
18 See Helmut K. Anheier and Yudhishthir Raj Isar, eds., *Cities, Cultural Policy, and Governance* (London: Sage, 2012).
19 See Roland Robertson, "Glocalization: Time–Space and Homogeneity–Heterogeneity," in *Global Modernities*, ed. Mike Featherstone et al. (London: Sage, 1995), pp. 25–44.
20 For such an understanding of governmentality, see Michel Foucault, *Security, Territory, Population: Lectures at the Collège de France, 1977–1978*, trans. Graham Burchell (New York: Palgrave Macmillan, 2007).
21 See Scott, *A World in Emergence*; and Paul Knox, ed., *Atlas of Cities* (Princeton University Press, 2014).
22 See Hilpert, *Die funktionelle Stadt*.
23 See Robert Imrie and Mike Raco, eds., *Urban Renaissance? New Labour, Community, and Urban Policy* (Bristol: Policy Press, 2003).
24 See Löw, *Soziologie der Städte*; and Helmut Berking and Martina Löw, eds., *Die Eigenlogik der Städte: Neue Wege für Stadtforschung* (Frankfurt am Main: Campus, 2008).
25 Regarding this distinction, see Yi-Fu Tuan's book *Space and Place*.
26 It is therefore no surprise that the late-modern urban renaissance often relies on the architecture, use models, and aesthetics from the time *before* industrial modernity (the bourgeois city) or on clear movements *against* industrial standardization (metropolises, trendy neighborhoods).
27 On this process, see the case studies presented in Sharon Zukin's *Loft Living* and Richard D. Lloyd's book *Neo-Bohemia: Art and Commerce in the Postindustrial City* (New York: Routledge, 2010).
28 See Paul M. Bray, "The New Urbanism: Celebrating the City," *Places* 8/4 (1993), pp. 56–65.
29 For a detailed discussion of this process, see Mónica Montserrat Degen, *Sensing Cities: Regenerating Public Life in Barcelona and Manchester* (London: Routledge, 2009).
30 Since the 1980s, one piece of evidence for the fact that cities are concerned with their own valorization has been the lively public interest (especially among the educated class) taken in large-scale municipal projects. Think of the controversies surrounding the renovation of Frankfurt's and Dresden's city centers or

the reconstruction of the Berlin Palace. These debates were largely about the authenticity or inauthenticity of the cities in question.
31 This singularization can take place, for instance, through a unique ensemble of architecture and streets, through a heterogeneity and richness of available activities, or through a complex visual language that draws vitality from historical references.
32 Richard Florida discusses this topic at length in his books *Cities and the Creative Class* and *Who's Your City?*
33 See Reinhard Bachleitner and H. Jürgen Kagelmann, eds., *Kultur/Städte/ Tourismus* (Munich: Profil Verlag, 2003).
34 On various aspects of this phenomenon, see Charles Landry, *The Creative City: A Toolkit for Urban Innovators* (London: Earthscan, 2008); Stephanie Hemelryk Donald et al., eds., *Branding Cities: Cosmopolitanism, Parochialism, and Social Change* (New York: Routledge, 2009); John Punter, ed., *Urban Design and the British Urban Renaissance* (New York: Routledge, 2010); and Löw, *Soziologie der Städte*.
35 Regarding city branding and architecture, see Anna Klingmann, *Brandscapes: Architecture in the Experience Economy* (Cambridge, MA: MIT Press, 2007); on the cultivation of creative scenes, see Bastian Lange, *Räume der Kreativszene: Culturpreneurs und ihre Orte* (Bielefeld: Transcript, 2007); and, on the topic of high culture, see Kylie Message, *New Museums and the Making of Culture* (Oxford: Berg, 2006).
36 See Sharon Zukin, *Naked City: The Death and Life of Authentic Urban Places* (New York: Oxford University Press, 2011).
37 It is telling that – analogous to the situation in the creative economy – the qualitative features of cities have also been translated into quantifications: think of city rankings.
38 Regarding cities on the rise, see Harald Simons and Lukas Weiden, *Schwarmstädte: Eine Untersuchung zu Umfang, Ursache, Nachhaltigkeit und Folgen der neuen Wanderungsmuster in Deutschland* (Berlin: Empirica, 2015). Regarding those in decline, see Philipp Oswalt, ed., *Atlas of Shrinking Cities* (Ostfildern: Hatje Cantz, 2006).
39 See Chris Anderson's book *The Long Tail*.
40 In Germany, a good example of the latter would be the town of Görlitz.
41 See Scott, *A World in Emergence*, pp. 145–60.
42 Many of these problems are often discussed in terms of gentrification. See Loretta Lees et al., eds., *The Gentrification Reader* (New York: Routledge, 2010). The city of Venice is perhaps the most drastic example of "attractiveness overkill." See the documentary *Das Venedig Prinzip*, directed by Andreas Pichler (Vienna: Filmladen, 2012).

2 The Rise of Cultural Essentialism

1 On the concept of neo-communities, see the discussion above in Part IV, Chapter 2.
2 See Maffesoli, *The Time of the Tribes* (the original French book was published in 1988).
3 On this topic, see also Castells, *The Power of Identity*; and Benjamin Barber's rather oversimplified discussion in his book *Jihad vs. McWorld: How Globalism and Tribalism Are Reshaping the World* (New York: Ballantine Books, 1995).
4 The concept of communitarianism has long been discussed in terms of political theory. See, for instance, the articles collected in Axel Honneth, ed., *Kommunitarismus: Eine Debatte über die moralischen Grundlagen moderner Gesellschaften* (Frankfurt am Main: Campus, 1995). Here, however, I will use the term in a sociological and non-normative manner. Moreover, I will also use the terms "neo-community" and "community" synonymously.
5 On the classical model of community, see Ferdinand Tönnies, *Community and*

Civil Society, trans. Jose Harris and Margaret Hollis (Cambridge University Press, 2001), which was originally published in German in 1887. More recent theories of community are more differentiated; see Roberto Esposito, *Communitas: The Origin and Destiny of Community*, trans. Timothy Campbell (Stanford University Press, 2010).

6 See Robert Wuthnow, *Meaning and Moral Order: Explorations in Cultural Analysis* (Berkeley: University of California Press, 1989); Bernhard Giesen, *Kollektive Identität: Die Intellektuellen und die Nation II* (Frankfurt am Main: Suhrkamp, 1999); and Mary Douglas's classic study *Natural Symbols: Explorations in Cosmology* (New York: Pantheon Books, 1970).

7 This is a classic topic. See, for instance, Maurice Halbwachs, *On Collective Memory*, trans. Lewis A. Coser (University of Chicago Press, 1992); and Pierre Nora's *Realms of Memory*.

8 One might ask whether there are (or could be) other forms of community formation that are not cultural-essentialist. This question has been addressed repeatedly in works of social philosophy, among them Jean-Luc Nancy's book *The Inoperative Community*. The ideal of a heterogeneous community suggested by Nancy corresponds quite well with the concept of "heterogeneous collaborations" that I outlined in Part III.

9 See Anderson, *Imagined Communities*; and, for further discussion of this topic, Eric Hobsbawm and Terence Ranger, eds., *The Invention of Tradition* (Cambridge University Press, 1984).

10 See Hobsbawm, *Nations and Nationalism since 1780*.

11 See Fredrik Barth's foundational book *Ethnic Groups and Boundaries: The Social Organization of Cultural Difference* (London: Allen & Unwin, 1969); and, more recently, Richard Jenkins, *Rethinking Ethnicity: Arguments and Explorations* (London: Sage, 1997).

12 See Cornel West, *Race Matters* (Boston, MA: Beacon Press, 1993); and Anthony Appiah and Louis Gates, eds., *Identities* (University of Chicago Press, 1996).

13 See John David Skrentny, *The Minority Rights Revolutions* (Cambridge, MA: Harvard University Press, 2002); and, on identity politics in general, Mary Bernstein, "Identity Politics," *Annual Review of Sociology* 31 (2005), pp. 47–74.

14 Since the 1970s, the mechanisms of self-culturalization have been especially striking within the framework of the so-called ethnic revival in the United States. There, white segments of the population have also been rediscovering their historical roots as singular ethnic communities – for instance, as Italian-Americans, Irish-Americans, Greek-Americans, or Scandinavian-Americans. See Matthew Frye Jacobson, *Roots Too: White Ethnic Revival in Post-Civil Rights America* (Cambridge, MA: Harvard University Press, 2008).

15 See Kevin Kenny, *Diaspora: A Very Short Introduction* (New York: Oxford University Press, 2013).

16 This topic has been addressed in a number of case studies. Regarding the situation in Germany alone, see Sigrid Nökel, *Die Töchter der Gastarbeiter und der Islam: Zur Soziologie alltagsweltlicher Anerkennungspolitik – Eine Fallstudie* (Bielefeld: Transcript, 2002); and Sabine Mannitz, *Die verkannte Integration: Eine Langzeitstudie unter Heranwachsenden aus Immigrantenfamilien* (Bielefeld: Transcript, 2006).

17 Werner Schiffauer rightly emphasized this point in his book *Parallelgesellschaften: Wie viel Wertekonsens braucht unsere Gesellschaft?* (Bielefeld: Transcript, 2008).

18 There are many indications that such homogenizing processes are facilitated by certain social and spatial situations. Belonging to a spatially segregated social underclass encourages cultural exclusion from the inside, as Didier Lapeyronnie demonstrated in his book *Ghetto urbain*.

19 On this topic, see Steven Vertovec, *Super-Diversity* (London: Routledge, 2014). Regarding hybridization, see Jan Nederveen Pieterse, "Globalization as Hybridization," in *Global Modernities*, ed. Mike Featherstone et al. (London: Sage, 1995), pp. 45–68.

20 In the field of political theory, a foundational study of this topic is Will

Kymlicka's *Multicultural Odysseys: Navigating the New International Politics of Diversity* (Oxford University Press, 2007).

21 See Étienne Balibar and Immanuel Wallerstein, *Race, Nation, Class: Ambiguous Identities*, trans. Chris Turner (London: Verso, 1991); and Mark Terkessidis, *Die Banalität der Rassismus: Migranten zweiter Generation entwickeln eine neue Perspektive* (Bielefeld: Transcript, 2004).

22 On this topic, see Frantz Fanon's classic work *Black Skin, White Masks*, trans. Charles Lam Markmann (New York: Grove Press, 1967).

23 See Anderson's classic study *Imagined Communities*; Hobsbawm, *Nations and Nationalism since 1780*; and Ernest Gellner, *Encounters with Nationalism* (Oxford: Blackwell, 1994).

24 On this topic, see also Armin Nassehi, "Zum Funktionswandel von Ethnizität im Prozeß gesellschaftlicher Modernisierung: Ein Beitrag zur Theorie funktionaler Differenzierung," *Soziale Welt* 41/3 (1990), pp. 261–82.

25 See Montserrat Guibernau, *The Identity of Nations* (Cambridge: Polity, 2007).

26 In addition to Quebec, other noteworthy regional-national movements are those within Spain (Catalonia, Basque Country), Great Britain (Scotland), and Belgium (Flanders), as well as the somewhat weaker movements in Italy (Venice) and France (Corsica).

27 One could also interpret these two variants in class-theoretical terms, with the sedentary old middle class and the underclass on one side and the mobile new middle class on the other. Accordingly, regionalist movements can potentially be supported by either side.

28 The case of Scotland is an example of both: the authentically Scottish against the globalist British and, at the same time, the European-Scottish against the provincial English.

29 See Sebastian Conrad, "Der Ort der Globalgeschichte," *Merkur* 68 (2014), pp. 1096–1102. This includes Russia as well, which, of course, does not belong to the global South.

30 Thus, the new Sinocentrism regularly refers to the allegedly Confucian heart of China, which implies a strong appreciation of education, a strong work ethic, the primacy of general welfare over individual interests, and the ideal of harmonious social life. The self-culturalization of Russia, which can draw upon a long tradition of Slavophilia, is based on orthodox Christianity, the value of the family, and a close connection to the "body of the people" and the natural environment. Regarding Russia, see Felix Philipp Ingold, "Russlands eurasische Geopolitik," *Merkur* 70 (2016), pp. 5–18; and Katharina Bluhm, "Machtgedanken," *Mittelweg 36* 25/6 (2016), pp. 56–75. On China, see William Callahan, "Sino-Speak: Chinese Exceptionalism and the Politics of History," *Journal of Asian Studies* 71 (2012), pp. 33–55.

31 An anti-Western attitude comes through especially clearly, for instance, in the work of the Russian author Aleksandr Dugin. See his book *The Fourth Political Theory*, trans. Mark Sleboda (London: Arktos Media, 2012).

32 See Hans Joas and Klaus Wiegandt, eds., *Secularization and the World Religions*, trans. Alex Skinner (Liverpool University Press, 2009); and Roland Robertson, "Humanity, Globalization, and Worldwide Religious Resurgence: A Theoretical Exploration," *Sociological Analysis* 46/3 (1985), pp. 219–42.

33 See Zinser, *Der Markt der Religionen*.

34 See, for instance, Hubert Knoblauch, "Das unsichtbare Neue Zeitalter: 'New Age', privatisierte Religion und kultisches Milieu," *Kölner Zeitschrift für Soziologie und Sozialpsychologie* 41/3 (1989), pp. 504–25.

35 The best analysis of contemporary fundamentalism is Olivier Roy's *La sainte ignorance: Le temps de la religion sans culture* (Paris: Seuil, 2008). See also Martin Riesebrodt, *Rückkehr der Religionen? Zwischen Fundamentalismus und der "Kampf der Kulturen"* (Munich: Beck, 2000); and Thomas Meyer, *Was ist Fundamentalismus? Eine Einführung* (Wiesbaden: Verlag für Sozialwissenschaften, 2011).

36 At the same time, Germans raised as Christians have also converted to Salafism,

and evangelical Christianity has been attracting more and more people in traditionally Catholic Latin America. In regard to religion, however, it is also not uncommon for external culturalization to take place through social discourses, which can portray religion as a sort of ascribed neo-ethnicity. This makes it possible, for instance, to describe all immigrants in Europe from Turkey or North Africa as representatives of the "Islamic cultural sphere."

37 Max Weber, "Religious Rejections of the World and Their Directions," in *From Max Weber: Essays in Sociology*, trans. H. H. Gerth and C. Wright Mills (New York: Oxford University Press, 1946), pp. 323–62.

38 Martin Riesebrodt has shown (in *Die Rückkehr der Religionen*, pp. 59–94) how parts of the old middle class, which has lost its status as a moral authority, and parts of the underclass have become important representative groups in religious fundamentalism. One can presume that the religious interests of the new middle class, in contrast, rather lie in the non-fundamentalist "new religions" or in engaging with official churches.

39 See Roy, *La sainte ignorance*.

40 In certain circumstances, religious communities can take the form of particular cultural communities with a "religious identity" that, within the framework of a multicultural system of identity politics, claim and exercise cultural rights. The intertwined nature of religious, ethnic, and national identities is a topic in and of itself. See Roy, *La sainte ignorance*.

41 Examples include the Front National in France, the Freedom Party of Austria, the parties of Fortuyn and Wilders in the Netherlands, and Fidesz in Hungary. For a general overview, see Ruth Wodak et al., eds., *Right-Wing Populism in Europe: Politics and Discourse* (London: Bloomsbury Academic, 2013).

42 See Julian Bruns et al., *Die Identitären: Handbuch zur Jugendbewegung der neuen Rechten in Europa* (Münster: Unrast, 2014).

43 On the theory of political cleavage, see Seymour Martin Lipset and Stein Rokkan, "Cleavage Structures, Party Systems, and Voter Alignments: An Introduction," in *Party Systems and Voter Alignments: Cross-National Perspectives*, ed. Lipset and Rokkan (New York: Free Press, 1967), pp. 1–64.

44 The ascribed "authenticity" of top candidates has likewise gained significance.

45 See Kriesi et al., "Globalization and the Transformation of the National Political Space"; and Peter de Wilde et al., "The Political Sociology of Cosmopolitanism and Communitarianism: Representative Claims Analysis," *WZB Discussion Paper SP 2014-102* (2014), online.

46 Here I am following Jan-Werner Müller's lucid interpretation of populism in his book *What is Populism?* (Philadelphia: University of Pennsylvania Press, 2016), though I push his ideas further in the direction of cultural essentialism.

47 As one of the pioneering thinkers of populist democracy, Carl Schmitt formulated this succinctly: "Democracy requires [...] first homogeneity and second – if the need arises – elimination or eradication of heterogeneity." Quoted from Carl Schmitt, *The Crisis of Parliamentary Democracy*, trans. Ellen Kennedy (Cambridge, MA: MIT Press, 1985), p. 9.

48 This "social" interpretation of homogeneity is also characteristic of left-wing populism.

49 In his book *Realm of Lesser Evil*, Jean-Claude Michéa uses the term "common decency," which he borrows from George Orwell, to denote the foundation of left-wing populism, even though it is rather typical of the right-wing sort.

50 See Mark Terkessidis, *Kulturkampf: Volk, Nation, der Westen und die neue Rechte* (Cologne: Kiepenheuer & Witsch, 1995).

51 Some of these policies (trade restrictions, for instance) are not "right-wing populist" in themselves. They can also be supported by the left or by proponents of regulatory liberalism. They only become right-wing populist causes because they are framed as such. It is no surprise that the two most important groups of voters who support right-wing populist parties come from segments of the two social classes that can perceive themselves to be losers in the processes of modernization and culturalization: the new (non-migrant) underclass and the

old middle class. See Inglehart and Norris, "Trump, Brexit, and the Rise of Populism"; and Sylvain Barone and Emmanuel Négrier, "Voter Front National en milieu rural: Une perspective ethnographique," in *Les faux-semblants du Front National: Sociologie d'un parti politique*, ed. Silvain Crépon et al. (Paris: Presses de Sciences Po, 2015), pp. 417–34.
52 See Terkessidis, *Kulturkampf*.
53 There is, however, a second possibility. A particular group identity can become non-exclusive and thus amenable to combinations. The communities then are non-essentialist and can, in the sense of a super-diversity, participate in multiple collectives that do not exclude one another. This is a constellation that no longer corresponds to the ideal type of the neo-community but, instead, to that which I referred to above as a heterogeneous collaboration.
54 This has already been a topic of widespread philosophical debate. See, for instance, the articles collected in Charles Taylor et al., *Multikulturalismus und die Politik der Anerkennung* (Frankfurt am Main: Fischer, 1993).
55 Such a state of conflict has also been proclaimed, for instance, by Aleksandr Dugin in his book *The Fourth Political Theory*.
56 See, for instance, Arthur Schlesinger, *The Disuniting of America: Reflections on a Multicultural Society*, 2nd edn. (New York: W. W. Norton, 1998); Guibernau, *The Identity of Nations*, pp. 58–88, 159–88; and the much-discussed commentary by Mark Lilla, "The End of Identity Liberalism," *The New York Times* (November 18, 2016), online.
57 See Dieter Thränhardt, "Integrationsrealität und Integrationsdiskurs," *Aus Politik und Zeitgeschichte* 46 (2010), pp. 16–21.
58 See Terry Eagleton, *The Idea of Culture* (Oxford: Blackwell, 2000).
59 The critical debate about neoliberalism has become especially intense since the financial crisis of 2008. See, for example, Piketty, *Capital in the Twenty-First Century*; and Wolfgang Streeck, *Buying Time: The Delayed Crisis of Democratic Capitalism*, trans. Patrick Camiller (London: Verso, 2014).
60 For a discussion of these challenges, see David Goodhart's book *The Road to Somewhere*.
61 On terrorism, see Thomas Kron, *Reflexiver Terrorismus* (Weilerwist: Velbrück Wissenschaft, 2015); and Michael Frank and Kirsten Mahlke, eds., *Kultur und Terror* (Bielefeld: Transcript, 2010). Regarding mass shootings, see Heiko Christians, *Amok: Geschichte einer Ausbreitung* (Bielefeld: Aesthesis, 2008); and Joseph Vogl, "Der Amokläufer," in *Figuren der Gewalt*, ed. Daniel Tyradellis et al. (Zurich: Diaphanes, 2014), pp. 13–18. On the topic as a whole, see Martin Altmeyer, *Auf der Suche nach Resonanz: Wie sich das Seelenleben in der digitalen Moderne verändert* (Göttingen: Vandenhoeck & Ruprecht, 2016), pp. 135–84.
62 See Elias, *The Civilizing Process*; and, for the latter view, Bauman, *Modernity and Ambivalence*.
63 Examples of such violence include spousal abuse, child abuse, discriminatory language, sexual harassment, bullying, etc.
64 See Cas Wouters, *Informalization: Manners and Emotions since 1890* (London: Sage, 2007).
65 For a sociological interpretation of violence that does not immediately explain the matter in socio-structural terms but, rather, takes its immanent form seriously, see Trutz von Trotha, "Zur Soziologie der Gewalt," in *Soziologie der Gewalt*, ed. Trotha (Wiesbaden: Westdeutscher Verlag, 1997), pp. 9–56.
66 Here I am referring to the attack on the World Trade Center in 2001, the massacre on the Norwegian island of Utøya in 2011, and the shooting that took place at the Parisian club Bataclan in 2015.
67 See my discussion of negative singularities above in Part IV, Chapter 2.
68 Walter Benjamin, "Critique of Violence," in Benjamin, *Reflections: Essays, Aphorisms, Autobiographical Writings*, trans. Edmund Jephcott (New York: Schocken Books, 1978), p. 294.
69 It is for this very reason that violence has had such a strong public presence

in the media, in popular culture, and in art since the 1980s – whether in news reports about child abuse, in certain computer games, or finally in the extent to which films have focused on violent phenomena (from popular action films to the aesthetically sophisticated representations of violence in films by directors such as Michael Haneke or Quentin Tarantino).

70 I have adapted this fitting formulation from Jan Philipp Reemtsma, *Gewalt als Lebensform: Zwei Reden* (Stuttgart: Reclam, 2016). Conversely, however, there has also been a tendency in late modernity to singularize (known) victims. See Klaus Günther, "Ein Modell legitimen Scheiterns: Der Kampf um Anerkennung als Opfer," in *Strukturwandel der Anerkennung: Paradoxien sozialer Integration in der Gegenwart*, ed. Axel Honneth et al. (Frankfurt am Main: Campus, 2012), pp. 185–248.

Conclusion: The Crisis of the General?

1 See Francis Fukuyama, *The End of History and the Last Man* (New York: Free Press, 1992).
2 See Reinhart Koselleck, "Fortschritt," in *Geschichtliche Grundbegriffe*, vol. II, ed. Otto Brunner et al. (Stuttgart: Klett-Cotta, 1975), pp. 351–423; and Jürgen Habermas, "Modernity: An Unfinished Project," trans. Nicholas Walker, in *Habermas and the Unfinished Project of Modernity*, ed. Maurizio Passerin d'Entrèves and Seyla Benhabib (Cambridge, MA: MIT Press, 1997), pp. 38–58.
3 See Urry, *Sociology Beyond Societies*; and Reckwitz, *The Invention of Creativity*, where I discuss this topic at length.
4 On the concept of recognition in general, see Axel Honneth, *The Struggle for Recognition: The Moral Grammar of Social Conflicts*, trans. Joel Anderson (Cambridge, MA: MIT Press, 1996).
5 Some of the problems associated with this were discussed as early as the 1950s in books such as Michael Young's *The Rise of the Meritocracy*.
6 See Neckel and Wagner, *Leistung und Erschöpfung*.
7 Within the framework of what Ingolfur Bühdorn has called "simulative democracy," moreover, the *performance* of the political has become the center of late-modern politics, which is in turn measured according to the standard of authenticity. See Ingolfur Blühdorn, *Simulative Demokratie: Neue Politik nach der postdemokratischen Wende* (Berlin: Suhrkamp, 2013).
8 This is also why there are such high levels of government debt (and, in part, why there is so much private debt as well). Regarding the recent history of debt accumulation, see Wolfgang Streeck's book *Buying Time*.
9 See Rosanvallon, *The Society of Equals*.
10 For a discussion of how present-day culture, too, might still be connected in certain ways to the general and universal, see Terry Eagleton's book *The Idea of Culture*.
11 See Reinhart Koselleck, "Krise," in *Geschichtliche Grundbegriffe*, vol. III, ed. Otto Brunner et al. (Stuttgart: Klett-Cotta, 1982), pp. 617–50.
12 See also the theoretical sketch by Sabine Hark et al., "Das umkämpfte Allgemeine und das neue Gemeinsame: Solidarität ohne Identität," *Feministische Studien* 33 (2015), pp. 99–103.
13 In light of certain progressive ideas, it could be said that the society of singularities needs a new form of social politics that, beyond merely caring for people, increases their chances to develop and, to that end, promotes the improvement of general social goods such as education and security. See Amartya Sen, *The Idea of Justice* (London: Penguin, 2010).
14 See Robert Fuller's enlightening book *Somebodies or Nobodies: Overcoming the Abuse of Rank* (Gabriola Island, BC: New Society Publishers, 2003); and David Goodhart's *The Road to Somewhere*, which is interesting in a different way. On its own, the expansion of education has obviously not solved this problem. In fact, its meritocratic spirit has even exacerbated it, given that those who are

unsuccessful at school now face an even greater risk of being marginalized. See Young, *The Rise of Meritocracy*.
15 Such is the case, for instance, with the transgender movement. See Jami Taylor and Donald Haider-Markel, eds., *Transgender Rights and Politics: Groups, Issue Framing, and Policy Adoption* (Ann Arbor: University of Michigan Press, 2014).
16 On this topic, see Adam Phillips's instructive book *Missing Out: In Praise of the Unlived Life* (London: Hamish Hamilton, 2012); and Rainer Funk's *Der entgrenzte Mensch*.
17 See, for instance, David Brooks's book *The Road to Character*.
18 See, for instance, Silke Helfrich, ed., *Commons: Für eine neue Politik jenseits von Markt und Staat* (Bielefeld: Transcript, 2012). A central aspect of such movements is the social form that I have referred to throughout this book as "heterogeneous collaborations."
19 Although several observers have spoken of the need for "*post*-liberalism," I would persist in using the term "liberalism" in order to underscore the relative continuity from classical to apertistic liberalism, whose orientation toward removing boundaries and promoting difference should not, in my opinion, be discarded but, rather, moderated. At the present time, however, the most powerful international rival of regulatory liberalism is indeed post-liberal: this is the anti-liberal right-wing populism that I discussed above in Part VI, Chapter 2.

Bibliography

Adam, Barbara. *Time and Social Theory*. Cambridge: Polity, 1994.
Adorno, Theodor W., and Max Horkheimer. *Dialectic of Enlightenment*. Trans. John Cumming. New York: Verso, 1979.
Aersten, Jan A., and Andreas Speer, eds. *Individuum und Individualität im Mittelalter*. Berlin: De Gruyter, 1996.
Albrecht, Clemens. "Die Substantialität bürgerlicher Kultur." In *Bürgerlichkeit ohne Bürgertum: In welchem Land leben wir?* Ed. Heinz Bude et al. Munich: W. Fink, 2010. Pp. 131–44.
Alkemeyer, Thomas, et al., eds. *Aufs Spiel gesetzte Körper: Aufführungen des Sozialen in Sport und populärer Kultur*. Konstanz: UVK, 2003.
Alkemeyer, Thomas, et al., eds. *Ordnung in Bewegung: Choreographien des Sozialen – Körper in Sport, Tanz, Arbeit und Bildung*. Bielefeld: Transcript, 2009.
Allmendinger, Jutta. *Das Land, in dem wir leben wollen: Wie die Deutschen sich ihre Zukunft vorstellen*. Munich: Pantheon, 2017.
Altmeyer, Martin. *Auf der Suche nach Resonanz: Wie sich das Seelenleben in der digitalen Moderne verändert*. Göttingen: Vandenhoeck & Ruprecht, 2016.
Amin, Ash, ed. *Post-Fordism: A Reader*. Oxford: Blackwell, 1996.
Anderson, Benedict. *Imagined Communities: Reflections on the Origin and Spread of Nationalism*. 2nd edn. London: Verso, 1991.
Anderson, Chris. *The Long Tail: Why the Future of Business is Selling Less of More*. New York: Hyperion, 2014.
Anderson, Chris. *Makers: The New Industrial Revolution*. New York: Crown Business, 2012.
Anheier, Helmut K., and Yudhishthir Raj Isar, eds. *Cities, Cultural Policy, and Governance*. London: Sage, 2012.
Anheier, Helmut K., and Yudhishthir Raj Isar, eds. *Heritage, Memory, and Identity*. London: Sage, 2011.
Appiah, Anthony, and Louis Gates, eds. *Identities*. University of Chicago Press, 1996.
Arnold, Matthew. *Culture and Anarchy: An Essay in Political and Social Criticism*. London: John Murray, 1949.
Aron, Raymond. *18 Lectures on Industrial Society*. Trans. M. K. Bottomore. London: Weidenfeld & Nicholson, 1967.
Arsel, Zeynep, and Jonathan Bean. "Taste Regimes and Market-Mediated Practices." *Journal of Consumer Research* 39 (2013). Pp. 899–917.
Assmann, Aleida. *Mnemosyne: Formen und Funktionen kultureller Erinnerung*. Frankfurt am Main: Fischer, 1993.
Augé, Marc. *Non-Places: Introduction to an Anthropology of Supermodernity*. Trans. John Howe. New York: Verso, 1995.
Austin, Rob, and Lee Devin. *Artful Making: What Managers Need to Know About How Artists Work*. Upper Saddle River, NJ: Prentice Hall, 2003.

Autor, David H., et al. "The Polarization of the U.S. Labor Market." *American Economic Review* 96/2 (2006). Pp. 189–94.
Bachleitner, Reinhard, and H. Jürgen Kagelmann, eds. *Kultur/Städte/Tourismus*. Munich: Profil Verlag, 2003.
Bachmann-Medick, Doris. *Cultural Turns: New Orientations in the Study of Culture*. Berlin: De Gruyter, 2016.
Badinter, Élisabeth. *Man/Woman: The One is the Other*. Trans. Barbara Wright. London: Collins Harvill, 1999.
Baethge, Martin. "Arbeit, Vergesellschaftung, Identität: Zur zunehmenden normativen Subjektivierung der Arbeit." *Soziale Welt* 42 (1991). Pp. 6–19.
Bahl, Friederike. *Lebensmodelle in der Dienstleistungsgesellschaft*. Hamburg: Hamburger Edition, 2014.
Bakhtin, Mikhail. *Rabelais and His World*. Trans. Hélène Iswolsky. Bloomington: Indiana University Press, 1984.
Balibar, Étienne, and Immanuel Wallerstein. *Race, Nation, Class: Ambiguous Identities*. Trans. Chris Turner. London: Verso, 1991.
Bandt, Jacques de, and Jean Gadrey, eds. *Relations de service, marchés de services*. Paris: CNRS, 1998.
Banks, Mark. *The Politics of Cultural Work*. New York: Palgrave Macmillan, 2007.
Barber, Benjamin. *Jihad vs. McWorld: How Globalism and Tribalism Are Reshaping the World*. New York: Ballantine Books, 1995.
Barck, Karlheinz, ed. *Aisthesis: Wahrnehmung heute oder Perspektiven einer neuen Ästhetik*. Leipzig: Reclam, 1998.
Barlösius, Eva. *Dicksein: Wenn der Körper das Verhältnis zur Gesellschaft bestimmt*. Frankfurt am Main: Campus, 2014.
Barlösius, Eva, et al., eds. *Ernährung in der Armut: Gesundheitliche, soziale und kulturelle Folgen in der Bundesrepublik Deutschland*. Berlin: Edition Sigma, 1995.
Barney, Darin. *The Network Society*. Cambridge: Polity, 2004.
Barone, Sylvain, and Emmanuel Négrier. "Voter Front National en milieu rural: Une perspective ethnographique." In *Les faux-semblants du Front National: Sociologie d'un parti politique*. Ed. Silvain Crépon et al. Paris: Presses de Sciences Po, 2015. Pp. 417–34.
Barth, Fredrik. *Ethnic Groups and Boundaries: The Social Organization of Cultural Difference*. London: Allen & Unwin, 1969.
Barthes, Roland. *The Language of Fashion*. Trans. Andy Stafford. London: Bloomsbury, 2005.
Basáñez, Miguel E. *A World of Three Cultures: Honor, Achievement, Joy*. New York: Oxford University Press, 2016.
Bataille, Georges. *The Accursed Share: An Essay on General Economy*. Trans. Robert Hurley. New York: Zone Books, 1988.
Bätschmann, Oskar. *Ausstellungskünstler: Kult und Karriere im modernen Kunstsystem*. Cologne: DuMont, 1997.
Baudrillard, Jean. *Symbolic Exchange and Death*. Trans. Iain Hamilton Grand. London: Sage, 1976.
Bauman, Zygmunt. *Liquid Modernity*. Cambridge: Polity, 2000.
Bauman, Zygmunt. *Modernity and Ambivalence*. Cambridge: Polity, 1991.
Baur, Bruno. *Biodiversität*. Bern: Haupt, 2010.
Baym, Nancy. "Interpersonal Life Online." In *The Handbook of New Media: Social Shaping and Consequences of ICTs*. Ed. Leah Lievrouw and Sonia Livingstone. London: Sage, 2006. Pp. 35–54.
Beck, Ulrich. "Jenseits von Stand und Klasse? Soziale Ungleichheiten, gesellschaftliche Individualisierungsprozesse und die Entstehung neuer sozialer Formationen und Identitäten." In *Soziale Ungleichheiten*. Ed. Reinhard Kreckel. Göttingen: Schwartz, 1983. Pp. 35–74.
Beck, Ulrich. *Risk Society: Towards a New Modernity*. Trans. Mark Ritter. London: Sage, 1992.
Becker, Howard Saul. *Art Worlds*. Berkeley: University of California Press, 1984.

Bibliography 373

Becker, Howard Saul. *Outsiders: Studies in the Sociology of Deviance.* New York: Free Press, 1963.
Becker, Rolf, and Wolfgang Lauterbach, eds. *Bildung als Privileg: Erklärungen und Befunde zu den Ursachen der Bildungsgleichheit.* Wiesbaden: Springer, 2010.
Beckert, Jens. "The Transcending Power of Goods: Imaginative Value in the Economy." In *The Worth of Goods: Valuation and Pricing in the Economy.* Ed. Jens Beckert and Patrik Aspers. Oxford University Press, 2011. Pp. 106–30.
Beckert, Jens, and Patrik Aspers. *The Worth of Goods: Valuation and Pricing in the Economy.* Oxford University Press, 2011.
Beckert, Jens, and Christine Musselin, eds. *Constructing Quality: The Classification of Goods in Markets.* Oxford University Press, 2013.
Belasco, Warren J. *Appetite for Change: How the Counterculture Took On the Food Industry.* New York: Pantheon Books, 1989.
Bell, Daniel. *The Coming of Post-Industrial Society: A Venture in Social Forecasting.* New York: Basic Books, 1973.
Bell, Daniel. *The Cultural Contradictions of Capitalism.* New York: Basic Books, 1976.
Bendl, Regine. *Diversität und Diversitätsmanagement.* Vienna: Facultas, 2012.
Benjamin, Walter. "Critique of Violence." In Benjamin, *Reflections: Essays, Aphorisms, Autobiographical Writings.* Trans. Edmund Jephcott. New York: Schocken Books, 1978. Pp. 277–300.
Benjamin, Walter. "The Work of Art in the Age of Its Technological Reproducibility: Third Version." In *Selected Writings: Volume 4, 1938–1940.* Ed. Howard Eiland and Michael W. Jennings. Cambridge, MA: Harvard University Press, 2003. Pp. 251–83.
Berghoff, Hartmut, and Jörg Sydow, eds. *Unternehmerische Netzwerke: Eine historische Organisationsform mit Zukunft?* Stuttgart: Kohlhammer, 2007.
Berking, Helmut, and Martina Löw, eds. *Die Eigenlogik der Städte: Neue Wege für Stadtforschung.* Frankfurt am Main: Campus, 2008.
Berlin, Isaiah. *The Roots of Romanticism.* Ed. Henry Hardy. Princeton University Press, 2014.
Bernard, Andreas. *The Triumph of Profiling: The Self in Digital Culture.* Trans. Valentine A. Pakis. Cambridge: Polity, 2019.
Bernstein, Mary. "Identity Politics." *Annual Review of Sociology* 31 (2005). Pp. 47–74.
Bhatti, Anil, et al. "Ähnlichkeit: Ein kulturtheoretisches Paradigma." *Internationales Archiv für Sozialgeschichte der Literatur* 36 (2011). Pp. 261–75.
Biebricher, Thomas, ed. *Der Staat des Neoliberalismus.* Baden-Baden: Nomos, 2016.
Bilton, Chris. *Management and Creativity: From Creative Industries to Creative Management.* Malden, MA: Blackwell, 2006.
Bismarck, Beatrice von. "Introduction." In *Cultures of the Curatorial.* Ed. Jörn Schafaff et al. Berlin: Sternberg Press, 2012. Pp. 7–20.
Blühdorn, Ingolfur. *Simulative Demokratie: Neue Politik nach der postdemokratischen Wende.* Berlin: Suhrkamp, 2013.
Bluhm, Katharina. "Machtgedanken." *Mittelweg 36* 25/6 (2016). Pp. 56–75.
Blumenberg, Hans. *The Legitimacy of the Modern Age.* Trans. Robert M. Wallace. Cambridge, MA: MIT Press, 1983.
Blumenberg, Hans. *Schriften zur Technik.* Berlin: Suhrkamp, 2015.
Böhme, Gernot. *The Aesthetics of Atmospheres.* Ed. Jean-Paul Thibaud. London: Routledge, 2017.
Bohrer, Karl Heinz. *Das absolute Präsens: Die Semantik ästhetischer Zeit.* Frankfurt am Main: Suhrkamp, 1994.
Bohrer, Karl Heinz. *Der romantische Brief: Die Entstehung ästhetischer Subjektivität.* Frankfurt am Main: Suhrkamp, 1989.
Bollenbeck, Georg. *Bildung und Kultur: Glanz und Elend eines deutschen Deutungsmuster.* Frankfurt am Main: Suhrkamp, 2001.
Boltanski, Luc, and Ève Chiapello. *The New Spirit of Capitalism.* Trans. Gregory Elliott. London: Verso, 2005.

Boltanski, Luc, and Arnaud Esquerre. *Enrichissement: Une critique de la marchandise*. Paris: Gallimard, 2017.
Bonß, Wolfgang. *Vom Risiko: Unsicherheit und Ungewißheit in der Moderne*. Hamburg: Hamburger Edition, 1995.
Bourdieu, Pierre. *Distinction: A Social Critique of the Judgement of Taste*. Trans. Richard Nice. Cambridge, MA: Harvard University Press, 1984.
Bourdieu, Pierre. "The Forms of Capital." In *Handbook of Theory and Research for the Sociology of Education*. Ed. John G. Richardson. Westport, CT: Greenwood Press, 1986. Pp. 241–58.
Bourdieu, Pierre. "The Market of Symbolic Goods." In *The Field of Cultural Production: Essays on Art and Literature*. Trans. Rupert Swyer. New York: Columbia University Press, 1993. Pp. 112–45.
Bourdieu, Pierre. *The Rules of Art: Genesis and Structure of the Literary Field*. Trans. Susan Emanuel. Stanford University Press, 1996.
Bourdieu, Pierre, and Jean-Claude Passeron. *The Inheritors: French Students and Their Relation to Culture*. Trans. Richard Nice. University of Chicago Press, 1979.
Boutang, Yann Moulier. *Cognitive Capitalism*. Trans. Ed Emery. Cambridge: Polity, 2011.
Brackert, Helmut, and Fritz Wefelmeyer, eds. *Kultur: Bestimmungen im 20. Jahrhundert*. Frankfurt am Main: Suhrkamp, 1990.
Brand, Klaus-Werner, ed. *Die neue Dynamik des Bio-Markts*. Munich: Oekom Verlag, 2006.
Brandt, Mathias. "Bevölkerungsanteil mit Hochschulabschluss," *Statista: Das Statistik-Portal* (September 9, 2014): https://de.statista.com/infografik/2686/bevoelkerungsanteil-mit-hochschulabschluss-in-ausgewaehlten-laendern.
Braudel, Fernand. *Civilization and Capitalism, 15th–18th Century*. Trans. Siân Reynolds. Princeton University Press, 2002.
Bray, Paul M. "The New Urbanism: Celebrating the City." *Places* 8/4 (1993). Pp. 56–65.
Bredies, Katharina. *Gebrauch als Design: Über eine unterschätzte Form der Gestaltung*. Bielefeld: Transcript, 2014.
Brighenti, Andrea Mubi. *Visibility in Social Theory and Social Research*. Basingstoke: Palgrave Macmillan, 2010.
Bröckling, Ulrich. *The Entrepreneurial Self: Fabricating a New Type of Subject*. Trans. Steven Black. London: Sage, 2016.
Bröckling, Ulrich, et al., eds. *Gouvernementalität der Gegenwart: Studien zur Ökonomisierung des Sozialen*. Frankfurt am Main: Suhrkamp, 2000.
Brooks, David. *Bobos in Paradise: The New Upper Class and How They Got There*. New York: Simon & Schuster, 2000.
Brooks, David. *The Road to Character*. New York: Random House, 2015.
Brown, Tim. *Change by Design: How Design Thinking Transforms Organizations and Inspires Innovation*. New York: Collins Business, 2009.
Bruns, Axel. *Blogs, Wikipedia, Second Life, and Beyond: From Production to Produsage*. New York: Peter Lang, 2008.
Bruns, Julian, et al. *Die Identitären: Handbuch zur Jugendbewegung der neuen Rechten in Europa*. Münster: Unrast, 2014.
Brusco, Sebastiano. "The Emilian Model: Productive Decentralisation and Social Integration." *Cambridge Journal of Economics* 6 (1982). Pp. 167–82.
Bude, Heinz. *Die Ausgeschlossenen: Das Ende vom Traum der gerechten Gesellschaft*. Munich: Hanser, 2008.
Bude, Heinz. *Bildungspanik: Was unsere Gesellschaft spaltet*. Bonn: Bundeszentrale für politische Bildung, 2011.
Bude, Heinz. *Gesellschaft der Angst*. Hamburg: Hamburger Edition, 2016.
Bude, Heinz, et al., eds. *ÜberLeben im Umbruch: Am Beispiel Wittenberge – Ansichten einer fragmentierten Gesellschaft*. Hamburg: Hamburger Edition, 2011.
Bull, Michael. *Sound Moves: iPod Culture and Urban Experience*. New York: Routledge, 2007.

Bultman, Bethany E. *Redneck Heaven: Portrait of a Vanishing Culture*. New York: Bantam Books, 1996.
Burgess, Jean, and Joshua Green. *YouTube: Online Video and Participatory Culture*. Cambridge: Polity, 2009.
Burkhardt, Marcus. *Digitale Datenbanken: Eine Medientheorie im Zeitalter von Big Data*. Bielefeld: Transcript, 2015.
Burns, Tom, and George M. Stalker. *The Management of Innovation*. Oxford University Press, 1994.
Busemann, Hanna. *Das Phänomen Marke: Betrachtung und Analyse aktueller markensoziologischer Ansätze*. Saarbrücken: VDM, 2007.
Caillois, Roger. *Man, Play, and Games*. Trans. Meyer Barash. Chicago: University of Illinois Press, 2001.
Callahan, William. "Sino-Speak: Chinese Exceptionalism and the Politics of History." *Journal of Asian Studies* 71 (2012). Pp. 33–55.
Callon, Michel, ed. *The Laws of the Market*. Oxford: Blackwell, 1998.
Callon, Michel, et al. "The Economy of Qualities." *Economy and Society* 31 (2002). Pp. 194–217.
Canter, David. "Offender Profiling and Investigative Psychology." *Journal of Investigative Psychology and Offender Profiling* 1 (2003). Pp. 1–15.
Carrier, James G., ed. *Ethical Consumption: Social Value and Economic Practice*. New York: Berghahn Books, 2015.
Castells, Manuel. *The Internet Galaxy: Reflections on the Internet, Business, and Society*. Oxford University Press, 2001.
Castells, Manuel. *The Power of Identity*. 2nd edn. Oxford: Blackwell, 1997.
Castells, Manuel. *The Rise of the Network Society*. Cambridge, MA: Blackwell, 1996.
Caves, Richard. *Creative Industries: Contracts Between Art and Commerce*. Cambridge, MA: Harvard University Press, 2000.
Ceruzzi, Paul E. *A History of Modern Computing*. Cambridge, MA: MIT Press, 2003.
Chandler, Alfred D. *The Visible Hand: The Managerial Revolution in American Business*. Cambridge, MA: Belknap Press, 1977.
Chevalier, Louis. *Laboring Classes and Dangerous Classes in Paris During the First Half of the Nineteenth Century*. Trans. Frank Jellinek. New York: Howard Fertig, 1973.
Christensen, Jens. *Global Experience Industries: The Business of Experience Economy*. Aarhus University Press, 2009.
Christians, Heiko. *Amok: Geschichte einer Ausbreitung*. Bielefeld: Aesthesis, 2008.
Ciompi, Luc. *Die emotionalen Grundlagen des Denkens: Entwurf einer fraktalen Affektlogik*. Göttingen: Vandenhoeck & Ruprecht, 1997.
Coates, Del. *Watches Tell More Than Time: Product Design, Information, and the Quest for Elegance*. New York: McGraw-Hill, 2003.
Cohen, H. Floris. *Scientific Revolution: A Historiographical Inquiry*. University of Chicago Press, 1994.
Conrad, Sebastian. "Der Ort der Globalgeschichte." *Merkur* 68 (2014). Pp. 1096–1102.
Counihan, Carol, ed. *Food and Culture: A Reader*. 2nd edn. New York: Routledge, 2008.
Crary, Jonathan. *Suspensions of Perception: Attention, Spectacle, and Modern Culture*. Cambridge, MA: MIT Press, 2001.
Crouch, Colin. *The Strange Non-Death of Neoliberalism*. Cambridge: Polity, 2011.
Currid, Elizabeth. *The Warhol Economy: How Fashion, Art, and Music Drive New York City*. Princeton University Press, 2007.
Dahrendorf, Ralf. "Die globale Klasse und die neue Ungleichheit." *Merkur* 54/11 (2000). Pp. 1057–68.
Davies, Rosamund, and Gauti Sigthorsson. *Introducing the Creative Industries: From Theory to Practice*. Los Angeles: Sage, 2013.
Degen, Mónica Montserrat. *Sensing Cities: Regenerating Public Life in Barcelona and Manchester*. London: Routledge, 2009.

Deleuze, Gilles, and Félix Guattari. *A Thousand Plateaus: Capitalism and Schizophrenia.* Trans. Brian Massumi. Minneapolis: University of Minnesota Press, 1987.
DeSoucey, Michaela, and Isabelle Techoueyres. "Virtue and Valorization: 'Local Food' in the United States and France." In *The Globalization of Food.* Ed. David Inglis and Debra L. Gimlin. London: Routledge, 2008. Pp. 81–96.
Deuze, Mark. *Media Work.* Cambridge: Polity, 2007.
Dewey, John. *Theory of Valuation.* Chicago: University of Illinois Press, 1939.
Diederichsen, Diedrich. "Kreative Arbeit und Selbstverwirklichung." In *Kreation und Depression: Freiheit im gegenwärtigen Kapitalismus.* Ed. Christoph Menke et al. Berlin: Kadmos, 2010. Pp. 118–28.
Diederichsen, Diedrich. *Über Pop-Musik.* Cologne: Kiepenheuer & Witsch, 2014.
Diederichsen, Diedrich, and Anselm Franke, eds. *The Whole Earth: Kalifornien und das Verschwinden des Außen.* Berlin: Sternberg Press, 2013.
Dietrich, Marc, and Martin Seeliger, eds. *Deutscher Gangsta-Rap: Sozial- und kulturwissenschaftliche Beiträge zu einem Pop-Phänomän.* Bielefeld: Transcript, 2012.
Dijck, José van. *The Culture of Connectivity: A Critical History of Social Media.* Oxford University Press, 2013.
Donald, Stephanie Hemelryk, et al., eds. *Branding Cities: Cosmopolitanism, Parochialism, and Social Change.* New York: Routledge, 2009.
Dormer, Peter. *Design since 1945.* London: Thames and Hudson, 1993.
Douglas, Mary. *Food in the Social Order: Studies of Food and Festivities in Three American Communities.* New York: Russell Sage Foundation, 1984.
Douglas, Mary. *Natural Symbols: Explorations in Cosmology.* New York: Pantheon Books, 1970.
Drucker, Peter. *Post-Capitalist Society.* New York: Harper Business, 1994.
Duckworth, Angela, et al. "Grit: Perseverance and Passion for Long-Term Goals." *Journal of Personality and Social Psychology* 92 (2007). Pp. 1087–1101.
Duffett, Mark. *Understanding Fandom: An Introduction to the Study of Media Fan Culture.* New York: Bloomsbury, 2013.
Dugin, Aleksandr. *The Fourth Political Theory.* Trans. Mark Sleboda. London: Arktos Media, 2012.
Dülmen, Richard van, ed. *Entdeckung des Ich: Die Geschichte der Individualisierung vom Mittelalter bis zur Gegenwart.* Cologne: Böhlau, 2001.
Durkheim, Émile. *The Elementary Forms of Religious Life.* Trans. Joseph Ward Swain. London: G. Allen & Unwin, 1915.
Dyk, Silke van, and Stephan Lessenich, eds. *Die jungen Alten: Analysen einer neuen Sozialfigur.* Frankfurt am Main: Campus, 2009.
Eagleton, Terry. *The Idea of Culture.* Oxford: Blackwell, 2000.
Eco, Umberto. *The Open Work.* Trans. Anna Cancogni. Cambridge, MA: Harvard University Press, 1989.
Ege, Moritz. *Ein Proll mit Klasse: Mode, Popkultur und soziale Ungleichheiten unter jungen Männern in Berlin.* Frankfurt am Main: Campus, 2013.
Ehrenberg, Alain. *Le culte de la performance.* Paris: Calmann-Lévy, 1991.
Ehrenberg, Alain. *The Weariness of the Self: Diagnosing the History of Depression in the Contemporary Age.* Trans. Enrico Caouette et al. Montreal: McGill-Queen's University Press, 2010.
Elias, Norbert. *The Civilizing Process: Sociogenetic and Psychogenetic Investigations.* Rev. edn. Trans. Edmund Jephcott. Oxford: Blackwell, 2000.
Elias, Norbert. *The Court Society.* Trans. Edmund Jephcott and Stephen Mennell. New York: Pantheon, 1983.
English, Bonnie. *A Cultural History of Fashion in the Twentieth Century: From the Catwalk to the Sidewalk.* New York: Berg, 2007.
English, James F. *The Economy of Prestige: Prizes, Awards, and the Circulation of Cultural Value.* Cambridge, MA: Harvard University Press, 2005.
Eribon, Didier. *Returning to Reims.* Trans. Michael Lucey. Cambridge, MA: MIT Press, 2013.

Esping-Andersen, Gøsta. *Changing Classes: Stratification and Mobility in Post-Industrial Societies*. London: Sage, 1993.
Esposito, Elena. *Die Verbindlichkeit des Vorübergehenden: Paradoxien der Mode*. Frankfurt am Main: Suhrkamp, 2004.
Esposito, Roberto. *Communitas: The Origin and Destiny of Community*. Trans. Timothy Campbell. Stanford University Press, 2010.
Etzemüller, Thomas. *Die Romantik der Rationalität: Alva & Gunnar Myrdal – Social Engineering in Sweden*. Bielefeld: Transcript, 2010.
Faludi, Susan. *Stiffed: The Betrayal of the American Man*. New York: William Morrow, 1999.
Fanon, Frantz. *Black Skin, White Masks*. Trans. Charles Lam Markmann. New York: Grove Press, 1967.
Featherstone, Mike. *Consumer Culture and Postmodernism*. London: Sage, 1991.
Feifer, Maxine. *Going Places: The Ways of the Tourist from Imperial Rome to the Present Day*. London: Macmillan, 1985.
Ferry, Luc. *Learning to Live: A User's Manual*. Trans. Theo Cuffe. Edinburgh: Canongate, 2010.
Feyerabend, Paul. *Against Method: Outline of an Anarchist Theory of Knowledge*. 4th edn. London: Verso, 2010.
Fischer-Lichte, Erika, ed. *Performativität und Ereignis*. Tübingen: Francke, 2003.
Fitoussi, Jean-Paul, and Pierre Rosanvallon. *Le nouvel âge des inégalités*. Paris: Seuil, 1996.
Flaßpöhler, Svenja. *Wir Genussarbeiter: Über Freiheit und Zwang in der Leistungsgesellschaft*. Munich: Deutsche Verlags-Anstalt, 2011.
Flew, Terry. *The Creative Industries: Culture and Policy*. London: Sage, 2012.
Flew, Terry. *Global Creative Industries*. Cambridge: Polity, 2013.
Florida, Richard. *Cities and the Creative Class*. New York: Routledge, 2005.
Florida, Richard. *The Rise of the Creative Class: And How It's Transforming Work, Leisure, Community, and Everyday Life*. New York: Basic Books, 2002.
Florida, Richard. *Who's Your City? How the Creative Economy is Making Where to Live the Most Important Decision of Your Life*. New York: Basic Books, 2008.
Floridi, Luciano. *The Fourth Revolution: How the Infosphere is Reshaping Human Reality*. Oxford University Press, 2014.
Floridi, Luciano. *Information: A Very Short Introduction*. Oxford University Press, 2010.
Foucault, Michel. *Abnormal: Lectures at the Collège de France, 1974–1975*. Trans. Graham Burchell. New York: Verso, 2003.
Foucault, Michel. *The Birth of Biopolitics: Lectures at the Collège de France, 1978–1979*. Trans. Graham Burchell. New York: Palgrave Macmillan, 2011.
Foucault, Michel. *Discipline and Punish: The Birth of the Prison*. Trans. Alan Sheridan. New York: Vintage, 1977.
Foucault, Michel. *Security, Territory, Population: Lectures at the Collège de France, 1977–1978*. Trans. Graham Burchell. New York: Palgrave Macmillan, 2007.
Foucault, Michel. "What is Enlightenment?" In *The Foucault Reader*. Ed. Paul Rabinow. New York: Pantheon Books, 1984. Pp. 32–50.
Fourastié, Jean. *Les trente glorieuses, ou la révolution invisible de 1946 à 1975*. Paris: Fayard, 1979.
Franck, Georg. *Mentaler Kapitalismus: Eine politische Ökonomie des Geistes*. Munich: Hanser, 2005.
Franck, Georg. Ökonomie der Aufmerksamkeit: Ein Entwurf. Munich: Hanser, 1998.
Frank, Manfred, and Anselm Haverkamp, eds. *Individualität*. Munich: Fink, 1988.
Frank, Michael, and Kirsten Mahlke, eds. *Kultur und Terror*. Bielefeld: Transcript, 2010.
Frank, Robert, and Philipp Cook. *The Winner-Take-All Society: Why the Few on the Top Get So Much More than the Rest of Us*. New York: Penguin, 2010.
Frank, Thomas. *Listen, Liberal: Or, What Ever Happened to the Party of the People?* New York: Metropolitan Books, 2016.

Frede, Frederik, et al, eds. *Freunde von Freunden: Berlin*. Berlin: Distanz, 2011.
Freeland, Chrystia. "The Rise of the New Global Elite," *The Atlantic* (January/February 2001): www.theatlantic.com/magazine/archive/2011/01/the-rise-of-the-new-global-elite/308343.
Freiberger, Paul, and Michael Swaine. *Fire in the Valley: The Making of the Personal Computer*. New York: McGraw-Hill, 1999.
Friedrich-Ebert-Stiftung, ed. "Gesellschaft im Reformprozess." Berlin, 2006: www.domradio.de/sites/default/files/pdf/061017_Gesellschaft_im_Reformprozess_komplett.pdf.
Frisby, David. *Fragments of Modernity: Theories of Modernity in the Work of Simmel, Kracauer, and Benjamin*. Cambridge: Polity, 1985.
Frith, Jordan. *Smartphones as Locative Media*. Cambridge: Polity, 2015.
Fuchs, Martin, et al., eds. *Rethinking Gamification*. Lüneburg: Meson Press, 2014.
Fukuyama, Francis. *The End of History and the Last Man*. New York: Free Press, 1992.
Fuller, Robert. *Somebodies or Nobodies: Overcoming the Abuse of Rank*. Gabriola Island, BC: New Society Publishers, 2003.
Fumagalli, Andrea, and Stefano Lucarelli. "A Model of Cognitive Capitalism: A Preliminary Analysis." *European Journal of Economic and Social Systems* 20 (2007). Pp. 117–33.
Funk, Rainer. *Der entgrenzte Mensch: Warum ein Leben ohne Grenzen nicht frei, sondern abhängig macht*. Gütersloh: Gütersloher Verlagshaus, 2011.
Funken, Christiane, et al. *Vertrackte Karrieren: Zum Wandel der Arbeitswelten in Wirtschaf und Wissenschaft*. Frankfurt am Main: Campus, 2015.
Galbraith, John Kenneth. *The Affluent Society*. 2nd edn. London: Hamilton, 1969.
GamesCoop. *Theorien des Computerspiels zur Einführung*. Hamburg: Junius, 2012.
Gardner, Howard, and Katie Davis. *The App Generation: How Today's Youth Navigate Identity, Intimacy, and Imagination in a Digital World*. New Haven, CT: Yale University Press, 2013.
Gay, Paul du. *Consumption and Identity at Work*. London: Sage, 1996.
Gay, Peter. *Pleasure Wars: The Bourgeois Experience, Victoria to Freud*. New York: W. W. Norton, 1988.
Gebhard, David. "William Wurster and His Californian Contemporaries: The Idea of Regionalism and Soft Modernism." In *An Everyday Modernism: The Houses of William Wurster*. Ed. Marc Treib. San Francisco Museum of Art, 1995. Pp. 164–83.
Gebhardt, Winfried. *Fest, Feier und Alltag: Über die gesellschaftliche Wirklichkeit des Menschen und ihre Deutung*. Frankfurt am Main: Peter Lang, 1987.
Gebhardt, Winfried, et al., eds. *Events: Soziologie des Außergewöhnlichen*. Opladen: Leske + Budrich, 2000.
Gehlen, Dirk von. *Mashup: Lob der Kopie*. Berlin: Suhrkamp, 2011.
Gehlen, Dirk von. *Eine neue Version ist verfügbar: Wie die Digitalisierung Kunst und Kultur verändert*. Berlin: Metrolit, 2013.
Gellner, Ernest. *Encounters with Nationalism*. Oxford: Blackwell, 1994.
Gerhardt, Volker. *Pathos und Distanz: Studien zur Philosophie Friedrich Nietzsches*. Stuttgart: Reclam, 1988.
Gibson, James J. *The Senses Considered as Perceptual Systems*. Boston, MA: Houghton Mifflin, 1966.
Giddens, Anthony. *Modernity and Self-Identity: Self and Society in the Late Modern Age*. Cambridge: Polity, 1991.
Giedion, Siegfried. *Mechanization Takes Command: A Contribution to Anonymous History*. Oxford University Press, 1948.
Giesen, Bernhard. *Kollektive Identität: Die Intellektuellen und die Nation II*. Frankfurt am Main: Suhrkamp, 1999.
Giesen, Bernhard. *Nationale und kulturelle Identität: Studien zur Entwicklung des kollektiven Bewußtseins in der Neuzeit*. Frankfurt am Main: Suhrkamp, 1991.
Gilmore, James H., and Joseph Pine. *Authenticity: What Consumers Really Want*. Boston, MA: Harvard Business Review Press, 2015.

Glasenapp, Helmut von. *Die fünf Weltreligionen*. Cologne: Dietrichs, 1985.
Glatter, Jan, and Daniela Weber. "Die mediale Konstruktion des Stereotyps Szeneviertel in Reiseführern." In *Tourismusräume: Zur soziokulturellen Konstruktion eines globalen Phänomens*. Ed. Karlheinz Wöhler et al. Bielefeld: Transcript, 2010. Pp. 43–66.
Goffman, Erving. *Stigma: Notes on the Management of Spoiled Identity*. New York: Touchstone Press, 1986.
Goldthorpe, John, et al. *The Affluent Worker in the Class Structure*. Cambridge University Press, 1969.
Goodhart, David. *The Road to Somewhere: The Populist Revolt and the Future of Politics*. London: Hurst & Company, 2017.
Goodman, Nelson. *Languages of Art: An Approach to a Theory of Symbols*. Indianapolis, IN: Bobbs-Merrill, 1968.
Goodman, Richard A., and Lawrence P. Goodman. "Some Management Issues in Temporary Systems: A Study in Professional Development and Manpower – The Theater Case." *Administrative Science Quarterly* 21 (1976). Pp. 494–501.
Goody, Jack. *Cooking, Cuisine and Class: A Study in Comparative Sociology*. Cambridge University Press, 1982.
Goos, Maarten, and Alan Manning. "Lousy and Lovely Jobs: The Rising Polarization of Work in Britain." *Review of Economics and Statistics* 89 (2007). Pp. 118–33.
Goos, Maarten, et al. "Job Polarization in Europe." *American Economic Review* 99/2 (2009). Pp. 58–63.
Gottdiener, Mark. *The Theming of America: Dreams, Visions, and Commercial Spaces*. Boulder, CO: Westview Press, 2001.
Götz, Norbert. "Modernisierungsverlierer oder Gegner der reflexiven Moderne." *Zeitschrift für Soziologie* 26/6 (1997). Pp. 393–413.
Grabher, Gernot. "Ecologies of Creativity: The Village, the Group, and the Heterarchic Organisation of the British Advertising Industry." *Environmental Planning A: Economy and Space* 33 (2001). Pp. 351–74.
Graebner, William. *The Engineering of Consent: Democracy and Authority in Twentieth-Century America*. Madison: University of Wisconsin Press, 1987.
Gramsci, Antonio. *Selections from the Prison Notebooks*. Trans. Quentin Hoare and Geoffrey Nowell Smith. New York: International Publishers, 1971.
Granovetter, Mark S. "The Strength of Weak Ties." *American Journal of Sociology* 78 (1973). Pp. 1360–80.
Gratton, Lynda. *The Shift: The Future of Work is Already Here*. London: Collins, 2011.
Grauel, Jonas. *Gesundheit, Genuss und gutes Gewissen: Über Lebensmittelkonsum und Alltagsmoral*. Bielefeld: Transcript, 2014.
Graw, Isabelle. "The Value of the Art Commodity: Twelve Theses on Human Labor, Mimetic Desire, and Aliveness." *ARQ* 97 (2017). Pp. 130–45.
Greiner, Ulrich. *Schamverlust: Vom Wandel der Gefühlskultur*. Reinbek: Hamburg Rowohlt, 2014.
Grigg, Joanna. *Portfolio Working: A Practical Guide to Thriving in the Changing Workplace*. London: Kogan Page, 1997.
Groh-Samberg, Olaf. "Sorgenfreier Reichtum: Jenseits von Konjunktur und Krise." *DIW Wochenbericht* 76/35 (2009). Pp. 590–612.
Groys, Boris. *On the New*. Trans. G. M. Goshgarian. London: Verso, 2014.
Guibernau, Montserrat. *The Identity of Nations*. Cambridge: Polity, 2007.
Gumbrecht, Hans Ulrich. *Präsenz*. Berlin: Suhrkamp, 2012.
Gumbrecht, Hans Ulrich. *Production of Presence: What Meaning Cannot Say*. Stanford University Press, 2004.
Gumbrecht, Hans Ulrich, and K. Ludwig Pfeiffer, eds. *Stil: Geschichten und Funktionen eines kulturwissenschaftlichen Diskurselements*. Frankfurt am Main: Suhrkamp, 1986.
Günther, Klaus. "Ein Modell legitimen Scheiterns: Der Kampf um Anerkennung als Opfer." In *Strukturwandel der Anerkennung: Paradoxien sozialer Integration in der Gegenwart*. Ed. Axel Honneth et al. Frankfurt am Main: Campus, 2012. Pp. 185–248.

Habermas, Jürgen. "Labour and Interaction: Remarks on Hegel's Jena Philosophy of Mind." In *Theory and Practice*. Trans. John Viertel. London: Heinemann, 1974. Pp. 142–69.
Habermas, Jürgen. "Modernity: An Unfinished Project." Trans. Nicholas Walker. In *Habermas and the Unfinished Project of Modernity*. Ed. Maurizio Passerin d'Entrèves and Seyla Benhabib. Cambridge, MA: MIT Press, 1997. Pp. 38–58.
Hafeneger, Benno. *Jugendbilder: Zwischen Hoffnung, Kontrolle, Erziehung und Dialog*. Opladen: Leske + Budrich, 1995.
Halbwachs, Maurice. *On Collective Memory*. Trans. Lewis A. Coser. University of Chicago Press, 1992.
Han, Byung-Chul. *Hyperkulturalität: Kultur und Globalisierung*. Berlin: Merve, 2005.
Han, Byung-Chul. *In the Swarm: Digital Prospects*. Trans. Erik Butler. Cambridge, MA: MIT Press, 2017.
Hand, Martin. *Ubiquitous Photography*. Cambridge: Polity, 2012.
Handy, Charles B. *The Age of Unreason*. Boston, MA: Harvard Business School Press, 1989.
Hannerz, Ulf. "Two Faces of Cosmopolitanism: Culture and Politics." *Statvetenskaplig Tidskrift* 107/3 (2005). Pp. 199–213.
Hansen, Mark. "Medien des 21. Jahrhunderts, technisches Empfinden und unsere originäre Umweltbedingung." In *Die technologische Bedingung: Beiträge zur Beschreibung der technischen Welt*. Ed. Erich Hörl. Berlin: Suhrkamp, 2011. Pp. 365–409.
Hark, Sabine, et al. "Das umkämpfte Allgemeine und das neue Gemeinsame: Solidarität ohne Identität." *Feministische Studien* 33 (2015). Pp. 99–103.
Harper, Shannon, and Barbara Reskin. "Affirmative Action at School and on the Job." *Annual Review of Sociology* 31 (2005). Pp. 357–79.
Harris, Cheryl, and Alison Alexander, eds. *Theorizing Fandom: Fans, Subculture, and Identity*. Cresskill, NJ: Hampton Press, 1998.
Harrison, Rob, et al., eds. *The Ethical Consumer*. London: Sage, 2005.
Hartigan, John. *Odd Tribes: Toward a Cultural Analysis of White People*. Durham, NC: Duke University Press, 2005.
Hartmann, Michael. *Der Mythos von den Leistungseliten: Spitzenkarrieren und soziale Herkunft in Wirtschaft, Politik, Justiz und Wissenschaft*. Frankfurt am Main: Campus, 2002.
Harvey, David. *A Brief History of Neoliberalism*. New York: Oxford University Press, 2005.
Harvey, David. *The Condition of Postmodernity: An Enquiry into the Origins of Cultural Change*. Oxford: Blackwell, 1989.
Häseler, Jens. "Original/Originalität." In *Ästhetische Grundbegriffe*, vol. IV. Ed. Karlheinz Barck. Stuttgart: Metzler, 2002. Pp. 638–55.
Hausherr, Sven, and Nina Trippel, eds. *Cee Cee Berlin*. 2 vols. Berlin: Distanz Verlag, 2014.
Häußermann, Hartmut, and Walter Siebel. *Dienstleistungsgesellschaften*. Frankfurt am Main: Suhrkamp, 1995.
Hays, Priya. *Advancing Healthcare through Personalized Medicine*. Boca Raton, FL: CRC Press, 2017.
Hebidge, Dick. *Subculture: The Meaning of Style*. London: Routledge, 1979.
Heidegger, Martin. "The Age of the World Picture." In *The Question Concerning Technology and Other Essays*. Trans. William Lovitt. New York: Harper & Row, 1977. Pp. 115–36.
Hein, Dieter, and Andreas Schulz, eds. *Bürgerkultur im 19. Jahrhundert: Bildung, Kunst und Lebenswelt*. Munich: Beck, 1996.
Heinich, Nathalie. *L'élite artiste: Excellence et singularité en régime démocratique*. Paris: Gallimard, 2005.
Heintz, Bettina. "Numerische Differenz: Überlegungen zu einer Soziologie des (quantitativen) Vergleichs." *Zeitschrift für Soziologie* 39/3 (2010). Pp. 162–81.
Helfrich, Silke, ed. *Commons: Für eine neue Politik jenseits von Markt und Staat*. Bielefeld: Transcript, 2012.

Bibliography

Helms, Dietrich, ed. *Keiner wird gewinnen: Populäre Musik im Wettbewerb.* Bielefeld: Transcript, 2005.
Henderson, Richard. "Industry Employment and Output Projections to 2024." *Bureau of Labor Statistics: Monthly Labor Review* (December 2015): www.bls.gov/opub/mlr/2015/article/industry-employment-and-output-projections-to-2024-1.htm.
Hendrick, Harry. "Die sozialinvestive Kindheit." In *Kindheiten in der Moderne: Eine Geschichte der Sorge.* Ed. Meike Sophia Baader et al. Franfurt am Main: Campus, 2014. Pp. 456–91.
Hepp, Andreas, et al., eds. *Medienkultur im Wandel.* Konstanz: UVK Verlagsgesellschaft, 2010.
Hesmondhalgh, David. *The Cultural Industries.* London: Sage, 2002.
Hesmondhalgh, David, and Sarah Baker. *Creative Labour: Media Work in Three Cultural Industries.* London: Routledge, 2011.
Hettling, Manfred. "Bürgerliche Kultur: Bürgerlichkeit als kulturelles System." In *Sozial- und Kulturgeschichte des Bürgertums.* Ed. Peter Lundgreen. Göttingen: Vandenhoeck & Ruprecht, 2000. Pp. 319–40.
Heur, Bas van. *Creative Networks and the City: Towards a Cultural Political Economy of Aesthetic Production.* Bielefeld: Transcript, 2010.
Hewison, Robert. *Cultural Capital: The Rise and Fall of Creative Britain.* London: Verso, 2014.
Hilferding, Rudolf. *Organisierter Kapitalismus.* Kiel, 1927.
Hilpert, Theo. *Die funktionelle Stadt: Le Corbusiers Stadtvision – Bedingungen, Motive, Hintergründe.* Braunschweig: F. Vieweg und Sohn, 1979.
Hitzler, Ronald, and Michaela Pfadenhauer, eds. *Karrierepolitik: Beiträge zur Rekonstruktion erfolgsorientierten Handels.* Opladen: Leske + Budrich, 2003.
Hobsbawm, Eric. *The Age of Extremes: The Short Twentieth Century, 1914–1991.* London: Michael Joseph, 1994.
Hobsbawm, Eric. *Nations and Nationalism since 1780: Program, Myth, Reality.* Cambridge University Press, 1992.
Hobsbawm, Eric, and Terence Ranger, eds. *The Invention of Tradition.* Cambridge University Press, 1984.
Hochschild, Arlie Russell. *The Managed Heart: Commercialization of Human Feeling.* Berkeley: University of California Press, 1983.
Hochschild, Arlie Russell. *Strangers in Their Own Land: Anger and Mourning on the American Right.* New York: The New Press, 2016.
Hochschild, Arlie Russell. *The Time Bind: When Work Becomes Home and Home Becomes Work.* New York: Metropolitan Books, 1997.
Hohnsträter, Dirk, ed. *Konsum und Kreativität.* Bielefeld: Transcript, 2016.
Holland, John. *Hidden Order: How Adaptation Builds Complexity.* Reading, MA: Basic Books, 1995.
Holm, Andrej. "Die Karawane zieht weiter: Stationen der Aufwertung in der Berliner Innenstadt." In *Intercity Istanbul–Berlin.* Ed. Mario Pschera et al. Berlin: Dağyeli, 2010. Pp. 89–101.
Honneth, Axel. *The Struggle for Recognition: The Moral Grammar of Social Conflicts.* Trans. Joel Anderson. Cambridge, MA: MIT Press, 1996.
Honneth, Axel, ed. *Kommunitarismus: Eine Debatte über die moralischen Grundlagen moderner Gesellschaften.* Frankfurt am Main: Campus, 1995.
Hörl, Erich. "Die technologische Bedingung: Zur Einführung." In *Die technologische Bedingung: Beiträge zur Beschreibung der technischen Welt.* Ed. Erich Hörl. Berlin: Suhrkamp, 2011. Pp. 7–53.
Hormel, Ulrike, and Albert Scherr, eds. *Diskriminierung: Grundlagen und Forschungsergebnisse.* Wiesbaden: Verlag für Sozialwissenschaften, 2010.
Hörning, Karl H. *Doing Culture: Neue Positionen zum Verhältnis von Kultur und sozialer Praxis.* Bielefeld: Transcript, 2004.
Howkins, John. *The Creative Economy: How People Make Money from Ideas.* London: Penguin, 2001.
Hughes, Thomas P. *American Genesis: A Century of Invention and Technological Enthusiasm, 1870–1970.* New York: Viking, 1989.

Hurrelmann, Klaus, and Erik Albrecht. *Die heimlichen Revolutionäre: Wie die Generation Y unsere Welt verändert*. Weinheim: Belzt, 2014.
Hüther, Gerald, and Uli Hauser. *Jedes Kind ist hoch begabt: Die angeborenen Talente unserer Kinder und was wir daraus machen*. Munich: Btb Verlag, 2012.
Hutter, Michael. *The Rise of the Joyful Economy: Artistic Invention and Economic Growth from Brunelleschi to Murakami*. New York: Routledge, 2015.
Ihde, Don. *Technology and Lifeworld: From Garden to Earth*. Bloomington: Indiana University Press, 1996.
Illouz, Eva. *Why Love Hurts: A Sociological Explanation*. Cambridge: Polity, 2013.
Imrie, Robert, and Mike Raco, eds. *Urban Renaissance? New Labour, Community, and Urban Policy*. Bristol: Policy Press, 2003.
Inglehart, Ronald. *Modernization and Postmodernization: Cultural, Economic, and Political Change in 43 Societies*. Princeton University Press, 1997.
Inglehart, Ronald. *The Silent Revolution: Changing Values and Political Styles Among Western Publics*. Princeton University Press, 1977.
Inglehart, Ronald, and Pippa Norris. "Trump, Brexit, and the Rise of Populism: Economic Have-Nots and Cultural Backlash," *Harvard Kennedy School Faculty Working Paper Series* (August 2016): https://papers.ssrn.com/sol3/papers.cfm?abstract_id=2818659.
Inglis, David, and Debra L. Gimlin, eds. *The Globalization of Food*. London: Routledge, 2008.
Ingold, Felix Philipp. "Russlands eurasische Geopolitik." *Merkur* 70 (2016). Pp. 5–18.
Isenberg, Nancy. *White Trash: The 400-Year Untold History of Class in America*. New York: Penguin, 2017.
Izenberg, Gerald N. *Impossible Individuality: Romanticism, Revolution, and the Origins of Modern Selfhood, 1787–1802*. Princeton University Press, 2001.
Jacobs, Jane. *The Death and Life of Great American Cities: The Failure of Current Planning*. New York: Vintage Books, 1961.
Jacobs, Sue-Ellen, et al., eds. *Two-Spirit People: Native American Gender Identity, Sexuality, and Spirituality*. Urbana: University of Illinois Press, 2005.
Jacobson, Matthew Frye. *Roots Too: White Ethnic Revival in Post-Civil Rights America*. Cambridge, MA: Harvard University Press, 2008.
Jager, Michael. "Class Definition and the Aesthetics of Gentrification: Victoriana in Melbourne." In *Gentrification of the City*. Ed. Neil Smith and Peter Williams. London: Routledge, 1986. Pp. 78–91.
Jameson, Fredric. *Postmodernism, or the Cultural Logic of Late Capitalism*. Durham, NC: Duke University Press, 1991.
Jansen, Stephan A., and Stephan Schleissing, eds. *Konkurrenz und Kooperation: Interdisziplinäre Zugänge zur Theorie der Co-opetition*. Marburg: Metropolis, 2000.
Jenkins, Richard. *Rethinking Ethnicity: Arguments and Explorations*. London: Sage, 1997.
Jensen, Rolf. *The Dream Society: How the Coming Shift from Information to Imagination Will Transform Your Business*. New York: McGraw-Hill, 2001.
Jessop, Bob. *The Future of the Capitalist State*. Cambridge: Polity, 2002.
Joas, Hans, and Klaus Wiegandt, eds. *Secularization and the World Religions*. Trans. Alex Skinner. Liverpool University Press, 2009.
Jones, Owen. *Chavs: The Demonization of the Working Class*. London: Verso, 2016.
Julier, Guy. *The Culture of Design*. London: Sage, 2000.
Junge, Matthias, and Götz Lechner, eds. *Scheitern: Aspekte eines sozialen Phänomens*. Wiesbaden: Verlag für Sozialwissenschaften, 2004.
Kalkowski, Peter, and Otfried Mickler. *Antinomien des Projektmanagements: Eine Arbeitsform zwischen Direktive und Freiraum*. Berlin: Edition Sigma, 2009.
Kant, Immanuel. *Critique of Pure Reason*. Trans. Paul Guyer and Allen W. Wood. Cambridge University Press, 1998.
Kant, Immanuel. *Critique of the Power of Judgement*. Trans. Paul Guyer and Eric Matthews. Cambridge University Press, 2000.

Karpik, Lucien. *Valuing the Unique: The Economics of Singularities*. Princeton University Press, 2010.
Kelleter, Frank, ed. *Populäre Serialität: Narration, Evolution, Distinktion*. Bielefeld: Transcript, 2012.
Kelley, Tom, and Jonathan Littman. *The Art of Innovation: Lessons in Creativity from IDEO, America's Leading Design Firm*. London: HarperCollins, 2001.
Kenny, Kevin. *Diaspora: A Very Short Introduction*. New York: Oxford University Press, 2013.
Kerscher, Gottfried. *Architektur als Repräsentation: Spätmittelalterliche Palastbaukunst zwischen Pracht und zeremoniellen Voraussetzungen*. Tübingen: Wasmuth, 2000.
Kimmel, Michael. *The Gendered Society*. New York: Oxford University Press, 2000.
Kippele, Flavia. *Was heißt Individualisierung? Die Antworten soziologischer Klassiker*. Opladen: Westdeutscher Verlag, 1998.
Kirkham, Pat. *Charles and Ray Eames: Designers of the Twentieth Century*. Cambridge, MA: MIT Press, 1995.
Klein, Gabriele, ed. *Tango in Translation: Tanz zwischen Medien, Kulturen, Kunst und Politik*. Bielefeld: Transcript, 2009.
Klein, Maury. *The Flowering of the Third America: The Making of Organizational Society, 1850–1920*. Chicago, IL: Ivan R. Dee, 1993.
Klingmann, Anna. *Brandscapes: Architecture in the Experience Economy*. Cambridge, MA: MIT Press, 2007.
Knecht, Alban. *Lebensqualität produzieren: Ressourcentheorie und Machtanalyse des Wohlfahrtsstaat*. Wiesbaden: Verlag für Sozialwissenschaften, 2010.
Knellessen, Olaf, et al., eds. *Serialität: Wissenschaft, Kunst, Medien*. Vienna: Turia + Kant, 2015.
Knoblauch, Hubert. "Das unsichtbare Neue Zeitalter: 'New Age', privatisierte Religion und kultisches Milieu." *Kölner Zeitschrift für Soziologie und Sozialpsychologie* 41/3 (1989). Pp. 504–25.
Knorr-Cetina, Karin, and Urs Bruegger. "Traders' Engagement with Markets: A Postsocial Relationship." *Theory, Culture & Society* 19/5 (2002). Pp. 161–85.
Knox, Paul, ed. *Atlas of Cities*. Princeton University Press, 2014.
Koelbl, Herlinde, et al. *Das deutsche Wohnzimmer*. Munich: C. J. Bucher, 1980.
Köhler, Andrea. *Scham: Vom Paradies zum Dschungelcamp*. Springe: Klampe Verlag, 2017.
Kohli, Martin. "Gesellschaftszeit und Lebenszeit: Der Lebenslauf im Strukturwandel." In *Die Moderne: Kontinuitäten und Zäsuren*. Ed. Johannes Berger. Göttingen: Schwartz, 1986. Pp. 183–204.
Koppetsch, Cornelia. *Das Ethos der Kreativen: Eine Studie zum Wandel von Arbeit und Identität am Beispiel der Werberufe*. Konstanz: UVK, 2006.
Koppetsch, Cornelia, ed. *Körper und Status: Zur Soziologie der Attraktivität*. Konstanz: UVK, 2000.
Kopytoff, Igor. "The Cultural Biography of Things: Commoditization as Process." In *The Social Life of Things: Commodities in Cultural Perspective*. Ed. Arjun Appadurai. Cambridge University Press, 1986. Pp. 64–91.
Koschorke, Albrecht. *Fact and Fiction: Elements of a General Theory of Narrative*. Trans. Joel Golb. Berlin: De Gruyter, 2018.
Koselleck, Reinhart. "Fortschritt." In *Geschichtliche Grundbegriffe*, vol. II. Ed. Otto Brunner et al. Stuttgart: Klett-Cotta, 1975. Pp. 351–423.
Koselleck, Reinhart. *Futures Past: On the Semantics of Historical Time*. Trans. Keith Tribe. New York: Columbia University Press, 2004.
Koselleck, Reinhart. "Krise." In *Geschichtliche Grundbegriffe*, vol. III. Ed. Otto Brunner et al. Stuttgart: Klett-Cotta, 1982. Pp. 617–50.
Kraemer, Klaus. *Der Markt der Gesellschaft: Zu einer soziologischen Theorie der Marktvergesellschaftlichung*. Opladen: Westdeutscher Verlag, 1997.
Krajewski, Markus, ed. *Projektemacher: Zur Produktion von Wissen in der Vorform des Scheiterns*. Berlin: Kulturverlag Kadmos, 2004.

Krämer, Hannes. *Die Praxis der Kreativität: Eine Ethnographie kreativer Arbeit.* Bielefeld: Transcript, 2014.
Kratzer, Nick. *Arbeitskraft in Entgrenzung: Grenzlose Anforderungen, erweiterte Spielräume, begrenzte Ressourcen.* Berlin: Edition Sigma, 2003.
Krieger, Verena. *Was ist ein Künstler? Genie – Heilsbringer – Antikünstler: Eine Ideen- und Kunstgeschichte des Schöpferischen.* Cologne: Deubner, 2007.
Kriesi, Hanspeter, et al. "Globalization and the Transformation of National Political Space: Six European Countries Compared." *European Journal of Political Research* 45 (2006). Pp. 921–56.
Kristeva, Julia. *Powers of Horror: An Essay on Abjection.* New York: Columbia University Press, 1982.
Kron, Thomas. *Reflexiver Terrorismus.* Weilerwist: Velbrück Wissenschaft, 2015.
Kron, Thomas, and Martin Horáček. *Individualisierung.* Bielefeld: Transcript, 2009.
Kruse, Horst H., ed. *From Rags to Riches: Erfolgsmythos und Erfolgsrezepte in der amerikanischen Gesellschaft.* Munich: Goldmann, 1973.
Kucklick, Christoph. *Die granulare Gesellschaft: Wie das Digitale unsere Wirklichkeit auflöst.* Berlin: Ullstein, 2014.
Kuhlen, Rainer. "Allgemeines/Besonderes." In *Historisches Wörterbuch der Philosophie*, vol. I. Ed. Joachim Ritter et al. Basel: Schwabe, 1971. Pp. 181–3.
Kuhn, Thomas S. *The Structure of Scientific Revolution.* 4th edn. University of Chicago Press, 2015.
Kumar, Krishan. *Prophecy and Progress: The Sociology of Industrial and Post-Industrial Society.* New York: Penguin, 1978.
Kurtz, Thomas, and Michaela Pfadenhauer, eds. *Soziologie der Kompetenz.* Wiesbaden: Verlag für Sozialwissenschaften, 2010.
Kurzweil, Ray. *The Singularity is Near: When Humans Transcend Biology.* New York: Penguin, 2005.
Kymlicka, Will. *Multicultural Odysseys: Navigating the New International Politics of Diversity.* Oxford University Press, 2007.
Labadi, Sophia. "World Heritage, Authenticity, and Post-Authenticity." In *Heritage and Globalization.* Ed. Colin Long and Sophia Labadi. New York: Routledge, 2010. Pp. 66–84.
Laclau, Ernesto. "Why Do Empty Signifiers Matter to Politics?" In Laclau, *Emancipation(s).* London: Verso, 1996. Pp. 36–46.
Lahire, Bernard. *La culture des individus: Dissonances culturelles et distinction de soi.* Paris: La Découverte, 2004.
Lambert, Joe. *Digital Storytelling: Capturing Lives, Creating Community.* New York and Abingdon: Routledge, 2013.
Lamont, Michèle. *The Dignity of Working Men: Morality and the Boundaries of Race, Class, and Immigration.* New York: Russell Sage Foundation, 2000.
Lamont, Michèle. "Toward a Comparative Sociology of Valuation and Evaluation." *Annual Review of Sociology* 38 (2012). Pp. 201–21.
Landow, George P., ed. *Hyper/Text/Theory.* Baltimore, MD: Johns Hopkins University Press, 1994.
Landry, Charles. *The Creative City: A Toolkit for Urban Innovators.* London: Earthscan, 2008.
Lange, Bastian. *Räume der Kreativszene: Culturpreneurs und ihre Orte.* Bielefeld: Transcript, 2007.
Lapeyronnie, Didier. *Ghetto urbain: Ségrégation, violence, pauvreté en France aujourd'hui.* Paris: Robert Laffont, 2008.
Lareau, Annette. *Unequal Childhoods: Class, Race, and Family Life.* Berkeley: University of California Press, 2003.
Larkin, Brian. "The Politics and Poetics of Infrastructure." *Annual Review of Anthropology* 42 (2013). Pp. 327–43.
Lasch, Christopher. *The Culture of Narcissism: American Life in an Age of Diminishing Expectations.* New York: W. W. Norton, 1978.
Lash, Scott, and Celia Lury. *Global Culture Industry: The Mediation of Things.* Cambridge: Polity, 2011.

Lash, Scott, and John Urry. *Economies of Signs and Space*. London: Sage, 1994.
Lash, Scott, and John Urry. *The End of Organized Capitalism*. Cambridge: Polity, 1987.
Latour, Bruno. *Reassembling the Social: An Introduction to Actor-Network-Theory*. Oxford University Press, 2005.
Laux, Henning. *Soziologie im Zeitalter der Komposition: Koordinaten einer integrativen Netzwerktheorie*. Weilerwist: Velbrück, 2014.
Law, John. *Organizing Modernity: Social Ordering and Social Theory*. Oxford: Blackwell, 1994.
Lazzarato, Maurizio. "Immaterial Labor." In *Radical Thought in Italy: A Potential Politics*. Ed. Paolo Virno and Michael Hardt. Minneapolis: University of Minnesota Press, 1996. Pp. 133–48.
Lears, T. J. Jackson. *Fables of Abundance: A Cultural History of Advertising in America*. New York: Basic Books, 1993.
Lees, Loretta, et al., eds. *The Gentrification Reader*. New York: Routledge, 2010.
Legnaro, Aldo. "Performanz." In *Glossar der Gegenwart*. Ed. Ulrich Bröckling et al. Frankfurt am Main: Suhrkamp, 2004. Pp. 204–6.
Leinberger, Paul, and Bruce Tucker. *The New Individualists: The Generation After the Organization Man*. New York: Harper Collins, 1991.
Leiris, Michel. *Ethnologische Schriften I: Die eigene und die fremde Kultur*. Ed. Hans-Jürgen Heinrichs. Frankfurt am Main: Suhrkamp, 1985.
Leistert, Oliver, and Theo Röhle, eds. *Generation Facebook: Über das Leben im Social Net*. Bielefeld: Transcript, 2011.
Lepecki, André. *Singularities: Dance in the Age of Performance*. New York: Routledge, 2016.
Lévi-Strauss, Claude. *The Raw and the Cooked*. Trans. John Weightman and Doreen Weightman. University of Chicago Press, 1983.
Lévi-Strauss, Claude. *Totemism*. Trans. Rodney Needham. London: Merlin Press, 1964.
Liessmann, Konrad Paul. *Das Universum der Dinge: Zur Ästhetik des Alltäglichen*. Vienna: Paul Zsolnay Verlag, 2010.
Lilla, Mark. "The End of Identity Liberalism," *The New York Times* (November 18, 2016): www.nytimes.com/2016/11/20/opinion/sunday/the-end-of-identity-liberalism.html.
Link, Jürgen. *Versuch über den Normalismus: Wie Normalität produziert wird*. 5th edn. Göttingen: Vandenhoeck & Ruprecht, 2013.
Lipovetsky, Gilles. *L'esthétisation du monde: Vivre à l'âge du capitalisme artiste*. Paris: Gallimard, 2016.
Lipset, Seymour Martin, and Stein Rokkan. "Cleavage Structures, Party Systems, and Voter Alignments: An Introduction." In *Party Systems and Voter Alignments: Cross-National Perspectives*. Ed. Seymour Martin Lipset and Stein Rokkan. New York: Free Press, 1967. Pp. 1–64.
Lister, Martin, et al. *New Media: A Critical Introduction*. New York: Routledge, 2009.
Livingstone, Sonia, and Ranjana Das. "The End of Audiences? Theoretical Echoes of Reception Amidst the Uncertainties of Use." In *A Companion to New Media Dynamics*. Ed. John Hartley et al. Chichester: Wiley-Blackwell, 2013. Pp. 104–21.
Lloyd, Richard D. *Neo-Bohemia: Art and Commerce in the Postindustrial City*. New York: Routledge, 2010.
Lorey, Isabell, and Klaus Neundlinger, eds. *Kognitiver Kapitalismus*. Vienna: Turia + Kant, 2012.
Louis, Édouard. *The End of Eddy*. Trans. Michael Lucey. New York: Farrar, Straus & Giroux, 2018.
Löw, Martina. *Soziologie der Städte*. Frankfurt am Main: Suhrkamp, 2008.
Luhmann, Niklas. "Komplexität." In Luhmann, *Soziologische Aufklärung 2: Aufsätze zur Theorie der Gesellschaft*. Opladen: Westdeutscher Verlag, 1975. Pp. 204–20.

Luhmann, Niklas. *Legitimität durch Verfahren*. Frankfurt am Main: Suhrkamp, 1969.
Luhmann, Niklas. *Die Wissenschaft der Gesellschaft*. Frankfurt am Main: Suhrkamp, 1992.
Lupton, Deborah. *The Quantified Self: A Sociology of Self-Tracking Cultures*. Cambridge: Polity, 2016.
Lutter, Mark. "Soziale Strukturen des Erfolgs: Winner-take-all-Konzentrationen und ihre sozialen Entstehungskontexte auf flexiblen Arbeitsmärkten." *Kölner Zeitschrift für Soziologie und Sozialpsychologie* 65 (2013). Pp. 597–622.
Lutz, Ronald. *Laufen und Läuferleben: Zum Verhältnis von Körper, Bewegung und Identität*. Frankfurt am Main: Campus, 1989.
Lyotard, Jean-François. "The Sublime and the Avant Garde." Trans. Lisa Liebmann. *Artforum* 22/8 (1984). Pp. 36–43.
MacCannell, Dean. *The Tourist: A New Theory of the Leisure Class*. New York: Schocken Books, 1976.
MacGregor, Neil. *A History of the World in 100 Objects*. New York: Penguin, 2013.
Maffesoli, Michel. *The Time of the Tribes: The Decline of Individualism in Mass Society*. Trans. Don Smith. London: Sage, 1996.
Mainzer, Klaus. "Singulär/Singularität." In *Historisches Wörterbuch der Philosophie*, vol. IX. Ed. Joachim Ritter et al. Basel: Schwabe, 1995. Pp. 798–808.
Makropoulos, Michael. "Massenkultur als Kontingenzkultur." In *Lautloses irren – Ways of Worldmaking Too ...*. Ed. Harm Lux. Berlin: Harm Lux, 2003. Pp. 151–73.
Makropoulos, Michael. *Modernität und Kontingenz*. Munich: Fink, 1997.
Mannitz, Sabine. *Die verkannte Integration: Eine Langzeitstudie unter Heranwachsenden aus Immigrantenfamilien*. Bielefeld: Transcript, 2006.
Manovich, Lev. *The Language of New Media*. Cambridge, MA: MIT Press, 2001.
Manovich, Lev. *Software Takes Command*. New York: Bloomsbury, 2013.
Manske, Alexandra. *Kapitalistische Geister in der Kultur- und Kreativwirtschaft: Kreative zwischen wirtschaftlichem Zwang und künstlerischem Drang*. Bielefeld: Transcript, 2016.
Manske, Alexandra. "Zum ungleichen Wert von Sozialkapital: Netzwerke aus seiner Perspektive sozialer Praxis." In *Soziale Netzwerke und soziale Ungleichheit*. Ed. Jörg Lüdicke and Martin Diewald. Wiesbaden: Verlag für Sozialwissenschaften, 2007. Pp. 135–62.
Mareis, Claudia. *Theorien des Designs zur Einführung*. Hamburg: Junius, 2014.
Maslow, Abraham H. *Motivation and Personality*. New York: Harper & Row, 1954.
Maslow, Abraham H. "A Theory of Human Motivation." *Psychological Review* 50 (1943). Pp. 370–96.
Maslow, Abraham H. *Toward a Psychology of Being*. 2nd edn. New York: Van Nostrand Reinhold, 1968.
Massumi, Brian. *Parables for the Virtual: Movement, Affect, Sensation*. Durham, NC: Duke University Press, 2007.
Mau, Steffen. *Lebenschancen: Wohin driftet die Mittelschicht?* Bonn: Bundeszentrale für politische Bildung, 2012.
Mau, Steffen. *The Metric Society: On the Quantification of the Social*. Trans. Sharon Howe. Cambridge: Polity, 2019.
Mayer-Schönberger, Viktor, and Kenneth Cukier. *Big Data: A Revolution that Will Transform How We Live, Work, and Think*. London: John Murray, 2013.
McClintock, Anne. *Imperial Leather: Race, Gender, and Sexuality in the Colonial Contest*. New York: Routledge, 1995.
McRobbie, Angela. *Be Creative: Making a Living in the New Culture Industries*. Cambridge: Polity, 2016.
McRobbie, Angela. *British Fashion Design: Rag Trade or Image Industry?* London: Routledge, 1998.
Menger, Pierre-Michel. *La différence, la concurrence et la disproportion: Sociologie du travail créateur*. Paris: Fayard, 2014.

Menger, Pierre-Michel. *The Economics of Creativity: Art and Achievement Under Uncertainty*. Cambridge, MA: Harvard University Press, 2014.
Menger, Pierre-Michel. *Portrait de l'artiste en travailleur: Métamorphoses du capitalisme*. Paris: Seuil, 2002.
Merton, Robert K. "The Matthew Effect in Science." *Science* 158/3810 (1968). Pp. 56–63.
Merton, Robert K. *The Sociology of Science: Theoretical and Empirical Investigations*. University of Chicago Press, 1998.
Message, Kylie. *New Museums and the Making of Culture*. Oxford: Berg, 2006.
Meyer, Thomas. *Was ist Fundamentalismus? Eine Einführung*. Wiesbaden: Verlag für Sozialwissenschaften, 2011.
Michéa, Jean-Claude. *Realm of Lesser Evil: An Essay of Liberal Civilization*. Trans. David Fernbach. Cambridge: Polity, 2009.
Milanović, Branko. *Global Inequality: A New Approach for the Age of Globalization*. Cambridge, MA: Harvard University Press, 2016.
Miller, Vincent. *Understanding Digital Culture*. Los Angeles: Sage, 2011.
Miller, Walter. "Lower Class Culture as a Generating Milieu of Gang Delinquency." *Journal of Social Issues* 14/3 (1958). Pp. 5–20.
Mills, Charles Wright. *White Collar: The American Middle Class*. New York: Oxford University Press, 1951.
Mintz, Steven, and Susan Kellogg. *Domestic Revolutions: A Social History of American Family Life*. New York: Free Press, 1988.
Mirzoeff, Nicholas. *An Introduction to Visual Culture*. New York: Routledge, 1999.
Mishra, Pankaj. *From the Ruins of Empire: The Revolt Against the West and the Remaking of Asia*. London: Penguin, 2012.
Mixa, Elisabeth. "I Feel Good! Über Paradoxien des Wohlfüls-Imperativs im Wellness-Diskurs." In *Un-Wohl-Gefühle: Eine Kulturanalyse gegenwärtiger Befindlichkeiten*. Ed. Sarah Miriam Pritz et al. Bielefeld: Transcript, 2015. Pp. 95–132.
Moebius, Stephan. *Die Zauberlehrlinge: Soziologiegeschichte des Collège de Sociologie*. Konstanz: UVK Verlagsgesellschaft, 2006.
Moldaschl, Manfred, and Günter Voß, eds. *Subjektivierung von Arbeit*. Munich: R. Hampp, 2002.
Morin, Edgar. *The Stars*. Minneapolis: University of Minnesota Press, 2005.
Moscovici, Serge. *Essai sur l'histoire humaine de la nature*. Paris: Flammarion, 1968.
Moyn, Samuel. *The Last Utopia: Human Rights in History*. Cambridge, MA: Harvard University Press, 2010.
Müller, Jan-Werner. *Contesting Democracies: Political Ideas in Twentieth-Century Europe*. New Haven, CT: Yale University Press, 2011.
Müller, Jan-Werner. *What is Populism?* Philadelphia: University of Pennsylvania Press, 2016.
Müller-Hilmer, Rita. "Gesellschaft im Reformprozess: Umfrage im Auftrag der Friedrich-Ebert-Stiftung," *TNS Infratest Sozialforschung* (2006): www.kantartns.de/sofo/_pdf/2006_fes_ergebnisse.pdf.
Mundhenke, Florian, et al., eds. *Mashups: Neue Praktiken und Ästhetiken in populären Medienkulturen*. Wiesbaden: Springer, 2015.
Muniesa, Fabian. "A Flank Movement in the Understanding of Valuation." In *Measure and Value*. Ed. Lisa Adkins and Celia Lury. Oxford: Wiley-Blackwell, 2012. Pp. 24–38.
Muniesa, Fabian. *The Provoked Economy: Economic Reality and Performative Turn*. London: Routledge, 2014.
Muniesa, Fabian, and Claes-Fredrik Helgesson. "Valuation Studies and the Spectacle of Valuation." *Valuation Studies* 1/2 (2013). Pp. 119–23.
Murcott, Anne, et al., eds. *The Handbook of Food Research*. London: Bloomsbury Academic, 2013.
Murray, Susan, and Laurie Ouellette, eds. *Reality TV: Remaking Television Culture*. New York University Press, 2009.
Nachtwey, Oliver. *Germany's Hidden Crisis: Social Decline in the Heart of Europe*. Trans. David Fernbach and Loren Balhorn. London: Verso, 2018.

Nancy, Jean-Luc. *The Inoperative Community*. Trans. Peter Connor et al. Minneapolis: University of Minnesota Press, 1991.
Nassehi, Armin. "Zum Funktionswandel von Ethnizität im Prozeß gesellschaftlicher Modernisierung: Ein Beitrag zur Theorie funktionaler Differenzierung." *Soziale Welt* 41/3 (1990). Pp. 261–82.
Neckel, Sighard. *Flucht nach vorn: Die Erfolgskultur der Marktgesellschaft*. Frankfurt am Main: Campus, 2008.
Neckel, Sighard, and Greta Wagner, eds. *Leistung und Erschöpfung: Burnout in der Wettbewerbsgesellschaft*. Berlin: Suhrkamp, 2014.
Nelson, Theodore H. *Literary Machines*. Sausalito, CA: Mindful Press, 1981.
Neustadt, Jeannette. *Ökonomische Ästhetik und Markenkult: Reflexionen über das Phänomen Marke in der Gegenwartskunst*. Bielefeld: Transcript, 2011.
Newcombe, Suzanne. "The Development of Modern Yoga: A Survey of the Field." *Religion Compass* 3 (2009). Pp. 986–1002.
Nierhaus, Irene, and Andreas Nierhaus, eds. *Wohnen-Zeigen: Modelle und Akteure des Wohnens in Architektur und visueller Kultur*. Bielefeld: Transcript, 2014.
Nipperday, Thomas. *Wie das Bürgertum die Moderne fand*. Stuttgart: Reclam, 1998.
Noble, David F. *America by Design: Science, Technology, and the Rise of Corporate Capitalism*. New York: Oxford University Press, 1979.
Nökel, Sigrid. *Die Töchter der Gastarbeiter und der Islam: Zur Soziologie alltagsweltlicher Anerkennungspolitik – Eine Fallstudie*. Bielefeld: Transcript, 2002.
Nora, Pierre. *Realms of Memory*. 3 vols. Trans. Arthur Goldhammer. New York: Columbia University Press, 1996-8.
Nullmeier, Frank. *Politische Theorie des Sozialstaats*. Frankfurt am Main: Campus, 2000.
Nullmeier, Frank. "Wettbewerbskulturen." In *Der Sinn der Politik: Kulturwissenschaftliche Politikanalysen*. Ed. Michael Müller et al. Konstanz: UVK Verlag, 2002. Pp. 157–76.
Nünning, Vera, and Ansgar Nünning, eds. *Erzähltheorie transgenerisch, intermedial, interdisziplinär*. Trier: Wissenschaftlicher Verlag, 2002.
O'Neill, Paul. *The Culture of Curating and the Curating of Culture(s)*. Cambridge, MA: MIT Press, 2012.
Osten, Marion von, ed. *Norm der Abweichung*. Zurich: Edition Voldemeer, 2003.
Oswalt, Philipp, ed. *Atlas of Shrinking Cities*. Ostfildern: Hatje Cantz, 2006.
Ott, Michaela. *Affizierung: Zu einer ästhetisch-epistemischen Figur*. Munich: Edition Text + Kritik, 2010.
Pallagst, Karina M., et al., eds. *Shrinking Cities: International Perspectives and Policy Implications*. New York: Routledge, 2015.
Pariser, Eli. *The Filter Bubble: How the New Personalized Web is Changing What We Read and How We Think*. New York: Penguin, 2011.
Park, Hyung Hu. "Heritage Tourism." *Annals of Tourism Research* 37 (2010). Pp. 116–35.
Parker, Martin. *Organizational Culture and Identity: Unity and Division at Work*. London: Sage, 2000.
Parkins, Wendy, and Geoffrey Craig. *Slow Living*. New York: Berg, 2006.
Parsons, Talcott. *Societies: Evolutionary and Comparative Perspectives*. Englewood Cliffs, NJ: Prentice Hall, 1966.
Passoth, Jan-Hendrik. *Technik und Gesellschaft: Sozialwissenschaftliche Techniktheorien und die Transformation der Moderne*. Wiesbaden: Verlag für Sozialwissenschaften, 2008.
Passoth, Jan-Hendrik, and Josef Wehner, eds. *Quoten, Kurven und Profile: Zur Vermessung der sozialen Welt*. Wiesbaden: Springer, 2013.
Pearlman, Alison. *Smart Casual: The Transformation of Gourmet Restaurant Style in America*. University of Chicago Press, 2013.
Perez, Carlota. "Technological Revolutions and Techno-Economic Paradigms." *Cambridge Journal of Economics* 34 (2010). Pp. 185–202.
Peters, Meike. *Eat in My Kitchen: To Cook, to Bake, to Eat, and to Treat*. Munich: Prestel, 2016.

Peters, Thomas J., and Robert H. Waterman. *In Search of Excellence: Lessons from America's Best-Run Companies*. New York: Harper & Row, 1982.
Peterson, Richard. "In Search of Authenticity." *Journal of Management Studies* 42 (2005). Pp. 1083–98.
Peterson, Richard A., and Roger M. Kern. "Changing Highbrow Taste: From Snob to Omnivore." *American Sociological Review* 61 (1996). Pp. 900–7.
Phillips, Adam. *Missing Out: In Praise of the Unlived Life*. London: Hamish Hamilton, 2012.
Pias, Claus. *Computer Game Worlds*. Trans. Valentine A. Pakis. Zurich: Diaphanes, 2017.
Picot, Arnold, et al. *Information, Organization, and Management*. Berlin: Springer, 2008.
Pieterse, Jan Nederveen. "Globalization as Hybridization." In *Global Modernities*. Ed. Mike Featherstone et al. London: Sage, 1995. Pp. 45–68.
Piketty, Thomas. *Capital in the Twenty-First Century*. Trans. Arthur Goldhammer. Cambridge, MA: Harvard University Press, 2014.
Pikulik, Lothar. *Romantik als Ungenügen an der Normalität: Am Beispiel Tiecks, Hoffmanns, Eichendorffs*. Frankfurt am Main: Suhrkamp, 1979.
Pine, Joseph B., and James Gilmore. *The Experience Economy: Work is Theatre and Every Business is a Stage*. Boston, MA: Harvard Business School Press, 2006.
Piore, Michael, and Charles Sabel. *The Second Industrial Divide: Possibilities for Prosperity*. New York: Basic Books, 1984.
Pollan, Michael. *Cooked: A Natural History of Transformation*. New York: Penguin, 2014.
Pollesch, René. "Lob des litauischen Regieassistenten im grauen Kittel." In *Kreation und Depression: Freiheit im gegenwärtigen Kapitalismus*. Ed. Christoph Menke and Juliane Rebentisch. Berlin: Kadmos, 2016. Pp. 243–9.
Pongratz, Hans, and Günter Voß. *Arbeitskraftunternehmer: Erwerbsorientierungen in entgrenzten Arbeitsformen*. Berlin: Edition Sigma, 2003.
Pörksen, Bernhard, and Wolfgang Krischke, eds. *Die Casting-Gesellschaft: Die Sucht nach Aufmerksamkeit und das Tribunal der Medien*. Cologne: Halem, 2010.
Posch, Waltraud. *Projekt Körper: Wie der Kult um die Schönheit unser Leben prägt*. Frankfurt am Main: Campus, 2009.
Poster, Mark. *The Second Media Age*. Cambridge: Polity, 1995.
Pott, Andreas. *Orte des Tourismus: Eine raum- und gesellschaftstheoretische Untersuchung*. Bielefeld: Transcript, 2007.
Potts, Jason, et al. "Social Network Markets: A New Definition of the Creative Industries." *Journal of Cultural Economics* 32/3 (2008). Pp. 167–85.
Powell, Walter W. "Neither Market nor Hierarchy: Network Forms of Organization." *Organizational Behaviour* 12 (1990). Pp. 295–336.
Pradtke, André. *Casting Shows als Märkte für Marktpotenziale*. Marburg: Metropolis, 2014.
Pratt, Andy. "Creative Cities: Cultural Industries and the Creative Class." *Geografiska Annaler: Series B – Human Geography* 90/2 (2008). Pp. 107–17.
Prebish, Charles S., and Martin Baumann, eds. *Westward Dharma: Buddhism Beyond Asia*. Berkeley: University of California Press, 2002.
Price, Derek J. de Solla. *Little Science, Big Science*. New York: Columbia University Press, 1963.
Pricken, Mario. *Die Aura des Wertvollen: Produkte entstehen im Unternehmen, Werte im Kopf – 80 Strategien*. Erlangen: Publicis, 2014.
Die Prüfung. Directed by Till Harms. Berlin: Lichtblick Media, 2016.
Punter, John, ed. *Urban Design and the British Urban Renaissance*. New York: Routledge, 2010.
Putnam, Robert. *Our Kids: The American Dream in Crisis*. New York: Simon & Schuster, 2015.
Raschke, Joachim. "Politik und Wertwandel in westlichen Demokratien." *Aus Politik und Zeitgeschichte* 36 (1980). Pp. 23–45.

Rasfeld, Margret, and Stephan Breidenbach. *Schulen im Aufbruch: Eine Anstiftung.* Munich: Kösel, 2014.
Raunig, Gerald. *Fabriken des Wissens.* Zurich: Diaphanes, 2012.
Ravasi, Davide, et al. "Valuing Products as Cultural Symbols: A Conceptual Framework and Empirical Illustration." In *The Worth of Goods: Valuation and Pricing in the Economy.* Ed. Jens Beckert and Patrik Aspers. Oxford University Press, 2011. Pp. 297–318.
Ray, Krishnendu. *The Ethnic Restaurateur.* London: Bloomsbury Academic, 2016.
Ray, Paul, and Ruth Anderson. *The Cultural Creatives: How 50 Million People Are Changing the World.* New York: Three Rivers Press, 2001.
Rebentisch, Juliane. *Theorien der Gegenwartskunst zur Einführung.* Hamburg: Junius, 2013.
Reckwitz, Andreas. "Ästhetik und Gesellschaft: Ein analytischer Bezugsrahmen." In *Ästhetik und Gesellschaft: Grundlagentexte aus Soziologie und Kulturwissenschaften.* Ed. Andreas Reckwitz et al. Berlin: Suhrkamp, 2015. Pp. 13–52.
Reckwitz, Andreas. *Das hybride Subjekt: Eine Theorie der Subjektkulturen von der bürgerlichen Moderne zur Postmoderne.* Weilerwist: Velbrück Wissenschaften, 2006.
Reckwitz, Andreas. *The Invention of Creativity: Modern Society and the Culture of the New.* Trans. Steven Black. Cambridge: Polity, 2017.
Reckwitz, Andreas. "Practices and Their Affects." In *The Nexus of Practices: Connections, Constellations, Practitioners.* Ed. Allison Hui et al. London: Routledge, 2017. Pp. 114–25.
Reckwitz, Andreas. "The Status of the 'Material' in Theories of Culture: From 'Social Structure' to 'Artefacts.'" *Journal for the Theory of Social Behaviour* 32/2 (2002). Pp. 195–217.
Reckwitz, Andreas. *Subjekt.* Bielefeld: Transcript, 2013.
Reckwitz, Andreas. "Toward a Theory of Social Practices: A Development in Culturalist Theorizing." *European Journal of Social Theory* 5 (2002). Pp. 243–63.
Reckwitz, Andreas. *Die Transformation der Kulturtheorie: Zur Entwicklung eines Theorieprogramms.* Weilerwist: Velbrück Wissenschaft, 2000.
Reckwitz, Andreas, et al., eds. *Ästhetik und Gesellschaft: Grundlagentexte aus Soziologie und Kulturwissenschaften.* Berlin: Suhrkamp, 2015.
Reemtsma, Jan Philipp. *Gewalt als Lebensform: Zwei Reden.* Stuttgart: Reclam, 2016.
Reese, Stephen, et al. "Mapping the Blogosphere: Professional and Citizen-Based Media in the Global News Arena." *Journalism* 8/3 (2007). Pp. 235–61.
Reich, Robert. *The Work of Nations: Preparing Ourselves for 21st-Century Capitalism.* New York: Vintage Books, 1991.
Reichert, Ramón. "Facebooks Big Data: Die Medien- und Wissenstechniken kollektiver Verdatung." In *Big Data: Analysen zum digitalen Wandel von Wissen, Macht und Ökonomie.* Ed. Ramón Reichert. Bielefeld: Transcript, 2014. Pp. 437–52.
Reichert, Ramón. *Die Macht der Vielen: Über den neuen Kult der digitalen Vernetzung.* Bielefeld: Transcript, 2014.
Rheinberger, Hans-Jörg. *Experiment, Differenz, Schrift: Zur Geschichte epistemischer Dinge.* Marburg: Basilisken-Verlag, 1992.
Rheingold, Howard. *The Virtual Community: Homesteading on the Electronic Frontier.* Cambridge, MA: MIT Press, 2000.
Rhodes, Gillian, and Leslie Zebrowitz, eds. *Facial Attractiveness: Evolutionary, Cognitive, and Social Perspectives.* Westport, CT: Ablex, 2002.
Riesebrodt, Martin. *Rückkehr der Religionen? Zwischen Fundamentalismus und der "Kampf der Kulturen".* Munich: Beck, 2000.
Riesman, David. *The Lonely Crowd: A Study of the Changing American Character.* New Haven, CT: Yale University Press, 1950.
Rifkin, Jeremy. *The Age of Access: The New Culture of Hypercapitalism, Where All of Life is a Paid-for Experience.* New York: Putnam, 2000.
Rifkin, Jeremy. *The Zero Marginal Cost Society: The Internet of Things, the*

Bibliography 391

Collaborative Commons, and the Eclipse of Capitalism. New York: Palgrave Macmillan, 2014.
Robertson, Roland. "Glocalization: Time–Space and Homogeneity–Heterogeneity." In *Global Modernities.* Ed. Mike Featherstone et al. London: Sage, 1995. Pp. 25–44.
Robertson, Roland. "Humanity, Globalization, and Worldwide Religious Resurgence: A Theoretical Exploration." *Sociological Analysis* 46/3 (1985). Pp. 219–42.
Robinson, Ken, and Lou Aronica. *Creative Schools: The Grassroots Revolution That's Transforming Education.* New York: Penguin, 2016.
Rogers, Richard George. *Towards an Urban Renaissance.* London: E. & F. N. Spon, 1999.
Rojek, Chris. *Celebrity.* London: Reaktion, 2001.
Rosa, Hartmut. *Resonance: A Sociology of Our Relationship to the World.* Cambridge: Polity, 2019.
Rosa, Hartmut. *Social Acceleration: A New Theory of Modernity.* Trans. Jonathan Trejo-Mathys. New York: Columbia University Press, 2013.
Rosanvallon, Pierre. *The Society of Equals.* Trans. Arthur Goldhammer. Cambridge, MA: Harvard University Press, 2013.
Rose, Nikolas S. *Governing the Soul: The Shaping of the Private Self.* 2nd edn. London: Free Association Books, 1999.
Rosen, Emanuel. *The Anatomy of Buzz: How to Create Word-of-Mouth Marketing.* New York: Doubleday Currency, 2002.
Rosen, Sherwin. "The Economics of Superstars." *American Economic Review* 71 (1981). Pp. 845–58.
Roßler, Gustav. *Der Anteil der Dinge an der Gesellschaft: Sozialität – Kognition – Netzwerke.* Bielefeld: Transcript, 2015.
Roth, Lutz. *Die Erfindung des Jugendlichen.* Munich: Juventa, 1983.
Roy, Olivier. *La sainte ignorance: Le temps de la religion sans culture.* Paris: Seuil, 2008.
Ryan, Camille, and Julie Siebens. "Educational Attainment in the United States: 2009," *United States Census Bureau* (February 2012): www.census.gov/prod/2012pubs/p20-566.pdf.
Safranski, Rüdiger. *Nietzsche: A Philosophical Biography.* Trans. Shelley Frisch. New York: W. W. Norton, 2002.
Salenbacher, Jürgen. *Creative Personal Branding.* Amsterdam: BIS Publishers, 2013.
Salzbrunn, Monika. *Vielfalt/Diversität.* Bielefeld: Transcript, 2014.
Sammer, Petra. *Storytelling: Die Zukunft von PR und Marketing.* Cologne: O'Reilly, 2014.
Sassen, Saskia. "Dientsleistungs Ökonomien und die Beschäftigung von MigrantInnen in Städten." In *Migration und Stadt: Entwicklungen, Defizite und Potentiale.* Ed. Klaus Schmals. Wiesbaden: Verlag für Sozialwissenschaften, 2000. Pp. 87–114.
Saussure, Ferdinand de. *Course in General Linguistics.* Trans. Roy Harris. London: Duckworth, 1990.
Savage, Mike, et al. *Social Class in the 21st Century.* London: Pelican, 2015.
Schäfer, Alfred, and Christiane Thompson, eds. *Spiel.* Paderborn: Schöningh, 2014.
Schäfer, Hilmar, ed. *Praxistheorie: Ein soziologisches Forschungsprogramm.* Bielefeld: Transcript, 2016.
Schäfer, Robert. *Tourismus und Authentizität: Zur gesellschaftlichen Organisation von Außeralltäglichkeit.* Bielefeld: Transcript, 2015.
Schatzki, Theodore. *Social Practices: A Wittgensteinian Approach to Human Activity and the Social.* Cambridge University Press, 2009.
Schelsky, Helmut. "Die Bedeutung des Schichtungsbegriffs für die Analyse der gegenwärtigen deutschen Gesellschaft." In Schelsky, *Auf der Suche nach Wirklichkeit: Gesammelte Aufsätze.* Düsseldorf: E. Diederichs, 1965. Pp. 331–6.
Scherer, Michael. "Inside the Secret World of Data Crunchers Who Helped Obama

Win," *Time Magazine* (November 12, 2012): http://swampland.time.com/2012/11/07/inside-the-secret-world-of-quants-and-data-crunchers-who-helped-obama-win.
Schiffauer, Werner. *Parallelgesellschaften: Wie viel Wertekonsens braucht unsere Gesellschaft?* Bielefeld: Transcript, 2008.
Schilling, Heinz. *Kleinbürger: Mentalität und Lebensstil.* Frankfurt am Main: Campus, 2013.
Schimank, Uwe. "Lebensplanung!? Biographische Entscheidungspraktiken irritierter Mittelschichten." *Berliner Journal für Soziologie* 25 (2015). Pp. 7–31.
Schimank, Uwe, et al. *Statusarbeit unter Druck? Zur Lebensführung der Mittelschichten.* Weinheim: Beltz Juventa, 2014.
Schirrmacher, Frank, ed. *Technologischer Totalitarismus: Eine Debatte.* Berlin: Suhrkamp, 2015.
Schlegel, Friedrich. *On the Study of Greek Poetry.* Trans. Stuart Barnett. Albany: State University of New York Press, 2001.
Schlesinger, Arthur. *The Disuniting of America: Reflections on a Multicultural Society.* 2nd edn. New York: W. W. Norton, 1998.
Schluchter, Wolfgang. *The Rise of Western Rationalism: Max Weber's Developmental History.* Trans. Guenther Roth. Berkeley: University of California Press, 1981.
Schmid, David. *Natural Born Celebrities: Serial Killers in American Culture.* University of Chicago Press, 2008.
Schmid, Wilhelm. *Philosophie der Lebenskunst: Eine Grundlegung.* Frankfurt am Main: Suhrkamp, 2003.
Schmidt, Eric, and Jared Cohen. *The New Digital Age: Transforming Nations, Businesses, and Our Lives.* New York: Random House, 2013.
Schmitt, Carl. *The Crisis of Parliamentary Democracy.* Trans. Ellen Kennedy. Cambridge, MA: MIT Press, 1985.
Schroer, Markus. "Soziologie der Aufmerksamkeit: Grundlegende Überlegungen zu einem Theorieprogramm." *Kölner Zeitschrift für Soziologie und Sozialpsychologie* 66 (2014). Pp. 193–218.
Schroer, Markus. "Visual Culture and the Fight for Visibility." *Journal for the Theory of Social Behavior* 44 (2003). Pp. 206–28.
Schröter, Susanne. *FeMale: Über Grenzverläufe zwischen Geschlechtern.* Frankfurt am Main: Fischer, 2002.
Schultz, Duane. *Growth Psychology: Models of the Healthy Personality.* New York: Van Nostrand Reinhold, 1977.
Schultz, Tanjev, and Klaus Hurrelmann, eds. *Die Akademiker-Gesellschaft: Müssen in Zukunft alle studieren?* Weinheim: Juventa Verlag, 2013.
Schulz, Stefan. *Redaktionsschluss: Die Zeit nach der Zeitung.* Munich: Hanser, 2016.
Schulz-Buschhaus, Ulrich. "Klassik zwischen Kanon und Typologie: Probleme um einen Zentralbegriff der Literaturwissenschaft." *Arcadia* 29 (1994). Pp. 165–74.
Schulze, Gerhard. *Die beste aller Welten: Wohin bewegt sich die Gesellschaft im 21. Jahrhundert?* Munich: Hanser, 2004.
Schulze, Gerhard. *Die Erlebnisgesellschaft: Kultursoziologie der Gegenwart.* Frankfurt am Main: Campus, 1992.
Schütz, Alfred. *The Phenomenology of the Social World.* Trans. George Walsh and Frederick Lehnert. Evanston, IL: Northwestern University Press, 1967.
Schütz, Alfred, and Thomas Luckmann. *The Structures of the Life-World.* 2 vols. Trans. Richard M. Zaner et al. Evanston, IL: Northwestern University Press, 1973–89.
Scott, Allen. *A World in Emergence: Cities and Regions in the 21st Century.* Cheltenham: Edward Elgar, 2012.
Selke, Stefan. *Lifelogging: Wie die digitale Selbstvermessung unsere Gesellschaft verändert.* Berlin: Ullstein, 2014.
Semmelhack, Elizabeth, et al. *Out of the Box: The Rise of Sneaker Culture.* New York: Skira Rizzoli, 2015.
Sen, Amartya. *The Idea of Justice.* London: Penguin, 2010.
Sennett, Richard. *The Corrosion of Character: The Personal Consequences of Work in the New Capitalism.* New York: W. W. Norton, 1998.

Sennett, Richard. *Together: The Rituals, Pleasures, and Politics of Cooperation*. London: Allen Lane, 2012.
Sennett, Richard, and Jonathan Cobb. *The Hidden Injuries of Class*. New York: Vintage Books, 1972.
Shackle, G. L. S. *Epistemics and Economics: A Critique of Economic Doctrines*. London: Transaction Publishers, 1972.
Sheller, Mimi. "Automotive Emotions." *Theory, Culture & Society* 21 (2004). Pp. 221–42.
Shenhav, Yehouda. *Manufacturing Rationality: The Engineering Foundations of the Managerial Revolution*. Oxford University Press, 1999.
Shih, Clara. *The Facebook Era*. New York: Prentice Hall, 2011.
Shilling, Chris. *The Body in Technology, Culture, and Society*. London: Sage, 2005.
Shirky, Clay. *Cognitive Surplus: Creativity and Generosity in a Connected Age*. New York: Penguin, 2010.
Shirky, Clay. *Here Comes Everybody: The Power of Organizing Without Organizations*. New York: Penguin, 2008.
Simanowski, Roberto. *Facebook Society: Losing Ourselves in Sharing Ourselves*. Trans. Susan H. Gillespie. New York: Columbia University Press, 2018.
Simmel, Georg. "The Concept and Tragedy of Culture." In *Simmel on Culture: Selected Writings*. Ed. David Frisby and Mike Featherstone. London: Sage, 1997. Pp. 55–74.
Simmel, Georg. "Fashion." *The American Journal of Sociology* 62 (1957). Pp. 541–8.
Simmel, Georg. "Die historische Formung." In Simmel, *Aufsätze und Abhandlungen, 1909–1918*. Frankfurt am Main: Suhrkamp, 2000. Pp. 321–69.
Simmel, Georg. *The Philosophy of Money: Third Enlarged Edition*. Trans. Tom Bottomore and David Frisby. London: Routledge, 2004.
Simmel, Georg. *Sociology: Inquiries into the Construction of Social Forms*. Trans. Anthony J. Blasi et al. Leiden: Brill, 2009.
Simmel, Georg. "Sociology of Competition." Trans. Horst J. Helle. *Canadian Journal of Sociology* 33 (2008). Pp. 945–78.
Simondon, Gilbert. *On the Mode of Existence of Technical Objects*. Trans. Cécile Malaspina. Minneapolis: University of Minnesota Press, 2017.
Simons, Harald, and Lukas Weiden. *Schwarmstädte: Eine Untersuchung zu Umfang, Ursache, Nachhaltigkeit und Folgen der neuen Wanderungsmuster in Deutschland*. Berlin: Empirica, 2015.
SINUS Markt- und Sozialforschung GmbH. "Information on Sinus-Milieus" (2018): www.sinus-institut.de/en/publications/downloads.
Skeggs, Beverley. *Class, Self, Culture*. London: Routledge, 2004.
Skrentny, David. *The Minority Rights Revolutions*. Cambridge, MA: Harvard University Press, 2002.
Slater, Don. *Consumer Culture and Modernity*. Cambridge: Polity, 1997.
Somsen, Geert J. "A History of Universalism: Conceptions of the Internationality of Science from the Enlightenment to the Cold War." *Minerva* 46 (2008). Pp. 361–79.
Spreen, Dierk. *Upgradekultur: Der Körper in der Enhancement-Gesellschaft*. Bielefeld: Transcript, 2015.
Staab, Philipp. *Macht und Herrschaft in der Servicewelt*. Hamburg: Hamburger Edition, 2014.
Stäheli, Urs. *Spectacular Speculation: Thrills, the Economy, and Popular Discourse*. Trans. Eric Savoth. Stanford University Press, 2013.
Stalder, Felix. *The Digital Condition*. Trans. Valentine A. Pakis. Cambridge: Polity, 2018.
Stalder, Felix, and Christine Mayer. "Der zweite Index: Suchmaschinen, Personalisierung, Überwachung." In *Deep Search: Politik des Suchens jenseits von Google*. Ed. Konrad Becker and Felix Stalder. Innsbruck: Studien Verlag, 2009. Pp. 112–31.
Stampfl, Nora. *Die verspielte Gesellschaft: Gamification oder Leben im Zeitalter des Computerspiels*. Hanover: Heise, 2012.

Star, Susan Leigh. "The Ethnography of Infrastructure." *American Behavioral Scientist* 43 (1999). Pp. 377–91.
Statistische Bundesamt. "Arbeitsmarkt: Erwerbstätige im Inland nach Wirtschaftssektoren": www.destatis.de/DE/ZahlenFakten/Indikatoren/Lange Reihen/Arbeitsmarkt/lrerw013.html.
Stearns, Peter N. *American Cool: Constructing a Twentieth-Century Emotional Style*. New York University Press, 1994.
Stehr, Nico, and Richard Ericson, eds. *The Culture and Power of Knowledge: Inquiries into Contemporary Societies*. Berlin: De Gruyter, 1992.
Steinbrink, Malte, and Andreas Pott. "Global Slumming: Zur Genese und Globalisierung des Armutstourismus." In *Tourismusräume: Zur soziokulturellen Konstruktion eines globalen Phänomens*. Ed. Karlheinz Wöhler et al. Bielefeld: Transcript, 2010. Pp. 247–70.
Stern, Martin. "Heldenfiguren im Wagnissport: Zur medialen Inszenierung wagnissportlicher Erlebnisräume." In *Aufs Spiel gesetzte Körper: Aufführungen des Sozialen in Sport und populärer Kultur*. Ed. Thomas Alkemeyer et al. Konstanz: UVK, 2003. Pp. 37–54.
Stern, Martin. *Stil-Kulturen: Performative Konstellationen von Technik, Spiel und Risiko in neuen Sportpraktiken*. Bielefeld: Transcript, 2010.
Stichweh, Rudolf. *Inklusion und Exklusion: Studien zur Gesellschaftstheorie*. Bielefeld: Transcript, 2005.
Stinchcombe, Arthur L. "Some Empirical Consequences of the Davis–Moore Theory of Stratification." *American Sociological Review* 28 (1963). Pp. 805–8.
Streeck, Wolfgang. *Buying Time: The Delayed Crisis of Democratic Capitalism*. Trans. Patrick Camiller. London: Verso, 2014.
Stroobants, Marcelle. *Savoir-faire et compétence au travail: Une sociologie de la fabrication des aptitudes*. Brussels: l'Université de Bruxelles, 1993.
Tauschek, Markus, ed. *Kulturen des Wettbewerbs: Formationen kompetitiver Logiken*. Münster: Waxmann, 2012.
Taylor, Charles. *The Malaise of Modernity*. Toronto: CBC, 1991.
Taylor, Charles. *Sources of the Self: The Making of Modern Identity*. Cambridge, MA: Harvard University Press, 1989.
Taylor, Charles, et al. *Multikulturalismus und die Politik der Anerkennung*. Frankfurt am Main: Fischer, 1993.
Taylor, Jami, and Donald Haider-Markel, eds. *Transgender Rights and Politics: Groups, Issue Framing, and Policy Adoption*. Ann Arbor: University of Michigan Press, 2014.
Tenorth, Heinz-Elmar. *Geschichte der Erziehung: Einführung in die Grundzüge ihrer neuzeitlichen Entwicklung*. Weinheim: Juventa, 2010.
Terkessidis, Mark. *Die Banalität des Rassismus: Migranten zweiter Generation entwickeln eine neue Perspektive*. Bielefeld: Transcript, 2004.
Terkessidis, Mark. *Kulturkampf: Volk, Nation, der Westen und die neue Rechte*. Cologne: Kiepenheuer & Witsch, 1995.
Thévoz, Michel. *Art Brut*. Trans. James Emmons. Geneva: Albert Skira, 1995.
Thomä, Dieter. *Troublemakers: A Philosophy of Puer Robustus*. Cambridge: Polity, 2019.
Thomas, William I., and Dorothy S. Thomas. *The Child in America: Behavior Problems and Programs*. New York: Knopf, 1928.
Thompson, Michael. *Rubbish Theory: The Creation and Destruction of Value*. New York: Oxford University Press, 1979.
Thornton, Sarah. *33 Artists in 3 Acts*. London: Granta, 2014.
Thränhardt, Dieter. "Integrationsrealität und Integrationsdiskurs." *Aus Politik und Zeitgeschichte* 46 (2010). Pp. 16–21.
Thrift, Nigel. *Knowing Capitalism*. London: Sage, 2005.
Thrift, Nigel. "A Perfect Innovation Engine: The Rise of the Talent World." In *Cultural Political Economy*. Ed. Jacqueline Best and Matthew Paterson. New York: Routledge, 2010. Pp. 197–222.
Tichi, Cecelia. *Shifting Gears: Technology, Literature, Culture in Modernist America*. Chapel Hill: University of North Carolina Press, 1987.

Tönnies, Ferdinand. *Community and Civil Society*. Trans. Jose Harris and Margaret Hollis. Cambridge University Press, 2001.
Toulmin, Stephen. *Cosmopolis: The Hidden Agenda of Modernity*. University of Chicago Press, 1990.
Traue, Boris. *Das Subjekt der Beratung: Zur Soziologie einer Psycho-Technik*. Bielefeld: Transcript, 2010.
Trilling, Lionel. *Sincerity and Authenticity*. Cambridge, MA: Harvard University Press, 1972.
Trotha, Trutz von. "Zur Soziologie der Gewalt." In *Soziologie der Gewalt*. Ed. Trutz von Trotha. Wiesbaden: Westdeutscher Verlag, 1997. Pp. 9–56.
Tuan, Yi-Fu. *Space and Place: The Perspective of Experience*. Minneapolis: University of Minnesota Press, 1977.
Turkle, Sherry. *Evocative Objects: Things We Think With*. Cambridge, MA: MIT Press, 2011.
Turkle, Sherry. *Life on the Screen: Identity in the Age of the Internet*. New York: Simon & Schuster, 1995.
Turner, Victor W. *The Ritual Process: Structure and Anti-Structure*. London: Routledge, 1969.
Ullrich, Wolfgang. *Alles nur Konsum: Kritik der warenästhetischen Erziehung*. Berlin: Wagenbach, 2013.
Ullrich, Wolfgang. *Siegerkunst: Neuer Adel, teure Lust*. Berlin: Klaus Wagenbach, 2016.
Urban, Wayne J., and Jennings L. Wagoner. *American Education: A History*. London: Routledge, 2008.
Urry, John. *Sociology Beyond Societies: Mobilities for the Twenty-First Century*. London: Routledge, 2000.
Urry, John. *The Tourist Gaze: Leisure and Travel in Contemporary Societies*. London: Sage, 1990.
Valentine, James. *Attractiveness of New Communities to Industries and Workers*. Saarbrücken: Lap Lambert Academic Publishing, 2012.
Vannini, Phillip, and Patrick J. Williams, eds. *Authenticity in Culture, Self, and Society*. London: Routledge, 2016.
Vedder, Günther, et al., eds. *Fallstudien zum Diversity Management*. Munich: Rainer Hampp Verlag, 2011.
Das Venedig Prinzip. Directed by Andreas Pichler. Vienna: Filmladen, 2012.
Verganti, Roberto. *Design-Driven Innovation: Changing the Rules of Competition by Radically Innovating What Things Mean*. Boston, MA: Harvard Business School Press, 2009.
Vertovec, Steven. "'Diversity' and the Social Imaginary." *European Journal of Sociology* 53/3 (2012). Pp. 287–312.
Vertovec, Steven. *Super-Diversity*. London: Routledge, 2014.
Vogl, Joseph. "Der Amokläufer." In *Figuren der Gewalt*. Ed. Daniel Tyradellis et al. Zurich: Diaphanes, 2014. Pp. 13–18.
Volbers, Jörg. *Performative Kultur: Eine Einführung*. Wiesbaden: Springer, 2014.
Vormbusch, Uwe. "Karriererepolitik: Zum biografischen Umgang mit ökonomischer Unsicherheit." *Zeitschrift für Soziologie* 38/4 (2009). Pp. 282–99.
Vormbusch, Uwe. "Taxonomien des Flüchtigen: Das Portfolio als Wettbewerbs technologie der Marktgesellschaft." In *Quoten, Kurven und Profile: Zur Vermessung der sozialen Welt*. Ed. Jan-Hendrik Passoth and Josef Wehner. Wiesbaden: Springer, 2013. Pp. 47–68.
Voswinkel, Stephan. "Anerkennung der Arbeit im Wandel." In *Anerkennung und Arbeit*. Ed. Ursula Holtgrewe et al. Konstanz: UVK, 2000. Pp. 39–61.
Voswinkel, Stephan. *Welche Kundenorientierung? Anerkennung in der Dienstleistungsarbeit*. Berlin: Edition Sigma, 2005.
Wagner, Peter. *A Sociology of Modernity: Liberty and Discipline*. London: Routledge, 1994.
Walter, Franz. *Im Herbst der Volksparteien? Eine kleine Geschichte von Aufstieg und Rückgang politischer Massenintegration*. Bielefeld: Transcript, 2009.

Ward, Janet. *Weimar Surfaces: Urban Visual Culture in 1920s Germany*. Berkeley: University of California Press, 2001.
Warnke, Martin. *Theorien des Internet zur Einführung*. Hamburg: Junius, 2011.
Weber, Alfred. *Fundamentals of Culture-Sociology: Social Process, Civilization Process, and Culture-Movement*. Trans. G. H. Weltner and C. F. Hirshman. New York: Columbia University Press, 1939.
Weber, Max. "Author's Introduction." In *The Protestant Ethic and the Spirit of Capitalism*. Trans. Talcott Parsons. New York: Charles Scribner's Sons, 1930. Pp. 13–31.
Weber, Max. *Economy and Society: An Outline of Interpretive Sociology*. Trans. Guenther Roth and Claus Wittich. Berkeley: University of California Press, 1978.
Weber, Max. "Religious Rejections of the World and Their Directions." In *From Max Weber: Essays in Sociology*. Trans. H. H. Gerth and C. Wright Mills. New York: Oxford University Press, 1946. Pp. 323–62.
Weber, Max. *The Sociology of Religion*. Trans. Ephraim Fischoff. Boston, MA: Beacon Press, 1999.
Wellgraf, Stefan. *Hauptschüler: Zur gesellschaftlichen Produktion von Verachtung*. Bielefeld: Transcript, 2012.
Wellman, Barry. "Physical Place and Cyberspace: The Rise of Networked Individualism." In *Community Informatics: Shaping Computer-Mediated Social Relations*. Ed. Leigh Keeble and Brian Loader. New York: Routledge, 2001. Pp. 17–42.
West, Cornel. *Race Matters*. Boston, MA: Beacon Press, 1993.
Wetzel, Dietmar J. *Soziologie des Wettbewerbs: Eine kultur- und wirtschaftssoziologische Analyse*. Wiesbaden: Springer, 2013.
Wheaton, Belinda. *The Cultural Politics of Lifestyle Sports*. London: Routledge, 2013.
Whimster, Sam. "The Secular Ethic and the Culture of Modernism." In *Max Weber, Rationality, and Modernity*. Ed. Sam Whimster and Scott Lash. London: Routledge, 1987. Pp. 259–90.
Whitman, Walt. "Leaves of Grass." In *Walt Whitman and Emily Dickinson: Selections from the Norton Anthology of American Literature*. 5th edn. Ed. Hershel Parker. New York: W. W. Norton, 1998. Pp. 21–64.
Whyte, William H. *The Organization Man*. New York: Simon and Schuster, 1956.
Wiebking, Jennifer. "Event-Gesellschaft: Der Moment ist das Geschenk." *Frankfurter Allgemeine Sonntagszeitung* 34 (August 23, 2015). P. 9.
Wilde, Peter de, et al. "The Political Sociology of Cosmopolitanism and Communitarianism: Representative Claims Analysis." *WZB Discussion Paper SP 2014-102* (2014): https://bibliothek.wzb.eu/pdf/2014/iv14-102.pdf.
Wildförster, Ricarda, and Sascha Wingen. *Projektmanagement und Probleme: Systematische Perspektiven auf Organisationsberatung und Begleitforschung*. Heidelberg: Verlag für systemische Forschung, 2001.
Wilkinson, Richard. *Unhealthy Societies: The Afflictions of Inequality*. New York: Routledge, 1996.
Williams, Joan. *White Working Class: Overcoming Class Cluelessness in America*. Boston, MA: Harvard Business Review Press, 2017.
Williams, Raymond. *Culture and Society, 1780–1950*. London: Chatto & Windus, 1958.
Willke, Gerhard. *Neoliberalismus*. Frankfurt am Main: Campus, 2003.
Windolf, Paul. *Expansion and Structural Change: Higher Education in Germany, the United States, and Japan*. Boulder, CO: Westview Press, 1997.
Wittel, Andrew. "Toward a Network Sociality." *Theory, Culture & Society* 18/6 (2001). Pp. 51–76.
Wodak, Ruth, et al., eds. *Right-Wing Populism in Europe: Politics and Discourse*. London: Bloomsbury Academic, 2013.
Woodmansee, Martha. *Author, Art, and Market: Rereading the History of Aesthetics*. New York: Columbia University Press, 1994.
Wouters, Cas. *Informalization: Manners and Emotions since 1890*. London: Sage, 2007.

Wuthnow, Robert. *Meaning and Moral Order: Explorations in Cultural Analysis.* Berkeley: University of California Press, 1989.
Yanagihara, Hanya. *A Little Life.* New York: Doubleday, 2015.
Young, Edward. *Conjectures on Original Composition.* London: A. Millar, 1759.
Young, Michael. *The Rise of the Meritocracy, 1870–2033: The New Elite of Our Social Revolution.* London: Random House, 1959.
Yúdice, George. *The Expediency of Culture: Uses of Culture in the Global Era.* Durham, NC: Duke University Press, 2003.
Zanten, Agnès van. "A Good Match: Appraising Worth and Estimating Quality in School Choice." In *Constructing Quality: The Classification of Goods in Markets.* Ed. Jens Beckert and Christine Musselin. Oxford University Press, 2013. Pp. 77–99.
Ziemer, Gesa. *Komplizenschaft: Neue Perspektiven auf Kollektivität.* Bielefeld: Transcript, 2013.
Zinser, Hartmut. *Der Markt der Religionen.* Munich: Fink, 1997.
Zuboff, Shoshana, and James Maxmin. *The Support Economy: Why Corporations Are Failing Individuals and the Next Episode of Capitalism.* London: Penguin, 2004.
Zukin, Sharon. *Loft Living: Culture and Capital in Urban Change.* New Brunswick, NJ: Rutgers University Press, 1989.
Zukin, Sharon. *Naked City: The Death and Life of Authentic Urban Places.* New York: Oxford University Press, 2011.

Index

3D printers 188, 334n29
"1968" 74, 208, 209, 270

abjection 57
abstention, aversion to 247
acceptance 73, 192–3
accessories 231, 355n22
achievement 313
  and labor 146, 150, 152–3, 158–60, 344n33
activism, cultural 215
actualism, affective 194, 349n42
  see also self-actualization
aesthetics/aestheticization 61, 62, 67, 212, 308, 328n19
  and goods 89, 90–1, 93–4
  and lifestyle 229–30, 246
  and middle classes 68, 69, 280
affect/affectation
  affect goods 82, 88, 91, 101, 116
  affect machine 170–2, 173
  affective actualism 194, 349n42
  and cultural capitalism 75, 82, 88
  and culturalization 49, 57–9, 72–3
  and digitalization 170–2, 173, 191, 194–5, 349n44
  negative 57, 194–5, 302, 306, 307
African Americans 291
aggressiveness 255
aging 258, 285
agricultural industry 23, 84
algorithms 11, 49, 166–8, 176, 183–6
antiques 95
appropriation, practices of
  and everyday life 215–16, 218
  and generalization 20, 23, 31

  and religion 297, 366n36
  and singularization 47–8, 49
architecture 2, 67, 103, 279
arrangement 47
art/arts 68–9, 125, 171
  and cultural capitalism 84, 85, 91–3, 94, 100
  and cultural economization 111–12, 119, 337n20
  and labor 149, 156–7, 158–9
  and lifestyle 68, 214, 231
  and marketization 111–12, 156–7, 337n20
atmosphere 41, 90, 98, 171
attention
  and cultural economization 107, 118, 119–23, 338n40
  attention capital and reputation capital 122–3, 127
  attention distribution 126, 339n59
  attention markets 113, 114, 115–16
  and digitalization 172–3, 179, 182–3, 187
  and violence 307
attractiveness 295
  attractive lives 222, 352n37
  attractiveness competition 277–81, 283, 284
  attractiveness markets 83, 106–9, 141–2, 280, 317–18
  and cultural economization 107–9, 111, 115–16, 117, 122, 124, 127, 280–1
  and digitalization 177–8, 182, 190

and cities 280–1, 283, 284, 285
and digitalization 177–8, 182, 190, 195
and lifestyle 236, 262, 265–6, 362n38
personal/physical 182, 195, 221, 236
audiences 173, 307
Austin, Rob and Devin, Lee 137
authenticity 5
authenticity revolution 73, 208
and cities 280, 283–4, 285, 363n31
and cultural communities 287, 296, 297–8
and cultural essentialism 287, 296, 297–8, 299, 300–1
and digitalization 178–9, 181–2
and lifestyle 73, 222, 233–4, 236, 249–50
homes / interior design 228, 229, 230
and middle classes 74, 224–5, 228, 229
and middle classes 69, 73–4, 75, 217–19, 224–5, 228, 229, 244
performative 76, 98–100, 151, 178–9
plebian 260, 261, 265
and self-actualization 212, 217–19
and underclass 260–1, 265
author function 117
automated processes of singularization 49–50, 169, 176
automobile industry 84
award ceremonies 122, 125, 338n47

background, cultural 154
Bahl, Friederike 253, 254
Bakhtin, Mikhail 67
Baribar, Étienne 293
Bataille, Georges 58
Bauman, Zygmunt 199
beauty 182, 195, 221, 236
Beck, Ulrich 2, 199, 200
Bell, Daniel 132
Benjamin, Walter 39, 308
biodiversity 276
biographies 94, 290
bodies 235–8
body tracking 185–6
Boltanski, Luc and Chiapello, Ève 138

Boolean logic 167
Bourdieu, Pierre 121, 154, 255, 359n8
bourgeoisie 175, 207–10, 232, 246–7, 315, 352n6
and cultural capitalism 89, 333n11
see also middle classes
brands 40, 84, 93–4, 119, 120–1, 282–3, 338n40
breakthrough moments 117
Brexit 361n36
Bude, Heinz 253
buzz effect 114–18

Caillois, Roger 58
Canada 295
capital *see* attention; cultural capital; reputation capital; singularity capital; social capital
capitalism 7, 20, 29, 115, 272
see also cultural capitalism; subject capital
career paths 146, 155–6
Castells, Manuel 199
casting 151–2
centrism, cultural 295–6
charisma 40
children 2, 238–42, 256, 257, 356n47
see also parenting
China 296, 366n30
circulation, cultural 102–5
citation indexes 339n59
cities 2, 72, 277–81
and apertistic and differential liberalism 275, 277–85
and attractiveness 280–1, 283, 284, 285
and authenticity 280, 283–4, 285, 363n31
and competition 280–1, 282, 283, 284
and cultural economization 110, 280–1
and culturalization 280–5, 363n30
and devaluation 57, 283–4, 285
industrial 27, 30, 278–9, 283
and industrial modernity 278, 279, 282, 284
and interchangeability 280, 283
and lifestyle 229, 243, 360n17
and new middle classes 2, 110, 217, 279–81, 285
and quality of life 280–1, 283

and singularity of place 280–1,
363n30
and standardization 279, 283–4,
363n26
and uniqueness 279, 282
civil rights movements 276, 277, 291
civilization 57
classics, cultural production of 101,
102, 112, 119, 120–1, 338n44
cleverness 260
client relationships 96, 334n33
Clockwork Orange (Kubrick) 35
coaching, personality-oriented 155–6
coherence 148–9
coincidence 117, 248
historical 73, 75
collaboration 156–7
heterogeneous 76, 215, 311
and digitalization 189, 349n35
and labor 140, 141–2, 143, 144
and neo-communities 189, 349n35
collectives 27–8, 30, 70, 93–4, 140, 188–9, 260–1, 287
and singularity 42–3, 50, 57
see also communities; identity, collective; neo-communities
Collège de Sociologie 58
communication 140, 170, 191, 193–4, 341n18
communicative associations 189
communitarianism, cultural 269–70, 287–8, 301–2, 305
communities 27–8, 42–3, 270, 296–9
and collective identity 286–91, 294, 295
digital 190–1, 290
ethnic 286, 291–4, 295, 302, 304
and homogeneity 288, 292
religious 296–7, 298, 301, 303–4, 367n38
and value/valorization 191, 287–8
see also neo-communities
companies, small 134, 139
comparison 37, 124–5
competencies 44–5, 82, 147–8, 154
competition
and apertistic and differential liberalism 273, 275
attractiveness competition 277–81, 283, 284
and cities 280–1, 282, 283, 284
and cultural economization 107, 109, 127

hyper-competitiveness 83, 109, 114
and labor 153, 156–8
and physical activity 237, 238
competition state 274–7, 281, 305, 314, 362n7
complexity, inherent 35–6, 37, 43, 44, 59–60
computing 166–8
conformism 192, 193, 265
connoisseurship, cultural 218–19
consensus, social-democratic 201, 272–4, 362n1
construction industry 84
consumption, cultural 82, 90
consumption, mass 30, 71, 82
consumption/consumers 107, 314, 336n11
consumer profiles 176, 184
and labor 138, 340n13
and lifestyle 82, 215–16, 227, 254–5
cooking 225–8
cooperation 140, 341n18
coopetition 157
corporations, large 29, 84, 134
cosmopolitanism 245–6, 265, 300–1
cultural 76, 216–19, 245, 290, 295
and travel 232, 235
counter-movements 69, 279, 290, 298
courtly culture 67
craftwork 94
creative economy 81, 83–6, 111, 134, 135–44
creative industries 83, 111–12, 134, 199–200, 275
see also labor
creativity 63, 67, 82
bound 157, 188
creativity *dispositif* 116, 123, 283, 289, 302–3
and lifestyle 112, 215, 226–7, 354n7
see also labor
crime 193, 260, 306–7
criminal profiles 184
crisis-proofing 358n76
cultivation, concerted 239, 306, 356n47
cultural capital
and inequality 252–3, 259–60, 262, 263, 265
and labor 154, 159
and lifestyle 199, 201, 203–4, 205, 220, 240

and singularity markets 119, 122
cultural capitalism 1, 7–8
  and affect/affectation 75, 82, 88
  and art/arts 84, 85, 91–3, 94, 100
  and brands 84, 93–4
  and cultural economization 106–7, 122–3
  and digitalization 74, 75, 90
  and economy of singularities 74, 75–6
  and food 94, 104
  and goods 87–105, 122–3
    and art/arts 84, 85, 91–3, 94, 100
    and ethics 94, 99
    and events 87, 91, 97–8, 102, 334n39
    and experience 101, 102
    and fashion 101, 102
    and idiosyncrasy 102, 103
    and media formats 87, 90–1, 96–7, 334n35
    and memory 98, 101–2, 335n49
    and modernity, bourgeois 89, 333n11
    and objects 87, 103–4
    and profanity / the sacred 89, 90, 91
    and rarity 94–5, 96, 97–8
    and services 87, 90, 95–6, 334n33
    and style 88, 93–4, 96–7, 334n33
    and uniqueness 87–105, 122, 334n29
    and value 87–8, 101, 102
  and lifestyle 87, 89, 209, 220
  and post-industrial society 8, 74, 81–105, 106–27, 209
  and social class 205
    and middle classes 89, 220, 333n11
    and upper classes 262, 361n29
    and uniqueness 40, 87–105, 122, 334n29
    and value/valorization 87–8, 101, 102
cultural class 200, 201–6
cultural diversity 270, 275, 276
cultural economization 75, 106–27, 177–8, 280, 310–11
  and art/arts 111–12, 119, 337n20
  and attention 107, 118, 119–23, 338n40
    attention capital and reputation capital 122–3, 127

attention distribution 126, 339n59
attention markets 113, 114, 115–16
  and attractiveness markets 107–9, 111, 115–16, 117, 122, 124, 127, 280–1
  and brands 119, 120–1, 338n40
  and cities 110, 280–1
  and classics 112, 119, 120–1, 338n44
  and competition 107, 109, 127
  and cultural capitalism 106–7, 122–3
  and economic sphere 107, 108–11
  and evaluation practices 119–20, 121–2, 125–6
  and labor 131–4, 152, 156, 160
  and lifestyle 220, 238, 243, 248–9
  and marketization 108, 109, 111, 336n17
  and mass media 109, 117–18
  and names 117, 119, 120–1, 123–4
  and novelty 112–13, 116
  and production 115, 131
  and quality 123, 339n59
  and quantification 125, 126
  and recognition 107, 112
  and reputation 119–20, 122, 123
  and society 108, 109–10
  and speculation 114, 115
  and value/valorization 107, 115, 118–20, 121–2
  and visibility 116, 118
cultural formats 164, 165, 169–70, 171–2, 173–4
cultural markets 106–27, 190, 191, 220, 337n22
cultural resources 175, 277
  culture as a resource 216–19, 234
cultural rights 293
cultural spheres 65–78, 295–6
culturalization 17, 52–64, 269
  and affect/affectation 49, 57–9, 72–3
  and cities 280–5, 363n30
  and cultural communities 293, 296
  and digitalization 164, 165, 166–75
  of economy 74, 81, 109
  external 291, 293, 367n36
  of goods 71, 85, 87–93, 248, 332n2
  and inequality 206, 252–66
  and labor market 156, 248

and lifestyle 211–12, 213, 229–30, 246, 248
negative 252, 255, 259
and rarity 91, 92–3
and rationalization 52, 58–61, 65–6
and Romanticism 69–70, 71, 74
and self-actualization 211–12, 213, 246
self-culturalization 291, 292, 293, 294, 296, 365n14
vernacular 280, 281
culture, concept of 3–4, 52–5, 60, 61–2, 68, 327n4
culture, organizational 141–4, 148, 277
culture industry 71–2, 92, 111–12, 114
see also art/arts
culture machines 164, 165, 169, 171, 172–5
cyberbullying 195

dance 237, 356n40
data 169
data tracking 11, 49, 124
and profiles 176, 183–6, 187, 348n18
dating, online 109–10
decision-making 28
decontextualization 104
Deleuze, Gilles and Guattari, Félix 231
democracy 300
density, inner 35–6, 44, 59
density, spacial and cultural 282
depression 250, 251, 313
design 63, 157, 171
of goods 89, 90, 93
and labor 136, 137, 340n13
and lifestyle 228–9, 230–2, 355n19
de-singularization 31, 38, 284, 290
and devaluation 46, 56
and digitalization 167, 192
and labor 141, 148
devaluation 56–8, 192, 296–7, 324n10
and cities 57, 283–4, 285
and de-singularization 46, 56
and labor and qualifications 109, 150, 248, 254
and lifestyle 77, 206, 229, 235, 252
and social class 77, 206, 252, 254, 255–8, 264
difference 36–7

absolute and gradual 25, 26, 37, 45–6, 67, 127, 275
indifference 57, 66
politics of 277, 291
qualitative 33, 37, 45, 104, 127
quantitative 34, 127
differentiation, functional 19
differentiation, social 273–4, 288
digital communities 190–1, 290
digitalization 163–5, 168–72, 190–1
and affect/affectation 170–2, 173, 191, 194–5, 349n44
and attention 172–3, 179, 182–3, 187
and attractiveness markets 177–8, 182, 190
and authenticity 178–9, 181–2
and collective identity 189, 191
and communication 170, 191, 193–4
and cultural capitalism 74, 75, 90
and cultural environment 172, 174, 186, 194
and cultural formats 171–2, 173–4
and culturalization 164, 165, 166–75
and culture 73, 74
and culture machines 164, 165, 169, 171, 172–5
and data tracking 176, 183–6, 187, 348n18
digital media 126, 250
and media formats 167–8, 170–2, 346n10
digital revolution 8, 74, 90, 171
digital subject 177–9, 181, 182, 185, 193
and economy of singularities 173, 174, 179, 199
and generalization 167, 168, 193–4
heterogeneous collaboration 189, 349n35
and human subjects 177–9, 192
and industrial modernity 163–5, 185
and infrastructure 166, 176
and interaction 168, 176, 345n7
and lived experience 171, 181–2
and media formats 167–8, 170–2, 346n10
and neo-communities 188–93, 290
and networks 168, 189

social networking 117–18, 142, 153–4, 170, 189, 191–2, 250, 292
and novelty 174, 175, 180–1
and overproduction 172–5, 346n23
and performance 171, 172, 174, 178–9
and personalization of the internet 11, 164, 186–8
and polarizations 194–5, 349n42
and singularization
  automated 48–51, 176, 177, 185, 186
  compositional 179–83, 347n6
  de-singularization 167, 192
and social media 3, 164, 169, 170, 176, 177, 182, 194
and standardization 50, 165
and technology 73, 74, 75
and temporality 174, 194, 349n42
and uniqueness 178, 181–2, 185, 188, 190, 191–2
universality/universalization 167, 168, 189
see also profiles
disappointment 12, 235, 248–51, 313–14, 318, 359n83
discrimination 275, 276, 293–4, 318
diversity
  cultural 270, 275, 276, 277
  and labor 137, 144
Douglas, Mary 225
duty 73, 270

Eames Chair 38, 94
economic capital 201, 203, 204, 220, 261, 355n19, 355n27
economic sphere 108, 109, 141
see also cultural economization
economy 7–8, 81–195
  creative economy 81, 83–6, 111, 134, 135–44
  culture economy 7–8, 12, 77, 132, 152
  economy of the particular and of the standardized 86, 97, 332n19
  service economy 12, 254
  superstar economy 114, 158–9
  see also creative economy; culturalization
economy of singularities 7–8, 12, 14, 81–127

and crisis of the general 312, 315, 317
and cultural capitalism 74, 75–6
and digitalization 173, 174, 179, 199
and labor 147, 149, 152, 153, 156, 158, 160
and Romanticism 208
see also goods; singularity markets
education
  as a good 109, 241
  and lifestyle 2, 238–42
    and middle classes 68, 201, 209, 220, 242, 263–4
  and middle classes 2, 239, 361n34
  and educational opportunities 73, 74, 200, 202
  and lifestyle 68, 201, 209, 220, 241, 242, 263–4
  and status 242, 264
  and United States 350n5, 350n10
  and polarizations 202, 241
  and qualifications 202–3, 240
  and standardization 2, 7, 24, 238, 240–1, 357n44
  and underclass 202–3, 239, 256, 257
education system 240–1
educational achievement 33, 245
see also qualifications
educational mobility 201, 203, 205
efficiency 59, 60
Ehrenberg, Alain 250
elderly people 244, 285
"elevator effect" 351n20
  paternoster-elevator effect 204–5, 206, 257, 264, 284, 313
Elias, Norbert 67, 305
emotion 48, 100, 170–1, 228
  embarrassment and shame 192, 349n37
  enthusiasm 139, 147
employment, mass 278
engineers 29, 165
Enlightenment 28, 323n27
ensembles 140, 141, 142, 185
enthusiasm 139, 147
entitlement 211, 219
entrepreneurship 109, 273
  culturepreneurs 138
  intrepreneurs 131
  self-entrepreneurship 131, 220, 274–5

environment, cultural 172, 174, 186, 194
equality 30, 39, 315
  inequality 146, 252–66, 272, 319
  and social class 201, 203–4, 206
Esping-Andersen, Gøsta 202
essentialism, cultural 271, 286–309
  and apertistic and differential liberalism 303–4, 305
  and authenticity 287, 296, 297–8, 299, 300–1
  and cultural communities 287–9, 297
    and neo-communities 289–90, 302–3
    and religion 296–7, 298, 303–4, 367n38
  and ethics 289, 298
  and goods 288, 297
  and history 269–70, 288–9
  and homogeneity 288, 300, 301, 302, 304
  and hyperculture 289, 290, 302–3, 304–5, 309
  and identity 290, 302–3
  and middle classes, old 303, 305, 367n38
  and nationalism 290, 294, 299, 303
  and place 66, 67, 69, 289
  and politics 290, 303, 304–5
    and populism, right-wing 299–301, 304
  and profanity 296–7, 298
  and self-actualization 298, 302–3
  and underclass 303, 305, 367n38
  see also ethnicity; nationalism; neo-communities; populism, right-wing; religion
ethicization 212
ethics 261
  and cultural essentialism 289, 298
  and cultural praxis 61, 62–3, 66, 308, 328n19
  and food 94, 227, 256
  and goods 88–9, 94, 99
ethnicity 110
  and communities 286, 291–4, 295, 302, 304
  ethnic identity 276, 277
ethnopluralism 301, 304
evaluation, practices of 43–6, 77, 153
  and cultural economization 119–20, 121–2, 125–6
  and generalization 20, 23, 26–7, 31
  see also devaluation
eventification 121
events 41–2, 171, 353n37
  and cultural capitalism 87, 91, 97–8, 102, 334n39
everyday life 62
  and self-actualization 210–13, 214, 215–16, 218, 352n7
exceptionalism 4, 296, 298
excess 112, 172–3
exclusion 56, 192
experience economy 83
experiences 101, 102, 237–8
  lived experience 47–8, 49, 327n46
    and digitalization 171, 181–2
    and lifestyle 233, 234, 249
    and self-actualization 248, 249
  negative experience 248–51, 359n83
experts 120, 126
exploration 214

Facebook 177, 181–2, 186–7, 347n6
failure 250–1, 264
family life 255, 263
fashion 93–4, 101, 102
film industry 47, 71–2, 122
"filter bubbles" 191, 193
fitness, physical 221, 235, 236, 237, 238, 244, 256
folk culture 67
food 104
  and ethics 94, 227, 256
  and lifestyle 225–8, 354n4
Fordism 29, 30, 70, 71, 74, 108, 146, 254
formalization 23–5, 33, 145–6
  informalization 159–60
Frank, Robert and Cook, Philipp 114
Front National, France 361n36
Funken, Christiane, Rogge, Jan-Christoph and Hörlin, Sinje 151
furniture 230–1, 355n21, 355n22

games 63–4, 89
  computer games 97, 171
gender issues 244–5, 258, 264–5, 357n63, 357n65
general, crisis of 310–19
general, politics of 269, 270, 272
general, social logic of 4, 7, 17, 19–31, 32, 65, 311

and education 241
and industrial modernity 28–31, 82, 311, 314
and labor 49, 135, 150
general, system of 274, 275–6
generality, doing 19, 20, 23, 26, 68, 73, 166, 167, 168, 316
generalization 23–7, 319
 and appropriation 20, 23, 31
 and digitalization 167, 168, 193–4
 and evaluation 20, 23, 26–7, 31
 and observation 20, 23
 and production 20, 23, 173
 and rationalization 20, 23, 31, 33
general-particular 21, 26, 37–8, 103, 125
 social logic of the particular 33, 34–5, 324n10
genetic research 10–11, 50
gentrification 228, 279–80
Germany 361n34
Giddens, Anthony 199
globalism/globalization 11, 226, 245, 270, 277–8
Goodman, Richard A. and Goodman, Lawrence P. 139
goods 8, 71, 87–105, 241, 333n10
 and aesthetics/aestheticization 89, 90–1, 93–4
 affect goods 82, 88, 91, 101, 116
 and classics 101, 102, 112, 119, 120–1, 338n44
 and cultural capitalism 87–105, 122–3
 and art/arts 84, 85, 91–3, 94, 100
 and bourgois modernity 89, 333n11
 and ethics 94, 99
 and events 87, 91, 97–8, 102, 334n39
 and experience 101, 102
 and fashion 101, 102
 and idiosyncrasy 102, 103
 and media formats 87, 90–1, 96–7, 334n35
 and memory 98, 101–2, 335n49
 and objects 87, 103–4
 and profanity / the sacred 89, 90, 91
 and rarity 94–5, 96, 97–8
 and services 87, 90, 95–6, 334n33
 and style 96–7, 334n33
 and uniqueness 87–105, 122, 334n29
 and value 87–8, 101, 102
 and cultural communities 288, 297
 and cultural essentialism 288, 297
 and culturalization 71, 85, 87–93, 248, 332n2
 and design 89, 90, 93
 and ethics 88–9, 94
 and modes of praxis 88–9, 90–4
 narrative–hermeneutic quality 88, 90–1
 and originality 91–4, 96
 overproduction of 115, 172–3, 248
 and performance 87, 107
 and rarity/scarcity 91, 92–3, 94–5, 96, 97–8, 334n30
 standardization 74, 81–2
 and status 71, 88
 and uniqueness 82, 87–105, 122, 334n29
 and value/valorization 77, 87–8, 101, 102, 133, 256
goods, concept of 332n2
goods, functional 90, 101, 108–9, 113, 133, 333n10
 and singularization 38, 84, 103, 333n19
goods, luxury 95
goods, material 81, 90, 95, 131
goods, singular 91–105, 106–27, 136, 338n44
 and labor 131, 133, 135, 141
 see also novelty
goods, standard 119, 334n33
Google 186, 187
Goos, Maarten and Manning, Alan 132
government/governmentality 24, 270, 277–8, 281–5
Gumbrecht, Hans Ulrich 98

hairstyling 334n33
health/healthcare 185–6, 221, 227, 236, 250, 256, 348n22
 mental health 12, 221, 237, 313
 depression 250, 251, 313
Herder, Johann Gottfried 289
heritage, cultural 31, 276–7, 283, 285
heroism 238, 308–9
hierarchy 27, 132, 173–4, 346n23
high culture 121–2, 217
 see also social class

history 269–70, 288–9, 298
Hochschild, Arlie 95
homes 228–32
homogeneity 288, 292, 300, 301, 302, 304
housing 109, 228, 230, 257
Howkins, John 84
human resource management (HRM) 155
human rights 276
hyperculture 76, 102–5, 315
  and cultural essentialism 289, 290, 302–3, 304–5, 309
  and lifestyle 216–18, 234, 237

identity
  collective 3, 144
    and communities 286–91, 294, 295
    and cultural essentialism 290, 302–3
    and digitalization 189, 191
    and populism 12–13, 286, 300
    and religion 12–13, 286, 298
  cultural
    ethnic 276, 277
    and nationalism 12–13, 270, 286, 295, 302–3
  identity politics 270, 291–2, 295, 303
  online 193
  personal 157, 179–82, 193
    and lifestyle 228, 229, 235
idiosyncrasy 66, 160
  and cultural capitalism 102, 103
  and social logic of the particular 33, 34, 37–8, 39
  singularization practices 46, 326n40
illegal activity 193, 260
illumination of the earth 72
images 26, 67, 170–1
income, effortless 122, 123
incommensurability 37
indifference 57, 66, 288
individualism/individuality/ individualization 2, 27, 38–9, 40, 325n26
individuals 287
inequality 146, 252–66, 272, 319
  and post-industrial society 253, 259, 263, 313, 315, 316
  and social class 201, 203–4, 206

inevitability 250
information 62, 169–70
infrastructure, digital 166, 176
infrastructure, economic 50
inhibition, social 30–1
innovation 67, 113, 136, 273, 274–5
"instrumentality deal" 254, 256, 263
integration, cultural 304, 318
intellectual property 84–5
interaction 49, 140, 341n18
  and digitalization 168, 176, 345n7
interchangeability 20, 24, 25–6, 228
  non-interchangeability 35, 44, 96, 178, 280, 283
interior design 228, 230–2, 355n21
International Style 2, 7, 103
internet / world wide web 168, 172–3, 186–8, 191–5
  see also digitalization
intrinsic logic of place 41
Islamic Revolution, Iran 270

Jacobs, Jane 229
job descriptions 152
job satisfaction 254
justice 158, 313, 316, 317
juvenilization 243–4, 258

Kant, Immanuel 4, 6
Keynesianism 30, 272
knowledge 24, 53
  knowledge economy 85, 203
  knowledge society 12, 85, 132, 169, 317
Kristeva, Julia 57

labor 131–60
and achievement 146, 150, 152–3, 158–60, 344n33
and art/arts 149, 156–7, 158–9
and competencies 147–8, 154
and competition 153, 156–8
and consumption/consumers 138, 340n13
and creative economy 134, 135–44
and cultural capital 154, 159
and culturalization 156, 248
and design 136, 137, 340n13
and diversity 137, 144
and economy of singularities 147, 149, 152, 153, 156, 158, 160
and generality

and social logic of singularity /
    the particular 317, 319
  and social logic of the general
    49, 135, 150
  and goods 131, 133, 135, 141
  and industrial modernity 81, 108,
    131, 152, 159, 160, 254
  and lifestyle 215, 242, 248
  and organizational culture 141–4,
    148
  and performance 133, 146, 150–3,
    158–60, 344n33
  and personality 140, 151, 154, 155
  and polarizations 132–3, 158–9,
    344n33
  and post-industrial society 132,
    253
  and post-materialism 135, 148,
    149, 156, 343n3
  and production 131, 135–8
  and profiles 147–50, 153, 157
  and projects 138–41, 143, 144, 147,
    157
  and qualifications 29, 132, 133,
    134, 147, 154, 160, 340n7
    devaluation of 109, 150, 248, 254
  and self-actualization 156, 215
  and singularization 145, 149–50,
    153–6
    de-singularization 141, 148
  and social logic of singularity /
    the particular 142, 150, 317,
    319
  and social class 146, 149, 254
  and social networks 142, 153–4
  and status/prestige 133, 157, 158
  and uniqueness 146, 153
  and value/valorization 133, 150
  and work ethic 145, 156, 209, 264,
    342n3
  and work–life balance 131, 157,
    232, 242
labor, immaterial 47, 131
labor, normalization 133
labor forms 131, 132–3
labor market 81, 156, 248, 273, 331n1
Lareau, Annette 239
law/legal systems 24, 33, 84–5
laypeople 120, 126
Lazzarato, Maurizio 132
"left-behind" people 204, 206, 239,
  259
"left-behind" places 203, 284

legends, living 123
leisure 242–3
Lévi-Strauss, Claude 225
liberalism 362n4, 370n19
  apertistic and differential liberalism
    269–70, 271, 272–85, 296, 314,
    319
  and cities 275, 277–85
  and competition 273, 275
  and cultural essentialism 303–4,
    305
  and cultural heritage/resources
    277, 278
  and populism 299, 301
  and quality of life 275, 276
  and social-democratic consensus
    272–4, 319, 362n1
  and uniqueness 275, 277, 278,
    279
  and lifestyle 209, 245, 270, 275,
    276
  neoliberalism 110, 209, 301, 305
    and apertistic and differential
      liberalism 272–3, 274–7, 305
    and politics 269, 270
  new liberalism
    and lifestyle 245–6, 258, 358n69
    and politics 258
    and post-industrial society 273,
      278, 284, 301, 305
  regulatory 319, 367n51, 370
  social 270, 299, 301, 303
lifelogging 186
lifestyle 77, 224–51
  and aesthetics/aestheticization
    229–30, 246
  and art/arts 68, 214, 231
  attractive life 222, 352n37
  and attractiveness 236, 262, 265–6,
    362n38
  and authenticity 73, 222, 233–4,
    236, 249–50
  homes / interior design 228, 229,
    230
  and middle classes 74, 224–5,
    228, 229
  and bourgeoisie 207–10, 232,
    246–7, 352n6
  and cities 229, 243, 360n17
  and consumption/consumers 82,
    215–16, 227, 254–5
  and creativity 112, 215, 226–7,
    354n7

and cultural capital 199, 201, 203–4, 205, 220, 240
and cultural capitalism 87, 89, 209, 220
and cultural economization 127, 220, 238, 243, 248–9
and culturalization 211–12, 213, 229–30, 246, 248
curated life 3, 214–16, 226, 229–30, 233, 295
and design 228–9, 230–2, 355n19
and devaluation 77, 206, 229, 235, 252
and education 2, 238–42
  and middle classes 68, 201, 209, 220, 242, 263–4
  everyday life 62
  and self-actualization 210–13, 214, 215–16, 218, 352n7
and food 225–8, 354n4
  culture 225, 226, 354n4
and gender issues 244–5, 258, 264–5, 357n63, 357n65
and globalism/globalization 226, 245
good life 213, 220, 318
and hyperculture 216–18, 234, 237
and identity 228, 229, 235
and industrial modernity 225, 229, 232, 235, 242, 248
  and education 238–9, 241
  and interior design 228, 230–2, 355n21
and juvenilization 243–4, 258
and labor 215, 242, 248
and liberalism 209, 245, 270, 275, 276
  new liberalism 245–6, 258, 358n69
  and quality of life 245, 270, 275, 276
lifestyle-as-culture 221, 224
and lived experience 233, 234, 249
and location/locality 228–9, 248–9, 263
and neighborhoods 228–9, 231, 232
and parenting 238–42, 256–7, 305
and performance 227–8, 231, 235
and post-industrial society 200, 202, 209
and post-materialism 208, 220, 224, 245, 318
and profanity 224–5, 226–7

and professionalism 220, 232, 243, 245
and profiles 241, 244–5
quality of life 73, 220
  and cities 280–1, 283
  and liberalism 270, 275, 276
  and middle classes 245–6, 265
  and Romanticism 207–10, 232–3, 246–7
  and self-actualization 76, 222–3, 231, 246–51, 311
    and bourgeoisie 209–10, 246–7
    and education and parenting 238, 240, 242, 356n47
  everyday life 210–13, 214, 215–16, 218, 352n7
  lived experience 248, 249
  and social class 207–23, 246–51, 253–4
  and status 222, 246–7
  and travel 234, 235
and social class 204, 205–6, 259–60, 263–4, 360n22
  self-actualization 207–23, 246–51, 253–4
  upper classes 261–2, 361n29
and social logic of singularity / the particular 241, 311, 313–14, 317, 318
and space 230, 233–4, 237–8, 243
and standardization 224, 225, 226, 228, 235, 236
and status/prestige 76, 209–10, 231, 235, 236, 253
  and parenting 238, 240
  and self-actualization 222, 246–7
and temporality 233, 234
and travel/tourism 232–5, 355n22, 355n29
and uniqueness 224, 233, 234, 239–40, 245, 352n37
and urbanity 229, 243, 282
and value/valorization 205–6, 222–3, 224, 229, 231–2, 235
and work ethic 145, 156, 209, 264, 342n3
see also middle classes; underclass
lifestyle, Californian 83, 208, 225, 235–6
literature 36, 40, 67
living standards 30, 73, 245, 248, 272
  and social class 201, 203–4, 205, 254–5

location/locality 142, 278–80, 289
  and lifestyle 228–9, 248–9, 263
  and social class 257–8, 265, 360n17
"long tails" 284
Löw, Martina 279
luck 158, 260
ludic practices 89, 171
Luhmann, Niklas 19

machines 26
Maffesoli, Michel 286
Manovich, Lev 167, 187–8
market deregulation 109, 270, 273, 274
marketing 50
marketization 108, 111–12, 156–7, 274, 336n17, 337n20
markets *see* attention; attractiveness; cultural markets; niche markets; singularity markets; standard markets; valorization markets; visibility markets; winner-take-all markets
Marx, Karl 8, 20, 133
Maslow, Abraham 213
mass culture 170–2, 173, 175
  and industrial modernity 70–2, 74, 81, 103, 173, 278, 279
  and goods 81, 102, 108
materialism 73
  post-materialism 10, 76
    and labor 135, 148, 149, 156, 343n3
    and lifestyle 208, 220, 224, 245, 318
    and self-actualization 208, 270, 273, 281
materialities 63
Matthew effect 116, 122, 123, 126, 183, 284
meaning 61–2, 302
media, mass 109, 117–18
media formats 40
  and cultural capitalism 87, 90–1, 96–7, 334n35
  and digitalization 167–8, 170–2, 346n10
memory 42, 69, 231, 288–9
  and cultural capitalism 98, 101–2, 335n49
meritocratism 245–6, 313
meta-authenticity 100
metropolitan regions 95, 143, 243

see also cities
Michelin stars 125–6
Middle Ages, European 67
middle classes
  and aesthetics/aestheticization 68, 69, 280
  and authenticity 69, 73–4, 75, 217–19, 224–5, 228, 229, 244
  and cultural capitalism 89, 220, 333n11
  and education 2, 73, 74, 239, 361n34
  and educational opportunities 73, 74, 200, 202
  and lifestyle 68, 201, 209, 220, 241, 242, 263–4
  and status 242, 264
  and United States 350n5, 350n10
  and industrial modernity 207–10, 229, 248, 263
  and inequality 201, 203–4
  and lifestyle 68, 73, 238–42
    and authenticity 74, 224–5, 228, 229
    and education 68, 201, 209, 220, 242, 263–4
    and quality of life 245–6, 265
    and self-actualization 207–23, 246–51
    and uniqueness 224, 352n37
  and profanity 69, 224–5
  and professionalism 146, 202, 220, 264
  and religion 69, 217
  and self-actualization 10, 76, 207–23, 246–51
  and standardization 224, 265
  and status 205, 219–23, 242, 263, 264
  and tourism 217, 285
  and underclass 265, 361n36
  and uniqueness 76, 219–23, 224, 352n37
  and value/valorization 55, 73
  see also lifestyle
middle classes, levelled 30, 200
middle classes, new 12, 74–5, 285, 301
  and cities 2, 110, 217, 279–81, 285
  and lifestyle 73, 77, 199–219, 224–51, 353n31, 361n32
    and curated life 3, 214–16, 226, 229–30, 233

and self-actualization 76, 210–16
and status 205, 219–23
and upper classes 261–2, 361n31
and self-actualization 76, 210–16, 246–51
middle classes, old 261, 263–5
and cultural essentialism 303, 305, 367n38
and lifestyle 204, 263, 265, 313
and status 263, 264
migration 226, 290, 292, 293, 301, 318
Miller, Walter 260
Mitscherlich, Alexander 279
mobile devices 171–2, 173
modernity, bourgeois 28–9, 68–70, 71, 89, 314, 333n11
modernity, classical 7, 19, 27, 39, 145–6, 175, 311–13
modernity, industrial 28–31
and capitalism 7, 115
and cities 278, 279, 282, 284
and digitalization 163–5, 185
and labor 81, 108, 131, 152, 159, 160, 254
and lifestyle 225, 229, 232, 235, 242, 248
and education 238–9, 241
and logic of singularity 311–13, 316
and logic of the general 28–31, 82, 311, 314
and mass culture 70–2, 74, 81, 103, 173, 278, 279
and goods 81, 102, 108
and middle classes 207–10, 229, 248, 263
and rationalization 8, 9, 10
and social class 200–1, 204, 216, 225, 254
modernity, late 72–8
see also cultural capitalism; culturalization; digitalization; essentialism, cultural; labor; liberalism; lifestyle; singularity markets
modernity, organized *see* modernity, industrial
modernization 9, 253
mods and rockers 35
modularization 180, 185, 188
moment and duration 101–2

motivation 60, 145
muddling through 252–66
multiculturalism 290, 293, 295
Muniesa, Fabian 106
murderers 57
music / music industry 104, 171, 326n40

names 153
and cultural economization 117, 119, 120–1, 123–4
narrative/stories 69, 94, 288–9
narrative–hermeneutic quality 61, 62, 66, 67, 68, 88, 328n19
nationalism 70, 294–6
and cultural essentialism 290, 294, 299, 303
and cultural identity 12–13, 270, 286, 295, 302–3
and politics 294, 296, 300
Native Americans 329n2
Neckel, Sighard 152
negativity 57, 195, 288, 307
neighborhoods 228–9, 231, 232
neo-communities 3–4, 76, 286–91, 349n35
and cultural essentialism 289–90, 302–3
and digitalization 188–93, 290
and heterogeneous collaboration 189, 349n35
and social logic of singularity 311, 314
and uniqueness 190, 191–2
Neolithic era 66
network, communicative 168
network capital 220–1
networks, collaborative 189
networks, social 117–18, 143–4, 170, 189, 191–2, 250, 292
and labor 142, 153–4
see also social media
"New Deal" 272
niche markets 83, 158, 337n26
niches, cultural/social 31, 284
Nietzsche, Friedrich 9
"nobody-knows-anything" markets 283
nouveaux riches 262, 266
novelty 102, 136, 312
and cultural economization 112–13, 116
and digitalization 174, 175, 180–1

objects 25–6, 61, 67
  and cultural capitalism 87, 103–4
  and social logic of the particular 39–40, 41, 325n15, 325n17
observation, practices of 31, 43, 44
  and profiles 183–6, 187
  and rationalization and generalization 20, 23
openness 219, 244, 248, 273
opinion 121, 122
order/disorder, problem of 22, 24, 31, 59, 60
organizations 27–8, 29, 132, 139
  organizational culture 141–4, 148, 277
originality 91–4, 96, 192, 193
"other-directed character" 178
otherness 31, 57, 92, 111, 192–3, 291
  and social logic of singularity / the particular 37, 318
overpopulation 285
overproduction 190, 248
  and cultural markets 112–13, 115, 337n22
  and digitalization 172–5
  and hierarchy 346n23
  of goods 115, 172–3, 248

pacification 305
parenting 238–42, 256–7, 305
Pariser, Eli 191
particularity 1–15, 125, 270
  see also singularization; social logic of singularity / the particular
pathological tendencies 193
perception, sensory 47, 61–2, 89
performance
  and achievement 158–60, 344n33
  and digitalization 171, 172, 174, 178–9
  and goods 87, 107
  and labor 133, 146, 150–3, 158–60, 344n33
  and lifestyle 227–8, 231, 235
  and social logic of singularity / the particular 150, 315
performativity 48–51
periphery 258, 303, 305
personal relationships 249, 359n8
personality 82, 179–82, 242
  and labor 140, 151, 154, 155
personalization of the internet 11, 164, 186–8

Peters, Tom and Waterman, Robert 149
Peterson, Richard 99, 217
place, singularity of 41, 280–1, 363n30
  and cultural essentialism 66, 67, 69, 289
  see also location/locality; space
play 63–4
polarizations 77–8, 114, 241, 300–1
  and digitalization 194–5, 349n42
  and labor 132–3, 158–9, 344n33
  and social class 77, 202, 203–4, 252
  and social logic of singularity / the particular 313, 317
political campaigns 50
political polarization 78
political reform 208
politics 269–85
  and cultural economization 110
  and cultural essentialism 290, 303, 304–9
    and populism 299–301, 304
    and nationalism 294, 296, 300
  and neoliberalism 258, 269, 270
  and social logic of singularity 314
    and crisis of the general 315, 316
politics of cities 282, 283
politics of difference 277, 291
politics of identity 270, 291–2, 295, 303
politics of the general 269, 270, 272
politics of the local 272–85
politics of the particular 269–71
popular culture 121–2, 175, 217, 260
populism, right-wing 4, 12–13, 261, 286, 299–301, 304, 367n51
positions, working 146
positivity culture 182, 194, 195
post-industrial society 3
  and cultural capitalism 8, 74, 81–105, 106–27, 209
  and inequality 253, 259, 263, 313, 315, 316
  and labor 132, 253
  and liberalism 273, 278, 284, 301, 305
  and lifestyle 200, 202, 209
praxis, cultural 59, 60, 61–4
  aesthetic 61, 62, 67, 328n19
  goods 89, 90–1, 93–4
  lifestyle 229–30, 246
  middle classes 68, 69, 280

creative 61, 63, 66, 328n19
ethical 61, 62–3, 66, 308, 328n19
goods 88–9, 90–4
ludic 61, 63–4, 66, 328n19
and meaning 61–2, 302
modes of 28, 48–9, 56, 88–9, 90–1, 94, 171
narrative–hermeneutic 61, 62, 66, 67, 68, 328n19
premodern societies 21, 31, 60, 66–8
prestige *see* status/prestige
production
  cultural 58
    and creative economy 82, 83
    and labor 131, 135–8
    overproduction 101, 102, 112, 115, 119, 120–1, 131, 338n44
    and cultural economization 115, 131
    and generalization 20, 23, 173
    and industrial modernity 30, 31
    and labor 131, 135–8
    mass 1, 29, 30, 71, 81, 96, 131, 278
    overproduction 83, 115, 190
    and cultural markets 112–13, 337n22
    and digitalization 172–5, 346n23
    of goods 115, 172–3, 248
  practices of 31
    and generalization 20, 23
    and practices of singularization 46–7, 48, 326n40
    and rationalization 20, 23–6, 58
profanity 45, 66, 133
  and cultural capitalism 89, 90, 91
  and goods 89, 90, 91, 133
  and lifestyle 224–5, 226–7
  and middle classes 69, 224–5
  and religion 296–7, 298
  see also sacred, the
professionalism 77
  and lifestyle 220, 232, 243, 245
  and middle classes 146, 202, 220, 264
profiles 177–8
  and compositional singularity 179–83, 347n6
  consumer profiles 176, 184
  and data tracking 176, 183–6, 187, 348n18
  and labor 147–50, 153, 157
  and lifestyle 241, 244–5
  and practices of observation 183–6, 187

and subjects 183–4, 192
and uniqueness 82, 149, 178, 181–2, 185, 188
progress, social 23, 248, 312
projects 138–41, 143, 144, 147, 157
provinciality 219
public sphere 184, 193–4, 290, 314, 315, 318
Putnam, Robert 201

qualifications 85, 313
  and education 202–3, 240
  and labor 29, 132, 133, 134, 147, 154, 160, 340n7
  devaluation of 109, 150, 248, 254
  standardization of 81, 145–6, 238, 357n44
qualitative-competitive method 125
qualities of the social 55
quality 55–6, 59, 92, 123, 125–6, 339n59
quantification 24, 92, 124–7, 339n60, 364n37
Quebec 295
racism 293
rankings 125–7, 364n37
rarity/scarcity 22, 31, 59, 60, 172
  and goods 91, 92–3, 94–5, 96, 97–8, 334n30
rationalization 21–5, 58–61
  and appropriation 20, 23, 31
  cognitive 23, 24
  and culturalization 52, 58–61, 65–6
  formal 10–11, 17, 19–20, 21–5, 33, 65, 155, 315
  and generalization 20, 23, 31, 33
  and industrial modernity 8, 9, 10
  and law / legal systems 24, 33
  normative 22, 23, 24–5, 57, 62–3
  and order/disorder problem 22, 24
  and production 20, 23–6, 58
  and rules 27, 28
  and standardization 23–4, 26, 27, 29, 33
  technical 23–4, 163
real estate 95, 248–9, 285
Reckwitz, Andreas 14
recognition 44, 133, 159
  crisis of 312–13, 315, 316–17
  and cultural economization 107, 112
recombination 175

"redneck culture" 261
Reich, Robert 134
religion 61, 110
   and appropriation 297, 366n36
   and collective identity 12–13, 286, 298
   and cultural communities 296–7, 298, 301, 303–4, 367n38
   and cultural essentialism 296–7, 298, 303–4, 367n38
   and profanity 296–7, 298
   religious fundamentalism 3–4, 270–1, 286, 296–9, 303–4, 309, 366n36
   and social class 69, 217, 298, 367n38
   and society 66, 67
religious texts 40
repression 30–1, 209, 352n6
reputation 119–20, 122, 123, 153
reputation capital 122, 123
restaurants 227
reviews 119
Riesman, David 2, 30, 178, 192
risk 114–15, 250
Romanticism 9–10, 39, 99, 289
   and culturalization 69–70, 71, 74
   and lifestyle 207–10, 232–3, 246–7
   and self-actualization 210, 213, 246–7
Rousseau, Jean-Jacques 99
routinization 214
Roy, Olivier 298
Russia 296, 366n30

sacred, the 45, 66, 69, 89
   see also profanity
Scandinavia 272
scarcity *see* rarity/scarcity
Schelsky, Helmut 200
Schimank Uwe, Mau, Steffen and Groh-Samberg, Olaf 220
schools 2, 7, 241
   see also education
Schumpeter, Joseph 274
science 24
Scotland 295, 366n28
secularization 296
self, late-modern 147, 177, 178, 199–201, 213
self, unlimited 247
self-actualization 157, 270, 298
   and appropriation 215–16, 218
   and authenticity 73, 212, 217–19
   and cultural essentialism 298, 302–3
   and culturalization 211–12, 213, 246
   and labor 156, 215
   and lifestyle 222–3, 231, 311
      and bourgeoisie 209–10, 246–7
      and education and parenting 238, 240, 242, 356n47
      everyday life 210–13, 214, 215–16, 218, 352n7
      lived experience 248, 249
      and social class 207–23, 246–51, 253–4
      and status 222, 246–7
      and travel 234, 235
   and middle classes 10, 76, 207–23, 246–51
   new middle class 76, 210–16, 246–51
   and post-materialism 208, 270, 273, 281
   and Romanticism 210, 213, 246–7
   and singularization 211, 212, 213, 246
   and social logic of singularity / the particular 313–14, 315, 317–18
   and value/valorization 212, 222–3
self-culturalization 291, 292, 294, 296, 365n14
self-development 12, 73, 213, 240, 250, 253, 318
self-discipline 254, 263
self-employment / freelance workers 134
self-exploitation 157
self-limitation 317, 318
self-optimization 159, 221, 236
self-presentation 177
self-representation 178
Sennett, Richard 199
sensuousness 61–2, 302
seriality 27
service class 132, 202, 203
service sector 77, 81, 86, 131, 133, 317, 331n1
   and cultural capitalism 87, 90, 95–6, 334n33
   service economy 12, 254
Shackle, George 87
shame 192–3
shootings, mass 305–9
similarities, zones of 21
Simmel, Georg 9, 30, 181

and individualism 39, 325n14
Philosophy of Money 8
Simondon, Gilbert 164
singularities, circulation of 102–3
singularities, contradictory 100
singularities, definition 32, 323n2
singularities, interactive 97
singularities, negative 56–7, 58, 100, 184, 284, 307–8
singularities, plurality of 76, 137, 140, 215
singularities, serial 97
singularity, compositional 77, 177, 179–83, 213, 347n6
singularity capital 120–4, 149–50, 222, 282–3
singularity management 281–5
singularity markets 75–6, 83, 119, 122, 190–1, 349n35
singularization 2, 5
  and appropriation 47–8, 49
  de-singularization 31, 38, 284, 290
  and devaluation 46, 56
  and digitalization 167, 192
  and labor 141, 148
  and functional goods 38, 84, 103, 333n19
  and idiosyncrasy 46, 326n40
  and labor 145–60, 317, 319
  de-singularization 141, 148
  and production 46–7, 48, 326n40
  and self-actualization 211, 212, 213, 246
  and social logic of singularity / the particular 35
  and idiosyncrasy 46, 326n40
  and labor 142, 150, 317, 319
  and technology 7, 8, 164
  and uniqueness 176, 177
  and value/valorization 6–7, 8–9, 45–6
  see also cultural capitalism; culturalization; digitalization; essentialism, cultural; labor; liberalism; lifestyle; neo-communities
singularization, radicalized 317–18
singularization processes 176–95, 310
  automated 49–50, 169, 176
social capital 220, 262–3
social class 199–201, 261–6
  class divide 201–6, 350n8
  and cultural capitalism 205

  and middle classes 89, 220, 333n11
  and upper classes 262, 361n29
  and devaluation 77, 206, 252, 254, 255–8, 264
  and education 239, 263–4
  and industrial modernity 200–1, 204, 216, 225, 254
  and middle classes 207–10, 229, 248, 263
  and inequality 201, 203–4, 206
  and labor 146, 149, 254
  and lifestyle 259–60, 263–4, 360n22
  self-actualization 207–23, 246–51, 253–4
  and living standards 201, 203–4, 205, 254–5
  and location/locality 257–8, 265, 360n17
  and polarizations 77, 202, 203–4, 252
  and religion 69, 217, 298, 367n38
  and cultural essentialism 298, 367n38
  and value/valorization 55, 73, 205–6
  see also middle classes; underclass; upper classes
social logic of singularity / the particular 4, 32–51
  crisis of recognition 312–13, 315, 316–17
  and culture 52, 55–6, 65, 73, 316
  and generality 25, 310, 311, 314, 315, 316, 317–18, 319
  and idiosyncrasy 33, 34, 37–8, 39, 46, 326n40
  and individualism/individuality/individualization 38–9, 40, 325n26
  and labor 142, 150, 317, 319
  and lifestyle 241, 311, 313–14, 317, 318
  and neo-communities 311, 314
  and objects 39–40, 325n15, 325n17
  and otherness 37, 318
  and performance 150, 315
  and polarizations 313, 317
  and politics 314, 315, 316
  and public sphere 315, 318
  and self-actualization 311, 313–14, 315, 317–18
  and self-limitation 317, 318
  and value/valorization 73, 317–18

social media 3, 164, 169, 170, 176, 177, 182, 194
  see also networks, social
social mobility 259–60
social movements 318
socialism 29, 30, 108, 146, 270
sociality 32, 188–91
socialization 52
society 42–3, 65, 66, 67, 108, 109–10
sociology 32
softwarization 186, 187–8
sound 171
Soviet Union 29
space 27, 77, 90, 285, 289
  and lifestyle 230, 233–4, 237–8, 243
  see also location/locality; place, singularity of
speculation 114, 115, 160
spill-over effect 121
sport 236–8
standard markets 75, 76, 82, 83, 106, 107, 109
standardization 11, 23–5
  and cities 279, 283–4, 363n26
  and digitalization 50, 165
  and education 2, 7, 24, 238, 240–1, 357n44
  of goods 74, 81–2
  and lifestyle 224, 225, 226, 228, 235, 236
  and mass production 30, 71
  and middle classes 224, 265
  of qualifications 81, 145–6, 238, 357n44
  and rationalization 23–4, 26, 27, 29, 33
  and Romanticism 208, 213
stardom 262, 266, 361n30, 362n38
starification 114
status/prestige
  and education 242, 264
  and goods 71, 88
  and labor 133, 157, 158
  and lifestyle 76, 209–10, 231, 235, 236, 253
    and parenting 238, 240
    and self-actualization 222, 246–7
  and middle classes 205, 219–23, 263, 264
  and self-actualization 222, 246–7
  singularity status 112, 183, 308
  and underclass 253, 254, 260
Stinchcombe, Arthur L. 344n33

student protests 270
style 40, 88, 93–4, 96–7, 334n33
subject capital 221, 236
subjects 26–7, 66, 67, 72, 87
  digital 49–50, 177–9, 181, 182, 185, 193
  and profiles 183–4, 192
  human 39, 40, 69, 168, 169
  immobile 247–8
  working see labor
success 152–3, 158, 159, 219, 222
superstar economy 114, 158–9
systematization 22, 311

tableau, modularized 180–1
talent 82, 149, 158, 241, 260
tango 237, 356n40
teachers 344n35, 357n52
teamwork 137, 138
technicians 29
technology 7, 8, 137, 163–4, 166–75
  and digitalization 73, 74, 75
  intelligent 50–1
rationalistic 50
technical culture 29, 163
temporality 27, 41–2, 69, 101–2, 118–19, 139, 312
  and digitalization 174, 194, 349n42
  and lifestyle 233, 234
terrorism 270, 305–9
text 26, 170
Thatcher, Margaret 270
things 93–5
  see also objects
Thomas theorem 6
traditional societies 19, 60, 66–7, 70, 190, 289
transgressions, social 171, 172
travel biographies 234
travel/tourism 1, 91, 277
  and lifestyle 232–5, 355n22, 355n29
  and middle classes 217, 285
tribal societies, archaic 66, 329n2
Trump, Donald 362n38
Turing machine 167
typifications 21–2, 66

underclass
  and authenticity 260–1, 265
  and cultural essentialism 303, 305, 367n38

and devaluation 252, 254, 255–8
and inequality 77, 252–5, 258–61
"left-behind" people 204, 206, 239, 259
and lifestyle 77, 206, 219, 252–5, 256–8, 313
  and education 202–3, 239, 256, 257
  and locality 257–8, 360n17
  and middle classes 265–6, 361n36
  respectable 255, 256–7, 265
  and status/prestige 253, 254, 260
uniformity 26, 30
uniqueness 52, 72, 307
  and apertistic and differential liberalism 275, 277, 278, 279
  and cities 279, 282
  and cultural capitalism 40, 87–105, 122, 334n29
  and cultural heritage/resources 31, 277, 278
  and cultural singularity markets 122–3, 190
  and digitalization 178, 181–2, 185, 188, 190, 191–2
  and generality 31, 318
  and goods 82, 87–105, 122, 334n29
  and labor 146, 153
  and lifestyle 224, 233, 234, 239–40, 245, 352n37
  and middle classes 76, 219–23, 224, 352n37
  and neo-communities 190, 191–2
  and profiles 82, 149, 178, 181–2, 185, 188
  quantification of 124–7, 339n60
  and singularization 34, 38, 40–1, 176, 177, 315, 318
United States 29, 70, 239, 272
  and education 350n5, 350n10
universality 25, 294, 296, 318–19
  and digitalization 167, 168, 189
upper classes 66, 203–4, 261–3, 361n29
urbanism 277–81
  urbanity 229, 243, 282
Urry, John 232
use value 87, 101
utility 55

valorization markets 107, 110, 159, 173
valorization spectacles 122, 127
valorization techniques 45, 118–20, 126
valorization transfer 223
value/valorization 52–8, 59–60, 182–3
  and communities 191, 287–8
  and cultural capitalism 87–8, 101, 102
  and cultural economization 115, 121–2
  and goods 77, 87–8, 101, 102, 133, 256
  and labor 133, 150
  and lifestyle 205–6, 222–3, 224, 229, 231–2, 235
  and practices of singularization 6–7, 8–9, 45–6
  and self-actualization 212, 222–3
  and social class 55, 73, 205–6
  and social logic of singularity / the particular 73, 317–18
  and violence 308, 368n69
  see also devaluation; evaluation, practices of
Vespa scooters 93, 103
violence 305–9, 359n83, 368n69
visibility 114–18, 173, 179, 182–3
visibility markets 176, 190, 283, 302, 307, 310
Voswinkel, Stephan 133

Warhol, Andy 308
waste 112
Weber, Max 7, 9, 20, 40, 60, 67, 107, 298
well-roundedness 148
Whyte, William 30
winner-take-all markets 111, 114, 204, 248, 260, 284, 313, 317
work ethic 145, 156, 209, 264, 342n3
work–life balance 131, 157, 232, 242
workers, industrial 81, 331n1
working classes 259, 261
working conditions 77, 132, 157, 313
working hours 152
World Trade Center attacks, New York 270

youth culture 244, 260–1, 357n60
youthfulness 243–4, 258

Zuboff, Shoshana and Maxmin, James 90
Zukin, Sharon 283